W9-AEX-996

China in the Age of Xi Jinping

This book presents a concise introduction to China in the Xi Jinping era. It is intended as a first book for those coming new to the subject, providing the essential information that most people need to know, without going into excessive detail. Its coverage includes the economy, society, politics, and international relations; China's history, especially the twentieth century; and Taiwan and Hong Kong, as well as the People's Republic of China. It will also be useful for more advanced students who need to understand developments in China outside their own primary disciplines.

The book provides an up-to-date and clear guide to the changes which have taken place in China in the late twentieth and early twenty-first centuries, including the recent further changes which are taking place under Xi Jinping's regime. It draws on the enormous body of empirical and theoretical research that is being carried out by economists, political scientists, and sociologists on China, but is itself written in non-technical and accessible language. It does not assume any previous knowledge of China and explanations of Chinese terms are provided throughout the book. It includes a map, a chronology, a glossary of Chinese terms, biographical notes on key figures, and a guide to further reading.

Michael Dillon is Professor of History and Affiliate of the Lau China Centre at King's College, London. He was formerly Director of the Centre for Contemporary Chinese Studies at the University of Durham and Visiting Professor at Tsinghua University, Beijing. He is the author of *Contemporary China – An Introduction* (Routledge 2009).

China in the Age of Xi Jinping

Michael Dillon

Routledge
Taylor & Francis Group
LONDON AND NEW YORK

First published 2021
by Routledge
2 Park Square, Milton Park, Abingdon, Oxon OX14 4RN

and by Routledge
52 Vanderbilt Avenue, New York, NY 10017

Routledge is an imprint of the Taylor & Francis Group, an informa business

© 2021 Michael Dillon

The right of Michael Dillon to be identified as author of this work has been asserted by him in accordance with sections 77 and 78 of the Copyright, Designs and Patents Act 1988.

All rights reserved. No part of this book may be reprinted or reproduced or utilised in any form or by any electronic, mechanical, or other means, now known or hereafter invented, including photocopying and recording, or in any information storage or retrieval system, without permission in writing from the publishers.

Trademark notice: Product or corporate names may be trademarks or registered trademarks, and are used only for identification and explanation without intent to infringe.

British Library Cataloguing-in-Publication Data
A catalogue record for this book is available from the British Library

Library of Congress Cataloging-in-Publication Data
A catalog record for this book has been requested

ISBN: 978-0-367-34301-9 (hbk)
ISBN: 978-0-367-34790-1 (pbk)
ISBN: 978-0-429-32521-2 (ebk)

Typeset in Times New Roman
by Apex CoVantage, LLC

Contents

Preface   vii
Acknowledgements   xii
Chronology   xiv

PART 1
Introduction   1

1   Land, people, and culture   3

2   China's past in the present   10

PART 2
Politics   21

3   Government and politics of China   23

4   Seeking a harmonious society: fourth-generation leadership of Hu
   Jintao and Wen Jiabao   48

5   Murder and corruption in the leadership: Bo Xilai and Zhou Yongkang 55

6   Rise of Xi Jinping: fifth generation or new authoritarianism?   61

PART 3
The economy   87

7   Economic growth and the changing economy   89

8   Rural economy   96

9   Urban and industrial economy   112

10 Banking, finance, and foreign trade   117

11 Tourism and transport   126

12 Western development   131

13 Belt and Road Initiative   144

PART 4
Society   149

14 Social change: rural reforms and urbanisation   151

15 Education and health   158

16 Law and human rights   179

17 Mass media   195

18 Religious and ethnic minorities   203

19 Gender and modernisation   223

20 The environment   229

PART 5
China's periphery   239

21 Tibet   241

22 Xinjiang   252

23 Inner Mongolia   266

24 Hong Kong   271

25 Taiwan   299

PART 6
International relations   311

26 China and the world 1: strategic relationships   313

27 China and the world 2: neighbours to the west   347

PART 7
Prospects: struggle between two new lines   363

28 After Xi: harmonious society or new authoritarianism?   365

List of abbreviations   369
Glossary of selected Chinese terms   370
Biographical notes   373
Index   380

Preface

Into the Xi Jinping era

China does not stand still. *Contemporary China – an Introduction*, my previous overview of the politics, economics, and society of China, was published in 2009; the information and analysis in that book were current when the manuscript was completed in the summer of 2008. In August of that year, China was host to the summer Olympics, which was deemed a success and boosted the country's image. The international banking crisis began in 2007 with the failures of sub-prime mortgages in the United States and entered its most dangerous and dramatic phase in September 2008 with the collapse of the Lehman Brothers investment bank. Since 2008, there have been major changes in China, some of which were in response to the financial crisis which was unfolding as *Contemporary China* went to press. This had a significant if indirect impact on the Chinese economy and a profound effect on the confidence of the elite in the Western financial model. The most significant changes, however, some of which were entirely unexpected, result from the rise to power of Xi Jinping in 2012.

It is now a commonplace that China is a major, even dominant, international economic force and an increasingly influential actor on the international stage. An informed understanding of the rapid, and often bewildering, changes in the Chinese world is not the exotic indulgence that it was once thought to be – although it never really was – but a practical necessity. Chinese studies, in common with the rest of the academic world, remains fragmented in disciplinary silos, with the attendant risk of failure to see the wood for the trees. This book, like its predecessor, aspires to compensate for that risk by offering an overall picture of China's development, set in the context of its contemporary history.

Xi Jinping takes control

Xi Jinping became General Secretary of the Chinese Communist Party (CCP) on 15 November 2012, and President of the People's Republic of China (PRC) on 14 March 2013, by which time he had also assumed the role of Chairman of the twin Central Military Commissions formally answerable, respectively, to the CCP and the government. Xi has been described as the most powerful leader of China since Mao Zedong, and this position was strengthened when he was acknowledged as a 'core leader' in October 2016. Xi rose to power on the dual platforms of alleviating poverty and combating corruption, but his administration will be remembered for authoritarianism and the intolerance of even the mildest forms of dissent. This has been accompanied by an aggressive assertion of China's position in the world and greater reliance on nationalist rhetoric. None of this was predictable in 2008 during the administration of General Secretary Hu Jintao and Premier Wen Jiabao.

China in the Age of Xi Jinping addresses these dramatic changes in the PRC, which celebrated its 70th anniversary in 2019, and offers a comprehensive picture of the state of that nation in as concise a form as possible. Although the book will be useful while the Xi Jinping administration remains in power, it should also have an afterlife as an account of that administration once Xi eventually stands down. It is not just an updated version of *Contemporary China – an Introduction*, although it draws on the material from that book and some factual passages that do not require updating have been retained. All chapters have been revised to reflect the changes of the past ten years, and several are completely new. The entire text has been either completely rewritten or thoroughly updated; the opportunity has been taken to consult sources that have become available since 2008 and to incorporate material and impressions from the author's research visits to China, including Xinjiang, Shanghai, Suzhou, Hangzhou, Chongqing, and Hong Kong, and to Mongolia during the same period.

Analysing contemporary China

In *Contemporary China – an Introduction*, I posed one of the fundamental problems faced by the serious student of Chinese affairs. Should the PRC, as some would argue, be characterised primarily as a nightmare realm of human rights abuses? China can be criticised on many human rights grounds. It has one of the highest rates of death sentences and executions in the world; many peasants and workers in both the countryside and the cities still suffer desperate exploitation; dissenting opinions and unorthodox political, religious, or social attitudes are severely repressed; there is no independent judicial system; the track record of the state in dealing with ill treatment or torture in prison and police custody is at best mediocre; some of the poorest children in the country are still in ill-equipped orphanages; no genuine independence for Tibet or Xinjiang can be countenanced or even discussed; corruption exists on a vast scale at all levels of society; and there is nothing that approaches political democracy as it is understood in the West. China is, however, also a country with a dynamic economy, has liberated millions of its people from desperate poverty, and has finally allowed its population to break out of a decades-old torpor, making it possible for millions, both peasants and urban dwellers, to improve their opportunities for work, education, travel – including overseas – and family life.

The banal answer, but the only appropriate one in 2009, when *Contemporary China – an Introduction* was published, and again in 2020, is that both perspectives are valid. Chinese society and the state are a mass of contradictions and complexities that render any attempt at a simplistic analysis futile and irresponsible. That does not prevent commentators and analysts from attempting to characterise the PRC as either heroic (less frequently now) or villainous, according to their own political or cultural perspectives and prejudices.

The public image of China changed dramatically following the rise to power of Xi Jinping. After an initial period of uncertainty about his intentions and pious hopes that, as the son of a leading CCP cadre purged by Mao Zedong even before the Cultural Revolution, he might reject Mao's autocratic approach and favour reform and liberal policies, it became clear that the converse was true. Since 2012, and even more so since 2017 when Xi's second term of office began, official China has become increasingly conformist and less tolerant of even the mildest dissent. Xi's genuine commitment to eliminating poverty and corruption has been marred by an authoritarian political culture, attempts to enforce social homogeneity, and centralisation of power; these have led commentators to compare him to Mao, an evaluation that Xi has done nothing to discourage.

This introduction to China in the age of Xi Jinping focuses primarily on the People's Republic, including Hong Kong, but also covers developments in Taiwan. Hong Kong became technically part of the PRC in 1997 as a Special Administrative Region. After over six months of often violent demonstrations in 2019 and the subsequent decision in May 2020 to impose a new National Security Law on the territory, it is now more firmly under the control of Beijing than at any time previously. Taiwan remains *de facto* independent but is faced with constant threats of Beijing's avowed determination to 'reclaim' the island.

This book draws on empirical and theoretical research carried out by economists, political scientists, anthropologists, and sociologists on contemporary China, but deliberately avoids the technical, and at times inaccessible, language of some specialists. It does not assume any previous knowledge of China or the Chinese language: any Chinese terms used in the text are explained as they occur and romanised versions of some terms are included for the convenience of readers who have some knowledge of Chinese. One of the most important assumptions underlying the approach of this book is that contemporary China cannot be understood adequately without an appreciation of both its immediate historical past and how this past is perceived by Chinese people today. Today's China of repression, but also reform, is a land of concrete, glass, and steel, but it is still the same China as the China of Mao Zedong and the Red Guards. Many of the students and secondary school pupils of the Red Guard generation grew up to be the managers, teachers, CCP officials, or senior civil servants of today. Their past – China's recent history – continues to influence their thinking.

Although the study of contemporary China has been well-served by many humane and balanced enquiries, it has also been bedevilled by simplistic and ill-informed, but nonetheless strongly held, political opinions and allegiances. In the tradition of the Cold War, China watchers have often been divided – frequently with little justification – into pro-China and anti-China. That automatically assumed that they were, respectively, anti-Taiwan or pro-Taiwan. This created serious professional anxieties. Scholars and analysts of the Chinese world can find themselves spending too much time looking over their shoulders for fear that they might be accused of being too hard or too soft on China. Such oversimplified classifications do not encumber studies of, say, Indonesia, the Philippines, or India (and developing China has many similarities with those countries), so why should they be considered so important in China studies?

In recent years, this situation has been complicated by increasing Chinese sensitivity towards Western scholars, journalists, and other commentators who are critical of Chinese policies. Some have been refused permission to carry out research in China, and others barred from even entering the PRC. These restrictions, often arbitrary, have been applied even more stringently in the case of outsiders taking an interest in the most politically sensitive areas of Chinese life: Tibet, Xinjiang, Taiwan, the Tian'anmen Square massacre of 4 June 1989, and anything to do with dissidents and the justice system. Hong Kong is now probably on that list. For those accustomed to the increasing freedom of access to archives, informants, and publications that began in the 1980s, this was an unwelcome and problematic reversal.

It is essential for the Western analyst or observer to be able to step into the shoes of the people of China, including those who are in positions of power, and to endeavour to understand how they perceive their country, their society, and their institutions. This does not imply sympathy with, or support for, those in power: the converse is frequently the case. However, not even attempting to see the world from Chinese points of view is both arrogant and dangerous. There is, of course, no single Chinese point of view: the way that peasant farmers in Henan, Western-trained intellectuals in Beijing, and Tibetan nuns in Lhasa think and feel about China and the world are far from identical. It is essential to appreciate this range of viewpoints, however inconsistent and mutually incompatible they seem.

China over 50 years: a personal perspective

This book, like its predecessor, has grown out of a critical engagement with China, its language, culture, history, and politics, that stretches back over 50 years of study, teaching, and research. During that period, the PRC has experienced the rise and fall of the Cultural Revolution; the death of its founding leader, Mao Zedong; a war with its former Communist ally, Vietnam; the introduction of the 'reform and opening' policy under Deng Xiaoping; the brutal suppression of the Democracy Movement in Beijing on 4 June 1989; the search for a 'harmonious society' in the Hu Jintao period and the authoritarian rise of Xi Jinping. As a backdrop to these events, the people of China have been witnesses to – and participants in – a dramatic process of urbanisation and modernisation; the migration of millions of men and women from the countryside to the cities in search of work; conflicts in the villages over taxation, land ownership, and the one-child policy; the escalation of underlying ethnic and cultural frictions between the Han majority and minority groups; the constant tension between the mainland and Taiwan; and a growing awareness of the dreadful potential of military conflict with the United States as China emerges as the second superpower of the twenty-first century. All of this happened in the presence of the international media, which had only restricted' access to China between 1949 and 1980.

More Chinese people than ever before have travelled abroad for work, study, or leisure; they take back to China (and to Taiwan) informed opinions, both positive and negative, about the West and detailed information about the outside world – a level of knowledge and understanding of which the preceding generation could not have dreamt. The dramatic transformation of the mainland has brought into sharp focus enduring questions about the nature of the Chinese state and Chinese society. China today does not look or behave like a traditional Soviet-style Communist state – and yet, the CCP remains firmly in control. Neither is it anything approaching a liberal democratic system with a completely free-market economy. The economy remains mixed, but state-owned enterprises still dominate key sectors. Migration and changes in working and living patterns are fundamentally and rapidly altering the social structure of cities, towns, and villages.

In the same period, Taiwan has evolved from a one-party state dominated by the former mainland government party, the Kuomintang (Guomindang), and its military adjuncts into a multi-party democracy, albeit one racked with discord, corruption, and ethnic and social divisions. There has been an upsurge of popular support for a formal declaration of the legal independence of Taiwan from China, associated particularly with the rise of the Democratic Progressive Party (DPP) and its President Tsai Ing-wen; this angers Beijing. Without careful management and sophisticated diplomacy, the independence issue has the potential to develop into a serious political, and even military, conflict.

Hong Kong, the last British colony in Asia, was returned to China in 1997 and became a Special Administrative Region of the People's Republic. While it retains its individual character and much of its old colonial charm under the mushrooming growth of shopping malls, it constantly grapples with the challenge of retaining its distinctive identity and traditions while operating within the PRC. It is subject to closer scrutiny by the Chinese government than at any time since 1949 and has come under increasing pressure to conform to Beijing's values, especially since the disturbances of 2019.

The observations offered in this book have been informed by the regular visits to China and other parts of the Chinese world since the early 1980s, not only to major urban centres such as Beijing, Shanghai, Chongqing, Suzhou, Hangzhou, and Guangzhou, but also to undertake intensive programmes of fieldwork during the 1990s in the rural areas and small towns of Jiangxi and Anhui in southern China; in the remote (their word, not mine) Hui Muslim regions of Shaanxi, Gansu, and Ningxia in the northwest, and the border regions of Xinjiang and Inner Mongolia. Other visits included Hong Kong and Taiwan, and China's Inner Asian neighbours, Mongolia and Kazakhstan.

The range of topics covered in this book is such that no individual can possibly claim to be an authority on all; the assessments and interpretations have been influenced by the work of many commentators, including academics and serious journalists, not all of whom will agree with the conclusions drawn from their efforts. Condensing complex and controversial topics into a few pages may well have resulted in some oversimplification, although strenuous efforts have been made to avoid misleading the reader. Every attempt has been made to make this book as up to date as possible, but economic, social, and cultural changes in twenty-first century China are rapid and often unpredictable.

Acknowledgements

I began the serious study of what was then a completely different contemporary China in the departments of Chinese studies and sociology at the University of Leeds in the United Kingdom during the late 1960s and early 1970s. It was the era of the Cultural Revolution, and there was virtually no opportunity for direct contact with the People's Republic of China. Staff in the departments, who came from diverse backgrounds in China and in Western Sinology, had between them an extraordinary range of expertise, experience of China, and interests which they communicated in their teaching. I am happy to acknowledge the inspiration of all the staff in Leeds who introduced me to Chinese studies.

In China, I have been fortunate over a period of 40 years to work with historians and other scholars at the Institutes of Modern History, Economics, World Religions, and Minorities of the Academy of Social Sciences in Beijing, and its regional academies in Shanghai and Guangzhou, and in the provinces or autonomous regions of Anhui, Jiangxi, Gansu, Ningxia, and Xinjiang. I have also found great profit and pleasure in cooperation with colleagues in many universities, including Renmin University of China and Tsinghua University in Beijing, Fudan University in Shanghai, the universities of Xinjiang in Urumqi and Ningxia in Yinchuan, and the Hong Kong University of Science and Technology. In Taiwan, I have carried out research at Academia Sinica in Taipei and have benefited from cooperation with colleagues at National Chengchi University.

These academic partnerships have been vital in shaping my understanding of China; my visits to many of these institutions in the 1990s were made possible with financial and organisational support from the British Academy and the Universities' China Committee in London. This book, and the other publications which have resulted from these exchanges, would have been much poorer without these academic exchanges, and I acknowledge with gratitude the generous support of these organisations over many years.

*

Since the publication of *Contemporary China – an Introduction*, I was Visiting Professor of Modern Chinese Politics in the Global Journalism Institute at Tsinghua University in Beijing (2009), for which I am grateful to Steven Dong; carried out fieldwork in the Xinjiang Uyghur Autonomous Region of China (2010); and researched the background to Deng Xiaoping's life in Chongqing and rural areas of Sichuan Province (2011). Most recently I have carried out research in Mongolia (2016), and in Shanghai and the surrounding area (2017 and 2018). These visits, and associated documentary research, have resulted in several publications on which I have drawn for this present book. They include: *China: A Modern History* I.B. (Tauris, 2010; paperback August 2012 and long-listed for ICAS Humanities Prize 2013), *Xinjiang in the Twenty-first Century: Islam, Ethnicity and*

Resistance Routledge (2018); *Lesser Dragons: China's Ethnic Minorities*, Reaktion Books (2018; listed as one of Top Five Books, in *International Affairs*, Chatham House, Royal Institute of International Affairs, December 2018); *Mongolia: A Political History of the Land and its People*, I. B. Tauris (2020), and *Zhou Enlai: the enigma behind Chairman Mao*, I.B. Tauris (in press 2020).

Invitations to comment in the media have obliged me to keep up to date with rapidly changing developments in China; for these I am grateful to various programmes on BBC World Service and Radio 4, and particularly to Jan van der Made of Radio France International.

Last, but certainly not least, Peter Sowden of Routledge has skilfully steered this book, like previous volumes, though the production process with exactly the right combination of encouragement, firmness, and tact. I am also grateful to anonymous reviewers who have been both critical and constructive and to the eagle-eyed and tactful copy editors. The sole responsibility for any inaccuracies and omissions in the text rests, as it properly should, with the author.

Michael Dillon
Sherwood Forest
January 2021

Chronology

Key imperial dynasties

Qin 221–207 BC
Han 206 BC – 220 AD
Tang 618–907
Song 960–1127
Yuan 1271–1368 (Mongol)
Ming 1368–1644
Qing 1644–1911 (Manchu)

Modern period

Qing dynasty 1644–1911
Republic of China 1912–1949
Republic of China on Taiwan 1949 to the present day
People's Republic of China 1949 to the present day

1839–1842 Opium War
1842 Treaty of Nanjing – Hong Kong ceded to Britain
1898 New Territories ceded to Britain
1899–1901 Boxer Rebellion
1908 Death of Empress Dowager
1911 Revolution overthrows Qing dynasty
1912 Republic of China proclaimed
1912 Sun Yat-sen relinquishes presidency to Yuan Shikai
1915 Japanese Twenty-One Demands for control over China
1919 May Fourth Movement – modern Chinese nationalism born
1921 Chinese Communist Party founded
1923 Guomindang GMD (Kuomintang) reorganised.
1923 CCP and GMD cooperate in First United Front
1925 Death of Sun Yat-sen
1926 Northern Expedition to unify China
1927 CCP and GMD split after Shanghai massacre
1928 GMD National Government in Nanjing
1929–1934 CCP establishes rural bases in Jiangxi province
1931 Japanese invasion of Manchuria

1934–1936 CCP Long March to Yan'an base

1937 (July) Japanese invasion of China Proper

1937 (September) CCP and GMD Second United Front

1945 Japanese surrender

1946 Civil War breaks out between CCP and GMD

1949 People's Republic of China founded

1950–1953 Korean War

1955 Bandung Conference of non-aligned nations

1956 Hundred Flowers Movement

1957 Anti-Rightist Campaign

1958 Great Leap Forward and creation of People's Communes

1959 Lushan conferences and dismissal of Peng Dehuai

1966 Cultural Revolution begins

1969 Ninth Communist Party Congress

1971 Death of Lin Biao

1972 US President Nixon visits China

1975 Death of Chiang Kai-shek

1976 (September) Death of Mao Zedong

1976 (October) Arrest of Gang of Four

1978 Third Plenum of 11th CCP Central Committee

1978 Reform period begins under Deng Xiaoping

1980–1981 Trial of Gang of Four

1987 Hu Yaobang dismissed as CCP General Secretary

1987 Zhao Ziyang replaces Hu as CCP General Secretary

1989 (4 June) Tian'anmen Square demonstrations suppressed

1989 (24 June) Jiang Zemin replaces Zhao Ziyang as CCP General Secretary

1989 Deng Xiaoping retires

1997 (February) Death of Deng Xiaoping

1997 (July) Hong Kong returns to China

1999 (May) Chinese embassy in Belgrade hit by NATO bombs

1999 (July) Falungong demonstrations

2001 (April) US fighter plane incident off Hainan island

2001 (December) China enters WTO

2002 (November) SARS epidemic

2002 (November) CCP 16th Congress – Hu Jintao General Secretary

2003 Hu Jintao President

2003 Avian influenza epidemic

2006 (January) Agricultural taxation abolished

2007 (October) CCP 17th Congress – Xi Jinping tipped as future leader

2008 (August) Olympic Games in Beijing

2012 Xi Jinping CCP General Secretary

2013 Xi Jinping President

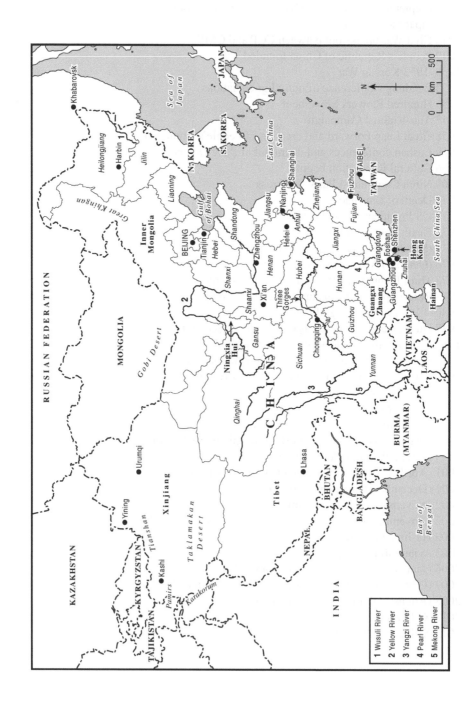

Part 1
Introduction

1 Land, people, and culture

China as a sub-continent

Although China is in many ways a country like any other – Denmark, say, or Ecuador or Nigeria – in view of its size and diversity, it is more realistic to think of it as a sub-continent. It is commonplace to speak of the countries of South Asia as the Indian sub-continent, a term which accurately reflects the size of the landmass; the geographical diversity; the variety of peoples, languages, religions and cultures; and the political differences of the states of which that region is composed. China has all of these, including the political division between the mainland and Taiwan, but it is usually treated, by Chinese and foreign observers, as a single homogeneous entity. If it is viewed as a sub-continent, as well as a nation, the geographical and cultural complexity underlying its history and the evolution of its political structures become clearer.

There is resistance, often intense resistance – by the government of the People's Republic of China (PRC), and by many Chinese people – to suggestions that China is, or ever has been, anything other than a single unified entity. This is invariably motivated by a sense of national pride or patriotism. From that point of view, to regard China in any other way leaves open the door to federalism or, worse still, to separatism – the possibility, however unlikely, that Tibet, Xinjiang, Inner Mongolia, or even one of the more prosperous southern provinces might achieve independence from the mainland: Taiwan's *de facto* independence is not recognised by Beijing. Citizens of China are acutely aware of the historical legacy of division and weakness that made it possible for a disaggregated China to be colonised partially by the West in the nineteenth century and subsequently, after a period of division between warring provincial military governments in the early twentieth century, to be invaded by Japan, which occupied much of Chinese territory between 1931 and 1945. A strong, unified China, it is argued, is the only way of preventing a repetition of that period of national humiliation. There is merit in that argument, but it severely inhibits discussion of possible alternatives to the historical and contemporary configurations of China's polity, such as regionalism and federalism.

Size

China is vast by any standards: it extends from a point 54° north latitude, on the Wusuli (Ussuri) river in the northern part of Heilongjiang province, which has a border with the Russian Far East, to 18° north, the southern point of the semi-tropical island of Hainan. It stretches for 3,000 miles across the eastern part of the Eurasian land mass from the most westerly part of Xinjiang at 74° east longitude to a point 135° east longitude, which is just to the west of the city of Khabarovsk. Westerners, especially Europeans, tend to assume that all of Russia lies to the west of China, but it is also a northern neighbour. China occupies an area of 3,657,765 square miles and has a land border of some 13,800 miles, mostly with Central Asia: it has a coastline that is over 9,000 miles long and functions as an important maritime frontier. Some of these figures may be disputed because of long-standing and unresolved boundary disputes, but they give a clear sense of the orders of magnitude involved in considering the geography of China. Because of the size and diversity of the country, it is essential that great care is taken when making generalisations about any aspect of Chinese society.

The population of China, which was 582 million when the 1953 census was carried out (the first in the entire history of China that had any degree of credibility),[1] has grown at a rate which is either impressive or alarming, according to the observer's point of view: it stood in 2019 at approximately 1.4 billion. This makes China the most populous nation on earth, a distinction it has held for decades, although India with a total population of 1.37 billion is gradually catching up. It is instructive to compare figures for China's population with other countries and regions. In 2019, the United Kingdom had an estimated population of almost 67 million, compared with the population of the Chinese province of Hubei, which is about 60 million; the whole of Europe, depending on how it is defined, is home to 747 million people who live on 6.5 million square miles of land shared by 44 separate nation-states; the United States has a total population of 329 million. The total land area of North America is 9.45 million square miles, and it has a combined population of over 514 million. In 2020, Taiwan had a population of 23.7 million and a declining birth rate, while in the former British colony of Hong Kong, there are only 7.5 million inhabitants.[2] Population size is far from being the only determinant of a nation's character and prospects for development and stability, but it is a critical factor.

Great rivers of China

In common with all civilisations of great antiquity, China owes the earliest development of its agriculture and settlement to the great rivers that flow through its territory. The two best known, and by far the most important in the story of China's development as a nation, are the Yellow River and the Yangzi.

The source of the Yellow River (Huanghe) is at a height of 14,000 feet in the mountains of Qinghai province close to the Kokonor: in the Mongolian language, Kokonor means Blue Lake, which is also what Qinghai means in Chinese. The Yellow River runs for over 3,000 miles through northern China and into the Gulf of Bohai to the north of the promontory of Shandong province. On its long journey to the ocean, the Yellow River describes a magnificent arc through the deserts and plains of China's borders with Mongolia and then bends sharply into the low-lying farmland of the eastern seaboard, farmland that the might of the river has been instrumental in creating. It is called the Yellow River because of the yellow or brown silt that it carries from the mountains down to the plains. The silt contributes to a fine grained, easily worked loess soil that has enabled China's farmers to till the land for centuries. The Chinese word *huang* covers a wider spectrum of colour than the English 'yellow' and includes light to medium browns. Similarly, the Chinese character for *qing* in Qinghai can be dark blue, or green or even black.

The waters of the Yellow River irrigate this loess terrain. However, the silt that has been such a boon to rural China has also destroyed it periodically: the accumulation of silt deposits builds up over time and causes the river to burst its banks, flooding the farms and villages of the North China Plain and causing great loss of life, as well as physical devastation and economic and social disruption. In one fateful year, 1851, the spectacular intensity of the flooding forced the river to change its course. Before the inundation, it flowed into the ocean south of the Shandong peninsula; after the flood it emerged to the north, at its present exit point. Not for nothing has the Yellow River been called 'China's sorrow'.

The river that the world calls the Yangzi (Yangtse) is known in China as the Changjiang; this simply means Long River, which it is, at a total length of 3,964 miles. It flows from its source high on the Tibetan Plateau through spectacular gorges, passes through the very centre of China and spills out into the Yellow Sea just to the north of Shanghai. Its great breadth is as significant as its great length. For centuries it was impossible to bridge the torrent along hundreds of miles of its length and, in many places, it is still necessary to use a ferry to cross from one bank to the other. The construction of the great bridge at Nanjing, which was completed in 1969 during the Cultural Revolution, was proclaimed a major triumph for Chinese engineers and for the collective spirit of the PRC.

Because of the difficulty that there has always been in crossing the Changjiang, the river was a major physical barrier; it is the natural boundary between northern and southern China, a separation that accounts in part for the pronounced cultural differences between the north and the south. The productive rice-growing areas of the south were traditionally known as Jiangnan ('south of the river', that is to the south of the Changjiang) and these areas have retained distinctive spoken languages and cultures which, especially in the more remote rural areas, are quite unlike those of the northern, Mandarin-speaking part of China.

The Three Gorges hydroelectric project which dams the upper reaches of the river is a colossal and controversial feat of engineering which began in 1993 and has submerged some 1,200 towns and villages, and displaced thousands of local residents. It has been criticised by environmental campaigners, and many have blamed it for the increased pollution of the river. A more detailed consideration of the Three Gorges project can be found in Chapter 20.

The Pearl River, or Zhujiang, is vital to the regional economy of south China. It is China's third longest river and is formed from the confluence of three smaller rivers: the Xi Jiang (West River), the Bei Jiang (North River), and the Dong Jiang (East River). The river and its tributaries flow through the provinces of Hunan, Jiangxi, Guizhou, Yunnan, Guangxi, and Guangdong before draining into the South China Sea in the great Pearl River Delta.

The Pearl River Delta is home to some of the most dynamic and enterprising urban economies of contemporary China, including the pioneering Special Economic Zone of Shenzhen, where Deng Xiaoping's reform policies were first displayed to the outside world; Zhuhai with its modern high-tech industries; and the old iron and porcelain town of Foshan. The delta has grown into one of the economic boom centres of post-Mao China and specialises in manufacturing, notably electronics and other consumer goods for the export market. This region is increasingly known in China as the Guangdong-Hong Kong-Macao Greater Bay Area (*Yue Gang Ao Dawanqu*). This is as much a political statement as a geographical description, and reflects the intention of the government of the PRC to integrate Hong Kong with the existing areas of southern China under the 'one country, two systems' model.

Mountains

Mountain ranges have always been the historical and natural boundaries between provinces in southern China. Mountainous terrain, which is difficult to farm and challenging to cross, has hampered communications and economic development over the centuries, although the lack of land routes has been compensated for by the abundance of natural waterways – lakes and rivers – which have played an important role in communications and commerce in the south.

The Tianshan (Mountains of Heaven) and the Pamirs mark the geographical frontiers of western China and the PRC's borders with Kazakhstan, Kyrgyzstan, and Tajikistan, although the Tianshan range (Tengri Tagh in Uyghur and other Central Asian languages) also extends into northern Xinjiang to the north of the Taklamakan Desert. The Karakorum mountain range, part of the Himalaya chain and home to K2, the second highest peak in the world, separates China from Kashmir and Pakistan; the eastern ranges of the Himalayas are the boundary between China and India. In the northeast of China, the Great Khingan (Xing'an in Chinese) range of volcanic mountains forms the geographical boundary between the plains of Manchuria and the high plateau of Mongolia.

Geography and development

Economic and social development in China have never been uniform; there are major differences between the north and south, partly because of geographical factors. The northern climate is drier; it is difficult to guarantee regular sources of water for agriculture and there is a constant underlying threat of desertification. The south experiences rainfall in much greater abundance. This makes it possible to grow sufficient rice to feed large populations, in some areas by multiple cropping, but the drawbacks are the risk of flooding and the threat of tropical storms and typhoons which regularly assault the coastal regions of the southeast, often with devastating effect on settlements, lives and crops.

Throughout recorded history, almost all the capitals of unified Chinese states have been in the north; the paramount strategic necessity of defending agricultural China from the nomads of the steppes of Inner Asia shaped communications and settlement for centuries.

There is a striking contrast between the relatively high level of development in the eastern and southeastern coastal regions and the economic and cultural backwardness of the interior (the western regions). Although this disparity has a historical pedigree that can be traced back for hundreds of years, it was exacerbated by the creation of the treaty ports and their hinterlands under the influence of Western colonisation in the 19th century. The discrepancy in levels of development between eastern and western China has increased dramatically during the economic expansion that has taken place since 1978. One economic marker that illustrates the different level of development is Gross Domestic Product (GDP), which broadly speaking represents the total value of all goods and services produced. Per-capita figures for the GDP of individual provinces and cities illustrate the difference between the coastal (the first group) and inland western (the second group) regions of China.

GDP per capita in RMB 2019[3]

Shanghai	157,279
Jiangsu	123,607
Zhejiang	107,624
Fujian	107,139
Shaanxi	66,644
Gansu	32,994
Ningxia	54,217
Guizhou	46,433

Provinces, autonomous regions, and municipalities

The major administrative sub-divisions of China are its 22 provinces and five autonomous regions (ARs) – Tibet (Xizang), Xinjiang Uyghur, Inner Mongolia (Nei Monggol), Ningxia Hui, and Guangxi Zhuang – which are provincial-level administrations that exercise a degree of autonomy (in reality only token autonomy) in deference to the large populations of non-Han Chinese people who have lived in them for centuries. Provinces and autonomous regions are further subdivided into prefectures and then counties: prefectures and counties are always based on urban administrative centres. In provinces that are not autonomous regions, but where there are concentrations of ethnic minority communities, there are also autonomous prefectures and counties.

Towns and cities may serve as provincial, prefectural, or county centres, but the largest cities – Beijing, Chongqing, Shanghai and Tianjin – are municipal administrations in their own right. In addition to the central urban areas, they have responsibility for surrounding tracts of rural land.

Languages and cultures

Chinese is the principal language of China, but it is not the only language and, more importantly, it is not even one single language. The official language of the country and its lingua franca is known today as *putonghua*, which translates as 'common language' and which purists tend to call Standard Chinese. In Taiwan, it is still known as *Kuo-yu* (in pinyin, *Guoyu*) which translates as 'national language', a term that was common on the mainland in the 1930s and 1940s and in recent years has reappeared in the PRC. Singaporeans refer to it as Huayu, 'Chinese language'. Standard Chinese is almost universally known in the English-speaking world as Mandarin, an even more old-fashioned term than Kuo-yu and one which was used of the court language of the Qing period (1644–1911). This language, indispensable for administrative discourse by imperial officials, was known in Chinese as *guanhua* 'official language'. The English name, Mandarin, is often said to derive from *mandar*, meaning 'to give orders' in the language of the Portuguese colonisers but probably originates in the Malay *Menteri*, derived in turn from Sanskrit *mantrī*, both of which mean 'minster' or 'counsellor'.

Mandarin, or Standard Chinese, is in fact a standardised form of the spoken language of the region of northern China that includes the capital, Beijing. It is not, however, spoken universally, even in the capital itself where there is a Beijing dialect (*Beijing tuhua*) which is used by the local people and which can take some time for even seasoned speakers of Standard Chinese to get used to. Mandarin is the official spoken language of television and radio and is taught in all schools: in theory, everyone in China should understand *putonghua* even if they are more comfortable speaking a dialect of Mandarin or one of the southern variants of Chinese.

There are various dialects of Mandarin throughout the north and northwest of China, the most noticeable difference being between the northern and southern dialect areas. Anyone who has ventured far from the major urban centres will have become aware of the great variations in pronunciation within the rural population of the Mandarin-speaking area. Because of the awareness of the existence of dialects within Mandarin, it has become more usual to see the other varieties of Chinese, which were once referred to as dialects, now promoted to the status of languages. This recognises the linguistic reality since they are as different from each other as the languages of say the Romance family in Europe – Portuguese and Romanian, for example. Regional forms of speech that are spoken a great distance apart, especially in the rural areas, are mutually incomprehensible, have quite distinct vocabularies, and to some extent, different grammars.

The most important non-Mandarin Chinese languages are: Cantonese, which is the principal language of Guangdong province and Hong Kong and is also used very widely as a lingua franca among the communities of the Chinese diaspora in Europe and North America; the Shanghai or Wu language of eastern China; and Fujianese or Hokkien from the southeastern province of Fujian, which is also spoken by a majority of the population of Taiwan, whose ancestors migrated from Fujian in the eighteenth and nineteenth centuries. In Taiwan, this form of Chinese is often referred to as Taiwanese to distinguish it from the Mandarin or *Kuo-yu* spoken by the ruling mainlander elite. Technically, it is Minnan or Southern Min: both Northern Min and Southern Min are spoken in Fujian on the mainland. Fujianese is also important in the Chinese communities of Indonesia, Malaysia, and other parts of Southeast Asia. Hakka is unusual in that it is a language with distinctly northern features that is spoken in several provinces of southern China, possibly as a result of migrations in centuries past. There are many speakers of Hakka in Taiwan and the Chinese diaspora.

What is unusual about the condition of language in China is that, while each of these regions has its own distinct spoken vernacular, they all use one single form of written Chinese – based on the grammar and vocabulary of Mandarin Chinese – for most practical purposes. This is possible because Chinese characters are not essentially phonetic. Written characters do include some elements to indicate phonetic values, but these are not regular enough to be a reliable indication of the pronunciation of characters: pronunciation must be learned separately for each character. Since a high level of literacy requires familiarity with thousands of characters, this is a demanding task. There are in existence variant written forms which are used in certain circumstances to represent the local idiom in, for example, popular regional drama, but all newspapers, magazines, books (including textbooks for schools), and the internet use the standard written language.

However, this standard written language appears in one of two forms of script: the older form, which is retained in Taiwan (where Mandarin is the main language) and Hong Kong (where spoken Chinese is primarily Cantonese), as well as in many expatriate communities; and the simplified script, which was created in the PRC as part of a programme of language reform in the 1950s. This reform was part of the CCP's efforts to grapple with the serious and enduring problem of illiteracy, especially in the countryside. Simplified Chinese characters, which are based on the original characters – sometimes their informal or cursive forms – but with a reduced number of brush or pen strokes, are disliked and even rejected by many Chinese who live outside the mainland. They are avoided in Taiwan because of their association with the CCP, although these objections are often couched in terms of aesthetics and readability rather than politics. Written styles also vary: Taiwan and Hong Kong favour prose styles that retain echoes of the classical Chinese tradition and tend to be terser and arguably more elegant, whereas writing on the mainland has deliberately remained closer to the spoken vernaculars as part of a policy of popularisation and in the hope that this would assist the spread of literacy. As China opened culturally to the rest of the Chinese world, there has been greater contact between these styles. Writers on the mainland have felt able to use more complex styles of writing that would once have looked out of place. The simplified script is also seen in Hong Kong, although the traditional version predominates.

Chinese is not unique in this separation of standard written and local spoken forms: the near universal use of a standard form of written Arabic throughout the Middle East disguises the fact that there exists a variety of very different and often mutually unintelligible spoken vernaculars, but the separation between spoken and written Chinese is much greater than that between spoken and written Arabic.

Notes

1 Leo A. Orleans *Every Fifth Child: The Population of China* London: Eyre Methuen, 1972, p. 17; *Handbook on Peoples China* Beijing: Foreign Languages Press, 1957, pp. 13–15; National Statistics, Republic of China (Taiwan) https://eng.stat.gov.tw/point.asp?index=9; Census and Statistics Department, Hong Kong Government https://www.censtatd.gov.hk/hkstat/sub/so20.jsp.
2 Central News Agency, Taipei, 15 November 2006.
3 National Economic Census, National Bureau of Statistics. The Western Development Plan to counteract these discrepancies is discussed in Chapter 12.

2   China's past in the present

Some appreciation of the historical background is essential for an understanding of the colossal changes in China during the twentieth and twenty-first centuries. The historical legacy, which continues to influence attitudes in contemporary China, includes: the Opium War and the impact of the West in the nineteenth century; peasant rebellions; cultural nationalism, which was in part a response to challenges posed by the West; the abortive Republican experiment of 1912–1913 and the collapse into Balkanised regional warlord regimes; the military occupation by Japan during the Second World War; Civil War between Communists and Nationalists; the rise of Mao Zedong; and the radical experiments of the Great Leap Forward and the Cultural Revolution. Some of these events remain fresh in the minds of the older generation. They are also familiar to younger people from studies at school, although mediated through the officially approved analysis, and in popular culture, notably films of wartime heroism at the cinema and on television.

The CCP has been in power on the mainland of China since 1949 and remains so at the time of writing. There has been no effective opposition and, until the suppression of the Democracy Movement in and around Tian'anmen Square in June 1989, CCP rule appeared to be completely unassailable. The CCP recovered from even that trauma: it reformed and restructured itself and has every intention of retaining power indefinitely. Whether it will succeed, and what will happen if it does not, are of fundamental concern for anyone interested in the future of China and, as China's global influence spreads, of the world.

The rise of the CCP and the revolutionary movement it spearheaded can be traced back to the colonisation of parts of Qing dynasty China by European powers, and later the United States and Japan, in the late nineteenth and early twentieth centuries. This encroachment culminated in the scramble for territorial concessions in 1898, the suppression of the Boxer uprising by foreign troops in 1900–1901, and the 1911 collapse of not only the Manchu Qing dynasty, which had demonstrably failed to resist pressure from the foreign powers, but the 2,000-year-old Chinese imperial system.

Two thousand years of imperial tradition

From 1644–1911, China was ruled by the Manchu Qing dynasty, the last in a long line of ruling houses that, by Chinese convention, stretches back in an unbroken line to the unification of the feudal warring states by the First Emperor, Qin Shi Huangdi, in 221 BC. A list of all the dynasties of imperial China in chronological order provides a comforting illusion of continuity and stability, but the transition from one dynasty to another was rarely peaceful. Typically, the ruling elite of a declining dynasty lost the confidence of all or part of the population; its authority waned during a period of court scandals or peasant rebellion, and a new elite came to power. The victors would claim that they now possessed the Mandate of Heaven [*tianming*] which the vanquished regime was deemed to have lost by virtue of its defeat.

Not all the dynasties that ruled China were 'Chinese', in the sense that not all were of ethnic Han Chinese origin. The Chinese state and Chinese society evolved through the perennial conflict between the steppe and the sown; between the nomad stock breeders of the northern and western high pasture lands and the settled rice and millet farmers of the fertile basins created by the Yangzi and the Yellow River. Some of the most important dynasties in Chinese history were of 'non-Chinese' (or, as far as many Chinese were concerned, 'barbarian') origin. The court and aristocracy of the Yuan dynasty were Mongolian and, of the Qing dynasty, Manchu; both of these ruling elites had their origins in nomadic tribal confederations from the vast regions to the north of China. Their languages, cultures, and traditions were quite unlike those of the Han Chinese, although proximity, trade, and conflict over the centuries had led to linguistic and cultural borrowing in both directions. Realistically, and in spite of the compilers of genealogies, there were few 'pure' Chinese or non-Chinese ruling houses. Intermarriage and concubinage brought new blood into the elites, whether or not this was acknowledged.

Manchus, Chinese, and the West

The forces that led to the disintegration of the Chinese Empire had their origins in the relationship between the Manchu elite and the Han majority, and were the wellspring of the nationalist movement of the late nineteenth and early twentieth centuries. Although the Manchus brought able Mongols, Muslims, and Han Chinese into their administration – they had little option as it was impossible for them to rule on their own – their garrisons, which were stationed strategically throughout China, were a visible reminder that the country was under the control of alien rulers. Conflicts arose between the Manchu and Chinese elites (there were far fewer Mongols), particularly over the most important issues such as relations with the West and the development of the economy. When there were serious difficulties or dangers, blaming the alien Manchus was the obvious solution for sophisticated Chinese thinkers, as well as for less educated peasant leaders. The most popular target was the Empress Dowager, Cixi, frequently demonised but, on the basis of the available evidence, unquestionably culpable of many of the crimes of which she was accused. As a woman who ruled in what, according to Confucian orthodoxy, could only ever be a man's role, she could be blamed for bringing down the wrath of heaven on China and endangering the Qing dynasty's entitlement to the Mandate of Heaven. It was not forgotten that she was Yehonala, of the ruling Aisin Gioro clan of the Manchus, a foreign tribe holding sway over the sacred territory [*shenzhou*] of the Middle Kingdom.

As early as the late eighteenth century, notwithstanding the success of the Kangxi and (particularly) the Qianlong emperors in military conquest and territorial aggrandisement, the position of the Qing dynasty was already under attack from rural religious rebels influenced by popular religious traditions, many of them associated with Buddhism and Daoism. It was not, however, this internal conflict that precipitated a crisis of state and of confidence, but the increasing demands of the West for trade.

Unable to obtain by negotiation the trading privileges they desired, and after the failure of several costly diplomatic missions, including the Macartney Embassy of 1793, the West, principally Great Britain, engineered a military confrontation – the Opium War of 1839–1842. It was the determination of the Qing court to bring to an end the British sale of opium to China that led to hostilities: on both sides, however, it was widely accepted that the issues in contention were far greater than just the trade in a narcotic, however much this was resented by China. At stake were China's territorial integrity and the question of who should exercise control over its foreign trade.

Defeat in the Opium War forced the court in Beijing to sign the Treaty of Nanjing in 1842, the first in a series of what are known in China as 'unequal' treaties. Under this and subsequent agreements, most of which were imposed on China by force or the threat of force, a number of coastal and river cities – the treaty ports – were opened to trade with the West, Christian missionaries were permitted to proselytise among the predominantly Buddhist and Daoist population of the hinterland, and perhaps most important of all, the island of Hong Kong was handed over to Britain. For Britain, Hong Kong was to become a prized and productive colonial possession; to China, it was an ever-present reminder of defeat and humiliation which was not resolved until the handover of July 1997. China was never completely colonised in the way that Britain had earlier taken control of India, but European (and later American and Japanese) merchants, administrators, and military personnel established themselves in the foreign-controlled concession areas in ports such as Shanghai, Tianjin, and Guangzhou, governing great swathes of territory with embassy-style privileges and keeping the locals at arm's length, unless they were required for trade or menial work. This semi-colonialism, as some called it, rankled with many thinking Chinese, although it also provided a source of economic and social advancement for a small class of merchants and entrepreneurs – the compradors – who were prepared to transact business with the foreigners and who also remained on good terms with the local Chinese administration.

Republican failure

The revolution of 1911 began as a minor mutiny of army units in the garrison of Wuchang (part of present-day Wuhan) and spread like wildfire throughout the whole country, precipitating the disintegration of the centralised bureaucratic administration of Qing China. A Republic was proclaimed in 1912 to replace the Qing dynasty, but it never took a firm hold of the country: the Napoleonic attempt in 1916 of the first President, Yuan Shikai, who had seized power from Sun Yat-sen, to have himself declared Emperor exposed the fragile basis of the new system. The early Republic persisted in name but in practice collapsed into a network of regionally based warlord kingdoms which formed fluid alliances with each other but were also in constant conflict. From 1917–1927, these warlords were the *de facto* rulers of China: central government was either weak or non-existent. China, a predominantly peasant society, suffered endemic poverty and disease, as well as periodic and widespread famines, some of which had catastrophic effects on the land and the people. Educated Chinese were conscious of the plight of their country and many were deeply ashamed and angry at the depths of degradation and humiliation into which their great nation had fallen.

In response, a Nationalist movement arose, advocating the overthrow of the warlords and the restoration of a unified national political structure. Most of its supporters rejected the old imperial structure – even in a revised form such as a constitutional monarchy – and favoured a republic as the most appropriate form of government for China. Two strands of nationalism, one associated with the Guomindang (Kuomintang or Nationalist Party) and the other with the CCP, emerged in the early 1920s.

The catalyst for the upsurge of nationalism was the treatment of China by the major international powers in the peace settlement that followed the signing of the Treaty of Versailles in June 1919 after the end of the First World War (1914–1918). Most educated Chinese who followed international developments had assumed that territorial concessions secured by Germany at the end of the nineteenth century would be returned to China after the allied victory; China had, at least nominally, been an ally of Britain. However, these concessions were transferred to Japan, in recognition of Tokyo's pact with Britain, the Anglo-Japanese Alliance of 1902, and Japan's nominal alliance with France during the war. The Japanese army and navy had played little part in the conflict, but the parties drawing up the treaty were conscious of Japan's status as the emerging great power in the Pacific. In China, the widespread demonstrations of the May Fourth Movement which followed the announcement in 1919 of the treaty provisions were accompanied by the New Culture Movement, a profound questioning of the nature of Chinese society and China's place in the world.

Birth of the CCP and Guomindang

Trade unions had been developing in Hong Kong, Shanghai, Guangzhou (Canton), and many other major Chinese cities, and they flexed their muscles in a series of strikes that Marxist activists helped to organise. It was in this setting that the CCP was formally established in 1921 with advice and support from the Comintern in Moscow; it held its founding conference in the grounds of a girls' school in Shanghai from 13–21 July (although the official birthday of the Party is 1 July). The 12 delegates who attended represented a total membership of 57 and the conference was obliged to repair to a boat on a lake for fear of informers. This was a small and inauspicious beginning for the Party that was to take control of China within less than 30 years.

At the same time, Sun Yat-sen, the leading nationalist revolutionary in China, also accepted offers of support from the newly created Soviet Union and its international arm, the Comintern. This was not because of any ideological attachment to Marxism, but because he admired the discipline and organisation of the Communist Party of the Soviet Union (CPSU). The Guomindang (GMD) under Sun Yat-sen was reorganised along the centralist and Leninist lines of the CPSU in 1923. Sun died on 12 March 1925, and his place as political and military leader was taken by Chiang Kai-shek (Jiang Jieshi) who had been commandant of the Huangpu (Whampoa) Military Academy in Guangzhou, a college charged by Sun with the responsibility of creating a modern officer corps for the GMD's new army.

First United Front and the Long March

It is ironic, in the light of their subsequent history of conflict and enmity, that both the CCP and the GMD in their early days were supported by the Moscow-based Comintern. This was partly because Stalin's theories of national revolution required an alliance between a bourgeois and a proletarian party, and partly because of the practical consideration that the CCP was considered far too weak to be an independent political force. The policy of the Comintern was that the two Chinese parties should cooperate; during what was known as the First United Front (1923–1927), CCP members joined the GMD while still retaining membership of their own party. They supported the National Revolutionary Army (NRA), which was controlled by the GMD and which Chiang Kai-shek led on what he announced was to be the movement's Northern Expedition from his base in Guangzhou in southern China to recover China from the warlords and establish a national government. This alliance came to an abrupt and grisly end in Shanghai in April 1927 while the Northern Expedition was still underway. Nationalist troops, assisted by members of Shanghai's criminal underworld, imprisoned or killed Communists and suspected sympathisers and broke up the trade union organisations that had been their main source of support.

The immediate response of the CCP to what they condemned a historic betrayal was to launch a series of urban insurrections. When these failed disastrously, the CCP was forced to abandon its offices in the cities and gradually regrouped in China's vast rural interior. Cut off from the urban labour movement, from the Nationalists, and from Western and modern ideas, the CCP underwent a profound transformation, first in its base camp at Jinggangshan on the border of Jiangxi province in south-central China, and then during a period of experimental independent government in the Jiangxi Soviet, a region in the south of Jiangxi province governed by the CCP from 1930 to 1934. Guomindang siege tactics, known as encirclement campaigns, finally forced the CCP to abandon its base in Jiangxi and it embarked on its legendary Long March, the epic strategic withdrawal that took it to the remote mountainous region of Yan'an in northwest China's Shaanxi province.

Yan'an and Mao Zedong

The Communists – or, to be more precise, one contingent of the CCP – arrived in the small town of Yan'an between September 1935 and October 1936, and it was in the traditional peasant cave houses of this mountain redoubt that Mao Zedong consolidated his leadership over what was to become the most successful section of the Party. The CCP also acquired a new ideology in Yan'an – Marxism-Leninism-Mao Zedong Thought. This was a highly idiosyncratic synthesis of crude mechanical Marxism drawn from such editions of the works of Stalin (and other theoretical studies from the Union of Soviet Socialist Republics [USSR]) as had been available in Chinese translation, underpinned by the romance of the Chinese rebel and revolutionary tradition which particularly attracted Mao Zedong. This mixture of philosophy and political dogma is often known in the West as Maoism for the sake of brevity, although this usage has never been popular in China.

The CCP that emerged from these harsh experiences was quite different from the party that had grown up in the metropolises of Shanghai, Hong Kong, Tianjin (Tientsin), Guangzhou (Canton) and Beijing in the 1920s. Its orientation was almost entirely rural. There was a constant drive to recruit peasants through a series of campaigns for land redistribution and rent reduction and, after the Japanese invasion of China in September 1937, the emphasis shifted to patriotism and resistance. The transformation of the CCP was so profound that many orthodox Communists would not acknowledge it as a genuine Communist party. In 1927, the Communists also created the Workers' and Peasants' Red Army, which had a close and symbiotic relationship with the Party and an overlapping membership.

Japan and Civil War

The Japanese invasion of 1937 dramatically altered the balance of power in China. The Nationalist GMD government under Chiang Kai-shek was forced to flee from its capital, Nanjing (Nanking in the spelling current at the time), and establish a temporary base in Chongqing (Chungking) in the southwestern province of Sichuan. The Japanese armies of occupation controlled the most populous parts of China, the east and the southeast – or at least they held the main towns and cities, and the railway links between them. The Communists consolidated their power base in the northwest and developed a strategy of guerrilla resistance behind enemy lines. A formal agreement between the GMD and CCP to combine their forces in a Second United Front for the War of Resistance against Japan led to limited military cooperation. From 1937 onwards, the military units of the Workers' and Peasants' Red Army were nominally under unified national control, adopting neutral names such as the Eighth Route Army and the New Fourth Army, but in practice they retained considerable operational and political independence.

With the defeat of Japan in August 1945 following the atomic bombings of Hiroshima and Nagasaki, the War of Resistance metamorphosed almost imperceptibly into a bitter Civil War between the Guomindang Nationalists and the CCP which lasted from 1946–1949, although there were ill-fated attempts by US diplomats to broker a coalition government of the two parties. The Civil War ended with the defeat of the GMD and its flight to the island of Taiwan, where the Nationalists continued their government, led by Chiang Kai-shek until his death in 1975, and maintained their claim to be the only legitimate authority for the whole of China.

CCP in power

The CCP emerged victorious from the Civil War in 1949, largely because of the patriotic reputation it had acquired through its guerrilla resistance, albeit somewhat exaggerated, to the Japanese invasion; its land reform policies which earned it widespread support from peasants; and the sheer incompetence and corruption of the GMD political and military leadership. A close reading of sources published in the late 1940s indicates that there was no realistic alternative to the CCP, whatever anyone might have felt about its background or policies.

The CCP made the difficult transition from revolutionary military force to civilian administration, a transformation that had many historical antecedents in the rise and fall of Chinese dynasties. A series of ruthless political campaigns in the cities removed Guomindang supporters from influential positions, and the old urban elite was gradually replaced by a new cadre of CCP sympathisers. In the rural areas, land reform teams led by the military and educated young CCP activists secured Communist control over outlying areas by means of the land reform strategy of confiscating land from wealthy owners and redistributing it to the poor. This was implemented throughout almost the entire country and guaranteed for the CCP the support of the poorest people in the rural areas.

The authority of the CCP was strengthened by China's participation in the Korean War on the side of North Korea. The domestic prestige of the People's Liberation Army (PLA), already high after its victory in the Civil War, rose even higher. The perception of an external threat, and a genuine and justified fear that UN (United Nations) troops led by the United States might take the opportunity to restore Chiang Kai-shek to power on the mainland, created a combination of patriotism and paranoia that enabled the state to equate opposition to the CCP with treason. When the armistice that ended the Korean War was signed in 1953, China was isolated from the West but arguably more unified under a strong government, dominated by the CCP but with extensive popular support for the involvement of other interest groups in the creation of a 'New China'. Popular policies, which included land reform and a marriage law that aimed at equality between men and women, were followed by a Five-Year Plan to develop the economy on the Soviet model. This was the case for most of China Proper, where the Han were in the majority – the situation in Tibet, Xinjiang, and Inner Mongolia was more complicated.

This apparent cohesion and unity of purpose masked significant dissent and disputes, even within the CCP elite: during the 1960s, divisions began to appear over the appropriate strategy for developing China. The 1958 Great Leap Forward was an attempt by Mao Zedong, in his view, to drag China kicking and screaming into the age of industrialisation. His strategy was to speed up and consolidate the collectivisation of agriculture while simultaneously increasing the national output of iron, steel, coal, and electric power for industrial development. More cautious members of the CCP hierarchy opposed this audacious but impractical approach; there was forthright criticism and robust opposition, but it was mainly in private. Far from overtaking Great Britain – one of Mao's stated aims – the mismanagement of the Great Leap was the main cause of 20 million or 30 million excess deaths in 1959–1960, three years in which rural China was devastated by terrible famines. There had been catastrophic famines in China long before Mao and the CCP, but far from mitigating the effects of the famines, as some claimed at the time, government policies – including the transfer of farmers from agriculture to the production of iron and steel in the over-enthusiastic drive to industrialise – made it more difficult to produce food crops and to share what was available.

The 'Maoist' approach of mass mobilisation and the politicisation of daily life was temporarily replaced by the cautious and pragmatic approach of Liu Shaoqi, Deng Xiaoping, Zhou Enlai, and others who acted more like Soviet-style central planners. Mao was held personally responsible for the catastrophe, although he was never criticised publicly at the time, and for several years his power and influence were diminished. In the early 1960s, China appeared to be reverting to a more conventional planned economy under a conservative bureaucratic structure.

Cultural Revolution

The Great Proletarian Cultural Revolution was launched in the summer of 1966 as a mass movement to rid the country of old-fashioned bourgeois culture (although an authentic bourgeois culture of the type that flourished in Europe had never existed in China), and to replace it with genuine proletarian culture. This was exemplified by vituperative criticism of traditional Beijing opera with its mandarins, mannered scholars and beautiful but fragile heroines, and the creation of alternative revolutionary operas to replace them. The resilient heroes of the new operas were workers, peasants, and soldiers, and some were even women: their milieu was no longer the court or the wealthy landowning family estate, but the docks or the mountains during the War of Resistance against Japan.

The Cultural Revolution had never been primarily about culture, although attacking his political enemies in the cultural elite suited Mao Zedong's purpose. It was fundamentally an attempt to stage a political comeback. Mao planned to use the troops of the PLA, which he had been cultivating under the leadership of his protégé and 'close comrade-in-arms', Marshal Lin Biao, together with the poorer peasants and young and idealistic urban students, to overcome his factional opponents. With this backing, the ideological dispute spilt over into violent factional conflict in factories and universities across the land. Chaos ensued – and within a year, the PLA had been deployed to police many cities and control unreliable local governments; much of China in 1968–1969 was effectively under martial law. Lin Biao, in a spectacular and baffling escapade, attempted to seize power in 1971 and was killed when his aircraft crashed in Mongolian territory while flying towards the Soviet Union.

Zhou Enlai and Deng Xiaoping

After Lin's death, an alternative and more sophisticated political programme emerged under the guidance of the enigmatic but popular Zhou Enlai. Zhou had survived the Cultural Revolution relatively unscathed and without having been publicly criticised. His initial actions were in the field of international relations and diplomacy – and his willingness, in conjunction with Mao, to talk to the United States after China and the Soviet Union had fought a series of border skirmishes in 1969 was almost certainly the main cause of the fatal rift with Lin Biao. China replaced Taiwan in the United Nations in October 1971, ending Beijing's international isolation. Deng Xiaoping, whose mentor Liu Shaoqi had died in 1969 as a result of persecution during the Cultural Revolution, gradually became more influential as Zhou Enlai became seriously ill, but Deng's historic return to power could not immediately be made public for fear of offending Mao and his supporters.

Although many ultra-radical policies had been abandoned as early as 1969, the Cultural Revolution only came to a complete end in 1976 after the deaths of some of the key political figures of twentieth-century China. The Guomindang leader, Chiang Kai-shek, died in Taiwan in 1975, and Zhou Enlai and Zhu De (the veteran Long March military leader) died during the following year. Mao Zedong also died in 1976, on 9 September, following what was regarded by the more traditional and superstitious element of the Chinese population as a celestial portent – an earthquake that had devastated the northeast city of Tangshan the previous July. Within a month, Mao's closest Cultural Revolution supporters, including his wife Jiang Qing, had been arrested and accused of operating as a counter-revolutionary Gang of Four against the CCP.

Reform decade: 1979–1989

The Gang of Four were not put on trial until November 1980, by which time the CCP's internal political battles had, by and large, been won by reformers. The Gang of Four and many of their junior aides and acolytes were sentenced to long terms of imprisonment: this included a life sentence for Jiang Qing, who later died in prison, almost certainly by her own hand. Deng Xiaoping's position was now more secure: he began to implement the policies of Four Modernisations (agriculture, industry, science and technology, and defence) that had been bequeathed to him by Zhou Enlai. These policies, which evolved into the broader approach of reform and opening [*gaige kaifang*] that was Deng's political trademark, launched the reform decade that transformed Communist China.

Although it could never be admitted openly at the time, Deng's policies undid most of the work that Mao Zedong had done between 1949 and his death in 1976. Officially, the reforms were subject to the Four Basic Principles: the dictatorship of people's democracy, leadership by the CCP, socialism, and Marxism-Leninism-Mao Zedong Thought. In practice, the third and fourth of these principles were mere rhetoric. The only principles that mattered were the first two: whatever reforms were to be carried out, the CCP would remain in power.

The earliest and the most fundamental of the reforms was the implementation in 1979 of the Household Responsibility System in agriculture. This anodyne term concealed a programme to return land to individual families, essentially privatising Chinese agriculture and thereby ending 20 years of the People's Communes, the distinctive Chinese form that collectivised agriculture had taken in 1958 during the Great Leap Forward. Private trade, privatised industry, and the emergence of a new class of small entrepreneurs, the *getihu*, gradually reduced the state's absolute monopoly over industry and commerce, and the CCP withdrew from direct involvement in much of the economy. Special Economic Zones with preferential taxation and financial packages for foreign investors became a back-door way of introducing European, American, and Japanese capital into China.

Reforms did not proceed without opposition; during the 1980s, tensions continued between senior political figures who were pressing for deeper and faster reforms and others, many of them elderly former military officers, who could not accept that everything they had fought for against the Japanese and the GMD might be destroyed by the reforms. To many of the older members of the elite, modernisation looked too much like Westernisation.

One of the leading reformers, Hu Yaobang, who had been CCP Secretary General and a protégé of Deng Xiaoping, was dismissed in 1987, accused of being too accommodating to the organisers of December 1986 student demonstrations against corruption and the restriction of freedom of speech. He was too close to the liberal elements of the Chinese intelligentsia and, more bizarrely, was accused of leading a pro-Japan faction in the CCP. He was replaced by Zhao Ziyang.

Remembering and forgetting Tian'anmen Square: 4 June 1989

Hu Yaobang's death, from natural causes, on 15 April 1989 was the catalyst for a wave of demonstrations from which the Democracy Movement eventually emerged. The demonstrations, and the temporary camp that students and local citizens established in Tian'anmen Square, were crushed by troops and tanks of PLA units on the night of 3–4 June 1989: the whole endeavour was denounced afterwards by the Chinese authorities as a counter-revolutionary movement. Zhao Ziyang was ousted for being too weak in his dealings with the protesters. The brutal suppression of a predominantly youthful and entirely non-violent domestic political movement was a clear indication that the gerontocracy could still tip the balance of power in a crisis. The decision to use the military to clear the demonstrators from Tian'anmen Square was by no means unanimous; it left the CCP and PLA desperately divided for years. Deng Xiaoping, the man whose name will be linked indelibly with both the reform programme and the brutal suppression of the demonstrators in Tian'anmen Square (although the degree of his responsibility is still disputed), died on 19 February 1997.

The military suppression of a peaceful civilian movement on 4 June 1989 was one of the most traumatic events for China in the second half of the twentieth century, not only for those who suffered in the assault but also senior political and military leaders, for whom it was a matter of embarrassment and shame. The events of 4 June remain one of the most unmentionable political topics and are effectively excluded from the public discourse in the PRC. Each anniversary has been marked by heightened security and often the detention, usually temporary, of actual or potential dissidents to remote locations until the day has passed.

Security for the 30th anniversary in June 2019 was more rigorous than usual. In Hong Kong, demonstrations marked the anniversary, but none were permitted on the mainland. There was no discussion in the mainland media, but, speaking in Singapore at the Shangri-La Dialogue – a high-profile conference attended by defence ministers from a wide range of governments – the Tian'anmen Square suppression was referred to after a speech on 'China and International Security Cooperation' given by State Councillor and Minister of National Defence, General Wei Fenghe, the most senior Chinese military official to have attended such a conference.

In answer to a question, General Wei responded that:

> This marks the 30th anniversary of that incident, and 30 years have proven that, as the leadership of the CPC, China has undergone major changes. How can we say that China did not handle the Tian'anmen incident properly? There is a conclusion of that incident, that is, that incident was political turbulence and the central government took measures

to stop the turbulence, which is correct policy, and because of the propensity of the Chinese government China has enjoyed stability and development. If you visit China, you can understand that part of history.[1]

Note

1 *South China Morning Post* (*SCMP*) 18, 26 May, 4 June 2019; www.iiss.org/events/shangri-la-dialogue/shangri-la-dialogue-2019.

Part 2

Politics

3   Government and politics of China

The formal structure of China's government in the early years of the PRC closely followed the one-party state model of the Soviet Union. The Communist Party of the Soviet Union (CPSU) was the only political authority in the USSR; in China, only the CCP, wielded real political power, although there are eight minor parties known collectively as the Democratic Parties. The continuing existence of these political groupings reflects alliances that the CCP made during the closing years of the Civil War in the 1940s. They played an important role in the New Democracy period of the early 1950s, but their influence declined, especially after the Anti-Rightist Campaign of 1957, and is now negligible.

In practice, China was, and still is, governed under a dual party-state system in which organs of government are shadowed by CCP monitoring bodies which are paramount. This parallel system of checks and controls stretches from the very top of the central administration to the lowest level of the state, the government of the townships. There is a considerable overlap between personnel in the government and party bodies, as well as with membership of the armed forces, the PLA.

Formal government has frequently been overshadowed and undermined by mass political campaigns; these were a regular feature of China's political culture in the first 30 years of the PRC and were particularly associated with Mao's distinctive brand of revolutionary romanticism. The campaigns were a symbol of Mao's determination to press forward with the revolution and to destabilise institutions, even those set up by the CCP, if they were in danger of becoming entrenched and ossified. The culture of political campaigns has not completely died out, but campaigns are now directed at specific policy targets in a more sophisticated and focused way.

Informal political relations, including internal but officially unacknowledged CCP factions, play a role in the selection and promotion of officials but reliable information on these is elusive. Many of those who led the CCP and governed the PRC after 1949 had formed close and enduring personal and family ties during the years of war and revolution. As that generation died out, some of those relationships extended to their sons and daughters. These *gaogan zidi* (literally 'sons and younger brothers of high cadres' but generally meaning 'children') formed a new elite and many became successful in official positions or in business.

Constitutions of the PRC

The first constitution, or more accurately proto-constitution, of the PRC was the Common Programme, adopted in 1949 by a broad range of parties under the guidance of the CCP. By 1954, after the end of the Korean War and the conclusion of the most violent phase of the political campaigns used by the CCP to consolidate its power, the PRC was ready to move towards the adoption of a full constitution. The first constitution proper was adopted by the first National People's Congress (NPC) on 20 September 1954. It was drafted by a constitutional committee and drew heavily on the 1936 Constitution of the Soviet Union. It enshrined the principle that the PRC would be led by the working class. This effectively guaranteed that the CCP, which viewed itself as the representative of the working class, would dominate China for the foreseeable future.

The Constitution outlined the structure of the Chinese government, known at the time as the Central People's Government, and its major organs of state. The highest authority was to be a quasi-parliamentary body, the NPC [*Quanguo renmin daibiao dahui*]; the State Council [*Guowuyuan*], headed by the Premier, was created as the executive body of the state, roughly equivalent to a cabinet in parliamentary democracies. Local People's Congresses were also established, creating a hierarchy of bodies in which, formally at least, the lower levels selected representatives to attend the higher. The Constitution also outlined the rights and duties of citizens and established the national flag – a red flag with five stars – and the national emblem – Tian'anmen, the southern gate of the Forbidden City, in the centre and under the light of five stars, surrounded by ears of grain and a cogwheel at the base.[1] The flag was chosen in a competition and represented the political symbolism of the time. The red background was intended to represent 'revolutionary enthusiasm' but, whether intentionally or not, echoed Ming imperial red, the colour of the last Han Chinese dynasty; the large star represented the CCP and the four smaller ones the four classes of 'the people' in alliance with the CCP in the period of New Democracy: the national bourgeoisie, the petty bourgeoisie, the working class, and the peasantry. It is also oddly reminiscent of the flag of the Guomindang's Republic of China and the Nationalist concept of the five nations of China: Han, Manchu, Mongol, Tibetan, and Muslim. There is some confusion in China today about the precise symbolism of the stars; many accounts avoid the issue and simply say that the stars represent the relationship between the CCP and the people of China.

Although the Constitution is couched in democratic terms with many references to elections, it does not require close reading to discern the considerable power wielded by the Standing Committee of the NPC and the Chairman of the State (President). Control of these positions ensures control of the government. Elections did and do take place, but the electoral processes, set out in separate legislation, make it possible for the CCP to control the nomination of candidates to elections at all levels and thus the entire process. The term Central People's Government gradually fell into disuse, but the executive arm of the government of China is still known as the State Council.

The Constitution was revised and simplified during the Cultural Revolution and a new version published in 1975 contained a great deal of Maoist rhetoric. A third version was promulgated in 1978, shortly after the death of Mao Zedong, but the Constitution currently in force is based on the one drawn up in 1982 at the beginning of the 'reform and opening' period. It reinstated the position of State Chairman (President), which had been removed during the Cultural Revolution when it had been held by Mao's political adversary, Liu Shaoqi. This is a role distinct from that of Chairman of the CCP, although both posts were at one time held by the same individual: Mao. The post of Chairman of the CCP was abolished in 1982 as part of the move to extirpate the influence of Mao Zedong, who was 'the Chairman' and replaced by the role of General Secretary. Hu Yaobang was the last chairman and the first of the new-style General Secretaries, a position held at the time of writing by Xi Jinping. The revised version of the Constitution restored clauses on the role of courts of law that had been expunged in the Cultural Revolution. It has been in operation ever since 1982, with amendments.

National People's Congress

Under the Constitution, the highest authority of the state is the NPC, a body of representatives elected by the provinces, autonomous regions, and the largest cities. It stands at the apex of a nationwide hierarchical network of People's Congresses. Members of the NPC serve for a term of five years, and the full NPC meets annually, normally for two weeks in Beijing in the first quarter of each year (that is, during the spring), and has the authority to amend the Constitution, enact legislation, elect a Premier (who is nominated by the State Chairman) and the heads of the Supreme People's Court and the Procuratorate (the state prosecution service), and rule on economic plans. When the NPC is not in session, its functions are exercised by a Standing Committee, which has very wide powers, including the authority to conduct elections, convene its own sessions, interpret legislation enacted by the full Congress, and supervise other state bodies including the State Council and the courts.

The NPC elects the Chairman of the PRC, the equivalent of a President, who has the power to nominate a Premier and senior ministers and officials, and has supreme authority to act in relations with foreign countries. The NPC also elects the Chairman of the government Military Affairs Commission – there is another CCP Military Affairs Commission – and the President of the Supreme Court. It maintains eight permanent special committees which have responsibility for drawing up legislation on key domestic and foreign policy areas: finance and economics; education, science, culture, and public health; ethnic minorities; foreign affairs; overseas Chinese; internal and judicial affairs; legal matters; and the environment. The operation of the NPC and its Standing Committee is governed by two documents, The Organic Law of the NPC and the Procedural Rules of the NPC, which were revised in 1982 and 1989, respectively.[2]

The degree of formality and tradition suggests that the functions and status of the NPC are equivalent to those of a parliament in a Western-style democracy; this is not the case. It has approximately 3,000 members and is too cumbersome to function effectively as a debating body. Many of its powers are delegated to the Standing Committee, which has 175 members (elected in March 2018 – the number can vary slightly) and meets on a bi-monthly basis. Although the NPC formally approves new legislation, it does not generally initiate it. Most legislation is originated by CCP bodies and passed to the NPC, in which the CCP has in any case a substantial built-in majority – over two-thirds.

During the 1990s, the NPC began to flex its muscles and for a time exercised a degree of independent judgement on technical aspects of legislation including tax laws. Increased attention was paid to the meetings of the NPC, which were more widely publicised. In addition to the work reports that the President, Prime Minister, and other senior figures have always presented in public, press conferences were opened to foreign print and media journalists.

The tenth NPC on 14 March 2004 introduced clauses on human rights, the mixed economy and private property. On 11 March 2018, during the 13th NPC, further amendments strengthened the position of the CCP, including the establishment of a National Supervisory Commission to combat corruption. The most significant amendments were the inclusion of 'Xi Jinping Thought' in the preamble to the Constitution and the removal of time limits for the posts of President and Vice-President of the PRC. These were interpreted as signs that

Xi intended to break with precedent and remain at the helm for longer than the ten years that had become customary since the retirement of Jiang Zemin in 2002.[3]

State Council

The State Council [*Guowuyuan*] was created as the executive organ of the government, under the Premier and with ministries and commissions subordinate to it. It is formally responsible to the NPC – the Standing Committee of the NPC when the NPC is not in session – but has far more authority than that might suggest. Its functions resemble those of a cabinet in a parliamentary system, and its members – who include the Premier, Vice-Premiers, members of the State Council and the Secretary General of the State Council – are the most powerful government officials; they also hold senior positions in the CCP. One of its most significant functions has always been the creation of the Five-Year Plans under which China's economy is still managed, but it also has broad responsibilities for law and order, and supervises the work of China's ministries and specialist commissions. The State Council has monthly meetings; its Standing Committee meets at least weekly.

Chinese People's Political Consultative Conference

The Chinese People's Political Consultative Conference [*Zhongguo renmin zhengzhi xieshang huiyi*] has the most cumbersome and unpronounceable English title of all Chinese political organs. It is usually referred to in English by its abbreviation the CPPCC and in Chinese as the *zhengxie*. It is a remnant of the attempts by the CCP in 1949 to create broad-based support for its policies in a united front, a term drawn from the USSR under Stalin. This nod in the direction of inclusiveness did not last long, but the CPPCC remains in place and includes delegates from ethnic minority groups, religious organisations, and a small number of legal non-CCP political organisations. It is useful to the CCP as a sounding board for the impact of its policies on minority groups and meets annually in Beijing in the spring at the same time as the NPC – they are generally referred to as the two meetings [*lianghui*].

Chinese Communist Party

The membership of the CCP [*Zhongguo gongchandang*] stood at 90.59 million on 1 July 2019. At one time it was the largest single political party anywhere in the world, but in August of that year, India's Hindu right-wing nationalist Bharatiya Janata Party claimed a membership of 180 million.[4] The great majority of CCP members are male (83%) and most are over 35 years of age (78%). Government officials, military officers, and carefully selected model employees from the state sector have traditionally been the most important component of the membership. In 2002, when reforms were introduced by Jiang Zemin to encourage previously unaligned businessmen and more women, scientists, academics, writers, and artists to join the Party, it was clear that the CCP was no longer (if it ever had been, since 1949 at least) the preserve of political militants and Marxist idealists. A report issued by the CCP's Organisation Department just before the Party's 17th Congress in October 2007 showed that, between 2002 and 2007, the size of the membership had increased by over six million: there were noticeable increases in the recruitment of women and people from the 'new social strata'; that is the business and managerial classes. The rate of increase of membership stabilised at about 1.5% per annum after new regulations were included in 2013 to restrict membership to applicants of the right quality. Of members recruited in 2017, over half were in 'front-line production roles', while 43.4% 'held junior college degrees or above'. Nearly two million 'non-public enterprises' had been persuaded to establish new Party organisations.[5]

The CCP provides the body of men and women on whom the state can draw for political, social, and economic leadership at all levels of society. It is a tightly disciplined, self-selecting elite group that is part of the career ladder for young Chinese people who aspire to important roles in government and society. Young aspirants can only become members after years of preparatory work, comprehensive tests, and the support of senior members of their local Party branch. The benefits of membership are considerable: in addition to the support provided by the Party for careers in public organisations, members have always enjoyed access to superior housing, better education for their children, and privileged sources of information denied to non-members. In a society where *guanxi* (connections) remain supremely important, those provided by the CCP are second to none.

Detention of Party members under the *shuanggui* and *liuzhi* systems

Although membership of the CCP confers many privileges and opportunities that are not open to non-members, members who break the law or Party rules have also been liable to extra-legal detention and interrogation by the CCP Central Commission for Discipline Inspection (for which see also in what follows) in addition to routine administrative and legal controls. This system, which operated until 2017, was known as *shuanggui*, which is best translated as double regulation – of time and place. Suspects were required to present themselves at a designated time and place to answer questions about their conduct. This procedure, which has in some cases led to long periods of detention without trial and allegations of confessions under torture, was little known until it was widely used during campaigns inspired by Xi Jinping against allegedly corrupt senior Party officials. Suspects could be detained at a time and place determined by the investigators, and many disappeared for long periods of time. The procedure was heavily criticised, as it was open to abuse for settling personal and political scores, and the government has acknowledged that some individuals were mistreated or tortured under investigation, leading in some cases to deaths.

According to Human Rights Watch,

> In his opening remarks to the 19th Chinese Communist Party Congress in Beijing on October 18, 2017, President Xi said shuanggui will be replaced by *liuzhi,* a new detention system, as part of broader reforms to the legal system.[6]

This new *liuzhi* system was intended to apply to all state officials and not just members of the CCP; it is not a liberalisation of the previous system, but another tool for Xi Jinping's crackdown on corruption. New regulations have been laid down for the legal operation of *liuzhi*, but information on how it operates is limited, and legal specialists have expressed concern that it simply constitutes a legal veneer to cover continuing bad practice.[7]

The CCP controls the public expression of opinions by its membership through the Leninist principle of democratic centralism. In theory, this means that policy is decided by mass democratic debate and, once decided on, is adhered to by all the members. In practice, in China as in the former Soviet Union, centralism has always taken priority and the democratic element was, and remains, difficult to discern.

The CCP has a top-down structure in which lower-ranking units are required to subordinate themselves to higher ones, and ultimately to the central bodies in Beijing: junior members subordinate themselves to senior members. This to some extent explains the continued influence during the 1980s and 1990s of Party elders who frequently restricted political developments and blocked policy changes long after they had retired from their formal positions. Deng Xiaoping, whose opinions were sought long after his retirement, and Jiang Zemin, who attempted to cling on to control of the Central Military Commission and then to manipulate the central Party organisations through his Shanghai faction, are the two highest-profile examples of this. Retired senior Party officials retain some privileges, and in many cases their sons and daughters, the *gaogan zidi* ['children of high cadres'], have taken advantage of these privileges to secure advances in their political or business careers.

Changing character of the CCP

The CCP is rather like grandfather's axe. Since its formation in 1921, it has had several new heads and countless new hafts to replace broken ones. Despite frequent destructive factional disputes that threatened to tear it apart and are now generally acknowledged in published accounts of Party history, it is often treated as a constant and unchanging organisation.

The longevity and tenaciousness of the Party are testimony to an underlying characteristic that has often been obscured by the political rhetoric of the day. Underneath the veneer of Marxism or Maoism (officially Marxism-Leninism-Mao Zedong Thought), there has been a constant emphasis on the national interests of China and the glory of the Chinese nation, past as well as present, and the promotion of patriotism. After the death of Mao Zedong in 1976 and the implementation of Deng Xiaoping's reform programme in the 1980s, there was a dramatic shift in policy which appeared to reverse or dispense with the entire previous economic policy of the CCP. It was primarily patriotism or nationalism that enabled the Party to retain its dominant political position.

Since the beginning of the reform period, there has been an attempt to broaden the base of the Party. Jiang Zemin's recruitment of men and women from the world of business was controversial in China and caused raised eyebrows among international observers, but it reflected the changing role of ideology in the Party. What had begun in the 1920s as an imitation of Soviet-style Marxism-Leninism, gradually adapted to Chinese conditions, led to the emergence of Mao Zedong Thought in the 1940s and its popularisation in the 1960s. After the death of Mao, the role of ideology diminished, gradually at first when radical economic reforms were launched under cover of a degree of ideological window dressing, and then dramatically. The CCP became a pragmatic and patriotic governing party, but the announcement of the death of ideology in China may have been premature. Domestic Chinese-language media, aimed primarily at Party and government officials, continue to use the same bureaucratic Marxist language and this increased, temporarily during the local rise of Bo Xilai in Chongqing (for which see Chapter 5), and more firmly after the coming to power of Xi Jinping in 2012.

The CCP maintains its own internal training and ideological programme, at the head of which is the Central Party School, an elite body that trains the next generation of the Party leadership, supported by a provincial network of subordinate institutions. In August 2020, Cai Xia, a prominent member of staff specialising in Marxism and CCP theory at the school, was dismissed and lost her membership of the CCP and her pension benefits after making speeches critical of the Party and its leadership. Her removal after investigations by the Central Commission for Discipline Inspection and its local officials alarmed the authorities who warned staff to be vigilant in not breaking Party discipline or losing their 'Party spirit'.[8] The Party also guards its secret historical archives with great care. Its academic department, the

Party History Research Centre, and its associated publishing house are responsible for the approved versions of Party history and past controversies.

At the base of the Party structure are the local branches, which can be found in villages, towns, and cities, but more significantly in schools, factories, large shops, offices, military units, and similar organisations. This penetration to the grassroots level has been one of the strengths of the CCP and one of the reasons for its ability to survive. The Party branches are not only the power base for the CCP in their locality and a reservoir to draw on when government officials are required, they have also been used as a powerful tool for the local implementation of national policies, whether economic plans or delicate matters of social engineering such as the one-child policy.

The government-run news agency, Xinhua, revealed that, in July 2007, as many as three million members of the CCP were employed by private firms, a considerable increase on previous figures. It was argued that this gave private businesses a voice in the corridors of CCP power, but it also provided the CCP with a remarkable source of information on the internal workings of private businesses. During the 1950s when the CCP, newly arrived in the cities after the Civil War, was implementing its policy of nationalising private firms, members of the CCP branches working in these firms were appointed to boards of directors as a prelude to the state taking control. During the Xi Jinping period, there has been renewed emphasis on Party branches in private industry for the purposes of monitoring the management of firms and ensuring their compliance with government policy.[9]

CCP Congresses

According to the Constitution of the CCP, the National Party Congress (Conference) – not to be confused with the quasi-parliamentary NPC – is its supreme policy making body. It is intended to meet regularly – every five years – although that was honoured more in the breach than the observance throughout the chaotic days of the Cultural Revolution and Mao Zedong's final years in power. The number of delegates varies but is usually in the region of 2,000. All have been elected by Party members in their constituencies, but it is an open secret that there is rarely, if ever, any choice of delegates and the election is rather a selection from, or an endorsement of, an approved list of Party members. In practice, far from functioning as the supreme authority in the CCP, the Party Congress gives formal and public approval to policies that have already been determined by those Party bodies that exercise genuine power – the Central Committee and the Politburo.

The 16th Party Congress under Jiang Zemin met in November 2002 and the 17th Party Congress under Hu Jintao convened on 16 October 2007. The 18th Party Congress, also presided over by Hu, ran from 8–15 November 2012 and confirmed Xi Jinping's appointment as General Secretary. Bo Xilai had been suspended from the Party before that conference opened (details of his case and that of Zhou Yongkang can be found in Chapter 5). The 19th Congress of 18–24 October 2017 was notable for the adoption of 'Xi Jinping Thought on Socialism with Chinese Characteristics for a New Era' as the guiding ideology which was written into the Party Constitution.

Central Committee and Politburo

Genuine political power, as has been noted, does not reside in the Party Congress, but in the two smaller bodies that are notionally subordinate to it, the Central Committee and the Politburo. The 200 full and 150 alternate members of the Central Committee [*zhongyang weiyuanhui*] are formally elected by the Party Congress, but this is not an open election and the names of candidates are approved in advance from a *nomenklatura* list in line with long-standing Chinese, and before that Soviet, practice.

The Politburo, the standard Russian abbreviation for Political Bureau [*zhengzhiju*], is the centre of power in the CCP. The Politburo is selected from the Central Committee and is therefore the elite of the elite. It includes powerful faction leaders and regional and provincial CCP secretaries. In October 2017, 25 individuals were elected to the 19th Politburo: these included only one woman and two military delegates.

There is an even smaller and more powerful group, the Standing Committee [*changwu weiyuanhui*] of the Politburo, which meets on a more regular basis. At the time of writing, it consists of seven people – although in the recent past, there have been as many as nine members and sometimes as few as five. It is the body that runs China on a day-to-day basis. The most senior Party and government leaders, including the General Secretary of the CCP, the Chairman of the NPC, the Chairman of the Central Discipline Inspection Commission, and the Premier are normally members of the Standing Committee. The deliberations and even the times of the meetings of the Standing Committee are not made public, and there are no formal minutes openly available. There is sufficient anecdotal evidence to indicate that meetings of these three bodies have often been contentious; that 'struggle' [*douzheng*] is more common than discussion; and that when a consensus or a majority decision is finally reached, this has often been after long and bitter dispute. Politburo Standing Committee members in August 2020 were, in order of seniority: Xi Jinping, Li Keqiang, Li Zhanshu, Wang Yang, Wang Huning, Zhao Leji, and Han Zheng.

Other influential CCP bodies

The Secretariat is the administrative arm of the Politburo and exercises considerable political influence in terms of access to the most senior leaders. It is the political power base and the tool of the General Secretary of the CCP. During the administration of Hu Yaobang in the early 1980s, the influence of the Secretariat briefly grew at the expense of the Politburo, which reasserted its authority after Hu was dismissed in 1987.

The Organisation Department is the bureaucratic heart of the CCP. It maintains a vast and comprehensive filing system, monitors the careers of all Party officials, assesses their performance, and collects evidence for promotions. Its authority extends to the thousands of officials who are appointed to provincial and lower government bodies.

The Central Commission for Discipline Inspection (CCDI) is the highest body in the network of Party discipline committees that monitors the management of the Party and adherence to policy; it is charged from time to time with rooting out corruption among the most senior officials. Its staff have access to their own network of moles and informers, and have been known to wield power ruthlessly. Their main role is ensuring the compliance of Party members with current policy decisions, but they are also deployed in factional disputes and even the most senior leaders are not immune from their investigation. In 1998, the former Secretary of the Beijing CCP, Chen Xitong, was investigated by the Central Discipline Commission and sentenced to 16 years imprisonment after having been found guilty of corruption during an internal power struggle. In 2000, Cheng Kejie, who had served as Deputy Chairman of the NPC, was executed after having been accused of accepting bribes to a total value of US$5 million, but this was an exceptional case. The CDI was the main instrument of Xi Jinping's wide-ranging anti-corruption campaign and was responsible for the administration of the *shuanggui* system for disciplining Party members that has been described previously in this chapter.

As its name suggests, the Communist Youth League (CYL – *Gongchanzhuyi qingnian tuan*) is the junior branch of the CCP. The CYL was originally modelled on the *Komsomol* of the Soviet Union and serves as one of the most important conduits for recruiting potential Party members. Its influence extends far beyond that role, and former members of the CYL have become one of the most important factional groupings within the Party. It has its own newspaper, *China Youth Daily*, which, at the end of the twentieth century, acquired a reputation for relative independence, radicalism, and attacks on corruption.

Factions within the CCP

There is no open acknowledgement of the existence of political factions within the CCP, although there is no doubt that they play a crucial role in intra-Party discussion and conflict, and in the careers of individuals. Most are not groups organised around clear political agendas. A more accurate term would be personal or patronage networks: individual members of the Party who seek promotion or preference will attach themselves to a more senior member with whom they can claim, or can develop, political *guanxi*.[10] In the early days of the PRC, these personal factions were often associated with the particular military unit, usually field armies, to which individuals had been attached in the Civil War of 1946–1949. In contemporary China, they are more likely to be political machines established in China's most prosperous regions. The Shanghai faction, which underwrote Jiang Zemin's rise to power as President from 1993–2003 and continued to exercise considerable influence within the Party and the government for some years afterwards, was the best known. Its influence apparently disappeared with the rise of Xi Jinping, although two members of Xi's Politburo, Han Zheng and Wang Huning, are sometimes identified with the faction. A resilient faction based on former members of the Chinese CYL was the power base on which Hu Jintao had built his candidacy. These are only the tip of the iceberg, since the entire Party apparatus is riddled with factions and interest groups, most of which do not have a name or an individual leader who is well known outside the corridors of power in Beijing.

Reformers have called for a recognition of the existence of internal Party factions as part of a commitment to a more open and democratic structure. This has been resisted as it is inimical to the fundamental principle of democratic centralism which insists that the CCP should always present itself as one body with one mind and one will.

The political transition from Jiang Zemin to Hu Jintao was noteworthy because it was accomplished without factional disputes spilling over into public conflict, in contrast with the Great Leap Forward and the Cultural Revolution. The leadership of Hu Jintao was at pains to avoid factional chaos, although this concern is not as central to the Xi Jinping administration. As a result of Jiang Zemin's awkwardly named Three Represents policy, which encouraged entrepreneurs to join the CCP, the potential for the proliferation of new factions increased greatly. It remains to be seen whether these can be contained within the CCP and whether there will be pressure from the newer members, either for their factions to be recognised publicly or for the creation of new political bodies.

Minority 'democratic' parties

There is a group of political parties, left over from the negotiations that took place at the time of the foundation of the PRC in 1949, which broadly agreed with the programme of the CCP at the time and have been allowed to remain in existence. They are the Revolutionary Committee of the Guomindang, a left-wing splinter group of the main Nationalist Party; China

Democratic League; China Democratic National Construction Association; China Association for the Promotion of Democracy; Chinese Peasants' and Workers' Democratic Party;
Chinese Party for Public Interest [*Zhigongdang*]; the Jiusan (3 September) Society, named
after the date China declared victory over the Japanese in 1945; and the Taiwan Democratic
Self-Government League.

The 'democratic parties' have been retained as they provided evidence of the CCP's willingness to engage in United Front politics and to consult a wider constituency than their
own members. In the early days of the PRC, there was genuine consultation, but, like other
non-CCP organisations, they fell foul of the intellectual repression of the Hundred Flowers
Movement and Anti-Rightist campaign in the second half of the 1950s. The 'democratic
parties' had provided much of the trenchant criticism of CCP practices that was published
during the Hundred Flowers Movement period, but at the end of the movement, members
of these parties who were most sympathetic to the CCP, or who even had dual membership,
were given the task of identifying and denouncing 'rightists' in their own ranks – and these
names were handed over to the Public Security Bureau during August–September 1957. As
a result of these acts of betrayal, perhaps as many as 12,000 members of the 'democratic
parties' were identified as rightists, dismissed from their posts, and sent to the countryside
or to industrial complexes for re-education through labour. Any vestige of genuine political
influence that these parties had exercised was destroyed in this campaign. They were unable
to attract new members and, although they continue to exist, they are irrelevant to the political process.

Illegal and underground political parties

There are no legal opposition parties in China – the 'democratic parties' described previously do not oppose the CCP – and it has been almost impossible for dissidents, or anyone
wishing to express an alternative political voice, to organise openly. During the chaotic days
of the Cultural Revolution, when political controls were removed or relaxed, some Red
Guard factions that had responded to Mao Zedong's call to 'rebel' began to look like political parties, but these were suppressed as the CCP rebuilt its structures after 1969. One of
the most interesting of these was the leftist umbrella grouping in Hunan province – Mao's
home province – that went by the name of *Shengwulian*, an abbreviation for Hunan Province
Revolutionary Great Alliance Committee [*Hunan sheng wuchanjieji gemingpai da lianhe
weiyuanhui*]. *Shengwulian* issued a manifesto *Whither China* in March 1968 which attacked
Mao and his supporters as a new type of bureaucratic ruling class, and called for a social
revolution against them led by the workers and peasants. It proposed the establishment of
a national version of the People's Communes as a form of mass democracy. This idea was
swiftly condemned by Party leaders, who denounced it at a mass rally in the Hunan capital
of Changsha. In the late 1960s and 1970s, it was the system of Revolutionary Committees,
largely controlled by the military, which the CCP used to bring the Cultural Revolution to an
end and not organs modelled on the mass democracy of the Paris Commune.

During the Cultural Revolution, there were attempts to form political parties in the ethnic
minority border regions. Inner Mongolians created a movement for an independent Southern
Mongolia, and in Xinjiang, the Eastern Turkistan People's Party was launched with covert
assistance from the Soviet Union. These organisations were short-lived and could not exist
openly after the authority of the CCP and its government was re-established.

The only real opposition movement of any significance to emerge since the Cultural Revolution was the China Democratic Party, which argued for the democratic reform of the

Chinese political system: this Party can be traced back to the 'democracy wall' activists of the late 1970s who argued for genuine democracy in the years immediately after the death of Mao Zedong and, in its more recent incarnations, to the Democracy Movement which was suppressed by the military on 4 June 1989. The China Democratic Party, which emerged around 1998, was declared illegal in China – the fact that its name was identical to one that had been created in Taiwan during the period of martial law did not help – and its best-known activist, Xu Wenli, spent over 16 years in prison for his political activities. A version of the party exists in exile in Europe and in the United States of America.

There have been reports of other initiatives to establish opposition parties: in December 2007, a New Democracy Party was formed by Guo Quan, a former academic at the Nanjing Normal University (Teachers' College). New Democracy – its name echoed the more inclusive and more broadly-based politics of the early 1950s – advocated the abolition of the CCP's single-party dictatorship in favour of a multi-party system. It failed to take root, and with the advent of the authoritarian regime of Xi Jinping in 2012, even discussing alternatives to the single-party rule of the CCP became taboo.[11]

People's Liberation Army

The roots of the modern PLA, which has played a significant role in PRC politics, lie in the armed defence units created by the CCP during the uprisings of 1927 that were precipitated by the breakdown of the Party's political alliance with the Guomindang. These units were known as the Workers' and Peasants' Red Army [*Gongnong hongjun*] and 1 August, the date of the formal creation of this Red Army in the Jiangxi city of Nanchang, is still celebrated as Army Day in the PRC. Throughout the second period of cooperation (Second United Front) between the CCP and the GMD during the Japanese invasion and occupation that lasted from 1937–1945, Red Army units did not use their own titles but went under names such as Eighth Route Army and New Fourth Army to imply that they were part of a single national military organisation: in fact they functioned to a large extent as independent units with their own command structures and political commissars. The independence of these units was reasserted at the beginning of the Civil War that followed the capitulation of the occupying Japanese Army in September 1945: CCP forces were re-designated the Chinese PLA [*Zhongguo renmin jiefang jun*] on 1 May 1946.

Power did grow out of the barrel of a gun, as Mao famously observed: both Sun Yat-sen and Chiang Kai-shek had taken a similar view. If it had not been for the victory of its armed units during the Civil War, the CCP could not have formed the government of the PRC in 1949. After the Civil War, the PLA established its position in China through military campaigns to bring the outlying territories, including Tibet and Xinjiang, under the control of Beijing. It enhanced its prestige greatly during the Korean War when, under the flag of the Chinese People's Volunteers, it was pitted against the technically superior forces of the United States which was at the head of a UN coalition. More controversial were its roles in the fighting with Soviet troops at the Ussuri River on the border with the Russian Far Eastern region in 1969, China's military invasion of Vietnam in 1979, and, above all, with the suppression of democracy demonstrations in Beijing on 4 June 1989.

Historically, the relationship between the PLA and the CCP was close and symbiotic. Although the institutions remained formally separate, it was often difficult to distinguish between their senior personnel during the war years. After 1949, PLA officers continued to serve in Party organs, and a CCP structure within the PLA is designed to ensure that the military remains fully informed of, and compliant with, CCP policies. At the time of writing, two senior military officers, General Xu Qiliang of the PLA Air Force and army General Zhang Youxia, are members of the ruling 19th Politburo by virtue of their service as Vice-Chairmen of the Central Military Commission. Notwithstanding Mao's dictum that 'the Party always commands the gun: the gun shall never command the Party', the military and its ethos have in the past played a significant – and at times dominant – role in the political direction of the CCP. During the final chaotic months of the Cultural Revolution, the military dominated the political structures to such an extent that much of China was effectively under martial law.

Service in the PLA is regarded as proof of loyalty, discipline, and patriotism, and therefore became a useful step on the road to Party membership. Many former soldiers returned to their villages with the prestige, authority, and ideological training that would set them on the road to a Party and government career, even if only at the local level. Since the end of the Cultural Revolution, the role of the PLA in politics has been downgraded. With increased professionalism came a separation from national politics and, in spite of the generals on the full Politburo, there is no longer a representative of the army on its Standing Committee, which is the key decision-making body in China. During the 1980s, the military was allowed, and even encouraged, to develop business interests; for some individuals, these were extremely lucrative. This policy was curbed during Jiang Zemin's presidency because of the prevalence of corruption and the fear that the army was losing its focus on defence; the size of the military was drastically reduced.[12]

Although the existence of a Communist Party organisation within the military and a strong sense of common interest bind the Party and the army together, it cannot be assumed that the views of the CCP and the PLA are identical. There is evidence that the PLA are far more hawkish on certain key issues of international relations than the main body of the CCP and that, in certain foreign policy debates, there is considerable tension between the two groups. Members of the PLA, and in particular its officer corps, are deeply imbued with a powerful sense of what they would regard as patriotism, but outsiders might view as nationalism, in their determination to protect the motherland [*zuguo* – a more accurate translation would be something like ancestral homeland]. Many senior and middle-ranking officers in the military are deeply attached to what they perceive as their highest patriotic duty – the recovery of Taiwan for the PRC.

The formal link between the army and the Party is the CCP's Central Military Affairs Commission (CMAC, also referred to as the Central Military Commission or CMC), which exercises political control over the military and is the body from which Deng Xiaoping and Jiang Zemin were, in turn, reluctant to resign as Chairmen: this is an indication of the authority of that committee. Technically, there are two Military Affairs Commissions, the second being a government body that is operated under the auspices of the NPC. It is the CCP's CMAC that exercises real authority over the armed forces, but the membership of the two bodies overlaps and they function to all intents and purposes as one organisation. At the time when all CCP leaders had at least some military experience, as was the case in the first 20 or 30 years of the PRC, there were direct and informal personal and individual relationships between the Party and the military. In contemporary China, few of the most senior political figures have a military background (many of them being university-trained engineers and technologists who have also had a thorough political education within the CCP), and the military has developed its own separate professionally trained cadre of officers; the formal institutional relationship is increasingly important.

The CMAC normally has a membership of 11, most of whom are senior military officers of general rank. However, the Chairman and Deputy Chairman are always from the highest echelons of the CCP, and the Chairman of the CCP automatically becomes the Chairman of the CMAC, although this is formally subject to ratification by the NPC. The remit of the

CMAC is the oversight of all matters military, including the appointment of senior officers, budget allocations, the size of the PLA, and the deployment of its forces.

The CMAC also controls the Peoples Armed Police (PAP), which is a strategic paramilitary police service (paralleled to some extent by the Gendarmerie in France or the Carabinieri in Italy) that was established in 1983 and is best known for its deployment in riot control and in the most politically delicate situations such as operations against pro-independence groups in Tibet and Xinjiang. The PAP is also charged with the duty of guarding senior members of the government and the CCP, and with protecting the most significant state installations, notably Zhongnanhai – China's Kremlin – where the senior leadership live and work in a walled area to the west of the Imperial Palace. There is a clear boundary between the People's Armed Police (PAP), which is part of the military and recruits many former soldiers, and the civilian police authorities, the *Gong'anju*, who are the responsibility of the Ministry of Public Security [*Gong'anbu*].

In March 2003, the NPC was presented with a budget for increasing military expenditure by 9.6%, the lowest increase for over a decade. China has increased its expenditure on the PLA each year, although it is widely assumed by Western analysts that the publicly announced budget represents only perhaps a quarter of the real total expenditure once the cost of the purchase of armaments and research and development are included.[13]

The PLA has also played a part in economic development, particularly in the outlying areas, and has been called upon for support by the civil authorities in times of natural disasters, for example during the great earthquake which devastated the Tangshan region in 1976 and in the many episodes of severe flooding in southern China. The military played a major part in the rescue and relief efforts after the Sichuan earthquake of 2008. The PAP operates fire and rescue services throughout China.

Xi Jinping's anti-corruption campaign and the PLA

The importance to CCP leaders of a military connection is illustrated by Xi Jinping's insistence on wearing PLA uniform on military occasions and even battledress (fatigues) when reviewing troops, even though his own military experience has been very slight. It emphasises his crucial role as Chairman of the CMC, through which he exercises authority as Commander-in-Chief of all China's military forces.

Under Xi Jinping, the PLA has been subjected to the most comprehensive reform and reorganisation in 30 years. Before he could implement these reforms, Xi had to assert his authority and the military were a prime target of Xi's campaign against corruption. As with parallel campaigns against individuals in government and the CCP, charges of corruption were more common against those who were directly opposed to Xi's policies or seen as an impediment to his reforms.

The anti-corruption campaign in the military began with Lieutenant-General Gu Junshan, who was deputy director of the PLA General Logistics Department from December 2009–February 2012; in this role, he was responsible for the management and sale of military land and buildings. He amassed vast personal and family wealth, connected, among other dealings, with his younger brother's factory which supplied the military with furniture for offices and housing. Gu was charged with 'embezzlement, bribery, misuse of state funds and abuse of power',[14] and was sentenced to death with a two-year reprieve, the deprivation of his military ranks and his political rights, and the confiscation of his personal property. Suspended death sentences usually mean life imprisonment, and this sentence was regarded as lenient and only passed as Gu had given evidence against others accused of corruption.

This opened the door to the investigation of General Xu Caihou, Gu's mentor who had been second in command of the PLA and Deputy Chairman of the CMC under Hu Jintao. Xu was politically close to former leader Jiang Zemin, but he had been responsible for bribery within the highest echelons of the PLA, where the most senior ranks could be purchased for huge sums of money. By the time of his arrest in March 2014, he was already in hospital following a diagnosis of terminal bladder cancer, and he died on 15 March 2015. The criminal investigation did not proceed, but he was expelled from the CCP and his vast fortune was confiscated. The third, and even more senior, high-ranking officer to fall foul of the campaign was General Guo Boxiong, who had also been a Deputy Chairman of the CMC. He was convicted of bribery and other forms of corruption and sentenced to imprisonment for life on 25 July 2016. By targeting such powerful 'tigers', Xi Jinping had publicly demonstrated his political authority over the PLA.[15]

Modernising and managing the PLA (2008–2019)

Detailed technical and strategic considerations of changes in the PLA are beyond the scope of this book, but it is important to note the broad outlines of the modernisation of the military and how this process was managed by the political elite.[16]

Xi Jinping's plan was that the initial reorganisation be completed by 2020 and the full modernisation by 2035. By 2050, the Chinese military should be 'world class and able to win any war anywhere'.[17] The balance of forces would alter with a reduction of 300,000 in the land forces, which stood at roughly two million in 2019. The size of the air arm would remain roughly the same, while the navy would see a modest increase. Traditionally, the PLA was dominated by senior officers of the land forces, but the navy and the air force play increasingly important roles, and the role of the navy in particular has become more vital to China's Pacific defence strategy in the future.

In addition to these three existing arms, the units responsible for strategic and conventional missiles would come under a new separate arm, the Rocket Force, and a Strategic Support Force would concentrate on electronic warfare.

It was envisaged that the higher command, which is directly responsible to the CMAC, would have a flatter structure with fewer levels of bureaucracy; the existing seven military regions would be replaced by five theatre commands. These are Northern, based in Shenyang to cover Northeast and Inner Mongolia; Western, based in Chengdu and covering Xinjiang, Tibet, Qinghai, and the western provinces of China Proper; Central, based in Beijing and covering points south; Eastern, in Nanjing for the coastal provinces from roughly Shanghai to the south of Fujian; and Southern, in Guangzhou for Guangdong and Guangxi. Joint Operations Commands would be created in the coastal theatre commands to facilitate combined operations for China's projection of power into the Yellow Sea and the East and South China seas.

Xi Jinping has constantly emphasised the need for the PLA to enhance its combat readiness and in his well-publicised first order of 2019, in a speech to the CMC that was also broadcast on television, he insisted that they must be prepared for a 'comprehensive military struggle from a new starting point'. This emphasised the point made in the title of the Chinese defence White Paper, *China's National Defence in the New Era*, that China was preparing for a new style of defence for a world in which the major parameters had changed.[18]

A programme of relocating the headquarters of its service branches away from Beijing was part of Xi's response to past corruption and nepotism. Plans to relocate the command headquarters of the Ground Force, Navy, Air Force, Rocket Force, and Strategic Support

Force were being discussed by the general staff in 2015, but a decision was not reached until 2017 or 2018. While the CMC will remain in the 1 August building in the west of Beijing with small administrative departments of each of the five forces, the headquarters of individual units will be relocated away from the capital to smaller cities. The reasons for the redeployment are to reduce cronyism and nepotism within the military, and improve combat readiness. Concern had been expressed that the most senior officers were too preoccupied with developing relationships with the political hierarchy in Beijing and not directing their energies towards combat training. The relocation will also involve the streamlining of the command structures with redeployments and redundancies, and was expected to face resistance from senior officers and their families for whom an appointment to Beijing was a prized posting. It was argued that facing redundancy in a smaller city outside Beijing would be less problematic than in the capital itself.[19]

Conscription and volunteers

Although all citizens of the PRC are formally required to be available for military service, this is entirely voluntary in peacetime, and there is generally no shortage of recruits, most of whom come from the rural areas. Service in the PLA still confers status – and not only is it a way for young peasants to leave their home villages and travel around China; it is also a sound basis for securing a government job later in life. At the age of 18, everyone is obliged to register with the government authorities unless they have a place at a university, in which case they will be required to undertake a programme of military training at the beginning of their course.

The PLA conducts its nationwide recruitment exercise once a year during the winter and the formal basis for recruitment and conscription is the Military Service Law of 1984 which provides for compulsory and voluntary elements of military service and for the operation of a militia in addition to the regular armed forces. All citizens between the ages of 18 and 22 are technically eligible for military service. They become eligible on 31 December of the year in which they reach their 18th birthday, are required to register before 30 September of that year, and they then remain eligible for conscription until they are 22 years of age. The assumption is that most recruits will be men, but women are also enlisted. No-one who is the sole breadwinner for their family or is a full-time student can be required to enlist.

Out of almost ten million men who reach military age in any given year, fewer than 10% are recruited into the army; the number of women who are recruited annually is small. During the 1980s, the PLA modified its conscription policies in an attempt to increase the quality of recruits. The higher educational standards that have been required since then went some way to counter the previous dominance of rural recruits, and there is now significant recruitment from the towns and cities.[20] The PLA recruitment office issued two interim regulations in 2006, requiring that all applicants for the armed forces should take psychological tests. This was in response to concerns that had been expressed by senior military officers about the suitability of recruits in the past.[21]

The demands of increasingly technological sophistication of warfare precipitated a change in China's military recruitment process. New priorities were outlined as a National Conscription Work Video Conference on 27 June 2018: an increase in the proportion of recruits to the air force and navy rather than the army, higher calibre and better educated recruits with a preference for university and senior high school graduates, and the establishment of regional recruitment stations to process recruits and match candidates to operational requirements. In January 2020, the State Council and CMAC announced that recruitment would henceforth take place twice a year rather than once. The Ministry of Defence maintained that the aim of the new system was to sustain a smooth flow of recruits and that the total number recruited would not be increased.[22]

China's military future

The PLA celebrated its 80th anniversary on 1 August 2007. To mark that milestone, a sizeable and well attended exhibition was mounted by the Military Museum of the Chinese People's Revolution, which is on Fuxing Road in the Haidian district of Beijing and is dedicated to the history of the PLA. The aim of the exhibition was to demonstrate not only the longevity of the PLA and its central role in the construction of the PRC – and thus the legitimacy of its contemporary political influence – but also its transformation from a highly politicised peasant army into a modern professional force. The twenty-first century Chinese military machine is equipped with advanced weaponry, including nuclear weapons, and is determined to extend its global reach, particularly into the Pacific, with its fleet of five long-range Type 094 Jin class nuclear ballistic missile submarines and, in the longer term, aircraft carriers.[23]

Ten years later, Xi Jinping marked the 90th anniversary of the PLA by reviewing troops in the field for the first time, consciously following the example of both Mao Zedong and Deng Xiaoping. On 30 July 2017, and wearing battledress, he reviewed 12,000 troops in combat outfits at a massive military parade near the Combined Tactics Training Base of Zhurihe in the grasslands of Inner Mongolia, the largest and most modern training establishment in China and possibly the largest in Asia. Two days later, on the precise anniversary, he wore his normal civilian clothing to address a celebratory meeting in the Great Hall of the People in Beijing. 'While hailing the PLA's great achievements over the nine decades, Xi said the Chinese military has reshaped its political environment, organizational form, system of military strength and work style over the past five years'. He called for continued improvement to ensure that China has a world-class military.[24]

Political campaigns

A list of the formal decision-making bodies within the CCP or the Chinese government gives only a partial, and in a sense a misleading, picture of the way that politics has dominated China since 1949. A series of dramatic mass political movements or campaigns [*yundong*], designed to persuade or coerce the populace into accepting the policy or political trend current at the time, began in the 1950s and lasted until after the Cultural Revolution. These movements began with a series of mainly urban political campaigns in the 1950s, of which the most important were the Campaign for the Suppression of Counterrevolutionaries and the Three-Anti and Five-Anti campaigns. They followed on from each other and to some extent overlapped and they took place at a time of great international tension – the outbreak of the Korean War – during which the isolation of the PRC became almost complete.

The first targets of the campaigns for suppressing counter-revolutionaries were individuals deemed to have been active opponents of the CCP, but as the campaign unfolded, it drew in thousands of minor officials, most of whom were associated with the defeated Nationalist government, and their past conduct was investigated in detail. Many were exonerated, but others were convicted and imprisoned or executed. The campaign was carried out in part through the courts, but it was also a mass movement that involved 80% of the population. At mass meetings, alleged counter-revolutionaries were denounced before they were executed, and individuals were put under pressure to betray people they knew had been involved with the previous regime.

The Three-Anti [Sanfan] campaign was publicised as a mass movement to counter corruption, waste, and the culture of bureaucracy. It was aimed primarily at officials employed in government departments responsible for financial and economic affairs and who were suspected of corruption using official contacts with the old commercial and banking elite. At the same time as the Three-Anti campaign, a parallel campaign was being mounted against another set of evils, this time five in number: bribery, tax evasion, fraud, theft of government property, and the leakage of state secrets. This was the Five-Anti [Wufan] movement directed against the 'national bourgeoisie', the industrialists and powerful merchants who had until then been treated as allies; only those who had not collaborated with the Japanese could be included in that category.

Hundred Flowers Movement, Anti-Rightist Campaign

A movement to bring educated Chinese into line with CCP policies was framed around the celebrated call to 'let a hundred flowers bloom and a hundred schools of thought contend' [*baihua qifang, baijia zhengming*], a phrase that had echoes of the glorious days of ancient Chinese philosophy. The slogan was vague enough to allow for a range of interpretations, but implied that in the PRC, there was room for a plurality of views. The fact that it was conveyed with a classical slogan was intended to reassure traditional scholars and older professionals, and to bolster the idea that this was a distinctively Chinese way of resolving differences. It appeared to promise greater intellectual freedom, including criticisms of the bureaucracy. It eventually led to the denigration and isolation of much of China's educated class and this was formalised in the subsequent Anti-Rightist Campaign, which stigmatised and punished tens of thousands of professionals who were identified as opponents of Mao. The damaging effect of this campaign on the families and careers of people accused of being 'rightists' lasted for decades.

Great Leap Forward

In the late 1950s and early 1960s, the Great Leap Forward dominated the Chinese press, newsreels, and the nascent television industry. There were constant images of the mass mobilisation of people from all walks of life, leaving their routine jobs and delighting in voluntary labour in the service of the state to complete some essential public works project. The drab and uniform clothing that men and women wore at the time – approximating to military uniforms in blue, or sometimes green or grey, denim – gave rise to the notion of an 'army of blue ants' on the move. The images of labour mobilisation were accompanied by overt political slogans and increasingly by portraits of Mao Zedong, a manifestation of the growing 'cult of personality' borrowed by Mao and his supporters from Stalin. The Great Leap Forward ended in catastrophe. Famine stalked the countryside and millions died from hunger and disease, but for decades, the scale of the disaster was concealed from the outside world and from China's urban population.

Cultural Revolution and after

On one level, the Cultural Revolution was the last of the major campaigns associated with Mao's ideas of continuous revolution. The campaign for converting bourgeois art into proletarian art which began the movement rapidly degenerated into a major factional conflict with violent clashes between Red Guard groups and the collapse of political order. The Cultural Revolution did not, however, see the end of political campaigns. The campaign against Lin Biao and Confucius of the early 1970s masked a factional battle aimed specifically at Zhou Enlai.

Bourgeois liberalisation

The final political mobilisation that was organised in the familiar Maoist manner was the campaign against 'bourgeois liberalisation' [*zichanjieji ziyouhua*] of 1985–1987. It was launched by conservatives in the Party hierarchy, notably Chen Yun, Peng Zhen, and Hu Qiaomu, who were opposed to the pace of Deng Xiaoping's reform programme, but particularly to what they perceived as the excessive Westernisation and democratisation that accompanied economic reforms. The conservatives believed that the increasing influence of the West was a genuine threat to the 'four cardinal principles' that Deng had agreed to prioritise as a counterbalance to his 'reform and opening' and undermined the leadership of the CCP. The principal target of the campaign was Hu Yaobang, who was ahead of his time in his support for democratisation and political pluralism.

The campaign was, to some extent, prompted by the appearance in China of limited examples of Western culture which displeased the older generation. Colourful clothes, new hairstyles, beauty parlours, and rock music all made their first appearance: the pop group Wham! played to a youthful audience of 15,000 in the People's Gymnasium in Beijing in April 1985, none of which would seem remarkable in the twenty-first century. It was the movement for democracy that began the following year with demonstrations in Hefei, led by the astrophysicist and dissident Fang Lizhi, that prompted the campaign. 'Bourgeois liberalisation' was identified as an evil by the CCP Central Committee in 1986, and in January 1987, an authoritative article criticising this iniquitous deviation appeared in *People's Daily*. Hu Yaobang was forced to resign as General Secretary of the CCP and many renowned intellectuals, including Fang Lizhi, were expelled from the CCP, some seeking refuge abroad.

Political campaigns of this type died out, but they were a powerful and pernicious presence in Chinese society from the 1950s to the 1970s, and the aftereffects linger on – people learned how to survive, but were always looking over their shoulders waiting for the next salvo. In addition to the losses of family members to prison, or sometimes to execution, and the damage to careers, a protective culture of self-censorship evolved that has stifled debate and creativity. Whatever criticisms Chinese citizens today might have about the political system under which they have to live in the twenty-first century, they have reason to be grateful for the absence of these campaigns.

Village committees: democracy from below?

Outbreaks of rural disorder beginning in 2004, and especially the violent suppression of the demonstrations in Guangdong province, raised the question of the role of village committees in the minds of Chinese political leaders and thinkers, as well as international observers. The Chinese government began promoting the development of directly elected village committees in the early 1980s, and serious attempts to introduce direct elections began in 1987. Rural unrest escalated in the 1990s, and Beijing considered strengthening these committees as a way of creating bodies that would resolve conflict and assure the Party's control over the countryside. How effective and how democratic they have been is a moot point, but their function was to ensure the consolidation of state power rather than the spreading of democracy for its own sake.

When the People's Communes were dismantled in 1978 at the beginning of the reform era, this was not only the end of collective agriculture, but also of a system of rural local government that had been in operation for 20 years. The idea of village committees, or more correctly 'villager committees' [*cunmin weiyuanhui*], was introduced to fill the vacuum. These committees are subordinate to the Ministry of Civil Affairs [*minzheng bu*], but operate below the lowest level of the formal government structure, the township. The evolving relationship between the committees and the township was not precisely defined.

The 1982 Constitution of the PRC included provisions for the direct election of committees by village residents. This was strengthened by the Draft Organic Law on Villager Committees, which was provisionally adopted by the NPC in November 1987 and which set out detailed regulations for the organisation and role of the committees and the procedures to be adopted in elections. During the trial period that followed, 25 provinces established committees. Many observers were highly sceptical about the election process. The government claimed that the election procedures were independent of the CCP and a shining example of rural democracy. In many cases, however, it was simply a case of the CCP providing a slate of candidates for the village residents to approve. In some elections, independently minded candidates did secure election, and this posed a challenge to the supremacy of the Party in the countryside. There was considerable opposition to the law within the CCP, and a significant body of opinion saw it as a threat by Western-style ideas of democracy to China's political system and to the power of the CCP, but in November 1998, an amended version of the legislation was passed by the NPC.

Typically, village committees consist of between three and seven villagers elected for a three-year term. They have a wide range of administrative responsibilities which include taxation and the management of budgets, public property and services, public order, social welfare, and the resolution of local disputes. This gives the committee considerable local power, but it is overseen by a village representative assembly which is supposed to be able to check abuses.

During the 1990s, rural China experienced a serious social crisis that was in part caused by budgetary decentralisation, the decline in funding from central government, and the search by local authorities to find new ways of generating revenue. Peasant families that had expected to receive land were dispossessed as wealthier families acquired large landholdings. Many were impoverished by the high taxes set by local government, often illegally. Resistance to these taxes and protests at corruption by local officials led to thousands of incidents of serious disorder in the countryside. These were aggravated by conflicts between farmers over land ownership. Subsequently, the forced – and some claim illegal – seizure of land by local officials and businessmen for the construction of non-agricultural enterprises exacerbated the situation. This was particularly the case in rural areas on the outskirts of major urban centres.

During these conflicts and protests, a new generation of peasant activists acquired political and organisational experience. Autonomous organisations with names such as the Peasant Burden Reduction Group and Peasant Rights Preservation Committee proliferated. The CCP has never been comfortable with independent political organisations, and has sought either to incorporate them into structures they could control or suppressed them. They have, however, been obliged to accept that the peasants represented by these organisations had genuine grievances that it was necessary to address.

It was hoped that the revised 1998 Organic Law on Village Committees which made provision for them to be run democratically and to be financially accountable would solve some of these problems. The law required:

1   The open nomination of candidates by individuals rather than a Party slate.
2   More than one candidate for each position.
3   Secret ballots in private voting booths.
4   A public count.
5   The immediate announcement of the result.
6   A recall procedure if the electors were not satisfied with the performance of the committee members.

In spite of this formally democratic system, the CCP did not abandon its attempt to control the process. It provided its own candidates and recruited able and popular village activists to the Party. The committees were a way of legitimising the Party in the rural areas, and this is particularly important for its power base. The roots of the modern CCP lie in the peasant movement of the 1930s and 1940s, and the leadership are keenly aware of the potential power of that peasantry. They recognise the need to keep the rural poor on their side rather than risk the development of independent organisations led by intellectuals from the countryside. It is important to note that, however open and democratic the village committee elections are, the CCP secretary in the village is not elected but is appointed by more senior Party bodies. There have been many reports of conflict between elected village heads and appointed Party secretaries: in the final analysis, the Party secretaries can override other bodies because they are able to call on more powerful support from higher CCP organisations.

The village committees do not automatically represent the interests of the peasants. They have taken the side of developers and local officials in many cases, and this gave rise to demonstrations and disorder, especially in Guangdong province. There have also been concerns that the committees are being taken over by rural groups based on extended families or clans that operate outside the law, and in some cases by criminal gangs and mafia-style organisations. On its own, the strengthening of village committees is unlikely to solve the problems of rural unrest. A genuinely independent judicial system would give poor farmers a legitimate outlet for their grievances, but that is unlikely at present. In the wake of recent protests, the few independent lawyers who have been willing to represent peasants have been barred from the courts.

The legal rights of peasants are far from clear. Theoretically, all land still belongs to collectives, but it is parcelled out to families who have the right and responsibility to farm it. The state is effectively the owner, but it is the new generation of landlords who have real power in the villages. They are involved in increasingly complex land disputes, and the poorer peasants are excluded from ownership and political power.

Some Chinese scholars have argued for the reintroduction of Peasant Associations. These were organisations used by the CCP in its campaigns for rent reduction and land redistribution from the 1920s to the 1940s. They were abandoned when the Party came to power and were effectively replaced by cooperatives, and subsequently the People's Communes. While their historical role was as revolutionary organisations, it is now being argued that they could function as representative organisations for peasants and play an important role in social integration in the countryside. It is interesting that one major outbreak of rural disorder in 2006 took place in Dongzhou and Shanwei which are only a few miles from Haifeng and Lufeng, the centres of the first Peasant Association movement in China in 1922.[25]

Central state, local state

The village committee system reflects general problems of governance faced by the Party-state in the reform period. As the CCP has reduced its control over the economy, it has also lost its authority over the regions. The relationship between the central state – Party committees and government ministries in Beijing – and the local state – the town and district councils – is an intriguing and evolving process.

Although it is not possible for central government to manage all aspects of the operation of local government directly, this is an issue that has absorbed many politicians in Beijing since the early years of the reform programme. Overall, control of policy and style of government is achieved not only by exhortation and political persuasion but also by a systematic programme of cadre evaluation. Local cadres are trained, evaluated, and rotated between lower- and higher-level posts in an effort to ensure continuity and consistency in the interpretation and implementation of policy. The cadre evaluation system is not new, but it has been overhauled and strengthened to reflect the demands of economic and fiscal decentralisation and the devolution of decision making to the regions.

Cases in which this system has failed tend to be highlighted, notably when there is local corruption or when political problems lead to disturbances. On balance, the system has enabled the central state to retain a great degree of control over the actions of local officials.

From local democracy to surveillance: the case of Wukan

A standoff that began on 21 September 2011 between the villagers of Wukan on the coast of Guangdong province and local officials after protests against land seizures and corruption was one of many 'mass incidents' during the period of dramatic economic growth. It took place in a historically significant part of China, and the protests took on an unusual political form.

Wukan is a coastal fishing village in the rural district administered by the city of Lufeng. The area has a history of peasant activism and resistance that goes back to the 1920s, when with neighbouring Haifeng it was part of the Hailufeng Soviet, a peasant government organised by Peng Pai, one of the most influential leaders of the CCP among the peasantry, predating Mao Zedong's peasant activism in Hunan province. The rural Soviet in 1920s Guangdong was part of the wider movement that eventually led to the victory of the CCP in 1949 and the establishment of the PRC. Leaders of the CCP in the early twenty-first century were concerned that a similar rural movement could become the agent of their downfall.

The discontent of the farmers dated back to the 1990s, when 400 hectares of farmland were sold to property developers. The deals were far from transparent, and did not adequately compensate those who had previously farmed the land, but it was widely believed that officials of the local government and CCP had made excessive profits from the sales. Petitions to central government in 2009 and 2010 went unanswered.

The Wukan demonstrations began on 21 September 2011 as villagers picketed local government buildings, the police station, and an industrial park. A detachment of 400 riot police was deployed, and several villagers were injured, some seriously. Following the intervention of the Guangdong provincial Party Secretary, Wang Yang, who favoured a non-confrontational approach as part of his 'Happy Guangdong' policy, a group of 13 villagers was permitted to negotiate with the local authorities, but after the arrest of three of them and the death in police custody on 11 December of a protester, Xue Jinbo, these negotiations broke down. Villagers attacked the local police station, and officials were forced out of the village.

Wang Yang's intervention led to an agreement to suspend the sale of farmland, the dissolution of the existing village committee, and a rare free ballot to elect a new committee. At the election held on 1 February 2012, one of the leading protesters, Lin Zuluan, who had been heading a shadow village government from the local temple to Mazu, the goddess of the sea traditionally revered by fisherman in the south China Sea, was elected village chief.

The dismissed committee members refused to accept defeat, and sought revenge and retribution through the courts. As government attitudes became more authoritarian under Xi Jinping and Wang Yang, in spite of his liberal reputation, rose in the hierarchy to become a member of the Politburo Standing Committee, most of the protest leaders were prosecuted – including Lin Zuluan, who was imprisoned after being convicted or corruption. Villagers insisted that the charges were fake and that a televised confession that he had taken bribes made by Lin had been under duress and demands for Lin's release led to further disturbances which lasted for several months. In December 2016, nine more villagers were accused of 'illegal assembly, disrupting traffic and spreading false information', and imprisoned for between two and nine years by the People's Court at Haifeng. By the end of 2017, the protest was no more; the government's policy of security above all was applied to Wukan. Security cameras had been installed, residents were unwilling to talk to visiting journalists, and the streets were lined with propaganda hoardings and posters proclaiming peace and stability.[26] The Wukan crisis illustrates the limitations of the village committee system.

The Mao problem

Assessing the role of Mao Zedong in the political history of China has always been problematic, both within China and among outside observers and analysts. As the leader of the most successful CCP grouping in the 1940s, hailed as the victor in the Civil War of 1946–1949 and as the founding Chairman of the PRC, Mao was the dominant figure on the mainland from 1949 until his death in September 1976.

His shadow continues to hang over contemporary China. His portrait still hangs above the southern entrance to the old Forbidden City, just below the rostrum on Tian'anmen Gate and overlooking Tian'anmen Square, which lies to the south, from where he proclaimed the establishment of the PRC on 1 October 1949. His likeness also remains on China's banknotes, even though his economic policies were rejected long ago. Although Mao memorabilia are now mainly sold to curious Westerners, he is still, if not revered, at least respected by many ordinary Chinese.[27]

On 8 September 2006, the eve of the 30th anniversary of his death, the Chinese language website of the official newspaper of the CCP, *People's Daily*, led with photographs taken from 1965–1974 showing Mao with world leaders and other prominent figures including US President Richard Nixon, UK Prime Minister Edward Heath, King Sihanouk of Cambodia, and Malaysian Prime Minister Mahathir Mohammed. The accompanying commentary was a reassessment of Mao's international influence and by no means a negative one, emphasising his role as an international statesman and the part that he had played in putting China on the world map.[28] Assessments of his contribution to China's modernisation and his own character are many and varied. Was he simply China's Stalin, a replica of the Soviet autocrat, or was there something different about him, something that could be called peculiarly Chinese? Was he a new-style version of the traditional Chinese emperors?

During the 1970s, Mao and Maoism had attracted the attention of radical Third World movements and a body of left-wing intellectuals, primarily in Europe. Third World radicals were also attracted by Mao's approach, as they saw the success of the peasant-based CCP as a model for their own political aspirations. Many peasant movements in Asia and Latin America declared themselves to be followers of Mao, or at least to have been influenced by his analysis of the potential of peasant revolution. What attracted many was the simplistic version of this analysis which had been popularised, at first in the PLA and then in China at large, by Lin Biao, who was at the time designated as Mao's 'close comrade-in-arms' and was his presumptive heir. Much of the image of Mao that the West perceived in the 1960s and 1970s was manipulated and popularised by Lin, a spin doctor before the concept had been invented. Lin's vision postulated the encirclement of the cities of the world by the countryside of the world in the same way that the CCP, it was argued, had encircled China's cities from its rural bases.[29] In an era when there was widespread support and sympathy, particularly on the political left, for peasant movements of national liberation, this appealing but unsophisticated argument won many devotees.

Time has not been kind to either these ideas or the movements that espoused them, but even in the early twenty-first century, when there are few Maoists in China apart from small groups sustained by internet publications which cling to Maoist formulae to resist economic modernisation, there are groups declaring themselves to be Maoists in Asia and Latin America. In India, the Naxalite insurrection of 1967 in the district of Naxalbari in West Bengal was inspired by Maoism and, in spite of severe government repression which almost eradicated them in the 1970s, their ideas live on and the Communist Party of India (Maoist) can maintain, with considerable justification, that it has the support of large numbers of the poor and dispossessed. 'Maoist' ideas are particularly influential in the regions inhabited by groups that are usually thought of as ethnic minorities but are known in India by the quaint term 'tribals', with all its archaic echoes of the British Raj.[30] Maoist rebels attacked a freight train at Latehar in the northeastern Indian state of Jharkhand on 26 June 2007, destroyed railway tracks, and abducted the driver and the guard of the train. They also called for an economic blockade in the region to protest against the development of Special Economic Zones, arguing that these would further impoverish many poor villagers. Similar attacks were reported in the state of Bihar, from which Jharkand was carved in 2000.[31]

In Nepal, a Maoist insurgency had challenged the troubled monarchy of that Himalayan kingdom for decades until the government took steps to try to bring it into the political mainstream in April 2006. In Peru, a major guerrilla movement which – like many of the radical groups in South America – is largely supported by indigenous or minority peoples is known as the *Sendero Luminoso* (Shining Path) and declares its allegiance to Mao and Maoism.

In Europe, the *événements* of May 1968 in Paris and the radical student and worker movement that accompanied them were contemporaneous with the most dramatic period of the Cultural Revolution: some European radical thinkers and activists, notably Jean-Paul Sartre, sought to ally themselves with Maoism. Most of those who did so had little direct knowledge or experience of Mao Zedong's policies or the Cultural Revolution in China, which was hardly surprising since China was off limits to most outsiders at that time. There was no real understanding of the authoritarian and Stalinist nature of Mao's regime, and some young Western radicals were attracted to the libertarian and anti-bureaucratic rhetoric that was emanating from the Red Guard movement.

The publication of *Mao: The Unknown Story* in 2005 brought a contentious and highly publicised version of Mao's life before the English-speaking general public for the first time.[32] This polemical and sensational work was published by a commercial firm rather than a serious academic press, and the authors claimed to have used sources that had been neglected by previous biographers, including documents from archives in Russia that had been previously unavailable. The book focuses on the negative qualities of Mao and his unpleasant personal characteristics and habits, and it has planted in the collective consciousness of the non-specialist public the idea that Mao was personally responsible for as many as 70 million deaths in China during the period of his rule.

Scholars of the Mao period and specialists in Mao's writings and activities have taken issue with this biography, not in any spirit of sympathising with Mao or support for his policies, but because the citations do not add up. Many sources which could have been used have been omitted. Individuals who knew Mao well were not interviewed, including foreigners who had worked with him closely and had acted as his translators or interpreters. Many of the sources chosen are partial or highly suspect. Is it sensible to believe that documents written by members of the Soviet government, the CPSU, and the former Soviet security services, which are lodged in the archives in Moscow and Leningrad, are accurate and factual because they show China and Mao in a negative light, when during the Cold War years they would have been regarded with the deepest suspicion?

Clearly, Mao was not the sort of person to be invited to dinner parties, and it may not have been advisable to introduce one's daughter or favourite niece to him, but was he a monster? He was almost certainly an egomaniac of the highest order, a man who had no compunction about blighting the careers of anyone who opposed him and had very little regard for the sanctity of human life, especially the lives of the peasants whose cause he was supposed to espouse. However, there is a problem in trying to match the image of Mao that has been purveyed in the West – a sadistic monster who had no education or ideas of his own – with what appears to have been the genuine reverence shown to him by huge numbers of Chinese people, including some of the most highly educated. He continues to be regarded with a great deal of pride as the leader, albeit a highly flawed leader, who made it possible for China to 'stand up'. The good old days of Mao are looked back on with a degree of nostalgia by some who contend that, in spite of the prevalent poverty, there was no corruption and that social problems such as prostitution and drug abuse were unknown. This view through rose-tinted spectacles, however short-sighted and ill-informed it might be, is still widespread. There is sufficient evidence of, if not corruption, at least the abuse of privilege among senior Party and government officials that goes back decades, but it was not public knowledge at the time – and the opportunities for financial corruption were in any case small, since there was very little money available.

People who knew Mao in his early days, including some who suffered under his regime, still contend that he was most comfortable with peasants and liked and respected them. He had his finger on the pulse of rural China, and he clearly had a talent for framing policies and ideas in a way that peasants would respond to positively: in his speeches and writings, he mixed idioms from several Chinese traditions including Daoism and Buddhism with a veneer of Marxism. To a large extent, Mao (and many of his supporters in the CCP) retained a narrow-minded outlook. Mao's only travels abroad were to Moscow; he was not an enthusiast for sophisticated urban culture, and even less for foreign society, and he seemed most at home in the peasant heartlands of China. He never made the transition from revolutionary political heavyweight to international statesman, and he did not transcend his romantic attachment to the tradition and legends of rural peasant rebels.[33]

Notes

1 *Constitution of the People's Republic of China* Beijing: Foreign Languages Press, 1954. Chinese text in *Jianguo yilai* Volume 5, pp. 520–42.

2 A formal statement of the NPC's own view of its work and its status can be found on its website at http://english.gov.cn/links/npc.htm.

3 https://npcobserver.com/2018/03/11/translation-2018-amendment-to-the-p-r-c-constitution/.

4 *China Daily* 1 July 2019; *Times of India* 29 August 2019. A useful single volume account of the CCP is Richard McGregor *The Party: The Secret World of China's Communist Rulers* London: Penguin, 2011.

5 Xinhua 12 October 2007, 30 June 2018.

6 Human Rights Watch, 18 October 2017.

7 *SCMP* 26 July 2018.

8 *SCMP* 17 August 2020; *Global Times* 20 August 2020; *Guardian* 21 August 2020.

9 *Financial Times* (*FT*) 17 July 2007; Xinhua 12 October 2007, 30 June 2018.

10 This is remarkably similar to factions in the Liberal Democratic Party (a conservative party in spite of its name) that has ruled Japan for most of the period since the Second World War.

11 *FT* 27 December 2007.

12 Yuan Houchun *The Great Disarmament* Beijing: Writers' Publishing House, 2009.

13 *SCMP* 6 March 2003.

14 *SCMP*, 10 August 2015.

15 *SCMP* 10 August 2015, 17 March, 30 July 2015; Ben Lowsen 'The True Crimes of Chinese PLA General Guo Boxiong' *The Diplomat* 15 June 2016.

16 An accessible and detailed analysis, although from a US defence point of view, is Phillip C. Saunders, Arthur S. Ding, Andrew Scobell, Andrew N.D. Yang, and Joel Wuthnow (eds.) *Chairman Xi Remakes the PLA: Assessing Chinese Military Reforms* Washington, DC: National Defense University Press, 2019.

17 *FT* 28 January 2019.

18 *SCMP* 5 January 2019; Katherine Hille 'China's Army Redoubles Modernisation Effort' *FT* 28 January 2019; Manoj Joshi 'Raisina Debates' Observer Research Foundation, New Delhi, 25 July 2019.

19 *SCMP* 17 April 2019.

20 *People's Daily* website.

21 Xinhua 29 September 2006.

22 Adam Ni 'What Are China's Military Recruitment Priorities?' *The Diplomat* 10 August 2018; *China Daily* 16 January 2020.

23 BBC News, *FT* 31 July 2007.

24 Xinhua 30 July 2017.

25 Tony Saich *Governance and Politics of China* Basingstoke: Palgrave Macmillan, 2004, pp. 195–201; Yawei Liu 'Assessing China's Villager Self-Government' *Carter Centre China Elections Project*, 3 November 2006; 'Victory for Villagers in Battle over "Rigged Poll" for Chief' *SCMP* 2 May 2006; 'Police Tackle "Rural Mafia"' *SCMP* 7 November 2006.

26 Reuters 10 November 2017; *SCMP* 6 October 2012.

27 The author was the subject of considerable derision from Chinese colleagues in a village outside Xi'an in 2005 when he bought a ceramic ornament of the Cultural Revolution period depicting Mao and Lin Biao.

28 *Renmin Ribao* 8 September 2006.

29 Lin Biao *Long Live the Victory of People's War* Beijing: Foreign Languages Press, 1965. This pamphlet was originally published as a leading article in *Renmin Ribao* on 3 September 1965 to commemorate the 20th anniversary of the defeat of Japan at the end of the Second World War.

30 Sunil Janah *The Tribals of India* Calcutta: Oxford University Press, 1993; 'A Spectre Haunting India' *Economist* 19 August 2006.

31 BBC News 27 June 2007.

32 Jung Chang and Jon Halliday *Mao: The Unknown Story* London: Jonathan Cape, 2005.

33 More balanced and authoritative assessments of Mao's status and his place in the history of modern China can be found in Philip Short *Mao: A Life* and Roderick MacFarquhar and Michael Schoenhals *Mao's Last Revolution*. Julia Lovell *Maoism: A Global History* London: Bodley Head, 2019 is a recent treatment of the international impact of Mao's ideas.

4   Seeking a harmonious society

Fourth-generation leadership of Hu Jintao and Wen Jiabao

The published agenda for the full meeting of the Central Committee of the CCP, from 9–11 October 2000, emphasised the Tenth Five-Year Plan for the development of the national economy and, in particular, the Western Development Programme, the grand plan for developing the impoverished western regions of the country. (For details of this programme, see Chapter 12.)

The participants were, however, more concerned to establish the basis for a smooth transition from the generation of leaders led by Jiang Zemin to what would become known as the fourth-generation [*di sidai*] leadership of the PRC. The impending retirement of President Jiang Zemin, Premier Zhu Rongji, and the Chairman of the NPC, Li Peng, within two years was confirmed and the names of the men who were to lead the new generation were given new prominence: Hu Jintao was confirmed as Vice-President, Wen Jiabao as Vice-Premier, and Zeng Qinghong, a prominent member of Jiang's Shanghai faction, was promoted to be the head of the CCP's Organisation Department.

This fourth-generation leadership that emerged from the 16th CCP Congress in November 2002 showed the Party in flux, fully committed to economic modernisation, but unswervingly dedicated to maintaining its own central and unchallengeable role in preserving the stability of the state. It also marked the beginning of the political decline of the Shanghai faction headed by Jiang Zemin. This was reinforced by the enforced resignation of Zeng Qinghong in October 2007, ostensibly because he had reached retirement age. Zeng had worked hard to liaise between Party factions, but he had been Jiang's preferred successor.

Generations of leadership in the PRC

The concept of generations of leadership in the CCP and the PRC did not appear in the public discourse until the 1990s during the final years of Deng Xiaoping's life. The issues of succession, and the balance of change and continuity, were always in the minds of the Party hierarchy and its collective memory in the Secretariat. Once the concept of a 'fourth generation' had become commonplace, it became necessary reclassify previous leaders in three predecessor generations.

First generation (1949–1976)

The key figures of the first generation, although that term was never used at the time, were Mao Zedong, Liu Shaoqi, Peng Dehuai, Lin Biao, and Zhou Enlai. They were the founding generation of the CCP in power and brought with them the legacy of the Long March, the revolutionary struggle in the countryside, the guerrilla resistance to the Japanese occupation, and the battlefields of the Civil War on which they defeated the armies of the Nationalists. They also carried with them the baggage of factional, political, and personal differences that were to bedevil China's domestic politics during the 1950s and which came to a head in the Cultural Revolution.

Second generation (1978–1992)

The second generation were Deng Xiaoping and the group of veteran Party leaders (often designated simplistically as moderates or conservatives) who came to power following the death of Mao Zedong in 1976 and the elimination of his political supporters, notably the Gang of Four. The major contribution of the second generation of leaders to the political development of the country was their willingness to tackle the thorny problem of economic reform as China emerged from the years of the Cultural Revolution.

Among the key members of this group were Chen Yun, respected as the Party's economics supremo, and Hu Yaobang and Zhao Ziyang, who both served as Premier, one after the other. This coalition came to grief after the military suppression of the Democracy Movement in Beijing on 4 June 1989.

The demise of the Soviet Union and the Communist states of Eastern Europe weighed heavily on Deng and his colleagues of the second generation; the lessons they took from this collapse included the need to ensure the legitimacy of the CCP by creating strong economic growth and maintaining close Party links to the growing business sector, while simultaneously consolidating the Party's authority over the military apparatus. This combination was far from the liberal regime that some Western observers hoped for, but the pragmatism Deng and his supporters demonstrated guaranteed the stability and continuation of the regime, which was above all else the main aim of the CCP.

Third generation (1989–2002)

Jiang Zemin, who succeeded Deng, was often derided as a nondescript caretaker Chairman of the Party. His administration followed Deng's prescription for stability and growth, but he will be remembered particularly for his initiative in admitting senior people from the business community to the Party. At the end of his term of office, Jiang was reluctant to relinquish the authority and influence of his office, to an extent that was extraordinary even for a CCP leader. This was assuaged somewhat by the possibility that his ideas would be preserved for posterity, partly as a result of a strange biography written by an American investment banker, Robert Kuhn, but approved by the Chinese authorities, which tried to present Jiang, in the eponymous title, as *The Man Who Changed China*. This was followed in 2006 by a multi-volume compilation of Jiang's speeches and writings in a *Selected Works* that ran to 654 pages.[1]

Although Jiang Zemin retired as General Secretary of the CCP in 2002 to make way for Hu Jintao and the fourth generation, his withdrawal from the leadership was gradual; he did not finally relinquish his last appointment as Chairman of the State CMC until 2005. He was the 'core' of the third-generation leadership and remained a shadow member of the fourth generation, a position strengthened by his leadership of the Shanghai faction within the CCP. His ability to influence the policies of the fourth generation from behind the scenes is illustrated by the consternation caused by rumours that circulated in 2011 that he was seriously ill or even that he had died. He had made no public appearances since December 2010 but appeared on television with Hu Jintao on 9 October 2011 during the celebrations of the centenary of the 1911 revolution. At the time of writing in August 2020, Jiang was 94 years old and no longer active in politics, although he did appear on ceremonial occasions.

Jiang's Premier, Zhu Rongji, was more noteworthy. Zhu, like Jiang, was a former Mayor of Shanghai. He was renowned for the bluntness of his manner and the shortness of his temper, but highly respected for his competent management of China's transition to a semi-market economy. He was largely responsible for the technical aspects of China's successful application to join the World Trade Organisation in 2001.

Fourth generation (2002–2012)

The two most prominent fourth-generation figures in the Politburo Standing Committee were President Hu Jintao and Prime Minister Wen Jiabao. The Vice-President, Zeng Qing-hong, part of the powerful Shanghai faction associated with former President Jiang Zemin, had a much lower profile but exercised considerable influence and had the reputation of being a shrewd political operator. He was also widely assumed to have seen himself as Hu's successor as President until his reluctant retirement at the 17th Party Congress in October 2007. There had been much speculation on whether a Hu–Zeng axis was emerging, which would eventually eliminate Wen Jiabao, or whether Wen was successfully consolidating his own position by embracing populist causes such as the reduction of poverty, opposition to political corruption and environmental protection. By the end of the 17th Party Congress in the autumn of 2007, Zeng had been removed and Hu and Wen were still in post.

Hu Jintao was born in Anhui province in southern China in 1942. He studied hydroelectric engineering at Qinghua (Tsinghua) University in Beijing and joined the CCP in 1964 while a student. He was a classic product of the 'double burden' system under which China's future potential leaders were simultaneously educated in technology and trained as politicians. His early career was in the Ministry of Water Conservancy and Power, not a glamourous post but one in which he managed some of the fundamental issues in the development of China's economy.

The most important positions Hu occupied were low profile, in the west of China and out of the political limelight. He was best known for the authoritarian style with which he ruled Gansu, the poor and remote province in the northwest, in the 1970s and 1980s and for his role as CCP Secretary in Tibet in the 1980s and 1990s, when he imposed martial law. He was also head of the Central Party School. One of his power bases was a group of former members of the CYL, of which he had been First Secretary in 1984–1985. He was recalled to Beijing in 1992 as a member of the Politburo Standing Committee under Jiang Zemin, but Deng Xiaoping continued to exercise considerable influence. When Hu became President of China in 2003, he brought officials from the CYL to Beijing and promoted them to key positions.

Like previous leaders of the CCP, Hu realised that he needed to ensure that the military remained firmly under the control of the Party and guarantee their support for him personally in order to consolidate his power. When Jiang Zemin retired, somewhat reluctantly, from the post of Chairman of the CMC on 19 September 2004, Hu Jintao moved rapidly to strengthen his personal relationship with senior military officers. He was responsible for promoting several key officers, including members of the CMC, to the rank of general and appeared publicly at PLA functions and exercises. He also made a point of being photographed with senior officers while wearing the Sun Yat-sen jacket [*zhongshan zhuang* – often called the Mao jacket] in military green rather than his usual trademark Western-style suit with collar and tie.[2]

Hu Jintao also strengthened the CCP's links to the increasingly important business sector, continuing the process initiated by Jiang Zemin. His 2006 New Year broadcast address focused on his commitment to 'peaceful development', the consensus term for China's non-aggressive rise to power and multi-lateralism. However, he also made a point of stressing his continuing support for the 'One China principle' and the active promotion of the peaceful reunification of Taiwan and opposition to Taiwanese secessionists (that is, the DPP of Chen Shui-bian), the cause dearest to the heart of the military. His priority was to maintain the legitimacy and longevity of the CCP above all other matters. He was a cautious but determined politician, a steady hand on the tiller and not easily rattled. He was prepared to tolerate administrative reforms, but not fundamental political change.

Prime Minister Wen Jiabao's image was of a meticulous, perhaps even dull, functionary, more concerned about results than political slogans. He was trained as a geologist, also worked in Gansu province and, during China's long drawn-out period of applying to join the World Trade Organisation (WTO), was given the crucial task of developing policies on agriculture, finance, and the environment. Wen had previously worked with Hu Yaobang, Zhao Ziyang, and Jiang Zemin when they were successively Party chairmen and, in June 1989, he had accompanied Zhao Ziyang on his celebrated visit to the students on hunger strike in Tian'anmen Square. Unlike Zhao, who was sacked and placed under house arrest, Wen's political career survived.

Premier Wen identified himself publicly with popular causes, especially the environment, openness, decreasing the wealth gap, and attacks on corruption. He visited Harbin on 26 November 2005 to observe the recovery work after the pollution of the Songhua River, admonished local officials for not having acted quickly enough, and warned against attempting a cover-up. He stressed the need for putting the protection of the environment ahead of the push for economic growth at any cost. On the eve of New Year 2006, he visited the cities of Jiujiang and Ruichang in the northeast of Jiangxi province which on 26 November had been devastated by an earthquake that cost the lives of 13 people and left over 100,000 homeless. Wen emphasised the need for reconstruction, not only of housing but also schools that had also been damaged or destroyed. He came from a humble family background and had the reputation of being genuinely concerned for the welfare of the common people.[3]

Wen Jiabao was consciously populist and never missed an opportunity to associate himself with victims in times of tragedy and loss, and to align himself with the public against official corruption and incompetence. Although his man-of-the-people manner and ease with in dealing with the public and publicity gained him popularity, it also led critics to question his integrity and describe him as 'China's best actor'.[4]

Anniversaries of former politicians

The treatment by the CCP of former leaders often illuminates the internal balance of power. Commemorations of the deaths of Hu Yaobang and Zhao Ziyang revealed noteworthy tensions within the Politburo Standing Committee. In the final months of 2005, there was considerable debate behind the scenes in Beijing on how to mark what would have been the 90th birthday of Hu Yaobang, who had died in 1989, and the first anniversary of the death of his successor, Zhao Ziyang. In CCP terms, Hu, whose death provided the focus for the Democracy Movement which was crushed on 4 June 1989, and Zhao were liberal reformers; attitudes to their legacy give an indication of the state of internal Party politics in 2005 and 2006.

A meeting to mark the 90th anniversary of Hu Yaobang's birth was held in the Great Hall of the People on Friday 18 November. It was a low-key affair, described by *People's Daily* as a symposium, and attended by three members of the Politburo Standing Committee, including Wen Jiabao and Zeng Qinghong. Hu Jintao did not attend, although he had supported the decision to hold the meeting. This was perhaps surprising as Hu Jintao had been appointed head of the CYL by Hu Yaobang in the 1980s and continued to associate himself to some degree with the more liberal and tolerant ethos that his mentor encouraged.[5] Hu Yaobang was General Secretary of the CCP in the mid-1980s and not only was he open-minded, he was personally responsible for the rehabilitation of political figures who had lost their posts during the Cultural Revolution. He was dismissed as Premier in 1987 after a series of demonstrations by students which began as protests against the increasing involvement of Japanese business in the Chinese economy but went on to attack corruption and demand greater democracy.

Zhao Ziyang died on 17 January 2005, but there were no public ceremonies to mark the first anniversary, which would have been standard practice. Instead, it was commemorated by a small gathering of family and friends: campaigners for democracy were firmly excluded. The former Premier is honoured for his role in extending the market reforms he had developed in Sichuan province to the whole of China in the 1980s, but his role in the 1989 crackdown, when he appeared to side with the demonstrating students, led to his house arrest for 15 years and made him a powerful symbol for reformers within the CCP. Rumours persisted that he had left behind a manuscript giving his version of the bitter political battles behind the scenes that led to the unleashing of units of the PLA on unarmed demonstrators on 4 June 1989. His memoir, *Prisoner of the State: The Secret Journal of Premier Zhao Ziyang*, based on taped interviews during his house arrest, was published in English in 2009.[6]

The 30th anniversary of the death of Zhou Enlai, in many ways the model for both Hu Yaobang and Zhao Ziyang, on 8 January 1976 was commemorated by the publication of a substantial memorial volume *Pictorial Biography of Zhou Enlai* [*Zhou Enlai hua zhuan*]. The book was launched at a symposium in the Zhou Enlai Memorial Chamber in the Mao Zedong Memorial Hall and was presided over by the Deputy Chairwoman of the Standing Committee of the NPC, Gu Xiulian. The former Prime Minister is still venerated as a great revolutionary and the politician who ameliorated some of the harshest policies of the Cultural Revolution.

In their different ways, Hu Jintao and Wen Jiabao were both followers of the Hu Yaobang and Zhao Ziyang style of government. The subdued commemoration of the two former leaders indicated a determination to keep alive their legacy without seriously disturbing the delicate factional balance within the Party. The legacy of Zhou Enlai is less divisive, but benefits the reformers. Hu and Wen functioned as a team as well as being rivals. It is tempting to see them as, respectively, a hardliner and a liberal, but that would be simplistic. Wen enhanced his authority by his championship of popular causes.

Harmonious society

In common with previous leaders and following Jiang Zemin's much-mocked Three Represents policy, Hu Jintao felt obliged to create his own signature contribution to the ideology of the Party and the state. His Scientific Development outlook [*kexue fazhan guan*], unveiled at the NPC in 2005, was not taken any more seriously, but one aspect, the building of a 'harmonious society' [*hexie shehui*] attracted interest, as it was far removed from the familiar language of class conflict and progress. Hu's thinking was a response to the challenges resulting from the market reforms, notably inequality and associated social problems, and emphasised cooperation and persuasion rather than compulsion, and social stability above all else. Under the tougher Xi Jinping administration, the concept of 'harmonious society' has been derided by some for its rejection of the revolutionary traditions of the CCP. In spite of this, traces remain in the pastel tones and subtler designs of contemporary political posters that replaced the harsher primary colours of the socialist realist tradition, but above all in the name of China's high-speed trains *Hexie*. Xi Jinping began to use the concept of 'harmony' selectively during his second term in office.

It is difficult to assess Hu Jintao's legacy, which has been overshadowed by the adminis-tration of Xi Jinping. Xi's political style has been diametrically opposed to that of Hu, whose legacy he has been determined to reverse if not erase. As late as 2010, it was assumed that Hu would continue to play a significant role in Beijing politics.

Willy Lam, a commentator with an established reputation for insight predicted that,

> While Hu will be stepping down as General Secretary of the Communist Party of China (CCP), the official leadership position, he is expected to retain his position as Chairman of the Central Military Commission, or commander-in-chief of the armed forces. In this position, Hu is expected to continue to wield considerable influence over policy and in deciding who will fill the top positions of authority in the sixth generation.[7]

After Xi Jinping came to power, Hu withdrew completely from high-level political life.

17th Communist Party Congress: preparing for the fifth generation

On 12 November 2006, the CCP announced its programme for electing delegates to the 17th Communist Party Congress which was scheduled to meet in the autumn of 2007. The 70 million members of the Party would elect a total of 2,220 delegates in 38 electoral units throughout the country. This was an increase of about 100 in the number of delegates com-pared with those who were elected to the 16th Congress, which met in 2002 when Hu Jintao was confirmed as CCP Chairman. The Party also decreed that at least 30% of the delegates should be from the grassroots – that is, farmers and industrial workers rather than existing Party officials – and that women and members of the ethnic minorities should be better rep-resented. It was argued that these changes were necessary to accommodate the six million new members who had joined the CCP since the 16th Congress.[8]

As the 17th Congress of the CCP loomed in October 2007, there was fevered discussion of the new generation of leaders, the fifth generation which would succeed Hu and Wen. It became clear that Hu Jintao would not have the same authority as his predecessors to anoint a preferred successor. A long period of horse-trading resulted from the growing influence of provincial Party leaders. Initial leaks from the plenary meeting of the Cen-tral Committee preceding the conference even suggested a collective leadership with no individuals specifically named as potential successors to the most senior posts, but two names emerged, Li Keqiang of Liaoning province and Xi Jinping from Shanghai. At the end of the Congress, Xi emerged on the Congress platform ahead of Li and the succession became clear.

Notes

1 *FT* 9 August 2006.
2 For example, *Renmin Ribao* (Overseas edition) 27 September 2006.
3 *People's Daily* 1 January 2006.

4 Yu Jie *Zhongguo yingdi: Wen Jiabao* (subtitled in English *China's Best Actor: Wen Jiabao*) Hong Kong: New Century Press, 2010. The subtitle does not reflect the Chinese original entirely accurately; *yingdi* means 'leading actor' or 'film star', but also has suggestions of 'shadow emperor'.
5 *People's Daily* 18 November 2005.
6 *SCMP* 6 May 2006; Zhao Ziyang *Prisoner of the State: The Secret Journal of Premier Zhao Ziyang* New York Simon and Schuster, 2009.
7 'Not Much Will Change under China's Next Leaders: Scholar' Report of Willy Lam Lecture *China Post* Taiwan 13 May 2010.
8 *SCMP* 13 November 2006.

5 Murder and corruption in the leadership

Bo Xilai and Zhou Yongkang

Before the new team of Xi and Li could be confirmed at the 18th CCP Congress, which opened on 8 November 2012, the Chinese leadership became embroiled in a dramatic and squalid scandal that was both political and personal, and rocked the establishment. As the reform of the economy had unfolded and the involvement of the private sector increased, so had the opportunities for bribery, fraud, and other forms of corruption. Exposures of high-level corruption within the CCP and its government became more frequent. In 1998, Chen Xitong, the former Politburo member and Mayor of Beijing had been sentenced to 16 years imprisonment for embezzlement. Zheng Xiaoyu, the director of the State Food and Drug Administration, was executed in 2007 for corruption and allowing contaminated pharmaceuticals to enter the market.

There were many similar convictions, but the case of Bo Xilai, who once was considered a potential Premier, attracted an exceptional level of international attention. It implicated not only Bo but also his high-flying lawyer wife Gu Kailai, the senior Chengdu police officer Wang Lijun, and a British businessman, Neil Heywood, widely rumoured to have worked with British intelligence organisations. It eventually enmeshed the Minister of Public Security, Zhou Yongkang, and raised uncomfortable questions for local government and police officers in the southwestern metropolis of Chongqing about their relationship with organised crime.

On 14 November 2011, Neil Heywood arrived at the Nanshan Lijing Holiday Hotel, in a popular tourist area on an isolated wooded mountain to the southeast of Chonqing, to meet Gu Kailai. Over 24 hours later, his body was discovered in his room. There was no autopsy or inquest, but the cause of death was rapidly assessed as having been either a heart attack or alcohol poisoning. Since Mr. Heywood was known to drink little alcohol, doubts were immediately raised among his friends and family, and there were suspicions of foul play. An enquiry was launched, headed by Wang Lijun, chief of police in Chongqing and also a Deputy Mayor and a member of the CCP. Mr. Heywood was cremated, and his ashes returned to his family.

Wang Lijun's previous career had been in Liaoning in China's northeast, where he had forged a strong relationship with Bo Xilai, who was then Governor of Liaoning; when Bo was promoted to the post of Communist Party Secretary of Chongqing, a municipality with status equivalent to that of a province, he took Wang with him. Wang was crucial to Bo Xilai's model for running Chongqing.

Bo Xilai and the 'Chongqing model'

As China approached the 18th Congress of the CCP and the inauguration of a new leadership, there were serious concerns that under the administration of Hu Jintao and Wen Jiabao, the programme of economic reforms was beginning to stall and the growing income gap and rampant official corruption were out of control. Debate inside the CCP on the way forward for economic reform was polarised. The two main competing approaches were expressed in terms of a 'cake theory': 'liberals' advocated increasing the size of the cake and deepening political reform, which favoured the increasingly influential middle class; 'conservatives' favoured prioritising a more equal division of the cake and a return to some of the policies of the Mao era, thought to be more acceptable to the lowly paid. These two schools of thought were exemplified in the Guangdong model, espoused by the 'liberal' Wang Yang in the south and 'conservative' Bo Xilai's Chongqing model. In a year in which the PRC was celebrating both the centenary of the Revolution of 1911 and the 90th birthday of the CCP, the political atmosphere was unusually intense.

The Chongqing model was a throwback to the days of the Great Leap Forward of the 1950s or the Cultural Revolution of the 1960s; it was bizarrely anachronistic in twenty-first century China. It featured the promotion of 'red culture', especially the singing of 'red songs', drawn from the repertoire of the years of revolution, which were promoted on state-controlled radio and television. It was possible to download 36 key tunes from television websites; local newspapers printed one 'red song' each day. Revolutionary films eulogis-ing Mao again became *de rigeur*; quotations from Chairman Mao could be sent as texts to mobile phones, and some bureaucrats were spending time in the countryside learning from the farmers. Bo Xilai, the son of Bo Yibo, a former guerrilla leader who became one of Deng Xiaoping's 'elders' in his influential Central Advisory Commission, espoused this 'red culture' campaign to accumulate revolutionary credibility in spite of his great wealth and power.[1]

This 'warm embrace of red culture to win the "new left"' was endorsed in *People's Daily* and praised by leading members of the Politburo, including Wu Bangguo, the Chairman of the NPC, when he visited Chongqing in April 2011. What 'stunned' Wu was the apparent success of a campaign against organised crime syndicates that Bo, through his chief of police, Wang Lijun, was running in parallel with the 'red culture' crusade. This campaign, which began in 2009, had netted almost 6,000 individuals accused of involvement in organised crime. The list included 'billionaire businessmen, government advisers, crime bosses and senior police offi-cers'; local gang bosses put a 'price tag of six million yuan' on the head of the outspoken and short-tempered Wang. Wu Bangguo may have been impressed but local lawyers were not; they complained that Wang's zero tolerance tactics, including torture to obtain confessions, had trapped many innocent individuals and were a threat to the rule of law.[2]

In early 2012, rumours began to circulate that Beijing had dispatched a team from the Cen-tral Commission on Discipline Inspection (CCDI), the CCP's powerful internal security unit, to Chongqing. It was suddenly announced that Wang Lijun had been stripped of all his police responsibilities and reassigned to duties connected with education and the environment. His replacement was announced as Guan Haixiang, a former CYL official aligned to the Hu Jintao faction. No reason was given but, four days after his dismissal, Wang fled Chongqing and reappeared at the US Consulate General in Chengdu, the Sichuan provincial capital. Fur-ther reports indicated that he stayed overnight at the consulate but was then flown to Beijing where he was given 'vacation-style treatment for stress'. Police vehicles surrounded the con-sulate and Wang was said to have offered the US Consulate staff confidential documents and requested political asylum. Consular staff refused to comment on this and insisted that there had been no threat to the building or its occupants. The incident threatened to undermine deli-cate US-China relations on the eve of a planned visit to Washington by then Vice-President Xi Jinping, to say nothing of its impact on Bo Xilai's political prospects.[3]

Wang Lijun was then officially replaced as police chief by Guan Haixiang, and all media outlets in Chongqing were placed under central government control. Bo Xilai and one of his closest colleagues, the Mayor of Chongqing Huang Qifan, were conspicuously absent from a public celebration of the success of law enforcement in the city, which received uncharacteristically low-profile treatment in the local media. Chinese commentators speculated that Bo was 'a second Gao Gang', the regional Party leader purged in the 1950s for establishing a semi-independent power base in China's northeast. As reports emerged about illegal detentions, torture, the imprisonment of a critical journalist, and other abuses in the anti-crime campaign, rumours spread that Bo had offered to resign. The crisis was interpreted as a high-level power struggle between supporters of Bo in Chongqing and Wang Yang in Guangdong.[4]

Bo emerged from his self-imposed silence on 12 March and declared that he had been wrong in appointing and relying on Wang Lijun. He appeared at a small meeting during the session of the NPC in Beijing where he promoted his 'Chongqing model', but his absence from a plenary session on criminal legislation prompted speculation about his position. On 15 March, the Xinhua news agency reported that Bo had been dismissed as Secretary of the Chongqing Communist Party and would be replaced by Zhang Dejiang; no statement was made about his Politburo seat. Wang Lijun was also dismissed and condemned as a 'traitor to his country and the Party'. 'Red' programming on Chongqing's television screens came abruptly to an end.[5]

Neil Heywood and the Bo family

Revelations that followed Bo's dismissal drew international attention to what had ostensibly been an internal power struggle: the Beijing authorities organised a concerted propaganda campaign to counter internet rumours of a possible coup d'état by Bo Xilai. On 27 March 2012, the *Daily Telegraph* in London, which has sources in the intelligence world, revealed that the British Embassy in Beijing had requested a new investigation into the death of Neil Heywood. Heywood was an Old Harrovian – a former student at the famous British public school, Harrow – who had worked with Hakluyt & Company, a British 'strategic intelligence and advisory' organisation founded by former officers of the United Kingdom's Secret Intelligence Service, MI6, and the Security Service, MI5. Mr. Heywood also had a business relationship with the Bo family, principally with Bo's wife, Gu Kailai, a connection either not known or not revealed at the time of his death in November 2011. By the beginning of April, Bo Xilai and his wife were both under house arrest in Beijing and their son, Bo Guagua, also an Old Harrovian who drove a red Ferrari in Chongqing, had returned in haste from Harvard University to be with his parents.

New rumours, which offered a possible explanation for Wang Lijun's attempted defection, began to circulate: Wang, it was said, had discovered that Gu Kailai was implicated in Heywood's death and had reported this to Bo, who was furious and demoted Wang. There were allegations that Bo had ordered the murder of Heywood after discovering a more personal relationship between him and Gu Kailai. The Xinhua news agency announced on 10 April that Bo's membership in the Politburo had been suspended while the Central Commission for Discipline Inspection carried out an investigation. Concurrently, police in Chongqing were investigating Gu Kailai (who was now referred to in the official press as Bogu Kailai, a most unusual form of naming in contemporary China but clearly designed to link her with her husband by combining their surnames) and Zhang Xiaojun, described as an 'orderly' working for the Bo household, who had been detained on suspicion of homicide.

Zhou Yongkang, who chaired the powerful Central Political and Legislative Affairs Committee of the CCP, had openly supported Bo Xilai's management of Chongqing during the NPC. At the end of March, Zhou was at a training camp for senior law and order officials, calling for Party unity.[6]

The case against Bo Xilai

With a major national leadership change planned within the next few months, the authorities in Beijing were desperate to see a rapid resolution to the Bo Xilai case. A government statement on 10 April announced the arrest of Gu Kailai on suspicion of having murdered Neil Heywood, and the suspension of Bo Xilai from the Politburo on the grounds of 'suspected serious violations of discipline', a frequent euphemism for corruption. Early indications of the likely outcome of the legal process were given to senior executives of key Hong Kong commercial and political institutions at a briefing by officials from Beijing at the Zijing (Bauhinia) villa in Shenzhen, just across the border from the former colony on or around 17 April. Gu Kailai was expected to take most of the blame, with Bo himself facing charges alleging lesser responsibility for the murder. In spite of Wang Lijun's defection to the US Consulate General, he was likely to be treated relatively leniently for assisting the investigation into Bo and Gu. Unofficial reports on the investigations indicated that, in addition to the three main suspects, as many as 40 other people had been detained, some at the seaside resort of Beidaihe which is favoured by the CCP leadership for key meetings. Rumours and leaked documents attributed Mr. Heywood's death to cyanide poisoning and revealed details of the lifestyle and financial complexity of the Bo family and their associates. Particular attention was also drawn to Bo's alleged closeness to certain military officers, hinting that they were planning a coup.[7]

The trial

Gu Kailai and her assistant, Zhang Xiaojun, were formally charged with murder on 26 July 2012. That August, Gu was convicted of the murder and sentenced to death, suspended for two years, a sentence later commuted to life imprisonment. Zhang was committed to prison for nine years as an accessory to murder. On 24 September 2012, Wang Lijun, Bo's chief of police, was sentenced to 15 years in prison for bribery, abuse of power, and attempting to conceal Gu Kailai's involvement in the murder of Neil Heywood.

The formal indictment against Bo Xilai, delivered in the Shandong capital of Jinan City Intermediate People's Court, included accepting bribes of RMB 20 million (RMB is renminbi, the normal Chinese currency) and embezzling a further RMB 5 million. His trial, in the same Jinan court, did not begin until 22 August 2013. It was not open in the Western sense and only carefully vetted journalists were permitted to report, but unusually, the proceedings were made available in real time through a microblog controlled by the court. Bo Xilai retracted the confessions which he was alleged to have made during the investigation, and declared himself not guilty of all the charges. There was little doubt about the verdict, which was awaited with anticipation and given on 22 September 2013. Bo was found guilty on all counts, although the court accepted two minor points which he had made in his defence. He was sentenced to imprisonment for life, a harsher outcome than many had predicted. An appeal by Bo's defence team the following month was rejected. The trial was followed closely in Chongqing, where Bo still had supporters, although others felt that he had received his just deserts after the persecution of so many innocent people.[8]

Zhou Yongkang

In Bo Xilai, the CCP had succeeded in caging a considerable tiger, who was undoubtedly a potential rival to members of the Politburo, if not a genuine coup plotter. The crime of Bo's wife and Bo's own overweening ambition had played into the hands of his rivals. The fallout from the trial implicated other officials who could be linked to Bo, the most important of whom was an even more formidable tiger, Zhou Yongkang, a member of the Standing Committee of the Politburo who was also head of the CCP's Central Commission for Political and Legal Affairs, the supreme authority for all policing and judicial matters and the security services. Zhou, born in 1942, had also been Party secretary for Sichuan province, of which Chongqing had formerly been a part, and served as Minister of Public Security from 2002–2007. He was also a staunch supporter of Bo Xilai and his policing policies in Chongqing, which he had defended in the early stages of the investigation. Rumours of close personal and financial ties between Zhou and the Bo family spread, as did suggestions that the Zhou family had benefited corruptly from his former roles with the China National Petroleum Corporation. In May 2012, Zhou Yongkang was obliged to surrender operational control over the security apparatus to Meng Jianzhu, his successor as Minister of Public Security.[9]

In a statement by the prosecution at Bo's trial, initially redacted and subsequently deleted from the official transcript, it was alleged that Zhou had issued orders to Bo on how he should deal with the attempted defection of Wang Lijun in Chengdu. The following month, it was announced that, after discussions at the informal but significant August meeting of leading Party members at Beidaihe, President Xi Jinping had established a special unit to investigate Zhou Yongkang, headed by the chief police officer of Beijing, and not by the Central Commission for Discipline Inspection, which would normally have handled the case. No member of the Politburo Standing Committee had been investigated for economic crimes since the Cultural Revolution. Zhou's case was investigated from August 2013–6 December 2014, when he was arrested and expelled from the CCP. In April 2015, he was charged with abuse of power, bribery, and deliberately leaking state secrets; his trial, in contrast to that of Bo Xilai, was in secret. Zhou pleaded guilty on 11 June, and the combined sentences of the court amounted to life imprisonment. In the final indictment, there was no mention of the Bo Xilai case. His shock of almost white hair in film of his final appearance contrasted dramatically with his sleek black hair in previous photographs and news footage.

The complex criminal, financial, and political scandal surrounding Bo Xilai unfolded in the twilight of the administration of Hu Jintao and Wen Jiabao, but was decisively resolved at the beginning of the Xi era. For Xi Jinping, the verdict not only removed his most dangerous political rival – it also marked an early success for his campaign against corruption in the Party and the government.[10]

Notes

1 Louisa Lim 'Cake Theory' *National Public Radio* 6 November 2011; *SCMP* 13, 20 April 2011.
2 *SCMP* 9 February 2012.
3 *SCMP* 8, 9, 10, 12 February 2012; *FT* 9 February 2012, BBC News 9 February 2012; *Duowei News* (Chinese) 8, 9, 10 February 2012.
4 Radio Free Asia 15, 21 February 2012; *SCMP* 18, 22 February 2012; *Duowei News* (Chinese) 15, 17, 19, 23, 25 February 2012; *New York Times* 16 February 2012; *FT* 5 March 2012.
5 *SCMP* 7, 9, 10, 13, 15 March 2012.

6 *Daily Telegraph* 26, 27, 29 March 2012; *SCMP* 27 March, 2, 3 April 2012; BBC News 20 March 2012; *Guardian* 30 March 2012; *FT* 31 March–1 April 2012; Xinhua 10 April 2012.
7 *FT* 11, 14, 18 April, 27 July 2012; *SCMP* 24 April, 4 June 2012.
8 *FT* 27 July 2012; *SCMP* 24 April, 4 June, 25 July 2012; Xinhua 25 July 2012, 22 August, 21, 23 September 2013; *China Daily* 24 September 2012.
9 *SCMP* 16 May 2012, 21 September 2013.
10 *SCMP* 1 September, 21 October 2013; *China Daily* 12 June 2015.

6 Rise of Xi Jinping

Fifth generation or new authoritarianism?

As the Central Committee of the CCP met in Beijing on Saturday 15 October 2011, the delegates sensed that this was not just the drawing to a close of one administration and the beginning of another dominated by the fifth generation of the leadership, but the dawn of an era of profound political change. Formally, the gathering was the 17th Central Committee of the CCP, meeting in its Sixth Plenary Session, and this nomenclature indicates the importance of continuity and tradition in what was once a revolutionary party. In the run-up to this session, and in anticipation of the incoming leadership of 2012 and 2013, there was a flurry of books in Chinese, many published in Hong Kong, on the likely composition of the emerging leadership, the process from which it would emerge, and the likely consequences of the changes in senior personnel. Decisions on the composition of the 'core leadership' of the fifth generation would be made public at the meeting of the 18th CCP Congress in October 2012 and reaffirmed at the NPC in March 2013. The battling for position had been underway for some time; 12 months in advance of the first of these key meetings, interest and expectation were at fever pitch within the CCP and in the domestic and international press.[1]

Change and continuity

Political appointments at the highest level are agreed by the most senior leadership, signposted well in advance; they are formally approved at the National Congresses of the Party, which take place in the autumn every five years, and are then ratified at the annual meeting of the NPC in the following spring. Although it is always possible for appointments that have been announced to be revoked, the expectation is that they will be confirmed. Since the death of Mao Zedong in 1976, there has been a broad consensus that conflict should be confined within the CCP and its decision-making bodies – the Central Committee and the Politburo – and that a united front with agreed appointments and policies should be made public. It was safe to say that, 'barring accidents, the CCP Eighteenth Congress will renew its Standing Committee with Xi Jinping and Li Keqiang as its leading members'.[2]

Promotion to the most senior positions in the PRC is normally the result of service in senior CCP and government positions in the regions (provincial Party secretary), with hardship postings in the troubled and deprived northwest (Tibet, Xinjiang, Gansu) attracting particular esteem. Overseas experience and knowledge are not valued in the same way. Willy Lam, one of the most respected analysts of Chinese politics, predicted continuity.

> The cultivation of Chinese leaders is a blend of traditional Chinese values, perceived devotion to the common people, superior knowledge of the nature of the party and above all, loyalty. The CCP wants to avoid at all costs the rise of a Chinese Mikhail Gorbachev who may introduce any kind of reforms that could threaten its iron grip on power.[3]

The current system of collective leadership was developed by the post-Mao CCP to create maximum political stability with minimum effect on China's society and the economy, while allowing for the routine change and renewal of senior personnel as the older generation retires. In 2012, the presumed outcome of the arcane processes that produced the new leadership was that changes in personnel would not affect the overall direction of policy. Willy Lam, speaking to the European Chamber of Commerce in Taipei, predicted that there would be no 'sweeping political or economic reforms in China within the fifth or sixth generations of leadership', arguing that the next generation of mainland leaders would make only moderate changes to the policies of the country. Change, he maintained, was more likely to come in the seventh generation as the Chinese officials who had studied or worked abroad became more prominent.[4]

Many Chinese commentators insisted that in the long run-up to the key 18th CCP Congress in 2012, there were bitter struggles for position and power within the Party, battles based on political commitment and the perceived direction of China's revolution as much as personal ambition and factional allegiance. Some, writing from Hong Kong, had contended for many years that the superficial smoothness of the planned transition masked deep and divisive conflicts. They argued that the Hu–Wen administration was in crisis and that changes at the top of the leadership would lead to a 'dangerous and unpredictable' [*fengyun xian'e*] mood in Zhongnanhai, the walled complex in Beijing that houses the offices of the CCP leadership and the State Council.[5]

Interest naturally focused on putative candidates for the top two positions, the assumption being that 'the fate of the Party and the state was in the hands of one or two individuals'. This was in spite of Deng Xiaoping's insistence that the future of China should depend on a new collective leadership; it was wrong, he argued, to exaggerate the role of individuals, and there should be no appointments for life. These arguments were designed to frustrate any possibility of an individual in the future having the power wielded by Mao Zedong; they were deployed in the discussions over the creation of a new leadership and seemed to account for the relatively unknown and seemingly uncharismatic individuals who emerged.[6] When the character of the new leadership was revealed, it was completely unexpected.

Starved of the type of information available in democratic societies, Chinese and Western commentators were obliged to speculate on the views of candidates for the top positions and their likely impact on policy. Two of the probable new entries to the Politburo, Wang Yang and Bo Xilai, were characterised as offering diametrically opposed models – the Guangdong and Chongqing models – for China's development. Wang Yang, as CCP Secretary of Guangdong province, the powerhouse of southern China, had promoted a 'Happy Guangdong' campaign that appealed to an emerging middle class that was believed to have 'a stronger appetite for political participation and rights protection', although there was little evidence for this. In Chongqing, the metropolis of Sichuan Province in China's west, Bo Xilai had run a campaign for 'red culture', marked by nostalgic television programmes harking back to the 'Maoist' era of the 1950s and 1960s and the singing of revolutionary songs evoking the Long March to power of the CCP. This campaign attracted far more attention in the West, as well as in China, than Wang Yang's, but the two together were oddly reminiscent of the 'struggle between the two lines' of the 1960s that culminated in the Cultural Revolution.[7] Whether these opposite perspectives reflected genuine differences of policy rather than regional interests and the personalities of the two governors is difficult to determine. Bo Xilai fell spectacularly after the scandal involving his wife and the British businessman Neil Haywood, and his 'red culture' campaign simply evaporated (see Chapter 5).

CCP factions and the succession process

Factions within the CCP that are acknowledged by Chinese and Western commentators include the CYL, the Shanghai clique, Qinghua clique, and princeling (crown prince) groupings. As the names suggest, these are based on local origins, education, or social connections, and have effectively replaced pre-Cultural Revolution factions that were based on service with field armies in the Long March and the Civil War of 1946–1949. As Willy Lam acknowledged, 'Factionalism is still a strong factor behind promotions in the CCP such as with the Communist Youth League faction versus the so-called "Gang of Princelings", descendants of heroes of the communist revolution'.[8]

The usefulness of factions as a guide to the workings of CCP – and specifically to promotions to the Politburo and Standing Committee – is questionable. As was suggested in Chapter 3, it is debatable whether the term faction is useful in the context of the CCP. These are not open groupings with distinctive political positions. In the context of the tight democratic centralism which prevails within the CCP, it goes without saying that they do not operate openly, do not publish manifestos or other policy statements on their own behalf, and do not operate open slates in Party 'elections'. Their existence is acknowledged off the record, as is the enormous influence they have in dictating the balance of leadership and formulating policy. Rather than being factions in the Western sense, it is more useful to consider them as patronage groups with common origins in a region, organisation, or social group which have common interests in preserving and enhancing the status of that faction within the Party.[9]

Rise to power of Xi Jinping

There were no serious challengers to Xi Jinping's promotion to head the CCP in succession to Hu Jintao. Xi had been the subject of several biographies and critical studies, and there were no public concerns about his ability to fulfil the role. There were reports that he had been reluctant to accept the position but that may have been just a formality. Willy Lam assessed his prospects in 2010:

> Xi is regarded as a candidate acceptable to all sides because of his lack of strong charisma or a large base in the party, not based on his achievements. As a loyal party member, Xi is expected to toe the party line and is unlikely to do anything radical while Hu Jintao remains commander in chief (until 2017). . . . As to how relations with China will proceed under Xi Jinping's leadership, Lam believes that there may be some degree of affinity for Xi in Taiwan given his long official stint in Fujian province and his contacts among Taiwanese firms that invested in the province. However, like all other senior party leaders, he is a strong nationalist who believes that greater economic integration across the Taiwan Strait will eventually lead to formal de jure reunification. He therefore will likely continue with the policies of Hu Jintao regarding Taiwan and for at least the first five years is likely to focus mainly on improving business and economic ties.[10]

Military experience

For the top leadership of the Party and state, relations with the military are vital, but by the end of the Fourth Plenum, Xi had not been named as Deputy Chairman of the CMAC; this caused surprise, especially among foreign observers, and strengthened rumours about his unwillingness to succeed. Xi was eventually appointed to the Deputy Chairmanship on 18 October 2010 at the Fifth plenum of the 17th Congress of the CCP. Hu Jintao retained his position as Chairman of the Party CMC when he stepped down as President in 2012 (although he remained head of the state CMC until the following year), following the precedent of his predecessor Jiang Zemin in 2007.

Xi was technically a serving officer when working in the offices of the CMC, but he has no combat or regular service experience. The Xinhua report of this appointment emphasised Xi's military connections, which were essentially political commissar attachments to military units.

Born in 1953, Xi has served in a number of positions related to the armed forces and military reserve affairs during his previous tenures at national and local levels. He was a military officer in active service when he worked as a secretary at the General Office of the Central Military Commission from 1979 to 1982. He served as the first political commissar and first secretary of the Party committee of people's armed forces department of Zhengding County, Hebei Province, from 1983 to 1985 when he was the secretary of the county's Party committee. Xi later served as the first secretary of the sub-military area commands' Party committees of Ningde and Fuzhou, both in Fujian Province, from 1988 to 1993.

From 1996 to 1999, he served as the first political commissar of the anti-aircraft artillery reserve division of Fujian provincial military area command, when he was deputy secretary of the CPC Fujian Provincial Committee. In 1999, Xi became vice director of the commission for national defense mobilization of Nanjing Military Area Command and director of Fujian Provincial commission for national defense mobilization, when he was promoted to acting Governor of Fujian Province. After a transfer to Zhejiang Province in 2002, Xi was appointed director of Zhejiang Provincial commission for national defense mobilization. When Xi was promoted to secretary of the CPC Zhejiang Provincial Committee, he was appointed the first secretary of the Party committee of Zhejiang provincial military area command. Xi was first secretary of the Party committee of Shanghai Garrison when he was transferred to serve as Secretary of the CPC Shanghai Municipal Committee in 2007.[11]

Crown prince

At the 17th Party Conference, Xi Jinping was treated as the crown prince, apparently put forward by Jiang Zemin and Zeng Qinghong – the leaders of the Shanghai faction – with the intention of countering Hu Jintao's protégé Li Keqiang, the candidate of the CYL faction, and pushing him in to the No. 2 position as 'assistant crown prince'. This was acceptable to many of the old guard because of Xi's political pedigree. His father was Xi Zhongxun (1913–2002), a former CCP guerrilla leader in Shaanxi, Deputy Prime Minister from 1959–1962 and later Governor of Guangdong who fell out with Mao Zedong (see in the following). Xi senior was also reputed to have been a mentor to both Hu Jintao and Wen Jiabao, and Xi Jinping had maintained good relations with Hu Jintao. In 2009, Xi Jinping had been sections entrusted with Project 6521 which established a nationwide network of taskforces to combat social instability during a series of sensitive anniversaries – 60th anniversary of PRC, 50th anniversary of Tibetan uprising, 20th anniversary of Tian'anmen, and 10th anniversary of Falungong suppression – the name of the project is taken from those numbers. This was an early indication of the style of his later policies.

Xi is usually included in the 'princeling' faction, but he also has a Shanghai background; he was Party Secretary in the city from 2007 after occupying senior posts in Fujian and Zhejiang. He was relatively unknown when he was assigned to the post of Secretary of the Shanghai Party Committee in March 2007 after the dismissal of his predecessor Chen Liangyu, who was subsequently sentenced to 18 years imprisonment for the misuse of social security funds. This was a brief sojourn for Xi, who was appointed to the Politburo Standing Committee in October 2007 and was succeeded in Shanghai by Yu Zhengsheng. When CCTV profiled the new Standing Committee that year, the contrast between the bespectacled Li Keqiang, always willing to discuss and explain policies, and Xi Jinping, who appeared to be lost in thought or listening attentively, was commented on. At a discussion on Scientific Development (Hu Jintao's signature theory outlook) with the Shanghai delegation at the 17th Party Congress that lasted over two hours, Xi did not make a speech; at the subsequent question-and-answer session with the media, he answered general questions but avoided details on policy. The Beijing correspondent of the South Korean daily, *Chosun Ilbo*, noted that, unlike Xi, Li Keqiang grasped the microphone and was willing to answer question after question.

Xi had powerful supporters within the Party bureaucracy, particularly He Guoqiang, who until October 2007 was head of the Central Organisation Department [*zhongzubu*] that controls the *nomenklatura* system of appointments and promotions; he subsequently became the head of the Central Commission for Discipline Inspection [*zhongjiwei*] which targets corruption inside the Party and can make or break political careers.[12] When Xi was appointed to lead Shanghai, He Guoqiang unstintingly praised him as 'politically strong and with a high level of ideology and policy' [*zhengzhi shang qiang, you jiaogao de sixiang zhengce shuiping*], and complimented him on his experience, leadership style, work methods and commitment to democratic centralism as well as his honesty and concern for the masses and his ability to unite people.[13]

Princeling with a common touch

Xi is associated with the 'princeling' [*taizidang*] faction, as he is the son of Xi Zhongxun, the former CCP guerrilla leader in Shaanxi and a Party elder and founding father [*yuanlao*] of the PRC. 'Princelings', a broad and vague category rather than a genuine faction, are the sons and daughters of previous senior leaders, and have a reputation – not always justified – for arrogance and corruption. Xi Jinping has been described as the 'princeling with the common touch' [*zui you pingmin qinghuai de taizidang*], whereas Li Keqiang is a quintessential product of the CYL. Xi does not like people to bring up the 'stars in the political firmament' [*zhengtan mingxing*] of the families of other senior cadres; if anyone 'violates this prohibition', he is known to become heated and flush with anger, not being a great communicator. In CCP political circles, he is well known for maintaining a distance between himself and other members of the 'princeling' class. Part of the reason for this is his father's political downfall in 1962 when Xi Jinping was only 10 years old. He grew up understanding that his father's generation had brought disaster on his own family; in spite of his apparently privileged background, he had to toughen himself up.[14]

In 1969, in the middle of the Cultural Revolution, when he was barely 16 years old, he went to the Liangjiahe (Liang Family River) Production Brigade in the Wen'anyi Commune in Yanquan County in northern Shaanxi as part of a school group taking part in agricultural labour. Recalling this experience with the peasants to a reporter in later years, he said,[15]

> For almost a whole year I did not rest at all unless I was actually ill. In rain and wind I chopped up hay for fodder in a cave with them and at night I watched over the animals.

I took the sheep out to pasture and did all kinds of jobs and at that time I would carry 200 jin (100 kilo) of wheat on my shoulders for ten *li* (5 kilometres) along a mountain road without shifting it from on shoulder to the other.

He was unable to cook for himself and preferred studying, so one of the villagers prepared his meals. In 1994, by which time he was a senior Party official in Fujian, he helped that poor villager with medical expenses. Together with almost 30,000 other Beijing students who had been rusticated [*xiafang*], he joined the CCP in Yan'an in January 1974 and became the first to become Party secretary of a Production Brigade branch. He was then approved as a 'Worker Peasant Soldier Student' and enrolled in the chemical engineering department at Qinghua University; his father had still not been rehabilitated. Years later, he took a doctorate in law at Qinghua after being a research student and working in the humanities and social science faculty.

During his time in Fuzhou, where he was Party secretary of the city form 1993–1995, he was noted for his lack of interest in prestigious construction projects and for his opposition to a new Fuzhou airport during the provincial airport boom of the 1990s. He preferred regular inspection visits to the countryside.

Like father, like son?

The tortuous path that brought Xi Jinping to power was connected not only to his father's political past, but also to Hu Yaobang, the reformist CCP Secretary General who was forced from power in 1987. His death on 5 April 1989 led to demonstrations that were the immediate precursor of the Democracy Movement which was suppressed on 4 June. Xi's background demonstrates how complex interpersonal ties are involved in political careers and is a warning against placing too much reliance on factional links.

Xi Zhongxun (1913–2002) was a member of the CCP from 1928 and operated guerrilla units in the Shaanxi-Gansu-Ningxia border region during the War of Resistance against Japan. His revolutionary track record led him to influential positions in the new government formed by the CCP in 1949, first as Acting Chairman of the Northwest Military Committee and then moving to Beijing in 1950 as both Director of the Central Propaganda Department and Deputy Director of the Culture and Education Committee of the Government Administration Council (forerunner of the State Council). He was also Secretary of the First GAC (Government Administration Council) and Vice-President and Secretary of the Second State Council. In the early 1960s, he was dismissed from his posts and arrested after having been implicated in a controversy over Mao Zedong's ironic criticism that 'using fiction to attack the Party is a great invention' [*liyong xiaoshuo jinxing fandang huodong shi yida faming*], a barely remembered campaign against a novel, *Liu Zhidan*. Xi Zhongxun was an associate of Gao Gang (1905–1954), who was the first senior CCP leader to be purged by Mao after Gao had apparently attempted to oust Liu Shaoqi and Zhou Enlai from the leadership in 1954. Gao Gang and Xi Zhongxun both served under Liu Zhidan, their divisional commander in the Shaanxi guerrilla underground and this association put them in opposition to the dominant Mao faction within the CCP and aligned them with the supporters of Peng Dehuai who was defeated in a conflict with Mao in 1959. That this was not simply a historical issue became clear when it was announced in 2008 that Gao Gang's widow Li Liqun, at the age of 87, was petitioning to have her husband exonerated. There were also unconfirmed rumours that she had visited Xi Zhongxun's widow (Xi Jinping's mother) at her home in Guangdong. Unlike many of the other internal conflicts of the 1950s and 1960s, many questions about the Gao Gang case remain unanswered and are potentially hazardous for the legitimacy of the current leadership.

Among his supporters, Xi Zhongxun had the reputation of being tolerant and even-handed. During the early 1950s, he argued that the methods of struggle against the CCP's opponents outlined in Mao Zedong's 1927 article *Report on an Investigation into the Peasant Rebellion in Hunan* should not be copied slavishly. He put this into practice in the Northwest Region that he governed during the Movement to Suppress Counterrevolutionaries by reducing the target for executions by 50% to 0.5 per thousand of the population, 60% lower than the general quota nationally. He did not target officials of the old regime at ward headman [*baozhang*] level, whereas in Sichuan under Deng Xiaoping, all at the level of headman and above were executed as enemies. He was a firm supporter of direct elections for people's representatives. During land reform, he had resisted what would later be classified as fanatical 'leftist' interpretations of Party policy. He prohibited 'digging out the hidden wealth' of landlords and wealthier peasants, physical punishments, and 'investigating three generations', and protected the 'enlightened gentry' and industrialists and merchants. This brought him criticism for not following the correct – that is, the Maoist – line in that campaign.

At the 10th Plenum of the Eighth CC held in Beijing from 24–27 September 1962, Mao declared that 'using fiction to attack the Party is a great invention' [*liyong xiaoshuo jinxing fandang huodong shi yida faming*], referring to the novels *Baowei Yan'an* (*Defending Yan'an*) by Du Pengcheng (1921–1991) and *Liu Zhidan* by Li Jiantong. Liu Zhidan (1903–1935) was a popular revolutionary and guerrilla leader and martyr in Shaanxi during the 1930s, and the biographical novel was regarded as undermining Mao's guerrilla strategies by praising Liu Zhidan. Li Jiantong, who had been asked to write the book by Workers' Press in 1956, was the wife of Liu Zhidan's younger brother, Liu Jingfan; her husband did not want her to write the book, surmising correctly that it would be impossible to write about Liu and Northern Shaanxi without writing about Gao Gang, whose 'anti-Party activities' had so recently been under investigation. Xi Zhongxun, by then a Vice-President of the State Council, advised her not to go ahead with the book. He understood the complicated history of the region and the difficulties the leadership were having in resolving the political, historical, and personal issues that surrounded it. Li Jiantong was adamant and wrote three drafts, the final one being submitted to Workers' Press in the summer of 1959. She did not submit it to Xi Zhongxun for his comments, and later conceded that this was a serious error.

Workers Press sent the manuscript to Xi Zhongxun before publication, just as the Lushan Plenum (at which Mao and Peng Dehuai famously clashed) was about to begin. Xi spotted the potential political traps and advised her to make changes and to publish the text in instalments rather than as a book in the first instance. Li Jiantong returned to North Shaanxi to collect further material, produced a fourth draft, still intent on publishing it as an entire book, and sent it again to Xi Zhongxun. Xi called a meeting with her; Ma Xiwu, who had participated in the Shaanxi campaign; and the publishers – he tried to persuade her that it needed to be restructured to make it clear that Mao's arrival in North Shaanxi had been the clinching factor. A sixth and final draft was sent to the publishers in the summer of 1962 and proof copies were produced. Li Jiantong sent a copy to Zhou Yang, who had been her teacher but was at the time the Deputy Director of the Party's Central Propaganda Department. He and his wife read it and praised it highly, as did Ma Xiwu; Xi Zhongxun relented and agreed that it could be published. Liu Jingfan, the author's younger brother, also came round to this point of view.

Gao Gang had been a close associate of Liu Zhidan in Shaanxi, and their political stance had been approved by Mao Zedong. Gao was purged and committed suicide in 1954; he could not be spoken of positively, if at all, and neither could his associates. The *Liu Zhidan* book was serialised in several newspapers, including *Workers Daily*, *China Youth Daily* and *Guangming Daily*, in July 1962, but Li Jiantong had also given a proof copy to Yan Hong-yan, a rival of Liu Zhidan and now a general and alternate member of the Central Committee who had been on his way to a Central Work Conference in the resort of Beidaihe. The Central Committee met in Beidaihe from late June until late September to discuss Mao's instruction to 'return to class struggle' [*chongti jieji douzheng*]. Yan Hongan saw the extracts during the work conference and asked Kang Sheng, the CCP security and intelligence supremo from the mid-1950s onwards, to have publication stopped. Kang chose to see the novel as an attempt to revive the political controversy over the Gao Gang affair, and he persuaded the Central Committee that the novel was a political tool of an ongoing anti-party bloc that included the deceased Gao Gang, Xi Zhongxun, and Peng Dehuai, whose Northwest Field Army Xi had served in as political commissar, and who was already under criticism for his opposition to Mao during the Great Leap Forward.

When Mao spoke at the opening of the 10th Plenum of the 8th Central Committee on 24 September and referred to 'using fiction to attack the Party is a great invention'[16] [*liyong xiaoshuo jinxing fandang huodong shi yida faming*], the quotation was apparently handed to him by Kang Sheng as he rose to speak. Kang persuaded the delegates to approve the establishment of a committee to investigate the crimes of Xi Zhongxun and his associates in this 'anti-Party group'. The committee reported in May 1963 and found the group guilty: Xi Zhongxun, as the most senior political figure, came in for the harshest criticism as the real 'first author' of *Liu Zhidan* and a plotter against Mao for decades. He was dismissed from all his posts and rusticated to Luoyang, where he worked as deputy manager of the machine shop in a mine. He had 'plunged from the ninth heaven into the eighteenth level of hell'.[17] The case continued to be discussed during the early years of the Cultural Revolution, and Xi was incarcerated for a total of eight years during that period. He was eventually released in the spring of 1975, but he was left to languish in the living quarters of a factory producing firebricks. Not surprisingly, this had a profound effect on his wife and children.

The real author, Li Jiantong, and her allies including Liu Jingfan, were imprisoned and later sentenced to periods of reform through labour, and the book was proscribed until 1978. On 14 July 1979, the verdict was reversed by the Central Organisation Department; it was decided that *Liu Zhidan* was after all a good novel praising the work of the older generation of revolutionaries and there was no basis for suggesting that Xi Zhongxun had been part of a 'secret anti-Party clique'. They had been framed by Kang Sheng. The decision was ratified by the Central Committee on 4 August 1979. Liu's role as a 'military strategist and high-ranking commander of the Chinese Workers' and Peasants' Red Army' is now acknowledged by the PRC Ministry of National Defence and Bao'an County in Shaanxi was later renamed Zhidan in his honour. The eighth CC meeting marked the beginning of the Socialist Education Movement, now regarded as a 'leftist' turn in CCP politics and a precursor of the Cultural Revolution.[18]

After his formal rehabilitation, Xi Zhongxun's case was raised by Hu Yaobang and Deng Xiaoping. On 22 February 1978, he was appointed a specially invited member [*teyao wei-yuan*] of the 5th CPPCC and chaired one of its meetings. He was sent to Guangdong province as Governor, to 'guard the southern gateway' [*bashou nandamen*] in Hu Yaobang's words,[19] where he established the conditions for the creation of Special Economic Zones in Shenzhen, Zhuhai and other districts. The economy of Guangdong at that time was in a poor state. The Cultural Revolution slogan 'take grain as the key link' had been taken literally and the production of non-staple foodstuffs including vegetables and fruit, for which Guangdong was well known, had declined dangerously; the peasants did not even dare to rear the 'three birds' [*san niao*], chicken, duck, and geese, which were their traditional sources of protein. Relations between Guangdong and its neighbours, including Hong Kong and Macao, were also causing concern for the new Party centre, which feared the social consequences of smuggling and other illicit links. Xi Zhongxun travelled widely in Guangdong, even in the hot summers, although he found it difficult to cope with the temperatures.

At the end of November 1981, Xi Zhongxun was recalled to Beijing and subsequently served as Deputy Chairman of the NPC, member of the Politburo and Secretary of the Central Secretariat. He was in tune with Hu Yaobang's reformist outlook and there were rumours that Hu had agreed that he should take over as Secretary of the Standing Committee of the Secretariat as soon as the idea of 'reform and opening' took hold. This was not supported by Deng Xiaoping, so Xi became an unofficial secretary to Hu and often acted as his office gatekeeper. People who went to see Hu often found themselves talking to Xi. In 1982, Xi Zhongxun, Peng Zhen, Nie Rongzhen, and others proposed that a Cultural Revolution compensation fund should be established at central and local levels to recompense those who had been wronged during that period. Although the proposal attracted some support, it was rejected by the Politburo on the grounds of the potential cost; they argued that most of the injustices had already been dealt with, but there was a reluctance to revisit the thousands of grievances from the Cultural Revolution, including some 380,000 cadres who had been classified as 'enemies in conflict with the Party' [*diwo maodun*].

Hu Yaobang, CCP Chairman (1981–1982) and then General Secretary (1982–1987) after the post of chairman had been abolished, spoke at the Twelfth National Congress of the Chinese Communist Party which was held in Beijing from 1–11 September 1982 and followed immediately by the First Plenary Session of the 12th Central Committee (12–13 September) of which Xi Zhongxun was a member, arguing for comprehensive modernisation and the creation of a democratic socialist China. Xi Zhongxun was one of Hu's strongest supporters and also continued to promote inclusive 'United Front' policies, although he had resigned from the Central Committee Secretariat in September 1985. In 1986, when differences between Hu and his mentor Deng Xiaoping began to emerge, Xi supported Hu's contention that it was time for Deng to step down. This political struggle was overtaken by events – the wave of student demonstrations which broke out in Anhui, Shanghai, and Beijing around demands for more democracy, an end to corruption and opposition to Japanese economic domination of China. Hu Yaobang was sympathetic to the students and was blamed for the disturbances; he agreed to step down as Secretary General during an unspecified meeting of senior Party officials held between 10–15 January 1987, although he was permitted to remain in the Politburo. This decision was essentially the responsibility of Deng Xiaoping with the support of senior political and military cadres who had concluded that Hu's calls for democracy and freedom had gone too far. Hu was replaced by Zhao Ziyang. Xi Zhongxun was so closely associated with Hu that he lost much of his influence, although he was elected Deputy Chairman of the 7th NPC Standing Committee in April 1988. He was re-elected in 1990 and personally criticised the military suppression of the Democracy Movement. He was, however, politically marginalised, his health worsened, and he died in 2002. Friends of Xi Jinping reported that he was determined to learn from his father's example and would avoid allying himself to a political cause that could destroy him. The families still had personal sympathies with the reformers; when Zhao Ziyang died in 2005, Xi and his mother Qi Xin sent a wreath to the funeral.[20]

Xi Jinping in Fujian province

When Xi Jinping graduated in 1979, he worked in an office in Zhongnanhai as Secretary to Geng Biao. Geng was a former ambassador and future Minister of Defence who at the time was a member of the Politburo, Vice-Chairman of the State Council, and Secretary General of the CMC. From 1982–1985, Xi was Deputy Secretary and then Secretary of the CCP Committee of Zhengding County in Hebei Province. In 1985, he was transferred to Fujian province, where he was to spend 17½ years. He took up his new posts as Deputy Mayor of Xiamen and member of the local CCP Standing Committee on his 32nd birthday. In contrast to his father's career, his progress seemed smooth. Within two or three years, he was on an upward career track, and after three years, he had advanced to the post of CCP Secretary of the prefectural level city, Ningde, which lies to the south of Fuzhou. In 1990, still only 37 years old, he became Party secretary of Fuzhou City and Chairman of the municipal People's Congress. In 1995, he also took on the role of Secretary of the Fujian Provincial Party Committee and two years later became alternate member of the CCP 15th Central Committee. In 1999, aged 46, he was appointed Fujian Deputy Party Secretary and Deputy Governor and Acting Governor. The following January, he was formally adopted as Fujian's Governor but transferred rapidly to the neighbouring province of Zhejiang as Deputy Party Secretary.

The Fujian cities of Xiamen and Ningde had a troubled history of corrupt relations between officials and local businesses; in several high-profile cases, officials had fallen from grace. Xi Jinping appears to have emerged from this without a stain on his character and with a reputation for incorruptibility. In 1988, when he took over the CCP Secretary post in Ningde, he immediately ordered that over 2,000 officials be investigated for building private houses in contravention of the regulations.

Zhejiang province

In 2002, Xi was appointed Zhejiang Party Secretary and became a full member of the Central Committee, replacing Zhang Dejiang, who had been promoted to membership of the Politburo and CCP Secretary of Guangdong province. The following year, Xi became Chairman of the Zhejiang People' Congress. People who knew Xi well reported that in 2002, when he was transferred from Fujian to Zhejiang, this promotion vastly exceeded his own expectations; he thought he might be sent to Shaanxi, a much less prestigious posting, because of his connections from the 1970s. He assiduously cultivated the local leadership of the Zhejiang region by travelling widely and visiting as many counties as possible. Even allowing for the hyperbole of the official media, it is clear that Xi had acquired a reputation for working tirelessly on behalf of his province and not enriching himself. One paper referred to his 'two planks' [*liang ban*] 'boss during the day, hard bed at night' [*baitian zuo laoban, wanshang shui diban*].[21] Xi's reputation and political standing benefited from the success of the Zhejiang economy, which was considered a model of provincial development. He was personally credited for building on a strong private sector of small businesses to develop industry and external investment, and for promoting the integration of all the economies of the Yangzi Delta region. This strategy was so highly regarded that he led a Zhejiang delegation to Shanghai to report on it in March 2003 and spoke again on the same topic in November 2006; this gave him the opportunity to demonstrate that his vision went beyond the purely provincial.

Mrs Xi: Peng Liyuan

Xi Jinping and his wife Peng Liyuan were introduced by friends when he was Deputy Mayor of Xiamen; they married in 1987, although her parents were unhappy about the consequences of her marrying into the political hierarchy. Peng did not have a political background, but she was well known as a singer of traditional folksongs and appeared regularly on television. She had joined the PLA at the age of 18, her career developed through military song and troupes, and she is said to be a civilian member of the PLA with a military equivalent rank of Major-General. Few of the rising generation of CCP leaders have direct military experience. As has been noted, Xi had worked for Geng Biao during his tenure at the CMC and his father had been a guerrilla leader in the 1940s, so he had some empathy with the military. His wife's connections enhanced this aspect of his curriculum vitae, and he took every opportunity to visit military units near his political bases in Fujian and Shanghai. Xi and Peng have lived apart for much of their married lives, and this often led to speculation that they are separated; it is, however, typical of many professional couples in China.

Shanghai

Xi Jinping was transferred to the powerful position of Shanghai Party secretary in March 2007 to replace the disgraced Chen Liangyu, who was imprisoned for fraud and bribery in connection with the corrupt management of the Shanghai pension funds. Xi had spent 22 years working in the developing economies of the east coast provinces; it was believed that this experience and his interest in integrating the Yangzi Delta would help Shanghai maintain its preeminent economic position.

Although he had close connections with the political elite of Shanghai, he had never been part of the 'Shanghai Clique' that dominated China's national politics during Jiang Zemin's tenure as CCP Secretary General, and he did not have his own coterie in the city. He had a reputation for cleaning up corruption and reforming official practices. Because his approach was low key, and his factional allegiances were unclear, he had few obvious opponents. The Shanghai faction was in retreat and the Communist Youth League (CYL) faction was unpopular for being overbearing and arrogant; Xi Jinping, with his 'princeling' background, was an acceptable compromise candidate.

The director of the Central Organisation Department, He Guoqiang, made it clear that Xi's appointment to head the Shanghai Party committee was made on the basis of the 'overall national interest'. The subtext of this remark would become apparent at the 17th Party Congress in October 2007, when Xi Jinping was elevated to the Politburo Standing Committee, apparently with the full support of General Secretary Hu Jintao, who wished to demonstrate that the higher reaches of the CCP were not entirely dominated by the CYL faction. With this promotion, Xi overtook the 'two Lis' of the CYL faction, Li Keqiang and Li Yuanchao (Head of the CCP Organisation Department since 2007 following He Guoqiang). Xi's ranking at No. 6 in the Politburo after the 17th Congress marked him out as the leading figure for the post Hu–Wen administration. The Shanghai post automatically qualified Xi for a seat on the Politburo at the 17th Congress, but it was assumed that he would remain in Shanghai for a decent interval before being moved to Beijing in the event that he was appointed to the Politburo Standing Committee within six months and by convention could not remain in charge of Shanghai. Some said that Jiang Zemin was the kingmaker, guiding Xi's meteoric rise; others insisted that the 'three Hus' of the faction – Hu Yaobang, Hu Qili and Hu Jintao – had all backed the Xis, father and son, so that in the end it was Hu Jintao who brought him into the top position.

Hu Jintao had been criticised by some of the 'princelings' who had worked in the CYL in the 1980s, and this may account for the fact that he had been sent to work in poor and distant Guizhou in 1985. However, he still had the support of the reformist Hu Yaobang, who made a point of spending the Spring Festival with him in Guizhou in February 1986, a visit that boosted Hu Jintao's morale and enabled Hu Yaobang to see for himself what progress was being made in China's poorest province. Hu Jintao greatly admired and respected his CYL mentor, Hu Yaobang, and after the elder Hu's death in 1989, visited his grave in Gongqing, Jiangxi to pay his respects. Hu Jintao was acutely aware of how highly Hu Yaobang thought of Xi Zhongxun, and his political integrity and had taken the decision early on to champion Xi Jinping in his political ambitions. Although he did not give his 'imperial endorsement' [*qin dian*] to any specific successor at the 17th Party Congress, neither did he indicate that he was unwilling to bestow his patronage on whoever was elected. Xi Jinping's success in his career was due not only to his own political connections, but also to those of his father's generation and his father's reputation.

Hu Jintao had frequently called for greater 'democracy within the Party' [*dangnei minzhu*], and some commentators argued that this assisted Xi Jinping's rise to power. In January 2006, before Li Datong, the managing editor of *Freezing Point* [*Bingdian*], a weekly supplement published by *China Youth Daily*, was dismissed and his publication temporarily suspended, he had argued that the political equilibrium achieved at the 17th Congress indicated that China was moving from autocracy in the direction of democracy and that internal democracy within the CCP was the first step in this direction. Li maintained that the basis for the legitimacy of CCP rule had changed; in the past, appointments had been based on 'nomination by the leadership' [*you lingdao timing*], but now 'everything could be changed by voting' [*you toupiao neng gaibian yiqie*].[22] This was clearly over-optimistic but represented the aspirations of many younger members of the CCP.

The Central Organisation Department carried out a survey by questionnaire of leading officials in Shanghai and members of the NPC and CPPCC, a total of 2,000 people; it found overwhelming support for Xi Jinping. Reuters cited sources that claimed Xi had gained the majority of votes in inner Party elections from the regions, and other sources indicated that he had obtained 90% of the votes in the first ballot in Shanghai and that he had unanimous support from the heads of Party committees [*dangwei shounao*]. His reputation within the Party was that of a virtuous official, and he was said to 'embody the traditional Chinese virtues of filial piety, respect for elders and caring for the young' and to have a clean record that was invaluable at a time when concern about official corruption was high on the Party's agenda.[23] It is tempting to link this evaluation to his father's track record of 'pursuing the ideals of democracy and freedom' [*zhuiqiu minzhu ziyou linian*] as well as 'reform and opening' and therefore to the reformist current exemplified by Hu Yaobang and Zhao Ziyang. In the light of the political fate of these two and their supporters, it would not have been surprising if Xi and others had kept their reformist powder dry or placed economic development and political stability ahead of democracy, at least in public. Optimists hoped that Xi was a reformist, but there was little evidence either way. Xi Jinping's public pronouncements at that time concentrated on familiar themes of the Hu and Wen administration such as measures to combat corruption and 'harmonious economic development' [jingji *hexie fazhan*]. There were no obvious signs of a tendency towards authoritarianism.

Xi Jinping was not without his critics; one Zhejiang official speaking off the record described Xi as 'simple and honest to a fault' [*hanhou youyu*] and not always consistent when problems arose. He tended to implement what his subordinates proposed if no major issues were raised in discussion. His grasp on power in Zhejiang had not been as firm as that of his predecessor, Zhang Dejiang. Others argued that his ability not to offend people created better and more stable relationships and that even if there were no great successes there were no great disasters. He was a safe pair of hands.

Insiders revealed how in March 2007, when Xi Jinping went to Shanghai to take up his post as Secretary of the Municipal Party Committee, he was met with 'sugar-coated bullets' [*tangyi paodan*]. On 28 March, the Shanghai Municipal Committee Hospitality Department offered him a detached 'British-style' three-storey house at South Xiangyang Road;[24] it was 800 square metres in area with a garden. Regulations limited the floor area of provincial-level officials to 250 square metres, and even members of the Politburo were not supposed to have more than 300 square metres. Xi took one look and left saying that it should be used as a convalescent home for elderly cadres. It is not possible to verify this account: was this the normal treatment of a new Party secretary? Did the officials misread Xi's reputation and his likely response? Were they trying to entrap this sea-green incorruptible? On another occasion, when Xi was due to visit Hangzhou, his subordinates had arranged for a private train to take him there from Shanghai, but Xi insisted on substituting a seven-seat bus. Relatives of his who had business interests in Shanghai moved their businesses elsewhere when he became Party secretary to forestall concerns about conflicts of interest. These stories reinforce his reputation for old-fashioned frugality and unwillingness to be compromised by corrupt practices.

Following his elevation to the Politburo, Xi Jinping moved to Beijing, where he was able to spend more time with his wife and daughter and devote more attention to his elderly mother, as would be expected with his filial reputation. In the capital, he also became more exposed to closer scrutiny and sharper criticism. Commentators wondered how he would work with Bo Xilai, whose father Bo Yibo had been diametrically opposed to the political approach of Xi Zhongxun, an enmity that may have continued into the next generation. This problem disappeared with the arrest and conviction of Bo Xilai in September 2013. Because Xi Jinping had benefited from the conflict between Hu Jintao under the CYL banner and Jiang Zemin under the banner of the Shanghai Clique, he was viewed as a counterweight to the two factions. More significant was the question of how Xi and the 'crown prince' of the CYL, Li Keqiang, would cooperate and compete in power.[25]

Li Keqiang

Although the relationship between Hu Jintao and Premier Wen Jiabao had not been one of equals, it was far more so than that between Xi Jinping and Premier Li Keqiang. Wen had a very public role and had no compunction in expressing controversial views openly. Li Keqiang, by contrast, has always appeared to be the loyal subordinate who has never been permitted to outshine his rival Xi in public. That does not accurately reflect either his ability or his role in policy implementation.

Li was born in 1955 in Dingyuan County, which is close to Chuzhou City in eastern Anhui. His father was a low-level CCP official in the county government. In 1974 at the age of 19, he was sent to live in the Dongling Production Brigade of the Damiao Commune in Fengyang County, Anhui as part of the 'rustication' [*xiafang*] programme of sending young city people down to the countryside as the Cultural Revolution drew to an end. Fengyang County, although a backwater, became famous in 1978; the move to end the People's Commune system and replace it with individual household contracts originated in one of its villages, Xiaogang. Within two years, Li had moved to become the Secretary of the Damiao Production Brigade committee and 'an individual advanced in the study of Mao Zedong thought in Anhui'.[26] Today, the village is still primarily engaged in agriculture, but many of its young people have joined the exodus to work as labourers in Jiangsu, Zhejiang, Guangdong, and Shanghai that was one of the results of the 1978 reforms. Li is remembered by older residents as a resourceful young man who moved stones to help build his own accommodation at the foot of a nearby hill, as there was nowhere else for him and his colleagues to live. He became Secretary of the local CYL branch and joined the CCP in about 1976 while still in the village.

He left Damiao in March 1978 as one of the first cohort to pass the entrance examinations for Beijing University when they resumed at the end of the Cultural Revolution. Li studied in the Faculty of Economics, where he was concurrently a research student and a member of staff [*zaizhi yanjiusheng*]; he graduated with the equivalent of a BA in law and a PhD in economics. An article on the Class of 1977 in the Beijing University Law Department – the Huangpu class, as they became known after the pioneering intake of the Huangpu Military Academy in the 1924 – appeared in the popular and independent weekly newspaper *Southern Weekend* [*Nanfang zhoumo*]. A group of students, including Li Keqiang, had planned to produce a book on 'legal culture' and, although this never materialised, it is an indication of his priorities at the time: after the lawlessness of the Cultural Revolution the students were examining ways of creating a society based on law. Of the 82 students in the Class of 1977, four including Li remained to carry out further studies, Li being assigned to the Economic Law Teaching and Research Section. Li became Secretary of the CYL branch for Beijing University; this marked his move away from the career in teaching and research for which he had seemed destined. While his colleagues became academics or lawyers, Li moved into politics.

Communist Youth League

Li owes his rise to power to his association with the CYL. On graduating in 1982, he remained at Beida, where after becoming Secretary of the university's CYL, he joined the national CYL Standing Committee as Secretary of the Universities Department and National University Liaison Committee. He retained the drive and enthusiasm he had shown as a student; although he had got on well with a great many students, he stood out from the crowd because of the independent and open-minded views he expressed on political and social issues, often incurring the criticism of CYL cadres from other fields. This outspoken attitude cost him the election as the Beijing City CYL representative to the 11th National Congress of the CYL in 1982. Wang Zhaohua, head of the CYL Central Organisation Department [*zhongzubu*], intervened and nominated him to the Congress; he was concurrently elected to the CYL Central Committee Standing Committee [*tuan zhongyang changwei*]. Li cultivated an interest in playing tennis, emulating senior officials including Wan Li, Hu Qili and Li Ruihan. Thus did patronage operate in the selection of leading cadres.

When Li became head of the CYL Universities Department in 1983, he was only 28 years old; he joined the CYL Secretariat at the same time as Li Yuanchao, who was also considered to be a rival rising star and who was secretary of the Secretariat and No. 4 in the organisation. Li Keqiang was 'candidate' secretary until he succeeded to the full post two years later at the Fourth Plenum of the CYL 11th Central Committee and then in due course became Secretary of the CYL Secretariat Standing Committee, where for two years he worked closely with the First Secretary of the CYL Hu Jintao, later President and CCP General Secretary, who had also risen through the bureaucracy of the CYL.

During the mid- and late 1980s, when there was an upsurge in student activism, Li Keqiang was in charge of liaison between the CYL and central and local bodies of the CCP. He advocated 'controlling student activism but without political persecution'[27] [*kongzhi xuechao dan bu gao zhengzhi pohai*]. According to Wang Juntao, a dissident arrested and tried for his part in the Democracy Movement of 1989, Li was 'not as aloof as he had some-times seemed at Beida but was wiser and steadier, as incisive as ever but still open minded in his outlook'.

In May 1993, at the age of 38, and after almost ten years in the CYL Secretariat, Li became First Secretary of the CYL for a five-year period. During his time in the CYL, he had fol-lowed a parallel academic career, taking his Beida master's degree in the Faculty of Eco-nomics and completing his PhD in 1995 while attempting to find ways for the CYL to implement Deng Xiaoping's 'theories' and wrestling with the implications of China's eco-nomic reforms. He also wrote articles including a 10,000-character paper, 'On the ternary structure of China's economy', for the influential journal *Chinese Social Science*, for which he was awarded a prize.[28]

Successive disasters in Henan

At the 15th Communist Party Congress in 1997, Li Keqiang was elected to the CCP Central Committee. He was transferred from the CYL Secretariat to Henan Province in June 1998 as deputy Party secretary; was later appointed deputy Governor, then acting Governor of Henan; and within six months Governor in his own right. At the conclusion of the 16th Party Congress in 2002, he was elevated to the position of Henan Party secretary and the following year Chairman of the Standing Committee of the Henan People's Congress. A move of this nature to establish a powerful position in one of the provinces is a *sine qua non* for potential senior leaders of the CCP. If his progress through the CYL had been smooth, the same could not be said for his time in Henan. One of the origins of Chinese civilisation, and one of China's most populous provinces, Henan had a history of conflict and natural disasters, and had been backward in modernising in the 1980s and 1990s. A series of unpredictable events in Hunan and difficulties with complex political relationships in the province left Li politi-cally bruised. He left his family behind in Beijing to shield them from inessential political socialising and moved on his own to the provincial capital, Zhengzhou. He soon acquired a reputation for declining invitations to banquets that had no connection with his official role; he dined simply, alone or with his private secretary.

Two serious fires occurred soon after Li's appointment as Governor. In Jiaozuo City on 29 March 2000, 74 people died while watching a film and on 25 December of the same year, 309 people perished when fire took hold of a dance hall in the city of Luoyang, where Christmas celebrations were taking place; in addition to partygoers, the dead included con-struction workers on other floors. Li attended personally to direct operations: since he had only been Governor for such a short time, he escaped direct blame for these disasters. The death toll (second highest in a fire since 1949) and the revelation that the local fire brigade had warned that the building was unsafe reflected on the provincial government: Li Keqiang accepted responsibility and wrote to the central government offering his resignation, but it was not accepted. He had had a narrow escape and the effects of these fires and a series of mining disasters taxed him mentally and physically between June 1998 and 12 December 2004, when he left Henan for Liaoning province.

During Li's tenure in Henan, there were other political headaches including a scandal of contaminated flour for noodles and the popularity of Falungong in the province. Outweigh-ing these, and the fire and mining disasters, was the corruption and wilful neglect by medi-cal authorities who failed to stop the illegal sale of blood which led to an unprecedented epidemic of HIV (human immunodeficiency virus) and AIDS (acquired immune deficiency syndrome). The commercialisation of blood supplies and the illegal sale of blood had begun before Li arrived in Henan, probably as early as 1992, but he was severely criticised for a news blockade and cover-up that contributed to an escalation of the outbreak. He did, however, enforce a clampdown on illegal sales and established a network of standardised [*biaozhunhua*] blood collection stations. In 2003–2004, he made three successive visits to one of the worst affected areas, Wenlou Village in Shangcai County in the south of the province, at a time when the newly installed administration led by Hu Jintao and Wen Jiabao was beginning to acknowledge publicly the need to deal with China's HIV/AIDS problem. Li publicly shook hands with AIDS sufferers, announced free medical treatment, and met in his office with AIDS activists who had previously been silenced by the authorities to discuss the problem of AIDS orphans and treatment. The timing suggests that he might have been waiting for a change of heart at the Party centre before he acted. At the beginning of 2004, he organised work teams of officials to go to the 38 worst affected villages to give 'help and support'. By 2004, the HIV/AIDS epidemic had been brought under control and the number of AIDS-related deaths had fallen significantly.

Commentators differ on Li's effectiveness in developing the economy of Henan. He boosted agricultural production and the processing of agricultural products, and Henan became known for well-recognised brands of foodstuffs, but critics argued that the 'cities of the central plains' were not well-managed and had difficulty attracting investment. Although these problems were not all the result of Li's policies, he was the top man [*yibashou*] at the time and much of the blame fell on him. His supporters point to an increase in the proportion of GDP contributed by Henan's growth and to an increase in the production of grains, metals, and other products. Li's parting shot at a 'meeting of leading cadres' to mark his transfer to Liaoning was to tell them that his decisions had not necessarily all been correct and that if in future they proved not to have been realistic [*bu fuhe shiji*], they should be modified. The cadres clapped, but Li put up his hand to stem the applause.[29]

Liaoning province

The morning after his send off from Henan, Li Keqiang flew to the Liaoning provincial capital of Shenyang, where he gave a formal 'speech on taking up his new appointment' [*jiuye jiangyan*] to a meeting of leading cadres. He was introduced at the conference by Li Jingtian, deputy director of the CCP's Central Organisation Department, himself a former CYL official, on behalf of the central leadership in Beijing; this was an endorsement of Li Keqiang by the centre after his tribulations in Henan.

Moving from Henan to Liaoning took Li Keqiang from a province associated mainly with agriculture and food processing to one of northeastern China's traditional industrial heartlands, known for oil and mining-related industries with an impressive record of growth in GNP. Liaoning's Party and government hierarchy had a track record of supplying members of the highest CCP bodies, notably the three Lis of Liaoning in the second half of the 1980s – Li Tieying (President of the Chinese Academy of Social Sciences from 1998–2003 and vice-chairman of NPC Standing Committee since 2003), Li Guixian (President of the Bank of China 1988–1993), and Li Changchun (Member of the Standing Committee of the Politburo since 2002) – not to mention the ill-fated Bo Xilai (later CCP Secretary of Chongqing 2007–2012). Liaoning was a fast track to the top, but the province faced severe economic and social challenges, mostly stemming from the legacy of state-owned enterprise, the pension burden of retired employees and changes in development strategies. Li Keqiang made full use of Beijing's policies of revitalising the northeast, which the Hu–Wen administration had initiated, to improve the living standards of local people. Liaoning was the focus of this policy, as it was regarded as the 'valve' or 'tap' [*longtou*] of the whole northeastern economy, as well as its principal outlet to the sea. Liaoning benefited from this policy, and so did Li Keqiang. Hu Jintao was happy for his protégé to take some of the credit for the success of this policy; this smoothed the way for his entry into high-level CCP politics.[30]

Li Keqing found a major project on which to concentrate: the shanty town districts [*penghu qu*] of Liaoning. Having learned the lessons of Henan, he became publicly associated with its success. The shanty towns were temporary buildings in declining mining areas, originally erected in the 1960s for mine and factory workers, but taken over by the poor and destitute who could not afford other accommodation. In December 2004, on only his 20th day in office, Li visited one settlement in Fuxin and vowed to do something about the problem as a matter of urgency. In a television interview with the well-known presenter Wang Xiaoya, he promised to transform the shanty town district if it was the last thing he did [*zaguo maitie*] ('even if he had to smash the pans and sell them as scrap'[31]). He quoted Archimedes and argued that his fulcrum to change the shanty towns was the CCP Centre and the power of the people; the shanty towns also functioned as a fulcrum for his own rise to power. He was able to raise RMB 500 billion from the State Development Bank and build new housing for 1.2 million people. Redevelopment started in 2005, and relocation was well underway by 2007. In January 2007, media outlets and others were invited to view the transformation and local officials praised Li to the skies for resolving such a long-standing problem; cynics suggested that it had been achieved only because of his powerful connections with the centre and sources of funding. Li included an account of the success of this programme in his report on the economic revitalisation of Liaoning to the 17th National Congress of the CCP on 17 October 2007.

> For instance, under the province's ambitious shanty town reformation plan, large expanses of slums dating back to the 60s have been replaced with rows and rows of low-rise residential buildings which now accommodate more than 1 million urban residents.[32]

On the eve of the 2007 Spring Festival, Wu Bangguo, Chairman of the Standing Committee of the Tenth NPC, secretary of its Leading Party Members' Group and a member of the Standing Committee of the Politburo, visited Liaoning. Premier Wen Jiabao followed hard on his heels in what was regarded as an unusual show of support for Li Keqiang and his policies in the province. According to Xinhua, 'This Spring Festival, after the conclusion of the official party and government ceremonies in Beijing, Premier Wen Jiabao travelled to Fushun in Liaoning, the site of China's earliest offensive on shanty towns'.[33] That was Wen's second visit to Liaoning in three years; Hu Jintao had used a meeting in Jilin about the Asian Games to make an unannounced visit to one of the shanty town sites. The project was lauded in the official media as a popular project [*minxin gongcheng*], a personal endorsement for Li Keqiang. Other actions designed to demonstrate public support for Li included a visit by Lee Kuan-yew, the elder statesman and 'Minister Mentor' of Singapore, to Liaoning.[34] Lien Chan, Chairman and then Honorary Chairman of the Taiwan-based Guomindang, spent four days in Henan during his 2007 visit to the PRC. Lian commented on the economic progress of the province and noted that, although Li Keqiang had moved to Liaoning two years previously, it was his name that always came up in conversations about economic development in Henan. *Liaowang* magazine, part of the Xinhua conglomerate, published a long article in early 2007, focussing on the economic successes of Liaoning under Li Keqiang.[35]

Li Keqiang's political luck did not hold; on 14 January 2005, shortly after he took office in Liaoning, 114 miners died in a disaster at a mine belonging to the Fuxin Mining Company.

The Deputy Governor of Liaoning, Liu Guoqiang, who had overall responsibility for industry and safety, was suspended pending an investigation, as were ten of the mine management. Other disasters followed, and some people even began to refer to Li Keqing as a 'disaster star' [*zaixing*] who was followed by calamities. He survived, but his reputation was more seriously damaged by incidents in early 2007: the mine disaster in Fushun which cost the lives of 29 miners, 32 lives lost in an escape of molten steel at a steelworks in Tieling, and finally the explosion at a dance hall in Benxi in which 25 people died. The fact that some of these disasters took place while the 'two meetings' – the NPC and the Chinese People's Political Consultative Conference – were in session in Beijing brought the issue to the attention of a wider public. Li handled the disasters well. At the time of the Fushun mine disaster, he was in Beijing, attending the NPC and the CPPCC; he ordered officials in Liaoning to report the circumstances in full to the media, thus avoiding a media storm. In the case of the Tieling and Benxi incident, he went to the scene and personally took charge of the rescue operations, avoiding criticisms from the relatives of those who had died. His abilities in crisis management won him approval, but the way this was presented in the media was limited by restrictions on local reporting and instructions that the media all use 'unified reports' [*tongyi de baodao*]. It was widely believed that such a blanket ban on criticism of Li could not have been arranged solely by the Liaoning authorities but must have been on the orders of the Central Propaganda Department. The only reason the Central Propaganda Department would have done this was on the orders of the highest-level leaders of the Party and government to protect the reputation of a man who was about to join their ranks.

Li Keqiang entertained progressive and enlightened views during his student years in the 1980s and had friends who were deeply involved in the Democracy Movement. China's Premiers have generally appeared more liberal or reformist than Party leaders, from Zhou Enlai through to Wen Jiabao (or have at least been given more licence to express their views); this encouraged hopes that he might be interested in pushing for greater openness and democracy. This reputation did not endear him to the older generation of CCP leaders, who remained highly influential behind the scenes. One of the chief concerns among the Party elders [*yuanlao*] was to ensure that there would never be a Chinese equivalent to Mikhail Gorbachev who might inadvertently bring about the downfall of the CCP regime by pushing a reform agenda.

While Li was a student at Beida, he had come under the influence of Gong Xiangrui (1911–1996), an academic lawyer who had studied at the London School of Economics in the 1930s. Gong specialised in comparative constitutional and administrative law and openly advocated political reform for China, including the separation of powers between the executive and the legislature and the introduction of a Western-style multi-party system: Gong's views are anathema to the old guard of the CCP, but they were of interest to Li Keqiang. Another member of staff who taught the Class of 1977, Yang Dunxian, who later became a journalist with *Southern Weekend*, was impressed by Li Keqiang, who he remembered taking a particular interest in the interaction between politics and legislation. In 2002, the Class of 1977 held a reunion at Beida and Li Keqiang, by then the Governor of Henan province, made a speech and also confirmed his reputation for never visiting Beijing without trawling the bookshops to augment his collection of books on politics, economics, law, management, and culture, including some published abroad.[36]

If Li retains feelings of nostalgia for the 1980s Democracy Movement, he has kept them well hidden. However, the intellectual ferment of Beida had a lasting effect on Li; he retained a love of learning and of the English language which he was able to use from time to time. The fact that he was a student at Beida and not Qinghua, which has been the cradle of the

CCP leadership, is important. There is a saying that means, on one level, 'Great world for Qinghua, Beida is a wasteland', and it is widely believed that Qinghua graduates in the Party look down on their colleagues who attended Beida. In the nine-man seventeenth Politburo Standing Committee, there were three Qinghua alumni – Hu Jintao, Wu Bangguo, and Xi Jinping (although that was one fewer than the four in the previous Standing Committee), but in the eighteenth, there was only Li Keqiang from the 'Beida wasteland'. Although he was the only Beida alumnus on the Standing Committee, there were others in the full Politburo (Li Yuanchao and Bo Xilai) and in the provinces at Deputy Governor level and above (and therefore eligible for Politburo status in the future). Overall, Beida alumni outnumbered those from Qinghua by 57–37.[37] Zhao Leiji, a Beida alumnus, was elected to the nineteenth Standing Committee. The Beida clique were beginning to catch up on the Qinghua clique, possibly auguring a future factional configuration.

Xi Jinping in power

Xi Jinping's rise to the top began with his confirmation as Vice-Chairman of the CMC in 2010. When he was elected General Secretary of the CCP at its 18th Congress in November 2012, he also became Chairman of the CMC. His appointment as President came with the NPC of March 2013: he then had authority over the Party, the army, and the state.[38] Although Li Keqiang was appointed as Premier to serve with Xi Jinping, up to the time of writing, it has been a Xi administration, rather than a Xi and Li administration. From the outset Li Keqiang was relegated to the side lines. Occasionally he has emerged from Xi's shadow, but General Secretary and President Xi continues to dominate the political scene.

'Document No. 9', March 2013

In a society governed through a complex bureaucracy, key documents illuminate government actions. 'Document No. 9' is the recognised shorthand for the Communique on the Current State of Ideology [*Guanyu dangqian yishi xingtai lingyu qingkuang de tongbao*], a CCP General Office classified document that originated in July 2012 but was widely circulated the following year, and specifically targeted at 'local divisional levels' of the Party and government. It was leaked to a Chinese website outside the PRC by Gao Yu, a journalist with a reputation for independent writing; she was sentenced to seven years imprisonment for publishing state secrets. 'Document No. 9' contains a detailed critical assessment of Western liberal and democratic thought, and ways of opposing it.

The document which was created in response to problems identified by the new leadership as emanating from the Hu Jintao and Wen Jiabao period specifies seven 'dangerous Western principles' or 'false ideological trends', which must be resisted:

1   Western constitutional democracy, including multi-party elections, which threatens to undermine the CCP's leadership, 'people's democracy', and 'socialism with Chinese characteristics'.
2   Universal values, in which Western values are believed to be the 'prevailing norm' as opposed to the theoretical underpinnings of the Party leadership.
3   Civil society and the idea that individual rights are paramount and should be immune from state actions, thus undermining the social basis of the CCP.
4   Neoliberalism 'under the guise of globalisation' and privatisation without controls, rather than the existing mixed economic system.

5   Western standards of journalism and freedom of the press, which weaken the role of Party discipline in controlling the media and publishing.
6   'Historical nihilism', which rejects scientific socialism and Mao Zedong Thought, and reassesses and undercuts the official history of the CCP and New China.
7   Questioning the authenticity of 'reform and opening' and 'socialism with Chinese characteristics' by using terms such as 'capitalist socialism', 'state capitalism', or 'new bureaucratic capitalism'.

These seven errors were followed by four remedies: the ideological sphere should be strengthened, Party members should be instructed in the difference between 'true and false theories', there must be 'unwavering adherence to the principle of the Party's control of the media', and the management of all propaganda in the ideological battlefield must be strengthened.

This was not a mass campaign, as the document was intended for limited circulation in Party and government circles at central and local levels, but the targets were remarkably similar to those of the campaigns against 'spiritual pollution' in October–December 1983, and against 'bourgeois liberalisation' in the late 1980s and early 1990s. The seriousness of the injunctions in 'Document No. 9' became clear as a campaign against all types of dissent unfolded. The crackdown affected human rights lawyers, private media outlets and a range of other independent thinkers. University staff were specially briefed that none of these taboo topics could be included in courses for students.[39]

Third Plenum 18th Central Committee, 9–12 November 2013

The first formal and public presentation of Xi Jinping's policies took place at the third full meeting of the CCP Central Committee (the 18th) from 9–12 November 2013. A year after Xi had been elected General Secretary, he announced the creation of two new bodies, the National Security Commission and Central Leading Group for Comprehensively Deepening Reforms. The National Security Commission effectively took over the security portfolio of Zhou Yongkang. Zhou had been under investigation for corruption since August 2013 in the wake of the Bo Xilai affair, although he was not formally charged and expelled from the CCP until December 2014. The Central Leading Group for Comprehensively Deepening Reforms, later rebadged as a commission, was established to oversee policy guidelines for tackling long-term issues in the reform process, but also to ensure the close control of the Party, and thus Xi, over the economy; this is normally the province of the State Council under the Premier, and the move downgraded Li Keqiang's role even further.[40]

Two specific, but no less important, social reforms were also announced: the abolition of the much-criticised penal system of education through labour [*laojiao* – see also Chapter 16], which was formalised by the Standing Committee of the NPC on 28 December 2013, and the relaxation of the one-child policy from 1 January 2016 with the announcement that two children would officially be allowed for all families.[41]

From 7–11 December 2013, Xi Jinping embarked on a visit to Guangdong province, one of the dynamos of the Chinese economy. This visit was regarded as a symbolic homage to Deng Xiaoping's 1992 'Southern Tour', during which he established nationwide political support for his reform programme.

Anti-corruption campaign

In parallel with his determination to alleviate poverty, one policy in which Xi Jinping genuinely believes is rooting out corrupt 'tigers and flies' in authority. Xi's campaign against corruption began immediately after the 18th National Congress of the CCP 2012 and ended the careers, and often the liberty, of tens of thousands of Party and government officials, executives, and military officers in the centre and the provinces, including over 100 at the highest level. Until 2017, this campaign was orchestrated by the Central Commission for Discipline Inspection, which had particular responsibility for Party members under the leadership of Xi's right-hand man, Wang Qishan. From 23 March 2018, that role was inherited by the National Supervision Commission, a new anti-corruption agency with authority that took precedence over even the Supreme Court.

While Xi's commitment to wiping out corruption is not doubted, the campaign was also a convenient way of eliminating political rivals. Of the thousands targeted in the campaign, a few will serve as examples. The case of Zhou Yongkang, the most prominent 'tiger', has been dealt with in Chapter 5. Xu Caihou had risen to the rank of general in the PLA and became a member of the Politburo and Vice-Chairman of the CMC. He was accused of having benefited from a 'cash for promotions' scheme within the military, in which the most senior ranks changed hands for millions of yuan. An investigation opened into his activities in the spring of 2014, but he was diagnosed with bladder cancer at about the same time. He was arrested from his hospital bed and expelled from the CCP in June 2014, and his ill-gotten gains were confiscated. He died on 15 March 2015, after which it was announced that no further action would be taken against him! Guo Boxiong, a retired PLA general and former member of the CMC was investigated for corrupt business dealings, expelled from the CCP on 30 July 2015, and on 25 July 2016 imprisoned for life after being convicted for bribery.

The case of Ling Jihua was more overtly political. A former aide to Hu Jintao and a product of the CYL, Ling had risen to be head of the CCP's General Office in 2007, a position of considerable influence and authority in the Party. In March 2012, his son, Ling Gu, was killed when the Ferrari he was driving crashed on Beijing's Fourth Ring Road. Two young women in the car survived, but the circumstances provided juicy gossip which reflected badly on Ling Jihua. In December 2014, he was investigated by the Central Commission for Discipline Inspection, dismissed from office, and expelled from the CCP. In July 2016, following a trial for corruption, the unlawful possession of state secrets even after he had left the General Office, and misuse of power, he was sentenced to life in prison. The campaign against the most senior 'tigers' continued. The arrest and trial of Meng Hongwei had international implications. Meng was a career police officer who had become Vice-Minister of Public Security but also the head of the Chinese section of Interpol. On 10 November 2016, he became the first Chinese president of Interpol, which should have been a feather in the cap of the PRC. In September 2018, his wife reported to French police that he had disappeared. It emerged that he had been detained by the Chinese authorities and was under investigation by the recently established National Security Commission. At a trial in June 2019, Meng pleaded guilty to bribery and in January 2020, it was announced that he had been sentenced to 13½ imprisonment and fined 2 million yuan RMB.[42]

Beidaihe meeting 2014

Xi Jinping emerged from the August 2014 summer summit that had convened on 4 August at Beidaihe, the Party's annual seaside retreat, in a stronger position than expected. Commentators had predicted that the meeting, which is not one of the highly publicised formal sessions but is politically more significant, would be a test of his authority and his ability to hold the CCP together; his anti-corruption campaign had affected more and more senior officials and implicated diverse Party factions, interest groups, and patronage cliques. The Beidaihe meetings were opportunities for members of the Politburo Standing Committee and other current members of the senior leadership to meet 'elders' from previous administrations for discussions that were not normally made public. Typically, other influential individuals are invited, depending on the topics to be discussed.[43]

As usual, no announcement was made of the end of the 'direction-setting gathering' at Beidaihe, but Xi's public appearance at the training venue of the Youth Olympic Games, where he met members of China's national athletic squad, signalled its conclusion. Reports of the agenda indicate that it had focused on the key domestic issues to be placed before the formal meeting of the Central Committee in October 2014, under the rubric of 'laws to modernise government'. The case of the disgraced Zhou Yongkang, under investigation since September 2014, was also discussed. In a more formal meeting of his Leading Group for Deepening Reform, Xi called for China to 'build a homegrown new media industry'[44] and the group approved a report on the 'integration of traditional and new media', so that they were 'diversified, advanced and competitive', and managed appropriately. It was also reported that the State Internet Information Office was restricting publication of its news content to news agencies and websites.

These meetings confirmed Xi's drive for control, his resolute opposition to any move towards diversity or openness, and above all his ability to concentrate power in his own hands. *People's Daily* on 13 August published an editorial comparing Xi's leadership with that of Deng Xiaoping in anticipation of the 110th anniversary of Deng's birth on 22 August.[45]

Political birthdays

In 2019, in a reversal of the style of the Mao period, members of the CCP were issued with guidelines on how they should celebrate their 'political birthdays' [*zhengzhi shengri*], the anniversaries of the day that they were admitted to the Party. The CCP's Central Discipline and Inspection Commission urged people to send political birthday cards to members who should retake the Party oath, re-read their application form to join the Party, and arrange a meeting with a senior Party official to discuss their shortcomings. For many Westerners, this has bizarre echoes of religious commitments such as renewal of marriage vows, rebaptism, or confession. The Party Branch Secretary in a state-owned enterprise in Jiangzi province reportedly organised joint ceremonies for all employees whose political birthdays occurred in the same month so that they could reaffirm their political vows together.

These moves came at a time when senior Party leaders feared that lack of discipline and loss of commitment in local-level Party organisations had become sufficiently serious to pose a threat to the Party's control. From 2016 onwards, a drive to establish CCP branches in private firms and foreign-owned businesses had enabled the Party to emphasise the spread of its influence, but this clearly was not having the effect on morale and dedication that Xi Jinping had anticipated.[46]

President Xi – for life?

Under informal conventions agreed when Jiang Zemin stepped down, Xi's term of office should end in 2022 (as General Secretary) and 2023 (as President). Many observers, inside China and beyond, doubt that Xi will respect these conventions, which have no legal force. Xi's term of office as President of the PRC was renewed in March 2018, but the term limits stipulated in the Constitution were removed and no successor was named; in theory, he could remain President for life. The respected journalist Wang Xiangwei reported that the rationale for the amendment was that it would 'uphold authority and the unified command of the Party leadership with Xi at the core'. The term limits had been added to the Constitution in 1982 with the specific aim of preventing leadership appointments for life, one of the lessons that Deng Xiaoping insisted should be learned from the Mao era.

The real basis of Xi's authority is not the presidency but his position as General Secretary of the CCP, and that should be decided first by the autumn of 2022. There was known to be concern about the Mao-style personality cult being constructed around Xi by the Party's propaganda organs and opposition within the Party to his remaining in power beyond the anticipated ten years; there were well-qualified candidates eager to succeed him. At the time of writing (summer 2020), it is not possible to predict whether the Xi Jinping era will come to an end in 2022 or 2023, or will be prolonged indefinitely following the example of Xi's neighbour, and perhaps ally, Vladimir Putin. Should he not step down, there will be serious conflict within the CCP, although it will not necessarily be visible to the naked eye.[47]

Opposition to Xi Jinping

There is much anecdotal evidence of opposition to Xi Jinping, including from within the CCP, but it is virtually impossible to quantify this or predict how successful it will be in preventing Xi from prolonging his presidency. From time to time, dissident individuals stick their heads above the parapet and are detained or disappear.

In 2016, Ren Zhiqiang, a CCP member and wealthy property magnate who owned the Huayuan Group, publicly challenged Xi Jinping's insistence that the media should always adhere to the Party line. On 12 March 2020, after criticising Xi's handling of the Covid-19 outbreak, he disappeared; on 7 April, the Central Commission for Discipline Inspection announced that Ren was being investigated for 'serious violations of law and discipline', the catch-all phrase indicating corruption. On 20 July, he was expelled from the CCP and on 22 September, he was found guilty of 'corruption, bribery and embezzlement of public funds', sentenced to 18 years imprisonment and fined RMB 4.2 million.[48]

In July 2018, an article by Xu Zhangrun, a professor of jurisprudence and constitutional law at the prestigious Tsinghua University, was published in which he criticised Xi Jinping's policies, including the abolition of presidential term limits. Xu was investigated and prevented from leaving the country. After the appearance in February 2020 of another article criticising the government's response to the Covid-19 outbreak, Xu was dismissed from the university, placed under house arrest, and detained by police on trumped-up charges of soliciting a prostitute. He was released after six days, but remained under surveillance.[49]

Such was the concern of the CCP leadership of political opposition within the political and legal system that in July 2020, a pilot campaign to purge the system of 'corrupt elements' and create an 'ironclad army' was launched by the Central Political and Legal Affairs Commission in five provinces. This was directed at law enforcement officers who had been acting as 'protection umbrellas' for criminals but, significantly, at 'two-faced officials' within the legal system who only paid lip service to the regulations of the CCP. A working group to counter 'political threats' was also established under the commission, a clear indication that the targets of the campaign were political opponents as well as criminals.[50]

The most dramatic evidence of opposition to Xi from deep within the CCP came in August 2020 with the defection of Cai Xia, a long-serving teacher of Marxism and CCP theory at the Central Party School which trains the most senior cadres in the country. In an interview not published until she had left China, Cai called Xi Jinping a 'mafia boss' and accused him of 'killing a Party and a country' and 'turning China into an enemy of the world'. Stunned officials at the Central Party School held an emergency meeting to 'strengthen discipline' and prevent 'major political incidents'. Cai's doubts had begun with attempts to formulate a credible Marxist theory around the risible and much-reviled Three Represents policy of Jiang Zemin in the 1990s, and were consolidated after 2012 as the authoritarianism of Xi became apparent. She gave speeches and wrote articles criticising Xu and supporting Ren Zhiqiang but cited as a turning point the death in police custody in May 2016 of the environmental campaigner Lei Yang. Lei was accused of involvement in prostitution, which family and friends rejected, and no charges were brought against the police.[51] Cai was expelled from the CCP, dismissed from the Party school, and deprived of her pension. Fearing detention if she returned to China, she remains in exile in the United States.[52]

Notes

1 Among other sources, this section draws on my chapter, 'China's Rulers: The Fifth Generation Take Power (2012–13)' in Kerry Brown (ed.) *China and the EU in Context: Insights for Business and Investors* London: Palgrave Macmillan, 2014, pp. 142–77.
2 Waican bianji bu (Editorial Department of Waican Magazine) *Zhong Gong shibada zhi zheng* (The Struggle for Chinese Communists' Eighteenth Congress) Hong Kong: Waican Publishers, 2011, p. 92.
3 'Not Much Will Change under China's Next Leaders: Scholar' Report of Willy Lam Lecture *China Post* Taiwan 13 May 2010.
4 'Not Much Will Change under China's Next Leaders: Scholar' Report of Willy Lam Lecture *China Post* Taiwan 13 May 2010.
5 Shi Hua *Hu Wen weiji* (*The Hu Wen Crisis*) Hong Kong: Hong Kong Cultural Press, 2004, p. 15.
6 Tan Tian *Shiba da qian de xiaoyan* (*Smell of Cordite before the 18th Party Congress*) Hong Kong: New Culture Press, 2010, pp. 16–17.
7 Tania Branigan 'China's Leaders Break Ranks in Readiness for New Dawn' *Guardian* 26 November 2011. The optimistic views on the middle class were those of Qiu Feng of the Unirule Institute of Economics, an independent think tank in Beijing.
8 'Not Much Will Change under China's Next Leaders: Scholar' Report of Willy Lam Lecture *China Post* Taiwan 13 May 2010.
9 There are intriguing parallels with the factional structure of the Japanese Liberal Democratic Party. The LDP, a conservative party, held power in Japan almost without interruption from 1955–2009. Although it has acknowledged factions, based on the patronage of powerful individual politicians, it is difficult to determine any differences of political ideology between them. The common thread between the two is the insistence of governing by consensus with dispute and policy differences being hammered out in private.
10 'Not Much Will Change under China's Next Leaders: Scholar' Report of Willy Lam Lecture *China Post* Taiwan 13 May 2010.
11 Xinhua
12 Xinhua 14 November 2009.
13 Tan Tian *Shiba da qian de xiaoyan* (*Smell of Cordite before the 18th Party Congress*) Hong Kong: New Culture Press, 2010, pp. 8–9, 17–18. Xinhua, BBC News 18 October 2010.
14 *Duowei Times* Beijing correspondent.
15 Xia Fei et al. *Taizidang he gongqingtuan: Xi Jinping PK Li Keqiang* (*Crown Prince Party and Communist Youth League Faction: Xi Jinping competes with Li Keqiang*) Hong Kong: Mirror Books, 2007, p. 92.
16 Shi Jian (ed.) *Gao Gang 'fan dang' zhenxiang* Hong Kong: Wenhua yishu chubanshe, 2008, p. 280.
17 Xia Fei et al. *Taizidang he gongqingtuan: Xi Jinping PK Li Keqiang* (*Crown Prince Party and Communist Youth League Faction: Xi Jinping competes with Li Keqiang*) Hong Kong: Mirror Books, 2007, p. 97.
18 Shi Jian (ed.) *Gao Gang 'fan dang' zhenxiang* Hong Kong: Wenhua yishu chubanshe, 2008, pp. 271–95 and passim; David Holm 'The Strange Case of Liu Zhidan' *Australian Journal of Chinese Affairs* no. 27 (January 1992); Jürgen Domes *The Internal Politics of China 1949–1972* London: Hurst, 1973, pp. 134–9; Jürgen Domes *Peng Te-huai: the Man and the Image* London: Hurst, 1985, pp. 42–7, 99–100, 125; http://eng.mod.gov.cn/Database/MilitaryFigures/2009-07/29/content_4016444.htm.

19 Xia Fei et al. *Taizidang he gongqingtuan: Xi Jinping PK Li Keqiang* (*Crown Prince Party and Communist Youth League Faction: Xi Jinping competes with Li Keqiang*) Hong Kong: Mirror Books, 2007, p. 98.

20 CCP Central Committee Party History Research Centre *History of the Chinese Communist Party: A Chronology of Events (1919–1990)* Beijing: Foreign Languages Press, 1991, pp. 428–30.

21 Xia Fei et al. *Taizidang he gongqingtuan: Xi Jinping PK Li Keqiang* (*Crown Prince Party and Communist Youth League Faction: Xi Jinping competes with Li Keqiang*) Hong Kong: Mirror Books, 2007, p. 115; Wu Ming *Xi Jinping zhuan* (Biography of Xi Jinping) Hong Kong: Wenwu yishi chubanshe. 2010, p. 297.

22 Xia Fei et al. *Taizidang he gongqingtuan: Xi Jinping PK Li Keqiang* (*Crown Prince Party and Communist Youth League Faction: Xi Jinping competes with Li Keqiang*) Hong Kong: Mirror Books, 2007, p. 120.

23 Xia Fei et al. *Taizidang he gongqingtuan: Xi Jinping PK Li Keqiang* (*Crown Prince Party and Communist Youth League Faction: Xi Jinping competes with Li Keqiang*) Hong Kong: Mirror Books, 2007, p. 121.

24 A building in the 19th century *shikumen* style that combined aspects of Western and Chinese architecture.

25 Xia Fei et al. *Taizidang he gongqingtuan: Xi Jinping PK Li Keqiang* (*Crown Prince Party and Communist Youth League Faction: Xi Jinping competes with Li Keqiang*) Hong Kong: Mirror Books, 2007, pp. 89–122.

26 Xia Fei et al. *Taizidang he gongqingtuan: Xi Jinping PK Li Keqiang* (*Crown Prince Party and Communist Youth League Faction: Xi Jinping competes with Li Keqiang*) Hong Kong: Mirror Books, 2007, p. 136.

27 Xia Fei et al. *Taizidang he gongqingtuan: Xi Jinping PK Li Keqiang* (*Crown Prince Party and Communist Youth League Faction: Xi Jinping competes with Li Keqiang*) Hong Kong: Mirror Books, 2007, pp. 141–2.

28 *Lun woguo jingji de sanyuan jiegou* (On the ternary structure of China's economy) *Zhongguo shehui kexue* (*Chinese Social Science*) Volume 3 May 1991.

29 Xia Fei et al. *Taizidang he gongqingtuan: Xi Jinping PK Li Keqiang* (*Crown Prince Party and Communist Youth League Faction: Xi Jinping competes with Li Keqiang*) Hong Kong: Mirror Books, 2007, pp. 131–63. For the 2008 celebrations of the 30th anniversary of the Fengyang reforms, see www.fengyang.gov.cn; *People's Daily* 27 December 2000. On contaminated blood supplies, see Pierre Haski *Le sang de la Chine: quand le silence tue* Paris: Grasset, 2005.

30 Xinhua 8 September 2004; Zhiyue Bo 'The 16th Central Committee of the Chinese Communist Party: Formal Institutions and Factional Groups' *Journal of Contemporary China* 13, no. 39 (May 2004) pp. 223–56. Bo identified Li Keqiang as the most well-connected member of this Central Committee.

31 Xia Fei et al. *Taizidang he gongqingtuan: Xi Jinping PK Li Keqiang* (*Crown Prince Party and Communist Youth League Faction: Xi Jinping competes with Li Keqiang*) Hong Kong: Mirror Books, 2007, p. 153.

32 *China Daily* 14 February 2007, 21 February 2007; english.cpcnews.cn/92375/6284736.html

33 Xia Fei et al. *Taizidang he gongqingtuan: Xi Jinping PK Li Keqiang* (*Crown Prince Party and Communist Youth League Faction: Xi Jinping competes with Li Keqiang*) Hong Kong: Mirror Books, 2007, p. 154.

34 *People's Daily* 15 May 2006.

35 *China Daily* 9 March 2007.

36 Xia Fei et al. *Taizidang he gongqingtuan: Xi Jinping PK Li Keqiang* (*Crown Prince Party and Communist Youth League Faction: Xi Jinping competes with Li Keqiang*) Hong Kong: Mirror Books, 2007, pp. 131–63.

37 *Da Qing shijie bei dahuang* can also be read as 'the great northern wastes of the Qing (Qinghua) dynasty world'. Xia Fei et al. *Taizidang he gongqingtuan: Xi Jinping PK Li Keqiang* (*Crown Prince Party and Communist Youth League Faction: Xi Jinping competes with Li Keqiang*) Hong Kong: Mirror Books, 2007, pp. 131–63.

38 Kerry Brown *CEO, China: The Rise of Xi Jinping* London: I.B. Tauris, 2016, pp. xxiii, 83, 90–2.

39 www.chinafile.com/document-9-chinafile-translation; *SCMP* 10 May 2013; Kerry Brown *CEO, China: The Rise of Xi Jinping* London: I.B. Tauris, 2016, pp. 165–6; Kai Strittmatter *We Have Been Harmonised: Life in China's Surveillance State* Exeter: Old Street, 2019, pp. 20–1.

40 *China Daily* 17 October 2017.
41 Xinhua, New China News Agency, reports throughout November 2013.
42 *Guardian* 21 January 2020, *FT* 22 January 2020.
43 *SCMP* 6, 8 August 2014.
44 *SCMP* 19 August 2014.
45 *SCMP* 13, 14, 18 August 2014.
46 *SCMP* 3 April 2019. David Daokui Li 'Lessons from the First 70 Years of the People's Republic' *FT* 2 October 2019.
47 Wang Xiangwei 'Why China's Silence on Xi's Term Limits Move Portends Trouble' *SCMP* 10 March 2018.
48 *New York Times* 7 April 2020; *SCMP* 24 July 2020; BBC News 22 September 2020.
49 BBC News 12 July 2020; *Guardian* 12 July 2020.
50 *SCMP* 20 April, 6 July 2020.
51 *FT* 29 December 2016.
52 *New York Times* 18 August 2020; *Guardian* 21 August 2020.

Part 3
The economy

7 Economic growth and the changing economy

Dramatic growth

The most dramatic aspect of China's reform programme since its inception in 1979 has been the rate of growth of the economy. International economic analysts have frequently used words such as 'breakneck' to describe the pace of reform, and concern has been expressed at regular intervals that the economy might overheat. Chinese economists and social planners have been acutely aware that this success in economic growth has been achieved at a price: the ever-increasing gap in income and standard of living between the rich and the poor; and between the wealthy eastern and coastal regions of China and the vast and often impoverished western territories.

After the plenary meeting of the CCP Central Committee that came to an end on Tuesday 11 October 2005, it was clear from the concluding communiqué that China would continue its economic expansion and that the CCP was determined that the country's GDP (the generally accepted measure of an economy's growth) should be doubled by the year 2010. However, the Central Committee also formally recognised the existing and potential social and environmental costs of the dash for growth, and the communiqué included a statement on the need to improve China's system of welfare and social security, and an indication that the leadership favoured the adoption of policies that were more responsive to environmental needs, almost certainly a sign of the influence of Premier Wen Jiabao.[1]

During 2006, there was no reduction in the speed of economic growth: the expanding export sector was the major contributor to an overall 10.4% increase in the size of the economy in the third quarter of the year, although domestic consumption also played a significant role. This was a reduction on the 11.3% growth of the second quarter, but all the indications were that, for the fourth year running, China's economy would still be growing by over 10%. At the same time the government had been restricting speculative investment. Some regional development projects did not receive the necessary government approval as part of a plan to slow what the leadership considers to be excessive growth in certain areas. This was achieved partly by the use of anti-corruption measures which allowed the central government to examine what it claimed was the misuse of public funds, including allegations of the abuse of pension funds in Shanghai which developed into a major scandal.[2]

Data from the National Bureau of Statistics that became available on 19 July 2007 revealed that, in spite of the government's measures, growth for the second quarter had not reduced but had in fact increased to 11.9%. This growth was accompanied by a higher level of consumer inflation, attributed mainly to the increase in food prices. Chinese analysts, including economists at the Chinese Academy of Social Sciences and members of a specialist committee reporting to the NPC, warned that the economy was on the brink of overheating. The response of the Chinese government, through the People's Bank of China, was a dose of fiscal engineering. The bank announced an increase in interest rates of 0.27% and a cut in the taxation of interest earned in savings accounts: these measures were designed to reduced consumption and promote savings; this reversed the policy that had been adopted in 1999.[3]

By the end of 2008, the National Bureau of Statistics was proudly reporting that, based on World Bank definitions, China was no longer a poor country but 'lower middle income'. The GDP of the PRC was US$3 trillion, roughly 6% of the world economy but still only equivalent to one-quarter of the US GDP. Although the average income of Chinese citizens had risen to US$2,360, poverty remained a major issue; 135 million Chinese still had a daily income of less than US$1 per day.[4] It was this sector of the Chinese population that Xi Jinping would target when he came to power in 2012.

China's economic growth in the third quarter of 2008 fell to 9%, the first time it had slipped to single digits in four years. This was a result of the global financial crisis, but also weakness in the domestic property market. Nevertheless, Xinhua news agency was able to announce on 10 October that the People's Bank of China, the central bank, had 'announced an interest rate cut in a coordinated global move to revive solvency in the international financial system'. Deposit and lending rates were reduced by 0.27% and reserve requirements by 0.5% and Beijing pledged further cooperation to help resolve the crisis.[5]

Economic legacy

China's economy when the CCP came to power in 1949 could be characterised as essentially pre-modern. The Middle Kingdom was predominantly an agricultural society, and in many parts of the country, peasants were still using traditional technology some of which had been in place with little change for hundreds of years.[6] This was not 'unchanging China', and there had been technical and organisational improvement in some regions and in the production of particular crops over the centuries, but the level of agricultural development was still far too low. The scarcity of arable land made it extremely difficult for China's farmers to produce sufficient food to meet the demands of population growth: this was a significant cause of the famines that the country had experienced in the 1920s and 1930s. War and Civil War had also played their part in this. In 1949, the amount of grain produced was a mere 113 million tonnes,[7] a quantity that was completely inadequate to feed the population. Urban China amounted to only some 20% of the total population of the country, but the towns and cities had to be fed from the surpluses generated from the countryside, surpluses that were seldom large enough even to feed the peasants.

Industrial development before 1949 had been patchy. There had been advances in modern heavy industry in the provinces of the northeast (Manchuria), largely as a result of the Japanese occupation in the 1930s and 1940s. Manchuria was considered by the government in Tokyo to be vital to the development of the Japanese economy since it possessed immense resources of coal and iron, resources that Japan lacked. Coal mines and iron workings had been developed by Japanese enterprises since the 1920s, as had the railway infrastructure which was required to transport their products back to Japan. There had also been significant developments in the treaty ports, which were spread along the southeast coast and inland along the banks of the Yangzi. The manufacture of textiles, food processing, and other light industries were widespread, but the development of these industries was hampered by the low level of technical skills among the workforce and by major problems in transport and distribution. The 'foreign matters' movement that followed the Tongzhi restoration in the early 1860s had also left a legacy of industrial development to underpin the naval and armament industries that had been created by the modernising proto-warlords of the late Qing period and which were the highest priority of the Qing government. This type of development was localised in certain of the treaty ports and other coastal cities, including Fuzhou and Shanghai.

The problems of underdevelopment and rural poverty had been further exacerbated, not only by decades of war and Civil War, but also by the hyperinflation of the 1940s. The first significant fiscal action taken by the new People's Government in 1949 was the centralisation of finance and taxation together with severe restrictions on the circulation of foreign currency. These measures, outlined in a Government Administration Council (GAC) document entitled *Decisions on the Unification of the Nation's Financial and Economic Work*, were published on 3 March 1950 and had the effect of breaking the inflationary spiral.[8] China had no inflation between that date and the beginning of the reform programme in 1978.

Planned economy to mixed economy

When it was established in 1949, the government of the PRC based its plans for economic development on the model that had been tried and tested (even if had often been found wanting) in the Soviet Union. It had no other significant allies, and was effectively obliged to follow this model. Essentially, this involved creating a national planning system with targets and production quotas that were set centrally: subsidiary quotas were allocated to regions, provinces, and, at the base of the planning hierarchy, to individual enterprises. These quotas were allotted on an annual basis; this was expressed within Five-Year Plans, a system that had been borrowed almost without change from the USSR. China's First Five Year Plan began in 1953 and from that time onwards, China has had a Five-Year Plan for the economy. No plans were as high profile as the first one: subsequent plans were overshadowed by political developments including the Great Leap Forward and the Cultural Revolution, and when the reform era began, they assumed less immediate significance in the day-to-day economic life of the country. They continue to exist, although they have not been referred to as frequently since the beginning of the economic reform programme in the 1980s. In 2007, China was working through the 11th Five-Year Plan.

The First Five-Year Plan (1953–1957) was regarded by many contemporary analysts, Communist and non-Communist alike, as having been broadly successful. It was the only Chinese plan during the Mao era that followed its natural economic course completely without interruptions by political upheavals, and it is therefore a good measure of the efficacy of this type of economic management in the Chinese context. Planning on a national scale could only begin in 1953 when the outlying provinces had been conquered and mass campaigns in rural and urban areas had assured the CCP that it was able to exercise political control. Initial attempts at long-term planning had been limited by lack of expertise in both planning and statistics, by the demands that the Korean War made on the Chinese economy, and by difficulties that China had encountered in negotiating an aid package with its ally, the Soviet Union. At first, plans had been made on an annual basis only, but by 1953, when the Korean War had ended and aid negotiations with the USSR had finally been concluded, realistic long-term planning was possible. The general principles of the First Five-Year Plan were published in 1953, but it was not until April 1955 that a full version was made publicly available.[9] In 1952, two government bodies were established to assist in the implementation of the plan, the State Statistical Bureau and the State Planning Commission, both of which were to become highly influential in the management of the Chinese economy. The fundamental role of the State Statistical Bureau was to generate the data needed for planning; the

State Planning Commission, which reported directly to the State Council under the 1954 Constitution, was responsible for both long-term and annual plans until 1956, when short-term planning was devolved to the State Economic Commission.[10]

The central body that oversaw the early plans, the State Planning Commission, was renamed the State Development Planning Commission in 1998 in recognition of its changing role in an economy that was becoming more mixed in character. In 2003, it merged with the Office for Restructuring the Economic System, a department established by the State Council with special responsibility for moving China towards a market economy, and with a section of the State Economic and Trade Commission. It was renamed again and became the National Development and Reform Commission, and its role was defined as overseeing 'the transition from the planned economy to a socialist market economy'.[11] Unlike the earlier bodies which had generated targets for local organisations, the NDRC is responsible for macroeconomic management, including the Five-Year Plans, which it is required under the terms of China's Constitution to present to the NPC on behalf of the State Council. It is also responsible for the structural management of the national economy; for regional development strategies, including for example the Western Region Development Programme; and for major construction projects which have implications for the national economy. It is a key government body, has almost 1,000 employees working in 26 departments, and is ideologically committed to economic reform under CCP control.[12]

An example of its specific, rather than its general, planning authority can be seen in the case of the steel industry in the province of Hebei, which is adjacent to the area directly under the control of the capital, Beijing. The NDRC accused the Hebei provincial government of having allowed the steel industry in the province to develop in an uncontrolled fashion and to expand in a way that was contrary to the national interest: in particular, it was argued that it duplicated industrial development in other regions. The NDRC instructed its office in Hebei province to prepare a report on overcapacity in Hebei which was due to be submitted to the NDRC and other central government bodies by the end of November 2006 and, in an unusual move, drew this to the attention of the central and the local media. The Hebei steel industry was seen as a test case, and it is a good example of the type of problems that have arisen in economic relations between the centre and provinces, and how they might be resolved. The measures proposed to bring Hebei into line included forcing the Hebei provincial government to decide on the closure of a number of steel plants in its own province.[13]

Economic growth after the 2007–2008 financial crisis

In the 1980s, observers could be excused for believing that China had abandoned the idea of a planned economy and wholeheartedly embraced Western-style capitalism. The degree to which this transformation is possible or desirable remains contentious, and the Western capitalist model has never been fully implemented for political as well as economic reasons. China constantly must decide on the balance between state control and the dangers of an untrammelled private sector, and the tension between economic expansion and social stability.

The global financial crisis of 2007–2008 was by common consent the most dangerous since the depression of the 1930s. It triggered a banking crisis and undermined confidence in the banks and other financial institutions of the Western world. China, however, remained relatively unaffected because its financial systems were still closed and insulated from external turbulence, although unsurprisingly, the level of Chinese exports to those countries worst affected was severely reduced, which required a nimble shift in policy.

According to the head of China's National Bureau of Statistics, Ma Jiantang, China's economy in 2009 grew by 8.7%, a figure that exceeded even the most optimistic predictions of the Chinese government. Analysts, particularly Western analysts, predicted that China was on course to overtake Japan and thus become the second largest economy in the world after the United States. Some even speculated that China would be the world's largest economy by 2030. Normally critical commentators conceded that this success in growth was due to China's swift and intelligent response to the 2008 international financial crisis. According to Jim O'Neill, then Chief Economist at Goldman Sachs,

> In November 2008 they came up with a quick, aggressive fiscal and monetary response which has worked. . . . They have replaced exports with domestic demand, both consumption and investment. . . . China has become more important as America [has become] less, which is what the world needs.

China recognised that it could no longer rely on American and other Western consumers to buy its products and began expanding its own domestic economic demand, including an emerging consumer base, which was largely responsible for its success in maintaining and improving its growth rate.[14]

The subsequent growth of China's economy was spectacular with annual rates of GDP increase between 6 and 9%, if not higher. Some Western analysts argued that the growth rate was not high enough – as appeared to be the case in 2008 when exports had dropped – and predicted that a slump was a possibility. Others expressed concern that the economy was overheating, and that inflation was a greater risk. When China announced on 21 January 2010[15] that the economy had grown by 8.7% over the previous 12 months, and, in the fourth quarter alone, by 10.7%, Western financial institutions emphasised the danger of overheating and inflation.

Price inflation was a reality in China for some time, and an increase in the price of winter vegetables in 2009–2010 was taken as an indicator of a general rise in the price of goods, although unusually low temperatures and poorer crop yields restricted the supply of fresh vegetables to the markets of northern China.[16] Inflation has historically been a sensitive political issue. During the period of the most tightly planned economy from the inception of the PRC in 1949 until 1978, China had experienced virtually no price inflation. Prices were controlled by the state and the role of the market was limited or non-existent, a reflection of the mechanisms of the Soviet-style planned economy and the experience of the Chinese leadership during the 1940s. Runaway inflation under the Nationalist Guomindang government, particularly towards the end of the 1940s, was a major cause of that regime's failure and the CCP was determined not to make the same mistake. Low inflation and price stability were promoted as great benefits of the planned economy until the late 1970s.

Although there was a significant growth in China's money supply in the late 1990s, after the Asian financial crisis, inflation remained relatively low. Some economists pointed to idle capacity in the economy which could therefore absorb the increase in money supply and resist inflationary pressure. In 2010, it was predicted that inflation might rise to a figure close to 3%. Yu Yongding, an economist working at the Chinese Academy of Social Sciences, considered that overcapacity was an important factor in containing inflation', which 'should not be too much of a problem as long as the government can control inflationary expectations'. One early indicator of inflationary pressure included a decision by Jiangsu province to raise minimum wage rates by 13% to attract migrant workers to the booking industrial region once the worst of the dangers of the global crisis had receded.[17]

The supply of money and the threat of inflation are related closely to the government's monetary policy and in particular China's attitude to the strength of the renminbi vis-à-vis the US dollar and other international currencies. This has become a matter of some acrimony in relations between China and the United States.

> China is being pressed to re-value its currency. It is a mistake to become obsessed by this. What the global economy needs is for China to grow and for its current account surplus to fall. . . . The singular focus on the exchange rate appears based on the assumption that it is the key cause of the surplus and the main policy instrument for removing it. The reality is more complex. Reducing the surplus in China involves deep structural change, much as reducing the US deficit does. The high savings in China are embedded in the structure of the economy. The government controls too much income directly through ownership of the state-owned enterprises.[18]

Michael Spence, the 2001 winner of the Nobel Prize in Economics and Chair of the Commission on Growth and Development, went on to argue that in order to convert excess savings into household consumption, which is essential for China's growth, it is necessary for China to have an appreciating currency. 'If the currency does not appreciate, the changes in the economy that are creating growth and prosperity are likely to come to a standstill. That will impact productivity, growth and incomes'.[19]

From 2010 onwards, China continued to wrestle with the relationship between the state and private sectors, the role of the market, and particularly the transition from an export-led economy undermined by the global financial crisis to one led by domestic demand. The crisis had a profound effect on Chinese attitudes towards Western capitalism, providing ammunition for those who wished to restrict marketisation and the opening of financial institutions. It raised fundamental questions about the future of Chinese capitalism, which some classified as state capitalism, and the underlying problems of inequality, the income gap, and poverty.

Covid-19 and the Chinese economy

In common with most of the world's economies, the Chinese economy was disrupted by the shutdown imposed by the Covid-19 epidemic in early 2020 which slowed the economy almost to zero. This was exacerbated by the evaporation of demand for international exports. The relatively swift recovery of Wuhan and Hubei province enabled an improved performance in March, but concerns remained that China faced serious challenges, including unemployment in double digits and the potential of a declared recession, which would have been the first since 1976.

The priorities of Premier Li Keqiang and his government were employment rather than growth. The administration's targets were the creation of as many as ten million new jobs in the cities. In spite of government instructions to enterprises designed to avoid redundancies, the official rate of unemployment in February 2020 was 6.2%.[20]

At the delayed NPC that opened on 22 May 2020, no GDP target was set for the growth of the Chinese economy, the first year that this had happened since the economic reforms of the 1980s. Li Keqiang argued that the main reason for this was the uncertainty of foreign markets: China's economy had declined by 6.8% in the first quarter of 2020, the most serious downturn for 40 years, and the decision not to set a target was a clear indication of lack of confidence in future growth.[21]

Notes

1 BBC News 12 October 2005.
2 *FT* 20 October 2006.
3 *FT* 20, 21, 22 July 2007.
4 BBC News 28 October 2008.
5 Xinhua 10 October 2008; *FT*/Reuters 20 October 2008.
6 Rudolf Hommel *China at Work: An Illustrated Record of the Primitive Industries of China's Masses, Whose Life Is Toil, and Thus an Account of Chinese Civilization* Cambridge, MA: MIT Press, 1969 [1937].
7 Xinhua 19 December 2020.
8 Cheng Jin *Chronology of the Peoples Republic of China 1949–1984* Beijing: Foreign Languages Press, 1986, pp. 2–3. The GAC functioned as the cabinet in the early 1950s.
9 Li Fuchun 'Bianzhi diyi ge wunian jihua ying zhuyi de wenti' Problems to be considered in drawing up the first Five Year Plan (15 September 1953) in *Jianguo yilai* Volume 1, pp. 402–6.
10 Audrey Donnithorne 'Economic Planning' in *China's Economic System* London: Allen and Unwin, 1967, pp. 457–95.
11 National Reform and Development Commission website https://en.ndrc.gov.cn/.
12 National Development and Reform Commission website https://en.ndrc.gov.cn/.
13 *Market News International*, Beijing.
14 'China Economy Sees Strong Growth' BBC News 21 January 2010; *FT* 21 January 2010.
15 *FT* 21 January 2020.
16 'Credit Binge Sparks Inflation Threat' *FT* 22 January 2010; BBC News 12 January 2010.
17 *FT* 7 February 2010.
18 Michael Spence 'The West Is Wrong to Obsess About the Renminbi' *FT* 21 January 2010.
19 Tom Mitchell 'China's Economy Has Yet to Feel Full Effects of Unemployment' *FT* 6 April 2010.
20 *FT* 7 February 2010.
21 *FT* 21 May 2020.

8 Rural economy

For most of the twentieth century, China could be described as a Third World country: its economy developed from a low base and its society is evolving rapidly with urbanisation on a colossal scale and the emergence of a prosperous middle class. China's status as a developing country was often forgotten or ignored because it was a Communist state. For thousands of years in the pre-historical period, and under the successive dynasties of the Empire, China was an almost exclusively rural and agricultural society: well into the twentieth century, as much as 80% of the population lived in the countryside and worked on the land.

That proportion declined significantly in the second half of the century. Since 1949, China has undergone a remarkable process of industrialisation and urbanisation, both in the age of the centrally planned economy of 1949–1978 and in the reform era that followed. At the start of the twenty-first century, Chinese society is changing rapidly and, as a result of industrialisation and migration, the rural economy today probably employs about 40% of the total population. If current plans for economic development are carried through, this proportion will continue to decrease.

Despite these profound and highly visible changes, China is still classified by the WTO as a developing country. It is anxious to retain this status because of the 'special and differential treatment' that it enjoys in trading relationships. In common with other developing countries, it subsidises agricultural production and imposes more stringent conditions for entries to its markets than fully developed economies. This status is increasingly seen as anomalous and some developed nations – especially the United States – have been pressing for a reassessment. Beijing has rejected these moves and Gao Feng, a spokesman for China's Ministry of Commerce, insisted that, 'China's position on WTO reform has been very clear, China is the largest developing country in the world'.[1]

Rural tradition and the village economy

The population of traditional China consisted almost entirely of peasants who owned their own land, tenant farmers, agricultural labourers and landowners. There was only a small urban sector.

County towns were established as the seat of magistrates [*zhixian*] who were civil servants entrusted with the dual role of administering their county on behalf of the Emperor and enforcing the law. The term 'magistrate', by which they are always known in the West, is misleading to anyone familiar to the English tradition in which magistrates preside in the lowest level of courts. The main function of magistrates in China was local administration: there was, however, no tradition of separating the legal system from government.

Some important towns grew up around specialised industries, such as the porcelain centre of Jingdezhen and Suzhou, which was renowned for its silk manufacture, but these were few and far between, islands of industry in an ocean of agriculture.

The village economy was the foundation and the backbone of rural Chinese society for centuries. It had a complex social structure that incorporated the individual household, the extended family or clan, neighbourhood groups that conventionally extended to five residences each side of a household, religious groups that worshipped local gods, and the village government under a headman who had probably risen to that position because of his seniority and experience. There were many regional differences which stemmed from land use, crops grown, and local cultures, but this structure, identified and described lucidly by the distinguished anthropologist Fei Xiaotong in the 1930s, persisted throughout the twentieth century – and although many believed that it had been eliminated during the CCP's programmes of land reform, collectivisation, and communes in the 1950s, it proved remarkably tenacious and re-emerged since the abolition of the People's Communes in 1978.

Agriculture was naturally the mainstay of the rural economy. It was the regular occupation of most of the population, and – in the traditional Chinese world view that, for convenience, is usually labelled Confucian – it was the only morally and socially acceptable calling for those born into peasant families. Almost all rural families grew crops, although some also raised livestock: in certain areas of southern China, fishing was important. Rice was, and remains, the main staple crop. It is especially abundant in the south and is also a powerful symbol of the Chinese rural economy, and indeed of Asian economies in general. In the north, wheat and millet are more easily grown, although there are also some productive rice-growing areas. People in the south fill up on bowls of rice; in northern villages and towns, the main source of carbohydrate is the steamed or baked roll or, in the far northwest, varieties of flat bread like the *nan* of Pakistan and Afghanistan.

In imperial times, the agricultural year was regulated according to the traditional Chinese calendar, a lunar calendar that takes into account the position of the earth in its solar orbit and should properly be termed a lunar–solar calendar. This calendar provided a framework for the seasonal cycles and was used to determine the correct time for the vital activities of the farming year such as sowing, transplanting, and harvesting. It also had a central social function as a reminder of the dates of local community and religious activities.[2] Even though the Western calendar is now used in China for most purposes, the dates of the traditional calendar are included on the mastheads of many newspapers. Almanacs that contain the lunar–solar calendar are widely consulted on the mainland, in Hong Kong and Taiwan, and in Chinese communities in the West. Chinese almanacs (in common with western publications such as *Old Moore's Almanach*) typically contain predictions, which in the case of China are likely to be of particular interest to farming communities such as trends in the weather and natural disasters; practical advice on crops and livestock, health, relationships, and business; and as much astrological material.

Handicraft industries were an important subsidiary occupation in rural areas, especially at quiet times for farming and when the weather made it impossible to work in the fields. Most handicrafts were produced by families at home or in small workshops rather than factory-sized units. The manufacture of farm tools and simple pots and pans was almost universal; some regions specialised in high-quality craft products that could be sold to outsiders for cash. These and other items were traded by peddlers or sold in the periodic and permanent markets with which traditional China abounded.

As the Civil War between the Communists and the Nationalists drew to a close in the 1940s, China's famers were suffering from severe poverty, backwardness, and underdevelopment.

It is no exaggeration to describe it as a rural or agricultural crisis. The need for reform was obvious to foreign and Chinese observers alike, whether or not they were sympathetic to the policies that the CCP eventually adopted to deal with these problems.[3]

Land reform

Of all the policies adopted by the CCP in the rural areas that came under its control during the periods of Civil War and the Japanese occupation, land reform [*tudi gaige*] was by far the most important. Without land reform and the support that the CCP derived from it, none of their other policies could have been implemented. It had initially been tried out in the Jiangxi Soviet during the early 1930s, and it later became part and parcel of the CCP's strategy for recruiting a mass army of sympathetic peasants during the dark days of the Japanese occupation. The term 'land reform' is sometimes used in a broad sense to indicate reforms that benefited the rural poor, including the reduction in rents and the interest rates on loans that the CCP compelled landlords and money lenders to accept during the 1946–1949 Civil War. In a more precise sense, it refers to the confiscation of land from landlords and rich peasants, and its redistribution to the poorest of the peasants. The economic rationale for compulsory redistribution was that the release of underused assets would be used by the poor to feed themselves. The political rationale, not always explicit, was that this would guarantee the support of the lowest socio-economic group in the countryside for the CCP. Land reform began in earnest, albeit in an uncontrolled and frequently forceful and brutal manner, in the areas that the CCP took from the Guomindang armies in the closing years of the Civil War. When the PRC was established in October 1949, one of the first pieces of legislation enacted by the new government was the Agricultural Reform Law, which came into force on 28 June 1950. Land reform then spread through almost the whole of China. The legislation set out precise regulations for methods of confiscation and redistribution; these were not universally observed, and the land reform movement was accompanied by much conflict and violence against landowners who resisted.[4]

Mutual aid teams, cooperatives, and People's Communes

Even before the land reform programme had been completed, the second phase of agricultural reform – building cooperatives – was introduced. On the face of it, there was a complete contradiction between redistributing confiscated land to peasant households and the subsequent policy of creating cooperatives, but the CCP argued that cooperation had always been its long-term goal. In the early 1950s, China's isolation from the West after the Korean War meant that its only allies were in the Soviet bloc: that alliance committed China to following, at least in broad terms, the style and approach of the Soviet Union in its development and management of the economy, albeit with modifications to take into account social and cultural differences. China did, however, attempt to avoid what the CCP believed to have been the errors and excesses of forced collectivisation in the USSR – above all, the attempt to exterminate the *kulaks*, the wealthiest peasant farmers, during the 1930s. Between 1949 and 1956, China to a large extent followed the Soviet model, but as relations between the two governments began to sour in the late 1950s, Beijing evolved independent strategies for agricultural development, as in other areas of policy.

The first stage was to combine small family-run farms into larger units that were deemed to be more productive and more efficient – mutual aid teams. These were family and village groups which were initially encouraged by CCP activists to cooperate in seasonal tasks by pooling their labour and farm tools, of which in many cases they had very few. Ploughing, spring sowing, and harvesting were among the key tasks undertaken by the teams. This was not an entirely new phenomenon: in many parts of the country, CCP activists could build on traditional forms of community and clan cooperation. Once teams were established, they were encouraged to become permanent and work together all year round.

Agricultural producers' cooperatives, or APCs [*nongmin shengchan hezuoshe*], the second stage in the programme of collectivisation, were created by amalgamating the permanent mutual aid teams. The first APCs appeared in 1954, but most were created during the movement that was dramatically launched as the High Tide of Socialism in the Countryside [*nongcun shehuizhuyi gaochao*], a political campaign orchestrated by the most enthusiastic supporters of Mao Zedong in the central bodies of the CCP. Documents published by activists during this campaign claimed that poorer peasant farmers were demanding to be included in the drive towards cooperation; Mao was persuaded by this and in turn demanded greater urgency in the creation of APCs. By the end of 1956, it was claimed that as many as 90% of rural households were members of an APC, but it is not clear how much genuine change in the management of agriculture this brought about. Members of this new interim body had an income derived in part from wages for the work they did for the cooperative and in part from rent payable for the land they had contributed, willingly or otherwise.

Higher-level producers' cooperatives (HPCs) were created during 1956 and 1957 by the further amalgamation of APCs to produce even larger collective units. In the HPCs, the land was deemed to be owned communally and no rental income was payable to the former owners of the land that had been collectivised.[5]

In 1958, the HPCs were in turn amalgamated into yet larger units that became known as People's Communes [*renmin gongshe*], a form of organisation favoured by Mao partly because he conceived of it as a distinctively Chinese-style administration for the countryside. For the next 20 years, the communes dominated the life of China's peasants. Not only were they responsible for managing the farming cycle and the production and distribution of agricultural goods; they were the basic administrative unit in the countryside. Education, childcare, retirement homes, medical clinics and hospitals, banking, and the building and maintenance of roads, bridges and many other public works and services were all the responsibility of the People's Communes.

To abolish market forces within the communes, it was planned to replace all wages in cash with work points. The work point system, in which jobs and responsibilities were graded in terms of points rather than cash, had been developed in the cooperatives and was formalised in the 1956 Regulations for Collectives. Peasant members of collectives at first received a portion of their income in rent, a portion in cash, and a portion in kind: that is they were entitled to an allowance from the grain harvest and other crops in proportion to the number of work points that they had earned. The rent element disappeared when higher-level cooperatives were created, and when the communes were established, it was assumed that the wage element would disappear. By the early 1970s, this was still in existence or, if it had been abolished, had since been reintroduced. Members of a family working in a Production Brigade in one commune in Henan were said to be receiving 'a share in the distribution of its income in the form of food grain, vegetables and other necessities and nearly 1,000 yuan a year in cash'. The level of cash income suggests a relatively prosperous family, but a publication by Foreign Languages Press indicates official recognition.[6]

Critics of the commune system point to the lack of financial incentives in a structure where it was possible to obtain the necessities of life by a system of work points. The work point system created a complex internal bureaucracy with specially trained commune accountants who became powerful by manipulating the supply of food and other products. The People's Communes had positive features, notably economies of scale when compared with small family farms and the ability to engage in the long-term planning of agricultural production. Under a government policy that emphasised 'grain as the key link' in its struggle to feed the urban population as well as the rural, this was essential.[7]

Responsibility System

Collectivisation and the communes were identified closely with Mao Zedong and his radical supporters and did not for long survive his death in 1976. Dismantling the commune system, which by then was widely regarded as inefficient and inimical to economic development, was the highest priority of Deng Xiaoping and his reformers when they took the reins of power in the late 1970s.

There had been a degree of decentralisation within the communes in response to the disastrous famines of the early 1960s, but Deng's CCP decided to dismantle them completely. The mechanism introduced to accomplish this was the Responsibility System for Agricultural Production [*nongye shengchan zeren zhi*], sometimes known as the Household Responsibility System or simply the Responsibility System, under which individual households were given contracts to cultivate land, although without titular ownership of the land they farmed. In effect, this was a complete repudiation of the commune system, but although Mao was dead and his most powerful supporters in the higher echelons of the CCP, the Gang of Four, had been arrested and were awaiting trial, there was considerable opposition within the Party to reversing Mao's polices so explicitly. A workable formula had to be found to embrace the formal retention of collective ownership while at the same time handing over the management of farms to families. This was not entirely a return to the system of family farms that had existed before the land reform programme of the 1950s. Although peasant families were still able to sell their surplus production, the new contract system was linked to local government, which was able to impose production and tax quotas on farmers.

After a pilot scheme in Anhui province's Fengyang County in 1979, the Responsibility System was implemented across the country. Contracts were originally issued on an annual basis and for a period of five years, but from 1984 a contract could remain in force for 15 years. In 1993, the term was extended to 30 years, although there was no legal support for this until the revision of the Land Administration Law of August 1998 in response to the second round of contracting that followed the expiry of the existing contracts.

The direct outcome of the new system was a dramatic (and immediately obvious) economic boom in the rural areas, especially in the southeast. The economy began to take off, building sites sprang up everywhere, and in the 1980s, it was common to see roads in the countryside partially blocked by piles of bricks and timber deposited close to bridges for transfer to boats on the rivers, and destined for building new houses in distant villages.

When a new post-Mao Constitution of the PRC was being drafted in 1982, it was openly acknowledged that, irrespective of their value for agriculture, communes had not been a success for local government because of an over-concentration of power and inappropriate management. The discarded system of township administrations, with their own People's Governments and People's Congresses, was reinstated as the basic level of state power, although the name commune persisted for some time as a form of agricultural management organisation.[8]

Rural-urban migration

The commune system had provided work and a livelihood for China's peasant population. The management bodies of the communes, the Revolutionary Committees, had also been able to discourage migration from the countryside to the cities, which was in any case diffi-cult because of poor rural transport facilities and the household registration [*hukou*] system. Under the *hukou* system, which is dealt with in more detail in Chapter 14, individuals were registered in families according to their place of residence and their occupational category, the most important distinction being between agricultural and non-agricultural categories. The *hukou* functioned as an internal passport system and registration was essential for access to rationed foodstuffs such as oil and rice. The *hukou* documents, which are still issued to every family in China with copies held in the local police stations, indicate where an individ-ual is registered and where he or she is allowed to live: in the past, it was extremely difficult for people from the countryside who had an agricultural *hukou* to find work, accommoda-tion, and even food in the cities without 'going black' [*zou hei*] and living on the fringes of the criminal underworld.

One of the most dramatic outcomes of the dismantling of the communes, and the eco-nomic reforms in general, was the creation of a vast population of migrant workers. This was unprecedented in the period since 1949, since the priority of the government had been to keep peasants on their farms to increase food production. The smaller decentralised farms created under the Responsibility System could not sustain the number of workers that the communes had been able to absorb, and the economic development that was taking off in the cities of the east and southeast created opportunities for the enterprising, the desperate, and the adventurous. In the mid-1980s, gangs of peasants from Shaanxi could be seen building new hotels and office buildings in Beijing, and the housemaid, nanny, or au pair [*baomu*] who was employed to look after the children and the households of the newly rich in the cities became an iconic figure. Most of the *baomu* in Beijing came from the south, particu-larly the province of Anhui, and they were even the subject of a popular film. However, the greatest migration was not northwards towards the capital but in the direction of the coastal provinces of the southeast, where the economic boom was most dramatic. Although it is dif-ficult to give precise figures for such a phenomenon, there is broad agreement that during the early years of reform, as many as 120 million rural residents may have been working in, or travelling to seek work in, the urban areas at any given time. That was the equivalent of the entire population of Japan being on the move in the interior of China, but migrant numbers continued to increase exponentially.

By early 2007, the wave of migration began to slow down. In some villages, everyone who was physically able to migrate had already left and new industries created in the coun-tryside absorbed as much surplus rural labour as they could. According to a survey by the Development Research Centre of the State Council, in as many as 74% of villages there were no longer any able-bodied workers available for employment in the cities. The Chinese Academy of Social Sciences warned that the Chinese economy was facing a labour short-age and that by 2009, this would generate wage increases in all sectors.[9] By late 2007, the potential rise in labour costs concerned foreign bankers and employers in China, for whom cheap labour was the major attraction in relocating factories to China. However, the number of migrant labourers continued to increase, peaking at 274 million in 2014, although it eased to 244 million in 2017. Many migrants now worked in the burgeoning service sector rather than in primary industries which employed the first generation.[10]

Land ownership in the reform era

The question of the ownership of land – and indeed, of property in general – remains unclear. In a formal and legal sense, land in the urban areas is the property of the state, while rural land is still considered to be collectively owned even though it has been almost 30 years since the dismantling of the People's Communes. In practice, this means that land in the countryside is also controlled by the state, although it is the local government – in the shape of the township administration – rather than central state bodies that has the authority to decide on its usage and disposal. The township is the lowest level of the hierarchical government structure. It normally has political and economic control over several villages, and in practice is not always strictly controlled by the higher tiers of government.

Peasant families were given the right to cultivate their farms under the Responsibility System of 1978 and were awarded long-term contracts. However, since they do not own the land that they farm, they do not have the inalienable legal right to sell it or to retain it. While this was an acceptable compromise in 1978, as the pace of development escalated and the demand for land for construction increased, it became problematic for farmers.

Because there is no private ownership, it has been relatively easy for agricultural land to be bought or requisitioned for industrial development, for the expansion of urban housing, or for extending the transport network. Although this type of expansion is deemed by the state to be essential for the overall process of urbanisation and rural development, it also generated opportunities for corruption. Local officials have been bribed by developers or have siphoned off compensation that was intended for peasants who had been forced off their land: this created a climate of dissatisfaction that frequently boiled over into violence. The reduction of the burden of agricultural taxation, and the final abolition of the land tax in 2006, assisted peasant families greatly, but it significantly reduced the income of local authorities and made the sale of land to developers an even higher priority for township officials. A survey of 1,962 peasant households in 1,773 villages that are located in 17 of the provinces of China found that 27% of farming families had been affected in some way by land seizures; there was a significant increase in the requisitioning of land from the late 1990s.[11] At the beginning of the twenty-first century, disputes over the sale of land began to replace protests against high taxation as the main source of unrest in the Chinese countryside, especially in the more prosperous villages close to urban centres.

Premier Wen Jiabao on rural stability

Towards the end of 2005, Premier Wen Jiabao, who was openly associating himself with populist causes, including opposition to corruption and the plight of the peasants, made a speech on the problems of stability in the countryside. The speech was unusually candid, and the text was not published until 19 January 2006, almost three weeks after he made the speech: speeches by the top leadership are normally made public immediately.[12]

Wen Jiabao observed that the development of the rural areas was a key factor in China's national revival and its stability in the long-term. The rural revival was characterised by Wen as 'the construction of a new socialist countryside', a policy that had been approved by the Fifth Plenum of the 16th Central Committee of the Communist Party. In practical terms, this involved the improvement of living standards and working conditions in rural areas, the implementation of 'institutional reform at township level and financial reform at county and township levels', and the success of the compulsory education policy. Wen pointed out that the popular abolition of agricultural taxes from 2006 did not resolve the problem of financial burdens on farmers and that it was necessary to 'guard against the re-emergence of random charging of farmers under various pretexts'.

Wen Jiabao indicated that preferential policies would encourage peasants to grow grain, a contemporary version of the 'grain as key link' argument of the Maoist era. He also argued that the acquisition of agricultural land for construction projects should be strictly regulated and that the rights of farmers to their own property should be respected. These issues were root causes of rural unrest in China in the early 21st century.

Acknowledging that migrant workers from the rural areas now played a key role in the country's industrial labour force, 'the Premier called for the improvement of their treatment, including pay, social security, vocational training opportunities and their children's education'. He also acknowledged that a range of public services in the rural areas, including education, medical care, and cultural services, would have to be improved.[13]

Fiscal decentralisation and local decision-making powers

Prior to the reforms of the 1980s, China's fiscal or budgetary system had been strictly controlled by central government. Taxes and other revenues were collected by the local authorities and passed on to the central government. A proportion of the tax that had been collected was then repaid to the local government according to formulae that were drawn up and controlled by central bodies.

During the 1980s, the fiscal system was gradually decentralised and local authorities retained more of the taxation they had collected. This decentralisation devolved responsibility for economic planning and decision making to local authorities. Some central control was retained to allow for the redistribute on of funds from poorer to wealthier provinces, but overall, decentralisation encouraged local authorities to search for ways to maximise their tax income. This was achieved by a variety of methods, some legal and some less so. The tax burden on farmers during the reform period had already been heavy and, after fiscal decentralisation, the potential for conflict between farmers and the local government and unrest increased.

Agricultural taxation and the roots of peasant unrest

The highly unpopular agricultural tax was gradually reduced in many areas of China, particularly in the poorest counties. Far from being an invention of the CCP, this tax was the continuation of a centuries-old tradition of taxing the peasants and a legacy of the Chinese Empire.

The Standing Committee of the NPC, at its meeting in Beijing in December 2005, decided unanimously (160–0, with one abstention) that the modern version of this tax, which had been introduced by the NPC on 3 June 1958, would finally be abolished from 1 January 2006. The main headline of *People's Daily* on that day read 'Chinese peasants bid farewell to the agricultural tax in the New Year'.[14] This move was intended to lessen the financial burden on farmers, to reduce the income gap between the rural and urban areas, and to combat the increasingly violent rural protests against heavy taxation and corrupt tax collection practices. Without the tax income, local governments were obliged to find other ways of raising revenue.

Peasant protest, 21st-century style

The rural protests that had flared up during the 1990s continued into the early 21st century. Expressions of peasant discontent were tolerated by the authorities to a far greater extent than previously, and between 2004 and 2006, there were frequent reports of demonstrations, sometimes violent. Disputes over taxation had affected the poorer and more remote interior counties, but conflict over land requisition and corruption was more prevalent in the wealthier and developed coastal areas, including Guangdong province, the economic dynamo to the north of Hong Kong where land for development was scarce and prices were at a premium. These protests were usually suppressed, often with considerable force, by police – or in some cases by armed private security units employed by local authorities who gained a reputation for brutality; many peasant protesters were injured, and some lost their lives.

Some major rural protests, 2004–2006

September 2004–February 2005: Yuncheng District, Yunfu City, Guangdong province. Farmers' land was requisitioned with little compensation. Fields and burial plots were bulldozed, and impoverished farmers were forced to withdraw children from school. Villagers sent petitions to the government in Beijing.

June 2005: Maxinzhuang village Shunyi, Beijing. Peasant farmers protested against the requisition of land to build a water sports complex for the Olympic Games.

11 June 2005: Shengyou, Dingzhou municipality in Hebei province. Villagers resisted armed private security guards who seized land on behalf of developers wanting to build a waste processing plant.

December 2005: Dongzhou, Guangdong province. At least three deaths were reported, but the total may have been as high as 20. Twelve villagers were sentenced to up to seven years imprisonment in May 2006 for illegal assembly, disturbing public order, and the illegal manufacture of explosives.

14–16 Jan 2006: Sanjiao township Zhongshan, Guangdong province. About 20,000 protesters blocked major roads after complaints that farmers had not been paid enough compensation for land that had been requisitioned to build a road.

29 April 2006: Zhaowenmin village, Ninghe County, Tianjin Municipality. At least 200 villagers clashed with police outside the offices of the Ninghe County government to protest against what they alleged had been rigged elections the previous day. They claimed that there had been intimidation and bribery, and that counterfeit ballot papers had been issued.

8 November 2006: Sanzhou village, Shunde Guangdong province. Villagers blockaded a warehouse built on land that they claimed had been requisitioned illegally. Officials had arrived for the opening and as many as 5,000 protesters were dispersed by riot police using tear gas.

10–11 November 2006: Further protests took place in Dongzhou when villagers were arrested after putting up posters against corruption.

These widespread outbreaks of unrest exposed serious problems caused by the failure of the government to resolve the complex question of rights to the ownership of rural land and the residential property that stands on such land. In particular, farmers and local government have disputed whether compensation for property should be at the market price if the land on which it stands is sold by the state.[15] Legislation on property rights was a constant concern of the Chinese government, and on Wednesday 18 January 2006, Sheng Huaren, the Vice-Chairman of the Standing Committee of the NPC, announced that a revised draft of this legislation was being prepared. The aim of the legislation was to protect assets owned by the state and clarify the status of collective and individual property and the rights of peasant farmers.[16]

Statistics from the Ministry of Public Security indicated that the number of protests during 2006 had declined in comparison with the unusually high number recorded in 2005. In the first nine months of 2005, there had been 17,900 'mass incidents', but the number of 'public order disturbances' – small-scale and less serious clashes – had increased by 6% to 87,000. It is not clear whether the reduction in serious disorder was a genuine figure or a result of under-reporting or redefinition by local officials, but the number of serious incidents that were acknowledged and the fact that they were being reported publicly, in a society where the tendency had been to keep silent about embarrassing issues, indicates the level of concern felt by the authorities.[17]

Since 2006, there was not the same concentration of protest in the countryside but similar conflicts continued to occur, especially after 2009 when local governments desperate for funds began selling land to developers: in 2010, 16 episodes of confiscation of land resulted in the death of at least one individual. In Yunnan province, farmers in Fuyou unsuccessfully fought developers supported by the local government in October 2014 and, after four violent clashes in 2013, thousands of villagers who lived around the scenic Dianchi Lake to the south of Kunming lost their land and livelihood to a gargantuan government plan to transform the area into a tourist attraction.[18]

Township and village enterprises

The disparity between poor and backward rural areas and rapidly developing cities is not as simple or as stark as it might appear. In response to the problems of rural unemployment and underemployment, and as part of a strategy for managing internal migration, China developed a nationwide network of township and village enterprises (TVEs), which, unlike the state-owned enterprises (SOEs), were primarily oriented towards the market. TVEs were generally small community enterprises which drew on the pool of surplus labour in the countryside; they were often engaged in businesses connected closely with farming such as the manufacture of farm tools and machinery, the production of fertiliser, and the processing of grain and other food products. Although publicised as a brand-new type of rural industrial development, they were clearly the descendants of the grassroots enterprises promoted by Chinese Industrial Cooperatives (Indusco or Gung Ho) in the 1930s and 1940s, and by the CCP in the early 1950s, and even small rural industries such as the backyard furnaces that were a much-criticised feature of the Great Leap Forward. The crucial difference between the TVEs of the reform period and their PRC predecessors is their orientation towards the market. The Household Responsibility System implemented for the management of agriculture from 1979 was adapted for TVEs which usually operate as cooperatives, although that term went out of favour because of its associations with the Mao period. Ownership rights in the cooperatives are distributed among employees who own shares in the business; some TVEs are privately owned.

TVEs were regarded as a major success story by the Chinese government, a distinctively Chinese response to the rural–urban divide. The International Labour Organisation referred to them as a 'leading force that has propelled China's market economy forward, a vital pillar of the rural economy and an important component of the national economy'.[19] According to statistics gathered in 2005, there were at least 22 million TVEs, employing over 138 million people.[20]

TVEs made an important contribution to the economy, although there were concerns about their impact on the environment and on the health and safety of their employees because of the low level of technology, education, and expertise available to them, the lack of regulation, and in many cases, their serious undercapitalisation. In spite of their early success, especially when compared to SOEs, they had effectively disappeared by 2020 and no separate TVE statistics were published. TVEs were integrated into other enterprises after property rights legislation and privatisation which became more acceptable.[21]

Rural reforms, 2008–2009

Two years of serious rural unrest persuaded the CCP leadership of the urgent need to reform the system of ownership and buying and selling of land, and to improve life in the countryside. Rural reforms were a priority in the final years of the Hu Jintao and Wen Jiabao administration.

The historic land reforms of 1978, which effectively abandoned collectivised agriculture, had allocated land to farming households but without the right to sell that land. Critics argued that this had led to small-scale and inefficient farming, but also to informal leasing, especially by those who had left the land to work in the cities. This leasing was illegal and unregulated, and was one of the main causes of corruption and abuse by local government officials. In October 2008, villagers in Bainitang near the Guangdong city of Heyuan – close to the revolutionary peasant bases of the 1920s – had protested against the acquisition, without compensation, of rural land for a hydroelectric power station. Building materials were destroyed, and two protesters and their lawyer were imprisoned.[22]

The CCP leadership, conscious of the risks of increasing the numbers of landless rural poor reviewed legislation on rural land sales; this became the primary focus of the Third Plenary Session of the 17th Central Committee that met in Beijing from 9–12 October 2008. In his work report, General Secretary Hu Jintao acknowledged that the rural infrastructure was weak, famers' income was not growing quickly enough, and support was needed to prevent rural development falling further behind that of the cities. The 1979 Household Responsibility System would remain in place to farm publicly owned land, but a 'strict and normative' land management system was needed.

Hu's communiqué was long on rhetoric but short on detail and prominence was given in the official accounts to the presence at the meeting of members of the Discipline Inspection Commission and agricultural specialists, leading to speculation that there had been considerable disagreement within the leadership. After the close of the meeting, Xinhua reported that the Central Committee had agreed on the establishment of 'markets for the lease of contracted farmland and the transfer of land-use rights, allowing farmers to subcontract, lease or exchange their rights'. These transactions had to be voluntary and carried out legally with adequate payment; the land transferred could only be used for its original purpose. Local 'land-use rights exchanges' were to be established: the first – Chengdu United Assets and Equity Exchange – was opened on 13 October 2008. On 27 June 2009, the Standing Committee of the NPC adopted legislation on the mediation and arbitration of land disputes, including 'measures and procedures' intended to provide a legal basis for dispute resolution.[23]

There had been considerable opposition to these reforms from senior CCP cadres who thought that the 1978 Responsibility System had gone far enough or should never have happened in the first place. Opponents were concerned that allowing the freer sale of land would lead to the re-emergence of a wealthy and powerful landlord elite and a class of poor and landless peasants. There was also a fear that as land was sold for non-agricultural purposes, there would be an absolute decline in the area of arable land and consequent risks for China's food security.

Substantial funds were transferred to county governments from the centre to enhance social services, improve the quality of life in the rural areas, and stem the tide of migrants heading for the major cities. According to Chen Xiwen, the government's influential adviser on rural affairs, the total number of rural migrants had reached 226 million, and this was creating a serious shortage of labour in the countryside. Consolidating land holdings and increasing capitalisation, initially through the Agricultural Bank of China – the recipient of an injection of funds equivalent to US$19 billion – would assist the reabsorption of migrants and provide additional financial security for the elderly and children who remained in the villages. The *hukou* system was also being relaxed, in line with the new regulations on land transfer.

Rural governance

Speaking in Zhengzhou on 10 November 2009, President Hu Jintao urged the establishment and improvement of 'democratic self-governance of villages that can both secure the CCP's leadership and safeguard villagers' rights'. This was echoed by other leaders including then Vice-President Xi Jinping. Rather than democracy in the Western sense, this was a demand for strengthening the CCP's grassroots governance organisations in rural areas and improving the existing limited village-level self-government. Ten years later, with Xi Jinping then in power, the Central Committee and the State Council were still grappling with the problem of 'enhancing rural governance'.

> By 2020, China aims to develop an institution structure and policy system for modern rural governance, with the primary-level CPC organizations playing a leading role, self-governance by villagers further enhanced, consultation systems about village affairs better established and the level of rural governance raised.

Longer-term aspirations included improvements in public services and security, and perfecting 'the Party-led rural governance model which combines self-governance, rule of law, and rule of virtue' by 2035. These guidelines confirmed that rural governance remained a priority for the CCP, but acknowledged that creating an effective institutional structure would still take many years.[24]

Eighteen red fingerprints and the end of collectivisation in Xiaogang village

Before the Central Committee meeting, Hu Jintao made a highly symbolic visit to Xiaogang, the village in Fengyang County, a deprived and backward rural area in the north of Anhui province which is celebrated as the cradle of post-Mao agricultural reform after a secret and illegal agreement by the villagers on dividing commune land, 30 years previously. Hu's visit emphasised the link between the 1978 reforms in the Deng Xiaoping era and his own 2008 proposals.[25]

Although credit for initiating the 'reform and opening' movement is normally accorded to the CCP leadership, and to Deng Xiaoping in particular, the villagers of Xiaogang should be recognised as the true pioneers, at least of the de-collectivisation of commune land which was the basis, and the essential precursor, of the nationwide reforms. Xiaogang is a was completely unknown outside of its immediate vicinity but it shot to prominence in 1978 when local peasant leaders, meeting in secret, agreed to divide up the collectivised land they had been working – in defiance of the CCP's regulations – and farm as individual households.

What could have been a political disaster for the village turned into triumph as the new leadership under Deng Xiaoping, recently restored to power after the death of Mao and the defeat of his political successors, the Gang of Four, was searching for ways to reform China's sluggish agricultural system. The grassroots initiative of the Xiaogang villagers provided a model for the reformers and, instead of political or criminal sanctions which they might have expected, their actions were honoured by the CCP and, in early October 2008 on the 20th anniversary of their local rebellion, with a personal and highly publicised visit by President Hu Jintao. The model they devised became the basis for the nationwide Responsibility System which was the death knell of the People's Communes that had been in place since 1958 and transformed the face of the Chinese countryside. While this process has been celebrated and applauded as the beginnings of a modern system of agriculture, there were serious misgivings that turning back the clock creates the danger of a sharply divided rural society with a wealthy and powerful landlord class and a poor and powerless peasantry, a situation uncomfortably analogous to the one that gave birth to the CCP from the 1920s to the 1940s.[26]

Anhui is a province in east central China which straddles both the Huai and the Yangzi rivers. It has an immense land area and is very densely populated, with over 61 million inhabitants in 2009.[27] It also has extremely diverse terrain: the north is a wheat-growing area, while the south is firmly in the southern China rice zone. In the far south, near the borders of Jiangxi and Zhejiang, lies the region of Huizhou, known in the past as Xin'an and home to a group of powerful merchant families who traded throughout the Empire (lacking, they said, the land to enable them to cultivate grain) and whose monumental commemorative archways [*paifang*] can still be seen in the villages of the region. The surrounding paddy fields give the appearance of being successful and productive, but in the 1980s, Anhui was notorious as one of the poorer parts of the otherwise rapidly developing east China region with pockets of poverty and severe deprivation. On a rail journey south in 1986, I vividly recall and encounter with the Deputy Governor of the province, looking lovingly out over the fields of his domain as the train trundled south and assuring me that Anhui was rapidly becoming one of the important grain-producing areas of China.

The Xiaogang villagers acted not out of ideological motives but desperation, seeking a practical solution for their own local problems. Their village was poor, even by the standards of northern Anhui, and natural disasters had been frequent. The village lies in the east of Fengyang County and is only 40 kilometres from the county seat of Fengyang, although it is administered by another township, Xiaoxihe. It is not far from the Beijing–Shanghai railway, a major road, and the commercial quays of the Huai River, and it is within striking distance of the city of Bengbu – yet somehow it had been left behind and ignored.

The lives of the villagers were difficult and had been for generations: poverty, gruelling work on the land, cold, and exhaustion were what they had come to expect. In spite of the political changes that had followed the establishment of the PRC in 1949, they had made little progress and many of the villagers went short of food and even lacked adequate warm clothing for the winter. Traditional feudal attitudes were entrenched in the village, and families took turns in nominating members to be village cadres, but even as late as 1978, local people described the village as 'dirt poor' and the villagers as penniless and frequently driven to begging.[28] The commune system of agricultural management and local administration was intended to cover the country uniformly, but it did not provide even the basic support necessary to drag Xiaogang the village out of poverty: by 1978, the villagers, in desperation, decided to act on their own initiative, defy the policy of collectivisation, and risk the wrath of local CCP officials.

In 1978, representatives of 18 peasant families in Xiaogang, meeting in secret, initiated the process of transferring control over agricultural production in the village from the production team (part of the commune) to individual households. The conspirators put their mark on a written agreement by pressing their fingers in red ink and then on the document. This Responsibility System [literally 'great work guarantee', or *dabaogan*] agreement became the model for the demolition of the entire People's Commune system and the return to family farms, although the fiction that this was achieved within the system of collective farming was retained for many years, latterly without much conviction.

The 30th anniversary of the Xiaogang revolution was celebrated locally, and the achievement of the villagers was acclaimed in the national press. In Xiaogang itself, the Responsibility System Memorial Hall, which had been formally opened on 19 June 2005, was extended with the help of funds totalling over RMB 3 million from local Party and government organisations. The hall was completed in time for the nationwide ceremonies held in December 2008 to commemorate the 30th anniversary of the 'reform and opening' programme. The calligraphy for the name of the new hall was provided by Wan Li, former chairman of the Standing Committee of China's parliamentary body, the NPC. The refurbished hall has a large and a small exhibition room, multi-function rooms, and a restaurant. The main exhibition hall features a group relief of the 18 rebels making handprints, and other objects and photographs connected with the village in 1978. In the long term, the intention was that the hall would serve as a base for patriotic education in the locality; village leaders hoped that it would also be a magnet for red tourism from the whole country and attract extra revenue for Xiaogang. At the opening ceremony of the refurbished Responsibility System Hall, 12 of the surviving members of the group of 18 who pressed their red fingerprints on the original agreement were presented with flowers by members of the Young Pioneers, the CCP's youth organisation.[29]

There was a sombre postscript to these celebrations in November 2009 when Shen Hao, the Communist Party Secretary of Xiaogang village, died suddenly at the age of only 45, apparently from a massive heart attack. Shen had taken over the village Party machine in 2004 and had been credited with the considerable economic success of the village in those few years as per-capita income had tripled. After his death, which followed an official banquet, local people said that he had burnt himself out working for them, but there were also suggestions that his death may have been due to alcoholic poisoning. Nevertheless, his legacy is now that of a model Party official, his exemplary life is studied at Party meetings, and villagers are said to have insisted that after his cremation, his ashes must be retained in the village.

Rural challenges in the Xi Jinping era

For 16 consecutive years, the first policy document issued by the central authorities each year, the No. 1 Central Document, had concentrated on agricultural and rural matters – and 2019 was no exception. The document jointly released by the Central Committee and State Council on 19 February referred to rural society as 'the ballast stone' for stability. As part of the continuing drive to build a 'moderately prosperous society', the term used in the Hu Jintao era, there were 'tough tasks' ahead in eliminating rural poverty, improving the environment in the countryside, and guaranteeing the supply of grain, which was critical given the size of China's population and the increasing demand for higher-quality food.

Although the CCP has concentrated on institutions for improving rural governance, there was also an assumption that improving the life and livelihood of the rural poor would reduce conflict in the countryside. As China attempted to replace lost export opportunities with domestic demand, it was expected that the consumer market in the rural areas, which was still largely untapped at the beginning of the Xi Jinping administration, would play a major role. That was predicated on an improvement in rural incomes and lifestyles, but it was clear by 2019 that the income gap between villages and cities was widening. In spite of a reduction in impoverished villages, there were still areas of extreme poverty. Rural incomes declined after 2014, and poverty returned to many villages. Rural disposable income per capita in 2014 stood at 13% of total income, but it had declined by 2018 to 9%.[30] Villages continued to lag far behind urban areas in level of income living conditions and public services. In spite of injections of funding from the centre, rural areas remained poorly served financially. Investment of RMB 7 trillion (US$1.05 trillion) was scheduled to revitalise rural China and unlock its potential for growth, which would in turn create a domestic consumer market.

Thirty-year leases provided a degree of security, but as farmers did not own their land, they could not sell what would otherwise have been a substantial asset or even be sure of securing loans against it. Small farms did not benefit from economies of scale, and as running costs increased – for fertiliser, electricity, and labour – grain prices fell, with a consequent decline in farmers' incomes. Pensions in the countryside were less adequate than in the cities: the existing scheme was funded by the government and the insured, but benefits were low and healthcare and education costs high.

One government response was to create an additional 10,000 primary supply and marketing cooperatives, bringing the total to 32,000. Funding for these coops, which were more in tune with traditional CCP philosophy of centralisation, was increased by the All-China Federation of Supply and Marketing Cooperatives from 2016. Although these were intended as an alternative to the privately privatised small farms, there were concerns that some were not genuine cooperatives.[31]

Notes

1 *SCMP* 6 April, 26 October 2019.
2 Hsiao-Tung Fei (Fei Xiaotong) *Peasant Life in China* London: Routledge and Kegan Paul, 1939.
3 Xu Xiuli and Wang Xianming (ed.) *Zhongguo jindai xiangcun de weiji yu congjian: geming, gailiang ji qita* (*Crisis and Reconstruction of Rural Society in Modern China: Revolution, Reform and More*) Beijing: Social Science Academic Press, 2013, pp. 3–112.
4 Xu Xiuli and Wang Xianming (ed.) *Zhongguo jindai xiangcun de weiji yu congjian: geming, gailiang ji qita* (*Crisis and Reconstruction of Rural Society in Modern China: Revolution, Reform and More*) Beijing: Social Science Academic Press, 2013, pp. 363–459.
5 Ma Shixiang *Nongye hezuohua yundong shimo: baiming qinlizhe koushu shilu* (*Complete Account of the Agricultural Cooperation Movement: Recorded Oral Testimony of One Hundred Participants*) Beijing: Dangdai Zhongguo, 2012.
6 Chu Li and Tien Chieh-yun *Inside a People's Commune* Beijing: Foreign Languages Press, 1975, pp. 55–6.
7 Ma Shixiang *Nongye hezuohua yundong shimo: baiming qinlizhe koushu shilu* (*Complete Account of the Agricultural Cooperation Movement: Recorded Oral Testimony of One Hundred Participants*) Beijing: Dangdai Zhongguo, 2012; Luo Pinghan *Nongcun renmin gongshe shi* (*History of Rural People's Communes*) Fuzhou: Fujian renmin chubanshe, 2006.
8 *Beijing Review* 3 May 1982. Weiguo Wang 'Land Use Rights: Legal Perspectives and Pitfalls for Land Reform' in Peter Ho (ed.) *Developmental Dilemmas: Land Reform and Institutional Change in China* London: Routledge, 2005, p. 66.
9 Xinhua 16 June 2007.
10 *China Daily* 25 December 2018.
11 *Wall Street Journal* 5 May 2006.
12 'Rural Area Development Key to Stability' Xinhua 19 January 2006.

13 State Council, 19 January 2006.
14 Xing Qinjiao 'Zhongguo nongmin xinnian gaobie nongye shui' *Renmin Ribao* (overseas edition) 30 December 2005.
15 NPC plenary session, 1 April 2004.
16 *People's Daily* 18 January 2006.
17 *FT* 8 November 2006.
18 FT 6 August 2015.
19 International Labour Organisation Report 1998; Cheng Jin (ed.) *An Economic Analysis of the Rise and Decline of Chinese Township and Village Enterprises* London: Palgrave Macmillan, 2017, pp. 1–3 and passim.
20 He Kang (editor in chief) *China's Township and Village Enterprises* Beijing: Foreign Languages Press, 2005.
21 International Labour Organisation report 1998; Cheng Jin (ed.) *An Economic Analysis of the Rise and Decline of Chinese Township and Village Enterprises* London: Palgrave Macmillan, 2017, pp. 1–3 and passim.
22 *FT* 8, 9 October 2008.
23 *Global Times* 28 June 2009.
24 Reuters, 23 October 2008; *China.org.cn* 11 November 2009; Xinhua 23 June 2019.
25 *SCMP* 10 September, 20, 26 October 2008; Xinhua 12 October 2008; *FT* 16 October 2008.
26 *SCMP* 20 October 2008.
27 *SCMP* 20 October 2008.
28 Fengyang Government website www.fengyang.gov.cn/travel_view.php?id=21&ty=6.
29 www.politics.people.com/GB/14562/3480083.html.
30 Fengyang Government website www.fengyang.gov.cn/travel_view.php?id=21&ty=6.
31 *SCMP* 26 October 2019; Xinhua 20 February 2019.

9 Urban and industrial economy

Until the late twentieth century, the urban industrial sector constituted only a small proportion of China's total economy. Towards the end of the first quarter of the twenty-first century, it is not only a major part of the economy, but a symbol of China's success in its drive for modernisation. China today possesses almost all of the types of industrial and manufacturing capacity found in other developed economies elsewhere, but the geographical spread of industries is patchy, and the level of development varies considerably. One of the greatest economic challenges faced by China in the twenty-first century is the successful transition from an industrial sector that was almost entirely state-owned to one dominated by private or mixed ownership.

State-owned enterprises

In common with the Soviet Union and other members of COMECON (the Council for Mutual Economic Assistance), the economic union of the Soviet bloc, China developed a large state-owned industrial base in the 1950s and 1960s. There is a widespread conviction, often based on little evidence or understanding, that the impact of these SOEs was wholly negative and that they hampered rather than assisted China's economic development. This belief is based on another assumption which is not always articulated clearly: that there is only one viable model for economic development, a Western individualistic and free-market model. The SOEs can certainly be criticised for inefficiencies, for conservative working practices, and for their inability to compete with international firms. They also limited the opportunity for individuals to develop their own careers, since most staff were directed into a firm on leaving school or college and did not leave unless they were transferred for some reason connected with the interests of the industry or the state. This system of lifetime employment which became known as the 'iron rice bowl' provided job security, but it inhibited movement between different types of employment and different parts of the country, and restricted the sharing of skills and information.

What the SOEs did provide was stability, security, and social cohesion; these were of great value in a country that had endured years of occupation by the Japanese military and a bitter Civil War. SOEs provided continuity and security of employment, cheap and decent accommodation, healthcare that was usually free of charge, and education for the children of employees. They were not able to provide social stability and competitiveness simultaneously; the CCP's ongoing programme of reform placed the need for international competitiveness over the need for security.[1]

Stages of SOE reform

In the 1980s, the reform of the SOEs was perceived – particularly by overseas business and finance interests – as the key indicator of China's ability and willingness to make a successful transition from a planned (some prefer the description 'command') economy to a mixed or wholly commercial industrial and financial system. Since these enterprises constituted the core of the industrial economy – mines, iron, steel and chemical plants, machine manufacture, automobile industries, and thermal, hydro, and nuclear power, for example – it was vital that they continued to function and produce materials needed to power China's economy even while being transformed. What is usually described as the reform of the SOEs is far more radical than that term suggests: at its fullest extent, the process involved the wholesale dismantling of a significant part of the state-owned industrial sector and the radical reform of the remainder.

Such a complex process had to be carried out gradually. Between 1980 and 1986, progressively more economic enterprises were given the authority to manage their own affairs autonomously – that is, without direct control from the ministries in Beijing. A 'dual price' system was established as part of the strategy of creating a market system that had not existed since the 1950s. Under this twin-track pricing system, some goods and services were made available at prices fixed by the state, while others were allowed to enter the market, which determined their prices. The proportion of goods available at market prices was gradually increased.

From 1987–1992, a 'contract responsibility' system was introduced and SOEs were then required to be profitable. A third stage in the reform process ran from about 1993–1997: the most significant change was the separation of ownership and control from management: managers of individual enterprises were given additional powers and profit incentives. A capital market was introduced to stimulate the reform of property rights. During the fourth stage, 1998–2001, although the state retained overall control of the largest SOEs, it was prepared to relinquish its authority over the more competitive small and medium-sized enterprises – and in 2001, the sale of these SMEs was seriously considered for the first time. This was not a simple process of privatisation, since state organs retained considerable control during what was intended to be a transitional period.

The standard method for reforming SOEs was the creation of a new board of directors and board of supervisors, and the issuing of shares in what was then deemed a new company. State organisations, however, retain a majority of the shares in the largest of the SOEs, so this process is not directly comparable with European privatisation programmes. Unreformed SOEs continued to play a considerable part in China's economic development, but their financial status changed. As direct funding from the state was reduced, financial support came from the banks, increasingly at commercial rates of interest.

The state retained complete control over SOEs in certain sectors, particularly those with a strategic role. All defence, telecommunications, and finance industries were ring-fenced for state-run organisations, although from 2003 onwards, the finance sector was partially opened to private firms as a condition of China's entry into the WTO. Foreign companies were generally not permitted to take over SOEs.

Social implications of SOE reform

One of the principal outcomes of the dismantling of the state-owned conglomerates was the winding down of the 'iron rice bowl' [*tie fanwan*] system, the arrangement which guaranteed employment for life in the major state enterprises. This system had provided a large measure of social stability since the 1950s, and employees benefited from a range of community provisions made by the SOEs, including housing, education, and medical and social care, and there was also a system of welfare provisions for the children of employees and elderly retired employees. On the debit side, as has already been noted, the SOEs did not provide any freedom of choice for employees, who were typically transferred to an enterprise at the conclusion of their secondary or tertiary education and remained there for the rest of their lives unless they were transferred to another plant. The concept of advertising opportunities for employment or applying for jobs was virtually unknown.

Labour unrest

The dismantling of the SOEs led to labour unrest in the cities, sometimes on a large scale, and there have been concerns about the impact of this dramatic change on the pensions of former employees. In October 2005, a protest by workers laid off from the Chongqing Steel Mill became violent. Employees made redundant at the plant, which had formerly been one of China's top companies but had declared itself bankrupt in July 2005, began a series of demonstrations on 12 August. They demanded severance payments of RMB 2,000 each, and alleged that the collapse of the company had been a consequence of corruption and malad-ministration by the management: the land on which the factory stood was said to have been sold for less than the current market price.

Hundreds of former employees of the steel mill blocked main roads in the city of Chongq-ing and brought traffic to a standstill. Negotiations between factory management and repre-sentatives of the workforce were deadlocked. The situation came to a head because protests were scheduled to continue during a summit meeting of town and city mayors from the Asia-Pacific region due to take place in Chongqing from 11–14 October. When police arrived in the early morning of 7 October, two police vehicles were overturned; the demonstrators alleged a provocation by plainclothes officers, but riot police were called. In the ensuing conflict, two women, aged 50 and 70, died.[2]

The Financial Times reported that in 2016 'Chinese labour unrest extended its foot-print . . . as workforce tensions that have long beset the manufacturing and construction industries began to hit the fast-growing sectors on which Beijing has pinned its hopes for future growth'.[3] The main challenges faced by the workforce in China remained the same as they had been for many years: relations between management and workers, employment conditions and wages, the limitations of labour legislation for dispute resolution, discrimina-tion against women and ethnic minorities in the workplace, social security and employers contributions, the special problems of migrant workers and their children, and safety in the workplace and a high rate of industrial accidents.[4]

Labour movement

In 1921, the CCP was born into a period of a young but vigorous labour movement with which it initially maintained close relations, as orthodox Marxist-Leninist thinking required. This relationship was shattered when the Guomindang massacred Communists and trade unionists in Shanghai and other cities in 1927 at the end of the Northern Expedition. Forced out into the rural areas, important sections of the Party lost contact with urban workers and forged close relationships with peasant farmers, although some CCP members like Liu Shaoqi managed to maintain clandestine links with organised labour.

Since 1949, there has been no officially tolerated independent labour movement in the PRC. The CCP, as the party of the workers and peasants, has substituted itself for autono-mous labour organisation. It create the state-controlled All-China Federation of Trade Unions as the only legal labour organisation; although Beijing claims that it is the continuation of the ACFTU founded in 1925, it is far from autonomous and serves to prevent workers from organising their own unions.

During the reform period, independent – and therefore illegal – workers' organisations emerged in many different parts of China, especially in the construction and service sectors in rapidly developing Guangdong, where there had been a series of uncoordinated protests and strikes. In many cases, the 'civil society labour organisations' were able to operate informally to 'resolve disputes through collective bargaining with management' which the ACFTU had not done. In December 2015, the Chinese government launched a crackdown on independent labour organisations in Guangdong. That summer it instructed ACFTU to carry out reforms that would enable it to represent workers more effectively and address inequality and persistent social and economic grievances. Although the independent organisations had provided models for dispute resolution it was by no means certain that ACFTU would build on these as it creates new top-down unions.[5]

State-owned Assets Supervision and Administration Commission (SASAC)

China's determination to press ahead with the reform of the SOEs, but to do so in a gradual and a controlled fashion, is demonstrated by the role of the State-owned Assets Supervision and Administration Commission (SASAC), a body operated by the State Council. In accordance with the Company Law of the PRC, SASAC was responsible for advancing the reform and restructuring of SOEs. Its formal duties include the preservation and augmentation of the value of state-owned assets in enterprises under its supervision and the development of modern business systems and methods in SOEs in general. It had the authority to dispatch supervisory panels to enterprises on behalf of the state, and could take control of the daily management of enterprises through these panels if it deemed it necessary. SASAC had authority to appoint and dismiss executives and to evaluate their performances: it could also draft legislation and administrative measures on the management of state-owned assets. On 24 January 2006, Huang Ju, one of China's Vice-Premiers, issued written instructions to SASAC, emphasising the importance of restructuring and calling for an increase in the pace of SOE reform.[6]

Private sector growth

In parallel with the dismantling of the state sector, there was a significant growth in private industry, initially on a small scale. The private sector had been almost eliminated in the early 1950s during the movement for the 'socialisation of industry', although some smaller-scale handicraft workshops remained outside state control. The importance of the private sector for the development of China during the reform era was formally recognised by the state: entrepreneurs were cultivated by local Party committees, and under Jiang Zemin were even encouraged to join the CCP. Restrictions on the areas of the economy in which private industry can operate remained in place for some time, notably in matters that involve defence and national security.

A new class of small entrepreneurs [*getihu*] emerged during the 1980s. Former employees of the SOEs were encouraged to cast themselves into the sea [*xiahai*] of private enterprise. This opportunity was seized by many entrepreneurially minded individuals who established new businesses, but there were also many social casualties.

The government was obliged to create a social security structure to support families living in towns and cities who did not have income from work, or whose income was below a certain level. There is an urban minimum living standard guarantee [*dibao*], and this miti-gated the problems of urban poverty. This benefit was payable to 22 million residents of the urban areas – the unemployed, those unable to work and the elderly without other means of support. The minimum income level varied from city to city – in Beijing in 2007, it was RMB 330 (£21.5 or US$43) per month – and eligible families received a payment to bring their income up to RMB 330 if their regular income was below that level. Inflation hit the urban poor hard, above all the steep rises in the cost of food. and the government authorised an increase of RMB 15 per month in these benefits to take effect from the end of August 2007.[7]

SOEs in the Xi Jinping era

The debate on how to deal with SOEs remains unresolved. In December 2012 at a forum organised by the influential *Caijing* [*Finance and Economics*] magazine, a Vice-Chairman of the Chinese People's Political Consultative Congress urged that most SOEs should with-draw from competitive markets to make way for private companies. President Hu Jintao had previously made it clear that public ownership would continue to dominate the economy.[8] During the Xi Jinping administration, mixed-ownership reform was the preferred mecha-nism. 'Non-state capital' was invested in two-thirds of the central SOEs, more than 50% of this in listed companies, according to Weng Jieming, deputy head of the SASAC, which supervises SOEs. As market operation mechanisms were adopted, 91 listed companies under the control of 45 central SOEs had adopted equity incentive schemes.[9]

Notes

1 Peter Nolan *China at the Crossroads* Cambridge: Polity, 2004, pp. 156–67.
2 *Chinese Labour Bulletin* 14 October 2005.
3 *FT* 2 February 2017, citing *Chinese Labour Bulletin*.
4 *Chinese Labour Bulletin* clb.org.hk, accessed 31 August 2020.
5 *The Workers' Movement in China (2015–17)* Hong Kong: Chinese Labour Bulletin, 2018.
6 Huang Ju died on 2 June 2007, only days after he had been selected as a Shanghai representative to the 17th CCP Congress due to be held in October 2007. He was only 69 years old and there had been rumours about his health for some time, but the manner in which his death was reported raised speculation that there was some mystery surrounding it.
7 Xinhua 10 August 2007.
8 *SCMP* 16 December 2012.
9 *China Daily* 19 September 2019.

10 Banking, finance, and foreign trade

Between the foundation of the PRC in 1949 and implementation of the major reforms of the 1980s, the banking system in China was relatively simple. In rural areas, markets did not operate to any extent and many transactions were made by administrative transfer within communes or between communes and state organisations. Money existed but was in fairly short supply, and there was no question of individuals investing or saving, other than secretly. Foreign trade was limited and carried out by means of transfers from the People's Bank of China.

Foreigners visiting China, including diplomats, business people, and other long-term residents, were not even officially permitted to use the normal Chinese currency, the RMB (renminbi): they were restricted to foreign exchange certificates (FECs), which as the name implies, were issued in exchange for the foreign currency that China desperately needed. This was a measure designed to protect the RMB in a hostile financial market. FECs were the only currency accepted in the Friendship Stores, special shops that sold high value and imported goods which only wealthy foreigners could afford and from which most Chinese were barred.[1] In theory, FECs were not supposed to be used in normal shops or by Chinese citizens, but they attracted a premium from Westerners who were working in Chinese organisations and from Chinese citizens who sought them to buy foreign imports.

As the overall standard of living improved in Chinese cities, people increasingly wished to acquire FECs so that they could buy the goods that had been the privilege of the foreigners, and a flourishing black market developed. It was impossible for a foreigner to walk for more than a few minutes in Beijing without being approached to 'change money', the one English phrase that everyone understood. As confidence in the RMB increased, the FEC system gradually became more trouble than it was worth and FECs were abolished in 1995 by the simple stratagem of the government setting the exchange value between FEC and RMB to 1:1. FECs had only really been usable in the major cities. Shopkeepers in the farther flung parts of China did not recognise them and some even assumed they were a foreign currency.[2]

People's Bank of China

The People's Bank of China [*Zhongguo renmin yinhang*] was established by the CCP on 1 December 1948 during the closing months of the Civil War. Inflation had reached such a level that the currency then circulating, the *fabi* [legal currency] issued by the Guomindang government was completely worthless. The first act of the new bank was to issue a new currency, the renminbi (people's currency, RMB). The unit of this currency is the *yuan*, usually referred to in speech as a *kuai*, a 'piece' of money.

The People's Bank was, and remains, the only bank allowed to issue notes and coinage. It functions as a central bank, albeit one under the strict control of the government and the

CCP. It is also the accounting arm of all government, military, and cooperative organisations, which are obliged to maintain accounts at the bank and to deposit reserves with it. In its early years, it effectively had a monopoly over credit for the non-agricultural sector and rapidly established a network of branches throughout the whole of the country in the 1950s.

The People's Bank came directly under the control of the State Council rather than the Ministry of Finance. In turn, it controlled two subordinate banks: the Bank of China, which had its origins in capital confiscated from a semi-official organisation run by the Guomindang government in the 1940s, and the Joint State-Private Bank, which was the result of the merger of dozens of private banks during the nationalisation of the private sector in the 1950s.

The special and critical needs of the agricultural sector were met by various specialist banks, the most important being the Agricultural Bank established in November 1963 after the decentralisation of management in the communes. Like the People's Bank, this was also directly answerable to the State Council. The People's Construction Bank of China functioned as a subsidiary of the Ministry of Finance, and its main role was managing the payment of state investment to construction units and other enterprises. The model for these banks was plainly the system of banking that had been created in the Soviet Union and had also been exported to Eastern Europe: it was also used in other Communist countries in Asia, including China's near neighbours, North Korea and North Vietnam.[3]

Reforming the state banks

The reform of the financial sector has been much slower than corresponding reforms in the agricultural and industrial sectors. As suppliers of credit to the SOEs, the banks are contractually and organisationally bound to these organisations which are being dismantled – and this has restricted their ability to function in the same way as banks in the developed world. The banks have a portfolio of non-performing loans and are considered by some economists to be technically insolvent according to international criteria: by some estimates, bad debts account for 40%–50% of total loans.

The process of reforming state-owned banks has been twofold. On the one hand, they have been reduced in size: the number of staff employed by the state-owned banks was reduced from a total of 1.6 million in 1997 to 1.4 million in 2001. On the other hand, the proportion of their dealings that involves loans to the SOEs has been reduced. Loans to private companies and to individuals, including mortgages and car loans, which previously were extremely rare, increased dramatically during the 1990s.[4] Concerns about abuses in the banking sector have been raised frequently, but the most direct criticisms were made in December 1999 by the deputy auditor-general of the Audit Office, Liu Jiayi, after an investigation into the operations of 4,600 branches of the Industrial and Commercial Bank of China and 1,700 branches of the China Construction Bank. The main problems highlighted were claims that assets had been overstated, but there were also allegations that some bank managers were running unofficial lending operations in parallel with the bank's legitimate loan transactions, and that they were diverting the interest from these illegal deals for their own use.[5]

Creating a modern financial sector

In December 1999, Zhou Xiaochuan, the president of the China Construction Bank (which was one of the old PRC banks and had been founded as the People's Construction Bank in 1954), outlined the options for banking reform being imposed on China by its application to gain admission to the WTO. He suggested that banks could become shareholding companies and that the major institutions – Bank of China, Agricultural Bank of China, and Industrial and Commercial Bank of China, which together controlled 80% of banking assets – could be decoupled. Joint ventures with foreign banks and listing on the stock market were also under consideration.[6]

When the government became concerned in 2003 that the Chinese economy was over-heating, it was to the central banks that it turned to operate one of the few effective levers available. Restrictions on lending were imposed, but with no certainty that these would be adhered to by bank managers who had been enjoying their newfound freedom to lend in the property and personal car loan markets.[7]

Stock market and stock exchanges

No stock market existed on the Chinese mainland between the founding of the PRC in 1949 and 1990 – during that time, the Chinese economy was a planned economy and the private sector was either non-existent or strictly regulated by the state.

China now has three official stock exchanges, one in Hong Kong and the others in Shanghai and in Shenzhen, which lies to the north of Hong Kong and was the first of the Special Economic Zones created at the birth of the reform era. There is also an informal and unregulated market for trading shares. The novelty of share buying has attracted a great deal of attention, not to say an atmosphere of mass hysteria, and the first bankruptcy of a listed company was treated by some sections of the Chinese media as if it were a rite of passage for China's entry into the market economy.

The Hong Kong Stock Exchange is the largest within China and one of the largest in the world: it has operated almost continuously since the end of the nineteenth century. It was established during the colonial period, and its traditions and its history are comparable with those of the London or New York Stock Exchanges or the Bourse in Paris, whereas the other two institutions, established recently on the mainland, have been obliged to create their own credibility and confidence.

The Shanghai Stock Exchange has a history which also dates back to the nineteenth century and it perhaps reached its peak during the 1930s when Shanghai, controlled to a large extent by European business interests, was the financial hub of China. It continued to operate in the early years of the Japanese occupation of China, but ceased trading in 1941 when the international settlement in which it was based was overrun by the Imperial Japanese Army. It reopened briefly in 1946 after the surrender of Japan, only to close again in 1949 when the CCP took control of China, including Shanghai. It has the history and the tradition, but it does not have the continuity that the Hong Kong exchange enjoys, and it is essentially a new organisation. In its most recent incarnation, as one of the flagships of Deng Xiaoping's economic reforms, it opened for trading in 1990 and a long-standing rivalry was reignited between Hong Kong and Shanghai for supremacy in financial markets. The Shanghai Stock Exchange deals in two types of shares which are designated 'A' and 'B' shares. The most significant difference between them is that prices for 'A' shares are quoted in renminbi (RMB), whereas 'B' shares are priced in US dollars. When the system was established, only Chinese investors were permitted to trade in 'A' shares: 'B' shares could be bought and sold by overseas investors, and from 2001 onwards by locals. There has been some relaxation of these restrictions, and the long-term plan is for the two types of shares to be consolidated.

Concern that China's stock exchanges were overvalued was reinforced by the revelation in November 2007 that PetroChina had suddenly emerged as the world's largest firm in terms of its market value. PetroChina began trading on the Shanghai Stock Exchange on 5 November 2007, and the price of its shares had tripled within hours. Stock market analysts had been expressing concern for some time that overly enthusiastic investors were pumping money into Chinese shares with unrealistic expectations of potential earnings and some were warning of a possible crash in the markets. A 'stock market frenzy' in 2007–2008 was caused by the dash of speculative traders into the market; the turnover in China's stock exchanges was briefly the second highest in the world. The overenthusiasm was cooled by the global financial crisis, and the markets in China stabilised.

Foreign exchange and renminbi convertibility

The reform of the foreign exchange system has played a critical role in China's economic modernisation. The high-profile disagreement between China and the United States over the convertibility and valuation of the renminbi, the currency of the PRC, is only the most public of the problems that has arisen with this complex reform.

Under the centrally planned economy, the state retained a complete monopoly of China's imports and exports. Import and export quotas were determined according to the needs of the Five-Year Plans, and there was hardly any scope for the operation of a price mechanism. The supply of foreign exchange before 1956 had been controlled by the People's Bank of China and by approved foreign exchange banks under the overall political direction of the government's Central Financial and Economic Committee. The system of control was further strengthened in 1956. The state had control over decisions on setting the rate of exchange of the RMB and the regulations that governed foreign exchange, and these were governed by the annual foreign exchange plan which was produced by the State Planning Commission. In the past, major changes to the rate of exchange could only be made with the specific approval of the State Council, but in 1993, it was agreed that the RMB would be 'pegged to a basket of international currencies'.[8]

There is a degree of consensus among international economists that the RMB has been undervalued, although economists working for Chinese state and banking organisations would not necessarily concede this in public. China has certainly had a long-term problem with a shortage of foreign exchange. Technical measures were implemented to resolve these problems: the RMB is now partially convertible, and decisions about the exchange rate and the allocation of foreign exchange are made to some extent on the basis of a price mechanism. China's reserves of foreign currency reached a total of US$1 trillion in October 2006.[9]

Since the RMB is not completely convertible, Beijing continues to face demands from the international banking community for currency liberalisation. China revalued the renminbi on 21 July 2005, discontinued the strict peg to the US dollar that it had been following and moved to a system that is known as the 'floating peg'. Since that date, the RMB has appreciated against the dollar, reaching its highest relative value on 4 December 2006 at 7.82 to the dollar, a gain of 3% since revaluation. Under the regulations set by China's central bankers for the 'floating peg', the dollar-RMB rate is not permitted to vary more than 0.03% in any single day's trading and the RMB can only move by 3% against other currencies in any single day. In spite of the power of the Chinese economy, the renminbi has still not become an international currency with the status of the dollar, the pound Sterling or the Euro.[10]

The United States and other countries remain dissatisfied with the valuation of the Chinese currency. They claim that the RMB is still undervalued, and that this allows China to sell its exports more cheaply, giving it a competitive edge and enabling it to develop a large trade surplus.[11]

Foreign trade

After the CCP took control of China in 1949, foreign businesses – many of which had been established in the country for decades, some of them for over 100 years – were targeted. Under the policy of the 'socialist transformation of industry', which was effectively the nationalisation of private companies and which reached its height in the mid-1950s, the assets of foreign companies were sequestered, and their businesses transformed into SOEs. Many foreign-owned companies, realising the possible implications of a takeover by the CCP, had already removed their assets and had relocated to Hong Kong or elsewhere. Between the 1950s and the 1980s, there were no foreign-owned economic enterprises in China, and this meant that when the reform programme was launched in the 1980s, there were no models and no recent or acceptable precedents for the involvement of Western companies in the Chinese economy.

China's external economic relations before 1980 had been almost entirely with the Soviet Union and other members of COMECON, which was established to promote cooperation between the economies of the Communist world. China had been accorded observer status in COMECON in the late 1950s, but never became a full member and withdrew in 1961 as relations between Beijing and Moscow soured.

Trade with the West did continue, although there were severe restrictions that affected both sides. The Canton (Guangzhou) Trade Fair, formally known as the Chinese Export Commodities Fair, which was first held in 1957, became the most important conduit for business between China and the West. It has taken place twice a year every year since then, in the spring and autumn. The irony of the setting in the city of Guangzhou, to which Western traders had been restricted until the Opium War of 1839–1842, was not lost on either side.

Part of the rationale behind the great political changes that were launched under the slogans of Four Modernisations and 'reform and opening' in the 1980s was the need to attract foreign investment, although without jeopardising state and CCP control over the economy as a whole.

This was initially achieved by the creation of joint-venture companies which combined Chinese management and foreign capital, often from overseas Chinese investors in Hong Kong (which was then still outside the PRC), Singapore, Taiwan and Southeast Asia, but also from Japan and the West. This method was initially successful in the development of large-scale enterprises which China had previously lacked, such as steel plants, factories for the volume production of automobiles of a Western standard, and high-quality hotels (such as the White Swan in Guangzhou) for both the business and tourist trade. However, joint-venture companies frequently encountered problems because of government regulation, tensions over management styles, and cultural differences. Wholly owned foreign enterprises were more attractive to overseas investors, and as China's foreign trade grew and the government became accustomed to the idea of sharing its economic power with private foreign companies, the joint-venture approach became less and less popular.[12]

China's accession to the WTO

China's application to join the WTO was deemed, both within the PRC and by the international community, to be the most important indicator of the modernisation of China's economy – or at least of the acceptance by worldwide opinion that it was a system that other advanced industrial economies could deal with.

The origins of the WTO were in the peace settlement that followed the Second World War. A conference was held in Bretton Woods, New Hampshire in the United States in July 1944 to set out the parameters for the post-war economic and financial order. It was attended by representatives of the victorious allied powers. The conference failed to agree on the creation of an International Trade Organisation, which had been one of its key objectives, but instead set up the General Agreement on Tariffs and Trade (GATT) and also the International Monetary Fund (IMF) and the International Bank for Reconstruction and Development. GATT's role was to regulate international trade and to encourage the growth of free trade by reducing tariffs and other barriers. Technically, it always remained an agreement rather than a fully-fledged international organisation, although it exercised much greater authority than this status might suggest. On 1 January 1995, GATT was replaced by the WTO.

Membership of the WTO confers many benefits, but there are also rigorous conditions, and China's accession to the organisation was delayed because of concern by both sides over the implications of these conditions, particularly the requirement that the PRC be opened to the international financial market. There were reservations as to whether China, as a 'socialist market economy', was in a position to fulfil the conditions. The thorny question of the status of Taiwan vis-à-vis the WTO was also a stumbling block. Nevertheless, China's accession was essential for the Chinese government, not only as a prerequisite for economic modernisation but as a matter of national pride. The PRC had been excluded from the United Nations for 22 years until 1971 and becoming a member of the WTO, this powerful new international economic club, was a matter of self-respect as much as economic necessity. It was also extremely important for the international community, as it was the only mechanism that was available to oblige China to open its commercial and financial sectors to overseas businesses and banks and to hold Chinese companies to international agreements.

The PRC finally joined the WTO on 11 December 2001 after protracted negotiations which were fraught with technical and diplomatic difficulties. The complete application process took a total of 15 years which was the longest on record in the history of either GATT or the WTO. Taiwan also became a member, but not until 1 January 2002. It did not join as the Republic of China, which would have been completely unacceptable to Beijing, but as the Customs Territory of Taiwan, Penghu, Kinmen, and Matsu (Penghu, Jinmen, and Mazu in the *pinyin* romanisation, although Jinmen is also known as Quemoy), the latter three being the names of islands under Taipei's control.

Foreign banks

As part of the negotiations to join the WTO, China was required to agree that it would open its financial markets to foreign banks within five years. Regulations for the operation of foreign banks in China were not published until 2006, and this publication followed a prolonged internal debate on the wisdom of allowing foreign banks into China at all. During the negotiations on China's accession to the WTO, there had been strong arguments against allowing international banks to establish themselves in China, even though this was a fundamental and necessary condition of accession. These arguments were to a certain extent inspired by patriotic or Nationalist sentiment, but there were also practical and realistic economic concerns, including the fear that because foreign banks had greater status and higher standards of service, they would attract investment away from the state-owned banks and the home-grown Chinese banking sector would be seriously undermined.

More optimistic supporters of economic reform hoped that competition with efficient foreign banks would oblige the state-owned Chinese banks to reform and adopt international norms. A more balanced scenario suggests that the banking sector might well divide into two, with smaller savers preferring to remain with the traditional Chinese banks while the larger corporations would incline towards the major international financial organisations which have greater capital and lending power at their disposal. Foreign trading partners, especially the United States, have consistently argued that China has failed to liberalise its financial markets and that it has effectively restricted the import of goods, partly by its determination to keep the RMB at a low level compared with the US dollar to increase its ability to export. Arguments over the degree of progress in the liberalisation of the banking sector are the next stage in negotiations between China and its foreign economic partners.[13]

With the advent of the reform period and the growth of foreign investment in China, overseas banks which had been prohibited from operating in the PRC began to establish a presence in the country. It was not, however, until China's accession to the WTO in 2001 that foreign banks could begin to operate effectively.

The operation of non-Chinese banks is overseen by the State Administration of Foreign Exchange (SAFE). It is part of SAFE's remit to control the flow of overseas capital into the country, because this is an important weapon in the government's armoury of measures to control the growth of the Chinese economy. In June 2007, it was reported that a number of international banks operating in China, including well-known names such as HSBC and Standard Chartered, had been penalised by SAFE, which accused them of ignoring regulations on the import of large amounts of capital and of speculative activity under the guise of investment. Many domestic Chinese banks also suffered penalties at the same time. Most of the capital involved was being invested in either the stock markets or in China's booming property market.[14]

The extent of financial links between Chinese and foreign banks was revealed in the wake of the crisis in the US banking industry caused by problems with high risk (sub-prime) mortgages for low-income would-be homeowners in the United States. In August 2007, the Bank of China revealed that it held securities that were underpinned by sub-prime mortgages to a value of nearly US$10 million. Although the total capitalisation of Chinese banks was high enough for this not to be a cause for concern, the degree of exposure to some of the more risky mechanisms in the international credit market surprised many financial analysts in the West, particularly since it had come relatively early in the process of reforming the Chinese banking system.[15]

HSBC and the PRC

The experience of HSBC (historically, the Hong Kong and Shanghai Banking Corporation) expanding its operations on the Chinese mainland is instructive. Relations with the government of the PRC were strained after the CEO of HSBC, John Flint, explained that he was obliged to provide information to US prosecutors on the case of Meng Wanzhou, Huawei's Chief Financial Officer (CFO), under the terms of an independent monitoring agreement (see Chapter 26).

The bank which had its roots in nineteenth-century China moved its headquarters from Hong Kong to London in 1993 after its purchase of the Midland Bank, one of the United Kingdom's most important banks. This was in spite of the completion in 1986 of its new building in Hong Kong designed by Norman Fosters, but was necessary to comply with the demands of UK banking regulators. While operating as one of the major clearing banks for the US dollar from its London base, it also attempted to expand into the Chinese mainland.

After criticism of the bank's behaviour in the Meng case by Liu Xiaoming, China's ambassador in London, John Flint stepped down, as did Helen Wong, the head of its Greater China operation; there were threats that HSBC could be listed by the Chinese government as an 'unreliable entity' on a list drawn up in retaliation for US attitudes towards China. Mark Tucker, HSBC chairman, emphasised the 'total alignment' of the banks with China's economic plans and its 'active involvement' in high-profile projects such as the planned internationalisation of the renminbi, the Greater Bay Area development and the Belt and Road Initiative.[16]

Shadow banking

The early 21st century saw the growth of a shadow banking system, defined by the *Financial Times* as a 'complex network of financing channels outside the formal banking sector'.[17] Estimates of the size of this network had ranged from RMB 13–24 trillion, which at the top level would make it equivalent to 50% of China's GDP. Although this network included loan sharks and other borderline operations, and some Chinese bankers warned of Ponzi schemes, the governor of China's central bank, Zhou Xiaochuan, insisted that the vast majority were regulated. Trusts, which operated like hedge funds in the West, loaned large sums of money to risky customers who may have been turned down by mainstream banks and promise high returns to investors. Much of the lending was into the property sector, where developers had been finding difficulty in securing loans. In an echo of the 2007–2008 financial crisis in the West, financial products were being created that regulators, banks, and customers did not properly understand.[18]

Responsibility for regulating banks, including shadow banking, is vested in the China Banking and Insurance Regulatory Commission – insurance was added to the portfolio after the arrest of the previous insurance regulator in 2017. The head of the commission, Guo Shuqing, who was appointed that year, particularly targeted shadow banks and in 2019, after a 'regulatory windstorm', the assets of institutions lending informally fell for the first time in ten years.[19]

Notes

1 These were based on the *valyuta* foreign currency shops of the Soviet Union.
2 The author experienced this as late as the 1990s in small shops and market stalls in Kashgar.
3 Audrey Donnithorne *China's Economic System* London: Allen and Unwin, 1967, pp. 402–33.
4 Stephen Green *Reforming China's Economy: A Rough Guide* London: Chatham House, RIIA, 2003; *FT* 28 August 2003.
5 *FT* 17 December 1999.
6 *FT* 13 December 1999.
7 *FT* 28 August 2003.
8 Zhang Zhichao 'China's Foreign Exchange Policy in a Time of Change' *Durham East Asian Papers* no. 11, Durham: University of Durham, 2000; *FT* 20 October 2006.
9 Zhang Zhichao 'China's Foreign Exchange Policy in a Time of Change' *Durham East Asian Papers* no. 11, Durham: University of Durham, 2000; *FT* 20 October 2006.
10 David Lubin 'Waiting, and Waiting, for the Global Renminbi' *Chatham House Expert Comment*, 15 February 2019.
11 *China Daily* 9 November 2006; BBC News 4 December 2006.

12 I am indebted to Yang Zhengming for information on the decline of joint-venture companies.
13 BBC News 11 December 2006.
14 *FT* 28 June 2007.
15 *FT* 25, 26 August 2007.
16 *FT* 20 August 2019.
17 *FT* 3 December 2012.
18 *FT* 3 December 2012.
19 *FT* 25 February 2020.

11 Tourism and transport

For centuries, inadequate transport had inhibited factor China's national economic development. In a country the size of a sub-continent, it was always easier to develop local systems of transport serving local economies than to construct long-distance systems nationwide. Imperial China had road networks and a national postal system, but in the south, most trade and travel was water-borne on the intricate and widespread network of rivers, lakes, and canals, including the Grand Canal that was used to transport grain from the rice bowls of the south to the imperial court and its city in the north.

In the 1920s and 1930s, the Guomindang Nationalist government began improving China's transport infrastructure – partly to enable the swift transfer of troops in their attempt to control the whole of the country, partly to develop of the economy. These developments were interrupted by Japanese colonisation, although some Japanese transport projects such as the South Manchurian Railway were eventually of use to the Chinese.

Railways had been a controversial development in the late nineteenth and early twentieth centuries. Conservatives regarded them as an alien development which would enrich the government and impoverish local businessmen; they were the focus of Nationalist or proto-Nationalist protest and disruption, much of it fuelled by superstitious fears that the construction of railways could damage the natural balance of the landscape.

When the PRC was established in 1949, development of transport was a vital factor under both the planned economy and Deng Xiaoping's reforms. The 1950s and 1960s saw significant growth in the rail network and domestic air travel: roads were relatively neglected, and there was no long-distance road network worth speaking of. Air travel was little used except by senior officials and later by foreign tourists. For most people in China, long-distance travel meant long hours on slow trains, travelling in hard seat, soft seat, or hard sleeper class; for the important, the relatively wealthy or the foreign tourist, there was the luxurious soft sleeper class.

Rail

China's railways have been transformed dramatically and are unrecognisable from pre-reform days. The magnificent black steam engines, some manufactured in the United Kingdom, that in the 1980s used to draw long-distance trains southwards from Beijing into the Yangzi Delta region and westwards out to Lanzhou and Urumqi are a thing of the past. Even the diesel and electric engines that replaced them are themselves being replaced by ultra-modern high-speed trains.

The Beijing–Shanghai Express Railway cut the journey time for the 800-mile journey between China's political capital and its commercial and financial centre from nine to five hours in a system designed to rival the Japanese Shinkansen Bullet Train. Construction of the line was due to begin in 2006, but was dogged with difficulties including budgetary disputes. *China Daily* reported in March 2007 that work on the line would begin later in the year. On 12 October 2007, the National Development and Reform Commission announced that a feasibility study had been approved by the State Council, and Xinhua news agency interpreted this to imply that the high-speed railway had finally been given the seal of approval. By September 2009, the section from Wuhan to Guangzhou was near completion and plans to construct 42 new lines were announced.[1]

Since 2008, the development of China's railway network has been nothing short of phenomenal. The first genuine high-speed line (HSL), between Beijing and Tianjin, was opened in 2008 and the journey of 70 miles at an average speed of 146 miles per hour was planned to take 30 minutes. After an extension of 27 miles in 2015 to Binhai, the Tianjin equivalent to Shanghai's Pudong, the line was carrying 88 million passengers a year. Both trains and signalling equipment were the result of cooperation between the Chinese rail authorities and Siemens.

By 2019, China could boast the largest HSL network in the world at 19,260 miles, with a further 4,000–5,000 miles under construction or planned. The original concept of a 4×4 grid of north–south and east–west lines was extended in 2010 to a planned 10×10 grid as the mainstay of the national rail network. About half of this grid was operational by 2015.

The construction of the HSLs was designed to accommodate speeds of up to 217 miles per hour, but high operating costs at these speeds have restricted operations. In September 2018, 'an accelerated service of nine trains in each direction'[2] was introduced for journeys between Beijing and Shanghai, the most important sector of the network. Travelling at an average of 181 miles per hour, these journeys take on average 4 hours, 31 minutes, with services leaving at 1900 hours in both directions shaving a further quarter of an hour off this time by achieving 192 miles per hour.

In 2019, the Shanghai–Guangzhou route was served by 11 trains a day and a new direct high-speed service from Shanghai to Hong Kong opened on 23 September 2018, linking the two cities in approximately eight hours. Many shorter routes were approved or were in the pipeline as rail became a serious competitor to air travel for covering the great distances across the Chinese mainland.

Rail links were crucial in the planning for the 2022 Winter Olympics which are scheduled to be staged in Beijing, Yanqing in the suburbs of the capital, and Zhangjiakou in Hebei province, the host for most skiing events. A Beijing North–Zhangjiakou inter-city link, under construction in 2019, will be fully automated, like the Docklands Light Railways in London, with driverless trains travelling at up to 217 miles per hour for a 50-minute journey.[3]

Roads

Roads began to emerge as a priority for development in the late twentieth century, and government plans to connect the major regions in a national motorway or expressway system have made great progress. This has been both driven by and resulted in an increase in the ownership of private transport, both cars and commercial vehicles. Whereas in 1988 a reasonably well-informed academic in Xi'an could say with some confidence that China would never become a society in which people owned their own cars because there was 'nowhere to park', in 2005, that same academic's university had a sizeable car park which had been created by demolishing local buildings because private car travel in the city had become such a high priority for the university's more senior staff.

China's network of national expressways is the largest in the world at 123,5000 kilometres, and road travel between regions is practicable for those who can afford cars. Beginning in

2004, the length of expressway was increased by 8,000 kilometres[4] a year and, in spite of the rapid increase in the number of private cars, fatalities on the road have been reduced by 50%.

Toll roads remain an inhibitor on the growth in the use of private cars, but the number of vehicles on the roads is still growing rapidly. The expansion of traffic in Beijing and other cities has been so rapid that the road network is at times scarcely able to cope. Frequent gridlock in Beijing during the 1990s was eased to some extent by the construction of four concentric ring roads, but this in turn has encouraged the use of cars. Similar developments have taken place in other major cities and the construction of inter-city highways proceeds apace, generating a comprehensive national network of highways, most of them radiating from Beijing and many of them of motorway or expressway standard.

Private cars are no longer the preserve of the wealthy minority, but are still seen mainly in the towns and cities: in the rural areas, while there are some cars belonging to wealthy individuals, there are still also many *danwei* [work unit] cars that are used by Party and government officials. For the poorest section of society, transport is overwhelmingly public. Cramped and overcrowded buses are still used for short and long-distance travel, but modern coaches and minibuses are increasingly replacing them.[5]

Underground and light rail

China has developing underground (subway) or light rail systems to help ease the crowded roads of its major cities. Beijing has had an underground system for many years. It was originally constructed with a view to securing communication between government offices during a possible conflict with the Soviet Union. It opened in 1969 for the use of government officials only, and it was not fully available to the public and foreign visitors until the 1980s. It is cramped and uncomfortable to travel in, but not much more so than the buses and trolley buses that were the only alternative for crossing the capital at the time of its construction. What began as a relatively small system linking a few stations in central Beijing was expanded, partly for the colossal construction programme for the 2008 Olympics. It is now the major means of commuting between the centre of the city and the suburbs for work, shopping, or leisure: in spite of the greatly increased number of trains, it is still so crowded that it is often impossible to find a seat.

Shanghai has an ultra-modern high-speed Maglev (magnetic levitation) railway built by a German company, which opened in 2004 and carries travellers on a short journey from the Longyang Road underground station to the main international airport in Pudong. It connects with the Shanghai Metro, an efficient and easy-to-use network with 17 lines that link almost all areas of the city and some towns beyond its boundaries.

Hong Kong's Mass Transit Railway (MTR), which came into service in 1979, is clean, efficient, and popular. Its 11 lines link the commercial districts of Central with the residential and rural areas of the New Territories and also the new airport at Chek Lap Kok, which is just north of the island of Lantau. New extensions include the South Island Line, which stretches to Ap Lei Chau or Aberdeen Island. The importance of the MTR to the smooth running of Hong Kong was highlighted when it became the main target of militant demonstrators during the protests of 2019 (See Chapter 24).

Aviation

Civil aviation developed in the 1980s and – after a number of serious accidents – was improved considerably in the 1990s. The first, and for a long time the only, Chinese airline, CAAC (Civil Aviation Administration of China, *Zhongguo minyong hangkong zongju*, and known universally by the abbreviation *minhang*) was established in 1949 as China's answer to Aeroflot and was responsible for all domestic civilian flights. It was initially under the control of the military, but responsibility for civil aviation was transferred to the government in 1980. As the national economic reform programme progressed, it was transformed into a regular airline operating both domestically and internationally.

In 1987, CAAC was broken up. CAAC itself retained overall control over the management and regulation of the industry, but the operational elements were divided into separate air-lines. Air China would operate international flights, and five regional airlines were created to operate domestic internal schedules: China Eastern Airlines, China Southern Airlines, China Northwest Airlines, China Northern Airlines and China Southwest Airlines. As international travel to and from China has developed, the main international air transport hub, Beijing Capital Airport, has been refurbished to international standards and many regional airports have been rebuilt and updated.

By 2017, there were 229 commercial airports and over 40 scheduled passenger airlines recognised by CAAC. Eight of these are regarded as major, and most serve China's many provinces; there are also eight authorised cargo airlines.

Tourism

One major and very visible development after China's opening was the expansion of tour-ism. Tourism for foreign visitors had been possible since the late 1970s, but only by a small number of organised tour groups and with considerable restrictions on the areas that could be visited. This changed year by year during the 1980s, and tour groups from Japan, overseas Chinese communities, and the West could be observed regularly in many parts of China. Individual tourism also developed, and it suddenly became possible to visit China as an independent traveller and to book hotels and hire cars (with drivers), as in most other coun-tries. The growth of tourism was assisted by the building of luxury joint-venture hotels in the main tourist centres and by improvements in transport – but mostly by changes in the official attitude towards foreigners who wished to travel independently and off the beaten track. At first this was done within the concept of the group tour booking, with the individual bizarrely treated as a group of one.

As China's economy developed, the number of people with disposable incomes increased and consequently, the demand for domestic tourism. Part of this was 'red tourism', focused on sites of political significance for the CCP, but for a generation, it was the first time that many were able to visit other parts of the country that had only been seen on television. This rapid increase in tourism contributed to a growth in the service sector of the Chinese economy. Subsequently, there was growth in overseas tourism and parties of Chinese tourists from the mainland mirrored the existing Taiwanese and Japanese tour groups in the major European tourist destinations.[6]

Notes

1 *FT* 12 October 2007; BBC News 9 September 2009.
2 Gordon Pettitt 'High-Speed Railway Developments' *Modern Railways* (June 2019), pp. 65–6.
3 Barry Naughton *The Chinese Economy: Adaptation and Growth* (2nd ed.) Cambridge: MIT Press, 2018, pp. 36–40. Gordon Pettitt 'High-Speed Railway Developments' *Modern Railways* (June 2019), pp. 65–6.

4 Barry Naughton *The Chinese Economy: Adaptation and Growth* (2nd ed.) Cambridge: MIT Press, 2018, p. 36.
5 Barry Naughton *The Chinese Economy: Adaptation and Growth* (2nd ed.) Cambridge: MIT Press, 2018, p. 36.
6 Barry Naughton *The Chinese Economy: Adaptation and Growth* (2nd ed.) Cambridge: MIT Press, 2018, p. 416.

12 Western development

The strategy of embarking on the long-term development of the Western region of the PRC emerged in 1999. It is legitimised as having been part of Deng Xiaoping's analysis of the 'two overall situations' [*liang ge daju*], which envisaged the economic development of the coastal regions as the priority, followed by the inland territories of China's west, regions that are remote from the centre of power and predominantly poor and backward. Development began under Jiang Zemin and his third-generation leadership, but after the 16th National Congress of the CCP in 2002, although Hu Jintao and the fourth generation continued to implement the policy of economic development in the region, there was far less rhetoric about Western Development as a programme.

For the purposes of the Western Development policy, the western regions were identified as the autonomous regions of Tibet, Xinjiang, Inner Mongolia, Ningxia, and Guangxi; the provinces of Sichuan, Guizhou, Yunnan, Shaanxi, Gansu, and Qinghai; and the municipality of Chongqing. This classification immediately suggests a number of problems: while some of these administrative units, notably Guizhou and parts of Xinjiang, contain some of the most deprived communities within the PRC, the same clearly cannot be said for Sichuan, which has been an economic success story for decades, and in particular the city of Chongqing, which, after a deft recalculation of the area under its administrative authority, overtook Shanghai as China's largest city in 1997.

The Western Development policy was also contentious in that it entailed a significant transfer of resources and personnel from the east of China, and that has raised concerns about the repopulation of ethnic minority areas by a mass resettlement programme of Han Chinese. Li Guantong, the Director of Regional Development for the State Council's Development Research Centre, issued a statement rebutting what he believed were inaccurate reports in the foreign media of a large-scale resettlement project and the aim of converting China's western regions into a 'container' for the increasing population of China as a whole, a total planned transfer of 300 million people. Li was attending an international symposium on the development of China's western regions in Chongqing, which had been designated as the lead city in the development programme. At the same symposium, Cai Fang, Director of the Institute of Population Science at the Chinese Academy of Social Sciences, made it clear that he was not in favour of a mass transfer of population, but he believed that the flow of people between the east and west should be allowed to develop naturally and regulate itself according to the market. Policies that were being adopted to permit the temporary migration of skilled workers to the west of China would, it was said, mean that these migrants would be able to retain all of their formal connections and registrations in the east and could return freely whenever they wished.[1]

Implementation in 2000

The year 2000 was designated as the date for implementing the plans that had been generated in 1999. The responsibility for implementation was given to a Leading Group for the Development of the Western Region under the overall direction of the State Council and it was agreed that specific plans for the west should be included in the national Tenth Five-Year Plan. The planners drew attention to the need for careful planning and explicitly warned against adventurist policies such as those carried out during the 1958 Great Leap Forward. They also acknowledged the economic and social backwardness of the western region and concluded that, since this backwardness was the result of a long process of historical development, it was reasonable to expect that it would also require a long process to change it.

For it to have any chance of success, the plan required the cooperation of a number of different agencies: the question of coordination was therefore vital. For example, to deal with ecological issues alone would involve government departments of forestry, water conservancy, agriculture, and land. Overall, planning would have to include a dozen provincial, municipal, and autonomous regions, as well as the quasi-autonomous Xinjiang Production and Construction Corps. Cooperation would also involve local government in neighbouring provinces, and the planners warned of the dangers of 'localism' which could impede the progress of the project.[2]

West China Forum 2004

On 18 November 2004, the West China Forum met in Nanning, the capital of the Guangxi Zhuang Autonomous Region. The forum is sponsored by the West China Development Office of the State Council, the State Development and Reform Commission, the Ministry of Commerce, the Information Office of the State Council, and the regional government of Guangxi. Over 300 participants represented the 12 western provinces and regions that are directly involved in the Western Development programme, and also the Xinjiang Production and Construction Corps (XPCC). The inclusion of the XPCC reflects its unusual status; it is considered to be equivalent in rank to a provincial level administration.

The keynote speech was given by Zeng Peiyan, member of the CCP Politburo and Vice-Premier of the State Council. He reiterated the influence of 'Deng Xiaoping theory' on the Western Development programme and emphasised the role of strategy in the state's coordinated plan for modernisation and the development of regional economies. He pointed to five key tasks in the programme which were later taken up in more detail by the Premier Wen Jiabao (see following section), but singled out two major developments, the Qinghai-Tibet railway and the construction of tarmac roads in every rural county, as being of particular significance.

Wen Jiabao on five years of Western Development

In February 2005, Wen Jiabao, the Premier, put his own personal imprimatur on the Western Development project in formal 'written instructions' issued under the less-than-snappy title *Blaze new trails in a pioneering spirit and do solid work to continuously bring about a new situation in the large-scale development of the western region*. Reaffirming that the underlying reason for the programme was the need to bridge the gap between the increasingly prosperous east and the underdeveloped west, he ordered that priority be given to agriculture and related rural issues but also to the protection of the environment of the western regions.

The gap between east and west, which has widened dramatically since the inception of the 'reform and opening' strategy of 1978/1979, is illustrated by that fact that approximately two-thirds of Chinese citizens living below the poverty line (defined as having an annual income of less than RMB 625 or US$75) live in the rural areas of western China.[3]

The introduction to this lengthy document was essentially a progress report on the first five years of the Western Development project. The priority of the state has been macro-level development with the emphasis on planning guidance, major construction projects and the allocation of substantial amounts of funding. According to Prime Minister Wen, the central government had committed RMB 460 billion for construction and a sum of RMB 500 billion in respect of transfer payments and special subsidies. As a result, the growth of the economy in the western regions had accelerated. Total output value had increased by 8.5%, 8.8%, 10%, 11.3% and 12% in 2000, 2001, 2002, 2003 and 2004, respectively, and these reported growth rates were higher than those claimed for previous years.

The development and modernisation of the infrastructure, a fundamental requirement evident to even the most casual visitor to the region, has been a major priority. Wen Jiabao claimed that state investment in fixed assets in the west had experienced an annual increase of more than 20% on average, a figure that is substantially higher than for China as a whole. Work started on 60 key construction projects for which the total investment has been RMB 850 billion. These include projects to improve major road and rail communications, water control, and the transmission of electricity and natural gas from the west to the east. Whether this last item is of significant benefit to the western regions is a moot point, but it does indicate one of the key underlying reasons for the strategy: the integration of the economy of the west into the national economy to secure resources that are essential to China's economic development as a whole.

Priority was also given to the protection of the environment of the west, a particular concern of Wen Jiabao, with emphasis on the return to forest conditions of land that had been previously cleared for agriculture and the reafforestation of barren mountain sides and wasteland. These projects are all designed to have wider benefits, including control over the dust storms from the north and west that regularly plague Beijing and Tianjin, conservation of farming land, and reduction in water pollution in the area around the Three Gorges Dam and in the headwaters of China's major rivers. There has also been an attempt to transfer scientific facilities to the west and in this way to improve educational and medical provision in the region.

Wen Jiabao also stressed the collateral benefits of the Western Development strategy. Equipment and technology required for the construction of major projects in the west had to be sourced in eastern China. Conversely, as has already been noted, energy and both raw and processed materials have been transferred from the west to the east. The net result is the strengthening of economic interdependence between the west and the east of China, which the CCP regards as an essential prerequisite for the maintenance of social and political integration and stability. In Wen's own words, the project has 'made it possible for people of various ethnic groups across the country, especially the people in the western region, to see the hopes and prospects for the development of the western region'.[4] However, he went on to acknowledge that 'we should also soberly note that the development of the western region is faced with many difficulties and problems and that the tasks are still very arduous'.[5] Among these problems, he listed the weakness of the existing infrastructure, environmental degradation, and the serious shortage of water resources, education, and cultural backwardness and the shortage of trained and qualified personnel. The overall tone is bland and optimistic, and Wen avoided specific details, but he did acknowledge the difficulties faced.

Wen Jiabao presented the development of the west as a *sine qua non* for the development of China as a whole. He drew attention to the fact that the population of the west of China (as defined for the purposes of this project) was 30% of China's total, but that its GDP per capita has been only 40% of the level achieved in the east. Net income in the rural west is approximately 50% of that in the east and, of China's rural poor, over 60% are to be found in the west. In the west, there are still 20 million people who 'have yet to solve the problem of food and clothing'. It is this inequality and the potential dangers for China's overall development and stability that have prompted the central authorities to place such a great emphasis on, and devote such a high level of resources to, the development of the west. 'There will be no well-off life in the country without a well-off life in the western regions, and there will be no modernisation in the country without modernisation in the western region', Wen continued. He pointed to the potentially powerful combination of the advantages possessed by the west in terms of market resources and labour with the east's advantages in capital, technology, and skilled personnel.

Wen stated explicitly that the 'large-scale development of the western region will constitute an important guarantee for the lasting political stability of the whole country'. Drawing attention to the complexity of the ethnic make-up of the region (50 of China's recognised ethnic minorities have a significant presence in the west) and its strategic position on China's land borders with a total of 14 states, he articulated the importance of gradually narrowing the 'development gap between the regions' and consolidating 'the favourable situation featuring ethnic solidarity, social stability and border security'. He did not single out any particular region in the west, but it should be noted that in 1996, a key policy paper, *Politburo Document No.7*, identified Xinjiang as the region in which stability was most under threat and called for economic development and an improvement in the lives of the people as an important component of the policies of combating instability.[6]

In this February 2005 speech, Wen Jiabao identified five major tasks for the Western Development programme.

1   Resolving the three rural issues [*san nong*]: peasants *nongmin*, agriculture *nongye*, and rural areas *nongqu*. This is an issue that applies throughout China and not just in the underdeveloped western region, but rural problems are particularly acute in the west. He argued that priority should be given to farming, to raising the income of peasants by increasing efficiency, moderating the tax burden and enabling them to earn more as migrant workers or in non-agricultural occupations. Wen set 2007 as the target date for alleviating basic poverty.

2   Improving the environment, primarily by returning agricultural land to forest and grassland, while preserving and improving the living standards of peasants and herdsmen in these areas.

3   Improvement of the infrastructure with an emphasis on water conservancy and transport, notably the construction of the western section of the national highway network.

4   Development of local competitive economies 'with distinctive local features'. He highlighted energy, mining, tourism, and specialised agriculture including the growing and processing of plants for Chinese medicine, but also pointed to the need for developing new high technology industries in the area.

5   Social programmes including education and public health. He argued that high priority should be given to making the standard system of nine-year education compulsory throughout the region and eliminating illiteracy, which was still a major problem among the young and middle-aged. This presumably refers to literacy in Chinese rather than,

say, Tibetan or Uyghur. He also called for mechanisms to attract and retain able and well-qualified personnel from outside the region, which would of course increase the westward migration of Han Chinese people and could deny employment to members of local ethnic minorities.[7]

This final issue highlights crucial omissions from Wen's speech – and indeed, from most discussions of the Western Development programme. The western region is treated as a unity with no real account taken of the ethnic mixture and potential ethnic conflicts in the region.

Economic development and migration

Although the greatest internal migration of China's population has been from the underdeveloped west to the prosperous and rapidly industrialising coastal areas of the south and southeast, there has also been a smaller but significant movement of population in the other direction, towards the northwest and particularly to the most northwesterly region of China, Xinjiang. Indeed, unlike the southwards migration which began relatively recently and is still increasing, the migration to Xinjiang has continued, virtually without interruption, since 1949 and has historical antecedents that go back thousands of years.[8]

There has been migration from the prosperous east to the underdeveloped west for centuries, but until recently, it has been on a relatively small scale. The question of large-scale migration raises the question of whether the economic development of China's west can ever be merely a neutral device for the alleviation of poverty or whether it is necessarily a conscious political tool, designed to stabilise the western regions, which are on China's sensitive borders with Mongolia, Kazakhstan, Kyrgyzstan, Takijistan, Afghanistan, and the Indian sub-continent. Stabilisation necessarily means the suppression, by political or military means, of any social or political movements that demand autonomy or independence. Foreign capital will not be attracted to China's western regions if there is a constant danger of riots, demonstrations, or sabotage in the areas that are being developed. In the long term, Beijing hopes that economic development will guarantee stability, but in the short term, this stability may have to be imposed – and that is likely to lead to repression, and possibly even bloodshed.

One of the greatest fears of the non-Han populations living in the western regions is that their societies, languages, and cultures will be threatened and eventually extinguished by the migration of educated and better qualified Han 'pioneers' from China Proper. This type of migration is not new: Chinese were allowed to move into southern Xinjiang to open up new land for cultivation as early as 1831, and there was large-scale migration and settlement by demobilised troops after the region came under the control of the PRC in 1949. However, the scale of the proposed developments suggests that they cannot be carried out without the transfer of at least hundreds of thousands more people from eastern China, where there is already a floating migrant population of perhaps 100–120 million, people from farming backgrounds who have been forced off the land and are looking for employment.

A social and ethnic transformation of the western regions on this scale will be resented and resisted by the local people. They will struggle to protect their languages, whether these are Turkic, such as Uyghur written in the Arabic script, and other related languages spoken by their neighbours even further west in Central Asia, or Tibetan, related to Chinese only distantly and written in characters derived from a script that was devised to write the Sanskrit of ancient northern India. They will also struggle to protect their religions, Islam in the case of Xinjiang and the Hui Muslims of Ningxia and Lama Buddhism in Tibet, both of which were suppressed during the Cultural Revolution of the 1960s but have proved extremely resilient and are enjoying a popular revival since the 1980s. Migration from China Proper would also be likely expand the existing educated middle class, predominantly Han, and further deepen the conflict with ethnic minority groups unless measures were adopted to spread employment to the minority communities.

What appears on the surface to be a laudable policy of developing a backward region and reducing poverty has a hidden agenda, and this could lead to further conflict between Han and non-Han rather than the stability it is designed to produce. An earlier scheme to resettle subsistence farmers from other provinces to Qinghai, which was to be funded by the World Bank, collapsed in July 2000 when it was pointed out that the plan involved the resettlement of Han Chinese on land that is now in a Chinese province but was part of old Tibet and formerly known as Amdo. After concerns were expressed about the possible dilution of Tibetan culture in the region and allegations of cultural genocide, the World Bank attached new conditions which China rejected.

There have been similar plans to relocate farmers from the land around the Three Gorges Dam to the southern Xinjiang city of Kashgar, where almost the entire population is ethnic Uyghur, and to move poor Hui Muslims away from the farmlands which contain the tombs of the *shaykhs* who founded the Sufi orders to which they belong. These policies show deep insensitivity to cultural and religious differences and are likely to increase, rather than reduce, the risks of inter-ethnic conflict.

Migration and Xinjiang

Although the Western Development project is targeted at the west of China in general with no real discrimination between the constituent parts, the impact on various areas is likely to differ considerably, depending on the ethnic make-up of the particular region and the relationship between non-Han and Han peoples who live there. In the case of Xinjiang, there is already considerable disquiet and resentment at the preferential treatment that appears to be given to Han migrants in employment.[9]

The policy of the CCP's government after 1949 followed very closely the imperial policy of garrisoning the frontiers with soldier-farmers to protect the borders. Quasi-military, administrative, and production organisations were set up with the approval of the central government, and the region attracted large numbers of migrants from a variety of backgrounds.

The pattern of migrating groups into Xinjiang since 1949 is quite clear and falls into a number of discrete types, although they overlap to some extent. The first group were ex-servicemen who were demobilised or transferred to civilian employment and who were resettled in Xinjiang from the 1950s onwards. Because they were predominantly Han and because of their connections with the PLA and frequently with the CCP, they have become the backbone of Chinese society in Xinjiang, and Beijing has often taken their loyalty for granted. When PLA General Wang Zhen took control of Xinjiang in September 1949, he had at least 89,000 troops under his command and this was increased by a further 80,000 when the Nationalist Guomindang forces under Tao Zhiyue surrendered and put themselves under his command. Agricultural production in Xinjiang was barely adequate for the indigenous population, let alone an occupying force, so the soldiers of the PLA were required to produce their own food supplies. During the early 1950s, there were over 100,000 troops engaged in agriculture and related occupations while still retaining their defence capability. This was the origin of the XPCC. During the 1950s, the original military colonists were reinforced by demobilised troops from other areas, including the northeast: these were often specialists with technical knowledge that was relevant to the key tasks of border protection and cultivation.

As Sino-Soviet relations grew more tense during the late 1950s and early 1960s, border security became an even higher priority, and more troops, specialist cadres, and demobilised ex-servicemen from central China were deployed on the frontiers including Xinjiang. This trend continued throughout the Cultural Revolution period and into the 1980s, and many brought their families and settled more or less permanently in the region. During the 1950s, military transfers amounted to perhaps 10,000 a year,[10] but this number reduced to 1,000 a year in the 1960s and slowed down even further in the 1970s and 1980s. Nevertheless, the total migration of military and military-related personnel to Xinjiang over the past 50 years is approximately 300,000. They also found themselves in the most powerful and influential positions in Xinjiang society and acquired a reputation for being both 'red' and tough.

The second group consists of criminals, who were brought into Xinjiang for 'reform through labour' [*laogai*], and political prisoners. As part of their sentences, they were required to work in the prisons or on the *laogai* farms for no, or little, wages, both during and after their sentences, and this provided a source of cheap labour for Xinjiang, although these labourers were far less reliable politically than the demobilised troops. This type of migration began as early as May 1951 when the Xinjiang Military Region accepted 10,766 prisoners from central China.[11] In 1954, a total of 27,643 criminals and 7,116 who had finished serving their sentences were allocated to the farms run by the XPCC [the *bingtuan*]. This figure rose to 97,673 in 1956 and 123,000 in 1975, and during the campaign against hooliganism in 1983, many serious criminals from the cities of eastern China were transferred to Xinjiang.

The supply of labour provided by demobilised soldiers and criminals was inadequate for the needs of the developing border region, and plans were drawn up to transfer more people. A campaign in the mid-1950s to 'Assist the border regions and protect the motherland' was followed by a central directive that was issued in August 1958 at the height of the Great Leap Forward to encourage the voluntary migration of young people to the borders and the minority areas to reduce the population pressure on the densely populated regions of Anhui, Jiangsu, Hubei, and the Shanghai area. It was estimated that two million young people would move and hundreds of thousands did indeed migrate in the late 1950s and early 1960s: the migrants were mostly peasants, but they also included students, workers, and unemployed people from the towns and cities. Many of the migrants, particularly those who came from the rural areas, were members of the CCP or the CYL. This flood of enthusiastic and patriotic 'educated youth' [*zhishi qingnian*] and 'youth supporting the border regions' [*zhibian qingnian*] continued until the mid-1960s, when it was subsumed into the nationwide *xiafang* campaign of transferring urban young people to the countryside, a process which continued during the Cultural Revolution.

In addition to those who moved westward under official government programmes, there were thousands of *mangliu*, or migrants who entered Xinjiang without government sanction. Statistics for what were essentially illegal migrants are necessarily unreliable, but *Xinjiang Daily* reported that there were at least 10,000 in Urumqi alone in July 1957 and the numbers increased dramatically as a result of the Great Leap Forward, with peasants moving west to escape the collectivisation or the famines. Xinjiang, and particularly the XPCC, was largely shielded from both the famine and collectivisation because of its special position.

The successors to these *mangliu* were the non-local labour [*wailai gong*, who were recruited to work in the west of China from the beginning of the 'reform and opening' period in 1979–1980]. The difference was that the new migrants had official sanction. There was a desperate need for new blood: most of the original demobilised military and ex-prisoners had reached retirement age and in many cases their children did not want to follow in their footsteps and continue to farm and open new land. Although far more attention has been paid to the migration of *wailai gong* labour from the central provinces to the southeast, where the economic boom has been most apparent, the exodus towards the northwest has also been extremely important in this period.

In 1983, the non-resident population, usually classified as 'mobile' or 'floating' population [*liudong renkou*] in Xinjiang was 179,100[12] and between 1981 and 1989, 625,800 people are recorded as having moved there from other provinces, an average annual entry of 78,000, many of them finding work in the service sector including low-level repair and maintenance jobs. In the 1990s, there was an upsurge in migration to Xinjiang. At the same time, the demand for labour changed and migrants found work in other sectors. These included agriculture (including the farms run by the XPCC), mining, and the oil industry, but also construction, handicrafts, and trade at all levels. As many as 500,000 migrants were travelling to Xinjiang each year: of these, perhaps 100,000 would become long-term residents, while the remaining 400,000 were typically short-term workers for picking cotton and other seasonal jobs and many are employed by the XPCC. Although the work is arduous and working conditions far from ideal, the potential income is sufficient to attract such large numbers of mainly rural people seeking work.

Other forms of relocation have included migration for marriage and family reasons, including the directed transfer of large numbers of young women from central China in the 1950s to redress the negative female-male balance of population in Xinjiang. There have also been transfers of cadres and specialist scientific and technical staff to assist in the development of the region, and some overseas Chinese who have 'returned' to China from Indonesia, Malaysia, Vietnam, and elsewhere, either as voluntary migrants or refugees, have been settled in Xinjiang.[13]

Migration to Xinjiang – and indeed, to other border and minority regions – is therefore far from being a new phenomenon. The migration that is being encouraged under the Western Development programme represents a modification of the existing pattern rather than a new initiative. However, the crude migration statistics obscure the important issue of the impact of migration on the ethnic composition of Xinjiang. Although there are no precise figures on the ethnic origin of the migrants, by common consensus they are overwhelmingly Han, as would be expected from their provinces of origin. The impact of this migration over the years since 1949 was to increase the Han population of Xinjiang to a total of at least five million by 1982. In percentage terms, the proportion of Han in Xinjiang has risen from 6.7% in 1949 to 10% in 1954, 28% in 1960, and 40% in 1970 – a level at which it remained for some years, partly because Uyghurs and other ethnic minority communities were exempt from the strict application of the one-child policy. The impact on the ethnic composition of Xinjiang has been significant, although it has not been homogeneous. Migration has been greatest to the areas of greatest industrialisation such as the oilfields in the north of the region, and much of southern Xinjiang has received a relatively low level of Han immigration.[14]

Oil and gas pipelines

As the Chinese economy continues to develop, energy – always a key component – has begun to loom even larger in the equation. China became a net importer of oil in 1993, and in 2003, it became the second largest country in terms of energy consumption, second only to the United States. The availability and security of its energy supply has preoccupied economic planners for decades. In the 1960s, the northeast was the major source of oil, but hopes are now pinned on what are believed to be colossal oil and natural gas resources in the Tarim Basin in Xinjiang, some of which have already been tapped. These reserves, above all other considerations, are the reason why Beijing is not willing to countenance any suggestion of independence for Xinjiang, and why it has clamped down on any hints of an Uyghur independence movement. To ensure security of supply, it must maintain political control over the region – and that requires a degree of social stability.

The importance of this factor is illustrated by the troubled history of the West-East Pipeline project, a major undertaking that was planned and executed by Chinese and foreign companies. This complex venture began in July 2002 with a total investment of over RMB 140 billion (US$16.9 billion) in a plan to transport natural gas from the Tarim Basin in western Xinjiang and the Changqing gas field in Shaanxi Province to Shanghai, the nerve centre of China's developing economy and a gas-guzzler of a city. The pipeline runs from Xinjiang through Gansu, Ningxia, Shaanxi, and Shanxi, which contain some of China's most challenging terrain, and onwards through Henan, Anhui, and Jiangsu to Shanghai and parts of Zhejiang province. When fully operational, the pipeline will supply 12 billion cubic metres of gas to the Shanghai region. The Changqing gas field in Shaanxi was initially the main source of supply, and this eastern section of the project was completed in October 2003 when trial operations were inaugurated. Supplies from Changqing were due to be replaced by gas from the Tarim Basin on 1 December 2004, and this western section, which runs from Lunnan in Xinjiang to Jingbian in Shaanxi, was able to begin transmission of gas on 6 September 2004. The formal opening of the pipeline was marked by Jiang Zemin, the President of China, on 1 October 2004, China's National Day, when he pressed a button at the gas compression facility in Jingbian to open valves controlling both the western and eastern sections of the pipeline, symbolising the full operation of the project. The intention was that commercial supplies of gas would be flowing by 1 January 2005. In his speech, Jiang Zemin declared that the opening of the pipeline would be a boon for both the east and the west of China. The east, which is desperate for energy, would get the supplies of gas that it needed, while the project would also be a boost to the economic development of the west as that region would be able to supply gas which would otherwise have to be purchased elsewhere.[15]

On 27 December 2004, the National Development and Reform Commission announced that commercial operations would in fact begin on 30 December.[16] By this time, the joint venture between PetroChina and the foreign companies with which it had been working on the creation of the pipeline had been dissolved as the two sides were unable to reach agreement on an investment strategy that was acceptable to all parties. Although the details of the disagreement have not been made public, among the issues at stake were the distribution of gas reserves and the length of the joint-venture contract. PetroChina had brought in foreign specialists in 2001 because, at the time, it wished to share the costs of investment in the project and the risks involved in what was one of the largest and strategically most sensitive projects of the reform period, but by late 2004, it had come to the conclusion that there was no longer any need to employ either foreign capital or foreign expertise, possibly because the scale of recent finds of gas reserves in northwestern China had given them confidence that they could go it alone. The companies that led the two foreign consortiums, Royal Dutch Shell and ExxonMobil, were notified of the termination of the agreement on 2 August 2004.[17] Members of the foreign consortiums were disappointed that they had been cut out of the deal at such short notice and at such a late stage after they had contributed to the planning and the engineering for several years. They had also contributed to programmes to alleviate poverty in China's west and environmental improvement work as part of what they conceived as their corporate and social responsibility.

The importance of this project, both for its economic and strategic value and for its role as a symbol of national development, can be adduced from the fact that the announcement was made on China's National Day. Although it was a grave disappointment for the foreign partners, it is perhaps hardly surprising that such a strategically important project, which is central to China's energy security and which has profound implications for China's economic development, should be brought entirely under the control of the government at a time when national sentiment is rising in China.

Regional autonomy and the ethnic dimension

Official statements on the Western Development policy have in general ignored or played down the ethnic dimension. However, *Regional Autonomy for Ethnic Minorities in China*, a White Paper issued by the Information Office of the State Council on 28 February 2005, indicated clearly that the government was still planning to rely on the existing structures of regional autonomy to manage this issue. The document reiterates the standard argument that of the 56 ethnic groups identified in China, the 55 – other than the Han – are 'relatively small, so they are customarily referred to as "ethnic minorities"'. It quotes the fifth national census carried out in 2000, in which the total population of the 55 ethnic minority groups was recorded as 104.49 million, which is 8.41% of the total population of the PRC. Regional autonomy it goes on to say is 'critical to enhancing the relationship of equality, unity and mutual assistance among different ethnic groups, to upholding national unification, and to accelerating the development of places where regional autonomy is practiced and promoting their progress'. The White Paper draws on the history of customary rule by non-Han communities during the imperial period and specifically mentions the system in Xinjiang under which local *begs*, leaders of Uyghur communities, were responsible for local government. It also praises Hui and inner Mongolian resistance to the Japanese invasion while castigating the separatists of Eastern Turkestan, Tibet, and Manzhouguo, thus clearly defining those who are inside and those who are outside the project of national unity represented by the CCP and the PRC. It acknowledges that 'the level of economic and social development in these regions [ethnic minority regions] is relatively backward'. Section I of the White Paper concludes by arguing that:

> Regional autonomy for ethnic minorities enables them to bring into play their regional advantages and promote exchanges and cooperation between minority areas and other areas and consequently quickens the pace of modernisation both in the minority areas and the country as a whole and helps achieve the common development of all regions and prosperity for all ethnic groups.

The development of ethnic autonomous areas is linked explicitly with the Western Development strategy in Section IV of the White Paper:

> To accelerate the development of China's western regions and ethnic autonomous areas, the Chinese government launched a grand strategy for the development of western China in 2000, which covers five autonomous regions, 27 autonomous prefectures and 83 of the 120 autonomous counties (banners). Three other autonomous prefectures enjoy the preferential policies that the state has adopted for the western regions.

This reinforces the impression that the development of the economies of minority areas and the promotion of prosperity of all ethnic groups are seen as key priorities for the state, and the White Paper proceeds to list a series of ten key measures designed to achieve these objectives:

1 *Speeding up development in ethnic minority areas*. The Western Development strategy is clearly the most significant example of this.
2 *Infrastructure projects*. Notable among these are the West-East Gas Pipeline, the West-East Power Transmission Project, and the Qinghai-Tibet Railway. Projects in Tibet and transport projects in general were singled out for special emphasis.
3 *Financial support for autonomous areas*. Subsidies and special funding for minority areas have been in place since 1955 and were maintained after the financial reforms of 1994, with additional funding being made available to minority areas in 1995.
4 *Environmental protection measures*. Environmental concerns are one of the major platforms of Premier Wen Jiabao.
5 *Educational projects*. Universal nine-year compulsory education remains a key target rather than a reality for many communities in the ethnic autonomous areas, and this is the responsibility of the Compulsory Education Project for Impoverished Areas. Special provision has been made to increase the number of ethnic minority students in universities and colleges by positive discrimination including the acceptance of lower entrance requirements.
6 *Poverty alleviation*. The desperate need for action on poverty in the ethnic minority regions is indicated by the decision of the state to establish the Food and Clothing Fund for Impoverished Ethnic Minority Areas in 1990 and the seven-year 'programme for delivering 80 million people from poverty' that was launched in 1994. The 'More Prosperous Frontiers and Better-off People' programme designed to address the problems of poor infrastructure and food and clothing supplies in the impoverished minority regions was initiated in 2000.
7 *Social welfare*. The state invested RMB 1.37 billion in public health and related projects in the minority areas. Radio and television coverage were also extended to these regions as and when electricity became available.
8 *External relations*. Wider access to trade with both neighbouring countries across the borders and neighbouring counties within China was encouraged by decentralising decision making to local enterprises.
9 *Twinning*. Developing regions are twinned with more developed regions in a practice that dates back to the late 1970s. Western regions received aid from the more advanced east.
10 *Preferential fiscal policies*. Preferential policies on loans and taxation for ethnic minority businesses were introduced in June 1997.

The official position is that the 'system and practice of China's regional ethnic autonomy have been immensely successful'. The White Paper rehearses statistics which demonstrate that the autonomous areas have enjoyed rapid economic growth. Living standards, as measured by per-capita net income and housing conditions, have improved. The infrastructure has improved. Traditional cultures have been protected and promoted, and this claim is supported by the publication of books in ethnic minority languages, the creation of computer software for use with these languages, and the establishment of research institutes specialising in the art, literature, and other cultural relics of the minorities. The level of education in the minority areas is said to have been raised significantly with increased enrolment. Similarly, health services have been improved. Foreign trade and tourism are also at an all-time high in the minority areas.

The evidence adduced is impressive, and it is clear that many improvements have been made in the infrastructure of the western regions, the most obvious being the construction of roads and the development of facilities for transporting water to the arid zones. These statistics are not always supported by independent studies. It is also significant that the issue of ethnic minority culture is at the end of the White Paper, giving the impression that it has been added as an afterthought.

Western Development, nation-building, and ethnicity

The Western Development programme contributes to the ongoing nation-building project of the CCP by addressing the economic base rather than the cultural and ethnic superstructure. The assumption, and it is usually an unspoken assumption, is that if the western region of China can be developed and brought up to an economic level that is the same as, or close to, that of the east and southeast, the problems of social unrest and ethnic separatism will either disappear or become insignificant.

The programme itself concentrates almost entirely on the economic benefits of integrating the underdeveloped west and the developed east, on the assumption that the development will benefit all citizens of China, whereas there is considerable evidence that not only are the benefits greater for the east, but that the western populations are aware of this and resent it. It makes passing mention of the ethnic differences of large parts of the western region, but the very definition of the west, to include Sichuan and Shaanxi provinces and the city of Chongqing, indicates that there has been an attempt to dilute ethic and cultural differences by subsuming them in a wider economic model. The particular problems of the border regions of Tibet, Xinjiang, and Inner Mongolia, where there are real or potential movements of cultural and ethnic nationalism, are not completely ignored, but they are minimised by this approach.

The tried and tested system of creating autonomous regions, prefectures, counties, and banners has been relied on to deal with these problems. It can be argued that these have been remarkably successful from the point of view of the central government in Beijing. All of the border regions have remained within the PRC since 1949; the revolts in Tibet in 1959 and the insurgency in Xinjiang since 1980 have been defeated and contained respectively; Inner Mongolian nationalism remains relatively passive. The system has created a political elite which includes members of the ethnic minorities, usually subordinate to their more senior Han Chinese colleagues, educated and trained by the CCP, and owing their careers to the Party. This elite has managed the difficult relations between the border regions and Beijing with some success.

The autonomous areas were created during the era of a tightly controlled political structure and a centralised and planned economy that was subject to rigid state planning. It is not at all clear whether they can meet the challenges of an economy that is opening up and is allowing the creation of a new private sector and an urban middle class. The Beijing-trained ethnic minority elites are in many cases coming under considerable pressure to choose between loyalty to the CCP and allegiance to their own communities.

The success or failure of the Western Development programme will depend on whether it can manage the growing ethnic tensions that are becoming apparent as the economy of the west develops and its people have more and more contact with both the rest of China and neighbouring countries. At present the indications are that although the economic development is showing signs of success, it is not addressing the ethnic issues but rather is ignoring them in the hope and expectation that, as they become prosperous, minority communities will be less concerned about their cultural and national identities and aspirations.

Notes

1 Xinhua (BBC Monitoring) 20 June 2000.
2 Xinhua (BBC Monitoring) 18 November 2004.
3 Xinhua (BBC Monitoring) 4 February 2005.
4 Xinhua (BBC Monitoring) 4 February 2005.
5 Xinhua (BBC Monitoring) 4 February 2005.
6 Chinese Communist Party Central Committee *Central Committee Document No. 7 1996: Record of the Meeting of the Standing Committee of the Political Bureau of the Chinese Communist Party Concerning the Maintenance of Stability in Xinjiang.*
7 Xinhua (BBC Monitoring) 4 February 2005.
8 Delia Davin *Internal Migration in Contemporary China* New York: St Martin's Press, 1999.
9 Michael Dillon *Xinjiang: China's Muslim Far Northwest* London: RoutledgeCurzon, 2004 and *Xinjiang in the Twenty-First Century: Islam, Ethnicity and Resistance* Abingdon, UK: Routledge, 2018.
10 Zhang Feng 'Qu da Xibei: 1949 yilai Xinjiang yimin' (Head for the Great North-West: Xinjiang Migration Since 1949) in Yu Zhen and Dawa Cairen (eds.) *Zhongguo minzu guanxi he minzu fazhan* (Ethnic Relations and Ethnic Development in China) Beijing: Minzu chubanshe, 2003, pp. 76–405.
11 Zhang Feng 'Qu da Xibei: 1949 yilai Xinjiang yimin' (Head for the Great North-West: Xinjiang Migration Since 1949) in Yu Zhen and Dawa Cairen (eds.) *Zhongguo minzu guanxi he minzu fazhan* (Ethnic Relations and Ethnic Development in China) Beijing: Minzu chubanshe, 2003, pp. 76–405.
12 Zhang Feng 'Qu da Xibei: 1949 yilai Xinjiang yimin' (Head for the Great North-West: Xinjiang Migration Since 1949) in Yu Zhen and Dawa Cairen (eds.) *Zhongguo minzu guanxi he minzu fazhan* (Ethnic Relations and Ethnic Development in China) Beijing: Minzu chubanshe, 2003, pp. 76–405.
13 Zhang Feng 'Qu da Xibei: 1949 yilai Xinjiang yimin' (Head for the Great North-West: Xinjiang Migration since 1949) in Yu Zhen and Dawa Cairen (eds.) *Zhongguo minzu guanxi he minzu fazhan* (Ethnic Relations and Ethnic Development in China) Beijing: Minzu chubanshe, 2003, pp. 76–405. Although described as 'returned', they might never have previously been to China, from where their ancestors had emigrated.
14 Zhang Feng 'Qu da Xibei: 1949 yilai Xinjiang yimin' (Head for the Great North-West: Xinjiang Migration Since 1949) in Yu Zhen and Dawa Cairen (eds.) *Zhongguo minzu guanxi he minzu fazhan* (Ethnic Relations and Ethnic Development in China) Beijing: Minzu chubanshe, 2003, pp. 76–405.
15 Xinhua (BBC Monitoring) 1 October 2004.
16 Xinhua (BBC Monitoring) 27 December 2004.
17 *SCMP* Hong Kong 4 August 2004.

13 Belt and Road Initiative

The Belt and Road Initiative (BRI) is more formally One Belt One Road [*yidai yilu*], being an abbreviation of the Silk Road Economic Belt and the Twenty-first Century Maritime Silk Road. The programme was revealed in the autumn of 2013 during visits by Xi Jinping to Kazakhstan and Indonesia. In May 2015, it was incorporated into 'Made in China 2025', a strategic plan for upgrading the manufacturing capacity of China's industries to produce goods and services of higher quality and higher value. Essentially, it was designed to invest Chinese capital in the infrastructure of neighbouring countries – initially in Asia to the west and east of China – but subsequently extended to Europe.[1]

First Beijing Forum, May 2017

International support was solicited for the first Belt and Road Forum in May 2017, which attracted leading political figures from 29 countries. It was a major diplomatic and media success for Xi Jinping although it did not produce many new proposals, apart from an announcement by President Xi that China would transfer a further RMB 100 billion (US$14.5 billion) into the project. The participants signed a joint communiqué pledging their allegiance to globalisation and free trade, and 68 states or international organisations signed bilateral agreements within the Belt and Road wrapper. Xi Jinping emphasised the alignment of Belt and Road with development strategies of China's neighbours, principally the Eurasian Economic Union led by Moscow and ASEAN (the Association of Southeast Asian Nations). His insistence on the need for regional and world peace and security as an essential prerequisite for the success of the project did not entirely mask the geopolitical thinking behind the project which would place China as the central kingdom in Eurasia. India's failure to send representatives indicated New Delhi's concerns about the prospect of this development.[2]

After Davos, 2019

The initiative has been controversial because of the control China could exert over foreign economies and the costs to those economies, including high interest rates on loans issued by the Asian Infrastructure Investment Bank and the separate Silk Road Fund, dedicated to investing in businesses under the Belt and Road Initiative. Chinese pronouncements on the initiative became more muted; at the World Economic Forum in Davos, Switzerland in January 2019, the panel that focused on the initiative was addressed by relatively low-ranking officials.

These criticisms were vigorously rejected during the 'Two Meetings' of March 2019. At the opening session of the NPC on Monday 4 March, Zhang Yesui, a former Deputy Foreign Minister, insisted that 'China attaches great importance to the problem of debt sustainability and will neither force others to cooperate on projects nor create any traps'. He pointed out that a total of 157 governments or international organisations had committed to contracts under the Belt and Road Initiative. This rebuttal was reinforced by Foreign Minister Wang Yi at a press conference the following Friday, arguing that far from being a 'debt trap' or a 'geopolitical tool', it provided 'an opportunity for many countries to develop together' and cited the number of agreements as 'a vote of support and confidence'. Wang's comments were understood to be in preparation for the second summit of the Belt and Road Initiative in Beijing in April 2019.[3]

The extension of the initiative to Europe obliged the European Union to consider its position in some haste. Towards the end of March 2019, President Emmanuel Macron of France received Xi Jinping in Paris for the final leg of Xi's European tour and invited Chancellor Angela Merkel of Germany and Jean-Paul Juncker, the President of the European Commission, to join them: their meeting resulted in an affirmation that all were committed to 'multilateralism and the pursuit of mutual trust'. Concerns about China's potential influence in European economies had been heightened when Italy became the first G7 country to join the BRI project when it signed a memorandum of understanding with Beijing on March 23, only days before this meeting. Michele Geraci, Undersecretary of State at Italy's Ministry of Economic Development, who had lived in China for ten years, insisted to the *Global Times* that projects entered into under the BRI programme were 'no different from those of the World Bank, Asian Development Bank and other international organizations'. Chinese officials saw Italy as opening the way for other European countries to participated in the scheme. Jean-Paul Juncker had previously referred to China as a 'strategic rival' to the European Union, but hastened to reassure Xi that this description was complimentary and referred to the strength of China's economic growth. This was in marked contrast to the view emanating from the United States which, with more bluster than analysis, dismissed BRI as a 'vanity project'.[4]

Other countries formerly supportive of the initiative were becoming more wary as the financial implications became clearer. Work was halted on a dam project in Nepal; after Mahathir Mohammed returned to power, Malaysia suspended BRI projects valued at US$40 billion, although construction was resumed on 12 April 2019 after the successful conclusion of year-long negotiations of a cost reduction in what was seen as one of the flagship BRI projects; the government of Myanmar asked Beijing to review the price of constructing a deep-water port; and both Pakistan and Sri Lanka were struggling with the repayment of loans to China. Chinese officials and investors in Indonesia had to overcome cultural barriers that resulted from clashes between their own assumptions of a hierarchical business environment, while Indonesian businesses rely on the development of cordial relationships between management and workforce. Chinese managers, most of whom would only be based in Indonesia for short tours, rarely acquired a sophisticated understanding of these cultural differences. Memories of the Indonesian massacre of the Chinese minority in the country during the 1960s contributed to resentment and suspicion of Chinese involvement in the local economy.

At a meeting with Xi Jinping on the sidelines of the June 2019 G20 summit in Osaka, Japan, Indonesia's President Jokoo Widodo asked that China establish a special fund for Jakarta within its Belt and Road Initiative, with the prospect of China being offered projects worth US$91 billion. Indonesia, which has the largest economy in Southeast Asia, has only benefited in a limited way from the BRI initiative, largely because of its reluctance to expose the Jakarta government to unsustainable debt with China and its insistence that loans be on a business-to-business basis.[5]

In Pakistan, the issue of Chinese investment in the port at Gwadar on the coast of the Arabian Sea close to the border with Iran was highlighted by an attack on the city's Zaver Pearl Continental Hotel during Ramadan in May 2019. The port of Gwadar was a key component of the China-Pakistan Economic Corridor element of the BRI and included a system of rail and road links and gas pipelines, including overland links to the Xinjiang city of Kashgar. The liberal English-language daily *Pakistan Today* reported that the attack was carried out by militants of the Balochistan Liberation Army (BLA) which had previously targeted the Chinese consulate in Karachi in November 2018, killing four people; the group maintained that Chinese involvement in Balochistan was not in the interests of the Baloch people whose language is related to the Persian of neighbouring Iran. The BLA maintained that Chinese and other investors were killed in the assault on the hotel – which was normally subject to the highest security as Chinese officials stayed there – although Pakistani sources insisted that the only casualties were a member of the Special Security Division commando team responding to the assault, four hotel staff, and the militants.[6]

As *South China Morning Post* put it, 'China's ambitious "Belt and Road Initiative" faces a host of difficulties – ranging from the complexities of local politics, geopolitical rivalries, fears of rising debts and commercial viability – even among neighbouring states which openly support the initiative'.[7]

Second Beijing Forum, April 2019

This second summit, a three-day event beginning on 25 April and following on from the 2017 forum, was intended to celebrate and promote Xi Jinping's Belt and Road Initiative but faced a more critical reception than its predecessor. As China extended the reach of Belt and Road eastwards towards Europe, there were increasing concerns about the financial costs to countries benefiting from Chinese investment, and Beijing was accused of using 'debt-trap diplomacy' to bind countries into dependant relationships with Beijing. Wang Yi, China's Foreign Minster, insisted that 'The "Belt and Road Initiative" (BRI) is not a geopolitical tool but a platform for cooperation',[8] but this was treated with scepticism. The level of concern was indicated by the number of governments that did not send representatives, notably Turkey, India, Sri Lanka, Poland, and Spain: the United States indicated that its delegation would be at a low level. There were serious proposals that the BRI should be internationalised and institutionalised so that it was not simply an initiative controlled by China, but there was no indication that Beijing was willing to countenance such a move.

Beijing has, however, rephrased some of its rhetoric on the BRI, insisting that, in addition to its role as a wrapper for international financial investment projects, it is also a vehicle for aid and humanitarian assistance programmes. Officials announced during the conference that international concerns about 'debt-trap diplomacy' would be addressed in the final communiqué.

As the forum opened, it was announced that the stalled East Coast Rail Link funded by China in Malaysia was 'back on track', although the financial arrangements had been changed considerably. In spite of the doubts and the criticisms, Beijing succeeded in ending the forum on a triumphant note. At a final press conference, Xi Jinping announced that 37 nations had agreed to sign a joint communiqué on cooperation with the BRI – eight more than at the 2017 inaugural forum – and deals valued at US$64 billion, which were listed in an annexe to the communiqué, had been concluded during the conference.[9]

After the second Belt and Road Forum, Wang Huiyao, founder of the Centre for China and Globalisation, a non-governmental think tank based in Beijing, argued in May 2019 that the BRI initiative had been misunderstood and needed rebranding or redefining, and made more 'multilateral', to dispel misunderstandings that had arisen. The global spread of China's trade and the protectionist response had created challenges that required addressing to define more clearly the scope of the BRI and secure its long-term success and sustainability of BRI. Wang proposed an international committee to assist the transformation of the initiative from a bilateral to a multi-lateral approach and counter allegations of Sinocentrism; closer engagement with international organisations, including the World Bank; and taking part in the Paris Club of creditor nations to help address allegations that the BRI is forcing poorer nations in to a debt trap. China is not a member of the Paris Club, but Chinese organisations have participated on an ad hoc basis. The Belt and Road Forum, Wang argued, could in the future rotate between global cities 'such as Geneva, Paris and Singapore' to demonstrate the openness of the programme and encourage wider participation by investors: it could even be rebranded as the 'Belt and Road International Development Plan'.[10]

Most of the expected world leaders attended the forum, but there were notable exceptions, notably India because of concerns about the China-Pakistan Economic Corridor. The Belt and Road Initiative has been most effective in the immediate periphery of China, particularly in Southeast Asia; of the ten heads of ASEAN states, only Indonesian President Joko Widodo, who was facing an election, failed to attend. Central Asian states were similarly supportive, with only Turkmenistan – the most distant from China – not attending. There was also genuine interest in Africa and the Middle East, and among the smaller countries of Europe. The two main areas where it had least impact were South Asia and East Asia, where only Mongolia was represented at the highest level.

Critics argued that, seven years after its inception, there was growing resistance to the Belt and Road Initiative. Some blamed overemphasis on the Maritime Silk Road element at the expense of the overland Silk Road Economic belt, which was linked to China's determination to strengthen its overall international maritime position. More generally, there were indications that the concentration on SOEs and infrastructure investment was limiting acceptance and that the entire initiative had drifted from economic projects to larger-scale geopolitical ambitions.[11]

Concern continued over the potential of BRI projects to generate sufficient revenue to clear the debts incurred by participant countries. This was exacerbated by the impact of the Covid-19 pandemic in the first half of 2020 as restrictions on travel and social distancing impeded progress in many ventures.[12]

Notes

1 Bruno Maçaes *Belt and Road: A Chinese World Order* London: Hurst, 2018 is a useful summary of the project at an early stage.
2 Shannon Tiezzi 'What Did China Accomplish at the Belt and Road Forum?' *The Diplomat* 16 May 2017.
3 *SCMP* 5 March, 8 March 2019; *New York Times* 22 January 2019.
4 *China Daily* 23 March 2019; *SCMP* 1 April 2019; *Global Times* 13 May 2019.
5 *SCMP* 3 May 2019; *FT* 13, 14 April 2019.
6 BBC News 11 May 2019; *Pakistan Today* 11 May 2019; *SCMP* 16, 18 May 2019.
7 *SCMP* 26 March, 5 July 2019.

8 Cao Dahsng 'Wang: BRI a Platform for Cooperation, Not Geopolitical Tool or Debt Trap' *China Daily* 19 April 2019.
9 *SCMP* 24, 25, 27 April 2019; *Guardian* 25 April 2019; Xinhuanet 27 April 2019.
10 *SCMP* 3 May 2019.
11 Shannon Tiezi 'Who Is (and Who Isn't) Attending China's 2nd Belt and Road Forum?' *The Diplomat* 27 April 2019; Chan Kung and Yu (Tony) Pan 'How China's Belt and Road Initiative Went Astray' *The Diplomat* 7 May 2020.
12 *SCMP* 19 July 2020.

Part 4
Society

14 Social change

Rural reforms and urbanisation

Until the late twentieth century, because China was a predominantly rural society, it was social change in the countryside that had the greatest impact on China's overall development. From the 1980s, urbanisation and industrialisation were accompanied by a mass migration from the countryside to the cities which radically changed the nature of Chinese society. In 2020, only about 40% of the population of China is classified as rural, although many urban residents maintain ties with their origins in small towns and villages.[1]

Social impact of land reform and collectivisation

During the implementation of the radical policies of land reform and collectivisation in the 1950s, the old pre-revolutionary rural social structure was attacked and, to all appearances, dismantled. In its place were installed social organisations that could be controlled more effectively by the CCP's bureaucratic and military machine. The history of these developments was outlined in Chapter 8.

Land reform, the confiscation of land in the possession of landlords and the wealthier peasant landowners and redistribution to the poorest farmers, was part of the CCP's successful strategy in the countryside during the 1940s. By the time it came to power as the government of the PRC in October 1949, the land reform process was already well advanced, and the Party and its cadres had amassed considerable experience in its implementation. The priority of the new government was to consolidate and codify the practice and, in many cases, to restrain overzealous activists who were redistributing land and killing people who they alleged were landowners with little regard to their status or conduct. The legislation designed to carry out this policy was the Agrarian Reform Law, which was promulgated in 1950. The general principles were expressed in Article 1 of the law:

> The land ownership system of feudal exploitation by the landlord class shall be abolished, and the system of peasant landownership shall be introduced in order to set free the rural productive forces, develop agricultural production and thus pave the way for New China's industrialisation.[2]

The campaign to implement land reform, led by work teams, was designed to break down the traditional social patterns of dominance, deference, and interdependence that had characterised rural China for centuries. Work teams identified landlords and sought to isolate them from the poorer members of their extended families. Landlord families often found ways to reduce their apparent standard of living dramatically so that they seemed to be no wealthier than middle-ranking peasants: some killed and consumed their livestock, rather than have cattle and sheep calculated as part of their wealth; others deliberately discontinued their customary participation in traditional social or charitable activities that clearly indicated their status as landlords. 'The old village institutions of clan, temple and secret society had been replaced by the new, which assumed their education, mediatory and economic functions'. A new elite of village cadres from the poorest peasant backgrounds emerged and the members of this new elite owed their positions entirely to the CCP.[3]

The policy of land reform led to collectivisation, but what were the social consequences of this economic policy, and what precisely did collectivisation mean for the families involved? In most cases, there may have been little physical displacement, if any: peasants continued to live where they had always lived, and they farmed the same fields. The changes that did take place were essentially in the management of agriculture and its impact on rural local government. Organisational changes ensured that control of agriculture was firmly in the hands of local supporters of the CCP. With the move to larger collective units, decision making was further divorced from the farming families so that planning could be carried out over a wider area. The names attached to the sub-divisions – brigades and divisions – are indicative of the changes in the style of management. They are essentially military terms and would have been familiar to peasants who had served in the PLA or even in the old GMD army. They certainly reflected the organisational style with which the PLA work teams that had spearheaded land reform would have been comfortable. The rhetoric that accompanied the push towards collectivisation was also frequently militaristic, although it could also be construed as patriotic or nationalistic. What might appear to have been the militarisation of the Chinese countryside was a movement towards the centralisation of decision making and control by the CCP and its local government.

After problems were encountered in the management of cooperatives, there was a move to decentralise the decision-making process and return a degree of control to the lower levels of management, but this tension between centralisation and decentralisation remained a constant feature of cooperatives, and of the even larger People's Communes that were to follow in 1958.

Demise of the People's Communes

The People's Communes were part of a broader politico-economic strategy devised by Mao, the Great Leap Forward [*da yuejin*], which was an attempt to galvanise China into speeding up its economic development and catching up with the West. Inspection tours in outlying regions of China, after the fashion of some of the Qing emperors, were an important part of Mao's style of leadership. They enabled him to claim that he was acting on the basis of first-hand knowledge of local conditions, and also gave him the opportunity to broaden his personal support by winning round local Party leaders to his own radical policies. At the beginning of August 1958, Mao was undertaking one of these tours in Hebei, Henan, and Shandong, three provinces in north-central China. While in rural Shandong, he discussed the creation of agricultural cooperatives with local Party leaders and said that, 'People's Communes are good. Their advantage is that they can combine industry, agriculture, commerce, education and military affairs, making it easier to exercise leadership'. This was the cue for an upsurge in the merger of cooperatives with local township administrations to create People's Communes. The term People's Commune [*renmin gongshe*] was probably not Mao's own creation. It had first appeared in the monthly theoretical journal of the CCP, *Red Flag*, on 1 July 1958 in an article written by his political secretary and adviser, Chen Boda, about the merging of cooperatives that was already being implemented by some county authorities in Henan province. When Mao spoke approvingly of the Commune idea, he was telling the Shandong leadership that they should adopt the model being tested just over the provincial border in Henan.[4]

Most communes were rural and were often identical to the previous *xiang* or township administrations, but there were also larger communes which were closer in size to a whole county. Urban communes were also created, mostly based on a large factory or a residential district, but they never achieved the support or status that rural communes enjoyed and died out very quickly.[5]

The rural People's Communes have been both mythologised and reviled. They were the normal way of life for the majority of China's farming families for 20 years. The manner in which communes were created and the way they operated across China varied greatly: all had their own local characteristics and idiosyncrasies that reflected geographical conditions, local agricultural traditions, and social and ethnic differences. The commune system came to an end in 1978 with the introduction of the Responsibility System and rural China reverted to a version of the system of landowners and peasants that had existed before the advent of the PRC and collectivisation. The role played by Party and government cadres in the lives of the peasants changed significantly. No longer in absolute command, although they still had considerable power through their ability to tax, members of local Party committees sought a new accommodation with the peasants, some of whom had become extremely wealthy, and some CCP officials joined in business ventures with the most influential landowners in their area. In the course of time some of these business ventures, wishing to expand, bought or requisitioned land that was being farmed by poorer or less influential peasant families. This has been a major factor in the outbreak of rural unrest that China experienced in the first years of the twenty-first century.

Migration and urbanisation

Urbanisation has been one of the most important features of China's development since the inception of the reform programme in the late 1970s. During the previous two decades, the CCP had sought to control the development of the metropolitan centres, partly for practical reasons and partly because of an abiding prejudice against the cities among an ageing leadership that had established its powerbase in the rural areas and felt that it owed a debt of loyalty to the peasant masses. When migration to the cities began in the 1980s, there were serious attempts to create buffer zones such as the designation of a ring of small towns around Shanghai as satellite towns to absorb the demand from the large numbers of rural people seeking a better and brighter life. The household registration system [*hukou*], which is considered in the following section, prevented rural people from moving to the cities in search of jobs; their agricultural role as producers of grain to feed the cities was seen as vital, 'the key link', by the government.

At the beginning of the reform period, approximately 18% of China's population lived in towns and cities.[6] By 2006, it was at least 40%, and by 2020, at least 60%. These figures are difficult to interpret precisely, as there is a vast floating population of migrant workers – estimated at something of the order of 120 million in the late 20th century but almost 290 million by 2018 – who were notionally rural residents but worked in the cities and whose remittance earnings formed a vital part of the income of their rural families. By 2007, the rate of migration from the villages was beginning to slow down, but many rural migrants remained in the cities, becoming part of a new emerging urban social structure. China is now home to some of the largest cities in the world, including Shanghai with a population of 26 million, Beijing with 21 million and Hong Kong with 7.4 million. The rise in population since the 1990s is staggering, but the boundaries of some substantial cities have been modified, and many cities include large areas of farming land in the territory under their jurisdiction.

The cities began to change in character with the rise of a new urban middle class and new urban workers who may have originated in the countryside, but in many cases were settling permanently in the cities and acquiring the new skills required for the modern economy. These included technical expertise and foreign languages, primarily English, which was increasingly viewed as an essential requirement in the tourist trade and for attracting foreign trade and investment.

New people needed new housing, and the Beijing skyline changed completely – and not necessarily for the better – with the appearance of blocks of high-rise flats. Houses and flats began to change hands (sometimes at exorbitant prices), and the Western concept of buying and renting replaced allocation by the *danwei*, at least at the top end of the market. The habits of urban residents also began to change. The *nouveau riche* rapidly acquired cars; the iconic Chinese bicycle, although still ubiquitous, became a symbol of the poor or the elderly. New restaurants and cultural amenities provided for the leisure activities of the rising new elite and internal tourism took off as people travelled to see the parts of their country that they had not been allowed, and probably could not afford, to visit for decades, often beginning with the ancestral homes [*guxiang*] of their extended families.[7]

The *hukou* system

At the centre of the restrictions on movement in pre-reform China was the *hukou*, or household registration system. Proposals to reform or even abandon the system stimulated an intense debate in Beijing political circles as China's urban population increased. The system of requiring the entire population to register as either rural or urban residents was criticised as discriminating against China's rural majority. It was also a barrier to the mobility of labour necessary to urbanise and modernise the country. Opponents of reform feared that the unfettered migration of rural workers to the cities would impose impossible strains on social services. They also predicted further rises in crime and disorder, which had in any event increased as the economy developed.

Origins of the hukou system

When the CCP emerged from its rural bases to take control of China in 1949, one of its major concerns was the threat of massive uncontrolled migration from the poor countryside to the cities. Provisional regulations for registering urban residents were introduced in 1951, and quotas for the urban and rural population ratio were fixed in 1955. The need for labour mobility to supply the demands of heavy industry ensured relatively free population movement until 1958. During the Great Leap Forward, which was launched in that year, the Regulation of Household Registration laws was passed to ensure strict control over internal migration.

For Chinese citizens, the *hukou* is represented by a maroon-coloured internal passport which records details of marriages, divorces, births, and deaths in the household of the holder, but also the town, city, or village in which he or she has the right to live. The *hukou* document is indispensable for proving entitlement to health, pension, and educational benefits, and is useful – sometimes essential – in other financial transactions. It is effectively a combination of residence permit and officially accredited family history, and has been particularly important in migration control and in the enforcement of the one-child family planning policy. It is not simply a creation of the CCP as it builds on elements of historical Chinese systems of social control that operated in different ways in most periods of imperial China and combines them with similar policies that were copied from the former Soviet Union. Taiwan, Japan, and the two Koreas also have similar systems, and this has led some observers to suggest that the *hukou* system reflects an East Asian or a 'Confucian' attitude towards social control.[8]

In order to live and work in the towns and cities, migrants were required to have an urban *hukou*, rather than the documents that were issued to members of farming families which restricted them to residence in the rural areas. Urban *hukou* became increasingly difficult to acquire. Without this permit, no access was possible to basic services such as accommodation, education, health, and welfare payments. This even extended to rationed food supplies during times of scarcity. The *hukou* system exacerbated the great disparity that already existed between living standards in the cities and in the countryside. It also reinforced a traditional urban prejudice against the rural population by forcing them to stay in their native villages where social, economic, and cultural services were at a low level if they existed at all.

Breakdown of the hukou system in the reform period

The system began to disintegrate as the reforms of the early 1980s took effect. Migrant workers left the rural communes – which were being dismantled and needed far less unskilled labour than under the previous system – and sought work in the cities. These workers were subject to quota systems and were often the victims of discrimination, intimidation, and violence by the authorities. They were also restricted to the most unpleasant and dangerous jobs – jobs that many of those who already possessed an urban *hukou* were not prepared to do. Employers were able to stipulate that the possession of an urban *hukou* was a prerequisite for the more desirable jobs. This was an effective way of excluding outsiders. Migrants to the cities who were unable to obtain the permit frequently had to pay higher prices for accommodation, education, and other services. Their lack of legal status often led to problems in getting paid and poor employment conditions.

By 1998, it had become clear that urbanisation and labour mobility were being stifled by the household registration system. The State Council introduced reforms, initially allowing outsiders to acquire urban *hukou* by marriage and permitting children to inherit this status from their parents. Centrally imposed urban and rural quotas were phased out in 2000, and in 2001, the responsibility for granting urban *hukou* was devolved to local governments. This led to inconsistency and confusion. Of the 23 provincial-level administrations, 11, mostly in the booming southeast, proposed abolishing the *hukou*. The large cities – particularly Beijing and Shanghai, which were the greatest magnets for the urban poor – resisted the reforms because of the potential pressure of migration and concerns about the impact on crime and security. At a conference on the problems of the floating population in November 2005, the Ministry of Public Security proposed the abolition of the demarcation between rural and non-rural residents in favour of a unified registration system.

Opponents of the reform pointed to problems that emerged during pilot projects. In 2001, the city of Zhengzhou, the major rail hub of north-central China, offered to issue residence permits to people whose relatives already lived in the city. This was reversed in 2004 because of claims that demands on the transport, health, and education systems had become unmanageable, and that crime had increased. Prejudice against rural migrants undoubtedly played a part.

Beijing's Public Security Bureau argued that reform of the system would lead to demands for places in the capital's schools that would be impossible to meet. They also predicted a rise in crime and disorder, and argued that the city could not meet the costs of medical care and social security. At worst, the local administrations of the biggest cities feared the development of shanty towns familiar in other parts in the developing world. The relaxation of *hukou* policies also risked increasing the impoverishment of the rural areas.

Changing hukou practice

The *hukou* has not been abolished, but it is no longer an absolute barrier to migration. Official sources estimate that the migrant population had mushroomed to at least 288 million by 2018.[9] Peasants in search of work and employers needing labour had found ways around the regulations, and the authorities relaxed enforcement. Some legal restrictions on workers without urban *hukou* were lifted, and in Beijing, the practice of fining or deporting migrants without a permit was discontinued. Some rural migrants were also permitted to transfer from a rural to an urban *hukou*. This reduced the level of discrimination and intimidation experienced by migrant workers at least temporarily, but uncertainly remained and restrictions were re-imposed when the Beijing authorities concentrated on presenting their city in the best light for the Olympic Games of 2008.

Rural migrant labourers have, however, become an underclass in the major cities. They have little security and are excluded from many benefits enjoyed by permanent residents. As such, they are at risk from exploitation, casual violence, and summary expulsion from the cities by the police. They are also vulnerable to being drawn into urban criminal gangs and prostitution. The problem of rural migrants is now a major concern for the authorities in the cities and fully integrating them is a high priority. Not all migrants settled in cities; many returned to poverty in the countryside. The reform, or even the complete abolition, of the *hukou* system will remove an outdated and unworkable formal barrier to migration.[10]

Relaxation but no abolition

In spite of decades of consistent criticism of the *hukou* system, including that of Xi Jinping, who had even argued for its abolition in his doctoral thesis, the government is not willing to abolish this formidable mechanism for controlling population movement. Proposed reforms have, however, mitigated negative impacts on the economy. On 8 April 2019, the State Council's powerful National Development and Reform Commission announced an urbanisation plan under which cities would relax requirements for residency to levels appropriate to their size. Cities with fewer than three million residents would 'completely lift all restrictions on domestic migrants obtaining residency permits'; cities with between three and five million should 'comprehensively lift or relax' existing restrictions; while the largest urban areas with more than five million should 'lower the threshold and boost the number of people gaining residency permits'. While this was a significant move away from earlier policies directly intended to restrict migration to the smaller cities, and a move towards the NDRC target of granting *hukou* to 100 million people by 2020, the distinctions between smaller and larger cities were maintained.[11]

Notes

1 World Bank Data website https://data.worldbank.org/indicator/SP.RUR.TOTL.ZS?locations=CN.
2 *Agrarian Reform Law of the Peoples Republic of China* promulgated by the Central People's Government of 30 June 1950, Chinese text in *Jianguo yilai* Volume 1, pp. 336–45.
3 Frederick C. Teiwes 'Establishment and Consolidation of the New Regime' in Denis Twitchett and John K. Fairbank (eds.) *Cambridge History of China Volume 14 The People's Republic, Part 1: The Emergence of Revolutionary China 1949–1965* Cambridge: Cambridge University Press, 1987 *Cambridge History of China* Volume 14, pp. 83–8. For detailed information on the evolution of land policies and their social consequences, see Chao Kuo-chun *The Agrarian Policy of the Chinese Communist Party 1921–1959* London: Asia Publishing House, 1960. Contemporary first-hand accounts of the movement in specific villages can be found in the classic *Fanshen* by William Hinton Harmondsworth: Penguin Books, 1972 and two books by Isabel and David Crook *Revolution in a Chinese Village: Ten Mile Inn* London: Routledge and Kegan Paul, 1959 and *Mass Movement in a Chinese Village: Ten Mile Inn* London: Routledge and Kegan Paul, 1979.
4 Jürgen Domes *Internal Politics of China 1949–1972* London: Hurst, 1973, pp. 97–9; Party History Research Centre, Central Committee of the CCP *History of the Chinese Communist Party: A Chronology of Events* p. 273.
5 Jürgen Domes *Internal Politics of China 1949–1972* London: Hurst, 1973, pp. 97–8.
6 Tom Miller *China's Urban Billion: The Story Behind the Biggest Migration in History* London: Zed Books, 2012.
7 Tom Miller *China's Urban Billion: The Story behind the Biggest Migration in History* London: Zed Books, 2012.
8 *Washington Post* 4 February 2020.
9 Chinese National Bureau of Statistics 28 February 2019. http://www.stats.gov.cn/english/Press Release/201902/t20190228_1651335.html.
10 Kam Wing Chan and Li Zhang 'The *Hukou* system and Rural-Urban Migration in China: Processes and Changes' Department of Geography University of Washington, 1996.
11 *SCMP* 11 April 2019; *Washington Post* 4 February 2020.

15 Education and health

The provision of education and health services is a recognised indicator of development in any society. Societies governed by Communist parties, as China has been since 1949, have always made a point of providing universal education, either free of charge or at a cost that could be afforded by the majority of the population. Educational provision in the early years of the PRC was limited, and the content of the curriculum was often weighted to serve a partial and partisan view of society. However, basic literacy was accorded a high priority and the government was able to point to this as a significant advance on previous systems.

Healthcare on a national scale was also a declared priority of the CCP, and some of the more idiosyncratic provisions, particularly the intriguingly named 'barefoot doctors' and the reliance on traditional indigenous medicine, attracted international interest. After the reform of the 1980s, both sectors were obliged to confront the impact of greater commercialisation. The costs of education and healthcare became priorities and challenges for the government and the majority of the population.

Education

Traditional education

Before the middle of the twentieth century, the provision of education in China was under-developed and uneven. For most of the imperial era, instruction had been provided only for the landed elite and its primary function was to ensure that potential administrators acquired a thorough grounding, not only in the literary Chinese language, the language of administration, which was a considerable challenge in its own right, but also in the philosophical and historical classical texts of the Confucian tradition, familiarity with which was believed to be essential for the correct governance of the Empire. This *literati* education proceeded through a series of examinations at local, provincial, and finally national levels, a process which took many years to complete. Only candidates who were able to devote themselves full-time to the study of the classics had any prospect of being awarded the degrees, and as a result the candidates were drawn almost exclusively from the landowning class, the gentry, and most were from families that were connected with existing official post holders. The process was one of indoctrination in the prevailing Confucian orthodoxy rather than anything approaching liberal, critical, or scientific education: questioning the conventional wisdom or advocating alternative approaches were on the whole discouraged as iconoclastic and dangerous.

There was no central or state-administered education: all teaching was provided at the local level and financed by individual families, clans (extended families), or other social organisations, including religious foundations. Teaching might be carried out in the home of the student or at the house of a private tutor, and could be at the student's own pace. It initially consisted of the directed reading of basic educational texts such as the *Thousand Character Classic [Qianziwen]* before the student was considered capable of proceeding to the *Four Books* and *Five Classics*, which collected together the major books of the Confucian canon of philosophy and literature. Girls were almost never allowed to attend school: exceptionally, the daughter of a wealthy family might be educated at home.

For the overwhelming majority of the population, whether farmers, craftsmen, or merchants, there was virtually no opportunity to gain a formal education, although some small traders did acquire the rudimentary skills in reading and writing that were necessary to run their businesses. There was no public education, but religious bodies did offer education to young novitiates. The Buddhist monasteries were notable for this, both in the Chinese tradition and the Tibetan; facility with spiritual texts was central to the performance of religious duties. For Muslims in some parts of China, the madrasas, religious schools that were run by mosques or Sufi orders, also provided an education. In all of these institutions, the education that the students received was essentially religious in nature. At the end of the nineteenth century as the Chinese Empire began to collapse, China was sadly lacking in secular, liberal and, above all, scientific and technical education. More seriously, a large part of the conservative elite did not even recognise that this problem existed.

Missionary contribution to educational reform

Christian missionaries arrived in China in considerable numbers in this period; the China Inland Mission alone had 641 missionaries on its books in 1895. The majority of missionaries in China were Protestant, although Catholic missions had established a small but influential presence much earlier, and education (together with medical care) was one of their most important activities after the initial task of establishing churches and preaching the gospel to attract converts. Although Christian missionary education, like that of the monasteries and mosques, had a substantial religious component, it did introduce other aspects of Western education to China. Missionaries who began to understand Chinese culture and sympathise with the predicament of the Chinese people embarked on a programme of secular education: to a certain extent, this was for altruistic and humanitarian reasons, but it was also part of a strategy to create a body of sympathetic followers. Missionaries supported schools, hospitals, libraries, and the press: some colleges and universities that were set up under the auspices of European and American churches were to become very influential, including the forerunner of Beijing University.

The traditional Chinese educational system fell into decline towards the end of the nineteenth century, and in 1905 the imperial examinations, which had been the cornerstone of the *literati* educational system, were abolished, signalling the final demise of the old educational order. Reforms that were introduced at this time reduced the role of the Confucian classics in schools and emphasised the ability to read and write the modern Chinese language. The new reformed schools had a strongly patriotic or even Nationalist ethos, and were to a large extent modelled on the successful educational reforms that had recently been implemented in Japan. Chinese students began to travel to Japan to complete their higher education, but many also studied in Europe and the United States.

Education and the New Life Movement

Education in the Republican period under the Nationalist Guomindang, which ruled most of China from its capital in Nanjing between 1928 and the Japanese invasion of 1937, was constructed to a certain extent on the model established by missionaries. Under the New Life Movement, which was inaugurated by the Guomindang in 1934, there was also an attempt to reintroduce the application of Confucian principles in a manner that was deemed appropriate to the society of that era in the belief that this would promote harmony and social order. This approach demonstrated a preference for indoctrination rather than education that followed the Confucian tradition, and although it was the creation of the Nationalists, it also laid the foundations for the educational system that was to develop later under the CCP.

The original ill-fated attempt at a Confucian revival gave way to a Western Christian and particularly an American style – and an American citizen, George Shepherd, became director of the New Life Movement in 1935. The day-to-day implementation of the aims of the movement such as courtesy, cleanliness, and social order, was to a large extent left to the police, the military, and even the Scouting movement. Gradually, the New Life Movement became more militaristic until it began to look uncomfortably like the right-wing youth movements that were springing up in Europe in the 1930s and showed signs of blatant borrowing from the style and trappings of European fascism.

Education and the CCP

When the CCP came to power, with an agenda that was radical but also at times xenophobic, the missionary schools fell under suspicion and a new type of education was created, an approach that was considered to be more suitable for a 'New China'. Schools and colleges that had been established by foreigners were the object of a campaign launched by the new Chinese government in 1951, and by the following year, all of these institutions had been brought under government control. The authorities encouraged students to criticise foreign, particularly American, cultural influences; this campaign was inspired by the conflict in Korea between China and UN forces which were dominated by the United States.

An important aim of the CCP's new strategy for education was to redress the social balance, to right a historical wrong and to create a system of schools for the peasant farmers who had been completely neglected by governments for centuries, in education as in so much else. Peasants had been the greatest supporters of the CCP in its rise to power, and the Party considered that it owed them a political, as well as a moral, debt.

Before 1949, the greatest educational problem was illiteracy: this may have been as high as 80% according to government data, although sources sympathetic to the GMD tend to claim that this figure was exaggerated. In any case, the combination of basic education with a programme to reform the use of the Chinese script dramatically reduced the level of illiteracy in China.

Basic education was in any case the top priority and establishing a universal system of education was one of the CCP's key aims. In the early 1950s, it was the Soviet Union that provided the model for China's system of primary, secondary, and higher secondary schools, and in the tertiary sector for colleges and universities. Soviet influence in the structure of education and the curriculum was strengthened by the presence in China of teachers from the Soviet Union and Eastern Europe (part of the larger group labelled 'Soviet experts' who provided technical and other expertise) who taught in schools and universities and who also trained many of China's teachers. Moreover, many Chinese students had studied in the Soviet Union, and Russian was by far the most important foreign language studied by young Chinese during the 1950s and 1960s.

Cultural Revolution period education

Within a few years of the establishment of the PRC, the differences between Mao and Moscow that were to lead to the Sino-Soviet dispute were already prompting some powerful CCP members to question the nature of the education being provided in China's schools. There was pressure for more political education, and there were demands that the schools should emphasise the importance of participation by students in physical labour. The chaos of the Cultural Revolution led to the breakdown of the centrally organised educational system, although schools did continue to function in spite of the difficult conditions.[1]

Education during the Cultural Revolution period was intensely political. Teaching and learning in all schools – from kindergartens to senior high schools, and also colleges and universities – was focused on the study of Mao Zedong Thought: it was an exercise in rote learning and the parroting of short texts that had been memorised rather than a critical approach, an uncanny echo of the imperial educational system. The school and college day was frequently disrupted by political demonstrations and periods of physical labour which were intended to express the closeness of students to the peasants and workers, but especially to the peasants. While some Western true believers who visited China during that period were impressed by the degree of political activity in schools, the vast majority of well-informed Chinese now view this as having been at best a complete waste of time and at worst an absolute disaster, both for their own educational opportunities and careers, and for the creation of a modern, educated Chinese society. It created a lost generation, whose education, either at secondary school or at university, was so disrupted by the Cultural Revolution that some individuals have never recovered.[2]

Educational reform in the 1980s and 1990s

When Deng Xiaoping's reform programme began in the 1980s, there was increased investment in public education with the aim of rebuilding a national system, although at this juncture, what the leadership envisaged was a system that would also be flexible enough to respond to varied conditions in different regions of the country. The political and ideological content that had dominated education in the 1960s and 1970s was drastically reduced: it was never completely eliminated, although the subject matter and the style have changed radically and there is now far less dogmatic Marxism and more material of a patriotic or nationalist nature in mainstream schools. On the other hand, the Young Pioneer [*Zhongguo shaonian xianfengdui*, or *shaoxiandui*] organisation, which recruits children of ages 7–14 and had a membership of 130 million in 2005,[3] exists in parallel with the school system to promote patriotic and socially responsible attitudes among children. Its function and approach are reminiscent of the Boy Scouts or Girl Guides and church Sunday schools, but the ethos is primarily political and patriotic.

Hu Jintao, speaking at a gathering of Young Pioneers in 2000 shortly before he was formally identified as the next leader of China, told them that they were 'expected to be strict with themselves, to be good students at school, good children at home and good children in society. They must strive to become talented young adults'. He went on to say that the Young Pioneer organisation was 'a cradle for nurturing China's children and provides a school where children can learn socialism and communism'.[4]

In April 1986, legislation setting out plans for a nine-year compulsory education system, a system similar to the one that exists in many other countries, was passed by the NPC. The intention was that this would be in force in the cities and the more economically developed rural areas by 1990 and that it would spread to the rest of the country by the year 2000. This nine-year system is the core of primary and secondary education: in addition to this, three years of pre-school teaching may be available before the compulsory core and three years of higher secondary afterwards: higher education is also available, but only for a talented minority. The reforms also permitted the reintroduction of private education, and by the end of 1993, there were 4,030 privately run primary schools, 851 secondary schools, and 800 higher secondary schools in operation.[5] By 2018, the total had soared to 183,500, the majority of which were kindergartens.

Primary education normally lasts for six years, although, in some poorer rural communities, children begin school at the age of 7 rather than 6 and follow a five-year curriculum. Primary schools teach for 40 weeks each year and the children usually attend classes for 24–27 hours each week. The study of the Chinese language necessarily occupies a high proportion of classroom time (up to 50%), and considerable emphasis is placed on moral and ethical education, but children also study mathematics, science, history, geography, physical education, music, and art.

Secondary education is compulsory for three years in junior high schools and the subjects studied are broadly the same as those taught in primary schools, with the addition of foreign languages and more specialised science subjects: the students spend approximately 30 hours in the classroom each week. In order to proceed from this junior level to senior high school, students must pass a competitive examination.

There is an attempt to run all schools throughout the country on exactly the same lines, although in practice, there is considerable variation, a situation that is oddly reminiscent of the system in France. Every morning, schoolchildren sing the national anthem as the national flag is raised on the flagpole that is found in every playground. Primary-age children throughout the country tend to wear the same practical standard green tracksuits as a school uniform, and they are rewarded for achievement with red stars rather than the gold or silver ones that were traditionally awarded in the West. For secondary schools, the uniform is a different colour, light blue tracksuits often being favoured. Some schools have provision for boarding pupils. Sporting activities are an important part of the curriculum, and basketball courts and table tennis tables are usually in evidence.

To European eyes, the system might appear regimented, but it would not be strange to Taiwanese or Japanese students and teachers: similar school regimes can also be found in other Asian countries. At the end of the school day when the children tumble noisily out of the gates of a school, it could be anywhere in the world.[6]

The reform programme conceded a degree of devolution to local authorities, but the idea of a centralised and standardised system has not been abandoned, and this was the responsibility of the State Education Commission which once again became the Ministry of Education in 1998 when the ministries of the State Council were restructured. Among its most important objectives were an expansion in the number of schools, especially at the middle school or junior high school level, and the training and certification of a body of appropriately qualified teachers. There was also a desire to maintain uniform national criteria for the curriculum, textbooks, and other teaching resources, and for examinations.

The key piece of legislation was the Compulsory Education Law of the PRC, which was approved by the NPC on 12 April 1986 and came into force on 1 July of the same year. The 18 clauses in this brief act included an outline of the nine-year compulsory education programme from the age of 6 years, or 7 where 6 is not possible: this alternative was offered in recognition of the problems involved in bringing education in the rural areas, particularly in poor or minority areas, up to the level of the urban areas. There were also instructions to local authorities to provide education in their own areas in accordance with local conditions. The law recognised that, of the two stages of compulsory education, the primary stage would become universal long before the middle or junior high school stage. It stipulated that *putonghua* [standard Chinese, but usually called Mandarin by Westerners] should be promoted in schools, but allows the use of non-Chinese languages in schools in ethnic minority areas. The law also specifies that there should be no tuition fees and that grants should be made available to support students from less wealthy families. It also provides for an expansion in the number of colleges to train teachers.[7]

While this in many ways has the appearance of an admirable and progressive approach to national education, the implementation of the policies has exposed many problems in the educational system, especially in the more remote rural areas. There are not enough schools; attendance is often very patchy, and although there is a clear prohibition on the levying of tuition fees, many schools have managed to circumvent this regulation by inventing other fees or charging for the provision of textbooks and other services. In some instances, this makes the cost of school attendance prohibitive for children from the poorest families, replicating conditions that existed in the rural areas and poorer towns before the government of the PRC first attempted to introduce compulsory education in the 1950s. For wealthier families, this is less of a problem, and it is widely acknowledged that many better-off families spend more on the education of their children that on any other single item of expenditure. The introduction of fees, both legal and illegal, is a direct result of the budgetary decentralisation that is a key feature of the economic reform programme. As central government funding has been reduced or withdrawn, schools have been faced with the need to find alternative sources of financial support.[8]

Key schools

Key schools emerged in the 1950s as a way of concentrating the most able students in schools that already had outstanding track records of achievement, and these institutions were provided with additional funding. This system was designed with the intention of steering the most able students into the higher education sector. Key schools were abolished during the Cultural Revolution because they ran counter to the prevailing mood of egalitarianism. They were reintroduced in the 1980s as part of the drive to reform the educational system, but rapidly fell out of favour as the creation of a universal national system of education was preferred, and they were abolished in the summer of 2006.

Private education in the reform era

With the advent of the reform era, private schools, colleges, and universities began to make their appearance, partly in response to the real or perceived inadequacies of the state sector and partly as newly liberated entrepreneurs spotted a business opportunity. It was not, however, until 1997 that the existence of the private sector was formally recognised by the Ministry of Education. There were conferences on independent or non-governmental education in a number of Chinese provinces in 2000 and 2001, and the NPC discussed its first draft legislation on private education in November 2001. Concerns were expressed about the standards of education provided by some of these institutions, and the government recognised the need to regulate the private sector. This was the topic of a heated debate at a meeting of the NPC Standing Committee held in June 2002 when members of the NPC clashed over whether the provision of education for profit, rather than as a public service, should even be permitted. Legislation on promoting what were termed Non-State Educational Institutions was passed by the NPC Standing Committee on 28 December 2002 and came into effect on 1 September 2004.[9] At a news conference held in Beijing in November 2005, the Minister of Education, Zhou Ji, emphasised the necessity for China to develop private education to reduce the pressure on the public system which was having great difficulty responding to the demands placed on it by the dynamic economic reform programme. Statistics produced by the Ministry of Education indicated that in 2005 there may have been as many as 70,000 independent schools in existence, catering to as many as 14 million students in all age groups from primary to college level.[10]

The growth of private schooling in China is a pragmatic response to the new demands created by the economic reforms rather than an attempt at constructing a political or ethical alternative to the existing state educational system. The creation of the independent sector has been almost entirely a result of practical needs and commercial opportunity, and does not appear to be explicitly ideologically driven.[11]

Further and higher education

China has a system of vocational and technical schools which recruit students of secondary age but provide the kind of education that is often the responsibility of the further education sector in the West. There are also colleges for agricultural and technical education, and a thriving and increasingly competitive university sector.

The higher education system ground to a halt during the Cultural Revolution of the 1960s. The time and energy of students was diverted into the conflicts between Red Guard factions that helped to facilitate the intra-Party struggle instigated by Mao Zedong, and it was impossible for most institutions to operate anything approaching a normal curriculum. When the universities and colleges were permitted to reopen, the spirit of the Cultural Revolution still prevailed and admissions were dependent, not on educational ability or potential, but on the political track record and family background of the applicants. Students who were blessed with good 'worker, peasant, or soldier' pedigrees took precedence over those who had enjoyed a bourgeois upbringing: this effectively precluded anyone from a family with any history of higher education. The result was a demoralised and largely ineffective higher education sector.

Scientific and technological advance was one of the cornerstones of the Four Modernisations programme put forward by Zhou Enlai and later by Deng Xiaoping. This prioritisation led to renewed investment in education and an emphasis on quality and professionalism rather than political attitude or family background. Universities were granted considerable autonomy in developing their own curricula and appointing their own staff, and a national examination system was established. These examinations are taken by all candidates for higher education establishments and are extremely competitive. In many households, all normal family activities are suspended during the examination season and the combined efforts of all family members are directed at getting talented sons or daughters into the right university. Elite institutions are able to select the most able applicants, which is a complete reversal of the position in the Mao era. During the 1980s, the system under which all graduates were allocated jobs by the state began to break down and employment choices expanded.

China has a total of over 2,000 universities, colleges, or other institutions of higher education: some are familiar names with international reputations, while others are virtually unknown – even within China. Among the universities that are consistently rated most highly are Beijing

University, Qinghua University (which is also in Beijing and has reverted to the older spelling of Tsinghua for international purposes), Renmin University of China (People's University, which was at one time a CCP training school), Fudan University in Shanghai, and the Chinese University of Science and Technology, which is based in Hefei, the capital of Anhui province, and which, according to some educationalists in China, aspires in the course of time to be a serious rival to the Massachusetts Institute of Technology in the United States. In addition to these, there are many provincial universities and teacher training colleges (normal schools), many of which are sound institutions, but there are also new names, many of them privately run, whose status and academic respectability is in considerable doubt.[12]

In the summer of 2006, the problems of private universities were brought to the attention of a wider public when there were serious disturbances among students at a college campus just outside the Henan provincial capital of Zhengzhou. There were angry demonstrations at the college, property was damaged, and police cars were attacked. Although there were reports that the trouble had been caused by student dissatisfaction at a spartan regime which included early morning physical exercises, prohibitions of drinking and smoking, and restrictions on when students could leave the campus, it was first and foremost the status of the degrees offered by the university that was behind the protests.

The college, the Shengda Economics Trade and Management College of Zhengzhou University, was developed by a partnership between Zhengzhou University and a Taiwanese educational foundation. Because it was sponsored by Zhengzhou University, which is a respected and prestigious establishment of national standing, it was presented as part of the public education sector. Students who were not able to gain admission to Zhengzhou University itself were able to pay for admission to Shengda. Their tuition fees were five times the normal level, but they claimed that they had been led to believe that their degree certificates would be those of Zhengzhou University. Government regulations imposed in 2003 made it mandatory for the name of any subsidiary college (Shengda in this case) to be included on the certificates, and when the cohort that graduated in 2006 discovered this, they took the view that they had been short-changed. The college principal resigned but the institution continues to operate as a college of Zhengzhou University. The Shengda case was the most prominent, but it was not an isolated incident. Demonstrations also took place in a textile college in Jiangxi province and in the PLA Artillery Academy in Hefei in Anhui province when changes to diplomas were announced.[13]

Hong Kong has several universities, including Hong Kong University (HKU), the Chinese University of Hong Kong, and the Hong Kong University of Science and Technology, as well as several which have been promoted from polytechnic or college status. Although they are formally within the PRC, they function and are administered independently, for the most part as they did when Hong Kong was a British colony and HKU played a key role in the Association of Commonwealth Universities.

Education in the Xi Jinping era

In common with other aspects of social policy, education under the Xi Jinping administration was marked by a retreat from tolerance and openness, although the basic structures remained the same. Education remained a high priority, but there were tensions over content and methods of delivery as academics and teachers struggled to maintain standards without falling afoul of government inspections.

By 2019, China probably had the most comprehensive system of education in the world. The Ministry of Education claimed that 99% of school-age children were receiving the full nine years of basic education that had been made compulsory by the legislation of 1986. The proportion of college-age young people in higher education was 20%, whereas in 1978 it had been only about 1.5%. In June 2019, over ten million students sat the fiercely competitive examinations for entry to higher education, the *gaokao*. In that same year, almost 500,000 international students were registered as schools and colleges in China, something unthinkable before the reform era. China's determination to create a comprehensive system of 'world-class' universities was expressed in Projects 211 and 285 and Plan 111, promulgated in 2006, to establish a network of 'innovation centres'. In a country the size of China, it is not surprising that there has been significant variation in delivery. Provision in the most advanced cities has far outstripped that of the remote rural areas.

Pre-school education had become more or less universal in the larger cities; elsewhere, provision varied, but even the most remote rural areas were served by special projects such as mobile teaching units. Primary schools operated on the basis of 38 teaching weeks in two semesters with a reserve week and 12 weeks' vacation. At secondary level, the two semesters consisted of 39 weeks of teaching (40 weeks for higher secondary), with one or two 'reserve' weeks and 10–11 weeks of vacation. Across the primary and secondary sectors, there were five days a week of teaching.

Subjects taught remained under the control of the Ministry of Education, whether compulsory – including Chinese language and mathematics – or optional, and there was a rigorous system of tests and examinations. The core curriculum was supplemented by a broad range of extracurricular or after-school activities which included drama, model building, handicrafts, creative writing, and outdoor activities. Textbooks were initially prepared and produced by the State Education Commission, which reverted to the title of Ministry of Education in 1998. Since then there has been a move to diversify textbooks to produce teaching materials appropriate to different areas of China, although ultimately, these are subject to the approval of the ministry.

By 2017, there were a total of 2,631 institutions of higher education in the PRC. Of these, 1,243 had university status, 265 were independent colleges and 1388 designated higher vocational colleges. During the reform period, there were moves to decentralise the system, allowing a degree of autonomy to individual institutions while the state retained oversight of content and quality. This decentralisation was slowed, if not reversed, under Xi Jinping in the interests of homogeneity. Tuition was no longer free, and students were required to make a contribution to the costs of their education: many took part-time jobs, but loans were available and scholarships were offered for academic excellence and character. A major concern of the sector was the development of a body of well-qualified teachers, to compete with international standards. Universities increasingly emphasised the importance of international cooperation and exchanges, and academics with qualifications from the PRC could be found in Western universities and vice-versa.[14]

As the Xi Jinping administration evolved, ideological control over education and particularly higher education emerged as the top priority. In 2016, Xi had indicated his intention of converting universities into 'strongholds of the Party's leadership',[15] and this included the development of courses on 'Xi Jinping Thought'. Renmin University in Beijing, well known as the original Party school, inaugurated the first Research Centre for the Study of Xi Jinping Thought, in October 2017, and by spring 2018, there were ten such centres across the nation.

The Ministry of Education announced plans for a new curriculum, new criteria for assessment, and better qualified teachers who would be specialists in ideological education. The ministry's guide for universities, issued in December 2017, made it clear that ideological and political performance would be the determining factor in the assessment of university

teachers and thus their career prospects. While there was deep unease and some open opposition to this in the universities, it is difficult to see how this trend could be reversed while Xi
Jinping remains in power, as the ideology to be taught is exemplified by the title of a new
master's course at a Yunnan University: 'Xi Jinping's Thought on Socialism with Chinese
Characteristics in the New Era'. This is the clearest and crudest example of a reversion to
cultural norms of the days of the Cultural Revolution, and the dismissal of the Tsinghua
law professor Xu Zhangrun (see Chapter 6) was a warning to academic staff unwilling to
conform.[16]

Confucius Institutes

One aspect of China's education system which overlapped with the foreign policy of the
PRC was highly visible and controversial. Under the auspices of the Ministry of Education,
Confucius Institutes were established in 2004 by the Office of the Chinese Language Council International [*Guójiā Hànyǔ guójì tuīguǎng lǐngdǎo xiǎozǔ bàngōngshì*], which is universally abbreviated as the Hanban. This is also subject to oversight by a governing council
chaired by Ms. Liu Yandong, a member of the State Council and Politburo who previously
headed the United Front Work Department, which has responsibility for supervising non-
CCP bodies at home and overseas.

The primary aim of the Confucius Institutes was to promote the study of the Chinese
language and culture through the provision of textbooks and native speaking teaching staff,
but it is also an instrument of soft power for the CCP and government of China. Institutes
were established in universities across the world with a particular concentration in Europe
and North America, where they were typically linked to a department of Chinese studies or
languages and literature. They were also popular in Asia, notably in South Korea and in Russia. Initially, this initiative was welcomed by teachers of Chinese who appreciated the input
of native speakers with experience of current conditions in the PRC and up-to-date teaching
materials, and by university administrations which were provided with financial support for
staff. The cultural outreach was compared with long-established institutions including the
British Council, the Alliance Française, and the Goethe-Institut.

After the initial enthusiasm, concerns began to emerge that agreements between the Hanban and Western universities were interfering with the content and design of courses and
that staff were censoring their courses or teaching to avoid offending Chinese colleagues.
It was feared that controversial areas of study were either being neglected or presented in a
form acceptable to Beijing. These topics included Taiwan, Tibet, Xinjiang, and the deaths
following the Tian'anmen Square demonstrations of 4 June 1989. Matters came to a head
in 2014. On 22 July, the Director-General of Hanban, Ms. Xu Lin, attempted to censor the
conference agenda of the European Association of Chinese Studies which was due to meet
in the Portuguese city of Braga the following day. She instructed staff to remove all reference to the Chiang Ching-kuo Foundation and other Taiwanese sponsoring bodies from the
conference papers, obliging the conference organisers to circulate separate documentation.

The following September, after undiplomatic comments by Xu Lin, and pressure from
its own academic staff, the University of Chicago declined to renew its Confucius Institute
contract with Hanban. Other universities in the United States followed suit, either because of
experience of Chinese interference in their curricula or pressure from right-wing politicians.
There were also increasing concerns that among the large number of PRC students studying
in the West was a significant number dedicated to promoting the agenda of the authorities in
Beijing, to the extent of pressurising other Chinese students to comply and reporting them to

the authorities if they did not. Academic response to the decisions to close Confucius Institutes was mixed: while staff typically abhorred the arrogance of the Hanban leadership and the bullying of students, there was a realisation that universities were losing a window into contemporary Chinese culture, with no obvious alternative in sight. In spite of the controversy, many Confucius Institutes continued in existence and new ones were created. By the end of 2018, there were 538 institutes situated around the world and almost 2,000 primary and secondary schools had teaching supported by the Hanban. The Hanban proved willing to renegotiate some contracts to address concerns of academic staff, but in July 2019, there were still complaints that contracts gave Chinese officials control over teaching.[17]

Health and family planning

Barefoot healthcare

In the pre-reform era, medical treatment and healthcare was generally provided free of charge or at least at a very low cost. For the majority of peasant farmers, it was provided by the commune clinic or by the legendary 'barefoot doctors', partly qualified medical auxiliaries who did sterling work in rural areas, often the more remote regions that had no Western-style professional medical provision. The term 'barefoot doctor' attracted a certain amount of derision in the West, but the work that they were doing was vital. Their role was similar to that of a district nurse or health visitor in the United Kingdom, combined with the first aid skills of the Red Cross or the St John's Ambulance Brigade. In communities where the alternative was no healthcare at all, they were a boon. In the towns and cities, medical care was generally much more advanced and was the responsibility of the work unit, the *danwei*, and diagnosis and treatment were generally provided free of charge for its employees.

Traditional Chinese medicine

The quality of care, and certainly the level of resources available, was usually very poor in comparison with the developed West, but it was no worse than in other developing countries in the same period and was better than in many. There was an emphasis on traditional Chinese medicine including herbal treatments, acupuncture, and moxibustion, which is the burning of the herb mugwort [*Artemisia vulgaris*] on the skin. This was partly a pragmatic response to the impossibility of providing Western scientific medicine in a vast, poor country and partly a patriotic response, taking pride in the traditional treatments that were distinctive or sometimes unique to China. Many Western specialists trained in conventional medicine initially dismissed Chinese claims for these treatments; some were impressed when it was demonstrated, for example, that acupuncture worked on livestock. It is ironic that clinics offering traditional Chinese medical treatments are now commonplace in many Western cities where they are offered as complementary to Western scientific medicine.

In the 1950s, the provision of healthcare was a high priority of the government and it was claimed that major endemic diseases such as cholera, typhoid, scarlet fever, and schistosomiasis (bilharzia), a debilitating disease caused by parasites that pass to humans through fresh water snails in drinking water, had been completely eradicated. Details of epidemic diseases and other health problems that beset rural China during the 1950s and 1960s are difficult to verify, but it is likely that epidemics played a large part in the high number of excess deaths recorded in the famines that followed the Great Leap Forward of 1958.

Reform era medicine

One of the consequences of the economic reform programme that began in the 1980s was that medical care was no longer free of charge, except for employees of state-run organisations and government and Party officials. Everyone else has to pay, and a recent but increasingly common way of doing so is by taking out medical insurance, either through a state-run system or, for an increasing proportion of the population, private insurance.

Paying for healthcare was not a serious problem for the newly rich elite, but the cost of consultations and medication became a heavy burden, even for relatively well-paid white-collar workers in the cities. In the rural areas, the premiums were often far beyond the means of the vast majority of the peasants and they simply pay cash if they could not avoid seeking medical treatment. Many people did not consult doctors at all, and this caused great concern, particularly in the light of epidemic health scares such as SARS (severe acute respiratory syndrome) and AIDS. For the unemployed and migrant workers, there was virtually no possibility of paying for healthcare. An additional source of disquiet was that under-attendance at clinics may result in under-reporting of serious conditions, and this in turn suggests that official statistics are even less reliable than they should be.[18]

In 1998, the government announced a plan for making medical insurance universally available for urban residents, the Decision on Establishing a Basic Medical Insurance System for Urban Employees, which, following the usual pattern, was implemented nationally after regional pilot studies. According to *People's Daily*, 'By the end of 2003, some 109.02 million people around China had participated in the basic medical insurance program, including 79.75 million employees and 29.27 million retirees'.[19]

Sichuan healthcare disturbances

The serious predicament that China faced in healthcare provision, especially in the rural areas, was graphically illustrated by a case in the southwestern province of Sichuan. Sichuan is a relatively prosperous province in what is otherwise the generally underdeveloped western region. It profited from the relocation of resources during the 1960s under the Third Front policy that was designed to protect China's strategic industries in the event of an attack from the United States or the Soviet Union. It was also the provincial political base of the reforming Premier Zhao Ziyang, who strengthened the economy of his region.

In November 2006, a 4-year-old boy was admitted to the No. 2 People's Hospital in Guang'an after having accidentally swallowed pesticide. Guang'an is in the east of Sichuan province and, coincidentally, also the birthplace of Deng Xiaoping. The boy's family and the hospital disagree about what happened, but the family claimed that he was refused treatment, in this case having his stomach pumped, because they did not have sufficient funds. They alleged that the hospital demanded RMB 800 and the family could only afford RMB 100. The boy died two hours after having been brought to the hospital. The hospital maintained that appropriate treatment had been given and that the family only paid RMB 123 after the child's death rather than the full fee of RMB 639 on which the hospital could have insisted.

The family set up a shrine outside the hospital, demanded compensation, and tried to petition the local government, but were rebuffed roughly by security staff. Believing that the boy had died because the hospital had refused to treat him, schoolchildren from a nearby secondary school and then other local residents began to demonstrate in front of the hospital. Up to 2,000 protesters came to the hospital, windows and equipment were broken, and the hospital was obliged to close. Police who were called to deal with the riot used tear gas and arrested at least 20 demonstrators. There were reports that three people had been killed during the disturbances, including one police officer. These deaths were never confirmed, but it was accepted by the authorities that a large crowd had gathered and that there had been a serious disturbance.[20]

The Guang'an city government investigated the incident in consultation with another hospital, the Huaxi, which is attached to Sichuan University. Their joint report concluded that the boy had drunk enough pesticide to kill '500 children' and that he might have done so because it had been in a soft drink bottle when bought by his grandfather. Staff at the Guang'an No.2 Hospital were exonerated: it was accepted that they had pumped the boy's stomach and put him on a drip; this was all that was possible in the circumstances. The willingness of local people to assume an injustice was a clear indication of the crisis of confidence in the healthcare system.[21]

Medical insurance for the countryside

In 2003, in an attempt to provide at least a partial solution to the costs of healthcare in poorer rural communities, the government launched a medical insurance scheme targeted at peasant farmers. As is the normal practice in China, this scheme underwent trials in selected counties before being extended nationwide after its popularity became clear. The scheme required large-scale government investment. Individual premiums were initially as low as RMB 10 per annum, the government provided matching funds and up to 50% of the medical fees incurred by patients were covered. Even though farming families still had to pay part of the cost of their medical care under the new scheme, it is intended that financial support from the government would ease the burden sufficiently to overcome the reluctance of many peasant families to seek medical advice. This rural medical insurance scheme was one of Premier Wen Jiabao's pet projects and in his speech to the NPC in March 2006, he announced his intention of making it available to 80% of the rural population by the end of the year.[22] The Minister of Health, Chen Zhu, claimed in October 2007 that 83% of the rural population, some 720 million farmers, had enrolled in the plan, now entitled the Rural Cooperative Medical Care programme, and that by 2008, it would have been extended to cover all of China's countryside.[23]

As not all medical costs were covered by the scheme, its success depended on the willingness of hospitals to limit their fees and the ability of the authorities to keep a tight rein on corruption. By 2008, it was becoming clear that Chinese citizens without health insurance were reluctant to spend their savings for fear of high medical bills: one hospital admission could cost as much of twice the annual per-capita income of the lowest fifth of the population. Rural cooperative health insurance covered less than one-third of the costs of an inpatient admission. Healthcare costs were so high that 35% of household in the cities and 43% in the countryside found them difficult or impossible to afford. The costs of treatment and medications continued to rise, and there was pressure on the government to make up the deficiencies from increased tax revenue.[24]

To bridge the gap between what the government was willing to pay and the cost of total coverage, the private healthcare business enjoyed a boom in the second decade of the twenty-first century. In 2018, its income was RMB 544.8 billion, an increase of 24% over the previous year and bolstered by the willingness of companies and other organisations to buy supplemental insurance for their employees.[25]

In spite of the problems that China has faced in developing an effective healthcare system, average life expectancy has risen from 32 in 1950 to 73 in 2006, and maternal mortality rates have been substantially lowered.[26] The escalating health problems of the reform era have put the system under strain; this was seen most clearly in the hospital sector, where escalating costs were exacerbated by corruption with surgeons expecting bribes for carrying out operations and long queues attended by touts who offered queue jumping for a fee. Low salaries for hospital doctors, in comparison with similar professionals, made the search for alternative incomes inevitable. The *New York Times* reported that international pharmaceutical companies, including GlaxoSmithKline, Eli Lilly, and Pfizer, had been fined or forced to come to a settlement with regulators for bribing doctors to use their products. Distrust of the professionals and the system had in some cases led to violence against doctors. The status and pay of general practitioners in the community were even lower than that of hospital specialists: medical graduates sought prestigious city posts and the primary care system remained understaffed and underused as it was less trusted than the hospitals.[27]

HIV/AIDS and SARS

International concerns about health in China focused on the major epidemic diseases, particularly HIV/AIDS and SARS, which was identified in 2002, largely because these were judged to present a significant risk to people living outside China. HIV/AIDS was a growing problem that was associated with greater mobility of the labour force, the re-emergence of prostitution on a large scale, and the appearance in certain areas of intravenous injection of heroin and other narcotics. The SARS epidemic began in Guangdong province in November 2002 and lasted until July 2003. Out of a total of perhaps 8,000 people identified as having been infected with the SARS virus, 800 died.[28] Both of these outbreaks generated criticism at the way the Chinese government has handled medical issues, and there was concern at the slowness with which resources were deployed to the affected areas and the lack of transparency about the prevalence of the diseases. Reporting of the problem within China was criticised for being inadequate, although the level of discussion in the media was consistent with the treatment of other controversial and difficult issues.

Smoking

Tobacco smoking was almost universal, at least among men, in China until the 1980s, and it was a taboo subject for many years because most of the CCP leadership – not least Mao Zedong – had been chain smokers. At academic and other meetings, it was routine for cigarettes to be handed out with the ritual cups of tea. After Mao's death in 1976, posters proclaiming the health risks of tobacco began to appear and the popularity of smoking has declined. The role of smoking in the rise of cancer and cardiovascular diseases was highlighted in the 'Healthy China 2030' strategy (see later in this chapter), which also raised the possibility of national smoke-free legislation to extend the regulations against smoking in Beijing that were enacted in 2015 and followed by other cities. At the time of writing, there was still no national legislation.

Contaminated blood

In 1995, a scandal emerged which highlighted both the shortcomings of the Chinese healthcare system in the countryside and the desperate poverty of many peasant families. Officials and businessmen in Henan province established a network of unofficial and illegal blood banks to supply hospitals and pharmaceutical companies with blood and plasma products. The creation of these blood banks coincided with the appointment of a new director of the provincial Bureau of Health, Liu Quanxi, who – among other projects – created a central blood collection facility and a pharmaceutical company. He encouraged health professionals in Henan to concentrate on providing services at a profit, an approach that was in tune with the early days of the reform programme. As many as 300 blood collection stations were set up in the south and east of Henan – the poorest regions of the province. Poor peasants were encouraged to sell their blood, and many did so.

Liu apparently argued that there would be an international market for Chinese blood since there was no HIV/AIDS in China, but whether this was from ignorance or simply a ruse to make money is not clear. Conditions at the blood banks were insanitary, needles were reused, and there were no facilities for screening donors for diseases. Much of the blood collected was contaminated with the HIV virus and Hepatitis B. This contamination was compounded by poor practices in processing the blood and by donors who presented themselves at multiple collecting points to maximise their income, often using false names to conceal the number of times they had given blood. In addition to the authorised blood banks, there were illegal collection points, some of which were eventually closed down by the local Bureaus of Health.

To add insult to injury, peasants were persuaded that it would be beneficial for their health to have own blood reinjected after the plasma had been removed. By the time this was done, the blood had already been mixed in centrifuges with other blood. They were charged RMB 5 for this procedure.

Not surprisingly, there was a major epidemic of HIV/AIDS and Hepatitis B in Henan: this outbreak was on a much greater scale than the spread of these diseases in the rest of China, which was already a serious cause for concern. The numbers involved cannot be determined with any certainty because of the culture of secrecy in China and attempts by the local authorities to cover up the disaster: some government officials have conceded that as many as 30,000–50,000 people were infected when they paid for contaminated blood, but academic researchers have argued that the total number of people who contracted HIV/AIDS or other diseases as a result of the contamination could be of the order of 300,000.

When the magnitude of the problem became apparent in 1995, the local government moved rapidly to close down the operation but also attempted to cover up the scandal, harassing and arresting journalists investigating unexplained sickness and deaths among rural families.[29] There is evidence that impoverished people had previously sold blood and possibly even organs, but it had never been organised on such an industrial scale before.

Although the most severe problems were in Henan province, there is concern that the blood supply in the rest of China was still not being monitored adequately more than ten years after the Henan scandal. The shortage of blood for transfusions increased the risk of illegal and unchecked blood being used in hospitals. In November 2007, reports began to emerge of demonstrations by victims of the Henan blood scandal demanding compensation from the hospital that had been responsible for infecting them. Campaigners for compensation, and doctors who attempted to publicised the problem and the cover-up, were harassed and threatened with prosecution, including the retired gynaecologist Dr Gao Yaojie, who became a national and international heroine for her activism. Dr Gao was nominated for international awards for her work, but was under increased surveillance and initially forbidden to travel abroad. She left China in 2009 to live in New York.[30]

Counterfeit vaccines

After the blood scandal and alarm about adulterated foodstuffs, including baby milk contaminated with melamine that poisoned over 300,000 children in 2008, questions were raised about the quality of vaccines.

The Chinese public's confidence in domestic vaccines hit rock bottom last year when Changchun Changsheng Bio-technology, one of the country's biggest vaccine makers, was found to have systematically manipulated data and produced hundreds of thousands of substandard DPT vaccines that were given to hundreds of thousands of babies.[31]

Thousands of babies had been vaccinated against diphtheria pertussis (whooping cough) and tetanus (DPT) with doses of vaccine that were either not safe or had expired. There was also concern about the quality of influenza vaccine. Many mainland families rejected local vaccines and sought them from Hong Kong, Taiwan, or Japan, prompting a government campaign to assure people that the scandal had been dealt with and that most vaccines produced in the PRC were safe. Dozens of officials were punished for failures in regulation and some lost their jobs. Legislation to prevent a repeat scandal with tougher regulation and supervision was passed by the Standing Committee of the NPC on 29 June 2019, providing for severe punishments for producing counterfeit or substandard vaccines, and compensation for those adversely affected.[32]

Healthy China 2030

The response of the Xi Jinping administration to the long-term problems of healthcare were unveiled at a national health conference in Beijing from 19–20 August 2016 and showcased at the World Health Organisation (WHO) 9th Global Conference on Health Promotion in Shanghai the following 21–24 November. China's strategy was encapsulated in the Healthy China 2030 planning outline produced by the Central Committee and State Council, which meshed neatly with the WHO's 2030 Sustainable Development Agenda. It was presented as the first comprehensive national strategy for health since the foundation of the PRC in 1949, and called for 'multisectoral collaboration and innovation' to respond to new challenges such as cancer and cardiovascular disease by stressing prevention rather than treatment. It also emphasised the development of primary healthcare and traditional Chinese medicine. On one level, this was a return to the values of the pre-reform era, but it drew on international evidence on the effectiveness of community health services close to the populations they served and staffed by well-qualified general practitioners. An action plan for implementing the strategy was publicised in July 2017.[33]

Coronavirus Covid-19 and Wuhan 2020

An outbreak of infection linked to a wholesale fish market in the great Yangzi port city of Wuhan in January 2020 threatened to be a repeat of the SARS epidemic of 2002–2003. As in the case of SARS, Chinese authorities downplayed the seriousness of the epidemic in the initial stages, making themselves vulnerable to allegations of a cover-up. A study at HKU estimated that between 1 and 17 January, the virus had spread to at least 20 mainland cities, with isolated cases in other countries. It was approaching the level of a full-blown epidemic even before the Lunar New Year celebrations during which hundreds of thousands of people were due to travel to family reunions. By 20 January, the authorities in Wuhan had acknowledged that four people in the city died from the virus and that 15 members of hospital staff were infected. By 24 January, the death toll had risen to 26, with over 900 known cases. Although no travel ban was imposed, all public transport, including rail and air, was suspended. Wuhan was effectively isolated and described by some residents as a ghost town, with shortages of basic supplies including food and medicines. Travel restrictions were also imposed in other cities in Hubei province, affecting approximately 40 million people, and the State Council assumed control over the response to the emergency. The WHO observed that such a lockdown of a major city was unprecedented, and its efficacy could not be predicted. The WHO did not declare an international emergency – although recognising that it was a national emergency for China – but its director-general, Tedros Adhanom Ghebreyesus, travelled to Beijing for an urgent meeting on Monday 27 January. The WHO finally declared a global emergency on 30 January.

The death toll had risen to 80, with 2,800 others infected, and Premier Li Keqiang was photographed in Wuhan wearing a face mask and blue medical gown as he took charge of crisis operations. The head of Wuhan's health commission was dismissed on 30 January. By the end of January 2020, the total number of deaths had risen to 279, with 11,791 known cases, but the authorities were more concerned at increases in the daily totals as an indicator of the speed of infection.[34]

The effect on the Chinese economy was severe, particularly since the increase in trading associated with Chinese New Year could not take place. This worsened as the numbers of people quarantined or otherwise isolated rose and economic activity in additional towns and cities declined, in some cases almost to zero. Some economists in China forecast that the growth rate in the first quarter of 2020 would be 1% lower as a result of the epidemic. As trading resumed on the stock exchanges on 3 February after the extended Lunar New Year holiday, the People's Bank of China made liquidity of RMB 1.2 trillion (US$173 billion) available to money markets and announced plans lower lending rates in order to safeguard the national economy.[35]

Speculation mounted on the political consequences of the way the government handled the crisis. Officials initially played down the severity of the epidemic, and police in Wuhan detained and threatened doctors who had tried to warn of the dangers and attempted to censor online discussion. This was a familiar bureaucratic reaction – cover up and silence critics. One of those threatened was Dr Li Wenliang, who had contracted the infection from his patients. After conflicting reports of his state of health, it was finally confirmed that he had died, and online criticism of the government rocketed. Many argued that if the authorities had taken notice rather than silenced the doctors, the epidemic could have been mitigated at an early stage. A group of academics circulated an open letter urging the government to 'protect free speech and apologise for the death' of Dr Li. Xi Jinping called for a more robust approach to the epidemic and dispatched to Wuhan a team from the Central Commission for Discipline Inspection to investigate the response of local officials – but arguably, his programme to recentralise political authority and regulate lower-level organisations more closely had triggered a return to the characteristic unwillingness of Party officials to take decisions until instructions had been received from higher authority.

In early February, after the dismissal of senior health officials, Jiang Chaoliang, CCP Secretary of Hubei province, and his counterpart in the Wuhan metropolis, Ma Guoqiang, were dismissed. These were the predictable scapegoats, to be sacrificed whether or not their actions had been appropriate. Other officials were summoned to explain their actions to a taskforce established by Premier Li Keqiang.[36]

Xi Jinping on Sunday 23 February gave instructions for an 'orderly resumption of work and production' which had been delayed since the beginning of the coronavirus crisis, but with severe precautions to restrict the spread of infection. The following day, 24 February, the Standing Committee of the NPC decided to postpone the full annual assembly of the NPC and the parallel session of the Chinese People's Political Consultative Conference – the 'two sessions' – due in March, to some unspecified date so that the government could concentrate on dealing with the epidemic. On 29 April, it was announced that they would take place on 22 May for the NPC and 21 May for the CPPCC: discussions were taking place on possible technological solutions to prevent infection.[37]

By the second week of March 2020, Chinese government figures indicated that the epidemic in Wuhan and its province of Hubei had reached a plateau and the number of new cases and deaths declined. A Vice-Premier and State Council member, Sun Chunlan, visited Wuhan on 5 March to inspect the work of the Neighbourhood Committees which had been charged with delivering food and other essential supplies to residential communities that had been locked down since the middle of February. Videos recordings of her visit, which circulated briefly on the Chinese web, featured barracking from residents who shouted from their windows that everything was 'fake' and a delivery taking place had been staged specifically for the inspection. A sycophantic attempt by Wuhan Party secretary, Wang Zhonglin, to drum up support for a 'gratitude campaign' to thank Xi and the CCP for their work in fighting the epidemic was met with scepticism and derision.

The following Tuesday, 10 March, President Xi Jinping visited Wuhan for the first time since the appearance of Covid-19. This was seen as a sign that the worst was over and Xi was taking credit for it whereas, during the crisis, he had allowed Premier Li Keqiang to shoulder responsibility. Xi 'vowed to resolutely fight for a victory in the war against the novel coronavirus disease (COVID-19)'. He went on to say that 'the situation in Hubei and Wuhan has shown positive changes with important progress, but the prevention and control task remains arduous'. Temporary hospitals constructed or converted to receive Covid-19 patients were no longer needed and were closed down and WHO officials praised the bold action of the PRC government.[38]

During the lockdown, the monitoring of the population of Wuhan was intensified but the surveillance was patchy. China is not monolithic, and coordination between different agencies is incomplete. No single government agency has responsibility for personal data, and much of it is in the hands of private companies, such as Alibaba and Tencent, that were reluctant to pass it on to state organisations, although pressure to do this increased as the epidemic worsened. Managers of buildings installed QR codes and residents were urged, but not obliged, to scan them with their mobile phones, thus linking to websites where they could register health status and travel. The much-reported health code that assigns red, amber, or green status to users was from a webpage established in Alibaba's base of Hangzhou. Voluntary completion of a questionnaire enabled those who were virus-free to be given codes that allowed them to use roads and public transport. This was later copied by the local government in Beijing. Surveillance cameras to check the movements of individuals supposed to be under quarantine and infra-red cameras to screen for high temperatures were also installed in some locations.

Wuhan remained under 11 weeks of complete lockdown until Tuesday 7 April when for the first time no deaths related to Covid-19 were recorded. From Wednesday 8 April, residents were permitted to leave the city provided that they had a QR code on their mobile phones to prove that they were free of the virus and had not been in contact with an infected person. As citizens returned to work, ID cards and temperatures were also checked. Although traffic built up rapidly, many people ventured out only with masks and other protective clothing. Although there was considerable relief at the relaxation, Western reporters could also find local people who were critical of the government's actions at the early stage of the crisis, especially the punishments of individuals for 'spreading rumours' when they warned about the dangers of the coronavirus.

Part of the Hankou district, where the virus is believed to have originated, remained under lockdown. Thousands of people from outside Wuhan had been trapped in the city, and the authorities only slowly made provision for accommodation and food and financial support. They also faced quarantine on arrival at their destinations.[39]

China declared the Wuhan lockdown over on Wednesday 8 April after 76 days, but there were still new clusters in May and local outbreaks in the northeast in May and in June in the Fengtai district of Beijing. Beijing assumed control of the narrative of the virus outbreak, claiming it as a major triumph and praising doctors such as Zhong Nanshan, a CCP member who had been able to raise the issue of the spread of the virus. The junior doctors who blew the whistle and were hounded for spreading rumours were airbrushed out of the narrative, including Li Wenliang, who succumbed to the disease.[40]

One-child families: population policy and family planning

Outside China, by far the best known – if not the best understood – policy of the PRC is the planned birth [*jihua shengyu*] policy which was introduced in 1979 and is universally known in the West as the 'one-child' policy. Mao Zedong had believed, at least in the early years of the PRC, that the more Chinese there were, the better: he refused to consider any artificial limitation on China's already spiralling population growth. The economic planners who came back into power in the Deng Xiaoping era saw population control as a vital part of their development strategy. The one-child family was promoted nationally as the ideal or 'model' family, and in the urban areas, the idea of planning to have only one child was enforced strictly as there was a serious shortage of housing and school places. As the economy developed, new urban professionals looked to career and wealth enhancement as an alternative to traditional large families.

In the rural areas, the situation was quite different and there was considerable resistance to the control of family size. What had started as an advisory policy was deemed mandatory in some areas, and families with more than one child faced punitive sanctions including fines and were made to pay for education and healthcare for second and subsequent children. The over-enthusiastic enforcement of the policy by local officials led to serious abuses including forced abortion and sterilisation. Families that wished to have more than one child devised a variety of subterfuges including travelling to remote villages to stay with relatives when a child was due to be born in order to avoid the family planning inspectors. In other areas, couples were allowed a second child if their first-born was not an able-bodied boy who could grow up to work on the farm.

The impact of the one-child policy varied from region to region, but it is generally accepted that it has exacerbated distortions in the sex ratio of the population. Boys greatly outnumber girls, in a ratio of 117:100.[41] A traditional preference for male children has meant that if families were obliged to have only one child, they would try to ensure that it was a boy, either by gender-selective abortion or by female infanticide, although it is extremely difficult to establish how widespread this latter practice was. The policy also led to public alarm at the creation of a generation of 'little emperors': one spoiled child in a family.

Following demographic changes in China that are associated with the economic reforms and increasing longevity that is leading to a greater proportion of older people, there has been a considerable relaxation of the policy. The revised policy was consolidated in legislation, the Law on Population and Family Planning, which was approved by the Standing Committee of the NPC on 29 December 2001 and came into force in September 2002. This legislation continued the existing policy of encouraging families to have only one child, but conceded that they were permitted to have a second child if their economic circumstances were suitable.[42] However, the State Family Planning Commission cautioned against the overhasty relaxation of the 'one-child' policy, emphasising the need for China to keep its population below 1.4 billion.[43]

Given what appeared to be a more relaxed attitude to the one-child policy following the abolition of many targets and quotas since 1998, news of demonstrations and riots related to the policy that erupted in May 2007 in the Guangxi Zhuang Autonomous Region in southern China came as something of a surprise. The disturbances took place in Bobai County in the southeast of the region. For many years, the family planning regulations had not been enforced in the county with any great enthusiasm, but in spring 2007, the authorities organised family planning work teams to crack down on families that had ignored the regulations: fines were increased and families that could not or would not pay faced the confiscation or destruction of their property. In one case, it was alleged that a farmer had his house bulldozed. To make matters worse, the work teams were intent on collecting fines retroactively, in some cases relating to births that had taken place in the 1980s. The new level of enforcement was carried out with a considerable degree of force, and the villagers responded by attacking staff in the family planning office, overturning cars and setting local government offices on fire.[44] In a further attempt to reinforce its commitment to the policy, the provincial government of Hubei has expelled many people from the CCP for disobeying the one-child rule.[45]

It is not clear whether these were intended to be local responses to a re-intensification of government policy at a national level or local initiatives to enhance the status and the finances of the family planning officials, whose regular income of fines had been drastically reduced by a more liberal interpretation of the policy. The overall finances of local governments had, in any case, suffered as a result of the policy of fiscal decentralisation.

The one-child policy was never intended to be permanent, and some of its supporters had predicted that it would only last for one generation. The government's aim – to control China's population – remained unchanged, and the policy appears to have delivered the goods. A consensus developed that the policy is outdated and draconian penalties are no longer necessary because of the pressure of social and economic realities in a developing and urbanising society. The third full session of the Central Committee in November 2013 announced that the one-child policy would be relaxed from 1 January 2016, and that two children would be officially permitted for all families. There were also strong indications that the legislation would eventually be abandoned completely.

The long-term impact of the abandonment of the one-child policy is unclear at the time of writing, but pessimistic predictions of a huge spike in births were not justified. Family planning officials had forecast that there would be 20 million births in 2018, but the action figure was just over 15 million, some two million fewer than in 2017. Economic factors had replaced government policies as the determinants of childbearing.[46]

Notes

1 R.F. Price *Education in Modern China* London: Routledge and Kegan Paul, 1979.
2 Peter Mauger et al. (ed.) *Education in China* London: Anglo-Chinese Educational Institute, 1974.
3 *People's Daily* 2 June 2000.
4 *People's Daily* 2 June 2000.
5 *China Daily* 27 July 2019.
6 Carrie Gracie BBC News 29 July 2006.
7 *Compulsory Education Law of the People's Republic of China* China Education and Research Network 2005.
8 Emily Hannum and Albert Park *Educational Reform in China* London: Routledge, 2007.

9 *People's Daily* 29 June 2002.
10 *PKU (Beijing University News)* 10 November 2005.
11 Julia Kwong 'The Reemergence of Private Schools in Socialist China' *Comparative Education Review* 41, no. 3 (August 1997), pp. 244–59.
12 Ministry of Education.
13 BBC News 30 June 2006; Jonathan Watts *Guardian* 26 October 2006; *International Herald Tribune* 30 November 2007.
14 Wang Xiufang *Chinese Education since 1976* Jefferson, NC: McFarland, 2010.
15 Nick Taber 'How Xi Jinping Is Shaping China's Universities' *The Diplomat* 10 August 2018; *China Daily* 11 September 2018.
16 Nick Taber 'How Xi Jinping Is Shaping China's Universities' *The Diplomat* 10 August 2018; *China Daily* 11 September 2018.
17 *FT* 26 October 2017; *Inside Higher Ed* 9 January 2019; BBC News 7 September 2019; Jennifer Hubbert *China in the World: An Anthropology of Confucius Institutes, Soft Power, and Globalisation* Honolulu: University of Hawai'i Press, 2020.
18 'China's High-Cost Health Care' BBC News 24 April 2003.
19 *People's Daily* 6 November 1999; 'State Council–China's Social Security and Its Policy' *People's Daily* 7 September 2004.
20 *SCMP* 13 November 2006; BBC News 12 November 2006.
21 *People's Daily* 14 November 2006.
22 BBC News 29 June 2007.
23 *FT* 4 October 2007.
24 *FT* 21 October 2008.
25 *China Daily* 30 October 2019.
26 *New York Times* 30 September 2018; Chaguan 'System, Heal Thyself' *Economist* 29 August 2020.
27 *New York Times* 30 September 2018; Chaguan 'System, Heal Thyself' *Economist* 29 August 2020.
28 BBC News 24 January 2020.
29 Pierre Haski *Le Sang de la Chine: quand le silence tue* Paris: Bernard Grasset, 2005. Haski's book is a remarkably detailed account based on the author's own investigations in the villages of Henan.
30 BBC News 20 April 2007.
31 *SCMP* 11 March 2019.
32 *SCMP* 22 February, 3, 11 March 2019; Xinhua 29 June 2019.
33 'Healthy China 2030' World Health Organisation, 2016; *China Daily* 17 July 2019.
34 *SCMP* 20, 21, 23 24, 27, 30 January, 1 February 2020; *Guardian* 23, 24 January 2020; *Al Jazeera Television News* 23 January 2020; *New York Times* 30 January 2020.
35 *FT* 3 February 2020.
36 *Guardian* 7 February 2020; *SCMP* 8, 11 February 2020; *FT* 6 February 2020; Reuters 11, 13 February 2020.
37 Xinhua 23, 24 February, 29 April 2020.
38 *Guardian* 5, 9, 10 March 2020; Reuters 6 March 2020; *SCMP* 10 March 2020; Xinhua 10 March 2020.
39 Yuan Yang, Nian Liu, Sue-Lin Wong and Qianer Liu 'Seizing the Moment for Surveillance' *FT* 3, 9 April 2020; *SCMP* 8 April 2020; BBC News 7 February, 8 April 2020; Xinhua 8 April 2020; Chaguan 'System, Heal Thyself' *Economist* 29 August 2020.
40 BBC News 8 April 2020.
41 *People's Daily* 30 December 2001.
42 *People's Daily* 30 December 2001.
43 *SCMP* 28 December 2002.
44 Jonathan Watts 'Chinese Villagers Riot over "One-Child" Policy' *Guardian* 21 May 2007.
45 BBC News 7 January 2008.
46 *Guardian* 2 March 2019; *Washington Post* 4 May 2019.

16 Law and human rights

Absence of the rule of law, lack of respect for human rights, restrictions on the freedom to dissent, and the absence of any tradition of independent print or broadcast journalism have been among the main criticisms of Chinese society, not only by Western commentators but by Chinese thinkers, many of whom do not feel able to express their views publicly. These issues are interconnected. Without the creation of a legal system that is both formally and, in practice, separate from the CCP and the state – a system with an independent judiciary – it is difficult to see how even the most basic human rights can be guaranteed in China.

Law

Traditional legal system

China has had a sophisticated legal system and a comprehensive written legal code for centuries: some of the earliest extant legal documents date from the Qin (221–209 BC) and Han (206 BC–AD 221) dynasties. The monumental legal code of the Manchu Qing dynasty (1644–1911) was the culmination of this long tradition. In addition to the *Da Qing huidian* [Administrative Statues] which set out the functions and authority of all the institutions of Qing government, the *Da Qing lüli* (Penal Code) was a comprehensive treatise on prohibitions, restrictions, crimes, and the appropriate punishments for these crimes. It also covered matters that in other societies would be treated as part of the civil law.[1]

Punishments were, by and large, administered by the local magistrate, whose functions, in spite of the usual English translation of the Chinese term, were primarily administrative: his role was essentially to be the Emperor's representative in local government. Punishments that could be imposed by the magistrate included imprisonment, flogging, the wearing of the cangue (a wooden halter) around the neck, and the death penalty. Trials were often perfunctory and the results arbitrary: pressure during interrogation, sometimes amounting to torture, could be used to extract a confession. There was no right to legal representation in court, although licensed notaries could submit a written defence to the magistrate.

When Westerners, particularly missionaries, came into contact with China in the nineteenth century, they stimulated a drive to reform the legal system, and some reforms were enacted in the early years of the twentieth century. After the revolution of 1911, the new Republican government continued to introduce reforms and began a system of registering lawyers, a system that was consolidated in the Lawyers Act brought in by the Guomindang (GMD) administration in 1941. The years of war and Civil War from the 1920s to the 1940s impeded the establishment of an effective legal system in the same way that they held back many other social reforms.

PRC legal system, 1949–1978

On coming to power in 1949, the CCP, under the terms of its prototype Constitution, the Common Programme, abrogated all laws that had been enacted by the defeated GMD and effectively dismantled what remained of the existing legal system. Lawyers as a category were viewed with deep suspicion because it was assumed that they were, or might have been, supporters of the old regime, and many were dismissed or not reappointed when the new system was created.

In 1950, the Central Ministry of Justice was established and work began to create a 'socialist legal profession' following the model of the USSR. The Organic Law of People's Courts was enacted in 1954 at the same time as the first full Constitution of the PRC, but the judicial system that it legitimised was not entirely new. It was based partly on courts, known as People's Tribunals, that had been in existence for many years in the revolutionary base areas controlled by the CCP and its armies during the Civil War. The lawyers that staffed the courts were appointed as public servants, and there was no attempt to separate government and judicial functions. In addition to the courts, a system of extra-judicial instruments evolved: these included provisions for administrative detention that did not require a decision by a court. The new legal profession that was beginning to find its feet was criticised during the Anti-Rightist Campaign of 1957, and after the onset of the Cultural Revolution, when all professions were regarded as suspect, there was effectively a legal vacuum that was not filled until the 1980s.[2]

Part of the 'reform and opening' programme, the major policy shift under Deng Xiaoping, was the restoration of a legal system and the development of a modern legal profession, although initially, all lawyers continued to be state-appointed officials rather than independent practitioners. During the 1980s and 1990s, the number of qualified lawyers increased substantially, and the quality of legal practice and the level of professionalism improved, although only in limited areas. China's rapid economic development created a new market for legal services, including a demand for practitioners in law relating to the operation and investments of foreign businesses in China. Private legal practice became possible, Chinese law firms were created, and major international legal practices began to establish branches in China. However, the operation of the legal system remained dependent on the state and ultimately on the consent of the CCP.

PRC legal system since 1978

China's modern system of law is still immature and underdeveloped. After 1978, a new legal system was established, and the NPC and its Standing Committee enacted a substantial body of legislation. The courts and the procuracy (the prosecuting authority) now operated across the whole of the country: both were originally staffed by former army and police officers with relatively little legal training, but have subsequently recruited large numbers of graduates from law schools.[3]

Although significant progress has been made, the system is still evolving and the operation of the rule of law as it would be understood in the West is still patchy. It is more highly developed in urban than in rural areas; the most advanced developments were in the major cities of Beijing, Shanghai, and Guangzhou (Canton). In the rural areas, particularly in the economically backward interior, there has been little progress. The lack of separation between the legal, government and Party structures remains a serious concern to both independent lawyers in China and the international legal community. The operation of the legal system remains subordinate to and – to a significant extent – controlled by central and local government, both of which are dominated by the CCP.

According to Jerome Cohen, one of the most respected Western specialists in Chinese law, legislation is frequently inadequate and many conflicts between national and local norms, and the proliferation of regulations, interpretations, and other edicts often produce incoherence and inconsistency. There are too few able lawyers and those who are not afraid to undertake sensitive cases sometime lose their licence to practice law or are detained and punished for 'damaging public order' and similar offences. Judges are often vulnerable to corruption, political control and the pressures of '*guanxi*' [social connections based on family, friendship, school, or local ties]. Since their appointment, promotion, assignment, compensation, and removal, are all at the pleasure of government and Party leaders rather than the Supreme People's Court or provincial High Court, they and the litigants who appear before them are subject to the abuses of 'local protectionism'.[4]

Chinese criminal law

> The weakest link in the PRC legal system is criminal justice. The codes of criminal procedure and criminal law . . . lend themselves to abuse by law enforcement authorities.[5]

Chinese citizens who are suspected, or accused, of criminal activities have none of the protection afforded to citizens in the developed West in relation to detention, bail, searches, or the right to silence. They do not have the right of access to lawyers as would be the case in the West. Frequently, neither the accused nor his or her family can afford to engage a lawyer. Even when a lawyer is appointed, access to the client and to information about the case being brought is regularly obstructed. Witnesses are rarely summoned to court for cross-examination. Although China claims that torture is not used in the interrogation of criminal suspects, there is a substantial body of evidence that this stricture is far from being universally observed.

On Wednesday 31 August 2005, the Chinese government signed an agreement with the UN High Commissioner for Human Rights, Louise Arbour, under which the United Nations agreed to assist China in improving the implementation of human rights policies that had already been agreed and facilitating China's 'ratification of the International Covenant on Civil and Political Rights'. The Special Rapporteur of the UN Commission on Human Rights with responsibility for investigating torture and other cruel inhuman or degrading treatment, Manfred Nowak, visited China for two weeks in November 2005 to meet officials of the Chinese government and representatives of non-governmental organisations (NGOs), and to inspect detention facilities. This visit had been requested by one of his predecessors in 1995, but it was not until 2005 that the terms of reference were finally approved by the two sides. He found that torture was 'on the decline – particularly in urban areas – [but] remains widespread in China' and complained of attempts by Chinese officials to obstruct his investigation. He concluded that it would be impossible to outlaw torture completely without reforming the legal system and creating an independent judiciary, and put forward a series of recommendations which included the abolition of programmes of forced re-education.[6]

Such reform, as there is, within the system is slow and cautious. Revisions made to legislation on the status and practice of lawyers that was approved at the end of October 2007 by the Standing Committee of the NPC stopped short of allowing legal organisations to operate independently, and had the effect of keeping them under the political control of the court bureaucracy. The new legislation did, however, formally concede the right of defence lawyers to have access to their clients without having to seek formal approval from a judicial department, a major concession. It was also formally acknowledged that,

> conversations between a lawyer and his client will not be monitored and neither will whatever a lawyer says in defence of his or her client in court be used as evidence leading to his or her prosecution. The amendment specifically stipulates that a lawyer has the right to consult all files and materials related to the case he or she is dealing with and also has the right to collect evidence himself or herself.[7]

These amendments reflected a significant shift in attitudes towards a more independent legal system, but there was no robust procedure to ensure that any of these rights would be enforced.[8]

People's Courts

The court system in China has four levels. The Supreme People's Court which sits in Beijing is the highest judicial organ in China, and is formally responsible to the NPC and its Standing Committee. It tries the most significant cases, hears appeals against the decisions of lower-level courts, and supervises the operation of local courts and special courts. The second tier consists of approximately 30 Higher People's Courts which sit in the capital cities of provinces, autonomous regions, and major cities which have been accorded independent municipal status.

In the third tier are the 400 or so Intermediate People's Courts based in the administrative centres of prefectures, certain other towns, and the districts of larger cities. Intermediate People's Courts try criminal cases and have jurisdiction in cases carrying the death sentence, subject to appeals to the Higher Court. Basic, or primary-level, People's Courts, of which there are over 3,000, are the lowest-level courts and sit in all counties and in many cities. They also have authority to establish People's Tribunals to handle local cases; it is estimated that there are as many as 20,000 such tribunals.[9]

Lawyers from China participate in cooperative training programmes with their counterparts from the United Kingdom, the United States, and Canada designed to examine ways of implementing a fairer and more transparent judicial system in China. The fact that such programmes exist and are considered necessary by both international and Chinese lawyers is an indication of the problems faced by China in creating a system that is considered fair and open by international standards. Until the recommendations that have emerged from these programmes have been fully implemented, there is no guarantee that criminal trials in China will be fair, and there is substantial evidence that many are not carried out fairly.

Prison and pre-trial detention

Prison conditions in China are generally acknowledged to be extremely grim. The few modern prisons in the more advanced cities may approach Western standards of hygiene and security, but this is far from the norm. Amnesty International and other organisations have consistently expressed concern about conditions in prisons and in the *laogai* [reform through labour and *laojiao* [education through labour] camps – although the latter were formally abolished in 2013. The harsh regimes in these camps have been uncovered by academics and human rights campaigners.[10] Information on conditions in prisons and labour camps is classified as state secrets, and it is therefore a treasonable offence to publish such information. Judgements about conditions have to be made on the basis of far less documentation than is desirable. Information collected from former inmates supports the view that conditions are harsh and there is no public scrutiny of the behaviour of prison staff towards inmates. There are regular reports of detention regimes that amount to inhuman or degrading conditions; without access to prisons and other detention facilities by independent inspectors it is extremely difficult to verify this. There are also frequent reports of unexplained deaths in custody, but this information is not published officially.

Political control and the reporting of court cases

Although there have been many changes in the Chinese media since the 1980s, the state still exercises firm control in many areas, particularly over matters judged to have an impact on national security. This is not restricted to the reporting of controversial political issues or questions related to defence: social disorder and organised crime and its consequences may also fall into this category. Whether a matter is reported and how it is reported may have to be approved by a senior political body.

Court cases are not routinely reported in the press in the way that they are in the West. They are only reported in the national and provincial daily press when of political significance and if the government intends that a lesson should be drawn from them. There are often more detailed reports in the local daily and evening newspapers, and on local television stations: local residents have access to some information about their own locality, but not necessarily about neighbouring provinces. Many trials, if not most, are effectively held in camera.

Local newspapers, particularly those published in the more remote regions, were classified as *neibu* [internal] rather than *gongkai* [open or public]. *Neibu* approximates to 'classified' or 'restricted' in Western government concepts of document availability and although these restrictions are frequently ignored in practice and local newspapers have regularly made their way abroad, high-profile cases have demonstrated that the government continues to regard the information published in them as state secrets. The transmission of state secrets to foreigners is considered to be a serious crime punishable by long terms of imprisonment.[11] Newspapers from Xinjiang and Tibet are subject to more stringent controls than, for example, those from Shanghai. However, other areas are also problematic, such as the southeastern coastal province of Fujian, from which many emigrants to the West originate. It is an especially sensitive area in military and political terms, not only because of the recent history of illegal emigration, but also because it faces the island of Taiwan, which has been in political (and occasionally military) conflict with China since 1949.

There is considerable local variation in the application of legislation, up to and including the death penalty, and the fact that there are agreements on good practice at national government level does not guarantee that the provisions of such agreements will be carried out at the local level.[12]

Petitioning the government

China may be working its way slowly towards the creation of a modern legal system influenced by advanced international practices, but an older and more traditional approach to redressing grievances, the petition to the government, is still in existence: it is often the preferred, and sometimes the only available, remedy for desperate individuals and communities from the most remote corners of the country. It is a system with a long historical pedigree and can also be found in societies in the Middle East and Africa which retain traditional systems of social control: however, it sits oddly with the formal structures of China under the control of a Communist Party. The Chinese term for petition is usually *shangfang*, which implies a visit to one's superiors, but there is also the *xinfang*, a letter of complaint to superiors. Party and government institutions usually have a petition department *xinfang bumen* which deals with both letters and visits.

Petitioners are typically peasant farmers from the more remote regions who make the long and uncomfortable journey to Beijing after having failed in attempts at persuading local officials that their grievances should be redressed. These grievances are often connected with the ownership and sale of land. Many petitioners have gravitated to the Fengtai district situated in the southwest of Beijing. Until the 1980s, Fengtai was mostly rural with many small farms. A petitioners' settlement has grown up in Fengtai and houses perhaps as many as 4,000 individuals, a small proportion of the thousands who attempt to petition the government each year. Many petitioners remain in the capital for extended periods in order to have their grievances heard. Conditions are poor and parts of the area resemble a shanty town. In September 2007, notices appeared requiring all petitioners to vacate their rundown accommodation by 19 September, and demolition began shortly afterwards. This was part of an operation to make the area look immaculate in advance of the beautification of Beijing for the Olympic Games of 2008, and attempts had already been made to clear out the transitory population in other parts of the capital. Petitioners are routinely harassed by police and detained, but desperation and possibly a naïve belief that the central authorities would be willing and able to deal with local maladministration continue to attract them to the capital.

In December 2012, there were reports that thousands of detainees had been released from the Jiujingzhuan Relief Service Centre in southern Beijing's Fengtai district just outside the Fourth Ring Road. This drew attention to one of China's notorious 'black jails' where petitioners and others were confined. According to Human Rights Watch, many of these illegal detention centres, which were created in 2003 when official detention centres in which police held individuals without proper *hukou* permits, were in hotels run by the government, nursing homes, or psychiatric hospitals. The release raised hopes that such illegal prisons would be closed, but they continued to be used for some years.[13]

Xi Jinping and rule of (or by) law

To outsiders, the Xi Jinping era saw a slowing down or reversal of the reform of the legal system, but the CCP leadership insists that continued reform is essential to the rule of law. Even before Xi Jinping came to power, there had been a reaction to the move towards judicial professionalism in 1990, with some arguing for a revival of populist ideas from the Mao period and an emphasis on mediation rather than court proceedings. This was accompanied by increased intolerance of independent 'public interest' [*weiquan*] lawyers who were seen to be undermining the supremacy of the Party over legal and constitutional matters. The re-emphasis of Party control was affirmed by the suppression in 2009 of the Open Constitution [*Gong meng*] Initiative that had been launched in 2003 by a group of lawyers and legal academics to promote genuine constitutionalism and human rights. In 2013, Zhou Qiang, the former Hunan Party Secretary and not a professional lawyer, was appointed head of the Supreme People's Court. The conflict within the legal profession and between lawyers and the political leadership is illustrated by a campaign to promote model judges, based on a deposed deputy president of the Shanghai People's Court who was praised for his academic qualifications, professionalism and expertise and experience in conducting trials. The increasing prominence of the CCP's CCDI meant that Party members accused of crimes or infractions were often dealt with by this powerful body under Wang Qishan rather than through the formal court system. The CCDI extended its remit to include high-profile non-Party figures.[14]

Speaking at a national conference on judicial reform in Guiyang in July 2017, the former Minister of Public Security, Meng Jianzhu, who at that time headed the Central Committee's Commission for Political and Legal Affairs and was explicitly conveying the instructions of Xi Jinping, insisted that China had to follow the 'socialist rule of law with Chinese characteristics'. This required 'trial-centred' reform of criminal procedure as well as reforms in 'public security, state security and judicial administration', and with the added input of modern technology. For the judicial system this involved a massive reduction in the number of judges from 210,000 before 2012 to 120,000. The best qualified and most able remained as judges, while the remainder were redeployed as assistants or court clerks to provide administrative and research support for the judges. It was believed that this would improve the quality of trial procedures.[15]

The basis for these changes can be discerned in a speech made by Xi Jinping on 24 August 2018, when the Central Committee inaugurated a Commission for Law-based Governance, headed naturally by Xi. An edited version of the article was published in the CCP theoretical journal *Qiushi* in February 2019 under the title 'Strengthen the Party's leadership over the overall rule of law'. Xi repeatedly emphasised the centrality of leadership, which had to be 'institutionalised and legalised' as it was the 'defining feature of socialism with Chinese characteristics'. Accordingly, it was necessary to build a 'socialist legal team' of judges and lawyers 'loyal to the Party, to the state, to the people and to the law': the order is significant. Xi reiterated his determination that China would never follow the path of Western constitutionalism, separation of powers and judicial independence, making it clear that the reforms were intended to create a smaller but powerful cadre of judges whose primary allegiance was to the CCP.[16]

Human rights

The question of human rights, or more precisely, the lack of human rights – in China did not become an issue of serious international concern until the 1980s when China became more open and accessible to foreign visitors including academics, journalists, and the employees of international NGOs. The military suppression of the Democracy Movement in and around Tian'anmen Square on 4 June 1989 concentrated Western attention on the more brutal aspects of the government of the PRC. The precise number of civilian deaths and injuries following the occupation of Tian'anmen Square by the army, instructed to 'protect the Party Centre', was never clearly established but certainly ran into the hundreds.

Subsequently, concern was raised about the suppression of political dissent, the repression of ethnic and religious minorities, the widespread use of capital punishment, the physical abuse of inmates in prisons and labour camps, and the treatment of orphans in nurseries. Attention also focused on shortcomings in the legal system more generally and the impossibility of fair trials, as has been previously outlined, particularly for impoverished litigants.

Human rights abuses did not begin in the 1980s. From the inception of the PRC in 1949, reports of mass trials during political campaigns and the incarceration and execution of people for what were essentially political offences had seeped through to the West, usually as a result of information gleaned from a steady flow of refugees from the mainland who escaped to Hong Kong and other places. Although there was scepticism and a suspicion that problems on the mainland were being exaggerated by Taiwanese propaganda organs for their own political ends, in time, the publication of PRC documents and the testimony of many eyewitnesses confirmed beyond any reasonable doubt the broad outlines of the repression.

There were also reports of the existence of a large-scale prison and labour camp system in China during the 1950s and 1960s and of the brutal regime that operated in China's *gulag*, but solid and reliable information did not begin to appear until after the end of the Cultural Revolution, when there was a significant change in attitudes towards the publication of official data. It should be remembered that widespread knowledge about the network of Soviet prison camps only dates back to the 1970s following the publication of Alexander Solzhenitsyn's *The Gulag Archipelago*.

Confucian tradition

Neither was human rights abuse in China purely a function of CCP rule since 1949. There had been no tradition of respecting individual rights in the imperial political and legal system. For the *laobaixing* [the mass of the population] in the Confucian worldview, what mattered was collective responsibility rather than individual rights – and indeed, collective culpability in the case of instances of individual wrongdoing. In spite of China's twentieth-century revolutions, these concepts have not been expunged.

'Confucian worldview' is a rough and ready shorthand for the complex traditional culture developed over 2,000 years that informed the policy decisions of the imperial court, its ministers, provincial governors, and local magistrates. This culture was based on detailed knowledge of vast collections of documents which contain deliberations on political and social issues by scholars and the ruling elite and which were selectively consulted when decisions were needed.

The modern Chinese word for 'human rights', *renquan*, did not appear until the end of the nineteenth century. In common with much of the modern vocabulary of science and social science, it migrated to China from Japan, where the concept of the Japanese equivalent, *jinken*, emerged from debates about Japan's modernisation during the Meiji period. The meaning of *renquan* in the late nineteenth and early twentieth centuries is ambiguous. At times, it was used to signify individual rights, but on other occasions, it meant something like 'popular power'. The republican revolutionary Sun Yat-sen did not employ the term in his writings on democracy, preferring 'people's power' [*minquan*].

Chinese values, Asian values, and world opinion

China's response to the criticisms of its human rights record was vigorous. Beijing argued that successive constitutions had made adequate provision for the freedoms of speech, assembly, and publication: technically, this is correct, although in practice these rights have always been honoured more in the breach than in the observance. The government of the PRC also argued that, as a revolutionary regime replacing the Guomindang, it was championing the rights of the peasants and other groups that had been disadvantaged under the former regime.

These arguments were deployed at a time when there was a backlash in Asia more generally against international demands for the universal application of Western-style human rights legislation. Many Japanese commentators contended that Japan was a unique form of society and did not fit into the normal Western social categories, and therefore should not be judged according to a Western value system. In Singapore, the ruling elite vigorously defended its paternalist and authoritarian attitudes, pointing to the economic success and social stability of the island city-state, and arguing that the suppression of dissent was a small price to pay. Malaysia, under its abrasive Prime Minister Mahathir Mohammed, and supported by many members of the political elite of Southeast Asia, professed a belief in the existence of a separate category of Asian values. Supporters of the idea of Asian values maintained that these were specific to Asia, although to what extent they were representative of the whole of Asia remained ambiguous. The implication was that they were of more lasting significance in East and Southeast Asia than were Western concepts of human rights and individual rights.

China's position was essentially a special case of this 'Asian values' argument, and official publications contended that 'Socialism with Chinese characteristics' [*juyou Zhongguo tese de shehuizhuyi*] was an alternative framework which would provide appropriate local solutions for China's social problems. The Asian values argument, which is probably best understood as part of a movement of cultural nationalism in response to the post-war economic and cultural dominance of the West, died down and international standards of human rights became more generally accepted in the region. In China, they are accepted privately by many individuals and increasingly recognised in some government and academic circles. There is an awareness within the political elite that many institutions in China do not live up to international standards, and the access of international observers to prisons and labour camps to inquire into allegations of torture or other physical mistreatment has been resolutely blocked. The obstruction has been greater in the most politically sensitive regions of China, notably Tibet and Xinjiang, where visits by foreign politicians, academics, and journalists, and the operation of NGOs, are more strictly controlled.

China issued a series of White Papers on human rights from 1991 onwards. These were unfailingly positive and emphasised China's economic development under the PRC and their benefits to the poorest sections of the population. The rights of ethnic and religious minorities were presented almost entirely in terms of economic progress; other social and political issues are discussed solely in terms of legislation, with little evidence of practical effects on social development. These White Papers have been dismissed by most international human rights organisations, although the very existence of documents of this nature, which are reported in the Chinese domestic press, means that there is at least a rudimentary debate on human rights within China.

In November 2006, the government of the PRC unveiled an exhibition in Beijing to demonstrate its commitment to the protection of human rights. The exhibition, which consisted of hundreds of photographs, legal documents, and published books, was organised jointly by the Information Office of the State Council, the Chinese Society for Human Rights, and the Chinese Foundation for the Development of Human Rights.[17]

China under Xi Jinping has continued this tendency, but there is increasing evidence that the CCP regards the Western emphasis on human rights as a serious threat to its existence. Beijing's propaganda organs moved from defence to attack and deployed its political and economic muscle in a determined attempt to undermine international organisations for the promotion and protection of human rights. The director of Human Rights Watch, Kenneth Roth, was denied entry by immigration officers to Hong Kong, where he intended to launch the organisation's *World Report 2020*, which was inevitably highly critical of the PRC's record on human rights.[18]

Political prisoners

There is no internationally agreed figure for the number of individuals imprisoned in China for political offences. This is partly because detailed information of this nature is regarded as an official secret in China, and the penalties for communicating it to foreigners are draconian. It is also partly because there is no agreement on the concept of political offences in China, and because many prisoners whose offences are political in nature may have been convicted on other, criminal, charges. It has been estimated that the number of individuals detained or imprisoned for political or other reasons that are contrary to the international understanding of fundamental human rights runs into the tens of thousands. Even people who have been tried under the evolving Chinese legal system may not have received a trial that would be accepted as fair under international norms. There is also considerable evidence of the existence of torture and ill treatment of prisoners in the network of labour camps which often appear to be run under brutal regimes.[19]

Death penalty

The death penalty has been applied widely in China; in some cases, the decision on whether a death sentence was appropriate appeared to be completely arbitrary. China executes offenders who are convicted of murder and other violent crimes, as do Japan (where at least ten convicted murders have been hanged with very little publicity since December 2006), Taiwan, and the United States, among other countries, but there are also death sentences for offences that involve no violence at all, including embezzlement, tax evasion, and drug trafficking. Political offences, including those associated with separatist movements in Tibet and Xinjiang, also attract the death penalty. Death sentences can be commuted by suspension for two years; this is equivalent to the sentence of life imprisonment in many Western legal systems.

The number of death sentences in the PRC, particularly for those crimes – including financial crimes – that have never carried the death penalty in most Western societies has been a matter of concern to international lawyers and human rights activists for decades. The total number of executions carried out in China is a closely guarded secret, although individual death sentences and the trials that precede them are reported by local newspapers, radio, and television. It has been estimated that in 2004, 6,000 people were sentenced to death, of whom 3,400 were executed. This is widely assumed to be an underestimate, and in 2005, a senior member of the NPC, China's legislative body, claimed in public that there were normally over 10,000 executions a year. There is a long-standing tradition in China of using seemingly precise numbers, especially large numbers, to indicate a vague figure so it cannot be assumed that this was based on precise statistics, but it was an unusual official acknowledgement of the scale of executions.[20] The state is able to use the broad and vague provisions of the criminal code to impose the severest sentences on anyone accused of 'endangering state security', a catch-all phrase which can be applied to any political and religious activities of which the government or the CCP does not approve, in addition to criminal activities.

During an official visit in August and September 2005, the UN High Commissioner for Human Rights, Louise Arbour, met the President of China's Supreme Court and government ministers, and called on China to release data on the extent of capital punishment. She also expressed concern about China's use of the death penalty for offences 'that do not meet the international standard of "most serious crimes"'.[21] Constant international pressure of this nature was influenced China's decision in 2006 that all death sentences would in the future be reviewed by the Supreme People's Court and would not be left solely to the discretion of the lower courts, which had been able to pass death sentences for decades. The ruling was a breakthrough, and compelling evidence indicates a subsequent significant reduction in the number of sentences of death. In September 2007, according to the English-language newspaper *China Daily*, which is aimed at expatriate foreigners living in China and overseas readers, officials of the Supreme People's Court declared that the number of executions was at a level lower than at any time in the previous decade. The Vice-President of the Supreme People's Court, Jiang Xingchang, indicated that criteria for applications by lower courts for capital punishment had been made stricter and court proceedings had become fairer and more efficient. Judges in lower courts were told that the death penalty should be restricted to 'an extremely small number of serious offenders' and should be avoided in the case of economic crimes and difficult personal and family cases.[22] There is no suggestion that China intends to abandon the death penalty in the foreseeable future: Jiang Xingchang indicated in January 2008 that China was intending to move to a system of execution by lethal injection rather than shooting convicted criminals in the back of the head, which has been the normal procedure for decades.[23]

Contrary to popular myth, there are no public executions in China. Sentences may be announced at public rallies, particularly during political campaigns, such as recent drives against corruption, when the authorities feel the need to use the execution and the threat of further executions to warn the populace against specific crimes such as embezzlement or separatism. There have also been persistent reports that members of the family of executed criminals are obliged to pay for the bullet that ended their relative's life. Although this story is so prevalent that it may well have happened, there is no real evidence that it is routine or that it is authorised. Reforms to the system of death sentences were carried out in 2006 and 2007, and there was an emerging consensus that the number of executions should be reduced, and that capital punishment should be rolled back over a period of time.

In 2011, 13 offences were re-designated as no longer capital offences. Under the Ninth Amendment to the criminal law, which was adopted on 29 August 2015, the number of crimes on the list of capital offences was reduced by nine to 46. Surveys indicate widespread support for capital punishment in the general population, and the government continues to use the threat of the death penalty as a method of control. In December 2017, thousands attended an open-air meeting at Lufeng in Guangdong province at which ten people were sentenced to death for narcotics offences. The dramatic and spectacular manner in which this was carried out was intended as a clear warning to local people. China did not hesitate to apply to death sentence to foreign nationals and a fourth Canadian citizen was sentenced to death on 7 August 2020; at least one of the four claims that evidence against him was fabricated. Death sentences are automatically referred to the Supreme People's Court, and at the time of writing, none of them had been carried out.[24] China is widely assumed to carry out the largest number of death sentences in the world – some thousands – but this information remains classified as a state secret.[25]

Torture and other ill treatment in custody

The anecdotal evidence of brutality and ill treatment throughout China's police and prison system is far too widespread to be dismissed or ignored, as the Chinese authorities often appear to wish. China formally proscribed torture in 1996, but evidence suggests that this has had little effect on practices at the township and village levels. Even if senior Party and government officials in Beijing wished to eliminate torture, the centre does not necessarily have the authority to compel the local organs of state to do so. The evidence for this could only be verified or countered by giving international organisations open access to police cells and prisons, and the Chinese authorities are unwilling to grant this type of access. In November 2006, in what was a most unusual admission by a senior legal official, Wang Zhenchuan, the Deputy Procurator General, agreed that at least 30 verdicts in the Chinese legal system that year might have led to wrongful convictions following illegal interrogation techniques, sometimes amounting to torture, because of local police and court procedures. Interrogations by police are already recorded in some instances, although the practice is not yet widespread.[26]

China's prisons

China has a prison system which is based both on the system that it inherited from the Nationalist Guomindang government and on its own prisons that were run in the Jiangxi Soviet in the 1930s and the border base areas that were under the control of the CCP in the 1940s. In addition to this largely urban prison system, it has a network of prison camps which are either 'education through labour' [*laojiao*] camps or 'reform through labour' [*laogai*] camps.

The *laojiao* [education through labour] camps were a Chinese innovation and were developed to deal with the tens of thousands of citizens who were designated as 'rightists' during the Anti-Rightist Campaign of 1957. Rather than handle their cases through the extremely rudimentary court and prison system that existed at the time, this new form of administrative detention enabled the police to send people who were accused of social or political offences directly to labour camps. The continued existence of the education through labour camps is criticised by international legal bodies, and many Chinese lawyers and legislators are aware of the international opprobrium that it attracts and are pressing for the abolition of this system, which is one of the main stumbling blocks to the establishment of the rule of law in China. Legislation to make this possible has been discussed by committees of the NPC for several years, but has never been enacted. It is widely believed that this is simply because of the opposition of the powerful Ministry of Public Security, which is reluctant to relinquish such a powerful instrument of control.

Education through labour institutions take prisoners mainly for short-term sentences, up to four years, and these are individuals who have been sentenced to undergo a period of administrative detention which has not normally been ordered by a court. The offences are usually minor and include prostitution, drug use, and small-scale theft, but detention in the *laojiao* camps has also been used for dissidents and the victims of political campaigns, although some of these have also been sent to the *laogai* camps. The regime in the *laojiao* camps is tough, but not as tough as in the *laogai* system, and time served in *laojiao* does not have the same stigma that is attached to a prison or a *laogai* sentence. International concern has led to pressure on the Chinese authorities, and in March 2007, it was announced that the future of this system was being reconsidered.

The reform through labour camps, *laogai*, also known as China's gulag (GULAG was the Russian acronym for the Main Administration for Collective Labour camps, the Soviet system of forced labour camps), were modelled on the prison system of the former Soviet Union. Just as the Soviet camps were typically located in Siberia and other regions far from metropolitan Russia, China's forced labour camps are mainly in the farthest-flung regions, with a significant concentration in the western part of China, especially in Xinjiang and Qinghai. The operation of these camps is a state secret, and the extent of the system was hardly known in the West until the 1990s, partly because the names of labour camps are similar to those of state farms or other non-penal institutions. There was much confusion, some of it deliberate: in many cases, labour camps operate under two names, one being the formal name within the penal system and the other the name used for commercial transactions. There is consistent evidence of brutal regimes and severe ill treatment in these institutions, but what is unusual about the Chinese labour camps, in comparison with other similar penal systems, is the way that they have been incorporated into the national economy. Labour camps produce a wide range of commodities, including tea, wine, coal, and industrial equipment, and are required to run at a profit or at least to be self-financing. Until the 1990s, there was little awareness that these goods, many of which were exported to the West, were produced by forced labour.[27]

Dissent, disappearance, and human rights activists

During Xi Jinping's term of office, the government of China has intensified its clampdown on freedoms of expression, association, and peaceful assembly, and its censorship of the media. Dissenters have been intimidated, have vanished without explanation, and have been subject to secret trials resulting in imprisonment on the basis of nebulous charges with little evidence of wrongdoing: 'picking quarrels and provoking trouble' [*xunxin zishi*] is a common catch-all charge under which rubric many activists have been imprisoned. Among prominent targets of the state were signatories of Charter 08, a petition demanding political and democratic reforms, that was signed in 2008 by hundreds of intellectuals and dissidents. A new term, 'residential surveillance at a designated location', which came into use in 2012, was evidence of an attempt partially to legitimise the black jails. Article 73 of China's Criminal Procedure Law was amended that year to allow 'residential surveillance' for crimes relating to 'endangering state security', 'terrorism', or 'serious crimes of bribery', but was applied very liberally. In 2014, Radio Free Asia reported that 80% of detainees in these 'black jails' were women petitioners.[28]

It is impossible to be certain how many individuals have been 'disappeared': a UN Working Group on Enforced or Involuntary Disappearances identified 20 new cases of enforced disappearance between February and May 2019. Two well-publicised cases of enforced disappearance are those of the lawyer, Gao Zhisheng, and the bookseller and publisher, Gui Minhai.

Gao Zhisheng served in the PLA and was a member of the CCP until his resignation in 2005. During the 1990s, he qualified as a lawyer under a new programme introduced by Deng Xiaoping to create a cadre of 150,000 lawyers for a reformed legal system. He developed a speciality in defending activists and minorities in cases that involved the abuse of human rights, often utilising the provisions of the Administrative Procedure Law of 1989 which enabled citizens to sue organs of the Chinese state. He moved to Beijing in 2000 and established the Zhi Sheng law firm, which was closed down by the authorities in 2005 following legal battles by Gao in support of protesters against illegal development. Gao was continually harassed and threatened, and was finally arrested in September 2006, convicted of subversion, and sentenced to three years imprisonment. He converted to Christianity and subsequently disappeared, apparently remaining in unofficial detention until he was released in August 2014. He was then subject to a period of house arrest then evaded the authorities in August 2017, but was rearrested that September. At the time of writing, his whereabouts were unknown and colleagues and friends were concerned about his safety.[29]

Gui Minhai was one of five booksellers from Hong Kong who suddenly disappeared in 2015 after the publication of books that were critical of the Chinese government or individual leaders. He was abducted in Thailand but returned to China for medical treatment in 2016 when he appeared on television, apparently confessing to a driving offence. On his return, Gui, who is a naturalised citizen of Sweden, was accompanied by Swedish diplomats; in February 2020, it was revealed that he had been sentenced to ten years imprisonment for 'illegally providing intelligence to foreign entities'.[30]

Surveillance and social credit

Among the most controversial and least well understood innovations in China's social policy under the Xi Jinping regime were the development of mass surveillance and a credit scoring system. Although the latter depends on the former, the two systems are not identical.

The network of cameras monitoring public spaces increased gradually in the early twenty-first century, but then exponentially. This surveillance was primarily the responsibility of local government organisations with the involvement of private technology companies. The main purpose was to maintain security in shopping malls and other public spaces, but with the development of sophisticated facial recognition software, the possibilities of monitoring the whereabouts and behaviour of targeted individuals increased. Surveillance was greatest in major cities, but spread more widely. There are parallels with similar surveillance programmes in Western societies which are promoted as tools for ensuring public safety and crime reduction. Those are typically under the control of commercial organisations as well as government, and although they have their critics, they are not subject to such wide criticism as surveillance in China. The specific case of Xinjiang, where surveillance cameras played a major part in controlling unrest in Kashgar in 2009, is considered in Chapter 22.

Critics feared that, when fully implemented, the social credit system would transform the nature of social control in the PRC, leading to what was referred to in the Asian business consultancy Dezan Shira's *China Briefing* as a 'dystopian capability to monitor and control individual behaviour'. In practice, by the end of 2019, the system was far from nationwide and local systems evolved their own criteria for punishments and rewards. Critics of the system from within the Chinese legal establishment raised concerns about the arbitrariness of judgements and the absence of legal regulation.

The idea of a social credit system originated in the Third Plenum of 2013 and was announced in 2014 when the Guidelines for the Construction of a Social Credit System were published by the State Council. At the heart of the system was the construction of a nationwide database, the National Credit Information sharing platform that would allow the monitoring of individuals, businesses, and government officials in real time. Although the intention was for the system to become operational, that database was still not in existence at the time of writing. Critics focused on the impact of social credit on individuals, but this was only one part of a three-part project which also focused on businesses and government officials.

The business arm of the social credit system was designed to collect and analyse data provided by businesses to the central government, integrate the data with government information and allocate performance scores to businesses. Scores could result in businesses being placed on blacklists and incurring penalties or achieving 'redlist' status, which would entitle them to benefits and preferential trading arrangements. The stated intention of the Chinese government is that this system would streamline the business environment and provide a sophisticated mechanism for regulating the market by encouraging businesses, including foreign enterprises, to follow regulations and implement government policies. Government bodies would also be subject to scoring on the basis of performance indicators.

Official sources insist that only about 20% of data stored in the social credit system related to individuals; most concerns business or government.[31] Moreover, data on individuals had only been collected and analysed in the pilot systems organised by local authorities and operated according to local conventions. Concerns were raised about the potential for abuse of the system and corruption, as a result of potential human error in data input and scoring.

At the time of writing, no nationwide system of scoring has been established, and it was not clear to what extent these experimental schemes will be adopted nationally. If the system is implemented nationwide as intended, it has the capacity for universal coverage and could subject businesses and individuals to a high level of surveillance which could deter people from conduct that the CCP deems hostile or objectionable. Many doubt whether this will be possible, given the 'technological and administrative challenges' posed by attempting to apply the system to a country the size of China.[32]

Notes

1 S. van der Sprenkel *Legal Institutions in Manchu China* London: Athlone Press, 1962.
2 Henry McAleavy 'The People's Courts in Communist China' *The American Journal of Comparative Law* 11, no. 1 (Winter 1962), pp. 52–65.
3 Jerome A. Cohen 'China's Legal System in Transition', *Testimony to the United States Congressional – Executive Commission on China*, Tuesday 26 July 2005, and reprinted in an edited form in *China Daily*, is a clear and concise account of the current legal system in China and its shortcomings (www.cecc.gov/pages/hearings/072605/Cohen.php); See also 'A Slow March to Legal Reform' by the same author *Far Eastern Economic Review* October 2007, pp. 20–4 and Hu Juan 'The Development of the Chinese Legal Profession since 1978' *Durham East Asian Papers* 9, East Asian Studies, University of Durham.
4 Cohen 2005, op. cit.
5 Cohen 2005, op. cit.
6 Press Release, United Nations Office of the High Commissioner for Human Rights, 22 August 2005, 2 December 2005; BBC News Online 2 December 2005.
7 *China Daily* 30 October 2007.
8 *Zhongguo xinwengang* (*China News* net) 28 October 2007; *China Daily* 30 October 2007.
9 Articles 199 and 200 *Criminal Procedure Law of the People's Republic of China* (Adopted on 1 January 1997).
10 Hongda Harry Wu *Laogai: the Chinese Gulag* Boulder: Westview, 1992; Harry Wu (with Carolyn Wakeman) *Bitter Winds: A Memoir of My Years in the China's Gulag* New York: John Wiley,1994; Jean-Luc Domenach *Chine: l'archipel oublié* Paris: Fayard, 1992 contains the most detailed research on the history of China's prison camps and the way they have become integrated into the Chinese economy. *Laojiao* camps are also referred to as 're-education' camps in some Western accounts.
11 Rebiya Kadeer, an Uyghur businesswoman from Xinjiang who was nominated for the Nobel Peace Prize in 2007, was sentenced to eight years imprisonment for sending such material to her husband in the United States. She has since been released and lives in exile in the United States.
12 *Criminal Law of the People's Republic of China* (extracts) in English and Chinese; *Country Report: China* Home Office Immigration and Nationality Directorate (April 2005); Jerome A. Cohen 'China's Legal System in Transition', *Testimony to the United States Congressional – Executive Commission on China*, Tuesday 26 July 2005; Hu Juan 'The Development of the Chinese Legal Profession since 1978' *Durham East Asian Papers* 9, East Asian Studies, University of Durham; *China: Profile of Asylum Claims and Country Conditions* Bureau of Democracy, Human Rights and Labor, US Department of State, Washington, DC 20520, June 2004; *Country of Origin Research, China: Update to CHN32869.EX of 22 September 1999 regarding treatment of illegal emigrants repatriated to China; particularly information regarding treatment of those repatriated from Canada in May 2000* Research Directorate, Immigration and Refugee Board, Ottawa, August 2000; Jerome A. Cohen 'A Slow March to Legal Reform' *Far Eastern Economic Review* October 2007, pp. 20–4.

13 BBC News 12 November 2009; *Global Times* 2 March 2010; *SCMP* 5 December 2012.
14 Carl Minzner 'Legal Reform in the Xi Jinping Era' *Asia Policy* no. 20 (2015), pp. 4–9.
15 *China Daily* 11 July 2017.
16 Charlotte Gao 'Xi: China Must Never Adopt Constitutionalism, Separation of Powers or Judicial Independence' *The Diplomat* 19 February 2019.
17 Xinhua 16 November 2006.
18 *SCMP* 12 January 2020; *Human Rights Watch* 14 January 2020.
19 Amnesty International Report 2005.
20 Amnesty International Report 2005.
21 *Mainichi Daily News* 2 September 2005.
22 BBC News 5, 14 September 2007.
23 BBC News 3 January 2008.
24 BBC News 29 July 2009; *Global Times* 5 November 2009; *Guardian* 18 December 2017, 7 August 2020.
25 Amnesty International 'Death Penalty in 2019: Facts and Figures' 21 April 2020, www.amnesty.org/en/latest/news/2020/04/death-penalty-in-2019-facts-and-figures/.
26 BBC News 20 November 2006.
27 Hongda Harry Wu *Laogai: the Chinese Gulag* Boulder: Westview, 1992; Jean-Luc Domenach *L'archipel Oublié* Paris: Fayard, 1992.
28 Reuters 15 January 2010; Radio Free Asia 21 October 2014; *Guardian* 3 January 2017.
29 Amnesty International 13 August 2019.
30 Amnesty International 25 February 2020; *Guardian* 25 February 2020.
31 Elyar Najmehci 'Correcting the Record on China's "Social Credit System"' *China Daily* 29 November 2019.
32 Zhu Ningning 'Women xuyao yibu shenmeyang de shehui xinyongfa' *Fazhi Ribao* (Legal Daily) 10 December 2019; Elyar Najmehci 'Correcting the Record on China's "Social Credit System"' *China Daily* 29 November 2019; Alexander Chipman Koty 'China's Corporate Social Credit System: What Businesses Need to Know' *China Briefing* (Dezan Shira and Associates) 5 November 2019; Human Rights Watch *World Report 2020*; Minxin Pei 'China's Social Credit System: Genesis, Framework and Key' *Provisions China Leadership Monitor* 63 (Spring 2020).

17 Mass media

Successive constitutions of the PRC have formally claimed that freedom of expression and the freedom of the press were guaranteed in China, but as with many other constitutional provisions, this has been honoured more in the breach than in the observance. Under the reforms of the 1980s, control over distribution and advertising was relaxed, but editorial content remained under the control of the CCP. Independent writing and broadcasting have been permitted as long as there was no perception of a threat to either the CCP or social stability. It has been difficult for Chinese citizens to express independent or controversial views publicly during even the most tolerant of political climates and even more difficult – if not impossible – for them to reach a wide audience if their views are at all individual or eccentric.

The CCP has maintained its ultimate control over the whole of the mass media [*chuanbo meijie*], from the press and domestic broadcasting to satellite television and the new media of the internet, fully recognising the force of the maxim that information is power. The main instrument of this control has been the National Radio and Television Administration (previously referred to as the State Administration of Radio, Film and Television), a ministry-level body reporting directly to the State Council. Since the onset of the reform era in the late 1970s, CCP control over certain aspects of the media relaxed appreciably and far more diversity and variety was permitted than during the Mao period. However, many topics, particularly controversial domestic issues, such as Tibet, Xinjiang, Falungong, and the suppression of the 4 June Democracy Movement in 1989, remained off limits. The mass media are far from being independent. Although its changed dramatically from the early years of the PRC when there were only two state-controlled national newspapers, a handful of state-controlled magazines, and a state-controlled radio network, it still does not stand comparison with the best of the Western media in terms of breadth, independence, and openness. It is far more diverse and livelier than it was in the pre-reform era, but it is still dominated by organs of the state, and more importantly, the state retains the ultimate sanction of closing down or censoring publications or other outlets of which it does not approve.

One apposite example was the reformist journal *Yanhuang Chunqiu* which carried articles on Chinese history and contemporary politics and championed the politics of Hu Yaobang and Zhao Ziyang, who ruled China in the 1980s. After months of harassment and an attempt by the state to replace the existing editorial team, it was finally closed down in July 2016.[1]

China has not been able to throw off the legacy of central control, even in the age of the internet and other new media, and although there has been a proliferation of information sources in print and other formats, the tension between the purveyors of information and the state has increased significantly under Xi Jinping's administration. While some areas, particularly entertainment, advertising, and fashion, remain relatively free from political restrictions, other fields are strictly controlled, notably the reporting, printing, and broad-casting of news. The reporting of issues that are considered by the CCP to be sensitive is constantly monitored and can be rapidly and effectively suppressed in the interests of state security. As has been noted previously, this concept encompasses a much wider field than would be found in the West. Not only are issues such as defence – which would be deemed to be genuinely sensitive in most countries – outlawed, it is not possible to report in any detail on the inner workings of the government or of the CCP, particularly in the case of internal conflicts or dissent, and it has been difficult to report openly on business relationships that involve any relatives of senior government figures, although information on these commer-cial involvements has surfaced from time to time as a result of corruption trials. Comment on developments in Taiwan, Tibet, and Xinjiang is also subject to rigorous scrutiny and restrictions, and during the demonstrations and riots in Hong Kong in 2019, coverage in the mainland media was restricted to a ludicrous extent, although it was fully reported in the Hong Kong media.

The greatest change in the media in the early twenty-first century was the removal of the substantial financial support that the state previously provided to many of the key outlets, with the result that they were compelled to find funding elsewhere, mainly from advertising. Journalists expressed concern that they were exchanging one patron for another and that news coverage had to be tailored so that it did not upset the advertisers. This did not apply to the major publications sponsored by the state and the CCP, including *People's Daily*.

Xinhua

Government news management is achieved primarily through the New China News Agency (NCNA), which is increasingly referred to outside China by its Chinese name of Xinhua. Xinhua is a colossal bureaucratic machine, said to have over 7,000 employees, and is directly under the control of the CCP's Propaganda Department: it has offices in every province of China, as well as branches abroad. Its wide coverage and its status and authority within China has obliged all Chinese newspapers to rely on it for national and international stories. As an agency of the CCP Propaganda Department, its international remit is to propagate news about China, as well as to gather news and information about the countries in which it is based.

Xinhua's close connection with the political establishment is illustrated by the peculiar case of Hong Kong, where for decades the Xinhua office functioned as the *de facto* Chinese embassy there because the PRC was unable to formally recognise the status of the colony. After 1997, the Xinhua office, which had played an invaluable role in negotiations with Beijing, was renamed the Liaison Office of the Central People's Government in Hong Kong, and it continues to function as a point of contact between a wide range of organisations and the government of the PRC.

China News Service is the second largest news agency, but is much less prominent than Xinhua. It was created in 1952 with the remit of communicating with Chinese communities overseas and the residents of Hong Kong, Macao, and Taiwan.

Newspapers

The main sources of news in the early days of the PRC were *People's Daily* [*Renmin Ribao*], the official gazette of the Central Committee of the CCP, and *Guangming Daily*, which was the only other newspaper published. The relationship between them was mod-elled on the relationship between *Pravda* and *Izvestia* in the USSR.

One of the earliest signs that reform was taking hold in the late 1970s was the change that could be detected in the style and format of *People's Daily*. *People's Daily* was revitalised in the late 1970s under its reforming managing editor Hu Jiwei. These changes were possible because of the improvement in the political climate and the positive influence of the reform-minded CCP Secretary General, Hu Yaobang, but according to Liu Binyan, one of China's best-known journalists who worked as an investigative reporter on the paper, none of this would have been possible without 'the moral courage of editor-in-chief Hu Jiwei and his deputy, the philosopher Wang Ruoshui, and their loyal staff', who came under constant pressure from conservatives in the CCP hierarchy opposed to the reforms.[2] The outcome was that *People's Daily* became more readable (or at least less unreadable) and, although it continued to cover major political and economic developments from the point of view of the CCP, the coverage became broader. Hu Jiwei also introduced a letters page, which at the time was regarded as nothing short of revolutionary.

Guangming Daily (*Guangming* means 'light' or 'bright' as in 'bright future', but the paper is invariably referred to by its Chinese name, even by foreigners) was originally published by the China Democratic League, one of the token minority parties still permitted to exist in the PRC, but it was taken over by the CCP Central Committee's Propaganda and United Front Work Department in 1959 when the minority parties lost all influence after the campaign against 'rightists', and it is now run by the CCP. It retains a distinctive tone which marks it out from *People's Daily*: its more sophisticated and literate style, and the wider range of topics that it covers makes it more appealing to educated professionals.

China's provinces all have their own daily newspapers, as do major towns and cities, and many also have evening newspapers with a small local circulation, such as the *Beijing Evening News* (*Beijing wanbao*), a chatty but readable small paper that circulates in the capital. In the past, these newspapers formed part of a centralised and hierarchical news organisation controlled by the CCP from Beijing: the provincial dailies would typically publish the same key policy articles that appeared in *People's Daily* with the addition of local editorial and news material. This tradition has not entirely died out, but there is less central control and a greater degree of independence in the local press: some regional newspapers acquired a reputation for fearlessness in the exposure of malpractice and corruption. The *Southern Metropolitan Daily* [*Nanfang dushi ribao*], the commercial counterpart of the CCP's *Southern Daily* [*Nanfang ribao*] in Guangzhou was noted for its trenchant and critical approach; its supplement, *Southern Weekly* [*Nanfang zhoumo*], had a track record of investigative journalism. Newspapers and magazines frequently carry stories of successful police actions against criminals, separatists, and organisations such as Falungong; publications issued by the police or legal bodies that specialise in that area are openly available. *Fazhi ribao* [*Legal Daily*] is the leading example of this type of publication. Criminal activity was rarely reported before the 1980s, and certainly not in the detail with which it is now covered.

These state-controlled newspapers are still published, although they do not have the monopoly that they used to enjoy. About 1,900 titles (February 2019 figures) are published in China today, many of them local, tabloid in style if not in format, and with a low cultural content.[3] Some sensational and shoddy publications are even published under the auspices of government or Party newspapers, and are used simply to generate revenue. The publication of magazines and books has increased exponentially with the principal control being the registration system under which all publications are required to register with the state, occasional campaigns against pornographic and other unacceptable material, and a highly effective culture of self-censorship. Chinese citizens are eager consumers of the print media: newsstands are ubiquitous and carry a range of both serious and popular titles.

It is possible to read English-language versions of the government's newspapers. *China Daily* has been published in English since 1983. It has no Chinese-language equivalent and is not the English version of *People's Daily*, although it does carry translations of articles from Xinhua news agency and from other Chinese newspapers. It has always had a relatively open and liberal approach, and its somewhat idiosyncratic English style has over the years been polished by a succession of staff from all over the English-speaking world. The tabloid *Global Times* was first published in Chinese as *Huanqiu shibao* in 1993 and concentrated on international affairs. An English version appeared in 2009 with more coverage of domestic events specifically to inform the foreign community in China; its online version is frequently consulted for the views of the Chinese government. Two spinoffs, *Metro Beijing* and *Metro Shanghai*, focus on developments in those two cities.

People's Daily itself is also available online in Chinese, both in the domestic edition which is circulated within China and the overseas edition which is significantly different. An online English-language edition contains a summary of the main news stories and editorials, but is not by any means a full translation of the paper that is still read by millions of members of the CCP and government officials every day. Both the content and flavour of the English version differ from the main Chinese edition.

China Youth Daily [*Zhongguo qingnian bao*] is the official organ of the Chinese CYL which created it in 1951; it built up a huge readership among young Chinese because all colleges universities and secondary schools were obliged to subscribe to it. In spite of its official connections, it established an important niche as a publication with an independent voice and published many articles critical of corruption and maladministration. It came into direct conflict with the government early in 2006 when its weekly supplement *Freezing Point* [*Bingdian*] published an article by a historian from Zhongshan University in Guangzhou, Yuan Weishi, who criticised the content of history textbooks used in Chinese secondary schools. Specifically, he complained about the treatment of the Boxer Rebellion of 1899–1901 which is always presented positively as a patriotic movement but which, he argued, should also be criticised for its violence and xenophobia. Publication of the supplement was suspended and the editor, Lu Yuegang, and the editor-in-chief, Li Datong, were transferred to other duties. When *Freezing Point* reappeared in March 2006, it appeared without Li and Lu in charge. The paper enjoys the patronage of the former head of the youth league, President Hu Jintao, but this did not prevent the suspension of the journalists; the episode reveals the strict limits as to what can be published.[4] Under the Xi administration, all newspapers have been more careful to stay close to the editorial line of the CCP.

Internal newspapers

For decades, China has operated a system of internal publications that were originally intended solely for Party and government officials, and contain news, analysis, and data that was not considered suitable for wider publication. These internal newspapers were graduated in terms of security and access; the best known were *Reference News* [*Cankao xiaoxi*] and *Reference Material* [*Cankao ziliao*], both of which are published by Xinhua. They have evolved and are no longer all distributed as restricted internal documents available only to certain cadres: *Cankao xiaoxi* is on sale to the public on newsstands. Other classified internal newsletters have included *Internal Reference* [*Neibu cankao*], which is only available to senior political leaders, and *Big Reference* [*Da Cankao*], which was circulated only to the very highest authorities.

Television and radio

Chinese Central Television (CCTV) is the largest media company in the PRC and is responsible for China's national television network of 16 channels. It is managed jointly by a Party and a government organisation: the CCP Propaganda Department oversees programme style and content, and the State Administration of Radio, Film and Television, an office of the State Council, has responsibility for day-to-day management. There are other broadcasters in China, mainly provincial stations which are extremely popular as they give considerable coverage to local events and personalities, and are available nationally via satellite, but only CCTV is allowed to import programmes from abroad.

While it no longer has the absolute monopoly on news broadcasting that it did before the reform era – there are over 3,300 channels, local, regional, and national – CCTV is able to dominate the news agenda. Channel 1, the main news channel, produces national news programmes three times daily and all regional networks are required to carry its main daily news broadcast which comes on air at 7 pm every evening. The other channels cover a wide range of topics including business, the arts, international affairs, sport, films, drama education, society, the law, and Beijing opera. Channel 9 is an international channel broadcasting English-language programmes. Regional television stations also originate their own programmes, often in the local variants of Chinese such as, for example, Cantonese and the Wu language of Shanghai. There are also programmes in ethnic minority languages: for example, in Yining in the far northwest of Xinjiang, it is possible to receive television broadcasts in Standard Chinese as well as the local Uyghur and Kazakh languages. Regional stations broadcast local news programmes in addition to the central news, and also feature cultural and educational programmes and, increasingly, light entertainment. Long-running soap operas and series based on traditional and historical themes are particularly popular.

When the reform era began in the late 1970s, there were probably fewer than 10 million television sets in China and many of these were only viewed by groups of people in work units, clubs, and other communal social facilities. Television is now almost universally accessible, even in the remotest rural areas and – as in the developed world – is mainly viewed in families and individual households.

The reception of international cable and satellite TV varies greatly. There is easy access in the topflight hotels that are run mainly for the benefit of foreigners, but coverage is otherwise very patchy. Attempts are still made to restrict the sale of satellite dishes capable of receiving broadcasts from Hong Kong and Taiwan, but these measures have been largely ineffective, and many Chinese viewers have access to programmes in Chinese from broadcasters such as CNN and Star TV. Cantonese speakers in southern China were ahead of their northern compatriots and had regular access to Hong Kong television programmes long before the handover in 1997.

Radio was by far the most common broadcast medium in the early years of the PRC and, although television is now almost universal, radio experienced a new lease on life and there are at least 2,600 radio stations which are all controlled by the government. There is still heavy coverage of political news, but it is now possible to listen to popular music for much of the day. Among the most popular programmes have been innovative phone-in shows which address personal and social matters that were almost completely neglected by the traditional media. Some of these programmes are hosted by agony aunts whose forthright style has turned them into national stars: because callers can be anonymous, there can be free and frank discussion about many controversial personal and social issues.

New media

The internet has proved extremely popular and official sources indicate that access is now available to 904 million users, 64.5% of the population, which would make it the largest population of internet users in the world.[5] The vast majority, 98.6%, have internet access through a smart phone, and 26.7% of users live in rural areas.

The Chinese internet is dominated by three powerful companies: Baidu, Alibaba, and Tencent. Baidu runs the most popular search engine; Alibaba is the leading e-commerce company and with Sina operates the microblog Weibo; Tencent is the proprietor of WeChat, the instant messaging app which is the nearest China has to WhatsApp. WeChat has a near monopoly of social media use in China, but has been compromised by official censorship.

Internet sites are monitored regularly by the authorities and many are blocked either permanently or temporarily if they are considered to be morally or politically suspect or otherwise unsuitable. The web filtering system that blocks banned URLs and suppresses sensitive keywords is known as the Great Firewall of China. Internet resources that are frequently blocked include Facebook, Twitter, YouTube, and websites relating to human rights. Internet users in the PRC became adept at circumventing these blockages through the use of virtual private networks and other devices, but in 2015, the authorities strengthened the firewall and made bypassing filters more difficult. Internet service providers practice a high level of self-censorship to avoid contravening severe government regulations on permitted content.

There are also government restrictions on the growth of internet service providers. There are many websites in Chinese, both in simplified and traditional characters, which carry news and comment on the Chinese world, some of them extremely well informed: among the most popular search engines are *Baidu Sina* and *Sohu*. There is also material for entertainment and much that is of a sensational or trivial nature. Access to the internet is also possible through internet cafes, although these often seem to be monopolised by teenagers playing online video games. Internet cafes are also subject to periodical crackdowns by the authorities whenever there are government concerns about unsuitable material being placed online.

The government is not solely concerned with the possibility of Chinese citizens having access to Western ideas on the internet. There is also a worry, voiced by the Deputy Director of the Chinese National Administration for the Protection of State Secrets, Cong Bing, that the internet could be used to leak state secrets, which are, as has been argued, defined far more broadly in China than they are in the West. Cong Bing specifically referred to the use of bulletin boards, chat rooms, and newsgroups on the internet as channels through which classified information could find a way out of China.[6] There was a significant reduction in government control over the media during the reform period, but this has slowed or even reversed under Xi Jinping.

Journalists

Chinese journalists in the past were state employees and, with a few honourable exceptions, did not enjoy a reputation for independence and fearless investigation. This changed, partly because Chinese journalists were exposed to Western media and in some cases had been trained in the West, but also because the expectations of their audience altered with increased commercialisation and competition. It became increasingly common for journalists from China to take qualifications in media studies in Western universities at both undergraduate and postgraduate levels.

The existence of an independent-minded tradition in the media was demonstrated in 1989 when groups of journalists were prominent among the demonstrators in Tian'anmen Square who were calling for greater democracy and openness. Inevitably they also suffered disproportionately in the political repression that followed the military suppression of the protests, but the tradition of independence persists in spite of the fact that journalists can be, and regularly are, fined or imprisoned for reports that criticise the government.

Globalisation and the Chinese media

Media academics in China are conscious of the tension between the CCP's attempts to control the mass media in the way that it has done for decades and the pressures of globalisation, which has exposed at least the educated portion of the Chinese population to foreign newspapers, magazines, radio, and – above all – satellite television and the internet. In 2002, Tsinghua (Qinghua) University published a collection of articles in Chinese under the English sub-title of *Globalisation and Mass Media: Clash, Convergence and Interaction*. Contributors included media researchers from Hong Kong and the West, in addition to academics working within the PRC. The discussion covered the impact of the global media on China and the global market for television products, protection and openness in the Chinese media, nationalism and internationalism in the media, the diffusion of the internet in China, and the reporting of China by foreign broadcasters. The breadth of issues discussed showed a keen understanding of the issues that faced Chinese media professionals.[7]

Foreign media

Since 1949, the PRC has sought to restrict the population's access to news from overseas, although not all Party members approved of this and the restrictions were relaxed considerably from the 1980s. Shortwave broadcasts, now obsolete, were regularly jammed, including those of the BBC, and rebroadcasting and the use of satellite receivers are controlled. Websites have been blocked, especially those in Chinese from outside China, and content deemed inappropriate has often been filtered.

Western journalists working in China are obliged to register with the authorities, the way they operate is restricted, and surveillance is often severe. From time to time, journalists have been expelled from China or their credentials not renewed. While these expulsions have been related to articles or programmes produced by the journalist, they have also been a result of the vagaries of diplomatic relations between Beijing and the home country of the journalists. During the Xi Jinping period, the restrictions on foreign journalists have increased significantly.

In February 2020, the *Wall Street Journal* (*WSJ*) published an article by Walter Russell Mead entitled 'China is the Real Sick Man of Asia' which warned of potential dangers in Chinese financial markets and the risk of an economic meltdown following the Covid-19 crisis. The headline was undoubtedly provocative, and the argument has to date not been borne out by events. On Wednesday 18 February, three *WSJ* reporters in China, Josh Chin, Chao Deng, and Philip Wen, were informed that they had been declared *persona non grata* and had five days to leave the country. This move came the day after the US State Department announced that five Chinese news agencies in the United States would be treated as official government bodies. Beijing indicated, however, that it was retaliation for the *WSJ* article. The Foreign Correspondents' Club of China protested at this draconian response; previously Beijing had allowed credentials to lapse rather than expel a journalist directly, which had not happened since 1998. The credentials of Melissa Chan of Al Jazeera were not renewed in 2012; *New York Times* staff were denied visas after publishing details of the family wealth of senior leaders; and Victor Mallet of the *Financial Times* was effectively excluded from Hong Kong after refusing to cancel a talk by a Hong Kong activist to the correspondents' club.[8]

Notes

1 *SCMP* 28 July 2016.
2 Liu Binyan *A Higher Kind of Loyalty: A Memoir by China's Foremost Journalist* London: Methuen, 1990, p. 155.
3 China Statistical Yearbook 2018.
4 *Washington Post* 24 January 2006.
5 *Global Times* 28 April 2020.
6 *People's Daily* 1 December 2006.
7 Yin Hong, Li Bin (Editors in Chief) *Quanqiuhua yu dazhong chuangmei: chongtu; ronghe; huxiang* (*Globalisation and Mass Media: Clash, Convergence and Interaction*) Beijing: Qinghua University Press, 2002.
8 BBC 'China Profile-Media' 6 March 2018; Walter Russell Mead 'China Is the Real Sick Man of Asia' *Wall Street Journal* 3 February 2020; *Washington Post* 19 February 2020.

18 Religious and ethnic minorities

Religion, which was supposed to have become irrelevant in a Communist state, emerged as a significant social issue and a challenge for the CCP and the government during the reform period. China has been criticised regularly by international human rights activists on its attitude to religious freedom in theory and in practice. While some religions are practised irrespective of ethnic affiliations, others – notably, Islam and Tibetan Buddhism — are closely tied to specific ethnic groups and are an integral part of their national and cultural identities.[1]

Religious movements in China

Religious institutions and religious movements have become more influential in China as the ideological and moral authority of the CCP (although not its political power) weakened. Religion survived decades of rule by an atheist government, against the expectations of many observers, and experienced a dramatic revival during the immediate post-Cultural Revolution period of 'reform and opening'. Religious leaders who were willing to work with the government and the CCP were appointed to advisory positions in local and central government, although their institutions were also subjected to surveillance and state control. Underground religious groups attract wide support in spite of (or possibly because of) the fact that their activities are officially proscribed.

Religious freedom is formally guaranteed under the Constitution of the PRC, but it is no secret that this applies only to bodies approved by, registered with, and monitored by the state. Individuals and congregations not registered with the government's Religious Affairs Bureau (the central body controlling the local bureau was renamed the State Administration for Religious Affairs in 1998) face significant restrictions. These can range from political pressure and obstruction to the compulsory closure of churches, temples, mosques, and religious schools, the seizure of devotional literature (books, audiotapes, and videotapes), and the imprisonment of priests, monks, nuns, and imams.

Since the 1980s, there has been a remarkable increase in overt religious activity. Religious buildings closed down or commandeered for secular use during the Cultural Revolution were reopened, and religious communities that had maintained their traditions and organisations informally and in secret emerged from the shadows. While many of these groups would be recognised as authentic religious bodies anywhere in the world, others exhibit the characteristics of religious cults with questionable spiritual and ethical values, particularly some of those that have sprung up in the more remote rural areas. Between these two extremes are the 'new religions', that have emerged from a selective synthesis of Buddhism, Daoism (Taoism), and traditional folk religions: Falungong is the most prominent of these. Although some of these groups are considered to be legitimate by both Chinese and

Western commentators, others are more questionable and it has been alleged that some sects practise psychological manipulation, the breaking up families, and economic and sexual exploitation.[2]

Daosim and Buddhism

Attendance at traditional Daoist and Buddhist temples and the presentation of votive offerings have increased since the end of the Cultural Revolution. In some remote rural areas, secret societies that draw on popular and often heterodox traditions of Daoism and Buddhism have also revived. In some cases, these are treated as criminal bodies by the police and local officials, but they persist. Their beliefs and organisation blend religious symbolism and rituals that are reminiscent of the secret societies of the nineteenth century. As the income and wealth gap between the cities and the villages widened, these societies appealed increasingly to the poor and marginalised. Some were involved in protests by villagers against unpopular land deals and corrupt officials.

Daoism is (together with popular and folk religions, from which it is sometimes difficult to distinguish) the indigenous religion of China. Shinto occupies a similar position in Japan, and there are parallels between the two religions, particularly in their sympathetic attitude towards the natural world. Daoism, especially in its popular form, overlaps with Buddhism, a second-century import from India that, in spite of its foreign origins, is also regarded as a native Chinese religion.

Daoism

Daoism (formerly spelt Taoism) has two aspects which sit uneasily together: on the one hand, there is the literary and philosophical tradition of the educated elite; on the other hand, the popular practices appertaining to China's folk religions. Literary and philosophical Daoism, exemplified by the oblique and often mystifying classical texts, the *Zhuangzi* and *Daodejing* [*Tao-te Ching*], advocated the belief that human beings should accommodate themselves to the flow of the natural world, the *Dao* or the 'way'. Popular Daoism, on the other hand, was a religion with its own particular texts and rituals, focused on 'immortals' and the quest for everlasting life. It was fragmented and frequently at odds with authority, and persists today. It is quite open in Hong Kong and Taiwan, but remained underground on the mainland until the 1980s and was frequently linked with new religious sects and clandestine organisations branded as criminal by the CCP.

Wing-tsit Chan, a distinguished expatriate Chinese scholar of philosophy who revisited China in 1948 and 1949 during the period when the Guomindang regime was collapsing and making way for the CCP, concluded that Daoism, together with folk religion in general, was defunct: 'Since [D]aoism underlies the religion of the masses, its decline is tantamount to the collapse of the people's religion as a whole'. Temples, shrines, idols, and priests were still in evidence, although their numbers were in decline and Chan felt that, 'the real spirit of the religion [was] dead, and its vitality [was] fast disappearing'. When the CCP established the Chinese People's Political Consultative Conference in 1949 to provide a forum for – and simultaneously a means of controlling – political, ethnic, and religious minorities, there were delegates representing Protestant Christianity, Buddhism, and Islam, but none from the world of Daoism. The Daoists had no effective leadership and no programme to address their needs in the mid-twentieth century: Daoist influence was limited largely to art, rituals, and festivals.[3]

According to the sceptical Chan,

> The chief reason for the Daoist collapse is, of course, its total devotion to the search for earthly blessings – wealth, health, longevity, happiness, children. With the advancement of science and education in China, the Chinese masses learn that the fulfilment of human desires does not come from chasing away evil spirits and praying to benevolent deities. Modern medical science is fast replacing the God of Medicine, and rural schoolchildren go to the temple of the God of Literature, not to pray but to play.

With hindsight, it is clear that Chan overstated the decline of Daoism; his negative view of the religion and its extinction in the twentieth century was in line with modernising Chinese scholars of his day. The collapse he witnessed was superficial: the importance of Daoism lies in its inseparability from the rituals of daily life in China, rather than its usefulness as a shortcut to wealth and longevity.

Daoism survived by metamorphosing into numerous sects and secret societies – some of which drew on Buddhist traditions – with their own political agendas. These included the White Lotus and the Guiyidao (the Way of Returning to – or Following – the One). Many of these religio-political associations had been in decline since the 1930s, but one, the Yiguandao (Way of Pervading Unity), had, as Chan put it 'gained strength and extended its activities during the Second World War'. It probably originated during the Boxer Rising (1899–1890) but developed rapidly under its teacher Zhang Tieran who died in 1947. Many religious groups, including the Yiguandao, flourished during the Japanese occupation of China and provided support and self-defence for the rural population.[4]

After the victory of the CCP in 1949, Daoism could not maintain an apolitical and detached position and was obliged to adapt to the new political conditions. Daoist temples lost much of their land during the land reform movement, as did other religious institutions, and this considerably weakened their economic position and their social authority. Monks had no option but to take manual jobs to support themselves: this was seen as a positive change by the CCP, but it undermined the mystique and prestige of the clergy among their followers. Even official CCP publications accept that during the Great Leap Forward of 1958, now acknowledged as an ultra-leftist deviation, many ancient and precious Daoist artefacts such as bells and cauldrons were melted down in 'backyard furnaces' to produce steel at any cost.[5] In spite of repression, the Daoist tradition continued, particularly in the countryside, sometimes underground and sometimes openly. In the 1980s, the police were openly reporting the arrest of members of the Yiguandao which the CCP claimed to have eliminated during the 1950s.

Daoist temples and monasteries reopened in the 1980s, some initially as tourist attractions, but they gradually regained their religious functions. Monks were recalled from retirement from the farms or other work units to which they had been assigned. Funds were raised to pay wages and buy materials to rebuild or repair temples; local seminaries revived the training of priests, and some novices were also sent to Beijing. The Chinese Daoist Association, which was originally founded in 1957 but had ceased to operate during the Cultural Revolution, was re-established in 1983 and based in Beijing at the Baiyunguan, the White Cloud Temple which is the largest Daoist temple in northern China. The Baiyun Temple was closed in 1966 with the Cultural Revolution and only reopened in March 1984, by which time it had over 30 resident monks who were training Daoists from over 100 monasteries registered with the Chinese Daoist Association.[6]

Daoism spread unobtrusively, sometimes in the most unlikely circumstances. In October 2000, there were reports that officials at a rural People's Court had engaged a Daoist priest to carry out a five-hour–long ceremony of exorcism after a guard had fallen to his death from a window. Higher authorities launched an enquiry into these activities, which contravened government policy on the avoidance of superstition. In the southeastern province of Fujian, one of the areas that has benefited most from the economic reforms of Deng Xiaoping, Daoist temples were re-consecrated by former monks who had returned from secular jobs. Rituals and local cults assumed to be extinct were revived and once again began to play a significant role in local politics. Ian Johnson has recorded the Daoism of the musical Li family of Shanxi province and the rituals of life and death at which they officiate; also the attempts by Daoist adepts at their temple, the Palace of the Bronze Ram in Chengdu, to interest educated citizens in Daoism by offering spiritual massages and readings from the classic *Daodejing*.[7]

Buddhism

Although Buddhism, which originated in ancient northeastern India, is technically a foreign religion, it has been established in China for so long that it is for all intents and purposes regarded as Chinese. Buddhist scriptures were translated into Chinese, its practices assumed a Chinese form, and it became an integral part of the lives of the majority of Chinese people.

Buddhism was well established in Central Asia by the first century BC and began to spread to China during the early Christian era. During the Han dynasty (206 BC–220 AD), the first great dynasty of the Empire and one of the formative periods of Chinese culture, the main centres of Buddhism in China were at Pengcheng in the south of what is now the province of Hebei and Luoyang. Another centre, Tonkin, is now in Vietnam. Buddhism acquired great political influence during the Tang dynasty (618–907) when it attracted support from the imperial court. In the words of Kenneth Ch'en, a leading scholar of Chinese Buddhism, in the Tang dynasty 'Buddhism finally came of age in China; it was supported by all elements of society – by the imperial household, the nobility, the great and wealthy families, and the common people'.[8] Temples became social and entertainment centres, as well as places for worship. Buddhist monasteries accumulated great wealth on the basis of donations from believers and acquired land: this gave them social influence and economic power in their immediate area. By the later years of the Ming dynasty (1368–1644), prosperity and stability had created a large landowning gentry class, far more than were needed for official positions, in either central or local government. For many people from this background, Buddhist monasteries became the focus of their social lives, either as patrons and supporters or as monks. Consequently, monasteries enjoyed immense wealth, prestige, and authority. In addition to the Buddhist establishment, there were many popular sects linked with secret societies, such as the millenarian and messianic White Lotus, which drew on the tradition of the Maitreya, the Buddha of the future, and which took part in rebellions against the Manchu Qing dynasty in the eighteenth century. White Lotus ideas were influential in the Boxer Rebellion of 1899–1901, and remain influential in parts of rural China to this day.[9]

In the early years of the PRC, hundreds of thousands of monks were compelled to leave their orders and to work in farms, workshops, or factories. At the same time, the CCP recognised Buddhism as an official religion and allowed two Buddhist delegates to attend the meetings of the Chinese People's Political Consultative Conference. Holmes Welch, the author of major studies of Buddhism in China, neatly summarised the official status of the religion in the first 17 years of the PRC: 'until the Cultural Revolution began in 1966, it was the policy of the Chinese Communist Party to protect Buddhism, while at the same time keeping it under control and utilizing it in foreign policy'.[10] This did not prevent damage to temples and their contents and physical attacks on Buddhist clergy during the campaigns for land reform (in spite of clauses in the land reform law specifically prohibiting this) and during the movement for the suppression of counter-revolutionaries. Although the general tenor of Marxist writing in China was anti-clerical, there was some ambiguity, even in the writings of Mao Zedong, where it is possible to detect some respect for peasant religious beliefs and an acknowledgement that if those beliefs were to be overturned, it should be the peasants themselves who decide to do so.

The career of Juzan (Chü-tsan) is instructive for an understanding of the position of Buddhism in the early years of the PRC. He was considered 'modern and progressive in outlook', and was one of the two Buddhist delegates to the CPPCC. Juzan became a monk in 1931, having studied under Taixu, 'the leading Buddhist reformer of the Republican era'. He moved to Hong Kong in 1948 and came into contact with a group of people who were to be extremely powerful in the PRC, including the writer Guo Moruo. As the CCP came to power, he lobbied for the preservation of a reformed school of Buddhism under the Communist state by placing the religion at the service of New China. In June 1950, he became the editor of the journal *Modern Buddhism*: this journal, unlike either its predecessors or other contemporary publications, was highly influential and became the nucleus of a powerful Buddhist organisation and the origin of the national Buddhist Association which was founded in 1953. The journal and the association were part of the CCP's system for controlling religious activity, and to a lesser extent, soliciting feedback from believers.[11]

Land reform was the single most important policy implemented by the CCP in its early years in power. Designed to alleviate dreadful rural poverty and to distribute land, albeit temporarily, to peasant families who had been the Party's power base, it also undermined the traditional social structure of rural China and effectively abolished the landowning class. Buddhist monasteries had acquired large holdings of land over a period of many centuries and were treated as landlords. During the land reform process, many lost all or part of their land, and thus their means of an independent livelihood, although the Agrarian Reform Law was implemented unevenly and not all monasteries suffered to the same extent.

As collectivisation succeeded land reform, some monks formed themselves into cooperatives and farmed or worked in craft industries to avoid being criticised as parasites. In 1958, the year of the radical Maoist Great Leap Forward, donation boxes at Buddhist temples and shrines were outlawed and monks were forbidden to carry out divination for money.

Many monks and nuns left their monasteries and became lay people, working in agriculture or industry. Monasteries and temples were taken over by the government and some were converted into schools, museums, administrative offices, or even army barracks. This was not unprecedented, as there were instances of the previous Nationalist Guomindang government having requisitioned monasteries. Some smaller temples were also destroyed during the 1950s. The net effect of these policies was a dramatic decline in the *sangha*, the community of Buddhist clergy which, along with the Buddha and the *dharma* [doctrine], are the Three Jewels – the essential components of Buddhism. However, monasteries and temples remained open and were visited by foreign Buddhists who travelled to China.

The destruction and neglect of sacred Buddhist sites in the early years of the PRC was not unique. Buddhism had experienced repeated repression and revival over the centuries. What followed in the 1980s was another phase in a historically familiar process of reconstruction, innovation, and adaptation. With the Cultural Revolution of 1966, the destruction of Buddhism had appeared almost complete. Mao Zedong's youthful political shock troops, the Red Guards, were encouraged to attack the Four Olds: old ideas, old culture, old customs, and old habits. Although Buddhism was not specifically named as a target, by the end of

September 1966, almost all Buddhist monasteries and temples had closed down (at least in the cities), as had mosques and churches. Many of these were converted into flats or for other secular purposes. Buddhist icons were damaged or destroyed, if they had not been carefully concealed, and monks were arrested and ill treated. Many were criticised in public meetings, and the work of the Chinese Buddhist Association came to a halt; it resumed some of its responsibilities in 1972 after the intervention of Premier Zhou Enlai.

When China began to return to some kind of stability in the late 1970s and early 1980s, Buddhist temples were once again opened, and, although initially there were very few monks in evidence, it was common to see votive offerings of money or fruit that had been left in the outstretched hands of the statues of Bodhisattvas. Official estimates suggest that there are now over 13,000 Buddhist temples in China and more than 200,000 monks and nuns. This total includes 120,000 lamas and nuns in the Tibetan Buddhist tradition which has over 3,000 temples and 1700 Living Buddhas.[12]

Tibetan and Mongolian Buddhism

Buddhism remains an especially potent force in Tibet and Inner Mongolia. Distinct from Chinese Buddhism, although drawing ultimately on the same inspiration and scriptural sources, it is also a means of expressing ethnic and cultural differences, and it has political and national dimensions. In the past, the traditional religious elite in both regions exercised temporal power in addition to spiritual authority: there is still considerable support for the Dalai Lama, who is venerated in Mongolia and Inner Mongolia, as well as in Tibet, and this is anathema to Beijing. Temples in Inner Mongolia remained closed well into the 1980s and some are primarily museums, although it is not uncommon to come across worshippers even in these.

The Yonghegong Lama Temple in Beijing, which dates back to the eighteenth century, reopened in the post-Cultural Revolution period and has a thriving community of monks, many brought in from Qinghai province. It is clearly a showcase designed to persuade visitors to Beijing that the CCP practices religious tolerance, but there is no doubting the genuine convictions of Tibetan, Mongol, and Chinese Buddhists visitors who prostrate themselves before the statues of the Buddha.[13]

Protests in Tibet by Buddhist clergy against the lack of religious freedom have been treated as nationalist disturbances by the government. Many monks and nuns have been imprisoned, and there are consistent and credible reports of brutal treatment.[14] The Tibetan issue is explored more fully in Chapter 21.

Islam

Islam has had a presence in China since the earliest days of the religion, but unlike Buddhism which is considered to be essentially Chinese in spite of its origins in India, it is treated as a foreign religion. Han Chinese often express negative stereotypes about Chinese-speaking Hui Muslims, suggesting that they are poorly educated, interested only in trade and not highly cultured. Some consider the older, traditional mosques to be dark, alien, and forbidding. Hui people are assumed by the state to be basically loyal to China, whereas the Uyghur Muslims of Xinjiang are suspected of sympathy for the independence movement. Not surprisingly, the reality is more complex.

Since the end of the Cultural Revolution, Hui Muslims were relatively free to worship in registered mosques and to study in registered madrasas (Qur'anic schools) in the areas of

Hui concentration in Ningxia and Gansu and elsewhere. They were also able to make the *hajj* pilgrimage to Mecca, subject to considerable monitoring and supervision by state bodies. Islamic organisations other than mosques, including the influential Sufi orders, which are usually based at the shrine of their founding fathers, were still treated with great suspicion. They prospered nevertheless, and pilgrimages to Hui shrines were generally permitted. Sufi organisations have a history of involvement in violent conflict, both with other Muslim groups and with the authorities, and have often been the focal point of activity against the state. They are carefully monitored by security organisations, but their leaders are also included in the deliberations of local government, often through membership of local branches of the Chinese People's Political Consultative Conference.

Xinjiang is different. The Uyghurs speak a Turkic language, and only have Chinese as a second language, if at all. There are severe restrictions on attendance at mosques, especially for anyone under the age of 18, and on formal religious education. Periodically, campaigns have been mounted to compel imams and other religious professionals to undergo training to ensure that they remain 'patriotic', and students and staff in schools and colleges are under pressure to eschew religion if they wish to have a career in public service. An interest in Islam by Uyghurs is believed by government organisations to be associated with the movement for independence. Although active support for an independent Xinjiang is not universal, there is some justification for this belief. Uyghurs have family, business, and religious ties with communities in the former Soviet Central Asian states, and the independence of these states after the collapse of the USSR in 1991 stimulated hopes for the revival of an independent Eastern Turkestan, which had existed briefly in the 1940s. Many Uyghurs do favour an independent state, and some have agitated for an Islamic state: most realise that this is unlikely – if not a complete impossibility – in the foreseeable future. Xinjiang is discussed more fully in Chapter 22.

Protestant Christianity

China treats Protestant Christianity [*Jidu jiao*] and Roman Catholic Christianity [*Tianzhu jiao*)] as if they are two completely separate religions, but in both cases the government attempts to restrict the participation of Chinese Christians in the wider religious community beyond China. Orthodox Christianity [*Zhengjiao* or *Dongzheng jiao* – Eastern Orthodox], which has a long history in certain ethnic Russian communities in the northwest and northeast of China, is also often treated as a separate religion.

The Three Self Patriotic Movement [*sanzi aiguo jiaohui*] – self-governing, self-supporting and self-propagating – which was established in the 1950s is the umbrella organisation for Protestant Christians who are willing to worship in churches that are approved and monitored by the state. Many Chinese Christians reject this system and belong to underground, or 'house', churches. Some of these churches are treated by the authorities as if they are cults: they are subject to periodic suppression, and their ministers who are not recognised by the authorities have been arrested and confined in labour camps. The geographical location of both types of churches, registered and underground, is related to the activities of pre-1949 missions: they were significantly stronger in the Yangzi valley which was within relatively easy reach of the nineteenth-century treaty ports.

Christianity was suppressed during the Cultural Revolution, as were other religions, but it was not entirely extinguished and began to reappear in the early 1980s. The first wave of this revival was most dramatic in the provinces of Zhejiang and Henan, and particularly in the poorer and more remote rural areas of Henan where a 'Christianity fever' was reported.

Because the leadership of the Three Self Patriotic Movement had lost its authority and credibility during the Cultural Revolution, in most cased the revival took the form of the recreation, or creation, of autonomous churches.[15]

Watchman Nee and the Lord's Recovery Church

The Lord's Recovery Church is an example of one of the underground Protestant churches, and its history illustrates the difficult relationship that unofficial congregations have had with the Chinese state. This church is one of the unregistered – and therefore illegal – underground Protestant groups, of which there are many in China, and its closest parallel in the West is something like the Plymouth Brethren. It belongs to the revivalist and ecstatic tradition of dissenting Christianity, hence its nickname – the Shouters, which is a name given to it by its critics and not one used in general, or particularly liked, by the church itself.

Watchman Nee, a legendary figure in the Chinese dissenting Christian tradition, is credited as the founder of the church and it acknowledges his religious legacy, although like many in the dissenting tradition, it has a complex history. Watchman Nee, Ni Duosheng (1903–1972), was born in Guangzhou but brought up and educated in Fujian province. He was influenced initially by Methodist missionaries but subsequently by members of the Church Missionary Society who were associated with the Exclusive Brethren, although he himself was later to be closer to the Open Brethren. He was baptised at the age of 19 and established a church in Shanghai, where he wrote what were to become important texts in the indigenising theology of Christianity in China. Watchman Nee's church was originally known as the Little Flock.

Watchman Nee came into conflict with the CCP very soon after the foundation of the PRC. Because of his conservative and fundamentalist theological stance, he was unable to comply with the CCP's policy on the registration and control of religious organisations. He was arrested in 1952 for his opposition to the CCP and also on charges of financial irregularities, was transferred to a labour camp in Anhui province during the Cultural Revolution, and died there in 1972.[16]

An autonomous and arguably more elitist Local Church broke away from the Little Flock: this was led by Witness Lee, Li Changshou (1905–1997), who had been a disciple of Watchman Nee. This sect became popular and spread through Christian communities in China and among overseas Chinese. Witness Lee moved to Taiwan in the 1940s in the wake of the military victories of the CCP and subsequently relocated to the United States. Chinese followers of the Local Church movement in the twenty-first century refer to their church as the Lord's Recovery [*Zhu de huifu*] Church, a term which to its members signifies the recovery or rediscovery of the true meaning and practice of the early church fathers. As it is primarily based in the United States, its involvement in China is seen by the government of the PRC as an example of outside interference in the religious policy of the Chinese state.

Repression of independent Protestant churches

Contact between the official church in China and the wider Anglican Communion has increased since China began to open to the outside world in the 1980s, although these contacts have been characterised by caution on both sides. Dr. Rowan Williams, then Archbishop of Canterbury and the head of the worldwide Anglican Communion, visited China in October 2006. His impressions of the development of Christianity in China were positive and his interviews in China inclined him to the view that estimates of 50–80 million Protestant

Christians in China were a reasonable guess. He acknowledged the existence of a cultural Christianity – that is, a sympathy for and interest in Christianity particularly among students and staff in institutions of higher education. He rejected the easy assumption that China was 'a field ripe for missionary harvest', arguing that the Chinese church should be permitted to manage its own development.[17]

The Protestant Shouwang church – the Chinese name translates as Watchkeepers and uses the same characters as found in 'watchtower' – was founded in Beijing in 1993 with ten original members by Jin Tianming, a chemical engineering graduate of the prestigious Tsinghua University, who was of Korean ethnicity. By 2011, it claimed 1,000 members, many from the educated professional middle classes, and did not have its own premises after an attempt to move into a property it had bought in 2009 was blocked, but it met in the houses of members or rented halls for services and Bible study. In April 2011, it held an outdoor service for the first time, and this was disrupted by police who detained 169 worshippers on the day and more during the week that followed. Many adherents were placed under house arrest. At a public service in the high-tech district of Zhongguancun on May 15, 13 members were arrested, including Pastor Jin, and many were placed in detention. Divisions within the church over the decision to hold outdoor services were reported to have led to senior members leaving the church.[18]

Another unregistered Protestant group, the Early Rain Covenant Church, based in Chengdu and described as Calvinist, was suppressed in December 2018. While most members detained at the time were released, its most senior figure, Pastor Wang Yi, remained in custody and one year later was sentenced to nine years imprisonment for 'inciting the subversion of state power' and operating a business illegally.[19]

Some groups exhibited behaviour that was more obviously cult-like. In December 2012, almost 1,000 members of a secretive apocalyptic Christian sect, Eastern Lightning [*Dongfang shanding*], which prefers the name Church of Almighty God, were arrested in the western provinces of Guizhou and Qinghai, charged with being members of a 'heterodox cult'. The group probably split from the Lords Recovery Church in the early 1990s and has been linked with civil disturbances, kidnappings, and murders. Leaders of the cult, including a 'female Jesus' who encouraged 'sex communication' to seduce unwary men, had predicted the end of the world with earthquakes, tsunamis, and three days of darkness during which the CCP would be overthrown. On 28 May 2014, a woman was beaten to death by six members of the church at a McDonalds's restaurant in the Shandong city of Zhaoyuan. A police crackdown resulted in the arrest of over 1,000 church members; five were charged with murder, two were executed, and the other three were imprisoned. A concentrated police campaign against the cult followed. The murders drew attention to the existence of the anti-cult 610 Office, which is discussed further in the section of this chapter on Falungong. In spite of the crackdown, the cult continued to exist, and 18 members were arrested in the summer of 2017.[20]

Catholic Christianity

Catholic Christianity in China is also divided. The Chinese Catholic Patriotic Association [*Zhongguo tianzhujiao aiguo hui*] is the official body and there is an underground Catholic Church, which is usually characterised as being loyal to the Vatican. During the papacy of John Paul II (1978–2005), the decision by Rome to canonise Chinese Catholic martyrs exacerbated the dispute between the two churches: given the Polish Pope's hostility to Communism, this was not surprising. In contrast, during the early days of the papacy of Benedict XVI (2005–2013), there was a mood of reconciliation and a move towards the re-establishment of diplomatic relations between the Holy See and Beijing which had been severed in 1951.

A papal letter addressed to Roman Catholics in China on 27 May 2007 initiated a fresh dialogue with both the Chinese Catholic Church and the secular authorities. It acknowledged the difficulties that had been faced by Catholics in China who had been put in the position of having to decide whether they should accept the authority of government bodies. It further affirmed that underground activities were not usual or desirable in the Catholic Church, but accepted that some Catholic bishops had 'felt themselves constrained to opt for clandestine consecration'. Pope Benedict's letter was couched in dense theological and legal language, and endeavoured to demonstrate that there was in fact a considerable element of continuity between his policy on China and that of the papacy of John Paul II, although the tone of the new Pope's approach was markedly different. Pope Benedict acknowledged that some bishops had 'consented to receive Episcopal consecration without the pontifical mandate' but had subsequently asked to be received into communion with the Vatican, and that these had been retrospectively legitimised as bishops. In some cases, this had not been made public; congregations and even priests were not aware of the legitimation, and this caused great confusion. Even bishops who had not asked for or obtained this legitimate consecration could be recognised as 'illegitimate but validly consecrated'. This acknowledgement confirmed rumours that had been circulating for some time and clarified oblique remarks that had been made by Pope John Paul II about covert consecrations *in pectore* [in the heart] during the final years of his papacy. These can now be understood to have referred to the appointment of three cardinals including Gong Pinmei, the Bishop of Shanghai. The process of reconciliation had been underway even before the papacy of Benedict XVI.

The relationship between the official and the underground Catholic Church has been complex: some Catholic bishops who were not formally approved by the Vatican, but were nevertheless considered to be acceptable to Rome because of their background and training, may have been selected and authorised by the Patriotic Association in what was probably both a gesture of accommodation and a face-saving exercise. Likewise, it appears that the Vatican has accepted the authority of many of the bishops who were consecrated by the officially recognised church.[21]

Cooperation and conflict in the consecration of bishops

An underground Catholic bishop, Han Dingxiang of Hebei province, who had spent almost 35 years in prison, died in September 2007 while still in custody. He had been suffering from lung cancer for some time and it appears that his funeral was arranged hastily and carried out without the presence of any Catholic priests. However, almost simultaneously in the southern city of Guiyang, a new bishop was consecrated jointly by clergy from the underground church and the state-sponsored Catholic Patriotic Association.[22] That was a low-profile ordination, but the ordination of Father Joseph Li Shan as Bishop in the Cathedral of the Immaculate Conception in Beijing (the Nantang or Southern Cathedral, as it is known in the city) on 21 September 2007 was a much more public occasion and, although he was the candidate of the Patriotic Association, his consecration was carried out with the express approval of Pope Benedict. This consecration marked a new phase in the relationship between the underground and official churches, and a recognition that the two were cooperating in shared activities. The Vatican hoped that this would herald a full unification of the Catholic Church in China and permit the establishment of full diplomatic relations with Beijing.[23]

There was further evidence for the trend towards closer relations between the official and underground Catholic churches late in 2007 when two bishops were installed with the approval of both traditions. Joseph Gan Junqiu was consecrated as Bishop of Guangzhou, the most important city in south China, while Lu Shouwang became Bishop of Yichang, a city in the west of Hubei province. In both cases the ceremonies were low key and not open to the press or television. A spokesman for the Catholic Patriotic Association insisted that the appointments had been made by Beijing, but he also expressed his satisfaction that the Vatican had approved of the individuals who had been chosen.[24]

The process of consecration of bishops did not run entirely smoothly and Guo Jincai became bishop of Chengde without Vatican approval – his excommunication, along with those of another five 'official bishops', was eventually revoked by Pope Francis in September 2018. In June 2011, it looked as if Joseph Shen Guo'an would be consecrated as bishop of Wuhan without the approval of the Vatican. In the end, the Vatican conferred papal authority without publicity.[25]

Overseas churches

Churches outside China that attempt to support churches on the mainland are viewed with great suspicion: these include evangelical Christians from South Korea, who have been involved in smuggling North Korean refugees into China, and the Cardinal Kung Foundation based in the United States, which is vociferously critical of the Catholic Patriotic Association. Some evangelical Christian organisations in the United States have an explicit policy of 'planting churches in China', a policy that is resented and resisted by the CCP, more from a sense of national pride and affronted dignity than for strictly ideological considerations. Outside interference of this nature is perceived as an attempt by foreign powers to undermine the state's policies on religion.

There is potential for considerable conflict between religious groups registered with the state and unofficial religions. The state tolerates religion if it is locally controlled, but abhors any suggestion of foreign interference. There are families whose members have been believers for generations, but religion has also found new adherents among social groups disillusioned with the CCP. Christianity appeals to some educated Chinese today, just as it did in the 1920s and 1930s: it is perceived as Western and modern, as well as anti-Communist. There is also the growing phenomenon of cultural Christians, individuals who identify themselves with Christianity to demonstrate that they are modern and fashionable but who do not necessarily believe or practice.

Unofficial branches of all religions continue to grow in popularity as confidence in the ideology of the state declines. While some of these groups have the familiar spiritual and social functions found in religious organisations in the West and elsewhere, others resemble messianic cults which may come into conflict with the Chinese state in the future as they have in the past.

Falungong – a 'new religion'

Falungong has been the *bête noire* of the government of the PRC since April 1999, when it organised large-scale demonstrations outside Zhongnanhai, the residential and administrative compound that is home to senior leaders of the CCP in Beijing.

Falungong, which draws on Buddhist and Daoist beliefs and on other spiritual traditions (or superstitions, depending on one's point of view) that have been popular among the less educated rural population, stands out as by far the most widespread of the many 'new religions' in China. It has, however, also attracted educated urban dwellers, including retired members of the CCP, police, and armed forces (which greatly alarmed the authorities), and spread rapidly across China. Its followers are typically middle-aged or elderly, and there appear to be many more women than men. It represents itself as primarily interested in achieving spiritual enlightenment through exercise and breathing techniques, and encourages particular combinations of *qigong* breathing and physical training, which links it to the martial arts tradition: it also propagates bizarre superstitions about health. Because it was ostensibly a Chinese organisation rather than a foreign import, it was not initially considered by Beijing to be a serious threat.

Falungong was formed by Li Hongzhi in May 1992, and at the time appeared to be just one of many newly organised or revived *qigong* groups. There is a great deal of uncertainty and obscurity about Li Hongzhi's background, much of it manufactured to give him an air of mystery or even sanctity, but he did serve in the PLA. *Qigong* is a traditional Chinese practice of exercise and deep breathing which, it is claimed, enhances physical, mental, and spiritual fitness, but it is also associated with ancient and esoteric Buddhist and Daoist religious practices. Groups of this nature were suppressed in the 1950s. After a brief revival, they suffered further repression during the Cultural Revolution, but many were allowed to operate with some restrictions in the more tolerant atmosphere that prevailed after the death of Mao Zedong in 1976. In 1985, the China Qigong Scientific Research Association was created as the national regulatory body for all *qigong* groups.[26] Falungong was initially recognised by this national body, and Li Hongzhi gave seminars in Beijing and in his place of origin, northeastern China, with official approval. Relations, however, broke down during the 1990s and Falungong withdrew, or was expelled from, the association, which continues to function. Falungong is no longer authorised by the association, and it operates outside of any government regulation.

Falungong attempted to establish its legality by registering with other government bodies, but was unsuccessful. In 1996, its publications were banned by the State Press and Publications Administration, partly because of concern at the rapidly growing number of advocates, but also because of the contents of its publications which attacked modern science and promoted what the Chinese government considered to be superstitious ideas. Particular concern was expressed about the Falungong attitude toward sickness and health, its rejection of modern medicine, and the substitution of *qigong* exercises for medical treatment, even in the case of severe and life-threatening illnesses. The philosophical vision which underlies Falungong's teachings sees humanity moving towards an apocalypse, after which only a small number of true believers will achieve salvation.

Having failed to secure legitimacy, Falungong decentralised into local associations and made its presence felt by dramatic demonstrations. It also acquired a large body of supporters outside China, both in the Chinese-speaking world and in the West, notably from people opposed to the CCP. It became clear from Falungong's own documents that it was not merely an organisation promoting *qigong* exercises, but was developing as a sect with apocalyptic ideas similar to those found in Buddhist and Daoist secret societies in China for many centuries, as well as in new religions and cults in the more developed world.

Li Hongzhi, the founder of Falungong, continued to spread his teachings in China after the publication ban, but relocated to the United States in 1998. This allowed the Chinese government to assert that Falungong was no longer a native Chinese religious movement, but rather an organisation with a foreign base and foreign funding which threatened the existence of the Chinese state.[27]

In China, Falungong attracted a significant number of professionals into its membership, many of them at or near retirement age but still part of China's educated and influential elite. Of particular concern to the authorities were reports of the level of interest in Falungong among senior officers of the PLA and the police. Following the demonstrations of 1999, many members of Falungong were arrested and detained. Accurate information on the scale and the nature of this detention is difficult to obtain, and almost all comes from sources close to either the Chinese government or Falungong supporters. There is little independent or objective data. Nevertheless, a coherent pattern has emerged. Very few members of Falungong were brought to trial under the normal judicial processes; those who were taken to court were the most senior activists and those associated with publishing and fund-raising. Far more Falungong supporters, numbering possibly in the tens of thousands, may have been subjected to administrative detention through the *laojiao* 'education through labour' provisions. These sentences do not require the intervention of the courts, and there are no public records of the numbers of Falungong supporters detained in this way.

Supporters of Falungong have claimed that members of the group have been tortured in detention and there have been a small number of high-profile instances when detained Falungong members have been reported to have committed suicide in prison, but it is extremely difficult to verify these. Foreign observers do not have access to prisons and labour camps, except on occasional, carefully controlled visits by international bodies. Although there is no evidence of a systematic policy of torture in any of these detention facilities, there is substantial and consistent anecdotal evidence of ill treatment and brutality towards minority groups, especially those that are designated as a threat to the state, which is certainly the case with Falungong.[28]

In Falungong, there is a core leadership, partly outside China, and a wide body of supporters or adherents within China, but also in Chinese communities elsewhere who are attached to local groups. The Chinese authorities were more concerned about the organisation of Falungong, both centrally and at the local level and its finances, than they were about the practice of individual adherents. By the summer of 2007, the number of reports of prosecutions simply for practicing Falungong had decreased.

The *Epoch Times*, published from an office in New York in hard copy editions in Chinese since May 2000, and in English since September 2003, represents itself as an independent newspaper for the communities of the Chinese diaspora. It also appears in Chinese and English internet editions, in addition to a number of other languages, and is distributed free of charge in Chinese-owned shops and supermarkets outside China. Its editorial perspective and news values are robustly in opposition to the CCP, and the activities of Falungong are reported favourably and in far more detail than in any other newspaper. Li Hongzhi has acknowledged that it was established to further the interests of Falungong adherents, but the paper hotly denies that it simply acts as a mouthpiece for the organisation. As Falungong's operations overseas expanded, it spread its beliefs through New Tang Dynasty Television, the Sound of Hope radio station, and the Sheng Yun Performing Arts dance and music company, which do not always make their connection with Falungong clear. After Li Hongzhi moved to the United States, the public security authorities proceeded to suppress the organisation ruthlessly. Following the mass demonstrations in Beijing in April 1999, Falungong was banned and formally designated as a heterodox cult [*xiejiao*]. Large quantities of its publications were seized and destroyed, and leading figures in the movement were arrested and imprisoned, which seriously restricted its ability to organise.

The perceived threat of Falungong to the CCP was so great that a special task force, the 610 Office, was established on 10 June 1999 (hence its name) to eliminate religious groups considered harmful, but primarily Falungong. This 'cult-busting office', as *China Daily* called it, was the executive arm of a CCP Leading Group for Dealing with Falungong (its title later expanded to include all 'heterodox religions') answerable to the powerful Political and Legal Commission of the Party. It operated outside the main legal and judicial framework, and there were consistent reports of excessive force and brutal treatment, often amounting to torture, in its drive to eliminate Falungong. In late 2008, the Ministry of Public Security was given more control over the 610 Office, that name no longer being used.[29]

Falungong continues to exist in China in spite of suppression by the state, but there are fewer demonstrations and it is no longer a major source of public controversy. It maintains a powerful voice in Hong Kong, Taiwan, and Chinese communities across the world.[30]

Sinicisation of religions in the Xi Jinping era

Religious policy under Xi Jinping followed the pattern of previous administrations, but much more stringently. Under the Hu Jintao and Wen Jiabao regime, Marxism-Leninism ceased to be a significant analytical tool, being replaced by nationalism and patriotism. Xi Jinping extended this but also attempted to impose maximum homogenisation on all aspects of society, including religion. As a result, the Chinese-ness of religions became the touchstone for how they were to be managed, and for Islam (especially in Xinjiang), Tibetan Buddhism, and Christianity, the extent to which, in Richard Madsen's words, they were willing to adapt to 'an idealised version of Han Chinese culture'. Xi's individual version of the Sinicisation of religion were set out in his keynote speech to the CCP's April 2016 National Conference on Religious Work and underlined in his lengthy speech to the CCP national conference in October 2017. The state-sponsored Protestant and Catholic association were instructed to draw up plans for Sinicisation within five years and even Buddhism, generally accepted as an integral part of Chinese culture, was obliged to ensure that the Chinese literary and architectural traditions had been assimilated into religious culture. It is not clear at the time of writing how effective these directives will be.[31]

Old Town God Temple, Shanghai

The Old Town God Temple [*Shanghai laocheng huangmiao*] is the most important Daoist temple in Shanghai and exemplifies the continuing interest in traditional religions, even in China's most enlightened and sophisticated city. The temple is located in the heart of the city, in one of the most visited tourist areas, close to a shopping complex and the Yu Garden. Official Shanghai chooses to emphasise the commercial activities of the whole area, and downplays the religious role of the temple, but many visitors are not tourists but local people paying their respects and making offerings to the traditional town gods. Daoist clergy officiate at ceremonies, and the temple and its courtyard are often thronged with crowds of visitors and worshippers; offerings, presented in orange bags, are piled in front of the massive images of the gods, sometimes as high as the faces.[32]

Ethnic minorities

The social position of many of the ethnic minority groups in China is closely linked to their religious beliefs and traditions, but they also have their own secular cultures, customs, and (in most cases) languages which are not all related closely to Chinese; they are also subject to the minority policies of the CCP. Previous governments of China had policies on minorities, but these were not always carefully considered or based on direct and thorough knowledge of the minority groups. In 1924, Sun Yat-sen, who is claimed as a formative political influence by both the CCP and the GMD, set out his position on minorities as follows,

> Although there are a little over ten million non-Chinese in China, including Mongols, Manchus, Tibetans and Tartars, their number is small compared with the purely Chinese population, four hundred million in number, which has a common racial heredity, common religion and common tradition and customs. It is one nationality![33]

On the surface, the people of China today might appear to be one single ethnic group, or one nationality in the wishful thinking of Sun Yat-sen, the father of the Chinese Republic. China's 1.4 billion citizens are no longer dressed in almost identical clothes as they were portrayed in the days of the Cultural Revolution, but they all seem to speak the same language and have a common culture. Dig a little deeper, however, and this façade of conformity and uniformity swiftly evaporates. China is a multi-ethnic, multi-lingual, and multi-cultural society. It is true that the language and culture of the Han Chinese people dominate, especially in the public arena, but even among the Han themselves, there are considerable cultural and linguistic differences. Although they are sometimes referred to as dialects of Chinese, spoken Mandarin and Cantonese are as different from each other as are Portuguese and Romanian.

Beyond the Han majority, China is home to a variety of ethnic groups which are categorised as minority nationalities [*shaoshu minzu*], a term derived from the system of ethnic classification used in the Soviet Union during the Stalin period. In most cases, their languages, cultures, and religions have little in common with those of the Han.

Minority people are found everywhere in China, including in Beijing and the other major cities, and they may work in the same kind of employment and live in the same areas as the Han. The distinctiveness of these communities is most apparent in their traditional homelands, some of which have been designated autonomous regions by the government of the PRC. The majority of these homelands are on, or close to, frontiers, notably China's western borders with Central Asia, but there are also many in the southwest, particularly in the province of Yunnan and in central China on the often mountainous borders between provinces.

Numbers

The Chinese state formally recognises the existence of 55 different minority nationalities: the people most recently acknowledged as comprising a distinct ethnic group are the Jinuo of Yunnan, who were granted nationality status in 1979. The largest group is the Zhuang of Guangxi in southern China, which has a population of 16 million. The smallest is the Lhoba of Tibet, of whom there are fewer than 3,000. The minorities number more than 106 million, comprising 8.4% of the total population of China, but occupy 60% of China's territory. The fact that minorities only amount to roughly 8% of the population is often used by the government or by some Han people to minimise, or even dismiss, the significance of the minority communities, many of which exercise an influence far greater than their relatively small numbers would suggest. They are often the majority communities in their home areas, which are often in strategic border locations.[34] Some ethnic groups have played a more prominent role in Chinese history and society than others.

Key ethnic groups

The 5.8 million Mongols who live mainly in Inner Mongolia and the northeast (Manchuria) are closely related to the Mongols of (Outer) Mongolia, and more distantly to the Buryat

Mongols of Russia. They are united by their language and culture, their nomadic heritage, and their devotion to Tibetan Buddhism. Today's Mongols are the descendants of the warriors of Chinggis Khan and Khubilai Khan, who conquered China, most of Central Asia, and much of the Middle East during the thirteenth and early fourteenth centuries. Mongol khans ruled China as the Yuan dynasty, but then lost power and retreated to the steppes. During the Cultural Revolution, many of the Buddhist monasteries of Inner Mongolia were destroyed by the Red Guards or fell into disuse. Some have become museums, but others are being restored. There is an active underground movement in support of an independent Inner Mongolia (or Southern Mongolia, as its supporters prefer to call it), but any public expression of this movement in newspapers and organisations has been ruthlessly suppressed by the Chinese authorities. More details on Inner Mongolia can be found in Chapter 23.

The 10.6 million Manchus, originally from China's northeast, gave their name to that region's former name of Manchuria. They were also originally tribal nomads, but when the Ming dynasty was on the point of collapse in 1644, Manchu khans invaded China and put their own Emperor on the Dragon Throne. The Manchus ruled China as the Qing dynasty until 1911, when they were replaced by a predominantly Han Chinese republican government.

Although they ruled in a coalition with Mongol bannermen and a small number of nobles and officials from the Han Chinese elite, the Manchus were the dominant group and Manchu garrisons were established throughout China to ensure their control over the Han majority. The Manchu language, which is completely unrelated to Chinese but has close connections with Mongolian, has largely died out as a spoken vernacular but continued to play a role as a language of the records of the imperial court until the end of the dynasty. The Xibo (or Sibe) people of Xinjiang, who are descendants of Manchu troops sent to the region in the eighteenth century, speak a form of Manchu to this day.

Many Tibetans would be uncomfortable to be classified as a Chinese ethnic minority, and some – possibly the majority – would prefer to be citizens of an independent Tibet. There are 5.4 million Tibetans living within the borders of the PRC, not only in the Tibetan Autonomous Region, which is ruled by Beijing from its administrative centre, Lhasa, but also in the provinces of Gansu, Qinghai, and Sichuan, parts of which belonged to old Tibet which was independent between 1911 and the creation of the PRC in 1949. Tibetan Buddhism, with its distinctive hierarchy of monasteries and lamas, functions quite separately from Buddhism as it is practised by Buddhists of Han Chinese origin. Its scriptures and liturgy are in the Tibetan language, which uses a writing system derived from one of the scripts of ancient India, probably one of the early systems of writing used for the classical language, Sanskrit – it does not use classical Chinese, which is the language of translated Buddhist sutras in China.

The 8.4 million Uyghurs of Xinjiang are a Muslim Turkic people and their language, religion, and culture have far more in common with the Uzbeks and also the Kazakhs and Kyrgyz people in former Soviet Central Asia than with the Han Chinese. The Uyghurs as a community are frequently referred to as 'restive', and have been collectively stigmatised as terrorists by the Chinese authorities since 2001 with very little justification: they struggle to maintain their cultural and religious identity in a state that is determined to assimilate them to Han norms.

The Hui are an interesting hybrid group in that they are Muslims of Central Asian and Middle Eastern ancestry, but their normal language at home and in their communities is one of the regional varieties of Chinese. They number about 10 million and have settled all over China, but they have had the greatest impact – both in terms of numbers and culture – in the northwest, particularly in Gansu province and in Ningxia, which is formally designated a Hui Autonomous Region. They speak the Chinese of their home region, but this is augmented by Arabic and Persian terms which have been incorporated into their discourse for centuries to convey religious and cultural meanings and to mark them out from the Han.

Yunnan province, which lies on China's border with Myanmar, Laos, and Vietnam, has the most complex ethnic mix of any part of China. The numerous groups, including the Dai, the Yao, and the Nakhi (Naxi), are relatively small and widely dispersed. They speak languages related to Thai, Vietnamese, and other languages of Southeast Asia. Unlike the minorities in the northern and northwestern border areas, no single group dominates the province. CCP officials attempting to classify the different cultures tended to regard them as primitive, and indeed their economic level and social organisation do in many cases resemble patterns found in Asia many centuries ago.[35]

Government policy, inequality, and discrimination

The CCP's policy on ethnic minorities was based on the practice of the Soviet Union, but also drew on its own historical contacts with minority groups during the Long March at a time when it was consciously seeking to distance itself from the policies of the Guomindang Nationalists, who had – to a large extent – neglected the ethnic minorities. It was on the Long March when many CCP members came into contact with some of these communities for the first time.

On paper, the Party's policies are designed to give equality to minority groups and to ensure that they enjoy at least a token representation in bodies such as the Chinese People's Political Consultative Conference, the national advisory body. In practice, ethnic minorities and their cultures have suffered considerable discrimination, especially during periods of Maoist radicalism such as the Great Leap Forward and the Cultural Revolution. There is little sympathy among the majority Han population for expressions of minority ethnic identity, and even less for demands for political independence by some Uyghurs and Tibetans.[36] The complex histories of the ethnic groups of Tibet and Xinjiang, and their relationships with China, are discussed in greater detail in Chapters 21–22.

China's ethnic minorities in the age of Xi Jinping

The more open-minded Chinese academic specialists and policy makers have conceded that ethnic conflict was likely to worsen as 'free-market forces and increased inter-ethnic communication and mobility [intensified] ethnic-based competition', and that current policies were inadequate to deal with them. Thus James Leibold, writing in 2013, pointed to the willingness of those Chinese intellectuals who were involved in ethnic minority affairs to consider a new range of solutions, discarding the old policies, which were effectively derivative of those devised in the Soviet Union during the Stalin period, and ushering in a 'second generation', a radical new direction of political thinking on minority affairs. Although the range of ideas put forward by this 'second generation' was wide, there was particular interest in adopting a version of what they understood as the famous 'melting pot' approach of the United States and implementing policy measures that would reduce the emphasis on ethnic identity to which great importance is attached and which is marked on identity documents.[37]

The work of the sociologist Ma Rong of Beijing University is central to this new thinking. Ma, who is of Hui (Muslim Chinese) origin, was a student of the great anthropologist Fei Xiaotong and, like Fei, studied in the United States. Ma's approach is broad-minded and 'liberal', but coincides with the underlying orthodox thinking of enhancing integration and encouraging movement towards a pan-Chinese identity. One of the underlying concepts of his approach is the depoliticisation of ethnicity; this was promoted as a new theoretical approach to the study of ethnic questions for over a decade. It aroused great interest, not only in the Chinese academic community, but also in government departments that deal with minority affairs. Ma's thinking involves the transformation of the language in which ethnic issues are discussed: this is intended to move discussion away from the highly politicised and outdated concept of 'minority nationalities' which for decades has restricted and stultified debate. In itself, it has not produced new policy solutions or impressed thinkers from the ethnic minority communities who perceive it as just another way of repressing the aspirations of their people. Ma's ideas attracted fierce opposition from those within the Chinese policy establishment who retain an attachment to the 'minority nationalities' approach, in the belief that it has worked and that to abandon it risks allowing the rise of destructive ethnic nationalism.[38]

The discourse on future ethnic policy with Ma Rong emerged during the period when Hu Jintao was President and CCP General Secretary and Wen Jiabao was Premier. The expression of some independent thought was permitted within the CCP and the government in those days.

After the rise to power of Xi Jinping in 2012, it became increasingly clear that even the limited open-mindedness of the Hu and Wen period would no longer be tolerated. Xi has attempted to impose an ideological straitjacket on the entire national discourse, particularly on contentious issues: there is no room for dissent or deviation from the government's rigid political position. Unconventional analyses and open discussion have been ruled out – the imprisonment of the noted economist and Central Minorities University professor, Ilham Tohti, for running a website to discuss alternative ways of resolving the conflict in Xinjiang is the clearest evidence for this. At the time of writing, the summer of 2020, the political climate has effectively imposed a freeze on the public discussion of any alternative approaches to minority issues.

The ideas associated with Ma Rong and his school are not really new; they are essentially a reiteration of the old concept of a *Zhonguoren* pan-Chinese identity that has been part of the state-building ideology of the CCP since 1949 and before that underpinned the thinking of the elites of the Republic. These ideas, like the older version, will continue find to favour with the Han majority but not among the minorities, particularly as they are frequently associated with reducing or abandoning such preferential treatment as ethnic minority groups have enjoyed.

Notes

1 Ian Johnson *The Souls of China: The Return of Religion after Mao* London: Allen Lane, 2017 is an authoritative on-the-ground report by an experienced China journalist.
2 The distinction between a religion and a cult is problematic, and not solely so in China – it is largely subjective. The Chinese authorities label Falungong a cult to deny it international legitimacy. Falungong leaders deny this and argue that they are a legitimate spiritual body.
3 Chan Wing-tsit *Religious Trends in Modern China* New York: Octagon Books, 1978.
4 Chan Wing-tsit *Religious Trends in Modern China* New York: Octagon Books, 1978, pp. 153, 156.
5 Gong Xuezheng et al. *Minzu wenti yu zongjiao wenti jiangzuo* (*Ethnic and Religious Issues*) Beijing: Zhonggong zhongyang dangxiao (CCP Central Party School), 1994, pp. 163–4.
6 D.E. MacInnis *Religion in China Today Policy and Practice* New York: Orbis, 1989, pp. 204–20.
7 K. Dean *Taoist Ritual and Popular Cults of Southeast China* Princeton: Princeton University Press, 1993; Ian Johnson *The Souls of China: The Return of Religion after Mao* London: Allen Lane, 2017, pp. 33–51, 201–4.
8 K.K.S. Ch'en *Buddhism in China: A Historical Survey* Princeton: Princeton University Press, 1964.

9 Yang Zengwen (ed.) *Zhongguo fojiao jichu zhishi* (*Fundamentals of Chinese Buddhism*) Beijing: Zongjiao wenhua chubanshe (Religious Culture Publishers), 1999; K.K.S. Ch'en *Buddhism in China: A Historical Survey* Princeton: Princeton University Press, 1964.
10 Holmes Welch *Buddhism under Mao* Cambridge: Harvard University Press, 1972, p. 6.
11 Chan Wing-tsit *Religious Trends in Modern China* New York: Octagon Books, 1978, p. 84; Holmes Welch *Buddhism under Mao* Cambridge: Harvard University Press, 1972, pp. 7–11, 389–407.
12 Yang Zengwen (ed.) *Zhongguo fojiao jichu zhishi* (*Fundamentals of Chinese Buddhism*) Beijing: Zongjiao wenhua chubanshe (Religious Culture Publishers), 1999, p. 73. Gregory Scott *Building the Buddhist Revival: Reconstructing Monasteries in Modern China* Oxford: Oxford University Press, 2020.
13 Author's visits to Beijing and Alashan, Bayinhot in Inner Mongolia 2001; author's interview with monks, Yonghegong 2005.
14 Interview with Buddhist nuns, London, May 2006.
15 John Gittings *Real China: From Cannibalism to Karaoke* London: Simon and Schuster, 1996, pp. 6–82.
16 Bob Whyte *Unfinished Encounter: China and Christianity* London: Collins, 1988.
17 Rowan Williams 'Christianity and the Reinvention of China', lecture, Chatham House, 1 May 2007.
18 *SCMP* 16 May, 6 June 2011.
19 *Guardian* 30 December 2019, Human Rights Watch World Report 2020.
20 *SCMP* 20 December 2012; *Guardian* 18 August 2014, 27 July 2017; *China Daily* 24 October 2014; BBC 2 February 2015.
21 BBC News 30 June 2007, 2 July 2007; 'Letter of the Holy Father Pope Benedict XVI to the Bishops, Priests, Consecrated Persons and Lay Faithful of the Catholic Church in the People's Republic of China' 27 May 2007 www.vatican.va.
22 *FT* 12 September 2007.
23 *FT* 20 September 2007; BBC News 21 September 2007.
24 BBC News 4 December 2007.
25 *SCMP* 3, 23 June, 4, 14, 16, 22 July 2011; 'Nota Informativa sulla Chiesa Cattolica in Cina' *Vatican bulletine* 22 September 2018.
26 Regulation of religious and quasi-religious groups by national bodies is standard practice in the PRC.
27 *Dangerous Meditation: China's Campaign against Falungong* New York: Human Rights Watch, January 2002. This is available at the Human Rights Watch website http://hrw.org/reports/2002/china. It is a particularly useful analysis of Falungong and the Chinese government's sustained attack on it because it is sceptical of source material that emanates from Falungong organisations in China and worldwide, as well as information from the Chinese government in Beijing, and subjects both to rigorous critical scrutiny. [This report was written by Mickey Spiegel, Research Consultant to the Asia Division of Human Rights Watch. Joseph Saunders, Deputy Director of the Asia Division; Sidney Jones, the division's Executive Director; Malcolm Smart, Human Rights Watch Program Director; and Jim Ross, Senior Legal Advisor, edited the report. Elizabeth Weiss, Fitzroy Hepkins, Veronica Matushaj, and Patrick Minges provided production assistance. A very special thank you goes to Julia Zuckerman, an indefatigable volunteer whose research talents and endless patience in locating and organising documentation were invaluable.]
28 *Dangerous Meditation: China's Campaign against Falungong* New York: Human Rights Watch, January 2002.
29 *China Daily* 24 October 2014.
30 Observations by present author in 2017 and 2018.
31 Richard Madsen 'The Sinicization of Chinese Religions under Xi Jinping' *China Leadership Monitor* no. 61 (Fall 2019), 1 September 2019.
32 Han Rongliang and Han Zhiyu *Shanghai daoyou* (*Guide to Shanghai*) Beijing: Zhongguo liuyou chubanshe, 2005, pp. 96–111; Observation by present author in 2017 and 2018.
33 Sun Yat-sen *Sanmin zhuyi* (*Three People's Principles*) (1924) in Leonard Shihlien Hsü *Sun Yat-sen His Political and Social Ideals* Los Angeles: University of Southern California Press, 1933, p. 168.
34 Xiaowei Zang 'Introduction: Who Are Ethnic Minorities and How Well Do They Do in China' in Xiaowei Zang (ed.) *Handbook on Ethnic Minorities in China* Cheltenham: Edward Elgar, 2016, pp. 1–19; Michael Dillon *Lesser Dragons: Minority Peoples of China* London: Reaktion Books,

2018, pp. 9–27; Michael Dillon *Mongolia: A Political History of the Land and Its People* London: I. B. Tauris, 2020.

35 Xiaowei Zang (ed.) *Handbook on Ethnic Minorities in China* Cheltenham: Edward Elgar, 2016, pp. 1–19 and passim; Michael Dillon *Lesser Dragons Minority: Peoples of China* London: Reaktion Books, 2018, pp. 28–44 and passim; Michael Dillon *Mongolia: A Political History of the Land and Its People* London: I. B. Tauris, 2020.

36 Colin Mackerras *China's Minority Cultures: Identities and Integration since 1912* London: Longman, 1995; Colin Mackerras *China's Ethnic Minorities and Globalisation* London: Routledge-Curzon, 2003; Metter Halskov Hansen *Frontier People: Han Settlers in Minority Areas of China* London: Hurst, 2005.

37 James Leibold *Ethnic Policy in China: Is Reform Inevitable?* Policy Studies 68 Honolulu, Hawai'i: East West Center, 2013, pp. xi–xii.

38 Lizhong Xie *Depoliticization of Ethnic Questions in China* Beijing: World Scientific, 2014; James Leibold *Ethnic Policy in China: Is Reform Inevitable?*, Honolulu, Hawai'i: East-West Center, pp. 13–22.

19 Gender and modernisation

All the economic, social, and political changes that have taken place in China have been experienced by men and women of all classes, but they have not necessarily been experienced equally or in the same way. According to the popular political cliché, women 'hold up half the sky', but it is very unlikely that most Chinese women would consider that they were treated as genuinely equal to men.

Three obediences

Any reasonable comparison between the lives of women in traditional China and their position in China today cannot fail to acknowledge the vast improvement in their status and, for many, their opportunities in life and work. For centuries the unquestioned assumption was that women were simply inferior to men. In this, China was no different from the other traditional peasant societies of Asia. Although there were philosophical attempts, drawing on Daoism, to emphasise the benefits of a complementary relationship between the male *yang* and the female *yin*, there is no doubt that this was a profoundly unequal relationship. More revealing were the 'three obediences' [*san cong*] which defined the relationships of women with the men in their families at different stages of their lives: it was, of course, assumed that they would not have any association with men outside their families. This manner of expressing social position was typical of the hierarchical attitude to society that is usually referred to for simplicity as Confucian: as a child, a woman would obey her father; on marriage, she would obey her husband; and when she produced a son (her primary social function), she would be obliged to comply with his wishes, at least once he had become an adult and certainly if she were widowed. Chinese society, however, was as complex and as muddled as any other, in spite of the attempts by the Confucian literati to impose a moral and social order: by no means did all families follow this prescription, but it was always there as a model for how women should behave.

Marriage

For a woman, marriage meant leaving the family home and moving into a new household with her husband. Indeed, the normal Chinese word for marriage when applied to a woman is *chujia*, 'to leave the family'. The new household belonged to her husband's parents and was typically dominated by her mother-in-law. For many women in traditional China, this relationship – not the relationship with their husband – was the most important in their lives: a good relationship with the mother-in-law could lead to a relatively happy and fulfilled life (albeit a severely restricted one), whereas a poor relationship could lead to desperation.

Social position made a great deal of difference: the majority of Chinese women, who were from farming families, were fated to spend their lives either in agricultural or domestic labour. For wealthier women, there was status and prosperity, but the price for rank was seclusion and social restriction. Chinese women of high social status, like women in other traditional Asian societies, were confined to the home and its immediate environs, a condition similar to the arrangement that was referred to as purdah in the Indian sub-continent and as the harem in the Muslim Middle East. This system had purportedly evolved to ensure the virtue of the women of the family, which was highly valued socially, and to demonstrate the wealth and status of the head of the household and his family.

In addition to wives, for men of means could take more than one wife, some women – concubines – had a relationship with men which was of a lower social status and did not formally entitle them to the same privileges and benefits of full family membership. Personality, intellect and opportunity made it possible for some women to transcend these social boundaries (as some women, notably celebrated courtesans, demonstrated in Europe). At the bottom of the social scale were women without husbands or families, some of whom made such a living as they could through prostitution. China was no different from any other pre-modern society in its snobberies and hypocrisy, and this applied to the status of women as much as to other aspects of the social order.

Bound feet

One custom which distinguished the position of Chinese women from all other societies was the practice of binding feet. Many, if not most, traditional societies exhibit or have exhibited some form of physical restraint on women, whether it be relatively minor ones such as corseting or fundamental and brutal ones such as the range of practices that are grouped under the misleadingly mild term of female circumcision. The socially approved foot fetish appears to have been unique to China. The bound foot, or 'lily foot', which is reputed to have been both aesthetically and erotically stimulating for Chinese men, was created by bending a young girl's foot while the bones were still malleable and binding the foot with cloth so that the toes were forced underneath. The foot grew to be deformed and much smaller than an unbound foot: the small foot, the Golden Lotus, which ideally was supposed to be not more than three inches in length, was prized by both women and men. Naturally, this practice severely restricted the mobility of those Chinese women who were subjected to it.

Some groups, notably the Hakka, have never practised the binding of feet. The practice was criticised by Western missionaries and was outlawed in 1902 under the Qing dynasty, but this was during its final years when it lacked the authority to enforce the prohibition; it was also strongly opposed by the government of the Republic. Sun Yat-sen supported legislation prohibiting the binding of feet in 1912 during his brief presidency. In spite of this, it persisted in the more remote rural areas, and it was still possible to see elderly women with bound feet towards the end of the twentieth century.

Seeking alternatives

It would be wrong to suggest that all Chinese women were completely confined and inhibited by the restrictive Confucian system. Some women were able to find an alternative life through membership of religious or quasi-religious secret societies, including the Boxers who rebelled in 1899. Western Christian missionaries who had been horrified by the practice of binding feet tried to ban it within their congregations, and European and American ideas about the position of women in society spread throughout the educated middle class in the early twentieth century. Women became aware of the possibility of new roles that they could play, but this was largely an urban phenomenon.

The legacy of subservience, mutilation, and restriction motivated a new generation of women to seek equality. In the 1920s and 1930s, many of them were attracted to radical movements, including the CCP, which actively recruited women and considered *funu gong-zuo*, 'woman-work', to be one of the Party's most important tasks. Woman-friendly policies were developed, both before and after the CCP took power in 1949, and both the motivations for and the outcomes of these policies are still widely, and hotly, debated in China today.

Women in the PRC

The most significant piece of legislation directed towards the condition of women in the early years of the PRC was the Marriage Reform Law of 1950. It was enacted to reject traditional 'feudal' marriage arrangements by outlawing all forced arranged marriages and the betrothal of children before they had reached the age at which they could reasonably be expected to understand what was being planned in their name. Both of these practices had been common, especially in rural communities. The new law did not outlaw all arranged marriages; it did, however, insist that there should be informed consent on both sides. The freedom of marriage and of divorce was set out in the legislation, but because of the persistence of conservative notions concerning the roles of women and the family (by women as well as men), the reality took longer to achieve.

During the years of Mao Zedong's chairmanship of the CCP, it was argued that women had achieved formal and official equality with men. This extended to work; women laboured in the fields and in the factories alongside men, and in theory earned equal wages. Westerners visiting China for the first time were frequently surprised to see women in labouring gangs on the roads and on building sites. A large number of women were appointed as Party cadres and government officials, although it did not require particularly keen observation to discern that the vast majority of women cadres occupied relatively minor positions in the Party, in the communes, or in the street committees of China's towns and cities. Nevertheless, since there had been very few opportunities for women to participate in government at any level before 1949 and virtually none at all before 1911, this can be considered as a major advance for women. Women also flourished in the professions of medicine, science, and education, thanks in large part to the example of the Soviet Union, where many women had become teachers and doctors.

Reform period

The introduction of economic reforms under Deng Xiaoping was a mixed blessing for women. Like men, they were in danger of losing their secure state employment following the collapse of the 'iron rice bowl' that had virtually guaranteed jobs for life, and many were forced into the private sector. Some took to this new life with enthusiasm and assurance, and there are many examples of successful women entrepreneurs. The class of professional women, building on the experience of doctors, teachers, and scientists, also began to grow in size and influence, and many were able to remain in official positions. The demands of the new society which provided these new career opportunities also created tensions in families, and the rate of divorce increased.

The application of market principles to the labour force has, on balance, had a detrimental effect on the employment prospects of women. In the rush for growth and competitiveness, many employers have ignored the legislation that protected the recruitment of women. As a result, many more women are in low-paid employment or are obliged to work for lower wages than men in the same jobs. The enrolment of girls and women in education has also declined. This is particularly the case in the poorer and most underdeveloped parts of China, but there are fewer girls than boys in primary education in general. At university level, fewer women are succeeding in gaining admission. This state of affairs is due partly to open discrimination by universities and colleges, and partly to the re-emergence of traditional prejudices against the education of girls.

For women in the countryside, the choice has often been to stay in their village with little or no work, or to travel, often great distances, in search of work. Many moved to the boom areas of the southeast to work in factories, some of them no better than sweat shops where they endured conditions that were similar to those that had been experienced by their grandmothers' generation in the 1920s – poor wages, unhygienic and dangerous working conditions, and in some cases, physical restriction to the accommodation provided by their employers.

As the need for agricultural labour declined, some women who remained in the country-side were able to move into handicraft production, food processing, and other small-scale industries. There were a number of government initiatives to assist in the creation of employ-ment opportunities: local branches of the All-China Women's Federation encouraged the development of family smallholdings and the production of craft goods such as baskets, cushions, and mats which could be sold in local markets. The federation had been set up in 1949 as one of the mass organisations under the control of the CCP and was given the task of promoting and protecting the rights of women. During the 1990s, it revised its view of its role and has claimed that it is now a non-governmental organisation.

In the 1980s, for the first time in decades, reports began to appear of the abduction of women and children in the countryside for sale as brides (or presumably, in some cases, into prostitution). The dissolution of the communes had liberated women from agricultural work, but alternatives were not always available. Although there is no reliable data on the traffick-ing of women and girls, this trade was given a new impetus in the 1990s when 'snakehead' gangs began to mastermind the emigration of large numbers of women, many of whom found their way into the sex trade in other countries.

Gender balance

For all women, but for rural women in particular, there was the added pressure of the one-child policy, which is discussed in more detail in Chapter 15. Not only has this policy had a profound effect on the lives of individuals and families, it has also contributed to a startling gender imbalance in the country as a whole. As a result of the age-old preference for boy children, there has been a significant increase in the abortion of female foetuses and female infanticide. These practices have been common knowledge since the 1980s, but they have become more widespread with the advent of ultrasound scanning technology and selective induced abortion, services that have been provided illegally by some doctors for fees of as much as RMB 1,000.

The whole process of scans and abortions is shrouded in secrecy, and it varies from region to region, but the impact on the gender ratio has been obvious and dramatic. The United Nations recommends a male-to-female ratio of no greater than 107:100, but the figure for

China was 116:100 in 2000 and 119:100 in 2005, according to figures issued by the Chinese Family Planning Association. In practical terms, this means that men will find it increasingly more difficult to find wives. When this is combined with the phenomenon of an ageing population, it raises the spectre of a new social problem: the likelihood of many single children having to support both of their parents and some of their grandparents for many years on a single salary.[1]

Women and the Xi Jinping era

On 2 November 2018, Xi Jinping addressed the recently appointed leadership of the All-China Women's Federation. He 'stressed upholding the socialist path with Chinese characteristics for women's development and mobilizing women to make achievements', according to Xinhua's report. He made it clear that 'the Chinese dream of national rejuvenation should be the theme of the contemporary women's movement', although there should be efforts to promote gender equality and enable women to 'contribute to the reform, development and stability of the nation on the frontline'. He emphasised the need to continue the previous submission of the federation to the authority of the Party, reinforcing his ideas of centralisation and homogenisation. He paid lip service to gender equality, work-life balance, and improving conditions for women in the workplace, but no specific proposals emerged from the meeting.[2]

It is not possible to give a sensible generalisation on the position of women in twenty-first–century China. For young female migrant workers in the sweatshops of the south, condition in some factories have been atrocious, at time leading to serious accidents and deaths. Conversely, women in affluent business families in Beijing, Shanghai, Guangzhou, and other large cities might be living lives of great luxury and privilege. Social conventions and conditions vary greatly from region to region, and the age-old divide between rural and urban women has, if anything, become wider.

In the job market, women continued to experience widespread and overt discrimination, against the formal requirements of the CCP and its government. Human Rights Watch[3] reported that, 'In the 2018 national civil service job list, 19 percent specified a requirement or preference for men, up from 13 percent from the previous year'. Major technology companies, which modelled themselves partly on international comparisons, including Alibaba and Tencent, were more forward looking and vowed to guarantee gender equality in their recruitment processes.

Chinese women were more willing to complain openly about sexual harassment, particularly in the workplace; this was not a new problem, but one that had been taboo in public discourse. It was extremely difficult for those who alleged harassment to obtain legal remedies. Chinese legislation prohibits sexual harassment, but as the term is not clearly defined, successful outcomes of legal action are rare. Nevertheless, the #MeToo movement gained traction in China. Leading public figures, including academics and journalists, found themselves accused of harassment or other misbehaviour on social media; the authorities covered up the cases when possible.

The preference for male children during the implementation of the 'one-child policy' led to a relative shortage of women for marriage and was a factor in the growth of the trafficking of women from the countryside to the cities and from China's near neighbours. After the relaxation of the 'one-child policy' (see Chapter 15), couples could legitimately have more than one child, but that affected different women in different ways. The sex ratio imbalance and the ageing of China's population have prompted a return to traditional gender roles as young women, especially in rural areas, increasingly came under pressure to marry young and bear children.

Notes

1 *People's Daily* 25 August 2003; BBC News 24 August 2007.
2 Xinhua 2 November 2018.
3 Human Rights Watch 2018 *World Report*. https://www.hrw.org/world-report/2018.

20 The environment

In spite of the ultra-modern appearance of its cities, China is still a developing country undergoing rapid economic and social changes. These developments are comparable with the transformation that took place in Europe during the industrial revolutions of the eighteenth and nineteenth centuries, and in the United States at a slightly later date. As an almost entirely agricultural society, traditional China was generally free from industrial pollution, although accounts of the porcelain centre of Jingdezhen during the Ming dynasty (1368–1644) refer to the constant smoke and flames emitted by the potteries and the noisy and dirty atmosphere that this created.[1] Coal and tin mining have existed for centuries, but the extraction of minerals was not on a scale comparable to that found in the West until relatively recently.

China has a great variety of landforms, from desert and grassland in the north to paddy rice fields in the south, in all of which land is used in different ways. Remnants of traditional methods of hunting and gathering, agriculture, and nomadic pastoralism continue to exist alongside modern farming and industrialisation, although they are dying out. Land use also varies according to local customs and the mores of different ethnic groups.

In so far as it is possible to speak of one single traditional Chinese view of the environment and humanity's relationship with it, the best example would be the concept of harmonisation with nature; of running with, rather than against, nature – an approach most closely associated with Daoism.

Since 1949, China's main priority has been industrialisation modelled initially after the development of the USSR and Eastern Europe, with which China was at least formally allied in the 1950s. China under Mao sought to catch up economically with the West, which had partially colonised it in the nineteenth and early twentieth centuries, and with Japan, which had occupied much of Chinese territory between 1931 and 1945. This drive for economic development was associated with the assertion of a Chinese national identity and a reaction to what Chinese Nationalists and patriots, including the CCP, conceived of as a century of national humiliation.

The CCP expressed no serious concerns about environmental issues in the early years of its administration. It concentrated on the development of heavy industry, particularly iron and steel plants and the oilfields of the northeast. Although the construction of these plants created a severe environmental burden, this was virtually ignored during the 1960s and 1970s. The environmental costs of industrialisation had also been ignored or downplayed in the Soviet Union and its allies in the drive to compete with the more advanced West. The modern environmental movement emerged slowly in Western Europe and the United States: two significant events were the publication of Rachel Carson's *Silent Spring* in 1962 and the launch of the Greenpeace organisation in 1971. As China opened up to visitors in

the 1970s and 1980s, journalists, academics, and business travellers travelled to the indus-
trialised areas of China, and reports of disturbing levels of pollution began to reach the
West. Chinese officials, and later academics and students, were once again able to travel
abroad; they took back with them ideas of environmentalism that were becoming prevalent
in the West.

Major environmental issues

Different geographical regions of China have suffered varying forms of environmental dep-
redation, some more significant and widespread than others. The spread of acid rain caused
by the sulphur dioxide that is emitted by factories and power plants affected much of China's
land mass: according to the Standing Committee of the NPC,[2] it has at time posed a threat to
the safety of the food supply, and more than half the 696 cities and counties monitored had
suffered, in some cases on a daily basis.

Sulphur dioxide emissions rose by 27% between 2000 and 2005, largely because of the waste
products of coal-burning power stations and coking plants, making China one of the principal originators of the chemical in the entire world. The pollutant was emitted at a rate that
was double the acceptable environmental limit and it affected 40% of Chinese cities. China
has subsequently put in place plans to reduce the sulphur emissions in its coal-burning power
plants as part of a drive to improve air quality. In the run-up to the 2008 Olympics, there
was particular concern about problems of pollution in Beijing and its environs because of
concerns about the effect of smog on athletes.[3] Atmospheric pollution, particularly in the
urban areas, was exacerbated by the exponential growth in the numbers of motor vehicles
on China's roads.

Between 2014 and 2017, research from University College London published in *Nature
Energy* indicated that after the implementation of an ultra-low emissions standards policy
for coal-fired power stations in 2014, there was a substantial reduction in sulphur dioxide
emissions. Researchers concluded that 'between 2014 and 2017 China's annual power emissions of SO_2 [sulphur dioxide], NOx [nitrogen oxides] and PM [particulate matter] dropped
by 65%, 60% and 72%, respectively'.[4]

There was also concern about increased water pollution, including the discharge of
untreated sewage and chemical waste products and the use of the rivers and the seas of China's
coastlines for disposal waste products. This had a deleterious effect on fish, prawns, and
other forms of marine life, many of which form an important part of the national diet. Industrial plants along the Yangzi became the target of government investigations as they were
considered to be particularly serious polluters and some, including three factories in Anhui
province, were closed after intervention by the State Environmental Protection Agency. The
agency was attempting to raise its profile after its deficiencies were revealed publicly in
the case of the pollution of the Songhua River in November 2005 (see 'Environmental case
study 2' section of this chapter).[5]

Deforestation was another major concern. In the early days of industrialisation, trees were
cut down in considerable quantities for building programmes, with little thought given to the
need for replanting. Logging had a serious impact on wildlife, and the impact of soil erosion and creeping desertification remains visible along hundreds of miles of railway track
in northern China, where trees that held back the desert were cut down. Netting holds down
the sand dunes and encourages the growth of plants to bind them together. The erosion of
soil from the hillsides and the expansion of the desert led to the silting up of rivers and consequent flooding.

Comprehensive Nuclear Test Ban Treaty (CTBT)

The environmental impact of the testing of nuclear devices has also been a matter of great concern, especially among the Uyghurs of Xinjiang: the region around Lop Nor in central Xinjiang has been the site of nuclear tests since the 1960s. For decades, there have been reports about the effects of radioactive contamination and pollution on the local population. Human rights activists from Xinjiang have assembled portfolios of photographs which present evidence of birth defects and other medical problems caused by nuclear testing and have attempted, unsuccessfully, to have the testing abandoned in their homeland. The nuclear industry, and in particular the testing of nuclear weapons, is covered by the strictest secrecy.

The Comprehensive Nuclear Test Ban Treaty (CTBT) was open for signature on 24 September 1996 after negotiations at the Geneva Conference on Disarmament and adoption by the UN General Assembly. Between 1945 and the adoption of the treaty, there had been a total of 2,000 nuclear tests, the majority carried out by the United States, with over 1,000 and the Soviet Union with at least 700.[6] France carried out over 200 and the United Kingdom and China each carried out 45. The majority of countries, 186, had signed the treaty at the time of writing, thus indicating their support and willingness not to undermine it. Of these, only 154 have ratified it by their legislatures, making it legally binding.

Eight countries listed in Annex 2 of the treaty – those with nuclear capability – had not ratified the treaty at the time of writing. These were China, Egypt, Iran, Israel, and the United States, which had signed but not ratified the Treaty; and India, North Korea, and Pakistan, which had not even signed it. The signature and ratification of these Annex 2 states is a precondition for the treaty coming into force.

In June 2004, the Chinese government indicated its support for the CTBT, pointing out that it had signed the treaty on the first day it opened for signature. The treaty was submitted to the NPC for consideration and ratification. At the time of writing, Beijing has not ratified the treaty but has cooperated with the Provisional Technical Secretariat of the CTBTO (Comprehensive Nuclear Test Ban Treaty Organisation) in building international monitoring stations, 11 of which are to be situated with the territory of the PRC. At the end of January 2018, China was presented with certificates by the CTBTO in recognition of four new nuclear monitoring stations, bringing the total in China to five. A radionuclide station had been established in Lanzhou, China's base for military operations in Xinjiang, in December 2016, and two more had been added in Guangzhou and Beijing, as well as primary seismic stations in Lanzhou and Hailar, which is in Inner Mongolia close to the border with Russia.[7]

The CTBT cannot become fully operational until the Annex 2 states have ratified it. Egypt, Iran, and Israel have not because of political tensions within the Middle East, in addition to internal problems in all three states; India and Pakistan are locked in a permanent dispute; and North Korea is resistant to normal diplomatic discussions. China is inclined to ratify if the United States also ratifies, but there is resistance within the United States, and especially the Republican-controlled Senate, to be seen to conceding anything to the PRC. The treaty is currently in a state of suspended animation.

Environmental case study 1: Three Gorges Dam

Judging by the degree of environmental concerns that it has generated, both within China and internationally, the development of the Three Gorges Dam has been the single most controversial of all the projects that have been initiated in contemporary China. The essence of the scheme is the creation of a large dam on the Yangzi at Sandouping in Yichang in the central region of Hubei province which will provide electricity for China's development and will also assist in the control of flooding. When completed, the Three Gorges Dam will be the largest hydroelectric project in the world when measured by its potential output of 18,200 megawatts, but it has been dogged by controversy: critics, both domestic and international, have focused on the environmental costs to what is one of China's outstanding areas of natural beauty and also the human costs for displaced communities.

The idea of damming the Yangzi at this point was not new. It was raised by Sun Yat-sen as part of his comprehensive plan for developing China's economy as early as 1919, and initial surveys were carried out in the 1930s, but it was not until the establishment of the PRC that a project on this grand scale became practicable: several feasibility studies were commissioned in the 1980s after the State Council's formal endorsement of the project in 1979.

Construction of the dam commenced with great optimism in 1994, and in 2003, the process was sufficiently far enough advanced to allow the water to begin to flow. By May 2006, the bulk of the work on the dam had been finished with the completion of the main wall. It was expected to start generating electricity in 2009 when buildings to house its 26 turbines, a two-way lock (which became operational in 2004), and a one-step ship lift would be finally completed. All of these projects were delayed: full operation did not begin until 2012 and the power plant was not certified as fully operational until November 2020.[8] The total cost of the project has been put at US$25 billion by the PRC official press releases. This is within the parameters of the government's stated budget limit, but critics in China have estimated that the real cost is much higher, and figures in excess of US$100 billion have been mentioned.

Criticism of the project fell into three categories: cost effectiveness, environmental degradation, and involuntary migration:

1   Because government statistics in China are not available for independent scrutiny, it is not possible to ascertain the genuine cost of the project. Opponents of the dam have argued that not only is the real cost much higher than the publicly quoted costs suggest, but that there has been corruption on a grand scale throughout the whole process, with contractors bribing the development corporation responsible for the project. It is also alleged that the potential output of the dam will be much less than claimed by the government. It had argued that by 2009, it would be capable of supplying some 10% of China's total electricity requirements. In addition, there is considerable resentment in China because the dam is designed to supply electricity to the eastern and southeastern provinces, which are already the most highly developed regions, and that it will contribute very little to the economic development of its own hinterland.

2   The issue of pollution is more complicated. It is possible to argue that in the longer term, whatever the immediate problems, the dam will reduce China's dependency on fossil fuels – coal, gas, and oil. However, in the short term, there is concern about potential damage to local ecosystems and in particular to vulnerable species of wildlife, such as the Chinese river dolphin, which are threatened by the degradation of their habitat.

3   The construction also has serious implications for communities living in the immediate area of the dam because the inhabitants of many local villages have been, or will be, relocated to other parts of China. Over a million people have already been moved and some 1,200 towns and villages will have to be abandoned to make way for the dam. The resettlement is being managed by a Three Gorges Resettlement Bureau, which, like other aspects of the project, has been accused of operating corruptly.

The environmental and other problems associated with the Three Gorges Dam are not peculiar to China, and similar issues have been raised in the case of other large power generation projects in developing countries. In September 2007, there were renewed warnings about the possibility of the construction of the dam triggering an environmental catastrophe. What made these warnings unusual and compelling was that they came from senior officials responsible for the construction.

The director of the State Council Three Gorges Construction Committee, Wang Xiaofeng, in a report published by the official Xinhua news agency after a discussion forum in Wuhan, raised concerns about inappropriate and unwise development in the region which, he contended, could lead to major ecological problems including soil erosion that might result in landslides on the steep hills that surround the dam. Landslips into the river had already caused unusually high waves that had damaged the river banks. The flow of the Yangzi had slowed above the dam, silting was becoming more acute, and water pollution – especially reduction in the quality of drinking water for local people – was also causing concern. Wang and a senior engineer, Huang Xuebin, who had responsibility for the control of geological problems associated with the construction, also expressed their disquiet at the impact that the development was having on the lives of local residents. This level of public concern would once have been unusual, but it reflects concern at a national level about the relationship between development and environmental problems. Wang was echoing concerns expressed publicly by Premier Wen Jiabao that China was in danger of sacrificing long-term environmental stability for short-term economic growth. In March 2007, when he was still deputy director of the Three Gorges committee, Wang had rejected allegations that the dam was causing major environmental problems and argued that the situation was stable. The change in his emphasis suggests a shift in the balance of environmental concerns in political circles at the national level.[9] It is also a feature of the Three Gorges cruises on the Yangzi that have been one of China's greatest tourist attractions, although for most visitors, the main reason for their visit it is the natural beauty of the gorges rather than the spectacular modern dam.

In spite of concerns about the stability of the dam and the acknowledgement by the Chinese authorities of the social and environmental damage created during the construction of the dam, it remains in operation. After extreme flooding during the summer of 2020 at a level not experienced for many decades, there were fears that the dam could collapse as it had almost reached capacity.[10]

Environmental case study 2: Harbin water pollution

A chemical spillage in November 2005 in the city of Jilin that polluted the Songhua River with benzene and threatened the quality of drinking water supplies to Harbin in neighbouring Heilongjiang province has significant implications for environmental policy, crisis management and openness in the Chinese media.

After the disquiet over China's handling of the SARS crisis, the way that different bodies handled the Harbin water pollution emergency sheds light on the effectiveness of China's crisis management systems. It also raises important questions about the degree of transparency in media reporting and how far an order made in September 2005 which lifted reporting restrictions on natural disasters has genuinely changed attitudes in the press and broadcasting.

A series of explosions (a total of 15 over a period of five hours) which began at 1.45 pm on 13 November destroyed the New Aniline Unit of the PetroChina petrochemical plant in Jilin. Five people were killed, over 70 were injured and the flames were so intense that they could not be extinguished until 4 am the following day. Water from the fire-fighting efforts contributed to the contamination of the Songhua River which flows through Jilin and on to Harbin before running into the Heilong (Amur) River at the border with the Russian Federation, turning what had been a local pollution problem into an international incident.

Managing the crisis involved many different national agencies, including the Chinese National Petroleum Corporation (PetroChina) itself; the State Environmental Protection Agency and its political master, the State Council; the provincial governments of Jilin and Heilongjiang; the city administrations of Jilin and Harbin; the military; and the Foreign Ministry, which had to apologise to Moscow for the impending pollution of the Amur River. China has different levels of contingency plans for emergencies – at the enterprise, county, regional, city, provincial, inter-province, and national levels – and these plans were put into effect immediately.

Reports in the official press which are confirmed by informal intelligence from the region suggest that the practical response to the crisis was impressive. Perhaps this is not surprising, since water conservancy and hydraulic engineering are the backgrounds of many senior Party leaders, including President Hu Jintao, under the 'double-load' system of technical and political training for CCP and government high fliers that has operated for decades in China. Drilling teams from the Daqing oil field were deployed to dig deep ground-water wells to provide alternative supplies of water. Bottled water was donated by organisations around the country until supplies outstripped demand. Heilongjiang province set aside funds of RMB 10 million to deal with the emergency, half of that sum being allocated to create new water supplies in residential areas. The PLA Air Force sent fire engines and personnel trained to deal with deep wells, and the army supplied water to hospitals and old people's homes. There has been no criticism of the speed or effectiveness of the aid and support to Harbin.

The handling of information about the crisis was less impressive. The immediate response of the Jilin authorities was the tried and tested one of saying nothing. When the Harbin municipal government discovered on 21 November that the Songhua River had been polluted, it initially covered up the problem, apparently on the instructions of central government, by claiming that the water had been cut off to allow maintenance work to go ahead. The degree of contamination was not acknowledged until the following day. Reporting of the incident in the Heilongjiang local press was restricted by the local bureaucracy. *People's Daily* in its domestic edition followed suit, and information was released very slowly and restricted to pages 4–5. The overseas edition of *People's Daily*, which is not aimed at a domestic readership, although it is available in some parts of China, covered the crisis more fully, as did its online English-language edition. *China Daily*, which is published only in English and has a tiny readership among Chinese citizens, covered the story in much more detail and on the front page, and this could have given the impression to foreign observers that there was far more openness than was actually the case.

The story was gradually taken up by the *China Youth Daily* and the *China Economic Times*, both of which have a track record of publishing more challenging material. Both voiced criticism of a cover-up and the dangers of 'irresponsible lies' by officials, and this was repeated in a *China Daily* editorial entitled 'Commentary: Cover-up can't hide murky water truth' on 27 November, the day that water supplies to parts of Harbin were due to be restored.

Wen Jiabao, the Prime Minister and (as the Chinese sources always point out) a member of the Standing Committee of the CCP Politburo, played a key role in the crisis. Without announcing his intentions in advance, he visited Harbin on Saturday 26 November to observe the level of water pollution and called for a full enquiry into the incident. This visit was seen as encouragement for local officials and staff in their relief efforts, but was also intended as a warning to local governments that they should act decisively on environmental matters. Significantly, he also called for the timely release of information when crises occurred.

Wen, who is a geologist and engineer by training, has made clear his own position that environmental protection should be given far greater priority in the rush for economic growth. He made a speech on scientific sustainable development at the 21st Century Forum in Beijing in September 2005 and, on 23 November, just before travelling to Harbin, he had presided over an executive meeting of the State Council, which was sitting to set medium-term targets for environmental protection.

Ironically, as the crisis was unfolding in the northeast, the First National Symposium on Inland Lakes was being held in the Jiangxi provincial capital of Nanchang. This conference heard that 70% of China's rivers were contaminated, and that this was affecting lakes and swampland. The causes of this, according to Chen Bangzhu, who speaks on population, resources, and environment for the advisory Chinese People's Political Consultative Conference, are the economic boom, the expansion of population, and irrational development, but also inadequate legislation and surveillance and insufficient media coverage of environmental issues. The environment is the one area in which the CCP has allowed a relatively uncontrolled political debate. Environmental NGOs have been allowed to operate with relatively little interference, and the support they have received created the first independent grassroots movement that has been tolerated since the CCP came to power in 1949.[11]

This crisis also had an international dimension as the contaminated water flowed towards the Amur River and eventually to the Khabarovsk region of the Russian Far East. China apologised to the government of Russia, but Moscow required assurances that everything possible has been done to prevent a recurrence of such pollution.

Questions have been asked about the causes of such a massive explosion in a strategically important industry, but also about the way in which the incident was reported. The relative openness in that section of the press that is aimed at an overseas readership could be extended to the domestic media, although that has not yet happened. Premier Wen Jiabao undoubtedly used the ensuing debate to enhance his environmental credentials and to increase his political support in the northeast.

The immediate impact for the administrations of Jilin and Heilongjiang was the arrival of an inspection team sent from Beijing to inquire into the contamination and to ascertain whether local authorities were remiss in not intervening earlier. The general manager of the Jilin petrochemical plant was dismissed, as were two of the plant managers who were judged to have been directly responsible for the initial explosions. Finally, in what was widely seen as an attempt by the government to demonstrate its commitment to accountability at the highest level, the director of the State Environmental Protection Administration (SEPA), Xie Zhenhua, submitted his resignation and it was accepted at the beginning of December 2005. SEPA was accused of having underestimated the seriousness of the explosions and their possible environmental and political impact.[12]

Environmental problems and multi-national corporations

A particularly complex and politically sensitive issue is the question of the contribution made to China's environmental problems by foreign multi-national companies. Concerns have been raised in China about the policies of some multi-nationals which are alleged to be exporting environmentally hazardous procedures to China, where the regulatory framework and the enforcement regime are still underdeveloped in comparison with the West.

In October 2006, Pan Yue, who is Deputy Director of China's Environmental Protection Agency and of Deputy Minister rank, published an essay entitled 'On Socialist Ecological Civilisation'. The title has a disconcerting Maoist ring about it, but the main thrust of his argument is important.

> With the rise of globalisation, developed countries have transferred their industry to developing nations as a form of environmental colonialism. In China, pollution has been moved from east to west and from the city to the rural areas. The rich consume and the poor suffer the pollution. The economic and environmental inequalities caused by a flawed understanding of growth and political achievement, held by some officials, have gone against the basic aims of socialism and abandoned the achievements of Chinese socialism.[13]

Other critics within China have gone further and have accused specific multi-national companies of pursuing a policy of 'eco-colonialism', focussing their attention particularly on the transfer of waste processing and waste disposal projects to China, while some Western commentators have accused China of blaming the multi-nationals for what is essentially a domestic problem caused by the expansion of China's economy.[14]

Environmental issues and Xi Jinping

There were no dramatic changes in China's policies on the environment during the Xi Jinping administration, although there was an increased emphasis on environmental protection and preservation of China's patrimony as a patriotic duty. At the NPC in March 2019, Premier Li Keqiang reported on the challenges faced by the Chinese economy in the time of a global economic slowdown and the destructive trade war with the United States. Xi Jinping chose to follow this by speaking to delegates from Inner Mongolia, where environmental issues were a constant concern, insisting that stimulus to the economy should not be at the cost of environmental degradation. The transition from 'high-speed growth to high-quality development' must be accompanied by reinforced environmental governance and firm control of pollution.[15]

Notes

1 Michael Dillon 'History of the Porcelain Industry in Jingdezhen' PhD thesis, University of Leeds, 1976; Michael Dillon 'Jingdezhen as a Ming Industrial Centre', *Ming Studies* no. 6 (Spring 1978), pp. 37–44.
2 Liu Li 'One third of nation hit by acid rain' *China Daily* 28 August 2006.
3 Xinhua News Agency, Beijing, 26 August 2006, via Reuters.
4 L. Tang, J. Qu, Z. Mi et al. 'Substantial Emission Reductions from Chinese Power Plants after the Introduction of Ultra-Low Emissions Standards' *Nat Energy* 4 (2019), pp. 929–38. https://doi.org/10.1038/s41560-019-0468
5 *FT* 10 July 2007.
6 PRC Foreign Ministry statement 2 June 2004 https://www.fmprc.gov.cn/mfa_eng/ziliao_665539/3602_665543/3604_665547/t18043.shtml.
7 PRC Foreign Ministry statement 2 June 2004; Xinhua 1 February 2018; CTBTO website, ctbto.org.
8 Xinhua 4 November 2020 http://www.xinhuanet.com/english/2020-11/04/c_139489698.htm.
9 BBC News 26 September 2007; *FT* 26 September 2007; *China Daily* 9 March 2007; *China View* (Xinhua) 26 September 2007.
10 *Guardian* 20 August 2020.

11 Lu Yiyi 'Environmental Civil Society and Governance in China' Chatham House research paper, London: RIIA, August 2005.
12 Xinhua 3 December 2005.
13 *China Dialogue* interview 27 October 2006.
14 Elizabeth Economy 'A Blame Game China Needs to Stop' *Washington Post* 3 December 2006.
15 *SCMP* 6 March 2019.

Part 5
China's periphery

Part 5

China's periphery

21 Tibet

The status of Tibet and its relationship with China remains one of the most intractable and emotive issues in Asian – and indeed, world – politics. The official Chinese stance is that Tibet, which it invariably refers to as Chinese Tibet [*Zhongguo Xizang*], has always been an integral part of China and always should be. Supporters of self-determination for Tibet point to its *de facto* independence between the collapse of the Chinese Empire in 1911 and the controversial Seventeen Point Agreement signed in 1951 between the Tibetan government and representatives of the newly victorious CCP. Many also believe that this independent status has a much longer history, and that Tibet was an autonomous and genuinely self-governing entity for centuries. It is therefore argued that Tibet was independent until 1951 and has since suffered an unlawful occupation by the Chinese.

This view is shared by the members and supporters of the Dalai Lama's government in exile in the Indian city of Dharamsala. The existence of this alternative focus of loyalty and authority has been a source of great solace for Tibetans inside and outside China, and simultaneously a cause of great irritation and anger for the Chinese authorities who have worked tirelessly to undermine the Dalai Lama's status as a major religious and political figure on the international stage.

The conflict has been highlighted by prominent and glamorous media and Hollywood figures who have rallied to the defence of Tibetan culture, and also by Western adherents of Buddhism. Whether this always reflects genuine spiritual conviction, deep knowledge of the religion, language, and culture of Tibet, or merely transient political fashion is a matter of judgement.[1]

Tibet and Qing China

The influence of the Qing dynasty in Tibet declined in the nineteenth century as its Manchu rulers became preoccupied with Western incursions on the coast and the domestic rebellions of the Taiping, the Nian, and the Hui Muslims in inland China, which were much closer to the capital, Beijing, than was Tibet. By the middle of the century, the authority of the Manchus in Tibet had decreased to the point at which Qing suzerainty was mainly symbolic. Tibet was effectively autonomous, and increasingly so as the century progressed. The 13th Dalai Lama (1876–1933) became known as the Great 13th not solely because of the extraordinary authority that he exercised, even for a Dalai Lama, but because Tibet unshackled itself from direct Chinese control during his rule.

In 1903, after an expedition under the command of Sir Francis Younghusband turned into a full-scale invasion of Tibet by the forces of British India, the 13th Dalai Lama left Lhasa, the Tibetan capital, and took refuge in Urga, the capital of Mongolia which was also a bastion of Tibetan Buddhism: Urga was renamed Ulaanbaatar (Ulan Bator) after the Mongolian revolution of 1924. The Dalai Lama arrived in Urga in October 1904 and, in his absence, the Chinese government pronounced him deposed. Tensions arose between the Dalai Lama and the Jebtsundamba Khutukhtu, the highest Mongolian spiritual authority, and the Dalai Lama returned to Tibet and attempted to arrive at an agreement with the Chinese government.

The Anglo-Chinese Convention of 1906 effectively repudiated the gains made by Younghusband's adventure and reaffirmed the Qing dynasty's suzerainty over Tibet. In 1908, Zhao Erfeng was charged by the Qing government with bringing the eastern province of Kham and eventually the whole of Tibet firmly under Chinese control and assimilating its institutions into the Chinese Empire. Troops under Zhao's command reached Lhasa in February 1910 and the Dalai Lama, believing that the Chinese government had reneged on an agreement with his officials, fled again – on this occasion to Darjeeling in India.

Independence after 1911

When the news of the Chinese Revolution of 1911 reached Lhasa, Tibetans rose against their Chinese masters, directed by a special group that the Dalai Lama had established in India.

> By April 1912, the Tibetans had prevailed: about three thousand Chinese troops and officers surrendered and were permitted to leave Tibet via India. In the fifth Tibetan month of the Water-Mouse year (1912), the Dalai Lama returned to Tibet, staying first in Chumbi and then, in January 1913, finally entering a Lhasa free of Chinese troops and officials for the first time since the eighteenth century.[2]

Although the new President of the Republic of China, Yuan Shikai, attempted to mend fences with the Dalai Lama by recognising his religious titles, the Dalai Lama insisted that he would exercise both spiritual and temporal authority in Tibet and 'cut even the symbolic tie with China'.[3]

The position of Tibet in the years following the collapse of Qing rule in 1911 was 'static and non-changing, living in splendid isolation and illusionary independence'[4] Its independence may have been an illusion, but it was a period of genuine political separation from China that lasted until 1951. The *de facto* autonomy of that period continues to inspire Tibetans who desire an independent state.

The political and legal status of Tibet has been a matter of international controversy since the middle of the twentieth century, when the long-standing but local question of borders and sovereignty achieved international prominence in Cold War disputes between the United States and China. To many Tibetans, the position was simple: Tibet is and always has been an independent state that was occupied illegally by the Chinese in 1951. For the government of the PRC, the position was equally simple: Tibet has always been and always will be part of China. The legal justification for this claim is questionable, but that is the premise on which Beijing's actions in Tibet are based. What is incontestable is that from the fall of the Qing dynasty in 1911 until the PLA marched into Tibet in 1951, Tibet functioned *de facto* as a fully independent state, ruled by a combination of secular and lamaist bureaucracies.[5] The situation is further complicated by the fact that the Tibetan Autonomous Region, as it is constituted today, is only the core region of what was Tibet before 1951; substantial parts of the territories of old, or ethnographic, Tibet have been transferred to the neighbouring Chinese provinces of Qinghai, Sichuan and Gansu.

Tibet incorporated into the PRC

When the CCP was victorious in the Civil War that ended in 1949, Tibet became part of the PRC, as did Xinjiang in a similar manner. The intention was that this would happen by means of a process of 'peaceful liberation' [*heping jiefang*]. This was achieved to a certain extent in Xinjiang, but Mao Zedong and the CCP acknowledged that the position of Tibet was different because of its isolation and because of the absence of a sizeable settled Han Chinese community. In December 1949, judging that Tibet could only be 'liberated' by military action, Beijing began to prepare for an invasion of the eastern provinces of Tibet, particularly Chamdo, while at the same time opening negotiations with the Tibetan government. The Tibetans failed to send a delegation to Beijing for these talks, and on 7 October 1950, the PLA Eighteenth Army crossed the frontier into Chamdo with the intention of rendering inoperative the Tibetan army units based there and cutting off Lhasa. The poorly led – and frankly, somewhat amateurish – Tibetan forces were no match for their battle-hardened counterparts in the PLA, and the entire Tibetan army was defeated within two weeks. The PLA could have moved directly to take control of Lhasa, as there were no significant military obstacles preventing it from doing so, but Mao's preferred strategy was to hold Chamdo and to try for a negotiated settlement that would win the approval of the Dalai Lama and thus the majority of the population of Tibet.

The Tibetans appealed to the United Nations, asking that the independent status of their country be recognised, but this was rejected after Britain and India vetoed any discussion on the issue. Britain believed that any demand for China to withdraw from Tibet would be unenforceable, and India was reluctant to compromise the close relationship it was hoping to develop with the PRC.

Reluctantly, the Tibetan government decided to send a delegation to negotiate with its new masters in Beijing, and the result was the Seventeen Point Agreement, signed in Beijing on 23 May 1951, which gave the Tibetan authorities limited autonomy within the PRC in return for agreeing to assist the PLA in its occupation of Tibet and ceding to Beijing the right to conduct foreign relations on its behalf. On 16 October, PLA troops moved to garrison Lhasa under the terms of the agreement. The circumstances under which this agreement was signed remain controversial, but it was clearly signed under duress. The Dalai Lama did not take part in the negotiations. He had moved from the Potala palace in Lhasa to the small town of Yadong, a Tibetan community close to Sikkim on the border with India, in preparation for a swift withdrawal should the PLA march on Lhasa. He returned to Lhasa in August 1951, and agreed to lend his support to the Seventeen Point Agreement in a telegram sent to Mao Zedong on 24 October. The Seventeen Point Agreement preserved most of the traditional political and religious structures of Tibet, including the unique role of the Dalai Lama, in exchange for the acknowledgement of Chinese suzerainty over the country. Beijing's strategy during this early period of the PRC was moderate and *laissez-faire*, in comparison with later policies, and the feudal and monastic economy remained intact – there was no confiscation of land from either the secular feudal landlords or the monasteries.

The agreement applied only to the Tibetan Autonomous Region – that is, the area around the capital Lhasa and Shigatse, the site of the Tashilunpo Monastery, and westwards into the high plains and the mountains. It did not apply to the Tibetan-speaking communities in Gansu, Sichuan and Qinghai; when land reform and collectivisation policies were carried out in these areas, they provoked great hostility from the Tibetan minorities and large-scale migrations westwards into central Tibet. In the mid-1950s, the radical programmes of collectivisation finally reached central Tibet and resistance to Chinese rule, largely organised by ethnic Tibetan refugees from outside the Tibetan Autonomous Region, was growing apace. Mao tried to reassure the Dalai Lama that Tibet would be protected from the radical reforms tearing apart the old rural society in the rest of China, but the resistance movement proved too powerful and the Dalai Lama found himself on the sidelines.

Tibetan insurgency

In March 1959, the attention of the leadership in Beijing was diverted from its factional disputes and the acrimonious internal debates over the Great Leap Forward and the communes by news from the far west of China that an armed revolt had broken out in Tibet against the administration that the CCP had established there in 1951. This was seen by Beijing as a serious assault on the integrity of the PRC, and the leadership of the CCP decided that it required an immediate and determined response.

The Tibetan revolt broke out on 10 March 1959 when the headquarters of the PLA and the Chinese government in Lhasa were surrounded by demonstrators. Forces loyal to the Tibetan government turned on the PLA garrison in the Tibetan capital on 19 March. The rising had little chance of succeeding; assistance from the CIA that some Tibetans believed they had been promised did not materialise in time. Over the next four days, the PLA suppressed the revolt, both in Lhasa and elsewhere in Tibet. The Dalai Lama had left Lhasa two days previously and crossed the border into India on 31 March, having renounced the Seventeen Point Agreement. The Tibetan government was dissolved, and a preparatory committee was set up to establish a new Tibetan Autonomous Region government. The Chinese decided that the Seventeen Point Agreement no longer applied and moved against the monastic and landed elites, confiscating the largest landholdings and closing down monasteries. The Dalai Lama established his own government in exile and the Panchen Lama, who was based at the Tashilunpo monastery in Shigatse, became the highest-ranking spiritual leader within Tibet. Historically, incarnations of the Panchen Lama have played an important role as a link between China and the Tibetans. The Panchen Lama was appointed Chairman of the Preparatory Committee for the Tibetan Autonomous Region on 28 March 1959 on the interesting but specious grounds that the Dalai Lama was being held by rebels against his will.

The Dalai Lama fled into exile in Dharamsala (a hill station in the northern Indian state of Himachal Pradesh). Tibet was designated an autonomous region of the PRC on 9 September 1965. The Dalai Lama and his senior religious and political officials remained in Dharamsala, depriving Tibet of the spiritual leadership that most of the population recognised.[6] The Prime Minister of India, Jawaharlal Nehru, formally invited the Dalai Lama to establish his government in exile in Dharamsala, an area that although predominantly Hindu had a tradition of Tibetan Buddhism that can be traced back to the eighth century. Dharamsala, and especially the part of Upper Dharamsala known as McLeod Ganj, grew into a substantial community of Tibetans in exile. The name McLeod Ganj [market] is a reminder of the history of the area as a nineteenth-century hill station of the British Raj which was popular as a summer escape for expatriate members of the Indian Civil Service working in Delhi.

Tibet after Mao

The Cultural Revolution of 1966–1976 increased the scale of political attacks on Tibetan Buddhism and its material culture that had begun during the suppression of the 1959 rising.[7] The death of Mao Zedong in September 1976 led to a period of relative liberalisation and in the mid-1980s, influenced by CCP General Secretary Hu Yaobang (whose premature death in

1989 precipitated the Democracy Movement and the demonstrations in Tian'anmen Square that were crushed on 4 June). The number of Tibetans participating in local government in Tibet increased, and the status of the Tibetan language and Tibetan culture in government and education was enhanced.[8] Hu Yaobang visited Tibet in 1980 on the 29th anniversary of the Seventeen Point Agreement and was openly critical of the condescending – and, in many cases, frankly racist – policies and attitudes of Han Chinese cadres in Tibet.[9]

In October 1987, partly in response to a major international diplomatic initiative by Dharamsala to procure a settlement to the Tibet question, a wave of demonstrations began in Tibet, led by monks and nuns who supported the creation of an independent Tibet under the Dalai Lama. The first demonstrations were led by monks of Drepung monastery, which lies to the west of Lhasa and is the senior monastery in the Gelug or Yellow Hat tradition. They carried out religious circumambulations of Lhasa and were arrested when they marched on government offices. The protests became violent after demonstrators were arrested and assaulted, and police fired on the crowds, killing some of the protesters.

Demonstrations continued, once more led by monks and nuns, whose courage and fortitude in the face of alleged brutality was recognised internationally. A further demonstration took place in 1988 when the Panchen Lama (who died unexpectedly shortly afterwards, on 28 January 1989) visited Tibet from Beijing in an attempt to ensure the success of the Great Prayer Festival traditionally held to accompany celebrations of the Tibetan New Year. Many monks believed that their festival had been hijacked by the CCP and a minor contretemps exploded into riots, followed by mass arrests and a political and religious clampdown. A nationalist Tibetan Buddhist movement had been formed, stimulated by – but isolated from and essentially independent of – the leadership in Dharamsala.[10]

Panchen Lama

The death of the 10th Panchen Lama in January 1989 and the search for his reincarnation precipitated another crisis. The Panchen Lama is second only to the Dalai Lama in the Tibetan spiritual hierarchy, and some Buddhists in Tibet even place his spiritual authority ahead of that of the Dalai Lama; in the twentieth century, successive Panchen Lamas have been closer to governments in Beijing than any other high lamas, and this has resulted in divisions and disagreements over spiritual and political precedence. Beijing tried to take control of the selection process, but the choice of a new Panchen incarnation also required the confirmation of the Dalai Lama. The Dalai Lama announced the name of his candidate, Gedhun Choeki Nyima, on 14 May 1995, but in November, Beijing endorsed a different contender, Gyaltsen Norbu, and the process collapsed in disarray.[11]

Conflict between the Tibetan religious leadership and Beijing concerning the succession of the Panchen Lama was highlighted when the Abbot of Kumbun monastery – in the province of Qinghai, part of old Tibet – was expelled from the Chinese People's Political Consultative Conference in June 2000 after leaving China for the United States in 1998. Agyo Lobsangtubdain Gyurma had been a member of the committee established by the Chinese that to locate the reincarnation of the Panchen Lama, but he spoke out in support of the Dalai Lama and rejected the Chinese choice of Gyaltsen Norbu.[12] The Dalai Lama gave an interview to the journal *Asiaweek* in 2000, and reflected on the effect his death would have on the Tibetan people, 'if I passed away, the reincarnation would logically come outside Tibet, in a free country. But China will choose a boy as the next Dalai Lama, though in reality he is not'. He added that Tibetans would reject any Panchen Lama who was nominated by Beijing.[13]

Reports of ill treatment and brutality continued to emerge from Tibet, and monks and nuns – the standard-bearers of Tibetan national and religious identity – were frequently the targets. Five nuns arrested after demonstrations in May 1998 were interrogated in Drapchi prison and beaten with belts and electric batons after calling out Tibetan nationalist slogans when ordered to sing Chinese patriotic songs. They committed suicide.[14]

Karmapa Lama

A young lama, virtually unknown outside the Tibetan community, left Tibet in December 1999 to join the Dalai Lama in Dharamsala. The 14-year-old 17th Karmapa Lama left the Tsurphu monastery to the northeast of Lhasa, saying that he was going abroad to buy musical instruments and black hats worn by previous incarnations of the Karmapa. Unusually, the Karmapa Lama, Ugyen Trinley Dorge, who was the son of nomads, had been recognised in 1992 by both Beijing and the Dalai Lama as a reincarnation of the previous head of the Kagyu sect.[15] The flight of the Karmapa Lama embarrassed the authorities and was followed by a renewed political offensive against monasteries in Tibet. Thirty monks were expelled from the Jokhang temple in Lhasa in June 2000 and the government threatened reprisals against anyone who had taken part in pilgrimages during the festival of Sagadawa. Children were told they would be expelled from school, officials that they would be dismissed, and pensioners that their pensions would be stopped. There were also reports of houses being raided and the seizure of religious objects and photographs of the Dalai Lama. Members of the CCP and teachers who had photographs of the Dalai Lama in their possession were fined.[16]

In September 2000, the Tibetan government in exile published a report, *China's Current Policy in Tibet*; it claimed that Beijing was aiming at the 'total destruction' of Tibetan culture. The report also argued that the Dalai Lama had moderated the more extreme elements of Tibetan nationalism and that China's refusal to have any contact with him could lead to more violent expressions of dissent.[17]

Qinghai-Tibet railway

Tibet's isolation has been a decisive factor in the development of its distinctive culture. It is physically isolated from China by distance and by the difficulty of developing land transport links from the lowlands to the high plateau. It is isolated from its near neighbour, India, to which it owes its historic Buddhist tradition, by the Himalayas. For some passionate supporters of the culture of Tibetan Buddhism, this seclusion has been wholly positive, and there are those who will argue that it is precisely Tibet's contact with the outside world that threatens its ancient religious culture. Others, including many thoughtful Tibetans, have concluded that, on the contrary, this isolation has been at the root of Tibet's problems at least since the early part of the twentieth century.

This being the case, the construction of a railway link between China Proper and Tibet could never be discussed simply in terms of transport and communications. The railway, which links Xining, the capital city of Qinghai province, to the Tibetan capital Lhasa, was in the minds of Chinese government planners for generations. It was regarded as an indispensable infrastructural project, without which the economic development of Tibet and its integration into China could not be guaranteed. It took so long to come to fruition largely because of the difficult terrain it has to cross and the altitude problems that affect not only travellers, but also engineers and labourers working on the roof of the world. Track, engines, and carriages all require special designs to be able to operate successfully at high altitude, and the coaches have to be equipped with an oxygen supply for passengers.

The Qingzang railway (Qing and Zang are the standard abbreviations for Qinghai and Tibet, respectively), which is mooted as the world's highest railway, runs for a total of 1,220 miles: the stretch from Xining to the city of Golmud has been operating since 1984, but the final section taking the railway to Tibet was not completed until it became part of the Western Development plan (see Chapter 12). Golmud is the principal city of the Haixi Mongol, Tibetan and Kazakh Autonomous Prefecture, the name of which gives an indication of the complex ethnic mix of this mountainous region. Construction of the key final stage from Golmud to Lhasa began in 2001 and was complete by the autumn of 2005. The formal opening ceremony took place on 1 July 2006 after months of testing of both track and rolling stock.

Services using this line include long-distance trains which run to Lhasa from Beijing, Chengdu, Chongqing, Xining, and Lanzhou. The journey from Beijing to Lhasa takes almost 48 hours, and the section from Xining to Lhasa alone takes 26 hours, in spite of journey speeds which are much higher than most of China's railway system.

Critics of the construction project argued that, far from improving the lives of Tibetans, the new rail link would serve to strengthen China's control over Tibet and would encourage the migration of young Tibetans away from their homeland in search of employment: it would also promote the migration from the east to Tibet of Han Chinese who are likely to obtain preferential treatment in employment opportunities. There were also concerns about the potential environmental impact of the increased flow of tourists and traders to the Tibetan Plateau. The Qinghai-Tibet highway which also brings in trade and migrants has not experienced the same level of criticism. Because the opening of the railway line was turned into such a high-profile event by the Chinese government, it became a symbol for the entire economic and political relationship between Beijing and Tibet.

Protests and self-immolation

Although protests by Buddhist clergy against the lack of religious freedom in Tibet were primarily of religious origin, they have been treated as nationalist disturbances by the Chinese government. Many monks and nuns have been incarcerated, and there are consistent and credible reports of their brutal treatment in detention.[18] In spite of the protests, talks on the future of Tibet between Beijing and the Dalai Lama's representatives continue behind the scenes, although this is not at all apparent from the rancorous rhetoric that is used by both sides in public, especially in statements emanating from Beijing. In October 2007, the Dalai Lama was awarded the Congressional Medal of Freedom by the President of the United States, George W. Bush. This was applauded by many Westerners as a sign of American support for religious freedom. Beijing was predictably outraged at what it viewed as outside interference in its domestic affairs and demonstrations to celebrate the award of the medal, which took place in Tibet, were crushed with considerable force by the Chinese authorities.

The cycle of repression and resistance in Tibet shows no sign of coming to an end. Monks and nuns persevere in leading the resistance to restrictions on their religious practice and teaching. Many have suffered unpleasant punishment and deprivation which they endure, supported by their Buddhist beliefs and monastic discipline.

The most shocking and controversial aspect of resistance is the willingness of a significant number of monks and nuns to set themselves on fire. In contrast to acts of violence against

people and property in other conflicts, including suicide bombings, self-immolation primarily affects the individual who undertakes the action; it also has a profound effect on the
monastic communities and the Tibetan Buddhist laity and is said to strengthen their spirit
of resistance. The Dalai Lama has not sanctioned the practice, but neither has he explicitly forbidden it; for this, he has been criticised from many quarters. The Chinese government blames the Tibetan leader for instigating, or at least inspiring, this self-sacrifice, even
though each case appears to be an individual act of protest. Self-immolation is not solely
a Tibetan phenomenon; it came to the attention of Westerners in 1963 when a Vietnamese
Buddhist monk set himself on fire in protest against the policies of the right-wing regime
in Saigon.

On 27 February 2009, Tapey, a young Tibetan monk of the Kirti monastery in the town
of Ngawa (Aba in Chinese), which is located in Nagwa County in Sichuan, attempted to
burn himself to death. He is believed to have survived, in spite of having been shot by
security personnel, and to be in detention. On 16 March 2011, another monk, Phuntsok, set
himself on fire in the same county and died the following morning.[19] The death of Phuntsok
prompted demonstrations by monks, nuns, and lay people in the local community, and a
campaign of self-immolations followed.

Sonam Topgyal, who had taken courses in advanced Buddhist studies at the Dzongsar
Monastery in Derge County, set himself on fire on 9 July 2015 in Gesar Square in the town
of Gyegu (Yushu in Chinese), which is in a majority Tibetan area in the south of Qinghai
province. The Chinese authorities surrounded the town with units of the PAP and other military units, isolated his home and family, and suspended telephone and internet services to
prevent the news from travelling.[20]

The last individual to set himself on fire in 2016, 33-year-old Tashi Rabten, lived with his
wife and three children in Maqu, a county in the Gannan Tibetan Autonomous Prefecture in
Gansu Province. Although witnesses insisted that he had called for freedom for Tibet and
the return of the Dalai Lama as he set himself ablaze during the evening of 8 December, the
authorities pressed his family to say that his suicide was not connected to the Tibetan cause
or Chinese policies but was the result of family problems. The 150th individual to sacrifice
himself was the monk Jamyang Losal, who died on 19 May 2017 in Gangca in the Tsojang
Prefecture of Qinghai province.[21]

Chen Quanguo's new initiatives

A new political initiative was launched in Tibet by Chen Quanguo, who was appointed Party
Secretary in Tibet in August 2011, although he had no previous experience of working in
ethnic minority areas. He remained in Tibet until August 2016, when he was transferred to
Xinjiang in a move widely seen as a vote of confidence in the way that he had managed
conflict in Tibet.

Chen's policies resulted in temporary and local successes, but did little to break the vicious
cycle of protest and repression. He announced his wish to work with the Buddhist clergy in
temples and monasteries, which some at least would have welcomed, and his intention to
transform their institutions into centres of learning that would support the CCP, which most
would not. He also declared that he would work to separate Tibetan Buddhism from the
Dalai Lama, a statement which could only result in the most fervent opposition. Although
these new policies were presented in a friendly and positive manner, the intended outcomes
were no different from those of previous hard-line CCP leaders in Tibet. Visiting the Jokhang
Temple on 10 January 2016 on the occasion of the Tibetan New Year, Chen made positive

comments about Buddhism but insisted that it must be patriotic and 'adapt to socialist society'. Chen's policies of enforcing 'patriotic education' ensured that all monasteries and temples had access to modern Chinese media outlets and were under surveillance by government work teams. Work teams were also deployed in Tibetan villages throughout the region, and this mass surveillance was credited with substantially reducing active Tibetan opposition to Chinese rule. It did not, however, end the wave of self-immolations.[22]

Tibetans were ordered to surrender their passports in 2012 and networks of 'convenience police stations' were established, initially in Lhasa, and then across the whole of the Tibet Autonomous Region. A system of 'double-linked households' was instituted: groups of ten households were required to watch over each other to guard against the twin evils of insecurity and poverty. The Henan provincial media, proud of a local boy made good, described Chen's policies in Tibet as 'measured' or 'orderly' [*youban youyan*]. In addition to this family surveillance system, Chen's plan for stabilising the region included the deployment of over 100,000 cadres to live in the villages. He also enforced tighter control over monasteries, replacing the Democratic Management Committees that had previously been run by monks with government-run bodies. He is credited with adopting a positive approach to the monks or lamas, indicating that he wished to treat them as 'friends of the citizens' [*gongmin de pengyou*], rather than inherently implacable enemies, and forged good personal relationships with some leading monks in Lhasa. That is unlikely to have altered their attitude to his policies – or the long-term aims of the CCP in Tibet.[23]

Destruction at Larung Gar

During the second half of 2016, there were major protests after the Chinese authorities decided to demolish buildings at the Serthar Buddhist Institute, a Buddhist academy and monastery in the valley of Larung Gar which lies in the Garze (Kardze) Tibetan Autonomous Prefecture of Sichuan Province. It is a colossal complex of religious and residential buildings, and may be the largest institution in the world for promoting the teachings of Tibetan Buddhism. The official reason given for the demolition was the overpopulation of the site caused by the number of monks and nuns wishing to study there. By the early twenty-first century, it had become home to as many as 10,000 monks, nuns, and other devotees: some reports indicated that the total number of students at the academy was in excess of 40,000, many of them living in makeshift accommodation which was turning into a shanty town. Demolition began in July 2016; by September, as many as 9,000 people had been evicted and the demolition of the temporary accommodation was well underway. Monks, nuns, and lay people who resisted were forcibly removed and some were imprisoned or subject to a course of 'patriotic re-education', an instrument of ideological control also used in other Tibetan communities. One group of nuns was moved to a remote military-style camp in the Gardze region. Officials announced that Buddhist education could restart in Larung Gar, but only under strict supervision by the state bodies that control religious activity. In June 2017, a senior lama claimed that a total of 7,000 buildings in the area had been demolished.[24]

Training Living Buddhas

As part of a programme for bringing all religious institutions in Tibet firmly under the control of the government, a training course was organised in late October 2016 for almost 400 Tibetan Buddhist clergy whose incarnations as Tulkus (Trulkus or Living Buddhas) had been included in a database compiled by the State Administration for Religious Affairs. The course, which was run by the United Front Work Departments of the CCP Central Committee and its Tibetan branch, included a visit to Changsha to see the newly built Mao Zedong Memorial Museum in Mao's home province of Hunan. The lamas were also taken to the former homes of Mao and Liu Shaoqi in Hunan and the Revolutionary Martyrs Memorial Hall in the Jiangxi hill town of Jinggangshan which celebrates the early activities of CCP in its rural bases. The object of the exercise was to inculcate 'national religious policies and socialist core values', and these were expounded at courses provided by the Tibetan Institute of Socialism.[25]

Notes

1 Patrick French *Tibet, Tibet: A Personal History of a Lost Land* London: HarperCollins, 2003 is a perceptive account of the relationship between Westerners and the Tibetan cause.
2 Melvyn C. Goldstein *A History of Modern Tibet, 1913–1951: The Demise of the Lamaist State* Berkeley: University of California Press, 1989, p. 59.
3 Melvyn C. Goldstein *A History of Modern Tibet, 1913–1951: The Demise of the Lamaist State* Berkeley: University of California Press, 1989, p. 60; See also Patrick French *Younghusband: The Last Great Imperial Adventurer* London: HarperCollins, 1994.
4 Dawa Norbu *China's Tibet Policy* Richmond: Curzon Press, 2001, p. 97.
5 Melvyn C. Goldstein *A History of Modern Tibet, 1913–1951: The Demise of the Lamaist State* Berkeley: University of California Press, 1989, pp. ix–xx and passim; Melvyn C. Goldstein *The Snow Lion and the Dragon: China, Tibet and the Dalai Lama* Berkeley: University of California Press, 1997, pp. 30–6.
6 Tsering Shakya *The Dragon in the Land of Snows: A History of Modern Tibet since 1947* London: Pimlico, 1999, pp. 163–211.
7 Tsering Shakya *The Dragon in the Land of Snows: A History of Modern Tibet since 1947* London: Pimlico, 1999, pp. 314–47.
8 Melvyn C. Goldstein *The Snow Lion and the Dragon: China, Tibet and the Dalai Lama* Berkeley: University of California Press, 1997, pp. 61–75.
9 Tsering Shakya *The Dragon in the Land of Snows: A History of Modern Tibet since 1947* London: Pimlico, 1999, pp. 381–2.
10 Melvyn C. Goldstein *The Snow Lion and the Dragon: China, Tibet and the Dalai Lama* Berkeley: University of California Press, 1997, pp. 79–83.
11 Melvyn C. Goldstein *The Snow Lion and the Dragon: China, Tibet and the Dalai Lama* Berkeley: University of California Press, 1997, pp. 100–11.
12 *SCMP* 29 June 2000.
13 Press Trust of India New Delhi 11 October 2000.
14 Personal communication from Tibetan nuns.
15 *FT* 5 January 2000; BBC News 8 January 2000.
16 Agence France-Presse (AFP) 17 August 2000.
17 *SCMP* 30 September 2000.
18 Interview with Buddhist nuns, London, May 2006.
19 *Phayul.com*, New Delhi, 17 March 2011.
20 *Free Tibet* 10 July 2015; Radio Free Asia 10 July 2015.
21 'Tibetan Self-Immolator Was Husband, Father of Three' Radio Free Asia 9 December 2016; 'Tibetan Monk Sets Himself Ablaze in Qinghai in 150th Self-Immolation' Radio Free Asia 19 May 2017.
22 Sophie Richardson 'China Poised to Repeat Tibet Mistakes: Abusive Policies Planned for Uyghur Region' *Human Rights Watch* 20 January 2017; *Tibet.cn* 13 January 2016. 'China: No End to Tibet Surveillance Program' *Human Rights Watch* 18 January 2016.
23 *Dahewang* (Great River Web), website of the Henan Provincial Government, from Chen's home province, 29 August 2016, http://news.dahe.cn/2016/08-29/107406757.html; 'Monasteries Placed Under New Controls' Radio Free Asia 16 March 2012; 'Passports Taken, More Police . . . New Party Boss Chen Quanguo Acts to Tame Xinjiang with Methods Used in Tibet' *SCMP* 12 December

2016. 'Party Boss Chen Quanguo Replicating his Tibet Policy in Xinjiang' *Tibetan Review* 13 December 2016.

24 'Larung Gar: China "Destroys Buildings" at Tibetan Buddhist Academy' BBC News 22 July 2016; 'China Slaps Ban on New Students at Larung Gar Tibetan Academy' Radio Free Asia 9 December 2016; 'Expelled Larung Gar Nuns Held in Camp in Kardze' Radio Free Asia 12 December 2016; 'Destruction at Larung Gar Greater than Earlier Reported' Radio Free Asia 22 June 1917.

25 'China Publishes "Verified Living Buddha" List' BBC News 18 January 2016; 'Training Course for New Living Buddhas Held' *Global Times* 6 November 2016.

22 Xinjiang

As the Xinjiang Uyghur Autonomous Region marked its 50th anniversary in 2005, Beijing was deploying both the carrot of economic development and the stick of political and religious repression to maintain its control of the region. In the past, Xinjiang has been described as both the 'pivot of Asia' and as a pawn of the Soviet Union. Today, it is the only part of Islamic Central Asia controlled by China, and it is China's land bridge to Eurasia; this is increasingly important since the inauguration of the Belt and Road Initiative. Xinjiang is both oil rich and politically unstable because of separatist sentiment among the indigenous Muslim and Turkic-speaking Uyghurs, many of whom would like a return to an independent Eastern Turkestan, a state which existed briefly in the 1940s. In Xinjiang, the Islamic traditions of Central Asia and China overlap, although the mosques of the Chinese-speaking Hui communities are separate from those of Uyghur Muslims.[1]

The network of mosques across Xinjiang provides the framework for the complex system of worship, education, and law that dominated the region before it came under the control of the CCP in 1949. It is difficult to obtain credible statistics on the total number of mosques; one estimate suggests that in 1949 there were 29,545 mosques in the whole of Xinjiang. By the start of the Cultural Revolution (roughly 1966–1976), this had been reduced to 14,119: many had fallen into disrepair, some had been requisitioned by the government and others had been demolished or closed down during anti-religious and other campaigns such as the movement for land reform. During the chaos of the Cultural Revolution, there were said to be only 1,400 active mosques; by 1990, the number had risen again to over 17,000, with over 43,000 other 'places of religious activity', shrines, and madrasas.[2]

Mazars – Sufi tomb culture

While mosques in Xinjiang are found in most villages, towns, and cities, the *mazar* tombs of the Sufi sheikhs and the religious complexes that have grown up around them are typically in isolated rural settings.[3] These tombs are the homes of the mystical Sufi orders, predominantly the Jahriyya and Khufiyya branches of the Naqshbandiyya. Devotees of these orders make pilgrimages to the tombs on the anniversary of the death of the founding *sheikh* and on major religious festivals. These pilgrimages have on occasion attracted crowds of such a size that the authorities have banned or restricted them.[4] The *mazar* culture is viewed by the Chinese state as a serious threat to its authority and has been the subject of frequent repression by the authorities: it has also been attacked by conservative Muslims and by Islamic reformers influenced directly or indirectly by Wahhabi teachings that have spread to Xinjiang from Saudi Arabia.

It is impossible to estimate with any confidence how many active *mazars* there are in Xinjiang, but a serious and authoritative study by an Uyghur scholar lists 73 major sites.[5] Because of the Uyghurs' dislike of the regulation of mosques by the government, this parallel Islam is becoming more popular. The fact that these sects are part of a trans-national Islamic movement (in particular the highly political Naqshbandiyya) is attractive to the isolated Turkic-speaking Muslims of Xinjiang, but troubles the Chinese authorities.[6]

Demonstrations and resistance in Xinjiang

Antagonism between Uyghur Muslims and the Chinese authorities, which had persisted since the suppression of insurrections in the 1950s, became more acute and more visible in the 1980s. It was most intense in two areas of Xinjiang: the southwest, which is dominated by the great Uyghur cultural and Islamic centre of Kashgar, and the Ghulja region in the northwest, which is close to the border between China and Kazakhstan. Major disturbances began in April 1980 with riots in the town of Aksu, which is midway between Urumqi and Kashghar, following clashes between local Uyghur people and members of the quasi-military XPCC and groups of demobilised Red Guards who were predominantly Han. This led to similar disturbances in Kashgar, student protests in Urumqi, and demonstrations by Uyghurs studying in the Central Nationalities Institute in Beijing who protested against racial and religious insults against Muslims. Generalised disaffection at Chinese rule was gradually evolving into a broad opposition movement.

On 5 April 1990 in the town of Baren, which is near Kashgar, the regular prayers at a mosque turned into demonstrations against the CCP's policies towards ethnic minorities. Some protesters called for a *jihad* against the unbelievers, and there were demands for the establishment of an Eastern Turkestan state. The demonstrators were able to ward off the police and it took the intervention of units of the People's Armed Police (PAP) and regular troops from the Kashghar garrison to subdue them. The Baren rising was not simply a spontaneous act of defiance: it was the result of a carefully planned and organised operation by a group which identified itself as the Eastern Turkestan Islamic Party and explicitly linked politicised Islam with the call for the independence of Xinjiang. The rebels attacked military vehicles and launched an assault on the town hall, which was the local symbol of Chinese administration. Police, troops, and the militia of the XPCC put down the rising after an early morning counter-attack on 6 April. The incident revealed the depth of anti-Chinese feeling, the degree of organisation of the rebels, and the Islamisation of the independence struggle. There were bomb attacks by separatist units on a bus in Urumqi in 1992 and on government buildings in the city of Kashgar in 1993.

The focus of opposition moved to the town of Ghulja in the Ili region, which is known as Yining in Chinese. It is an important symbol to many Uyghurs, as it was the seat of an independent East Turkestan government in the 1940s. Unrest in the spring of 1995 began with demonstrations calling for an end to Chinese rule in the region, and police stations and local government offices were attacked and looted. There were also verbal, and occasionally physical, assaults on imams who were considered to be compromised by their cooperation with the Chinese authorities. The government mobilised 20,000 troops under the command of the Lanzhou Military Region to put down the insurrection. Its parallel political response was to launch a nationwide Strike Hard Campaign, ostensibly a campaign against organised crime and hooliganism but, in the ethnic minority areas including Xinjiang, also designed to strike at the roots of opposition to Beijing's rule.

The Strike Hard Campaign in Xinjiang led to harsh and sustained repression during 1996, and there were public trials of large numbers of Uyghurs who were accused of serious criminal offences but who were also alleged to be linked to the separatist movement; many were executed. There were persistent reports of secret executions of separatists without trial. In this atmosphere of repression and anger, young Uyghurs took to the streets of Ghulja on 5 April 1997, attacking Han Chinese residents of the city. Police action to stop the violence led to an escalation of the protests, and the following day, there were further attacks on Han residents and their property. The Yining rising has become notorious for the violence with which it was suppressed. Official figures claim that fewer than 200 people were killed by the police and military, but eyewitness reports put the death toll much higher – into the thousands. The violence continued sporadically until 9 April, and there were bomb attacks by separatist groups in Urumqi on 25 February and, unusually, in Beijing on 7 March. Public security organisations were placed on the highest alert nationwide; they launched a major crackdown in Xinjiang, arresting thousands of people in what was essentially an intensification of the Strike Hard Campaign. The authorities also embarked on campaigns of political education utilising the theme of national unity.[7]

CCP policy and the Religious Affairs Bureau

The CCP has sought to regulate all religions, including Islam, through the Religious Affairs Bureau, which was established by the State Council in 1954; its successor organisation, the State Administration for Religious Affairs, was established in 1998. It created the Chinese Islamic Association with which all mosques, madrasas, and other Muslim organisations are legally obliged to register. Many groups, including some of the Sufi organisations, have refused to register on the grounds that an atheist state should have no authority over their doctrines and forms of worship. This has created conflict, not only between unregistered Muslim organisations and the government, but between registered and unregistered Muslim groups. The Chinese Islamic Association fell into abeyance during the Cultural Revolution but was resurrected after Deng Xiaoping came to power in 1978. New mosques were built, older ones that had been damaged during the Cultural Revolution were restored or even extended, and worship became more open and relaxed.

When the rise of political and ethnic dissent began to alarm the authorities in the 1990s, the situation changed abruptly. A confidential internal *Document No. 7*, issued by the CCP in 1996, identified separatism in Xinjiang as the greatest threat to the region and to the nation as a whole. *Inter alia*, it demanded a crackdown on illegal madrasas, a restriction on the construction of new mosques, and an end to independent classes in martial arts and Qur'an study sessions which were suspected of being covers for separatist activities. It called for a purge of Party cadres who were also devout Muslims and who had refused to give up their beliefs in spite of years of CCP ideological indoctrination.[8]

Religious restrictions in Xinjiang

State control over Muslims in Xinjiang was reinforced after the publication of *Document No. 7*, and further intensified after the uprising in Ghulja in February 1997. The attacks by Al Qaeda on New York and the Washington, DC area in September 2001 reinforced China's fears of links between separatism and political Islam, but the repression in Xinjiang had already been in place for five years.

Under the new restrictions, children under the age of 18 were prohibited from entering mosques, and the wearing of the hijab and other forms of Islamic dress was strictly forbidden in schools. Members of the CCP and the CYL, and employees of government organisations, including retired members of staff, were forbidden to enter mosques; notices outlining these restrictions appeared in Uyghur at the entrances to all mosques. Mosques were prohibited from becoming involved in disputes over marriage and family planning; there was a specific prohibition on reading out the Islamic marriage contract, the *nikah*, in the mosque before a couple getting married had been issued with a valid civil marriage certificate. The aim of these restrictions was to assert the primacy of civil laws over Islamic law and to restrict the authority of the local *qadi* judges. Printed or taped materials related to anything deemed to be religious extremism or separatism were also explicitly banned, and the teaching of religion anywhere other than in a registered mosque was outlawed. The new restrictions limited the sale of religious literature in general, and a list of banned books was issued to booksellers.

Training 'patriotic religious personnel'

It has been estimated that there were 54,575 imams or more senior religious leaders in Xinjiang in 1949; this had been reduced to 27,000 by the start of the Cultural Revolution in 1966.[9] Few were officially active during the Cultural Revolution, but imams continued to operate without the knowledge of the Chinese authorities.

The only organisation for training imams from the whole of China, including Xinjiang, in the 1950s and 1960s was the Chinese Islamic Academy in Beijing. In 1987, an Islamic academy was established in Urumqi specifically to cater to Uyghur-speaking imams; the first graduates left the academy in 1992 to staff the mosques of the region. The Qur'an was published in an Uyghur translation to cater to those whose grasp of Arabic was poor. The Religious Affairs Bureau exercised considerable control over the training and curriculum of Islamic education.[10]

In 2001, 8,000 imams from the mosques of Xinjiang were compelled to take part in a 'patriotic education campaign'. This was organised by a work team from the central government in Beijing and ran from 15 March–23 December. Imams were required to attend seminars for instruction in the CCP's thinking on legal, political, and religious topics; they were ordered to avoid any involvement with mosques or other groups deemed to be involved in separatist activities. This campaign was designed to strengthen government control over registered mosques and to increase the gulf between them and those that refused to register. Xinjiang remained tense, and Uyghur Muslims continued to experience severe and ongoing surveillance and repression, especially at work and in schools and colleges.

Economic reform in Xinjiang

Beijing's strategy for dealing with ethnic separatism in Xinjiang since the early 1990s has been twofold. On the one hand, there has been ruthless repression of unofficial religious activity and any political or cultural activities that could be classified as separatist. On the other hand, the CCP has embarked on an ambitious programme of economic reform, on the assumption that the principal underlying reason for the disaffection of the Uyghurs is not ethnic nationalism but poverty and underdevelopment. The decision was made to confront the problem of the relative underdevelopment of China's western provinces as a whole and the policy of the Great Development of the Western Regions [*Xibu da kaifa*], the Go West policy, was launched in 2000 in Chengdu, the capital of Sichuan province (this is examined more closely in Chapter 12).

The development of the energy resources of Xinjiang has been one of the notable consequences of the Go West policy. An oil pipeline which links the region with Kazakhstan and another pipeline which transports much-needed natural gas to fuel the industrial and commercial development of Shanghai are two of the most important enterprises, although the impetus for both projects predates the announcement of the Go West policy. Both were major infrastructure projects designed to ensure that Xinjiang's vast natural resources were deployed to support the overall development of China's economy. Both were financed through partnerships with foreign corporations, although China retained overall control.

There was substantial investment in the oilfields of northern Xinjiang; this region has enjoyed far greater development than the predominantly agricultural south. This was achieved with the import of modern technology, technical expertise, and labour, in some cases from abroad, but mainly from the east of China. This expertise and labour was provided by predominantly Han Chinese engineers, technicians, and workers, and their presence in the region in well-paid and high-status occupations increased the anxiety of Uyghurs, who are usually less well educated and less competent in the Chinese language, that they are being marginalised in their own land.

In spite of undoubted improvements in the economy of much of Xinjiang over the past five years, ethnic and political tensions remain unresolved. For the government of the PRC, the preservation of Xinjiang as an integral part of the PRC is non-negotiable: it is seen as a vital source of China's escalating energy requirements and is essential to the security of China's Inner Asian borders, especially since the establishment of US military bases in Central Asia and the Belt and Road Initiative. It is also a matter of national pride that no part of the existing territory of China should be lost.

Urumqi, July 2009: riots and deaths in the regional capital

For the Chinese government, the violence that erupted on 5 July 2009 in Urumqi, the administrative capital of the Xinjiang Uyghur Autonomous Region, and cost the lives of at least 200 people was a turning point that required a different, and harsher, political response. Bloodshed in the regional capital drew the attention of the world's media, and the violence was reported in far more detail than hitherto.[11]

The Urumqi riots were triggered by news of the deaths, in the city of Shaoguan in south China's Guangdong province, of two Uyghur migrant workers who had been wrongly accused of raping Han women. The violence did not come as a complete surprise; the Chairman of the Xinjiang People's Congress, Nur Bekri, an ethnic Uyghur, had previously cautioned that maintaining stability in Xinjiang would be a problem. Speaking at a fringe meeting during the NPC in Beijing in March 2009 he warned that unrest and militant activity in neighbouring states could spread into Xinjiang.

> We don't believe that hostile forces from home and abroad will give up. . . . I'm afraid that we will face a more severe situation in maintaining stability than last year, our task will probably be heavier, and the struggle will probably be fiercer.[12]

Urumqi had thus far been insulated from the worst of the conflict. This was not entirely surprising, as there is a large resident garrison of troops and PAP; the central area of the city is dominated by Han Chinese.

The demonstrations in Urumqi began when a group of some 300 demonstrators, mostly Uyghurs, organised a sit-down protest in People's Square in the centre of the city at around 5 o'clock on the afternoon of 5 July to demand an investigation and mourn the two Uyghurs reported to have been killed; some of the demonstrators claimed that the real number of casualties in Shaoguan had been higher. The crowd gradually grew to around 1,000 and when police arrived, the demonstrators refused to disperse. According to Uyghur sources, riot police attacked protesters with truncheons and electric cattle prods, fired shots into the air and pinned individuals to the ground before taking at least 40 of them away in police vehicles. Xinhua, the official Chinese news agency, reported that protesters had 'attacked passers-by, torched vehicles and interrupted traffic on some roads', but did not make it clear whether this took place before or after the police intervention. There were a number of casualties, including two deaths, and the demonstrators were forced to disperse by the police but regrouped later.[13]

Information about the disturbances began to appear online, including pictures of police vehicles, soldiers, and burning cars. At about 8 o'clock in the evening, as it was getting dark, there was still chanting from the crowds of people in the streets. Military vehicles, including armoured personnel carriers with machine guns mounted on top, moved through central Urumqi; soldiers emerged with riot shields and batons, and loudspeaker messages ordered residents to stop looking out of their windows. During the assault that followed, demonstrators were arrested and some may have been shot and possibly killed. When local people felt that it was safe to look out of the windows, they saw blood on the streets but no bodies. The soldiers were still there. By the following day, the blood had been cleaned away.[14]

On the following day, 6 July, local television news programmes carried their first reports of the violence in Urumqi, but claimed that Uyghur people had initiated it by attacking Han Chinese. This was the opposite of what eyewitnesses reported. The Communist Party Secretary of Xinjiang, Wang Lequan, and the Urumqi City Communist Party Secretary, Li Zhi (both of them Hans), appeared on television, blaming separatist groups organised by outsiders, and threatened that the authorities would 'strike hard' and arrest everyone involved in this organised political action and treat them as separatists.

On 7 July, armed gangs of local Han Chinese retaliated and Uyghurs were attacked and some killed in streets close to the city centre. The television news continued to show the same set of images from 5 July, all of which carried the official message that the conflict had been initiated by Uyghur violence.

After Urumqi: Kashgar and Khotan in summer 2011

The violent clashes in Urumqi were followed by the inevitable clampdown on social and religious activities, but repression did not quell the discontent and Uyghur resistance to the Chinese continued, often taking the form of an increased adherence to Islamic forms of dress.

In the summer of 2011, both Kashgar and Khotan were the scenes of conflict and bloodshed. On 18 July, a group of Uyghurs armed with knives and explosive devices attacked a police station in Khotan and took hostages to bargain for the release of family members who had been detained in the clampdown after the Urumqi disturbances. The Uyghurs of the Khotan area had many grievances: numerous young men had been detained without trial around the date of the second anniversary of the July 2009 Urumqi riots. Family members were unable to contact them, and there were serious concerns after news spread of the disappearance of young Uyghurs who had been held in police custody. Official sources simply reported an organised attack with explosive devices, Molotov cocktails, and grenades, as well as axes, knives, and 'jihadi flags'. In the operation that followed, at least one police officer, two of the hostages, and some of the attackers were killed.

A campaign to prevent women from wearing black headscarves and robes had been underway for months; in May and June, girls in the nearby county of Karakash (Moyu) were banned by the local authorities from wearing full-length black Islamic dress, which had become increasingly popular since the Urumqi disturbances. Stalls in the Grand Bazaar in Khotan were ordered to stop selling Islamic dresses or veils.

In Kashgar, violence broke out on Saturday 30 July 2011, the eve of the Ramadan fast. There were two explosions: the first blast came from a minivan at about half past 10 o'clock in the evening, and the second from a hijacked truck which was driven into a group of pedestrians on a crowded street where Han Chinese workers were known to gather at food stalls. Six or seven people died, and almost 30 were injured. Two suspects were later killed in a cornfield outside Kashgar, but others were detained and the government announced almost immediately that the attack was the responsibility of Islamic militants who had previously travelled from Xinjiang to Pakistan where they had joined the 'separatist East Turkestan Islamic Movement' and had undergone training in the use of firearms and explosives.

On the afternoon of 31 July, a restaurant in Kashgar was set on fire and the owner and a waiter were killed. The background to this attack was the resentment of the citizens of Kashgar at the demolition of the traditional Uyghur quarter in the centre of the old city and the failure to respect Ramadan.[15]

Jeep attack in Tian'anmen Square, October 2013

One extraordinary incident attracted immediate worldwide attention. A jeep or SUV was driven through a crowd of tourists and other pedestrians in Beijing's Tian'anmen Square on 28 October 2013. It crashed and burst into flames near the symbolic Tianan'men Gate, from where Mao Zedong had proclaimed the establishment of the PRC in October 1949 and where his portrait still hangs. The square was also the scene of the military crackdown of 4 June 1989 and is close to the CCP leadership compound of Zhongnanhai.

The vehicle was driven by Usmen Hesen, an Uyghur: he and his two passengers, his wife and his mother, were all killed in the crash; two pedestrians were also killed, and 40 others were injured. Local police said that they had discovered explosive gas containers, knives, and a jihadist flag inside the vehicle, but Uyghur sources have been sceptical about these claims and some have suggested that the police planted evidence after the incident to misrepresent it as a jihadist plot. Meng Jianzhu, the head of the Central Politics and Law Commission of the CCP, issued a statement accusing the East Turkestan Islamic Movement (a group which may or may not exist) of responsibility for the attack, and called on the Shanghai Co-operation Organisation (SCO) to assist China in combating the threat from this organisation.[16] It transpired that the motives for the attack were primarily personal and local; it was revenge for a heavy-handed raid on a mosque in the driver's home village of Yengi Aymak in Akto County one year previously and possibly for the death of a relative in the post-Urumqi clampdown.[17] Although there was a religious element to the attack, it was not a jihadist plot masterminded by forces outside China.

Immediately after the attack, the authorities launched a wave of reprisals, including detentions in the Yining (Ghulja) region and increased security checks and police searches. In Beijing, Uyghur residents and visitors were subject to increased surveillance, and Ilham Tohti, a respected economics professor at the Central Nationalities University [*Zhongyang*

Minzu Daxue] in Beijing, who ran a website that discussed Uyghur topics, was harassed and threatened by police.[18]

Seriqbuya, Kunming, and Luntai, 2013–2014

In April 2013, 21 people were killed in clashes between local Uyghurs and police and a house was burnt to the ground in the village of Seliqbuya in Maralbashi county in the southwest of Xinjiang. The following November, three auxiliary police officers were killed during an attack on a police station in the same area.[19]

At Kunming railway station on 1 March 2014, a group presumed to be Uyghurs, wielding knives and meat cleavers, left 31 people dead and 141 injured. It is far from clear why Kunming, in the southwestern province of Yunnan, was the setting for this attack, as there had been no history of serious inter-ethnic problems in the city, in spite of Kunming being on a recently established migrant route for Uyghurs trying to leave China. The Ministry of Public Security named the mastermind behind the attack as Abdurehim Kurban, but *China Daily* later reported that three men with Uyghur names – Iskandar Ehet, Turgun Tohtunyaz and Hasayn Muhammad – had been tried for the assaults in September 2014 by the Kunming Intermediate People's Court and executed.[20]

That same month, there were explosions (apparently coordinated) in at least three different locations of Luntai County, a remote area on the desert fringes of southern Xinjiang. Initially, two people were thought to have been killed and many others injured. As more detailed information emerged, it became clear that the violence was more serious: 50 people had died and at least 54 had been injured. The attacks had taken place at a shop, an open market, and two police stations, possibly after a failed attempt to attack the local government offices.[21]

The case of Ilham Tohti

The strongest evidence of the unwillingness of the authorities to tolerate even discussion of the conflict in Xinjiang was the trial of the Uyghur academic Ilham Tohti, also in September 2014. The trial, and the draconian penalty meted out to him, can only be interpreted as warnings that not only would the Beijing government ruthlessly suppress any secessionist activities by campaigners or militants in Xinjiang, it would not even permit any academic or theoretical debate of alternatives to the official government position, let alone any discussion of possible secession or independence; the term always employed by Beijing is *fenliezhuyi* ['splittism'], which is also translated as separatism.

Ilham Tohti is an Uyghur from Artush in Xinjiang, but the activities for which he appeared in court took place in Beijing where he worked as an established teacher of economics at the Central Nationalities University. This institute is now known in English by its Chinese name, Minzu University, and it is the leading institution of higher education in China for educating and training intellectuals from China's ethnic minorities and ensuring that they are integrated into the mainstream political culture that is controlled by the CCP and its government.

Ilham Tohti was part of the Beijing intellectual elite and openly criticised government policies on Xinjiang, but he had never advocated violence or supported separatist activities. His trial took place in Urumqi, the administrative capital of Xinjiang, a city in which he did not work or live, but where the riots of July 2009 had taken place; it was a crude attempt to link him to violent demonstrations in which he had taken no part. Foreign diplomats from Europe and North America and representatives of the media were refused access to the trial, but stood outside the courtroom. In his closing statement, Ilham Tohti insisted that 'he loved his country . . . and that his opinion [had] always been that it is in the best interests of Uyghurs to remain in China'. These are hardly the views of a separatist. Nevertheless, on 23 September 2014, he was sentenced to life imprisonment and the confiscation of all of his assets, an 'unusually harsh' sentence, according to the *South China Morning Post*.[22] An appeal was rejected on 21 November 2014 at a hearing held inside the prison where Ilham Tohti was detained and at a time when his lawyers were not able to be present.[23]

Terrorism and Xinjiang

Tibetans resisting rule by China have little difficulty in obtaining at least moral support from a wide range of opinion in the West. They are invariably presented as peaceful protesters, harming no-one but themselves. The same cannot be said of attitudes towards their counterparts in Xinjiang, Tibet's neighbour to the north. Militants in Xinjiang have all been classed as terrorists, particularly since the attacks by Al Qaeda on New York and the Washington, DC area in September 2001, and it is often assumed that their actions are solely a result of associations with international jihadist movements, although the movement for independence which many Uyghurs do support has a history which precedes modern jihadism by many decades.

Under the Terrorism Act 2000, the British government included groups acting for independence in Xinjiang in its list of proscribed organisations. This followed action taken by the United Nations after sustained lobbying by the Chinese government. The entry in the official Home Office (United Kingdom) list of Proscribed Terrorist Organisations reads as follows:

> Turkestan Islamic Party (TIP) also known as East Turkestan Islamic Party (ETIP), East Turkestan Islamic Movement (ETIM) and Hizb al-Islami al-Turkistani (HAAT) – Proscribed July 2016 TIP is an Islamic terrorist and separatist organisation founded in 1989 by Uighur militants in western China. It aims to establish an independent caliphate in the Uighur state of Xinjiang Uighur Autonomous Region of North-western China and to name it East Turkestan. TIP is based in the Federally Administered Tribal Areas (FATA) of Pakistan, and operates in China, Central and South Asia and Syria. The group has claimed responsibility for a number of attacks in China, the latest of these being in April 2014. TIP has links to a number of terrorist groups including Al Qa'ida (AQ). In November 2015, TIP released the 18th issue of its magazine 'Islamic Turkestan' through the Global Islamic Media Front (GIMF), detailing TIP's jihad against the Chinese authorities. Video footage from September 2015 shows TIP hosting training camps in areas controlled by the Pakistani Taliban in North Waziristan. More recently TIP has maintained an active and visible presence in the Syrian war and has published a number of video clips of its activities. Examples of this from March to April 2016 include:
>
> - TIP claiming a joint attack with Jund al Aqsa in Sahl al Ghab and published a video of a suicide bomb attack in April 2016;
> - a video published in March 2016 which promotes the victories of TIP in Syria and calls for Muslims to join jihad; and
> - a video slide show published in April 2016 which shows fighters and children in training.
>
> TIP has been banned by the UN and is also sanctioned by the USA under the Terrorist Exclusion list.[24]

Although this is presented by the Home Office as undisputed fact, there are reasonable doubts about the existence and the activities of these groups. There is no doubt that individuals and groups have carried out attacks within and outside Xinjiang that, by any definition, can be characterised as terrorist. What is less certain is whether these attacks are genuinely linked to the groups claiming responsibility on their web pages. Equally unclear is whether militant groups within Xinjiang have real links to jihadist groups based in the Middle East, such as Al Qaeda or Daesh (Islamic State, or ISIS). There has been long history of resistance by Uyghur militant groups to the Chinese authorities, long predating the foundation of the PRC in 1949 and the birth of Osama bin Laden, the founder of Al Qaeda, in 1957. Although activist groups inside Xinjiang have a history of seeking external support, they have for many years demonstrated their ability to act independently.

The Uyghurs of Xinjiang have been subject to even stricter strict controls since the Urumqi riots of July 2009, and there is no indication that these will be relaxed in the foreseeable future. A new regional counter-terrorism law was passed in May 2016; editors and contributors to Uyghur language websites have been detained for criticising government policies on religious observance; in some towns and cities, fences are being built around areas where large numbers of Uyghurs live to allow the police to carry out security checks more easily; more prisons are being built, and the security forces have been equipped with modern sophisticated equipment for counter-terrorism operations. Some local authorities have ordered Uyghurs to attend regular flag-raising ceremonies, evening classes, or public *taiji* exercises to demonstrate their loyalty to the state and to Chinese values. The confiscation and control of passports has also been reported, although initially, this was carried out in a piecemeal way by county governments. Educational establishments have been particular targets in an attempt to counter the Islamic education that is carried out in the mosques. Compulsory lessons in political education have been introduced into universities and colleges; new regulations, which were unveiled by the regional government in October 2016, provide for sanctions against parents who encourage their children to take part in religious activities.

To verify the effectiveness of this repression, 350 cadres in the Khotan region were deployed to monitor religious activities in mosques and elsewhere. The concentration on Khotan followed an explosion on 10 September 2016 near Kokterek in Guma County (Pishan in Chinese) in Khotan prefecture which resulted in the death of a senior police officer and injuries to others.[25] That incident followed a series of attacks on local government offices and police stations; these were relatively minor in comparison with the more dramatic and well-publicised attacks such as the knifing of passengers at Kunming railway station, but were serious enough for the communities that were affected. In the absence of a new approach to break the vicious circle, retaliation to the repression has continued

Chen Quanguo and new initiatives in Tibet and Xinjiang

A new political initiative to counter violent conflict was launched, first in Tibet and subsequently in Xinjiang, by Chen Quanguo, who was Party Secretary of the Tibetan Autonomous Region from 2011–2016 and was transferred to the same position in Xinjiang in August 2016. Chen Quanguo became more widely known after August 2016 when he succeeded Zhang Chunxian as Xinjiang's Communist Party Secretary. Zhang's performance had been low key and he had been criticised for being lacklustre and prioritising economic improvement over security. Chen introduced new and draconian methods of repression to Xinjiang, most of which had previously been rehearsed in Tibet.

A network of new 'convenience police posts' was constructed: they were to be manned day and night, and were equipped with first aid kits and other items to assist in emergencies but also with surveillance cameras; they could rapidly be converted to checkpoints in the event of disturbances. Numerous auxiliary police were recruited, and families were enrolled in a Xinjiang version of the 'double-linked household management system' that had been piloted in Tibet; groups of ten families were required to spy on each other to check on security threats and risks of poverty – the double link. Households could be monitored on a regular basis and rewarded or admonished, depending on reports.[26]

Although this and its predecessor in Tibet were described as innovations, they revived systems of local control practised in China under the Ming and Qing dynasties. The 'double-linked household management system' has been borrowed with little modification from the *baojia* system of social control in the later dynasties of the Chinese Empire. Increased surveillance is likely to increase tensions within the Uyghur communities and is not a useful long-term strategy for ending the conflict, but if the 'poverty alleviation' measures are genuine – and reduction of poverty is one of the genuine drivers of Xi Jinping's national political strategy – they could assist in conflict reduction.

These surveillance methods have been paralleled by a further onslaught on religious activities in Xinjiang, including forcing restaurants to remain open during Ramadan, billeting cadres in the homes of families to monitor their religious behaviour, and even attempts to prohibit parents from giving newborn babies names considered dangerously Islamic. Some of these repressive measures have been implemented by the regional government for the whole of Xinjiang, but others are local initiatives, and it is by no means clear that all government instructions will be obeyed. On the basis of previous experience, it is likely that this additional repression will curb overt religious activity and related acts of resistance in the short term – perhaps while Chen Quanguo remains in post – but in the longer term will be the source of great resentment which is likely to erupt into further conflict.[27]

The policy that initially attracted most international attention after Chen's move to Xinjiang was the confiscation of passports by local police. The holding of passports by police, to be released on request, was targeted at Uyghurs planning to travel abroad because of government concerns about outside influences on militant activists; all residents, including Hui Muslims and Han Chinese, were also affected.

In May 2017, the authorities in Xinjiang confiscated all copies of the Qur'an published before 2012, as part of a campaign against the ownership of 'illegal religious items'. Official translations of the Qur'an, published in 2012, were said to contain less 'extremist' material, but it is far from clear how different this translation is from earlier versions. The following June, Muslims in Kashgar and Khotan were fined heavily and forced to attend re-education classes if they had observed Ramadan against official instructions to ignore the religious duty of fasting during daylight hours. Officials were assigned to monitor families during the fasting period; some were said to be compelling Muslims to eat during the day.[28]

Internment camps

The level of repression increased dramatically; by the summer of 2017, a network of permanent 're-education camps' was under construction, designed to house thousands of Uyghurs detained by the authorities on suspicion of sympathising with separatist ideas. The existence of this hitherto undisclosed plan was initially tracked by satellite surveillance and confirmed when notices were published, inviting bids for new construction projects.[29]

Credible evidence that large numbers of Uyghurs (and members of other Muslim minorities) were being detained has been available for years – but bespoke 're-education camps', designed to deradicalise Muslims and turn them into patriotic citizens, were an innovation. Initially, official Chinese sources denied that these institutions existed but 'information from 73 government procurement and construction bids valued at around RMB 680 million (approximately USD$108 million), along with public recruitment notices for camp staff and other documents, provides contrary evidence from other official sources, albeit indirectly. Given the scope of these bids, there is no doubt that the network of camps is on a colossal scale and that the numbers to be detained are likely to increase.[30]

There are no reliable estimates for the number of people interned under this system, but human rights observers suggest that it runs into the hundreds of thousands and may reach one million. One former inmate estimated that his camp alone held almost 6,000 detainees.[31] The Communist Party secretary of the village of Aqsaray in the Qaraqash region near Hotan was ordered to target 40% of the population of the village as potential unreliable elements in need of re-education. In another village in Qaraqash, Yengisheher, it was reported that almost half the adult male population in the 1,700 or more households that constitute the village had been placed in detention camps. How long they were held was not clear, but their incarceration was having a deleterious effect on agriculture, on which local people rely, as only women, children, and the elderly were available for work in the fields.

On one level, this network of camps reproduces the system of 're-education through labour' [*laojiao*], an extra-judicial process for detaining minor offenders or dissidents that was heavily criticised by Chinese lawyers and formally abolished in 2013. Detention camps in Xinjiang to wean Uyghurs away from actual or potential 'extremism' appeared in 2014, possibly using the facilities of the old *laojiao* system. The new network evolved from these early models in response to Chen Quanguo's insistence that detainees should undergo 'transformation through education' [*jiaoyu zhuanhua*]. Information in the bids indicates that existing facilities are to be reinforced and security strengthened. They resemble prisons but, unlike regular prisoners, the intended detainees were not tried and sentenced for criminal activity.[32]

Anecdotal evidence of life in these new detention camps (and no other evidence is currently available) indicates harsh conditions, brutality by staff, solitary confinement, food deprivation, and physical assault for those who do not consent to be remoulded. Friends and relatives are frequently denied information about where individuals are detained, and there have been several reports of unexpected and unexplained deaths in the camps. The thinking behind the programme, according to the Associated Press news agency, is 'to rewire the political thinking of detainees, erase their Islamic beliefs and reshape their very identities . . . with almost no judicial process or legal paperwork'. This is grimly reminiscent of the 'thought reform' or 'brainwashing' programmes of the early years of the PRC.[33]

Not all 're-education camps' are closed prisons. In the Kashgar area, and probably elsewhere, 'open' camps hold those deemed to be minor offenders, or less of a threat to the state. Detainees in these camps are required to attend during the day, but can return home in the evenings. Periods of 'study' at these camps can last for months. Uyghurs under the age of 40 are particularly targeted, and anyone born in the 1980s and 1990s is regarded as a member of an 'unreliable and untrustworthy generation'. Although most of those detained are from farming families, writers and teachers have also been held, as have local officials deemed insufficiently enthusiastic about the re-education programme.[34]

Notes

1 There is some evidence of links between Uyghur and Hui members of the Khufiyya Sufi order.
2 Wang Wenheng *Xinjiang zongjiao wenti yanjiu* (*Studies on Religion in Xinjiang*) Urumqi: Xinjiang People's Press, 1993, pp. 93–5. These figures appear to reflect only the registered and officially sanctioned mosques and other bodies.
3 The Uyghurs use the Arabic and Turkic term *mazar* (tomb or shrine, *mezar* in Turkish) for the tombs of their founding sheikhs, but there is also a tomb culture among the Hui (both within and outside Xinjiang) who use the term *gongbei*, a Chinese transliteration of the Arabic *qubba* (dome or cupola, after the dominant architectural feature of these tombs).
4 The author attended one such festival at the Imam Asim shrine in the Khotan region as a participant observer in the summer of 2010. See Michael Dillon 'Religion, Repression and Traditional Uyghur Culture in Southern Xinjiang: Kashgar and Khotan' *Central Asian Affairs* 2 (2015), pp. 246–63. The shrine complex was reported to have been destroyed by the Chinese authorities in April 2019, Radio Free Asia 15 May 2019.
5 Reyila Dawuti (Rayila Dawud) *Weiwuerzu mazha wenhua yanjiu* (Studies of Uyghur Mazar Culture) Urumqi: Xinjiang University Press, 2001.
6 Thierry Zarcone 'Le Culte des saints au Xinjiang (de 1949 à nos jours)' *Journal of the History of Sufism* 3 (2001), pp. 133–72.
7 The Chinese authorities initially suppressed information about these disturbances, although details leaked out through émigré publications and the monitoring of local broadcast and print media by the BBC and FBIS. In-depth accounts, from the perspective of the Chinese government, were later published in Xu Yuqi and Chen Yishan (eds.) *Xinjiang fandui minzu fenliezhuyi douzheng shihua* (*Narrative History of the Struggle against Separatism in Xinjiang*) Urumqi: Xinjiang People's Press, 1999 and Ma Dazheng *Guojia liyi gaoyu yiqie: Xinjiang wending wenti de guancha yu sikao* (*The Interests of the Nation Are Above Everything: Observations and Reflections on the Stability of Xinjiang*) Urumqi: Xinjiang People's Press, 2003. See also Michael Dillon *Xinjiang: China's Muslim Far Northwest* London: RoutledgeCurzon, 2004 and 'Uyghur Separatism and Nationalism in Xinjiang' in Benjamin Cole (ed.) *Conflict, Terrorism and the Media in Asia* London: Routledge, 2006, pp. 98–116.
8 Chinese Communist Party Central Committee *Central Committee Document No. 7 Record of the Meeting of the Standing Committee of the Politburo of the Chinese Communist Party Concerning the Maintenance of Stability in Xinjiang* in Uyghur, 19 March 1996.
9 Wang Wenheng, pp. 91–2.
10 Wang Wenheng op.cit., pp. 91–2. A separate academy was also established in Yinchuan, the capital of the Ningxia Hui Autonomous Region to train Chinese-speaking Hui imams.
11 Some of the information used in this section has been provided in confidence and on the condition of anonymity. The author is particularly grateful for the assistance of those informants who had first-hand experience of the disturbances.
12 Reuters via BBC News 6 March 2009.
13 AFP (Beijing and Tokyo) 5 July 2009; *Times of India* 5 July 2009.
14 Uyghur eyewitness who must remain anonymous.
15 BBC News, 18 July 2011; *SCMP* 18, 19, 20, 21 July 2011; *Global Times* Xinhua, 19, 31 July 2011.
16 *SCMP* 1 November 2013; Radio Free Asia 27 November 2013.
17 Radio Free Asia 6 November 2013.
18 *SCMP* 3 November 2013; Radio Free Asia 4 November 2013.
19 *SCMP* 17 November 2013; Radio Free Asia 16, 20, 22 November 2013.
20 *China Daily* 24 March 2015.
21 Radio Free Asia 25 September, 3 October 2014; *SCMP* 26 September 2014.
22 *SCMP* 23 September 2014.
23 *Guardian* (via Associated Press [AP], Beijing) 21 November 2014.
24 Home Office *Proscribed Terrorist Organisations* 15 July 2016, www.gov.uk/government/uploads/system/uploads/attachment_data/file/538297/20160715-Proscription-website-update.pdf.
25 Radio Free Asia 13 June, 5, 16, 19 August; 18, 19, 27 September, 24 October, 14, 16 December 2016; *SCMP* 16 August, 12 October 2016.
26 *Dahewang* (Great River Web), website of the Henan Provincial Government, from Chen's home province, 29 August 2016, http://news.dahe.cn/2016/08-29/107406757.html; 'Monasteries Placed

Under New Controls' Radio Free Asia 16 March 2012; 'Passports Taken, More Police . . . New Party Boss Chen Quanguo Acts to Tame Xinjiang with Methods Used in Tibet' *SCMP* 12 December 2016; 'Party Boss Chen Quanguo Replicating his Tibet Policy in Xinjiang' *Tibetan Review* 13 December 2016.

27 *SCMP* 12 December 2016; Radio Free Asia 1, 8 June 2017.

28 'Xinjiang Authorities Confiscate "Extremist" Qurans from Uyghur Muslims' Radio Free Asia 25 May 2017; 'Muslim Uyghurs in China Fined, Sent to "Study Classes" for Observing Ramadan' Radio Free Asia 14 June 2017.

29 Roseann Rife 'A Police State in Xinjiang in Which Moderate Voices Are Silenced Is Not What China Needs to Achieve Stability' *SCMP* 17 January 2018.

30 Adrian Zenz 'New Evidence for China's Political Re-Education Campaign in Xinjiang' *China Brief* 15 May 2018.

31 Adrian Zenz 'New Evidence for China's Political Re-Education Campaign in Xinjiang' *China Brief* 15 May 2018; 'Nearly Half of Xinjiang Village's Residents Sent to "Political Re-Education Camps": Official *Radio Free Asia* 14 June 2018.

32 Adrian Zenz 'New Evidence for China's Political Re-Education Campaign in Xinjiang' *China Brief* 15 May 2018; 'Nearly Half of Xinjiang Village's Residents Sent to "Political Re-Education Camps": Official *Radio Free Asia* 14 June 2018.

33 AP 'Inside the camps where China tries to brainwash Muslims until they love the party and hate their own culture' *SCMP* 17 May 2018.

34 'Authorities in Xinjiang's Kashgar Detain Uyghurs at "Open Political Re-Education Camps"' Radio Free Asia 9 May 2018; 'Xinjiang Jails Uyghur Civil Servants Over Lack of Enthusiasm For Anti-Extremist Campaigns' Radio Free Asia 18 May 2018;'Nearly Half of Xinjiang Village's Residents Sent to "Political Re-Education Camps": Official' Radio Free Asia 14 June 2018.

23 Inner Mongolia

Mongolians in the PRC are one of 55 official ethnic minorities or 'nationalities' of China. They are also part of a much wider Mongol nation including the Buryats and Kalmyks of Russia. The most important is the independent nation of Mongolia [*Mongol Uls*], previously known as the Mongolian People's Republic [MPR, *Bügd Nairamdakh Mongol Ard Uls*] and, before that, as Outer Mongolia. Outer Mongolia became independent in 1911 after the collapse of the Chinese Empire and it became the MPR in 1924 after the Mongolian revolution, while Inner Mongolia remained within China.[1]

The current population of the Inner Mongolian Autonomous Region is just under 25 million. The four million ethnic Mongols constitute less than 20% of this total, but ironically even this is more than the total population of independent Mongolia, which in 2016 was approximately three million; in some administrative divisions – banners – of Inner Mongolia, however, Mongols are the overwhelming majority. The current population of Inner Mongolia is predominantly Han (80% of the total population of 25 million). Not only do the Han dominate in demographic terms, they also control most economic activity other than herding, particularly mining and other extractive industries which have been developed under the PRC and which have become the focus of increasingly acrimonious disputes between local Mongol herders, the Chinese government, and developers who are mostly Han.[2]

Inner Mongolian Autonomous Region

After the defeat of Japan in 1945, Inner Mongolia was re-occupied by Soviet, Mongolian, and finally Chinese Communist forces who moved in from their bases in Manchuria; the territory was returned to China. The Inner Mongolian Autonomous Region (in Chinese, *Nei Menggu zizhiqu*) was established by the CCP on 1 May 1947, two years before the foundation of the PRC. Like Tibet, Ningxia, and Guangxi, the other autonomous regions in China, the autonomy is primarily symbolic. Mongols are represented in government bodies, but overall authority rests with the regional CCP Committee which – with the notable exception of its leader, the loyal Communist, Ulanfu – has been dominated by Han Chinese since the late 1960s.

Ulanfu

The founding chairman of the autonomous region was Ulanfu (1906–1988), an ethnic Mongol of the Tumed Left Banner, an administrative area that lies close to the city of Hohhot which became the capital of Inner Mongolia. Ulanfu had been a member of the CCP since 1925, although he was simultaneously a member of the Guomindang, as was permitted during the United Front, and had attended the inaugural conference of the Inner Mongolia Nationalist Party. He studied in Moscow at the Sun Yat-sen University and the University of the Toilers of the East, and from 1929, he was engaged in clandestine work with the CCP in Inner Mongolia. For his military experience in the resistance to the Japanese and the subsequent Civil War, he was promoted to the rank of general in 1955.

Ulanfu was the individual most responsible for the negotiations that resulted in the creation of the autonomous region in 1947, and he remained chairman of the autonomous region and a loyal supporter of the CCP until 1966 when, like many of the old guard of CCP leaders, he became the target of political attacks during the Cultural Revolution. He was one of the senior political figures who survived the Cultural Revolution – under the protection of Zhou Enlai – and then served as Vice-President of China from his rehabilitation in 1983 until his death in 1988.

Traditional religion and culture

Mongols who are believers follow the Lama Buddhist tradition of Tibet, although both Tibetans and Mongols prefer to call their religion Tibetan (rather than Lama) Buddhism. It follows a different tradition from the Chinese schools of Buddhism and is based on scriptures in Tibetan and Sanskrit, although the extent to which these scriptures are used depends on the degree of literacy and scholarship of the monks and priests. Some Buddhist temples remain in use for worship in Inner Mongolia, many others were destroyed during the Cultural Revolution, and some are being restored at great expense and with great care.

Secular Mongol culture is inextricably entwined with the economy and lifestyles of nomadic herders. The felt tent that is the traditional home of Mongol nomads is often called a *yurt* in English, but that is a Turkic or Persian word used by Kyrgyz, Kazakhs, and other Central Asian peoples. In the Mongolian languages, it is a *ger*. The *ger* is easy to dismantle and reassemble during the migration from winter to summer quarters and back, but sturdy enough to withstand extreme weather conditions and provide shelter. The *ger* provides a protected living space for a large family unit; there is room for a fire and an outlet for the smoke, and *ger* etiquette is governed by strict rules which stipulate where family members and visitors may sit or sleep. The *ger* is less used in Inner Mongolia than further north in Mongolia, where there are *ger* communities in stockades on the outskirts of towns and cities including the capital Ulaanbaatar as well as out on the steppe, but it remains a symbol of the distinctiveness of Mongol culture. Mongols in contemporary Inner Mongolia are more likely to live in blocks of flats or other accommodation alongside their Han neighbours, but the *ger* is so flexible that it can also be used as a temporary structure, for example to house workers on construction projects.

Inner Mongolian resistance, nationalism, and development

Separatist or independence organisations have existed in Inner Mongolia since the 1950s, but have a much lower profile than in Xinjiang and Tibet. The breakup of the Soviet Union reawakened Mongolian's interest in secession, and in 1990, there were demonstrations in favour of the independence of what activists call Southern Mongolia; some secessionist groups openly pressed for the right to join the MPR, although this was not encouraged by the Ulaanbaatar government. In 1991, leaders of a group based near the regional capital, Hohhot, were imprisoned for two years for separatist activity and 26 others were placed under house arrest. A second group was also broken up and its leaders arrested in 1995 – one of the leading figures, Hada, was charged with separatist activities and espionage in 1996 after taking part in discussions about the possibility of the establishment of an independent Inner Mongolian People's Party. Hada was sentenced to 15 years imprisonment, after which he should have been released by 2011, but he was not finally freed from prison until 2014.

Most Mongols in Inner Mongolia accept that their future lies with China, and not the MPR. It has been the long-term aim of the CCP to oblige Mongols, and other nomads, to make the transition from a herding economy to modern agriculture and industry. In 2001, the Southern Mongolian Human Rights Information Centre reported that this policy was being accelerated by the enforced migration of 640,000 herders from the grasslands to urban centres. The ostensible reason for this 'ecological migration' was to reduce overgrazing and avoid sandstorms and the desertification of the region's delicate grasslands: these are real problems, but the causes and possible solutions are debatable. The displaced Mongols had little alternative but to move to unskilled work in agriculture or find employment in mining or in the towns; all of these options would place them under the control of Han Chinese businessmen and officials. Mongol activists argue that herding causes less damage to the environment than extractive industries or intensive agriculture.[3]

Since the 1990s, coal mining and the extraction of iron ore, copper, and rare earth minerals have transformed the landscape. Many Mongols complain that they have been 'marginalised, sidelined, ignored . . . ' and that their very identity has been threatened as the disappearance of grasslands removes their livelihood and their homes. Some Mongols have moved into 'modern' employment, but many more have been left behind by the rapid development of new economic sectors.[4]

May 2011 disturbances in Inner Mongolia

The death of Mergen, an ethnic Mongol herdsman, in the Xilingol League in northern Inner Mongolia on 10 May 2011 triggered large-scale demonstrations.[5] Xilingol is one of the few remaining areas of Inner Mongolia with a thriving nomadic culture, and Mergen was leading a group of 20 fellow herdsmen who were demonstrating against the noise and pollution produced during mining operations. The demonstrators maintained that their herds were being adversely affected. While attempting to prevent trucks carrying coal from taking a shortcut across traditional grazing lands, Mergen was dragged along by a coal truck which was being driven by a Han Chinese and was killed. Protests began outside the government offices of the Right Ujumchin Banner which administers that area, and children from a local secondary school demonstrated outside government offices in the regional centre, Xilinhot.[6]

As the protests escalated, riot police were deployed in the regional capital, Hohhot. Student activity in all colleges was monitored, and access to the internet was restricted. PAP reinforcements were deployed from Baotou, Inner Mongolia's main industrial city, and schools, colleges, and all organisations that employed a significant number of Mongols were warned against a 'political conspiracy of external hostile forces and a very few internal extremists'.[7]

In contrast to the heavy police and security presence on the streets in Inner Mongolia, the public response of the authorities was positive and conciliatory. The chairman of the company which owned the truck that had caused the death of the herdsman visited the victim's family; compensation was offered, and the Han Chinese driver was charged with murder. He was sentenced to death after a six-hour trial and reportedly executed.[8]

The official Chinese-language media played down the unrest, but *Global Times*, an English-language tabloid published by the *People's Daily*, argued that the 'reasonable grievances' of ethnic Mongols should be properly addressed'. The paper insisted that the protests were caused by economic worries not ethnic conflict and added with great emphasis that there were no links between the Inner Mongolia protests and recent disturbances in Tibet and

Xinjiang.[9] The government of Inner Mongolia promised to 'discipline the mining industry' and compensate herdsmen for damage to the environment caused by coal extraction. Hu Chunhua, then Secretary of the Inner Mongolian CCP Committee, recognised the public anger that had been aroused by the death of Mergen and announced the setting up of a programme to inspect mining sites throughout the region.[10] In spite of this, the clampdown on dissent in Inner Mongolia was harsh, and human rights activists inside China and elsewhere remained concerned about detentions without trial, deprivation of freedom of movement, and the loss of other liberties

Simmering discontent in Inner Mongolia

Continuing ethnic conflict in Inner Mongolia mainly concerns land, particularly traditional grazing lands, where clashes continue between developers and herding families whose traditional way of life is under threat. In April 2012, 22 demonstrators from the Naiman Banner were arrested after protesting against the illegal acquisition of land in eastern Inner Mongolia by a Chinese forestry firm. Pollution by smelting plants in Zaruud Banner began to poison sheep on traditional grazing lands in the spring of 2016; herders protested and several were detained, including one who had made a video showing the effects of pollution on the animals. The following June, herders in northern Inner Mongolia blocked roads in an attempt to prevent construction traffic from reaching a new major new road that would encroach on grazing lands.

In the Zaruud region in July 2016, farming families who refused to move when their land was requisitioned had their houses and farm buildings destroyed. That August, there were similar protests over eviction in Shin-Barag in eastern Inner Mongolia. These were followed by heavy-handed police checks and attempts to prevent news of the demonstrations leaking out, even to the extent of confiscating the herders' mobile phones. The difficulties of the herders were exacerbated by severe drought in the autumn of 2016. The price of scarce grass soared, leaving insufficient winter fodder for cattle and sheep; the selling price of livestock dropped, reducing the income of the Mongolian herders.

There were few explicitly political responses to this from the majority of Mongolians in Inner Mongolia. Hada had been sentenced to 15 years in prison for 'separatism', but was incarcerated for an extra four years and only released in December 2014; he remained under a form of house arrest in Hohhot, the capital of Inner Mongolia. In November 2016, he applied to China's Supreme Court for an injunction against the police who he accused of torturing and drugging him in order to extract a false concession.

On 5 December 2016, there were protests outside the local government offices in Ulaan hada (Chifeng in Chinese) against a decision that Chinese would be used in the city's kindergartens rather than Mongolian. This decision followed the appointment of two senior teachers who were Han Chinese and were alleged to have forbidden Mongolian teachers even to speak to each other in their own language. Parents demanded the appointment of ethnic Mongolian senior teachers.[11] In 2020, further east in Tongliao city, parents refused to send their children to school for the autumn term after the Inner Mongolia Department of Education announced that there would be no more classes in the Mongolian language for first-year primary schoolchildren. Mongolian-medium teaching would cease, and only materials in the Chinese language would be available. This was a reversal of the previous practice of prioritising Mongolian and introducing Chinese at a later stage in the curriculum. Similar protests were reported in the Shilingol League close to the border with Mongolia, and demonstrations were planned for the regional capital Hohhot and other major towns and cities.

Mongolian families complained that the new policies breached regional legislation on ethnic autonomy and the Constitution of the PRC. In September 2020, there were reports that four Mongolians had committed suicide as a result of the conflict over language teaching.[12]

Notes

1 Charles Bawden *The Modern History of Mongolia* London: Weidenfeld and Nicolson, 1968, pp. 1–39 and passim; Baabar (B. Batbayar), C. Kaplonski (ed.) *History of Mongolia: from World Power to Soviet Satellite* Cambridge: White Horse Press, 1999; Michael Dillon *Lesser Dragons: China's Ethnic Minorities* London: Reaktion Books, 2018.
2 Colin Mackerras *China's Minorities: Integration and Modernisation in the 20th Century* Oxford and Hong Kong: Oxford University Press, 1994, pp. 76–7, 121–2.
3 *SCMP* 2 April 2005. The Southern Mongolian Human Rights Information Centre is an émigré organisation based in the United States.
4 *SCMP* 7 June 2011; Personal observations by the author in Inner Mongolia in October and November 2001 confirm this analysis.
5 Michael Dillon 'Unrest in Inner Mongolia May 2011: Implications for Central Government Policy on Ethnic Minority Areas and the Career of Hu Chunhua', briefing paper commissioned by Europe China Research and Advice Network (ECRAN) for European External Action Service, June 2011.
6 *SCMP* 26 May 2011.
7 Southern Mongolian Human Rights Information Centre, website, 30 May 2011, 4 June 2011.
8 *SCMP* 31 May 2011.
9 *SCMP* 31 May 2011; BBC News 30 May 2011; *Global Times* 4 June 2011; *SCMP* 9 June 2011; *Global Times* 9 June 2011.
10 *SCMP* 3 June 2011.
11 Radio Free Asia 4 April 2012, 12, 18 April, 13 June, 19, 28 July, 12 August, 28 October, 23 November, 5 December 2016; *SCMP* 15 October 2016.
12 Radio Free Asia 28 August, 4 September 2020.

24 Hong Kong

Hong Kong became a British possession at the end of the Opium War (1839–1842). The island of Hong Kong was ceded to the British crown in perpetuity under the Treaty of Nanjing, which was concluded in 1842 and which marked the formal end of the war. The Kowloon peninsula, which is on the mainland, was acquired in 1860, and in 1898, Britain was given a 99-year lease to the New Territories which lie to the north of Hong Kong on the border with Guangdong province. This lease expired in 1997, and consequently 1997 was the date set for the return of the colony to China. In theory, Hong Kong Island could have been retained by Britain, but in practice, it could not have functioned independently without resources and labour from the mainland parts of the colony.

Between 1842 and 1997, Hong Kong was run as a crown colony with a British Governor and a civil administration that was dominated by expatriate British officials. It developed as a trading and manufacturing centre, and became one of the most important ports and financial centres of Asia. No attempt was made to create a system of political democracy; Hong Kong under the British was an unequal society, with most of its Chinese inhabitants, who were the majority of the population, taking no part in the running of the territory in which they lived. Nevertheless, it was an economic success story from which much of the population benefited. The Second World War and the post-war mood for decolonisation changed it significantly and set it on the long, slow road to its eventual return to China on 1 July 1997.

Japanese occupation

The occupation of Hong Kong by the Imperial Japanese Army during the Second World War lasted from the surrender of the British garrison by the Governor Sir Mark Young on 25 December 1941 to the capitulation of Japan in August 1945. This difficult and uncomfortable period is known to many Hong Kong residents simply as the three years and eight months. The colony was ruled under martial law, thousands of British servicemen and women and civilians were imprisoned in internment camps, and there were widespread food shortages which led to malnutrition, the spread of disease, and the consequent loss of life. Conditions were much harsher for the majority of the population of the colony, the Chinese, than for the Europeans. Japanese troops behaved towards the Chinese with at best callousness and at worst brutality, as they had in the rest of occupied China. Although some sections of the population, including elements of the business class of Indian origin, were initially seduced by the Japanese claim that they would liberate fellow Asians from the racist rule of European colonialists, this illusion did not last long and reality soon set in. Some members of the local business community, irrespective of ethnic background, cooperated with the Japanese occupiers, as in other parts of China. There was resistance, but it was in vain. Japan established its own colonial administration and Japanese specialists were brought in to occupy the most senior government and administrative posts, with Chinese employees remaining in subordinate positions.

Return of the British

In August 1945, after the unconditional surrender of the Japanese government and the collapse of Japan's dreams of empire, plans for the reoccupation of the colony were put into effect almost immediately and a British naval task force entered Hong Kong harbour on 30August 1945. Rear Admiral C.H.J. Harcourt, the commander of the task force, sailed into Hong Kong on board the cruiser *HMS Swiftsure* to re-establish the British government's control over the colony. A British military administrative office was set up in Victoria on Hong Kong Island on 1 September, and on 16 September, the new administration accepted the formal surrender of the Japanese garrison in the colony at Government House.[1]

The reoccupation was accomplished by means of a diplomatic sleight of hand because it did not entirely meet with the approval of Chiang Kai-shek. Chiang assumed that his Guomindang government was going to resume its control over the whole of China, control that had been so rudely interrupted by the Japanese attack on Nanjing in 1937. As Nationalists, the Guomindang were opposed to the occupation of Hong Kong by the British and wished it to be returned to China. Chiang had made it clear that he wished the surrender of the Japanese forces in Hong Kong to be taken by his own Nationalist troops, but circumstances obliged him to compromise and the surrender was in fact taken by the British but under his nominal authority as a courtesy. Sir Mark Young returned as Governor for a year; he was replaced by Sir Alexander Grantham in July 1947.

Even at this early stage, the shadow of the eventual handover had fallen over Hong Kong, and a division was beginning to emerge between those who thought they could somehow avoid the inevitability by economic and political reform and those who accepted it and tried to work towards the best possible outcome. In both cases, there was an agreement that the priority for Hong Kong should be economic development. The assumption was that prosperity would reduce demands from the Chinese population of Hong Kong for the return of the colony to China. It was also hoped that Hong Kong would be so valuable to China as an intermediary during the period of China's isolation after the Korean War, and later as a financial services centre with international connections and credibility, that Beijing would not wish to exert overwhelming pressure on the colony. Many in the administration and the populace in general simply avoided the issue and went about their normal business.

The British presented the new post-war administration as simply a case of carrying on where they had left off after a brief, ill-mannered interruption by the Japanese occupation. In reality, the character of Hong Kong society was never to be the same again: it changed subtly, but it changed profoundly. Some of the changes came about as a result of legislation: strict regulations on the Chinese language press were rescinded, and the exclusive residential areas of the Peak were no longer limited by law to Europeans. More significantly for long-term social change in the colony, there was a drive to recruit additional Chinese employees into government service at all levels. The colonial apparatus remained, but it was being opened up to the local majority population.

Hong Kong and the PRC

As the Civil War in China came to an end in 1948–1949 and it became clear that the CCP was going to form the next government, what had been a gradual flow of refugees moving south turned into a mass migration and thousands of Chinese citizens headed towards the colony. Most of the migrants were farmers who settled in the New Territories, the largest area of land in Hong Kong: it is in the north of the colony and is part of the mainland. The farmers were able to rent small parcels of land – market gardens – and grew vegetables for which there was an increasing demand in the urban areas of Hong Kong. This new market-oriented economy disrupted the older rice-growing economy of the New Territories which faced collapse. Emigration to the United Kingdom from Hong Kong began in this period, as many farming families chose to migrate rather than find different ways of earning a living in Hong Kong.[2]

The political and personnel changes that occurred in the PRC in the 1970s made it easier for progress to be made in its in relations with Hong Kong. After the death of Lin Biao in 1971, Zhou Enlai's more intelligent and conciliatory foreign policy permitted high-level contacts with the United States and other Western governments. Mao Zedong died in 1976, and the 'reform and opening' policy agenda of Deng Xiaoping incorporated an awareness of the need for China to engage with the wider world.

At the same time, the new Governor of the colony, Sir Murray MacLehose, who had been appointed in 1971, took a practical and positive approach to contacts with Beijing. He broke with all precedents by developing a cordial working relationship with the Xinhua (New China) news agency office in Hong Kong. Xinhua is the official news agency of the PRC and its office in Hong Kong was for many years the only form of representation that Beijing had in the colony: it acted both as an unofficial embassy and as an important conduit for information and informal and, in many cases unacknowledged, negotiations.

Preparing for the handover

Governor MacLehose made an official visit to China in 1979 to discuss an improvement in trade between Hong Kong and China, and in particular to take part in discussions with the government of the PRC on how the colony could assist in China's ambitious programme of economic modernisation. Although this was not the beginning of formal negotiations about the terms and timetable for the formal handover of Hong Kong to China, it was a useful reconnaissance mission and enabled the Governor and his closest colleagues to form an opinion of the attitudes of the new reform-minded leadership in Beijing on the Hong Kong issue.[3] One of Governor MacLehose's significant domestic policy initiatives was the establishment in 1974 of the Independent Commission Against Corruption (ICAC), which attempted to stamp out what was perceived to be an unacceptable level of corruption in the civil service and the police, which was an issue that had to be resolved before the handover.

The task of initiating the formal negotiations on the future of Hong Kong with Beijing fell to Lord MacLehose's successor as Governor, Sir Edward Youde, who took office in 1982, and these negotiations took place the same year, both before and during the visit to China of the British Prime Minister, Margaret Thatcher. Mrs Thatcher took an uncompromising stance on the continuation of a British presence in Hong Kong after what she regarded as her success in the Falklands War. However, the Chinese under Deng Xiaoping were equally, if not more, intransigent and were insisting on the return of Hong Kong to Chinese control. In theory, there was a difference between the legal status of the island of Hong Kong, which had been ceded to Britain in perpetuity in 1842, and the New Territories, which were British by virtue of a 99-year-lease that was due to expire in 1997. In practice, there was common consent that the two parts of the colony were not viable separately and would have to be treated as a whole. An accommodation between Britain and China was therefore essential for Hong Kong's continued economic success and social stability.

Negotiations between Britain and China continued until September 1984, by which time it was clear to the British negotiators that Beijing was not going to retreat on its determination that Hong Kong would return to China. Britain had hoped to be able to continue administering Hong Kong after the transfer of sovereignty, but this was completely unacceptable to the Chinese side. The Sino-British Joint Declaration on Hong Kong was agreed and initialled in Beijing on 26 September 1984 by Sir Richard Evans, Britain's ambassador to the PRC, and Zhou Nan, the Chinese Deputy Minister of Foreign Affairs. The formal signing ceremony by Mrs Thatcher and the Chinese Premier, Zhou Enlai, took place in Beijing on 19 December, and after a period of formal ratification, the agreement became effective from May 1985.

Joint Declaration

Under the terms of the Sino-British Joint Declaration, it was agreed that the sovereignty of the entire territory of Hong Kong would be transferred to China on 1 July 1997. Britain would continue to be responsible for administering the territory in the interim, and the PRC would cooperate in this. China agreed that it would create a Special Administrative Region (SAR) to govern Hong Kong and allowed that the SAR would enjoy a considerable degree of autonomy in all questions – with the exceptions of foreign policy and matters connected with defence. A SAR was a new concept, although Special Economic Regions, including Hong Kong's immediate neighbour Shenzhen within the PRC, were already in existence.

The Joint Declaration provided for a Chief Executive to be nominated by China in place of the Governor, but accepted that existing personnel, including foreign nationals, would be able to remain in post. Existing social and economic practices, the legal system, and the rights and freedoms that the colony had traditionally enjoyed would be respected. It was also announced that a Basic Law would be drawn up, and that this would be enacted and ratified by the NPC in Beijing. This law would guarantee the status quo in Hong Kong for 50 years under a formula that went by the name of 'one country, two systems'. In other words, although Hong Kong would be deemed to be a constituent part of the PRC, it would be governed according to the long-established capitalist system and in a manner that would take into account the distinctive way of life that prevailed there rather than the state-dominated economic system of the mainland. There had been great apprehension in Hong Kong about the outcome of these negotiations and, although there was still concern and lack of confidence in the willingness and ability of China to act on the basis of the Joint Declaration, the feeling overall was one of relief and an acknowledgement that things could have been much worse.

Basic Law

The Basic Law was drafted by a joint committee which included members from both Hong Kong and the PRC. There was considerable public consultation in Hong Kong, and rather less on the mainland. It was adopted by the seventh NPC on 4 April 1990 and became effective on the day of the handover, 1 July 1997. The text of the Basic Law concerned the autonomy of the SAR, the maintenance of the status quo for 50 years, and the preservation of the existing system of legislation, including protection from arbitrary detention or imprisonment and freedoms of speech, the press, and assembly. A number of issues remained contentious, notably the question of the right to abode of mainland residents who might wish to settle in

Hong Kong, the possibility of a move towards complete universal suffrage, and the length of the term of office of future Chief Executives.

Democracy in Hong Kong?

When the Joint Declaration became effective in May 1985, Hong Kong entered a period of uncharted waters. An issue that had concerned both residents and foreign observers for decades but had been largely avoided by the administration, Hong Kong's lack of democracy, suddenly acquired greater importance in this transitional period. It has been argued that the absence of democracy in Hong Kong in the post-war period was due to the lack of grassroots demand and a popular perception that, at least in economic terms, the government was delivering the goods. There was, however, a long-established core of activists who had argued for redressing the democratic deficit. The spilling over of the Cultural Revolution into Hong Kong in 1967 certainly did not help the cause of democracy, and the demonstrations provoked more alarm than sympathy. The colonial government did use the opportunity this presented to increase the degree of public participation in the processes of government, and the positive response that this generated suggests that democratisation was long overdue.[4]

Hong Kong did not have a democratically elected parliament. The legislative body of Hong Kong, the Legislative Council (Legco) was created in 1843 by the British colonial administration under the terms of the Charter of Hong Kong, Letters Patent of Queen Victoria. The members of the Legislative Council were not democratically elected, but were appointed to advise the Governor, who alone had the authority to enact legislation. When the 1843 Charter was replaced in 1917, the wording of the new Letters Patent was altered to clarify the relationship between the Governor and the Legislative Council by stressing that the council was not merely an advisory body but that its consent was required for legislation. Membership of the Legislative Council was increased from time to time until by 1976, it had 23 official and 23 unofficial members (the unofficial members were members who did not have government posts and were in large part drawn from the business community). The first elections to the Legislative Council did not take place until 1985, and the number of unofficial members was increased so that it exceeded the number of official members. In 1995, the final Legislative Council before the handover included 20 of its membership who had been returned by direct elections. The Legislative Council had evolved very slowly from an advisory to a legislative body, but resistance to the idea of elections by full universal suffrage continued to the very end.

The final colonial Governor, Chris Patten, was a British conservative politician who had lost his seat in the constituency of Bath in the 1992 elections. His governorship was controversial because of his abrasive manner towards officials in Beijing and the changes he made to the functional constituencies from which the unofficial members of the Legislative Council were elected. These changes effectively extended the franchise in the last elections before the handover, apparently against the understanding that had been reached in the negotiations and were against the wishes of Beijing: the final Legislative Council of the colonial era was dissolved after the handover and replaced by a provisional body. The new Legislative Council of the Hong Kong Special Administrative Region with 80 members was elected in May 1998.[5] Patten's reforms attracted a great deal of support within Hong Kong, especially but not exclusively among the expatriate community, and some considered that he had taken an important stand against Beijing.

The formal and peaceful handover of power to the PRC took place on 1 July 1997 in a ceremony which was attended by Prince Charles, the heir to the British throne. After the ceremony, the Prince and the last Governor departed from the last colony on the royal yacht *Britannia*, and Hong Kong became a Special Administrative Region of the PRC. The Portuguese colony of Macao, Hong Kong's near neighbour, agreed to revert to Chinese rule under similar conditions in 1999.

Hong Kong's limited democracy – Chief Executive and Legco

After the handover, the first Chief Executive was Tung Chee-hwa, a businessman with close ties to the government in Beijing. He was succeeded in 2005 by a former civil servant, Donald Tsang, who had served as the colony's Financial Secretary from 1995, and then by C.Y. Leung (Leung Chun-ying). Carrie Lam became Chief Executive on 1 July 2017, having been appointed on 31 March that year.

The Chief Executive is chosen not by a popular vote but 'by a broadly representative Election Committee in accordance with the Basic Law and appointed by the Central People's Government'. This ensures that only candidates acceptable to Beijing are considered. In December 2007, pressure from Hong Kong led to an agreement by the Standing Committee of the NPC in Beijing that direct elections could be considered from 2017 and that a Legislative Council [Legco] could be elected by universal suffrage by 2020. This was a disappointment to many who had hoped that direct elections would be introduced in 2012. After the protest movements of 2014 and afterwards, and wrangling between political parties in Hong Kong, reforms to the Legco election progress faltered. Direct universal suffrage remained and aspiration and the sixth term Legco was elected on 4 September 2016 based on both geographical and functional constituencies.[6]

Political differences in Hong Kong are typically represented as opposition between pro-Beijing and pro-democracy groups. A third group, the 'localists', are, as the name suggests, primarily concerned with local or sectional interests, and their influence is mainly confined to the district councils rather than the Hong Kong legislature. Twenty-six parties are represented at all levels, but six have no representation in the legislature. It was rarely possible for one party to form an administration, so coalitions have been the rule. On the basis of the number of seats held in the legislature, the most influential pro-Beijing parties following the elections of September 2016 were the Democratic Alliance for the Betterment and Progress of Hong Kong (DAB), the Business and Professionals Alliance for Hong Kong (BPA), the Hong Kong Federation of Trade Unions (FTU), and the Liberal Party. Pro-Democracy parties in the legislature are headed by the Democratic Party (DP) and the Civic Party (CP).

Occupy Central and Umbrella Movements 2014

Towards the end of 2014, concern at the unwillingness of the Hong Kong authorities to implement the ultimate aim of universal suffrage set out in the 1990 Basic Law led to demonstrations by the Umbrella Movement which 'occupied public spaces and streets outside the HKSAR [Hong Kong Special Administrative Region] government offices for 79 days'. Objections to a government 'moral and national education programme' led to a rally organised by Joshua Wong. Three people inspired by the Occupy movement against inequality and the global financial system that had begun in New York in September 2011 conceived the idea of an Occupy Central movement: they were Benny Tai, a law professor; Chan Kinman, a sociologist; and a Baptist minister, the Reverend Chu Yiu-ming. Two organisations, the Federation of Students and Scholarism, played a key role in the Occupy Central for Love and Peace, to give it its full name, which was a campaign of peaceful civil disobedience designed to persuade Beijing to allow Hong Kong to move forward to genuine universal suffrage. Specifically, they demanded that the then Chief Executive, C.Y. Leung should resign and that Beijing must

> retract its decision on the city's 2017 chief executive poll, which would restrict the number of candidates to two or three approved by a 1,200-strong nominating committee. They also called on workers and teachers to strike, students to boycott classes and shops to close for business.[7]

The State Council in Beijing responded with a White Paper that insisted that Hong Kong's 'two systems' must be subordinated to 'one country'. On 31 August, the Standing Committee of the NPC published the '8.31 Decision' on arrangements for the elections of a Hong Kong legislature in 2016 and a Chief Executive in 2017. The rules would allow 'one person one vote', but there were to be tight restrictions on who could be nominated.

The Umbrella Movement, created by students, emerged in late September 2014 in response to these two documents and merged with Occupy Central to organise occupations and demonstrations that would continue until the middle of December. This movement failed to gain the support of the wider public and was weakened by factional disputes. Young radicals began to generalise their arguments and link the lack of political democracy with problems of urban development and the lack of social welfare programmes. This emerged in the elections to district councils in 2015 and elections to the Legislative Council the following year. Candidates who could be identifies as broadly pro-democracy won seats in several constituencies, but six were disqualified on the grounds of their pro-independence views, including Edward Leung Tin-kei, who was imprisoned after resisting police actions against 'local food vendors'. A slogan associated with him, 'Reclaim Hong Kong, the revolution of our time', became popular in the summer 2019 demonstrations. In April 2016, the case of the Occupy Central trio came to trial; they were sentenced to 16 months in prison, although the Reverend Chu You-ming's sentence was suspended for two years. Six others sentenced on the same day included two elected members of the Legislative Council. Joshua Wong and others associated with the Umbrella Movement faced charges of illegal assembly and incitement, and were imprisoned. Wong's sentence was reduced to two months on appeal and he was released on 17 June, one day after the conclusion of Hong Kong's largest-ever political demonstration.[8]

Extradition bill crisis, 2019

In the spring and summer of 2019, attempts by the Hong Kong government to enact legislation on extradition to China divided public opinion in the former colony and resulted in the largest demonstrations since 1997. Organisers of the protest on Sunday 9 June claimed that over one million residents had protested against the proposed legislation; even the police acknowledged that the number of demonstrators may have reached 240,000.[9]

The 'Fugitive Offenders and Mutual Legal Assistance in Criminal Matters Legislation (Amendment) Bill 2019' was proposed in February 2019 in response to the case of a Hong Kong resident who was accused of killing his pregnant girlfriend in Taiwan and could not be extradited from Hong Kong to Taiwan because no extradition arrangements were in place. The proposed legislation aroused widespread opposition in legal and professional circles, and the media in Hong Kong, on the grounds that it would provide an opportunity for the extradition of Hong Kong citizens to other parts of the PRC. Critics of the bill pronounced it the 'last nail in the coffin' of Hong Kong's independence, arguing that extraditions could be requested solely on the basis of witness statements and that existing provisions for oversight by the Hong Kong Chief Executive's cabinet and Legco were being abolished. Concern was expressed that Beijing could use the legislation to target its political enemies, which would have a deleterious impact on freedom of speech in Hong Kong. The many foreign residents of Hong Kong could also risk arrest for political reasons. Critics pointed to the disappearance in 2015 of booksellers who had published material about the Chinese leadership deemed salacious: some had reappeared on the mainland, where they had confessed to non-political crimes such as traffic offences.

The bill become public knowledge in February and the first protest, a march of up to 12,000 people, took place on 3 March. As the implications of the legislation became clearer opposition grew, and tens of thousands (some estimated 130,000) people demonstrated on 28 April, the largest street demonstration in five years. On 28 June, 7,000 lawyers, symbolically dressed in black, marched silently and on 9 June, the numbers on the streets approached one million and there were outbreaks of violence.[10]

12 June demonstrations

Hong Kong's Chief Executive, Carrie Lam, insisted that the provenance of the bill was entirely Hong Kong's and not Beijing's, and that the government would not give in to pressure. Following the public expression of disquiet, the second reading of the bill, scheduled for Wednesday 12 June 2019, was postponed by the president of Legco, Andrew Leung Kwan-yuen, although there was a clear majority in the legislature in favour of passing the bill. Police units in the vicinity of the Legco building were reinforced, but no plans for dispersing the demonstrators were announced. In the words of the Hong Kong *South China Morning Post*,[11] the actions of the demonstrators were 'coordinated spontaneously on the ground and through encrypted messaging': Carrie Lam called them 'organised riots'. The protesters stockpiled water and food, and equipped themselves with 'face masks, goggles and makeshift body armour'. As the confrontation escalated, the police responded by firing tear gas canisters and rubber bullets and some demonstrators were injured.

By 14 June, opinion in Exco was divided. One of Carrie Lam's senior advisers, Bernard Chan, indicated that there had been far greater concern in the business community than had been anticipated: this was a critical factor in the level of support for the protests. Carrie Lam initially insisted that the bill could not be withdrawn, but the possibility was raised that a pause in the legislative process might allow time for the crisis to be defused.[12]

If this was a crisis for the Hong Kong leadership, it was also a predicament for Xi Jinping and raised awkward questions about Beijing's authority over Hong Kong. Any solution required face-saving devices for Lam and Xi and for Hong Kong pan-Democrats. The most vulnerable was Carrie Lam, criticised by veteran *SCMP* columnist Wang Xiangwei for her naiveté:

> [Her] plan to bulldoze through the local legislature with the bill is ill-timed, ill-advised and ill-thought-out, and she and her officials are ill-prepared for not seeing the bigger picture and for the extraordinary pushback from the general public in Hong Kong and the international community.[13]

A meeting of PRC officials who oversee Hong Kong affairs took place in Shenzhen, the city just across the border – to meet in Hong Kong itself would have signalled that the autonomy of the former colony was a mere façade. It was not clear whether this was attended by Han Zheng, Vice-Premier and member of the seven-man Politburo Standing Committee who holds the Hong Kong portfolio for the central government in Beijing, but *Singtao Daily*, which supports the Beijing government, reported that Carrie Lam met him in Shenzhen. In a speech on Saturday 15 June, Carrie Lam announced that the passage of the bill through Legco would be suspended indefinitely to allow time for further consultation to take place. Since no timetable had been announced, some sources close to the Hong Kong government suggested that the bill would be allowed to die a 'natural death' when the term of office of the sitting Legco expired in July 2020.[14]

Even this concession did not satisfy the protesters who were emboldened by the level of support and angered by what some Hong Kong commentators considered the arrogant tone of Carrie Lam's speech. On Sunday 16 June, organisers of the mobilisation claimed that the numbers on the streets had risen to two million, occupying much of Central district near the Central Government Complex and blocking main thoroughfares such as Harcourt Road. Many of the protesters wore black, and their resolve was further strengthened by the death of one of their number; although it was an accident as he fell from a high building, he was regarded as the first martyr of the cause. Police maintained a low profile, following criticism of violent tactics on previous days.[15]

Most media outlets on the Chinese mainland avoided covering the demonstrations, but the English-language *Global Times* carried a bland report on the suspension of the extradition bill, with a gesture towards 'one country, two systems' as an explanation and warned against outside interference. The *China Daily* headline, 'Stench of hypocrisy accompanies foreign meddling in Hong Kong', spoke for itself.[16]

Carrie Lam had initially described the 12 June demonstrations as 'riots', and as the protesters formulated their demands, reclassifying the violence of that day and an amnesty for those arrested were among their priorities. The resignation of the Chief Executive was at the top of their list, although she received support from the convenor of Exco, who asked that her 'achievements of the past two years' be taken into account and noted that the bill was technically defunct. Former Legco President Jasper Tsang pointed out that even if she resigned, there was no viable replacement who would have the confidence of both the people of Hong Kong and the central government of China. He pointed out that she had little say in decisions over her future; these rested with Beijing.

On Monday 17 June, Joshua Wong, one of the highest-profile leaders of the Umbrella and Occupy movements, was released from prison where he had been serving a sentence for his part in the occupation of Civic Square and Mong Kok, which he had refused to leave on 26 November 2014. He had served the customary portion of his two-month sentence for contempt of court, but the timing was significant. The demonstrations continued, although with reduced numbers and a new focus on the police headquarters in Wan Chai, which by Friday 21 June was effectively under siege in response to the heavy-handed police tactics on 12 June and the fate of those detained during the demonstrations. By the early hours of Saturday 22 June, most of the demonstrators had dispersed and the Justice Secretary Teresa Cheng had rejected calls for a public enquiry into the behaviour of the police. There was no suggestion that the protests were over – and significantly, members of the Hong Kong business community, often assumed to be aligned with Beijing in the interests of stability, began to voice their concerns about the implications of the extradition law more openly. As the protests declined towards the end of June, the astute and acerbic cartoonist of the *South China Morning Post*, Harry Harrison, depicted two of his favourite characters – the smug and cynical fat cats – in conversation. 'So, now things have settled down a bit, we can get back to business as usual'. 'Yes . . . with impunity from extradition'.[17]

Conscious of the eventual failure of the 2014 Umbrella Movement, the demonstrators refined their tactics, concentrating on non-cooperation but with minimum impact on essential public services. Smaller groups occupied specific locations or delivered petitions to foreign diplomatic missions and other bodies – 'peaceful guerrilla warfare' directed from virtual command centres'. The strongest protest was at the police headquarters in Wanchai, which 1,000 demonstrators – many wearing masks and hard hats and using umbrellas to foil security cameras – surrounded after 10 pm on Wednesday 26 June. At 4 o'clock the following morning, police in rioter gear dispersed the remaining 100 protesters, arresting some. The siege was over by 6.30 am, roads in Admiralty were reopened, and bus and MTR services were restored.

An election forum for the district and council ballots was cancelled on the grounds of public safety. The Chief Executive, Carrie Lam, maintained a low profile, but did issue a statement insisting that those involved in the violence of 12 June would be treated 'impartially and fairly'. Apart from a formal condemnation of violence by the Chairman of the Standing Committee of the NPC, Li Fei, there was no intervention by the authorities in Beijing; mainland social media, WeChat and Weibo, avoided discussions of the demonstrations.[18]

The storming of Legco

Monday 1 July 2019 was the 22nd anniversary of the handover by the British colonial authorities. Further demonstrations had been anticipated, but not the level of violence and destruction that ensued. Between 290,000 and 550,000 people – depending on which estimate was accepted – thronged the streets of Central, marching peacefully against the extradition bill. This march was, however, eclipsed in the media by a storming of the Legco building by up to 1,000 protesters. This ultra-radical spin-off was not planned, but the result of a hastily convened group of some 200 radicals at noon on the day of the march. Eighty per cent of those polled favoured an attack which began at 1.47 p.m and lasted until midnight. In complete contrast to the peaceful march, the assault on the Legco building was violent and destructive. Metal trolleys were used to smash doors and the glass frontage, and steel doors were ripped away. The Legco chamber was desecrated; the Bauhinia flag, symbolic of post-1997 Hong Kong, was replaced by a monochrome image; and photographs of Legco presidents, past and present, were defaced or damaged. The most striking image was the appearance of the pre-1997 colonial era flag with the Union Jack in the top left corner: this was calculated to goad the Chinese authorities and led to speculation that *agents provocateurs* had been involved in the violence. The occupation of Legco was ended after police in riot gear and firing tear gas canisters moved in at midnight. By 12.48 am, the protesters had either left voluntarily or been forced out, and the streets around Legco had been cleared. Television footage revealed substantial damage: members of Legco estimated that it might take six months to repair, necessitating the use of temporary premises to allow important legislation to be processed. Hong Kong Chief Executive Carrie Lam and the Beijing authorities issued statements criticising the violence: although there had been no active participation by PRC military or police, it emerged that a central government task force dispatched from Beijing had been stationed in neighbouring Shenzhen throughout June to monitor the crisis around the extradition bill and 'ensure that there was no bloodshed' in Hong Kong.[19]

There were international repercussions. The British Foreign Secretary, Jeremy Hunt, also at the time a contender for the recently vacated leadership of the Conservative Party, spoke out in support of demonstrators and freedom in Hong Kong as set out in the 12-point Joint Declaration of 1984. Liu Xiaoming, the Chinese ambassador to the United Kingdom, responded with an unusually blunt statement criticising 'interference' by the British government, which he accused of 'colonial-era' delusions. The head of the British diplomatic service, Sir Simon McDonald, described Ambassador Liu's comments as 'unacceptable and inaccurate' and summoned him to the foreign office, a universally understood diplomatic convention implying a severe protest or rebuke. On Sunday 7 July, protests continued across the harbour with thousands marching from the harbour front at Tsim Sha Tsui northwards along Nathan Road towards the Mong Kok shopping area popular with mainland tourists, where violence broke out among a small number of demonstrators. In a conciliatory gesture, Carrie Lam announced that the extradition bill was 'dead' and would automatically fall as the current session of Legco came to an end in 2020. This was not accepted by many protesters, who continued to insist on a formal withdrawal of the bill.[20]

The focus of the demonstrations shifted from Hong Kong Island across the harbour to Kowloon, with a mass rally that began on Friday 12 July in Tsim Sha Tsui close to the ferry terminals and proceeded northwards to the West Kowloon terminal of the rail link to Guangzhou. As many as 230,000 demonstrators (56,000, according to the police) took part in a largely peaceful march that passed through areas which attract shoppers from the mainland and spilled over into the lanes of Nathan Road. In the Sheung Shui district, close to the border with the PRC, placards and slogans criticised 'parallel traders' from the mainland who were accused of threatening the livelihood of local businesses by buying cheap in Hong Kong and reselling across the border. In contrast, violence that broke out in Shatin on Sunday 14 July left 22 people injured, some seriously, and dozens were arrested. Police tactics of blocking exits to shopping malls came under criticism. The main Shatin protest march (115,000 or 28,000, according to police) lasted several hours but passed off peacefully – but riot units were called in to rescue 20 officers from the Organised Crime and Triad Bureau trapped at the entrance to the Shatin MTR by a crowd of protesters.[21]

Crisis talks

The authorities in Hong Kong and Beijing realised that this was the deepest political crisis in the territory since the handover in 1997. Carrie Lam was said to have offered her resignation on several occasions; this was rejected by Beijing, partly on the grounds that her extradition bill had provoked the emergency and it was therefore her job to resolve it. The Hong Kong and Macao Affairs Office, a PRC government office, had been instructed to present a new strategy to end the crisis, and a Central Coordination Group for Hong Kong and Macao under Vice-Premier Han Zheng was formulating a strategy document. Military intervention was not on the table, but there were concerns about security in the light of a scheduled visit by Xi Jinping to Macao later in the year. PRC intelligence organisations were criticised for having failed to gauge the mood of the Hong Kong public.

Hong Kong businesses – generally conservative, willing to work with the PRC, and not wishing to alienate customers from the mainland – were in a quandary as neither did they wish to offend pro-democracy supporters. The implications of the extradition bill for businesses who could be caught up in a mainland anti-corruption campaign persuaded some to side tentatively with the demonstration.[22]

On the eve of a major march planned for Sunday 21 July, there were reports of explosives being found together with pro-independence propaganda in an industrial building in Tsuen Wan. During the march on Hong Kong Island, demonstrators had attacked and damaged the

PRC Liaison Office at 160 Connaught Road in Sai Ying Pun, but were repulsed by police with tear gas and rubber bullets. At the end of the march, demonstrators returning home and other commuters were attacked as they alighted from the MTR train at Yuen Long station in the northwest of Hong Kong by a group of over 100 men dressed in white shirts and armed with steel bars, while police refused to intervene. The assailants have never been clearly identified, but reports suggested that they were from 14K and Wo Shing Wo triad gangs based in Yuen Long and Tim Shui Wai, both new towns formed in the 1970s and 1980s with estates housing lower income residents. Following the violence, Yuen Long was reported to be a 'ghost town', its inhabitants apprehensive about a further demonstration planned for 27 July and with little confidence in the effectiveness or the conduct of the police.[23]

The demonstrations in central Hong Kong continued, but by mid-August, the attention of the protesters was directed towards the airport at Chek Lap Kok on Lantau Island. A rally on the evening of Tuesday 13 August turned violent after clashes with the police and the arrest of five demonstrators who potentially faced lengthy prison sentences. Demonstrators had detained and manhandled two men they believed to be undercover police: one who was beaten and had his hands tied turned out to be Fu Guohao, a reporter for the mainland English-language daily, *Global Times*. The protests at the airport, which took place for six consecutive days, led to the cancellation of over 1,000 fights and affected at least 55,000 passengers; the main local carrier, Cathay Pacific, cancelled 272 flights in two days.[24]

Five demands and military in Shenzhen

The enormous number of protesters was impressive and clearly indicated the strength of feeling across Hong Kong society. The protest movement, however, remained amorphous, sustained by social media consultations and without any openly declared leadership.

In early July, the movement coalesced around five demands presented to the Hong Kong government:

1 The complete withdrawal of the extradition bill.
2 Resignation of Chief Executive Carrie Lam.
3 Retraction of characterisation of demonstrations as 'riots'.
4 Independent enquiry into police actions.
5 Unconditional release of all arrested.[25]

These were maximalist demands to which the Hong Kong government, answerable to Beijing, could not agree: there was no effective group with which it could negotiate, and the demonstrators seemed in no mood for compromise.

Meanwhile, across the border in Shenzhen, from where senior PRC officials had been monitoring the crisis, reports of a military build-up were substantiated by film of large numbers of armoured personnel vehicles marshalled in a sports stadium. These were units of the PAP, a gendarmerie or carabinieri force, part of the Ministry of Defence rather than the Ministry of Public Security which has responsibility for the regular police in the PRC. The PAP have units which specialise in riot control and similar operations, and have been used in both Tibet and Xinjiang. Their presence was at least a warning that they could be brought into Hong Kong to reinforce the Hong Kong police or the existing PLA garrison in the territory. On Thursday 15 August, the Ambassador of the PRC to the United Kingdom, Liu Xiaoming, indicated firmly that China had both the ability and the will to intervene if necessary and reiterated complaints that foreign interests had become involved with the protest movement and that some UK politicians in particular still had a 'colonial mindset'.[26]

An unexpected casualty of the protests was the senior management of Cathay Pacific: the highly respected CEO, Rupert Hogg, and his deputy, Paul Loo Kar-pui, resigned after reports that employees of the airline, including pilots, had supported the anti-Beijing demonstrators. Cathay initially issued a statement that what employees did in their own time was their own business, but Merlin Swire, the chairman of Cathay's parent company, was then summoned to Beijing and a new CEO, Augustus Tang Kin-wing, was appointed.[27]

Demonstrations on Saturday 17 August, notably a teachers' march under the slogan 'Safeguard the next generation; let our conscience speak' passed off with little violence in persistent rain. Rubbish bins and other objects were thrown by a small group at the police in Mong Kok, but no tear gas was deployed. A counter-demonstration against the violence and in support of the police and the Hong Kong and Chinese authorities took place from Tamar Park on Hong Kong Island. Police estimated that over 100,000 attended, while organisers claimed almost 500,000. Another planned march the following day, which was expected to confirm the continuing level of support for the protest, attracted, according to the organisers, 1.7 million people to a legal rally in Victoria Park in driving rain. Some marched towards government buildings, defying a police ban, but there was little if any violence as protesters reflected on the backlash following the conflict at the airport. For the third night running, no tear gas was deployed.[28]

On 20 August, Chief Executive Carrie Lam announced her intention of establishing a 'platform for dialogue', 'listening to what the people have to tell us', although it was far from clear what form this would take. She rejected demands for an independent enquiry into the actions of the Hong Kong police during the demonstrations, insisting that the existing Independent Police Complaints Council was fully competent to deal with allegations of misconduct, although conceding that it would be supported by 'overseas experts' in a fact-finding study. She again refused to withdraw the extradition bill but reiterated that there were no plans to revive it. Although these proposals were welcomed as a step towards resolving the crisis, they did not answer the five demands raised by the informal leadership of the protests, but Hong Kong was temporarily calmer.[29]

Hong Kong Way and water cannon

From seven o'clock in the evening of Friday 23 August, thousands of protesters demanding democracy for Hong Kong formed human chains across the whole of the territory, mirroring the map of the MTR which took them to their assembly points, 'from Kennedy Town to Causeway Bay, from Kowloon Tong to Yau Ma Tei, along the Tsim Sha Tsui harbourfront, and from Tsuen Wan to Lai King, as well as further east along the Kwun Tong line'. Others climbed Lion Rock, a popular landmark, from where they used laser pointers and torches to simulate a laser light display. This 'Hong Kong Way' was in conscious emulation of the Baltic Way or Baltic Chain, in which two million people joined hands across the states of Latvia, Lithuania, and Estonia on 23 August 1989 to demand their freedom from the USSR, and subsequently the Catalan Way of 2013.[30]

When further violence broke out that weekend, the two overlapping currents of protest became clear. Clashes and arrests on Saturday 24 August were followed on Sunday by a mass demonstration in the Tsuen Wan district of the western New Territories, an area notorious as the traditional headquarters of the triad society, the Wo Shing Wo. Police fired tear gas cannisters, at least one revolver shot was heard, and water cannon were used for the first time in these protests. Many supporters of demands for more democracy dissociated themselves from the violence.[31]

On Monday 26 August, behind closed doors, Chief Executive Carrie Lam met representatives of selected youth organisations, including the Outstanding Young Persons' Association, the Hong Kong Playground Associations, and the Junior Chamber International Hong Kong. The Exco Secretaries for education and Home Affairs also attended. The 20 or so invitees, mostly in their 20s or early 30s, had taken part in the demonstrations but not in the violent protests. Other groups and individuals declined to participate in what was clearly an attempt to separate the peaceful and violent strands of the protests.[32]

In advance of demonstrations planned for the weekend of 31 August and 1 September, Hong Kong police arrested several high-profile figures in the pro-democracy movement, including Joshua Wong and Agnes Chow, who were released within hours. A peaceful protest for Saturday 31 August – the fifth anniversary of Beijing's rejection of demands for universal suffrage, which triggered the 2014 Umbrella Movement – was banned by the police, but this ban was disobeyed by thousands who assembled at Causeway Bay to march westwards along the north coast of Hong Kong Island towards the government buildings. Marches ended with barricades set on fire and Molotov cocktails and other projectiles being thrown at police, who responded with tear gas and water cannon spraying blue dye to identify participants in the disturbances. Units of the Special Tactical Squad, the 'Raptors', entered MTR stations and attacked passengers, seemingly at random – video from Prince Edward station showed passengers being attacked inside a stationary train. Prince Edward, Mong Kok, and Kowloon Bay MTR stations remained closed overnight. The night's violence left over 30 people injured, at least five seriously. At the end of the demonstration, detachments of riot police leaving Causeway Bay faced jeering crowds of protesters and residents. Police were losing the confidence of large sections of the community; discipline was under strain, and some units appeared out of control. Widely circulated footage of PLA vehicles moving into Hong Kong raised fears of a military intervention by Beijing, but claims that this was no more than the regular rotation of troops in and out of the 6,000-strong garrison may have been accurate: the prominence given to the footage was, however, an unambiguous warning that intervention remained an option for Beijing.[33]

By the end of Sunday 1 September, the focus had moved once again to the international airport at Chek Lap Kok which was occupied by protesters who built barricades and disrupted the working of the airport. There was violence and destruction at Tung Cheng MTR station on the route to the airport: station facilities were seriously damaged, and the Airport Express train service was suspended for a period. Police patrols at MTR stations prevented further disruption of Hong Kong's rail network.[34]

Strikes were planned for the following day: there were calls for a two-day general strike and, at the start of a new term for most schools and colleges, a student boycott of classes. The strike did not materialise, but thousands of students failed to attend classes in favour of a rally in Central's Edinburgh Place in front of City Hall in the name of Demosisto, a pro-democracy party established in April 2016 by associates of Joshua Wong and Agnes Chow. Participation was patchy with rallies affected by driving rain, but a sit-in at the Chinese University in Shatin, organised by the student unions of 12 Hong Kong universities, filled the University Mall in Shatin with up to 30,000 participants. A demand by teaching staff at the Diocesan Girls' School that students remove masks and other symbols of the protest attracted support from alumni.[35]

During what Chief Executive Carrie Lam believed to be a private lunch with business leaders in Hong Kong, she indicated that she would resign, 'given the choice', as she believed herself responsible for the chaos. An audio recording was leaked: Carrie Lam regretted the leak but insisted that she had never offered her resignation to the Chinese central government. A transcript of the 24-minute-long recording released on 3 September included the following statement:

> I don't want to spend your time, or waste your time, for you to ask me what went wrong, and why it went wrong. But for a Chief Executive to have caused this huge havoc to Hong Kong is unforgivable. It's just unforgivable. If I have a choice, the first thing is to quit, having made a deep apology, is to step down. So I make a plea to you for your forgiveness. This is something that no matter how well intended, I just want to put this message across. This is not something malicious. This is not something instructed, coerced by the central government. This is out of a good intention, myself and some of my key colleagues to try to plug legal loopholes in Hong Kong's system, very much prompted by our compassion for a single case, and this has proven to be very unwise given the circumstances.[36]

This ambiguous message, subsequently glossed to imply that the Chief Executive had no choice because of her loyalty to Hong Kong, led to speculation that she was distancing herself from Beijing in advance of a decision to invoke the Emergency Regulations Ordinance, which has not been used since 1967 when the factional conflicts of the Cultural Revolution spread to Hong Kong.

> Such regulations grant a wide range of powers, including on arrests, detentions and deportations, the control of ports and all transport, the appropriation of property, and authorising the entry and search of premises and the censorship and suppression of publications and communications.[37]

Hong Kong and Macao Affairs Office press conference

Yang Guang and Xu Yuling of the PRC State Council's Hong Kong and Macao Affairs Office gave a press briefing on the afternoon on 3 September. At an unusually long session, Yang emphasised the outbreaks of violence and the illegality of some marches, and said that the situation in the territory was still not under control. He warned against attacks on the Liaison Office, Foreign Ministry and PLA garrison – 'which represent the country' – and again raised the spectre of 'foreign forces', 'black hands harbouring political goals', plotting to separate Hong Kong from the motherland: the popular slogan, 'Liberate Hong Kong; revolution of our times' was evidence of this. On a more positive note, he urged Carrie Lam to carry out a dialogue with Hong Kong people, especially the young, to resolve critical social problems, notably the housing crisis.

Asked about the likelihood of special powers being taken under the terms of the Emergency Regulations Ordinance, Xu acknowledged that this had been discussed but indicated that no deadline had been set before its implementation. She insisted that the PLA could be deployed in Hong Kong in an emergency under the provisions of the Basic Law and insisted that mobilising the PLA garrison based in Hong Kong would not constitute an end to 'one country, two systems'. She maintained, however, that the prime role of the PRC central government was to support the government and the police of Hong Kong. However, when outlining the damage that had been done during the demonstrations Yang said, 'I can smell terrorism'. Yang rejected any possibility of political reform – particularly of the procedures for selecting a Chief Executive – in response to the five demands of the protesters and both deftly fielded shouted questions about the autonomy of Carrie Lam. In summary, Xu reiterated that,

> peaceful marchers and radical protesters have to be separated. Their demands reflect deep-rooted problems in Hong Kong, and attention should be paid to their concerns, she adds. She says Beijing has been supporting Hong Kong under the Greater Bay Area plan, which seeks to turn the city and 10 neighbouring cites into a world-class finance and technology hub.

Repeated visits by senior PRC officials to Shenzhen and other parts of Guangdong province, and frequent reference to plans for the Greater Bay Area, underlined Beijing's view that in economic terms, the future of Hong Kong would be as a constituent part of a developing region rather than a special semi-autonomous economic unit. Reports in the Chinese official media increasingly favoured the development of Shenzhen as a financial hub to rival Hong Kong.[38]

Extradition revisited

Reports on 4 September indicated that Carrie Lam would meet pro-government allies to inform them that she had decided to withdraw the derided extradition bill which was described as 'dead' but remained on the statute book and could possibly be resuscitated; this would respond to one of the five demands of the protesters. In a pre-recorded television message that afternoon, which followed an hour-long meeting with Exco colleagues, she announced four proposals:

1   Formal withdrawal of the Extradition Bill.
2   Full support for the Independent Police Complaints Council (IPCC), with two new members in addition to overseas experts previously announced.
3   Dialogue with communities to assess grievances and consider solutions.
4   An invitation to 'community leaders, professionals and academics to independently examine and review society's deep-seated problems and to advise the Government on finding solutions'. This was simply an iteration of the earlier offer of a 'platform for dialogue' with a little more detail.[39]

These proposals met with approval from some supporters of the pro-democracy movement; at least it bought Carrie Lam time to prepare longer-term solutions. The more radical elements inevitably rejected the proposals, and demonstrations – some violent – continued, with a renewed focus on allegations of police misconduct. On Friday 6 September, demonstrators attacked the police station in Mong Kok and there were battles with police at the Mong Kok and Prince Edward MTR stations. On the afternoon of Saturday 7 September, there were small-scale demonstrations at shopping malls in Kowloon Bay and Shatin. Tight security was in place at MTR stations and at the Chek Lap Kok airport, where operations were 'running smoothly'.

Although these developments permitted optimists in Hong Kong to hope that the crisis had been defused, Wang Xiangwei, former editor-in-chief of the *South China Morning Post*, who is based in Beijing as the paper's 'editorial adviser' and has access to the thinking of senior officials, warned that a nine-minute televised selection from an address to students at the Central Party School by Xi Jinping on Tuesday 3 September pointed to Beijing's intention of taking a tougher line as preparations are made for the seventieth anniversary National Day celebrations planned for 1 October. To Wang, Xi's rhetoric, which repeatedly emphasised the need for 'struggle', was reminiscent of speeches by Mao Zedong.[40]

On Sunday 8 September, thousands of protesters marched peacefully to the US Consulate to demand the support of the United States in 'liberating' Hong Kong. In moves that could have been calculated to infuriate the Beijing government, demonstrators carried the Stars and Stripes, and called for Washington to endorse a Hong Kong Human Rights and Democracy Act that would link US trade with Hong Kong to satisfactory progress in human rights. Smaller and less peaceful groups of demonstrators were involved in running battles with the police in Causeway Bay, and attempts to disrupt the transport network resulted in the closure of the Central MTR station. Rumours spread that three protesters had been killed in a police operation inside Prince Edward MTR station on 31 August, and 'mourners' who did not believe official denials burnt paper offerings outside the station. Some maintained this belief throughout the protests. This was a further indication of the public loss of confidence in the Hong Kong police force, which was already facing serious allegations of assault, including sexual assault, during arrests and detentions.[41]

Community dialogue and the PRC at 70

Towards the end of September, peaceful demonstrations were confined largely to the weekends and attracted tens of thousands of participants, although numbers were decreasing. Much smaller groups of increasingly violent militants damaged property and targeted enterprises and individuals associated with the mainland cause or the Hong Kong police. Some groups were filmed trampling on the PRC flag, and similar deliberate provocations assumed greater significance in view of the impending celebrations of the 70th anniversary of the PRC on 1 October 2019. These incidents occurred primarily in the outlying townships close to the border with the mainland, in particular Tuen Mun and Yuen Long.

Carrie Lam's first community dialogue took place on 26 September at the Queen Elizabeth Stadium in Wanchai with 150 participants chosen by lottery from 20,000 applicants. The meeting lasted for two hours and the Chief Executive was subjected to civil but unsympathetic questions and complaints from the audience. She announced two concessions, reflecting concerns raised at the meeting. Demonstrators who were arrested would no longer be held in the detention centre at San Uk Ling, where there had been serious accusations of abuse. although she continued to insist that the expanded Independent Police Complaints Council was the appropriate body to deal with complaints against the police, she accepted that this was only one way of ascertaining the truth and conceded that an independent enquiry might be held after some months if the IPCC investigation did not prove satisfactory. The stadium was surrounded by thousands of protesters, chanting slogans and waving placards. Most dispersed after the meeting, but a small masked group remained and Carrie Lam was not able to leave safely until 1 am.[42]

As the 70th anniversary of the foundation of the PRC approached, the 17th weekend of protest saw thousands of peaceful demonstrators in Tamar Park marking the fifth anniversary of the Umbrella Movement of 2014. Police monitored and questioned travellers on the MTR and buses, but militant protesters evaded these searches and violent attacks were met with police water cannon and pepper spray. *South China Morning Post* reported 'street fights and vandalism amid chaotic scenes of chaos' in Causeway Bay, Wanchai, and Admiralty after marches on Hong Kong Island on 29 September. The anger of the demonstrators, as violent as any since the outset of the disturbances, was directed against the police.[43]

On the morning of 30 September, as Chief Executive Carrie Lam and over 200 of Hong Kong's elite took flights to Beijing to participate in the National Day celebrations, police began a wave of arrests in connection with previous incidents, including prominent activists alleged to have been involved in the storming of the Legco building on 1 July.[44]

More than a quarter of MTR stations were closed on 1 October, as were thousands of shops and other businesses. As the military parade celebrating National Day went ahead in Beijing, violent clashes erupted in various districts. During one of the most violent days of the protests, a protester in Tsuen Wan in the New Territories was hit in the chest by a live round fired by police and taken to hospital. This marked an escalation in the response of the police, and in the Admiralty area close to government buildings the crowds fell silent as the news spread. The 18-year-old demonstrator was seriously injured and suffered a collapsed lung, but narrowly escaped becoming the first martyr of the 2019 protests.[45]

Carrie Lam's invocation of colonial-era emergency powers under the Emergency Regulations Ordinance to ban the sale and wearing of masks only inflamed feelings among the protesters and the weekend of 4–5 October saw increased vandalism, much of it directed towards institutions such as the Bank of China that were identifiable as mainland interests. Another protester was hit by a police bullet, this time a 14-year-old boy shot in the leg who was subsequently arrested, and the whole MTR network was shut down. On Sunday 6 October, many MTR stations remained closed as 24 Legco members favouring reform attempted to use the High Court to overturn the ban on masks: their plea was rejected by Mr Justice Godfrey Lam Wan-Ho. In the face of a declaration that their demonstration was illegal, tens of thousands marched on Sunday afternoon, and the entrances to several MTR stations were severely damaged. Thirteen protesters were detained and charged during the Sunday demonstrations, but thousands continued to wear masks. Much of the MTR remained closed the following Monday morning, but 39 stations opened during the day; the entire network closed down at 6 o'clock in the evening to allow time for repairs. By Tuesday, the MTR system was in 'recovery mode', although several stations remained closed. The following day, normal services were operating on seven MTR lines, including the Airport Express, but there were restrictions on the remainder. Carrie Lam maintained that she had not ruled out the possibility of requesting assistance from mainland forces. Protests continued on a smaller scale during the weekend of 12–13 October with associated violence from flash mobs of militant groups targeting businesses linked to the mainland, but also administrative buildings and the offices of politicians deemed to be pro-Beijing: ten MTR stations were also closed.[46]

The Hong Kong Chief Executive's annual speech to Legco, presenting the administration's policy review, was scheduled for Wednesday 16 October in the chamber of the legislature. Carrie Lam began as planned, but was heckled by opposition members of Legco chanting 'five demands, not one less', the main slogan of the protesters. She had to abandon the live speech, and it was transmitted by video link from a corridor in the Legco building. In the speech, and at a press conference that followed, she agreed to address economic issues highlighted during the demonstrations, particularly the housing problem. This failed to satisfy pro-democracy legislators and their supporters; heckling resumed in the legislature chamber the following day, and some pro-democracy Legco members were removed by security staff.[47]

South China Morning Post on 19 October reported 'a rare Saturday afternoon without any violent protests' as a peaceful prayer rally calling for 'international humanitarian aid' went ahead in Edinburgh Place, close to the PLA barracks. A Sunday march had been banned, but was awaited with some trepidation. Violence broke out again and petrol bombs were thrown at Tsim Sha Tsui police station and MTR stations, eight of which were closed. Police responded with tear gas and water cannon, one of which was deployed for no apparent reason against the entrance of the Kowloon Mosque and Islamic Centre on Nathan Road, spraying the building with water dyed blue. Carrie Lam and Commissioner of Police Stephen Lo visited the mosque the following day; their apology, for what they described as a mistake, was accepted by the mosque leadership.[48]

Reports began to circulate that Beijing planned to replace Carrie Lam as Chief Executive of Hong Kong as soon as the situation on the streets stabilised. Beijing immediately contradicted these reports, claiming that Western sources had 'ulterior motives'. With the release from prison on Wednesday 23 October of Chan Tong-kai, who was serving a sentence for money laundering but had admitted killing his pregnant girlfriend in Taiwan, and whose case prompted Carrie Lam's extradition bill, hopes were raised that tensions in Hong Kong might be eased. The bill was formally withdrawn from the legislative process the same day. Chan expressed his willingness to surrender to the Taiwan authorities, but the Hong Kong government rejected conditions stipulated by Taipei, particularly a request that Taiwan police be authorised to travel to Hong Kong to escort Chan back to the island. As an SAR of the PRC, Hong Kong is not permitted to recognise the authority of government or legal bodies in Taiwan.[49]

As marches and violence continued for the 21st consecutive weekend, one of the most prominent figures of the protest movement, Joshua Wong, chair of the Demosisto group that advocates self-determination for Hong Kong, was barred from standing in district council elections. The returning officer determined that his support for an independent Hong Kong, which he denied, disqualified him from standing; pro-Beijing sources accused him of being in the pay of the United States.[50]

On the Saturday of the 22nd weekend, demonstrators attacked and started a fire in the lobby of the Asia Pacific Regional Bureau offices of the official Chinese news agency, Xinhua, in Wanchai; the agency, which condemned the vandalism as 'barbaric', had been the unofficial link between Hong Kong and the government of the PRC before the 1997 handover. This followed indications from the meeting of the Fourth Plenary Session of the 19th Central Committee of the CCP in Beijing that serious consideration was being given to changing the procedure for appointing members of Hong Kong's administration, including the Chief Executive.

Carrie Lam announced changes in plans that had originally involved travel to Shanghai and Nanjing, but would now include Beijing. On Monday 4 November, while in Shanghai, she met President Xi Jinping, who was in the city for the opening of the China International Import Expo. Xi expressed his full confidence in and support for the embattled Hong Kong Chief Executive, although insisting on 'unswerving efforts to stop and punish violent activities in accordance with the law'. On the unscheduled Beijing visit, a statement from her office announced that:

> [On] the next day [Wednesday 6 October], she will be received by the Vice-Premier of the State Council, Mr Han Zheng, in the morning, and in the afternoon, she will attend the third plenary meeting of the Leading Group for the Development of the Guangdong-Hong Kong-Macao Greater Bay Area.

This was the first official meeting between Ms. Lam and Han Zheng, the central government leader responsible for Hong Kong affairs, since the disturbances began. The meeting, which was also attended by State Council officials with responsibility for Hong Kong affairs, took place on the morning of Wednesday 6 November. Following the lead of Xi Jinping, Han

Zheng did not raise the issue of foreign interference and spoke of 'disturbances' rather than 'riots'. In lengthy comments, he alluded to the problems faced by Hong Kong people, including the shortage of housing and land, and income disparity, but expressed concern that the violence had undermined progress towards economic development of the Greater Bay Area.[51]

On Saturday 9 November, a peaceful vigil was held in memory of Hong Kong University of Science and Technology student, Chow Tsz-lok, who died after falling from a multi-storey car park near a police dispersal site. The following day, sporadic violence by flash mobs on 'shopping tours' erupted across Hong Kong. The violence spilled over into Monday morning's rush hour and an unarmed demonstrator, who was shot with a live police round in Sai Wan Ho, was in intensive care but survived. Another man, believed to be sympathetic to the Beijing authorities, was doused with inflammable liquid and set on fire; he remained in hospital in critical condition. There was also a confrontation between protesters and police at the Chinese University of Hong Kong in Sha Tin, where all classes were suspended for at least three days. Police fired at least 1,000 tear gas rounds and deployed water cannon at the campus where a car was set on fire. Violence also erupted at City University, and HKU cancelled classes. Demonstrators described a new strategy of 'weekday violence' to involve more workers in the Central district in protests. In Causeway Bay, a shop was engulfed in flames, putting at risk the flats above.

On the morning of Wednesday 13 November, the city was described as 'paralysed' with public transport suspended and banks and universities closed: 80 students from the mainland were removed from the Chinese University for their own safety, and some Taiwanese students had also been persuaded to return home. District councillors were among those arrested as they met their student constituents, and there was renewed evidence of public disquiet at police behaviour. The MTR system reopened just before 3 o'clock in the afternoon, but Mong Kok station remained closed. The city was gridlocked; the Cross-Harbour Tunnel was blocked, and its tollbooths were set on fire.[52]

PLA troops from their East Kowloon barracks appeared on the streets to clear barricades and debris from the road between the barracks and Hong Kong Baptist University. They were dressed in T-shirts and shorts – some apparently military issue – rather than uniforms, but their presence was regarded as combination of community service and a warning that they could be deployed again in a policing function. There were reports that some troops in riot gear were monitoring the situation. As the weekend of 16–17 November drew to a close, the campus of Hong Kong Polytechnic University (PolyU) in the Hung Hom district of Kowloon became the main focus of activity, with hundreds of students effectively besieged by heavily armed police. Water cannon, a long-range acoustic device mounted on an armoured vehicle, rubber bullets, and live ammunition were all deployed in the most tense and chaotic confrontation since the conflict began. What were described as 'mass arrests' began around 10 o'clock on Sunday night: many of those trapped within police cordons feared arrest if they accepted police conditions for a peaceful evacuation of the campus. Police attempted to take control of the campus in the early hours of the morning, but retreated in the face of fires started by protesters. The management of PolyU issued an Emergency Message on 17 November, deploring the violence and vandalism and announcing the cancellation of all lectures and the suspension of all operations on the campus.

PolyU became the focus of all the discontent during 18–19 November as a student-led occupation turned into a siege. Police attempted to keep protesters inside the campus while many protesters tried to escape, some with help from supporters outside the university. By the morning of 20 November, most of the protesters had come out and been arrested, leaving a small group of between 20 and 50.[53]

District elections, 24 November 2019

District council elections went ahead as planned in spite of the protests and government warnings that they would be cancelled if violence persisted. Turnout was exceptionally high: by lunchtime, 1.5 million of the 4.1 million registered electors (out of a total population of 7.44 million) had already cast their votes, a higher figure than the final total of the 2015 elections. When polls closed, more than 2.7 million had voted, bringing the turnout to 71%. The outcome of the elections vastly exceeded the expectations or even the hopes of 'pro-democracy' supporters, who won 17 out of 18 districts and 347 out of 452 seats – a further 60 seats were independent, many sympathetic to the pro-democracy cause. Initial responses from Carrie Lam and her officials were cautious and unrevealing but newly elected councillors moved to try to extricate the final 20 or so protesters from the PolyU who remained in place the following Tuesday when the university organised 100 staff, led by an Executive Vice-President in 'safety teams' with medical and social work personnel, to bring them out before police entered the wrecked and besieged campus. After a four-hour search, they found no hard-core militants. Some had surrendered to the police or been arrested; others had escaped through the sewer system. The end of the siege came with the entry of police and firefighters into the campus at 8 o'clock on the morning of Thursday 28 November. Officers of the Explosive Ordnance Disposal Bureau searched for potentially hazardous materials, but the team also included trained negotiators, psychologists, and medical personnel, while the specialist riot squads remained outside the campus. The police cordon was formally lifted just before mid-day on Friday 29 November, concluding a search with fire brigade staff that had uncovered over 4,000 petrol bombs.

Much of Hong Kong was peaceful in the immediate run-up to the polls. The occupation of PolyU continued, although after the intervention of influential individuals and medical teams persuading demonstrators to come out, only a small hard-core group remained. Throughout the crisis, the international media had inevitably focused on the dramatic violence and vandalism on Hong Kong Island and in Kowloon, but residents and visitors reported that large areas of the territory remained completely untouched by the disorder, apart from graffiti. The main casualty for most people was the transport system; the closure of severely damaged MTR stations made it difficult for many to travel to work. MTR Corporation management and trade union representatives agreed that normal service would be resumed on Monday 2 December, provided that there was no further damage. Protests continued after the election, but on a smaller scale and more peacefully, although police deployed pepper spray against protesters on Pedder Street on Friday 29 November.[54]

A law signed by US President Donald Trump on 27 November, the Human Rights and Democracy Act, linked the preservation of Hong Kong's autonomy directly to trade agreements with the United States and provoked a ferocious response from Beijing, which threatened 'counter-measures'. Demonstrators held a 'Thanksgiving rally' on Friday 29 November to show their support for Trump.[55] Another rally, to express continued support for the pro-democracy movement, was organised at Chater Garden, a public park close to the Legco building in Central and a popular venue for political demonstrations or rallies, on Saturday 30 November by secondary school students and the 'silver-haired group' of the older generation; it was authorised by the police and remained peaceful. As a peaceful, authorised Sunday march to a point in Hum Hom, close to the PolyU, came to an end, a militant breakaway group vandalised shops and restaurants in the nearby Whampoa district. Police responded with pepper spray, tear gas, and rubber bullets to violent demonstrators and others who moved away from the authorised route.[56]

By mid-December 2019, after six months of protests, the division between supporters and opponents of the democracy protests showed no signs of dissolving. Lists appeared online of restaurants classified as 'yellow' for those known to support the protests and 'blue' for those believed to sympathise with the establishment or Beijing. An attempt to impeach Carrie Lam in Legco failed with a narrow majority in the geographical constituency and a vote against in the functional constituency, in spite of criticisms of the Chief Executive from 'pro-Beijing' Legco members. In the wake of the elections and the sense that government was taking no notice of the protesters, a mass demonstration from Victoria Park in Causeway Bay to Chater Park in Central was mounted on Sunday 8 December. The organisers, the Civil Human Rights Front, secured police approval and claimed a total of 800,000 participants. It was peaceful until darkness fell and a small group of militants staged a violent attack, by which time most demonstrators had returned home.[57]

One attempt to respond to protesters' demands for an independent enquiry into the behaviour of the police was the appointment of a panel of international experts to work with the existing watchdog, the IPCC, which was not respected by most protesters. On 11 December, the experts withdrew as they had not been able to agree on an acceptable process for the IPCC – which was not able to summon witnesses or force the police to hand over evidence – to carry out an investigation.[58]

Sporadic and scattered violence continued with the firebombing of the MTR station at Ngao Tao Kok in eastern Kowloon; escalators, ticket machines, and a Maxim's Cakes shop at the station were damaged. More strikes and protests were planned as the year came to an end, and Christmas Eve celebrations were marred by outbreaks of violence between black-clad protesters and police in Tsim Sha Tsui and Mong Kok. Further violence broke out in Mong Kok and Shatin on Christmas Day.[59]

Carrie Lam's annual 'duty visit' to Beijing took place on 16 December 2019. Xi Jinping commended her 'courage and commitment' in the face of the six months of protest. Li Keqiang's statement of support was more practical and more nuanced. Not only did he remind the Chief Executive that her task of resolving the violent protests was far from complete, he praised her approach and emphasised the need for the Hong Kong government to resolve fundamental social problems. The presence of Guo Shengkun, head of CCP Central Political and Legal Affairs Commission, at her meeting with Xi was seen as a reminder of Beijing's concern at the security implications for the PRC of unrest in Hong Kong.[60]

One of the notable features of the disturbances was the failure of the central government in Beijing to intervene directly. Many attributed this to the legacy of the Tian'anmen massacre of 4 June 1989; although the reasons were more complex, a major confrontation between a sizeable portion of the Hong Kong population and the PRC police or military was avoided. Beijing's influence was restrained, subtle, and discreet, but nonetheless formidable. On 19 November 2019, a new Commissioner of Police for Hong Kong, Chris Tang Ping-keung, was appointed by the State Council in Beijing, replacing Stephen Lo, who had been in charge for most of the troubles. Commissioner Tang visited Beijing at the beginning of December for meetings at the Ministry of Public Security to meet the Minister, State Councillor Zhao Kezhi, and Zhang Xiaoming, Director of the Hong Kong and Macao Affairs Office. According to *Global Times*, which praised Tang's purported 'tough guy' reputation in Hong Kong, 'Tang expressed his gratitude to the Ministry of Public Security for its strong support and help'. Most significantly, on the Saturday Tang met Guo Shengkun, a member of the CCP Politburo and head of the Central Committee's Commission for Political and Legal Affairs, the Party supreme authority on law and order. As dozens were arrested following violence on Christmas Eve, the chairman of the Junior Police Officers' Association, Lam Chi-wai, wrote to his members that non-violent protesters were as culpable as violent militants. On the same day, Lam expressed his appreciation for the support of the PRC central government and a group of secondary schoolchildren in the mainland city of Chengdu. Hong Kong police, estranged from much of the territory's public, increasingly identify with the mainland authorities.[61]

New Year, continuing protests

Sporadic violent incidents over the Christmas period were succeeded by a mass protest on New Year's Day. The event's organiser, the Civil Human Rights Front, claimed that over a million had taken part and initially it was authorised by the police. After objects were thrown, police responded with tear gas. When the organisers refused to call of the march, the police declared it illegal and conflict escalated in the Wan Chai area with Molotov cocktails thrown at the police, who responded with water cannons. The main targets of the militants were branches of HSB bank and the Sogo department store which, in spite of its Japanese name, is run by a Hong Kong–based company with branches in China. Over 400 people were arrested during the march, one of the largest totals in any one day, which brought the total for the whole protest period to over 6,000.[62]

Minor reshuffle: major refocus?

On 4 January 2020, it was announced by the State Council in Beijing that the head of the Liaison Office of the Central People's Government in Hong Kong, Wang Zhimin, was to be replaced by Luo Huining, the former Party secretary of the northern province of Shanxi. Luo has no connections with the Hong Kong political world, and had only visited the territory once previously. Although no official explanation was given for Wang Zhimin's removal, he had been criticised for misreading the seriousness of the situation in Hong Kong. According to *Global Times*, Luo's appointment was intended to signal the inauguration of a new era in Hong Kong, with an 'enhanced role' for the office which would involve a 'more active role in engaging with Hong Kong society in a more creative way instead of simply being a channel of communication'. Since its establishment in 1999 as the successor to the Hong Kong branch of the Xinhua news agency, its role has been principally communication and coordination with the Ministry of Foreign Affairs in Beijing and the PLA Hong Kong Garrison. Under its previous director, Wang Zhimin, the office was accused of having misjudged the situation in Hong Kong and become isolated from wider Hong Kong society with a very weak presence in the territory. The incoming director would emphasise sovereignty over local autonomy; that is, 'one country' over 'two systems'. He also signalled a 'changing relationship with the Hong Kong SAR government', being 'politically responsible for the government's decisions', and abandoning the principle of political neutrality which has guided the civil service since colonial times.[63]

In what may have been an indication of a new policy influenced by Beijing, on 12 January, the executive director of Human Rights Watch, Kenneth Roth, was barred from entering Hong Kong, which he had visited many times previously, and where he intended to present and in-depth report that would *inter alia* argue that the Chinese government was 'undermining the global system for enforcing human rights'.[64]

Speaking at a meeting of Hong Kong's Legislative Council for the first time since October 2019, Carrie Lam responded to a question by arguing that if the territory showed 'loyalty' to China, the degree of autonomy that the 'one country, two systems' allowed could be extended beyond the 50 year cutoff point of 2047 established in Article 5 of the Basic Law when Hong Kong was handed over to China in 1997. Whether this was a concession proposed by Beijing was not clear, but in response to demands from the floor, Carrie Lam refused to contemplate taking seriously accusations of police brutality. Pan-democratic protesters heckled during her speech, and some were ejected by security staff.[65]

Covid-19

The Wuhan Covid-19 coronavirus outbreak in January 2020 temporarily diverted attention from the democracy protests. The two issues merged in the minds of activists, who demanded that the border with the mainland be closed completely to prevent the spread of the virus. Rail and ferry services between the mainland and Hong Kong had already been suspended, but a complete closure was not recommended by the WHO. The demand for a complete closure was, however, backed by healthcare workers who were members of the Hospital Authority Employees Alliance, a trade union that emerged out of the 2019 protest movement, who registered for strike action if it were not closed. Over 3,000 'non-essential' staff took part in a strike on Monday 3 February, but thousands of front-line staff, including doctors and nurses, were due to strike on Tuesday 4 February if their demands were not met by 6 September. The response of the administration was to close land border crossing points at Lo Wu and Lok Ma Chao at midnight before 4 February. The Hong Kong Ferry Terminal remained closed, but the international airport, the new Hong Kong-Zhuhai-Macao Bridge, and the Shenzhen Bay joint checkpoint – through which some 60% of travellers enter or leave Hong Kong – remain open. Thousands of Hong Kong residents had left the territory to visit relatives on the mainland for the New Year; although they all had the legal right to return home, 2,100 were stranded in Hubei province.

As a further concession to the protesters, Carrie Lam announced that, with effect from Saturday 8 February, anyone entering Hong Kong from mainland China, including Hong Kong residents, would be placed in quarantine for 14 days. This measure would be enacted by employing special powers under the Prevention and Control of Disease Ordinance.[66]

Kindergartens and schools in Hong Kong were closed on 14 November 2019 as a result of safety concerns following the escalation of pro-democracy protests. Schools were due to reopen on 20 November, but there were delays for cleaning and repairs after the disturbances. In response to the Covid-19 outbreak, classes were again suspended after the Lunar New Year holiday, which ended on February 3, initially until 17 February. The Education Bureau extended this suspension for two weeks until March 16, but it was announced at the end of February that they would reopen on 20 April 2020 after the normal Easter break. Entrance examinations for universities were scheduled to go ahead as planned on 27 March.[67]

Beijing reasserts its authority

Throughout March and the beginning of April 2020, the coronavirus epidemic eclipsed all other considerations in Hong Kong as elsewhere, but in mid-April, Beijing began to reassert its authority. On 15 April, the head of the PRC's Hong Kong Liaison Office, Luo Huiming, called for the urgent passing of national security laws for Hong Kong to counter what he described as the threat posed to 'one country, two systems' by pro-democracy demonstrations. This followed criticism by the Liaison Office and the mainland Hong Kong and Macao Affairs Office of 'filibustering' by pro-democracy Legco members in arguments over control of the powerful Legco House Committee. These interventions raised the question of the authority of Beijing's organisations to intervene in Hong Kong politics under the terms of the Basic Law: confusing statements by Chief Executive Carrie Lam and the Hong Kong Government Information Services Department failed to resolve the controversy.[68]

Power, rather than authority, was demonstrated on 18 April when 15 pro-democracy activists and former members of Legco – described as 'riot leaders' by *Global Times* – were detained on suspicion of organising unlawful assembly. Those arrested included 81-year-old Martin Lee, a legislator and former barrister who had been one of the drafters of the Basic Law, and Jimmy Lai, the owner of *Apple Daily*, a Chinese-language newspaper critical of the PRC government. The arrests were designed to take advantage of the lockdown and undermine the authority of pro-democracy politicians ahead of Legco elections scheduled for later in the year. Three of the most senior judges in Hong Kong issued a statement on 14 April, warning that the independent judicial system of the territory was under attack. In a cabinet reshuffle reported on 21 April, Erik Tsang took over as Secretary for Constitutional and Mainland Affairs. Tsang, who had a good relationship with the authorities in Beijing and had attachments to security organisation in the Chinese capital, replaced Patrick Nip, who was obliged to apologise over confusion about the right of the PRC Liaison Office in Hong Kong and its Hong Kong and Macao Affairs Office to interfere in Hong Kong matters, contrary to Article 22 of the Basic Law.[69]

Article 22

No department of the Central People's Government and no province, autonomous region, or municipality directly under the Central Government may interfere in the affairs which the Hong Kong Special Administrative Region administers on its own in accordance with this Law.

If there is a need for departments of the Central Government, or for provinces, autonomous regions, or municipalities directly under the Central Government to set up offices in the Hong Kong Special Administrative Region, they must obtain the consent of the government of the Region and the approval of the Central People's Government.

All offices set up in the Hong Kong Special Administrative Region by departments of the Central Government, or by provinces, autonomous regions, or municipalities directly under the Central Government, and the personnel of these offices shall abide by the laws of the Region.

*For entry into the Hong Kong Special Administrative Region, people from other parts of China must apply for approval. Among them, the number of persons who enter the Region for the purpose of settlement shall be determined by the competent authorities of the Central People's Government after consulting the government of the Region.

The Hong Kong Special Administrative Region may establish an office in Beijing.[70]

National security legislation, April–May 2020

On 15 April, Luo Huining, who had been appointed to the Hong Kong Liaison Office the previous January, called for the urgent passing of national security laws by Hong Kong's Legco to combat radical violence, foreign interference and pro-independence forces in the region. Luo cited Article 23 of the Basic Law, which provides for legislation to 'prohibit any act of treason, secession, sedition, subversion against the Central People's Government, or theft of state secrets'. Attempts to pass legislation of this nature in 2003 were abandoned after mass demonstrations.[71]

On Friday 22 May, as the annual session of the NPC was about to get underway, the Chinese government announced without warning that a 'draft decision on establishing and improving the legal system and enforcement mechanisms for the Hong Kong Special Administrative Region (HKSAR) to safeguard national security was submitted to China's national legislature for deliberation on Friday'. Although Hong Kong Chief Executive Carrie Lam rapidly expressed her willingness to work with Beijing on this legislation, her demeanour when giving a statement to the press supported claims that even the Hong Kong delegation to the NPC had not been briefed about this announcement.[72]

The immediate reaction to this declaration that Beijing was going to bypass the Hong Kong legislature to enact such legislation was international condemnation, including a joint statement by 200 parliamentarians and other political leaders from 23 countries calling on the international community to protest China's decision. On 24 May 2020, protesters were met with tear gas and water cannon after setting up barricades on the main Gloucester Road in Causeway Bay; some 40 were arrested.[73]

Beijing's decision did not create a new law; it authorised the Standing Committee of the NPC to work on draft legislation, work which was probably already in progress and could be enacted in the summer of 2020. On 4 June 2020, as a prelude and in spite of the efforts of opposition members, some of whom were ejected from the chamber, Legco passed legislation making it an offence to jeer at, or otherwise insult 'The March of the Volunteers', the national anthem of the PRC, and officially of Hong Kong.[74]

At first, there was no sign of any weakening in the resistance to Beijing's pressure. On Friday 12 June, one year after the beginning of major violent clashes between protesters and police, crowds gathered illegally in Causeway Bay, Sha Tin, Mong Kok, Tai Po, Yuen Long, and Kwun Tong, many of them singing 'Glory to Hong Kong', the anthem of the protest movement and a rejoinder to Beijing's insistence on respect for 'The March of the Volunteers'.[75]

As the summer wore on, overshadowed by the Covid-19 crisis, the scale of protests lessened and the authorities took the opportunity to arrest individuals they identified as responsible for the demonstrations, including on 10 August Jimmy Chee-Ying Lai, the owner of the independent and popular Chinese-language newspaper *Apple Daily*, which had consistently supported the pro-democracy movement. Detainees were charged, some appeared in court, and others fled or tried to flee Hong Kong. Taiwan, which had invited dissidents, was a favoured destination, but some were apprehended en route by Chinese coast guards. Jimmy Lai was accused of having threatened a reporter from the rival *Oriental Daily*; he was cleared on 3 September, but continued to face charges in connection with the demonstrations.

On 31 July, Carrie Lam announced that the September Legislative Council elections, in which the opposition had realistic hopes of success, were to be postponed because of the Covid-19 virus. When the Hong Kong government announced the introduction of mass testing for the virus in August 2020, there were fears that the results might be misused by PRC authorities. The protests had (at least temporarily) halted – but not opposition by many people to the imposition of control by Beijing. On Sunday 6 September, the day on which cancelled legislature elections should have been held, there were new mass protests against the cancellation and the security legislation. At least 289 people were arrested, including a 12-year-old girl out buying art materials who was thrown to the ground by several police officers because she had been running in 'a suspicious manner'.[76]

Notes

1 Steve Tsang *Hong Kong: An Appointment with China* London: I.B. Tauris, 1997, pp. 51–3; Philip Snow *The Fall of Hong Kong: Britain China and the Japanese Occupation* Harvard: Yale University Press, 2003.
2 James L. Watson *Emigration and the Chinese Lineage: The Mans in Hong Kong and London* Berkeley: University of California Press, 1975.
3 Steve Tsang *Hong Kong: An Appointment with China* London: I.B. Tauris, 1997, pp. 83–94. Sir Murray became Lord MacLehose in 1982 on his retirement from the governorship.
4 Steve Tsang *Hong Kong: An Appointment with China* London: I.B. Tauris, 1997, p. 119.
5 The official history of the Legislative Council and an account of its current operation can be found on its website www.legco.gov.hk.
6 'Hong Kong: The Facts–Government Structure' www.gov.hk March 2019; BBC News 29 December 2007.
7 *SCMP* 23 May, 29, 30 September 2013.
8 Chaohua Wang 'Hong Kong v. Beijing' *London Review of Books* 13 August 2019, pp. 11–12.
9 BBC News 4 September 2019.
10 Radio Free Asia 26 June 2019.
11 *SCMP* 13 June 2019.
12 *SCMP* 9, 12, 14 June 2019, *Guardian* 7/12, June 2019. The full text of the bill can be found at: www.legco.gov.hk/yr18-19/english/bills/b201903291.pdf.
13 *SCMP* 15 June 2019.
14 *SCMP* 15, 16 June 2019; *Guardian* 15 June 2019; Carrie Lam announcement, *Al Jazeera TV Live*, 15 June 2019.
15 *Al Jazeera TV Live*, 16 June 2019; *SCMP* 16 June 2019.
16 *Global Times* 16 June 2019; *China Daily* 16 June 2019.
17 *SCMP* 17, 18, 19, 20, 21 June 2019; *Guardian* 22, 23 June 2019; BBC News 23 June 2019; 'Harry's View' *SCMP* 30 June 2019.
18 *SCMP* 25, 27 June 2019; *Guardian* 25, 26 June 2019; *FT* 26 June 2019.
19 *SCMP* 1, 3 July 2019.
20 *Guardian* 3 July 2019; BBC News 3, 9 July 2019; *SCMP* 9 July 2019.
21 *SCMP* 13, 15, 18 July 2019.
22 *FT* 15, 17 July 2019; *SCMP* 18 July 2019.
23 *SCMP* 20, 21, 27 July 2019; *Guardian* 22 July 2019.
24 *FT* 15 August 2019.
25 *SCMP* 10 July 2019.
26 *Guardian* 15 August 2019.
27 *SCMP* 18 August 2019.
28 *SCMP* 18 August 2019; *Guardian* 18 August 2019.
29 *SCMP* 20, 21 August 2019; *Guardian* 20 August 2019.
30 *SCMP* 23 August 2019.
31 *Guardian* 25 August 2019; *SCMP* 26 August 2019.
32 *SCMP* 27 August 2017.
33 *SCMP* 30, 31 August, 1 September 2019; *Guardian* 30 August, 1 September 2019; BBC Television News 31 August 2019.
34 *SCMP* 1 September 2019.
35 *SCMP* 2 September 2019; *Guardian* 2, 3 September 2019.
36 *SCMP* 3 September 2019.
37 *SCMP* 28 August, 4 September 2019.
38 *SCMP* 3, 8 September 2019; *Guardian* 3 September 2019
39 *SCMP* 4, September 2019.
40 *SCMP* 7, 8 September 2019; *Guardian* 7 September 2019.
41 *SCMP* 8, 9, 10 September 2019.
42 *SCMP* 27 September 2019; *Guardian* 27 September 2019.
43 *Guardian* 28 September 2019; *SCMP* 29 September 2019.
44 *SCMP* 30 September 2019; *Guardian* 30 September 2019.
45 *SCMP* 1, 2 October 2019.
46 *SCMP* 5, 6, 7, 8, 9, 13 October 2019.

47 *Guardian* 16, 17 October 2019; *SCMP* 16, 17 October 2019.
48 *SCMP* 19, 20, 21 October 2019.
49 *SCMP* 23, 26 October 2019; *FT* 23 October 2019.
50 *SCMP* 30 October 2019.
51 *Guardian* 2, 3 November 2019; Xinhua 2 November 2019; *SCMP* 3, 5, 6 November 2019.
52 *Guardian* 2, 3, 11, 13 November 2019; Xinhua 2 November 2019; *SCMP* 3, 5, 6, 10, 11, 12, 13 November 2019; *FT* 6 November 2019.
53 *SCMP* 17, 18 November 2019; *Guardian* 17, 18 November 2019; BBC News 18 November 2019.
54 *SCMP* 23, 24, 25, 26, 27, 28, 29 November 2019; *Guardian* 23, 24 November 2019; BBC News 23, 24 November 2019, personal communication from Hong Kong residents and visitors familiar with the territory.
55 *Guardian* 28, 29 November 2019.
56 *SCMP* 30 November, 1 December 2019.
57 *SCMP* 4, 5, 8 December 2019; Radio Free Asia 4 December 2019.
58 *Guardian* 11 December 2019; *SCMP* 11 December 2019.
59 *SCMP* 12, 25 December 2019.
60 *SCMP* 15, 17 December 2019.
61 *Global Times* 19 November 2019, 5, 6, 9 December 2019; *Guardian* 26 December 2019; *SCMP* 28 December 2019.
62 *Guardian* 1 January 2020
63 *SCMP* 4 January 2020; *Guardian* 4 January 2020; *Global Times* 4, 6 January 2020; *China Daily* 4 January 2020.
64 *SCMP* 12 January 2020.
65 *Guardian* 16 January 2020; *SCMP* 16 January 2020.
66 *SCMP* 1, 2, 3, 4, 6 February 2020; BBC News 3 February 2020.
67 BBC News 13 November 2019; *The Standard* (Hong Kong) 20 November 2019; *SCMP* 25 February 2020.
68 *Guardian* 15 April 2020; *SCMP* 19 April 2020.
69 BBC News 18 April 2020; *Global Times* 18 April 2020; *FT* 20 April 2020; *SCMP* 19, 20, 21 April 2020.
70 www.basiclaw.gov.hk/pda/en/basiclawtext/chapter_2.html.
71 *Guardian* 15 April 2020.
72 Xinhua 22 May 2020; *Al Jazeera News* 24 May 2020.
73 *SCMP* 24 May 2020.
74 *SCMP* 4 June 2020.
75 Zen Soo 'Hong Kong Protest Marks Anniversary of Violent Police Clash' *The Diplomat* 13 June 2020.
76 BBC News 31 July, 10 August 2020; *SCMP* 2, 3, 9 September 2020; *Guardian* 10 August, 7 September 2020.

25 Taiwan

The relationship between Taiwan and the PRC remains an enigma to outsiders. The existence of two separate Chinese states, neither of which recognises the other, is one of the more bizarre political hangovers from the Cold War. The situation makes no sense without some understanding of the historical process by which this situation arose in the 1940s and 1950s.

The government of the Republic of China on Taiwan chose to regard itself as Free China throughout the Cold War period, in spite of the fact that it was a one-party state (as was the PRC), that it ruled Taiwan under martial law for 38 years, and that it was largely a regime staffed by supporters of the Nationalist Kuomintang (Guomindang, but the older spelling and the abbreviation KMT is preferred in Taiwan), imported from the mainland, who governed the indigenous Taiwanese and aboriginal populations often against their will.

Economy of post-war Taiwan

From 1945, the economy of Taiwan grew at an unprecedented rate. Supporters of the Free China concept choose to attribute this either to the superiority of the Kuomintang's policies over their Communist rivals on the mainland or to the greater capacity of the island's population for hard work and creativity. However, the economic development and prosperity of Taiwan in the 1950s could not have been achieved without the generous financial support of successive US administrations, initially by means of aid packages as part of the US economic support for its Cold War allies and, when these were withdrawn in 1965, as a financial arrangement that acknowledged Taiwan's role in the provision of supplies for the US forces during the Vietnam War.

The government in Taipei implemented a programme of land reform at the same time that the CCP was carrying out its own policies of confiscation and redistribution of agricultural land on the mainland. For the Kuomintang, this programme of rural reconstruction was not a socialist policy as such, but a practical realisation of Sun Yat-sen's policies of 'land to the tiller'. It was a three stage programme which began with an overall reduction in the rent paid by tenant farmers, continued with the sale to farmers of publicly owned land that had originally been retained by the Japanese colonial administration to encourage immigration from Japan, and was completed with a compulsory purchase programme under which the government acquired land from large land holdings and resold it to farmers at cost plus interest. Agricultural productivity and the rural standard of living increased as a result of these policies.

Taiwan's industrialisation was even more successful than its agricultural transformation. A period of post-war reconstruction was followed by a four-year economic plan which provided investment for small and medium-sized enterprises. By 1956, the number of factories and factory workers and their per-capita income had risen dramatically. During the 1960s, Taiwan gradually moved towards a policy of encouraging the production of consumer durables for the export trade and established itself as a major participant in international export markets.[1]

Taiwanese and mainlanders

Since 1949, Taiwan (or Formosa, as it continued to be known in the West for many years, retaining the name of Ilha Formosa – 'beautiful island' – that had been given to the island by Portuguese traders) has been presented in contrasting political guises. To many Westerners, and to the government of Chiang Kai-shek during what it believed was its temporary exile on the island, it was Free China. The government, and its allies overseas, continued to regard Chiang's administration as the legitimate government of the whole of China and assumed that it would one day resume its rightful position and govern the mainland once more from its capital in Nanjing. To the newly established government of the PRC in Beijing, Taiwan was a bastion of the defeated Nationalist Kuomintang where they had been able to find short-term refuge. Beijing believed that in due course, the Nationalist rebels would be crushed, the island would return to being a province of China, and it would submit to the authority of the CCP's government.

The Cold War in Asia, exacerbated by the Korean War, ensured that these two positions became firmly entrenched. For the people who lived in Taiwan, it was never as simple as these arguments suggest. The group of military officers and civilian administrators who had crossed to the island, both in advance of and accompanying the retreating National-ist government during the Civil War of the late 1940s, gradually established themselves, not as members of a transitory administration but as a new ruling elite for the island. They displaced the colonial administration that had been controlled by Japan and replaced it with a Chinese government, but this Chinese government was not a government of Taiwanese but a government of mainlanders who spoke Mandarin and brought with them the cultural attitudes and political networks of the mainland.

The indigenous Taiwanese, the descendants of a much earlier generation of migrants from Fujian, who spoke the language of that southeastern province of China in a modified Taiwan-ese form, were effectively excluded from power. Their language is often called Taiwanese, but that name is unhelpful as it suggests that it is only spoken on the island. Linguistics spe-cialists know it as Minnan, which is also spoken in the southern part of Fujian province on the mainland. *Min* is the traditional single-character name for Fujian, and *nan* means south.

The ethnic and political conflict between these two groups has affected every aspect of the development of Taiwan's history from the 1940s until the present day, but for most of that time, it is a conflict that has been obscured and was rarely referred to and little understood by outsiders. If the confrontation with the CCP was the Kuomintang's major overseas challenge in the years after the Second World War, its confrontation with the movement for Taiwanese self-government was its greatest domestic challenge.

Taiwan gradually evolved into a one-party state, a mirror image of its Communist adver-sary on the mainland: the Kuomintang was the only political party legally permitted to exist until 1986 and martial law, which had been imposed in 1947, remained in force until 1987.

Movement for democracy in Taiwan

The beginnings of a movement for a democratic Taiwan can be traced to the periodical *Free China* [*Ziyou Zhongguo*]. In its inaugural edition in November 1949, the prominent liberal intellectual, Hu Shi, set out the journal's twin objectives of supporting the idea of a free and independent China based on Taiwan and opposition to Communism. Initially, the outlook of *Free China* chimed with the views of the Kuomintang, which was on the point of taking power on the island. However, when the Korean War broke out and Taiwan began to receive aid from the United States which strengthened its political position, the Kuomintang no longer felt able to tolerate the discordant voices of the liberal intelligentsia, began a rectification campaign, and arrested dissidents. *Free China* responded by attacking the economic and social policies of the Kuomintang administration in articles and editorials, including a special edition criticising Chiang Kai-shek on the occasion of his 70th birthday. It grew more and more unsympathetic to the government, and in 1960 opposed a proposal that Chiang Kai-shek should be appointed to a third term in office. The Constitution of the Republic of China specified that a President should be elected for a term of six years and that this could be extended for a second term, but not for a third. The National Assembly voted to suspend this constitutional requirement in February 1960 in the light of the tension between Taiwan and the mainland, and on 21 March, Chiang was elected for a third term in office as President. He subsequently served a fourth and a fifth term. *Free China* also called on the government to abandon the idea of a counter-attack on the mainland and proposed the establishment of a separate Democratic Republic of Chinese Taiwan to oppose the PRC. A group associated with *Free China* formed a political party, the China Democratic Party, to contest elections, but on the eve of the party's launch in September 1960, the leaders were arrested by troops of the Taiwan garrison headquarters on suspicion of involvement in an armed rebellion and the party was strangled at birth. *Free China* was outlawed and ceased publication that year.

The repression was so severe that an open and organised opposition did not reappear until the 1970s, by which time Taiwanese society was undergoing great changes as a result of the industrialisation of the island and the emergence of a new middle class. In the early 1970s, the periodical *University Review* [*Daxue zazhi*] took on the role of the government's main critic, although it did not actively engage in politics. It was joined by *Taiwan Political Commentary* [*Taiwan zhenglun*] in 1975.

The Extra-Party [*Dangwai*] Movement which developed in the 1970s became the major focus for dissidents. The term *Dangwai* [literally, outside the Party[had originally meant anyone who was not a member of the Kuomintang; it became used more widely for members of the opposition movement who did not necessarily belong to any political grouping. This group was coalescing into an influential movement. When issue No. 5 of *Taiwan Political Commentary* was banned in 1977, a number of opposition activists who were associated with it stood in elections. Some were elected, and the movement benefited from a higher profile and a more organised presence throughout the island.

Taiwanese politics after Chiang Kai-shek

Chiang Kai-shek died in 1975, having been effectively President of Taiwan for life, although he had never been acknowledged as such. On 6 April, he was succeeded by C.K. Yen (Yen Chia-kang) who had been his Vice-President, this succession being in accordance with the provisions of the Constitution. However, this was a presidential appointment in name only. Chiang Ching-kuo, Chiang Kai-shek's son, became Chairman of the Kuomintang in 1975, and it was he who exercised real power. In 1978, Chiang Ching-kuo formally succeeded Yen as President; he was elected to serve for a second term as President in 1984. His Vice-President in this second term was Lee Teng-hui, who was not a member of the mainlander elite but a Taiwan-born politician who had been Mayor of Taipei and Governor of Taiwan, and who had been educated at Cornell University in the United States, where he had completed a PhD in agricultural economics. Lee Teng-hui was the most significant of the group of native-born Taiwanese protégés of Chiang Ching-kuo, who had been strongly in favour of advancing the political careers of non-mainlanders who showed promise.

Now that there was no longer the powerful guiding or restraining hand of Chiang Kai-shek, divisions began to emerge within the Kuomintang between factions that can be characterised broadly as the old guard and the modernisers, although like all factional descriptions, these are oversimplified. The Kuomintang had been transformed from a revolutionary party with a strong link to the military into a mainstream political organisation concerned with policy and with the minutiae of the day-to-day running of an administration. As it became a more bureaucratic organisation, the requirement for unquestioning loyalty declined and the existence of a range of political views became more acceptable.

'Formosa' or Kaohsiung incident

In August 1979, a group of political dissidents who were opposed to the Kuomintang's monopoly of power, many of them lawyers and others who had been part of the *Dangwai* movement, launched a new journal. Its Chinese name was *Meili dao*, a literal translation of the Portuguese name Ilha Formosa (Beautiful Island) by which Taiwan had known until the mid-twentieth century and it is generally known in English as *Formosa*. During the autumn of 1979, it established 15 branch offices throughout Taiwan, offices that were effectively the branches of an embryonic political party, albeit a party without a name [*meiyou dangming de dang*] or an openly acknowledged existence: political parties other than the Kuomintang remained illegal under the martial law regime.

The magazine was harried by supporters of the Kuomintang, the police, and military intelligence, and this campaign of harassment culminated in simultaneous attacks on the home of the publisher in Taipei and the offices of the magazine in the cities of Kaohsiung and Pingtung on 29 November 1979.

On 10 December, opposition politicians organised a demonstration in Kaohsiung, a major industrial city, port, and naval base in southwestern Taiwan, in association with *Formosa* magazine to mark International Human Rights Day. What had begun as a peaceful demonstration turned into a serious disturbance after the intervention of police and undercover agents of the security services, and a number of the organisers were arrested. Among those arrested were Annette Lu, who was later to become Vice-President of the Republic of China and other opposition activists who were later to occupy senior positions in the Democratic Progressive Party (DPP).

Reforms of 1986

In March 1986, a commission that had been appointed by President Chiang Ching-kuo and consisting of 12 members of the Central Committee of the Kuomintang was convened to make recommendations on six major reform proposals. These were the repeal of the Emergency Decree on Martial Law, which by 1986 had been in force for 38 years; the legalisation of new political parties, some of which had already been operating illegally for years; the reinforcement of local sovereignty; the creation of a parliamentary system; the internal reform of the Kuomintang; and an onslaught on crime and corruption.

On 28 September 1986, six organisations applied to be registered formally as political parties. The biggest of these, the DPP, went on to capture 11 seats in the National Assembly and 12 seats in the Legislative Yuan in the elections that were held in December 1986. This election victory was a turning point in the political history of Taiwan; for the first time, it introduced to the legislature politicians who were openly in favour of a genuinely independent Taiwan with no claim to rule the mainland.

Martial law was finally lifted on 15 July 1987, and in November of the same year, residents of Taiwan were permitted to visit relatives across the Taiwan Straits in the PRC for the first time since 1949.

Lee Teng-hui era

Chiang Ching-kuo had been in poor health for some time and died on 13 January 1988. His protégé, Lee Teng-hui, was sworn in as President and, at the Thirteenth Congress of the Kuomintang in July 1988, he was also confirmed as Party Chairman, a notable achievement for a native Taiwanese. At the same meeting, many Taiwan-born politicians were elected to key posts in the new leadership. Of the 31 members of the Standing Committee of the Party, 16 were Taiwanese in origin, and Lee Teng-hui's first cabinet brought eight Taiwanese politicians into government.

The Thirteenth Congress had also agreed on a number of measures to improve relations with the mainland and to enable personal, family, cultural, and business exchanges between Taiwan and the PRC. The only proviso was that none of these exchanges should in any way suggest any recognition of the PRC or endanger Taiwan's security. There was no question that transactions between the two sides of the Taiwan Strait could be carried out on the basis of equal relations between two independent states. The government in Taipei, in common with the government in Beijing, remained formally committed to the idea of a reunified China at some point in the future and was not prepared to compromise on this fundamental principle.

However, in July 1999, President Lee Teng-hui issued a statement in which he argued that future contacts between China and Taiwan should be on the basis of 'special state-to-state relations'. This was much closer to asserting Taiwan's formal independence and was viewed by many commentators as dangerous brinkmanship which was bound to provoke the wrath of the government in Beijing. Lee was becoming detached from mainstream Kuomintang politics and was already planning his retirement at this time. Both of these factors were used to limit the damage that his remarks were believed to have caused and to reduce cross-straits tension which had escalated as a result of his statement. He was subsequently expelled from the Kuomintang in September 2001 when he broke Party discipline by publicly endorsing election candidates from another political party, the Taiwan Solidarity Union (TSU). This new party had been formed in August 2001 by defectors from the Guomindang, many of whom were personal supporters of Lee Teng-hui. The TSU was the first political party to use the name Taiwan in its official title, a deliberate move to emphasise its pro-independence credentials at a time when the DPP was being criticised by many supporters of complete independence for being too willing to reach an agreement with Beijing. Lee Teng-hui died in the Taipei Veteran's Hospital on 30 July 2020 at the age of 97. A memorial was established at the Taipei Guest House for the public to pay their last respects to the man credited with bringing parliamentary democracy to Taiwan.[2]

Chen Shui-bian's presidency

Chen Shui-bian, the leader of the DPP, was elected President in March 2000 in a historic election that ended 50 years of unbroken rule by the Kuomintang. Chen Shui-bian was born

into a poor farming family in the south of Taiwan, the heartland of the independence movement. He practised law and was drawn into pro-independence politics when he represented
several of the defendants in the *Formosa* incident in 1979. He became active in the *Dangwai*
opposition movement and served on the Taipei City council, where he became Mayor in
1994. His style is populist, and he is often referred to by the familiar soubriquet of 'A-bian' –
which can be either affectionate or slightly disdainful, depending on the context.

Although he had been a vociferous supporter of the idea of an independent Taiwan, he
moderated his calls for immediate formal independence in order not to provoke a military
response from Beijing. The DPP was one of the new parties that first registered in 1986
and it has been by far the most successful of the pro-independence groups. President Chen
defeated the Kuomintang candidate Lien Chan, a protégé of former President Lee Teng-hui,
and an independent contender, James Soong, but his government still did not have a majority
after this election. In the December 2001 parliamentary elections, the Kuomintang lost its
parliamentary majority for first time since 1949. The DPP secured 87 seats in the legislature,
the GMD had 68 members, and other parties had 70 between them.

China–Taiwan relations and the 1992 consensus

On 24 January 2001, Vice-Premier Qian Qichen of the PRC, who had been a widely respected
Foreign Minister, called on the Taiwan authorities to accept the 1992 consensus on the principle of One China.

This consensus was the result of a meeting between the two organisations established in
China and Taiwan to manage cross-straits relations. The Association for Relations across
the Taiwan Straits ARATS (PRC) and the Straits Exchanges Foundation SEF (Taiwan) met
in Hong Kong in 1992. The consensus, which was that both sides should abide by the One
China principle, may not have been a consensus at all, as the Taiwan side rejected it, but
since the rejection came after the election of the pro-independence DPP, the status of this
consensus is disputed.[3]

Political relations between China and Taiwan remain strained, but economic relations
have developed in a way that belies the degree of cross-straits tension that appears to exist.
Taiwanese firms have invested heavily in the mainland economy, and in 2002, there were
at least 50,000 businesses based in the island operating in the PRC.[4] In Shanghai, there is a
resident Taiwanese community that is at least 300,000 strong and runs its own schools and
a newspaper. At the same time, however, direct trade, transport, and communications are
banned, although there have been moves to relax these restrictions. The economies of China
on both sides of the Taiwan Strait are linked closely together, but closer economic integration is hampered by the lack of a political accommodation.

The role of the opposition Kuomintang – it continues to use the older romanisation –
has changed significantly since it went into opposition. In spite of the historical antipathy
between it and the CCP, the KMT was prepared to enter into discussions with Beijing and
continued to insist on a policy of reunification in the long term in the face of the growing
wave of sentiment in favour of independence. However, at a KMT Congress that was held
in the city of Taoyuan in June 2007, major changes were made to the Constitution of the
Party, enabling it to concentrate on the island of Taiwan and the 'people's welfare' (the old
reformist term used by Sun Yat-sen) rather than having reunification as its main objective.
The party leader, Ma Ying-jeou, the KMT's candidate in the presidential elections of 2008,
indicated that he would be willing to conclude a peace agreement with the PRC. These
moves reflect the party's willingness to bow to the contemporary political reality of Taiwan's

de facto independence rather than the historical commitment to One China which has both united and divided the KMT and the CCP since the 1920s.[5]

The tacit acceptance of the status quo for all practical purposes does not mean that Taiwan has abandoned all prospects of retaining its former position in international organisations. There has been continuous low-level diplomatic pressure by Taipei and its supporters, particularly in the United States, ever since the PRC replaced it in the United Nations in 1971; however, Beijing has maintained the upper hand and has far more supporters in the UN than does Taipei. On 20 July 2007, an application for Taiwan's membership of the United Nations, signed by President Chen Shui-bian, was sent to the Secretary General, Ban Ki-moon. In contrast to previous attempts to rejoin either the full UN or its subsidiary organisations (for example, the UN Convention on the Elimination of All Forms of Discrimination against Women [CEDAW] in March 2007 and the WHO in April 2007), all of which had been submitted under the name of the Republic of China, this application was in the name of Taiwan. This did not placate the PRC, which immediately responded that it would resolutely oppose the application, as it considered it to be yet another attempt to split China that was destined to fail. Not surprisingly, this attempt to overturn the decision of the United Nations to recognise the PRC in its resolution of 1971 was firmly and swiftly rejected by the United Nations. In spite of this clear rejection, the Taiwan government was not prepared to abandon plans to organise a ballot calling for the island to be admitted to the United Nations. A referendum took place in conjunction with presidential and parliamentary elections in March 2008: although a majority of voting were in favour of Taiwan being admitted to the UN, the vote was invalidated by virtue of the low turnout.[6]

In July 2007, supporters of a formal declaration of independence for Taiwan celebrated the 20th anniversary of the end of martial law. The name of the Chiang Kai-shek Memorial Hall, established in 1980, was formally changed to the National Taiwan Democracy Memorial Hall earlier in the year, but campaigners were demanding that the bulky statue of Chiang Kai-shek which still dominates the complex be removed to signify both a complete break with the past and a rejection of the psychology of the martial law era.[7] Although the role of Chiang was significantly downplayed, the statue was still standing as of December 2020.[8]

Constitutional change and the elections of 2008

The National Assembly, Taiwan's parliament, was elected on the mainland in 1947 on the basis of nationwide constituencies and moved to Taiwan after the KMT's defeat in the Civil War. Members of the assembly continued to hold their seats representing constituencies on the mainland, although after 1949, there were naturally no elections. The perpetuation of this system, which claimed to represent the people of the mainland, was widely regarded as absurd, and in 1991, a reformed parliament, the second National Assembly, was elected on the basis of direct elections in Taiwan only. It was this second National Assembly that approved the constitutional amendments that made direct elections to the presidency and vice-presidency possible in 1996. The Assembly then withdrew from political decision making and gradually devolved its authority to the Legislative Yuan [*lifayuan*]. In 2005, the National Assembly voted to abolish itself. The Legislative Yuan thus became the only parliamentary body and is often referred to as the parliament [*guohui*], although it can be argued that, constitutionally, it is not a genuine independent parliament but the legislative branch of a presidential system.

The Legislative Yuan is a body that has also existed since 1947 and is one of the six Yuans that together make up the administration of the Republic of China in a system that had its origins in the political thinking of Sun Yat-sen.[9] The Legislative Yuan is, as its name suggests, the main body for creating legislation, but until 2005 it was overshadowed by the National Assembly; the Executive Yuan is the Cabinet and the President serves as the head of that body; the Control Yuan is a monitoring body with particular responsibility for investigating allegations of corruption; the Judicial Yuan administers the courts and the justice system; and the Examination Yuan is responsible for the recruitment to the civil service through competitive examinations.

Politics in Taiwan in the early years of the twenty-first century is complicated and confusing, not surprisingly for a political system in transition. The main political parties have been the DPP, which is openly in favour of an independent Taiwan, and the Kuomintang, which has an interesting position in that it is in favour of One China (Taiwan and the mainland under one rule) while maintaining its absolute opposition to the CCP. However, because of its adherence to the idea of One China, it has been able to negotiate with Beijing more easily than has the overtly pro-independence DPP. There have been rifts and alliances, smaller parties have also played a role, and it has become common to discuss Taiwanese politics in terms of a Pan-Blue coalition around the KMT and a Pan-Green coalition based on the DPP. To a large extent, differences over policies have been overshadowed by allegations of corruption against leading members of both political camps, which have often led to lengthy court cases.

In the elections to the Legislative Yuan that took place in January 2008, the voters overwhelmingly elected representatives of the Kuomintang which had been in opposition since 2000. The KMT secured 81 out of a total of 113 seats in the parliament; the DPP, the party of the incumbent President Chen Shui-bian, was only able to take 27 seats, with the remaining seats going to minority parties. Chen Shui-bian responded to this defeat by resigning as leader of the DPP, although he remained President. In the immediate aftermath of this landslide victory, the presidential elections of 22 March 2008 were won by the leader of the KMT, Ma Ying-jeou.

Ma Ying-jeou administration

The return to power of the Kuomintang resulted in significantly improved relations between Beijing and Taipei. High-level visits by the leaders of the CCP and KMT led to announcements that restrictions on cross-straits air travel and currency exchange regulations would be relaxed. The first of a series of regular direct passenger air services across the Taiwan Straits took place on 4 July 2008, with a flight from Guangzhou to Taipei. In spite of concerns about Ma's conciliatory policies towards Beijing, and his handling of Typhoon Morakot in 2009, he was re-elected President in 2012, beating the DPP candidate Tsai Ing-wen with 51.6% of the vote to her 45.63%.

Ma's meeting with PRC President Xi Jinping, in Singapore on 7 November 2015, provoked anger from opposition politicians in Taiwan who considered it a betrayal. This insistence on a closer relationship with the PRC was the primary cause of a substantial decline in Ma's popularity. He lost support among those of the younger generation, who increasingly identified as Taiwanese rather than Chinese – as evidenced by the Sunflower Movement of 2014 when thousands demonstrated against closer economic ties with the mainland. Ma's trade policy was widely believed to have benefited large companies and widened the gap between rich and poor. Even within his own KMT, he lost influence, largely because of his inability to create a consensus as in the reform of pensions which disadvantaged his supporters in the military, the civil service, and education. Ma resigned as chairman of the KMT to take responsibility for the party's sizeable losses in the November 2014 local elections, and he was succeeded by Eric Chu, who was the unsuccessful KMT candidate in the 2016 presidential election.[10]

Tsai Ing-wen administration

Tsai Ing-wen became President of the Republic of China on 20 May 2016, representing the DPP and its partners in the Pan-Green coalition. She was the first woman to serve as President, and the first with both Hakka and Paiwan aboriginal antecedents. Her early career was in government posts with no political affiliation, and she served as a non-partisan Minister of the Mainland Affairs Council under Chen Shui-bian, not joining the DPP until 2004; she was Vice-Premier until the mass resignation of Chen's cabinet in 2007. She was elected leader of the DPP in 2008 and was defeated by Ma Ying-jeou in the 2012 presidential elections before achieving a landslide victory in the elections of 2016.

The United States and the Taiwan Strait

On April 28, 2019, the US Navy deployed two destroyers, the *USS William P. Lawrence* and the *USS Stethem*, on a voyage northward through the Taiwan Strait. In the words of Commander Clay Doss of the Seventh Fleet, this was to demonstrate 'the US commitment to a free and open Indo-Pacific'. The move was designed to assert the right of the US military to operate in the region, in the certain knowledge that it would provoke an angry response from Beijing.

China continued to maintain that as much as 80% of the waters of the South China Sea are legitimately its territorial waters, and these claims have been asserted with the support of the PLA Navy, but also an increasing number of coast guard and maritime militia vessels, both of which the US Navy has threatened to treat as if they were regular naval craft.[11]

The potential for the escalation of tensions in the Taiwan Strait or the wider South China Sea into armed conflict remained high.

> The China-Philippines Scarborough Shoal stand-off in 2012, the China-Vietnam oil-rig incident in 2014, China's island-building and militarisation operations, the Philippines' Permanent Court of Arbitration landmark victory in 2016 and the regular US-led freedom of navigation operations all highlight the inefficacy of the 2002 Declaration on Conduct (DOC) of Parties in the South China Sea and the complex interplay of economic, environmental, legal, political and strategic issues.[12]

Increasingly difficult relations with the United States prompted Beijing to reinforce links with its Southeast Asian neighbours, and China's strategy for managing these tensions in what could legitimately be termed its own back yard – by analogy with the Caribbean and Central and South America, which are often referred to as the back yard of the United States – was to draw up a Code of Conduct. A draft of this document, the 'Single Draft COC Negotiating Text', was agreed at a meeting between ASEAN foreign ministers in Singapore on Thursday 2 August 2018, following discussions with PRC officials the previous June in Changsha. China is not a member of ASEAN and does not have observer status; ASEAN is invited to attend the SCO which was established by China. The United States viewed China's Code of Conduct with scepticism: Randall Schriver, Assistant Secretary at the US Department of Defense, at a news conference in Kuala Lumpur on 26 April 2019, encouraged ASEAN states to insist on a code that was more clearly legally binding.[13]

Challenges to Tsai Ing-wen's presidency

Polls in the run-up to the 11 January 2020 presidential elections indicated that the incumbent, Tsai Ing-wen, was on course for a second term in office, but that in the concurrent parliamentary vote neither her DPP nor the opposition Kuomintang were likely to secure a majority because of the number of new parties that had emerged and the uncertain preferences of young Taiwanese voting for the first time.

The TVBS Taiwan commercial television channel published a poll on Tuesday 3 December which gave Tsai 46% of the vote, while her maverick and controversial KMT opponent, Han Kuo-yu, the Mayor of Kaohsiung who had benefited from an anti-DPP surge in the 2018 mayoral elections, had 31%. Tsai and Han took part in a television debate on 18 December with the third serious candidate, James Soong Chu-yu, whose centre-right People First [Qinmin] Party was formed in 2000, following his failed presidential bid as an independent. Many had written off Tsai after the humiliating defeat of DPP candidates in the local government elections of 24 November 2018, after which she resigned as party chair. The polls then put her at 30 percentage points behind the populist Han Kuo-yu, but by the end of 2019, the position had reversed dramatically: polls showed her at 20 points ahead on 31 December, the last day that polls could legally be published. Commentators attributed the rise in her fortune to the Hong Kong protests and a rejection of Xi Jinping's January 2019 proposal that talks should begin to discuss the application of the Hong Kong 'one country, two systems' model to Taiwan.[14]

Tsai's landslide victory with 8.17 million votes in the election of 11 January 2020 was attributed to her robust resistance to Beijing's persistent demands for Taiwan to be incorporated into the PRC on the basis of the 'one country, two systems' model that had been agreed for Hong Kong in the 1980s, and the rejection of closer control by Beijing by massed demonstrators in Hong Kong for the second half of 2019. In a provocative but carefully calculated interview with the BBC, President Tsai insisted that Taiwan had no need to declare independence since it was effectively an independent country as Republic of China, Taiwan and insisted that the people and government of Taiwan deserved respect from the PRC. While her insistence on Taiwan's *de facto* independence was bound to anger Beijing, this was balanced by her statement that there was no intention of declaring formal independence.[15]

In a speech to mark her swearing-in as President for her second four-year term, and as tensions intensified as a result of the Covid-19 epidemic and national security legislation in Hong Kong, Tsai invited Xi Jinping to stabilise relations across the Taiwan Strait. She once again rejected the application of 'one country, two systems' to Taiwan, but offered to resolve problems in the light of the island's Constitution and domestic legislation. She insisted that China must treat Taiwan as an equal, rather than a junior, partner. The immediate response from Beijing was that the Taipei administration's rejection of the 1992 consensus on treating both sides of the strait as part of One China – and which many argue was not a consensus at all – had 'unilaterally destroyed the political basis for peaceful development'.[16]

The Taiwan government and the DPP spoke out forcefully against Beijing's decision to impose national security legislation on Hong Kong, fully aware that a similar attempt could be made for Taiwan. The Kuomintang, which has sought closer ties with Beijing and accepts the 'One China' policy in principle, pointed out that 'the proposed legislation would hit a raw nerve with Hong Kongers'. They insisted that 'the Republic of China is an independent, sovereign nation and rejects the 'one country, two systems' framework, and called for Beijing to address the concerns of Hong Kong people constructively.[17] To add insult to injury, in June 2020, the defeated Kuomintang presidential candidate, Han Kuo-yu was also removed as Mayor of Kaohsiung when almost 940,000 citizens voted to have him recalled, the first recall of an elected official in Taiwan since democracy was introduced in 1986.[18]

Notes

1 This and subsequent selections rely on Chen Hongtu (ed.) *Taiwan shi* (*History of Taiwan*) Taibei: Sanmin, 2004; Huang Xiuzheng, Zhang Shengyuan, and Wu Wenxing *Taiwan shi* (*History of Taiwan*) Taibei: Wunan tushu, 2004; John F. Copper *Taiwan: Nation-State or Province?* Boulder, CO: Westview, 1996 and Simon Long *Taiwan: China's Last Frontier* Basingstoke: Palgrave Macmillan, 1991.
2 Central News Agency, Taipei, 31 July 2020.
3 Press release, Chinese Embassy in the UK, 25 January 2002.
4 *Economist* 3 January 2002.
5 *FT* 27 June 2007.
6 BBC News 20 July 2007; *FT* 21, 22 July 2007; BBC News 24 July 2007.
7 Personal communication from Taipei resident.
8 *Taipei Times* 16 July 2007.
9 The Chinese character *yuan* refers to a court or courtyard, a hall, a college, or other significant public buildings. It is not usually translated in the political context; administrative branches of government in Taiwan are normally known as the Five Yuan.
10 D.D. Wu 'Does Ma Ying-jeou Know Why He Is Unpopular in Taiwan?' *The Diplomat* 21 March 2017.
11 *SCMP* 28 April 2019.
12 *SCMP* 8 January 2019.
13 *SCMP* 2 August 2018; Radio Free Asia 26 April 2019.
14 *SCMP* 8 December 2019, 6 January 2020.
15 BBC News 14 January 2020; *SCMP* 15 January 2020; Shelley Rigger 'Taiwan's 2020 Election Analysis' *China Leadership Monitor* 63 (Spring 2020).
16 *FT* 21 May 2020.
17 *Taipei Times* 23 May 2020.
18 *Taiwan News* 6 June 2020; Nick Aspinwall 'Taiwan's "Han Wave" Comes Crashing Down' *The Diplomat* 10 June 2020.

Part 6

International relations

26 China and the world 1

Strategic relationships

International relations and the legacy of history

No country is more conscious of its history than China. The record of China's economic domination by the West and Japan from the middle of the nineteenth century to the middle of the twentieth is taught to all school children, and it is a central part of the discourse on China's national identity, whether at the formal or informal level. This was the period of China's 'national humiliation' [*guochi*]: an important source of the legitimacy of the CCP is its ability to demonstrate that it freed China from that humiliating state of being, as Mao Zedong would have put it, a 'semi-colony'. China was of course never completely colonised, and the degree of colonisation was much less that the process by which large parts of Africa, Latin America, South Asia, and Southeast Asia were brought under the economic and political control of European powers in the nineteenth century, but this has not made the resentment any less intense. Neither should the CCP take all the credit for liberating China from the influence of the West and from the Japanese occupation in the 1940s, but it does.

The 'unequal treaties', beginning with the Treaty of Nanjing, which was signed in 1842 at the end of the Opium War, were the initial focus of this resentment. Chinese thinkers of a patriotic or nationalist turn of mind insisted, not without justification, that the series of treaties concluded with Western powers from the end of that war onwards had been signed under duress: the repeal of these treaties became an important rallying cry for Nationalists. The unequal treaties were eventually repealed in 1943 under the wartime Guomindang administration, by which time they had become largely irrelevant in practical terms. The military occupation of their native soil by Japan was the main concern of most Chinese in that period. However, it was not until the return of Hong Kong to China in 1997 that many Chinese, and not solely those sympathetic to the CCP, could feel that the dishonour had been erased. These memories of subservience and humiliation have informed, and it can be argued that to some extent they have also hindered, China's development of a modern approach to foreign policy.

China was a member of the Communist bloc from 1949 until the collapse of the Soviet Union in 1991, but it was never a compliant member meekly following the political orders of Moscow. A Treaty of Friendship, Alliance and Mutual Assistance signed in Moscow on 14 February 1950 presented a picture of the PRC and Soviet Union united in a common purpose, but there were great strains from the outset. Mao Zedong's determination to be independent increased after the death of Stalin in 1953; he could then claim to be the senior world Communist leader, and by 1956, there was a considerable divergence between the approach of China and the USSR to domestic and international policy. These differences escalated when Mao launched the ill-fated Great Leap Forward in 1958 – and in 1960, the

USSR withdrew all technical assistance from China. The Sino-Soviet dispute became common knowledge in 1963, deteriorated even further during the Cultural Revolution, and was never resolved. By the time that Soviet power finally collapsed in 1991, China was demonstrably capable of acting independently.

The Chinese alternative to Moscow's policies of confrontation under Stalin and peaceful coexistence during Khrushchev's regime was 'revolutionary diplomacy', a concept that was attributed to Mao Zedong, as most major policy decisions were, but was probably at least as much the product of Lin Biao's military approach and strategic thinking. In broad terms, revolutionary diplomacy envisaged the encirclement of the capitalist nations (the cities of the world) by the developing peasant countries of the Third World, a strategy that mirrored the historical experience of Mao's CCP in rural China during the 1930s and 1940s. This is very revealing of the very limited awareness that the CCP had of international affairs at the time. The practical consequence of this view of the world was the cultivation by Beijing of national liberation and other radical movements in the Third World, often in opposition to similar bodies sponsored by Moscow. Most revolutionary diplomacy involved little more than rhetoric; the amount of useful support in terms of finance or weaponry that was given to revolutionary organisations outside China was limited.

Revolutionary diplomacy came to an end with the death in a mysterious aircraft accident of Lin Biao and members of his family in September 1971. Lin had been nominated as Mao Zedong's heir apparent in 1969, but Mao was afraid that Lin was trying to oust him, and it is possible that preparations were being made for an attempted coup d'état against Mao by Lin and members of his family. Lin had been adamantly opposed to any idea of a rapprochement with the United States; to Mao this was suddenly worthy of consideration because the Sino-Soviet dispute had escalated to the point that there were serious military clashes in the border areas of northeastern China.

Zhou Enlai, the most experienced and sophisticated international political actor in the CCP leadership, regained his formal power, protected the Foreign Ministry from the worst of the depredations of the Red Guards, and oversaw the return to more conventional diplomatic relations with other states in 1971 and 1972. The highlights of this normalisation, as it was called, and the dramatic indication that China was coming in from the cold were Beijing's accession in 1971 to the UN seat that had been occupied by the Guomindang-controlled Republic of China since 1945 and the visit by US President Richard M. Nixon to China in February 1972. Although Beijing's radical rhetoric continued for some years, this often served to obscure the Chinese government's real intention, which was to play a key role in international organisations and to replace Taiwan as the international voice of China.

Since the 'reform and opening' of the Deng Xiaoping administration in the late 1970s, China has steadily expanded its role in international organisations, especially in the United Nations and its subsidiary bodies. One of the most significant developments was the long drawn-out and eventually successful negotiations for membership of the WTO, which China was finally able to join in 2001. China's position in these organisations has evolved from that of an outsider, more concerned with rhetoric than reality, to a seasoned player with highly professional diplomats operating at all levels and determined to be taken seriously.

After its entry into the United Nations in 1971, China developed a network of diplomatic and economic relations, both with the major international players, including the United States and Japan, and with less powerful states. At the dawn of the twenty-first century, approaches were made to Latin America and Africa, primarily for economic reasons, as China sought both raw materials and low-cost labour. The collapse of the Soviet Union in 1991 compelled Beijing to establish new economic and diplomatic relationships with its immediate neighbours to the west in the great landmass of Central Asia and then with the Muslim states of the Middle East, as discussed in Chapter 27.

Ambassador Sha Zukang's interviews, August 2006

An extraordinarily forthright and no-holds-barred broadcast interview given to the BBC in August 2006 by China's Ambassador to the United Nations in Geneva, Sha Zukang, was either alarming or refreshing, according to the point of view of the listener.

> All the time I feel great. I always feel proud of my country. I don't have that kind of mentality of inferiority to anyone. I am so proud as a Chinese national and as Chinese Ambassador: I am not inferior to anyone in the world. . . . China's military build-up is not threatening anyone. It is for legitimate defence. So, we are not fighting anywhere; we are not killing innocent people in the world today anywhere and we have to be careful, careful to make sure no-one in the world can harm China. We are determined to defend our country with [a] little bit [of a] military increase. They are trying to make a huge story about it. . . . China's population is six times or five times that of the United States. Why blame China? No! Forget it! It's high time to shut up. It is the US's sovereign right to do whatever they deem good for them, but, don't tell us what is good for China![1]

Ambassador Sha's breathtakingly undiplomatic diplomacy, his heart-on-sleeve patriotism, and his impassioned defence of the rights of his country to defend itself may have startled those observers who chose to believe that China's move towards a market economy necessarily predicated a 'peaceful rise' and that it was becoming more and more like the West in its attitudes. To anyone who had heard the same views in conversations with Chinese thinkers, as well as the man in the street, it was refreshing to hear them again, in English, in public, and from a senior diplomat: the realisation that these views were widely held, if not always expressed so candidly, opened up the possibility of a more realistic analysis by Westerners of China's international position and role. Sha finished his career as Under Secretary-General in the Department of Economic and Social Affairs at the United Nations from 2007– 2012. In 2010, he was chosen to be Secretary General of the 2012 UN Conference on Sustainable Development.

China and the United States

The relationship between the United States and the newly created PRC got off to a bad start in the 1940s and slowly worsened – sometimes not so slowly. Although the United States had been a key player in the international efforts to mediate in the Civil War that broke out in China almost immediately after the defeat of Japan in 1945, its political loyalties were not in any doubt. In spite of the fact that US diplomats were engaged in negotiations for a coalition government and that many experienced American 'old China hands' were at best highly critical of Chiang Kai-shek's regime, when negotiations failed and it came to a choice that the United States supported the Nationalists – the Guomindang.

The Guomindang was forced off the mainland by its defeat in the Civil War and re-established its administration on Taiwan; it continued to claim to be the legitimate government of the whole of China. The formation of the PRC was announced on 1 October 1949, and by that time, Mao Zedong had already declared that China must 'lean to one side' and ally itself with the USSR. The expulsion of Western missionaries and the takeover by the Chinese state of foreign – including American – businesses exacerbated relations, but it was the Korean War that effectively prevented the establishment of normal diplomatic and commercial relations. Chinese troops fought Americans, who led the coalition of South Korea and other partners in the United Nations against China's ally North Korea. The war and the 'loss of China', as it was perceived in the United States, created problems for both sides. On the one hand, China endeavoured to exclude American influence; on the other hand, the United States, during its McCarthy period, forbade commercial dealings with the PRC and banned its citizens from travelling to China. McCarthyism dominated the US domestic political scene between 1950 and 1955. It was a period of anti-Communist paranoia dominated by the impression that the United States was under immediate and serious threat of internal subversion by agents of the Soviet Union and, increasingly, China. Distinguished American China specialists such as Owen Lattimore and John Service were excluded from their academic and government posts, and many other old China hands were accused of being sympathetic to Communism – a shameful case of guilt by association.

There were few contacts between the United States and the PRC in the 1950s and 1960s. Washington devoted its efforts to shoring up the Chiang Kai-shek regime in Taiwan, and the CIA mounted ineffectual and often incompetent attempts at subverting the new administration such as the parachuting of Tibetan exiles back into their homeland – from where they were never heard of again.

During the Cultural Revolution, the United States was condemned by China for its imperialist policies and Beijing consistently articulated its fears that it was being surrounded by American forces – or at least by forces sympathetic to the United States. This was not purely political paranoia: in addition to Taiwan and Japan, which were firm allies of the United States, American forces were present in large numbers in South Korea. The United States was also prosecuting its interests in Vietnam, fighting against both the North Vietnamese government in Hanoi, which was supported by Moscow and Beijing, and the guerrillas of the National Liberation Front. The NLF – the Viet Cong to the American military – was a coalition of nationalists and Buddhists, dominated by the Communists, which was active in the south of the country where it was attempting to destabilise and overthrow the government of America's allies in the capital, Saigon.

As the Cultural Revolution began to run out of steam in 1969 and 1970, Mao Zedong and the most influential leaders of the CCP and the PLA reassessed threats to their long-term survival. During the Cultural Revolution, they had already launched a barrage of vitriolic abuse against their erstwhile ally, the Soviet Union, in the press, referring to the Moscow leadership as the New Tsars and characterising their policies as 'social imperialism'. The combination of ideological and border disputes resulted in armed conflict on the China-USSR border in 1969.

Richard Milhous Nixon became President of the United States in 1969. His track record gave no hint of the changes that he was about to bring to Sino-American relations. His reputation was that of a tough – indeed, ruthless – right-wing lawyer who had played a key role in the anti-Communist witch hunt of the McCarthy period. However, once in office, his priority in foreign affairs was to disengage from overseas involvements, and from Asia in particular; to downgrade the overseas military commitments of the United States; and to avoid becoming enmeshed in future major military entanglements after the quagmire of the Vietnam War. The war was becoming increasingly unpopular among the American public at the same time that it was becoming impossible for the United States to achieve a military victory. The Nixon Doctrine of disengagement was the basis for a reassessment of America's policy in East Asia, and it was the conjuncture with a similar reassessment being carried out in Beijing that made such profound change possible.

Nixon visited Beijing in 1972, but the ground had been prepared by his Secretary of State, Henry Kissinger, in secret meetings and shuttle diplomacy throughout the previous year. The visit permitted the opening of negotiations for the normalisation of diplomatic relations. A US diplomatic liaison office was established in 1973, although the formal appointment of an ambassador was not ratified until 1976. The long drawn-out negotiations were dogged by the issue of Taiwan.

Since the normalisation of diplomatic relations, the main emphasis of both sides has been on economic relations, primarily trade: there have also been increasingly acrid disputes about the relative value of the renminbi and the US dollar. A series of political crises, however, underlined the seriousness of tensions between China and the United States. The three most potentially dangerous of these crises were the North Atlantic Treaty Organisation (NATO) bombing of the Chinese embassy in Belgrade in May 1999, the collision between a US Navy reconnaissance aircraft and a Chinese fighter over Hainan Island in April 2001, and allegations in 1999 that a Chinese-born American scientist had been passing nuclear secrets to Beijing.

Belgrade, Hainan, and espionage alarms

In May 1999, during NATO operations in the civil war in Yugoslavia, the Chinese embassy in the capital Belgrade was struck by bombs. The building was severely damaged, and three Chinese citizens – all journalists – were killed. The CIA took responsibility for the attack, maintaining that they had used an obsolete map. Rumours spread in China that the bombing had been deliberate because the embassy was being used to assist the Yugoslav army in its radio communications. In China, students demonstrated outside foreign embassies; on some university campuses, foreign students were the target for verbal abuse in an increasingly threatening atmosphere. Relations between the United States and China improved towards the end of the year, and the two parties came to an understanding on the payment of compensation to the families of the victims and recompense for the damage to the embassy. This did not finally resolve the matter, especially in the eyes of many Chinese who persist in believing that the attack was deliberate.

On 1 April 2001, a US Navy Lockheed EP-3E Aries II signals reconnaissance aircraft was patrolling close to Hainan, the large island off the southern coast of China. US sources claimed it was operating legitimately in international air space, but Shenyang-8 fighters of the PLA Air Force intercepted it on the grounds that it was carrying out an espionage mission within Chinese air space. The wing tip of one of the fighters touched the reconnaissance aircraft, the fighter crashed, and the pilot is presumed to have been killed, although his body has never been found. The Aries effected an emergency landing on Hainan, where US diplomats were hurriedly dispatched to negotiate for the release of their crew, all of whom had survived. The crew were released ten days later, but the Chinese authorities held their aircraft for several weeks, giving them time to assess or even remove its advanced technology.

The fact that the aircraft was intercepted was an indication of the tension between the Chinese and American military on the borders with Chinese airspace: the speed with which a negotiated settlement was reached is a mark of the importance attached by the two governments to maintaining diplomatic relations.

Several ethnic Chinese individuals working in the United States fell foul of either American or Chinese accusations of spying. In December 1999, Wen Ho Lee, who was born in Taiwan but was a US citizen and worked at the Los Alamos National Laboratory, was arrested on suspicion of having passed classified information about US nuclear weapons to the PRC. These allegations were subsequently dropped, although Dr Lee pleaded guilty to a less serious technical charge of downloading restricted data, but the length of time that he had been held, in solitary confinement and without charge, made his case a *cause celebre*.

Responding to rising China

Attempts to stabilise relations between Washington and Beijing during the Clinton presidency led to the US-China Relations Act 2000, which promised permanent normal trade relations – a necessary prerequisite to China's accession to the WTO. China was treated as a responsible stakeholder in the international arena and served as mediator with Pyongyang in difficult negotiations over the future of the Korean peninsula in 2005. Two years later, Beijing increased its military spending by 18%: by 2010,[2] the PRC was acknowledged to be the world's second largest economy. The United States responded to these military and economic challenges – actual or potential – with the announcement by President Barack Obama's Secretary of State, Hilary Clinton, of a 'pivot' towards Asia, the redirecting of much of Washington's diplomatic, economic, and strategic firepower away from its previous focus on the Middle East and South Asia.

Increases in the US trade deficit with China led to political tensions that were only partly defused by the Sunnylands summit between President Obama and the new Chinese leader, Xi Jinping, in June 2013. China's expansion of its naval strength in the South China Sea, and above all the construction of artificial islands that could house military bases, led to further conflict which was intensified after the inauguration of President Donald Trump on 20 January 2017. The Trump administration initially accepted Beijing's 'One China' formula and Xi, with whom Trump claimed a good rapport, was hosted at the President's Mar-a-Largo resort in April of that year, but relations soon deteriorated.[3]

Trade war, 2018–2020

Trade negotiations between the United States and China during the Trump administration can only be described as chaotic. Washington's negotiating style veered erratically from overconfident promises of deals to threats and the application of punitively high import tariffs. Beijing, in common with much of the rest of the world, struggled to determine the implications of Washington's policy statements, but resisted demands that implied major structural changes to China's fundamental economic policy and legislation. Washington targeted China with new tariffs in March 2018 and the escalation of the trade war over that summer was confirmed by a hard-line speech by Vice-President Mike Pence in October. In the summer of 2019, tariffs became more punitive and Washington revived the old accusation that China was a currency manipulator.[4]

In early 2019, hopes were running high that an agreement on trade was imminent, but this was premature; Beijing's frustration with US negotiators was barely concealed. For their part, the US side maintained that China had been backtracking on points previously agreed in a voluminous draft document, although no specific details were given. Some US demands required changes in Chinese legislation; specifically, cancelling subsidies to certain industries and SOEs would undermine China's development strategy and would, in the view of many Chinese economists, be suicidal.

Trump had threatened that, in the absence of an agreement, the tariffs already in place would be raised from 10% to 25% on Chinese products valued at US$200 billion. Comments in *Taoran Notes*, a social media account, described by *South China Morning Post* as a medium for Beijing to 'signal the leadership's thinking and manage domestic expectations' indicated that China was unwilling to make any further concessions. Xi Jinping vetoed some concessions proposed by his negotiating team and made it clear that he would take personal responsibility for the consequences of standing firm. A further round of negotiations led by Vice-Premier Liu He was scheduled for Thursday 9 May but with less time allocated than expected. No agreement was reached by the deadline of noon on Friday 10 May, and the US tariff increases became effective. Beijing immediately announced that it would take counter-measures and implemented a stimulus package.[5] The immediate impact of the trade conflict was dramatic; the *Financial Times* described global markets as 'rattled' and share values fell on the Shanghai and Shenzhen stock exchanges, and in New York, although there was a later rally.

It was becoming increasingly apparent that an agreement on tariffs and trade could not resolve the difficulties between Beijing and Washington. These were not purely economic issues, but resulted from competition for geopolitical ascendancy in the Asia-Pacific region and further afield.[6]

Huawei and digital commerce

Conflict over the Huawei electronics company threatened to undermine attempts to achieve a trade deal between the United States and China in 2018 and 2019, but underlying concerns about the security of Chinese digital technology had a wider impact.

The possibility of Huawei coming under pressure from the Chinese government was highlighted in discussions about China's National Intelligence Law of 2017. Huawei is believed to be connected closely with Chinese military and security organisations. It was established in 1987 by Ren Zhengfei, who had worked for 20 years in a PLA civilian research unit specialising in military information technology. From an initial staff of just three, it grew into a multi-billion-dollar enterprise. Ren had never held a military rank, but a former Vice-Chairwoman of the company had been an officer in China's Ministry of State Security.

The conflict became public when Meng Wanzhou, deputy chair of Huawei's board and its CFO, was detained by Canadian police at the request of US authorities in 2018 while changing planes in Vancouver, Canada on 1 December. Ms. Meng, who is the daughter of Reng Zhengfei and also uses the name Sabrina, faced extradition to the United States on criminal charges, including bank fraud and the theft of technology, that implicated her personally and the company corporately. During the 'two meetings' in Beijing in March 2019, China's Foreign Minister, Wang Yi, publicly professed his support for Huawei, telling Chinese firms that they should not allow themselves to be 'victimised like silent lambs', and making it a test case for China's right to compete in the development of advanced technology. Huawei instituted legal proceedings against the United States which had prohibited the use of its equipment, and Meng Wanzhou sued the Canadian authorities for illegal detention.[7]

In March 2019, the European Commission was considering critical communications systems that could be supplied by Huawei or other Chinese software companies. The consensus was that Huawei's technical specifications for 5G communications networks were excellent but there was concern over security implications. Unlike the European Union, the United States appeared determined to exclude Chinese firms from any areas of electronic infrastructure that were considered sensitive, concerned that legislation and political pressure in China required Huawei to use its technology to assist the Chinese state in intelligence collection. The European Union was prepared to consider the technology, as long as it was confident that security risks were manageable. As 5G technology would be more 'deeply embedded in daily life through its use in road and rail management to controlling household devices', there were concerns about the security of data in the systems and the possibility that the software might include secret 'back doors' through which external agents could effect access. Dr Ian Levy of Britain's Government Communications Headquarters (GCHQ), interviewed on the BBC Television technology programme *Click*, acknowledged that the security services were alert to the possibility of such vulnerabilities, but did not think that they had been deliberately inserted. Similar vulnerabilities already existed in 4G software; sensitive data was already encrypted and would continue to be encrypted in 5G systems.[8]

On 26 March, New Zealand Prime Minister Jacinta Ardern announced a visit to Beijing, truncated by the attacks on mosques in Christchurch, to discuss upgrading Wellington's existing free trade agreement and exploring the possibility of taking part in China's Belt and Road Initiative. Among potential points of disagreement was New Zealand's decision, on the grounds of national security, to prevent Huawei from supplying 5G equipment to Spark, the country's principal telecommunications provider.[9]

Concerns about security risk were reinforced two days later when the British government made public a technically authoritative report by the National Cyber Security Centre, which is part of Government Communications Headquarters, one of the British security services, in anticipation of a decision on whether Huawei would be an appropriate provider of 5G telecommunications services in United Kingdom. The report concluded that the centre could give 'only limited assurance that the long-term security risks can be managed in the Huawei equipment currently deployed in the UK'. The report did not indicate that Huawei was 'deliberately introducing backdoors or working to carry out any kind of espionage on behalf of the Chinese state', as had been alleged by some critics, but expressed concern about company practices in both software engineering and cyber security processes that resulted in potential vulnerabilities. Some of these problems had been raised with the company previously, but in the opinion of the report's authors, had not been adequately addressed.[10]

The controversy reached a new level after a meeting of the United Kingdom's National Security Council on Tuesday 23 April 2019 attended by selected members of the British Cabinet and senior officials of the security services. It was agreed that Huawei would be invited to contribute to the United Kingdom's 5G network by supplying 'non-core' telecommunications equipment. This decision was leaked to a conservative British newspaper, the *Daily Telegraph*, which revealed that Prime Minister Theresa May had forced through the agreement in the face of opposition by at least five cabinet ministers. This leak flouted established rules of Cabinet collective responsibility and official secrecy, and an enquiry was launched, raising the possibility of a cabinet minister facing prosecution under the Official Secrets Act. The Secretary of State for Defence, Gavin Williamson, who had acquired a reputation for gaffes and inappropriate comments, was abruptly dismissed by the Prime Minister for having leaked information from the National Security Council; he insisted that he was not guilty. The Metropolitan Police took the view that what had been disclosed did not amount to an offence under the Official Secrets Act, but Williamson insisted that there should be an impartial investigation into the affair.[11]

A pointed intervention by the PRC ambassador to the United Kingdom, Liu Xiaoming, highlighted the international implications of the Huawei decision. Writing in the equally conservative *Sunday Telegraph*, Ambassador Liu argued that Britain 'should resist external pressure over decisions on Chinese companies and make "independent" choices'. He urged the United Kingdom 'to defy "pressure" and "interruptions"', in a direct rebuttal of the position of the United States, insisting that Huawei had a 'good track record' on security. Liu Xiaoming underpinned his remarks with warnings about the possible impact of the disagreement on the United Kingdom's future trade relationship with China.[12]

Liu Xiaoming's article revived the position he had set out in a statement issued by the Chinese Embassy in January 2019 and also published in the *Sunday Telegraph*.

> The fact is that Huawei acts strictly in line with the laws and regulations of the UK and delivers what customers want. How to respond to the hyped allegation against Huawei is not an economic question but a political one. It is a question of 'to be, or not to be'. To answer the question, I believe the UK has to decide whether it wants to see China's development as an opportunity or a threat. To make the right choice, the UK needs to pursue independent policy based on its national interests, instead of drifting along with others. Staying open and inclusive is the key to maintaining UK's global influence. Clinging to an outdated Cold War mentality and taking 'national security' as an excuse for discrimination against foreign companies will not only bring harm to others but also backfire. Globalisation is an irreversible trend. China has resolved to embrace the world and engage in open cooperation. I expect the UK to carry on with its historic spirit of openness and make the wise choice that serves its interests, joining hands with China to deliver more benefits to the peoples of both countries.[13]

China's Minister of National Defence, General Wei Fenghe, answering questions after his presentation at the 18th Asia Security Conference of the Shangri-La Dialogue in Singapore on Sunday 2 June 2019, firmly rejected any suggestion that Huawei was anything other than a private company.

> Another question is about Huawei – in the interests of time, I will just answer some important questions. Huawei is a private company. China is opposed to the attempts of other countries to impose sanctions on private companies. Huawei is not a military company. Do not think that the head of Huawei used to serve in the army, the company that he has built is part of the military. That does not make sense; there are these kinds of ex-servicemen across the board. After their retirement from the military a lot of them have set up companies in countries across the board.[14]

Although much of Wei's response was incontrovertible, his insistence on the absence of military links was treated with considerable scepticism. In most countries, private companies operating in areas where there are security or defence sensitivities invariably have links, whether formal or informal, with military and government organisations, and the links between the Chinese state and industry are closer than most.

The United States remained firmly against any use of Huawei technology and on 28 April 2019, in an intervention in the UK debate, Robert Strayer, a Deputy Assistant Secretary at the US Department of State, reiterated the position of the Trump administration that Huawei 'was not a trusted vendor'[15] and that any including its technology in 5G networks was a security risk that could endanger the sharing of intelligence between the United States and the United Kingdom. Senior officials of US intelligence agencies briefed American companies and other organisations during May 2019 to underline their concerns about the dangers of cyber-attacks and intellectual property theft. In an unusual – and possibly unprecedented – move, company executives were shown classified material to reinforce these arguments.

After Google announced that it was limiting Huawei's access to its Android operation system, commentators expressed concern that what had begun as legitimate concern over cyber security had been transformed into a campaign to 'decouple the US and Chinese tech sectors'[16] which could be seen as 'opening salvoes in an emerging US-China cold war'. The opening demands of the Trump administration, as leaked in May 2018, were regarded by many outside the United States as outrageous, amounting to 'a list of surrender demands for China to acquiesce to', according to Friedrich Wu at Singapore's Nanyang Technological University. In Beijing, television stations began to screen old films about the heroic actions of the Chinese People's Volunteers during the Korean War of the early 1950s, reinforcing the sense that a trade war was evolving into a protracted economic and political conflict.

Huawei insisted that it would strongly resist pressure from the United States, and by the end of May 2019, the Huawei dispute and the Trump trade war were inextricably entwined. China openly considered restricting the export of rare earth minerals, which are essential for the manufacture of many electronic components for defence and communications, as well as consumer goods such as electric vehicles, cameras, and mobile telephones. The possible use of these restrictions as a threat in the trade war was emphasised by the high profile accorded to a visit by Xi Jinping to a rare earth mining and processing plant at Ganzhou in the south of Jiangxi province, especially as President Xi was accompanied by Vice-Premier Liu He, the industrial economist who leads the trade negotiations with the United States, was at school with Xi Jinping, and is one of his most trusted advisers.[17]

At the G20 summit in Osaka at the end of June 2019, Trump met Xi Jinping and unexpectedly reversed his position by announcing that US companies would henceforth be permitted to supply limited of equipment to Huawei, which had been placed on an 'entity list' of countries requiring government approval before sales could be agreed. In return, the US agreed not to impose additional tariffs on US$300 billion worth of Chinese imports and to continue with trade negotiations which had stalled at the February summit in Hanoi. Initial responses by officials from both sides indicated cautious optimism, but reaction from Chinese businesses expressed their concern at Trump's 'flip-flopping'.[18]

Confusion about the adoption of Huawei technology in the West continued. The head of the United Kingdom's Security Service (MI5), Andrew Parker, issued an unusual statement that he was 'confident that US intelligence sharing with the UK [would] not be jeopardised' if Britain used Huawei technology in future 5G mobile phone networks. He had 'no reason today to think that' the long-standing intelligence partnership would be affected – despite intensified US lobbying against using the Chinese company in a critical piece of national infrastructure. This view was endorsed by British Prime Minister Boris Johnson, but other cabinet ministers had reservations. This was in the face of pressure from officials in the US government to continue to exclude Huawei technology, a position that was supported by Australia, a key partner with the United States and United Kingdom in the 'five eyes' intelligence network.[19]

In May 2020, the US Department of Commerce amended the blacklisting conditions imposed the previous year in the light of concerns that sanctions against Huawei would put at risk not only the company itself, but its wider supply chain of computer chips, including enterprises in Taiwan. Businesses wishing to manufacture chips to Huawei's specifications using American equipment could do so, but only after applying for a licence. Huawei responded to the pressure from the United Kingdom with a spirited campaign that emphasised its contribution to the British economy for over 20 years, asking the government not to overestimate risks to security. In one of a series of controversial U-turns, and in line with US policy, Boris Johnson announced that no new Huawei equipment would be bought for the United Kingdom's 5G network, and by 2027, 5G and its 6G successor would have no Huawei components at all.[20]

'Phase one' trade deal, 15 January 2020

In mid-January 2020, the United States reversed its policy of labelling China as a currency manipulator in preparation for the signature of a partial trade agreement, designated as 'phase one' of a final accord. 'The US said it made the change because China had agreed to refrain from devaluing its currency to make its own goods cheaper for foreign buyers'. It was, however, a move for political rather than technical reasons. As the 'phase one' deal was signed on 15 January 2020 in the White House by President Trump and Vice-Premier and Politburo member Liu He, a trusted confidante of Xi Jinping, the American side hailed the signing as 'transformative', while for the Chinese, it was a 'win-win deal' that would benefit relations between the two countries. In concrete terms little was agreed: the United States reduced by half the recent tariffs it had imposed on Chinese imports, while China agreed to purchase more goods from the United States, particularly from the agricultural sector. This agreement failed to resolve most outstanding problems in trade relations between China and the United States; it was merely a lull in the trade war in the expectation of further talks to deal with the main issues. Trump urged a speedy move to 'phase two' of the negotiations, but Liu He rejected this as risking acting like 'a bear losing itself in a corn field'. He went on to say, 'We might get nothing if we rush to a second job before the first one is properly done. I don't think it is a wise choice to impatiently launch new stages of talks'.[21]

Economists welcomed the agreement but, in the words of the respected *Financial Times* analyst, Martin Wolf, it was 'a truce, not peace'. While the deal covered 'intellectual property, "forced" transfer of technology, agriculture, access for financial services and currency manipulation', and Beijing's commitment to 'import various US goods and services' at a rate approximately double that of existing imports, much of the detail was not new. Many of the PRC policies had already been implemented and Beijing no longer manipulated its currency. US policies were confused and contradictory, and continuing discord between the two economic giants seemed inevitable. EU officials were unenthusiastic about the agreement, which was likely to discriminate against EU trade with China and was potentially in breach of WTO rules.[22]

Trade negotiations were complicated, and at least temporarily supplanted, by international reactions to the Hong Kong demonstrations of 2019 and the pandemic of Covid-19 in early 2020. The confrontational Chinese 'wolf-warrior' approach was replaced by more conciliatory diplomacy, although Beijing insisted that it would adopt 'targeted, proportional and surgical responses' to US measures against Chinese firms such as ByteDance and WeChat. The most powerful foreign affairs official, Yang Jiechi of the State Council, argued against a 'disastrous' confrontation with the United States, and all indications were that Beijing was keeping its powder dry in anticipation of a change of administration in Washington.[23]

China and Russia

The PRC and the Soviet Union had in theory been close allies since the signing of the Treaty of Friendship, Alliance and Mutual Assistance in Moscow on 14 February 1950. In practice, that alliance was strained from the outset but weakened after the death of Stalin in 1953 when Mao Zedong increasingly insisted on following an independent political course. After the Great Leap Forward of 1958, relations deteriorated rapidly and Soviet technical assistance was withdrawn from China in 1960. During the 1960s, Moscow and Beijing clashed frequently in meetings of the Communist states; the Sino-Soviet dispute overlapped with the Cultural Revolution and culminated in armed conflict between Chinese and Soviet forces on their shared border in 1969.

A planned visit to Beijing from 15–18 May 1989 by Mikhail Gorbachev, the reforming General Secretary of the CPSU, was intended to heal the breach. Gorbachev met Deng Xiaoping and the General Secretary of the CCP, Hu Yaobang, but the summit was completely overshadowed by the protests by students and other residents of the capital in Tian'anmen Square, and the subsequent military crackdown in which many hundreds of civilians were killed. Moscow soon became preoccupied with the disintegration of its client regimes in Eastern Europe and finally with the breakup of the Soviet Union itself in 1991. Sino-Russian relations were reduced to necessary security and trading agreements as the new Russian Federation struggled to establish its relationships with Europe and Asia.

Disputed borders that had not been previously resolved were demarcated in a 1991 agreement and supplementary agreements in 1994 and 2004. The latter included the transfer of Amur River islands to China. China's demand for energy in its dramatic economic rise matched Russia's need to export oil and gas for many years, but as China's growth slowed, so did the demand for energy. Chinese investment was invaluable to Russia, especially in its Far Eastern Federal District bordering on China. China also supplied migrant labour, which was in demand but triggered discontent among the Russian population. China was also a major purchaser of Russian armaments, including combat aircraft, but conflict arose over the manufacture under licence of Chinese variants of Sukhoi and Tupolev aircraft, and eventually independent Chinese versions which appeared strikingly similar to Russian originals. China became a net exporter of armaments after decades of duplicating and adopting Russian technology.

China needed to cooperate with Russia, but this cooperation always included an element of competition. A new Treaty of Good Neighbourliness and Friendly Cooperation was signed in 2001: there was no longer any ideological alignment between China and Russia – and indeed, none had existed since the 1960s. In spite of mutual distrust, which had a long historical pedigree, China and Russia made common cause against a global order dominated by the West. This took the form of diplomatic cooperation in the United Nations and other international bodies, notably in opposition to the United States, against which both had grievances.

Vladimir Putin and Xi Jinping

Xi Jinping undertook a state visit to Moscow in 2013 shortly after taking office; it was his first foreign visit. He continued to visit every two years, returning in 2019 to attend the St Petersburg International Economic Forum. Vladimir Putin visited China on many occasions during these years, including a state visit in 2018.

The authoritarian mind-sets of Putin and Xi facilitated a commonality of interest, even though the development of Russia was put in the shade by the spectacular economic performance of its eastern neighbour. As relations worsened between China and the United States, following the launch of Trump's trade war in 2019, Russia and China moved closer together in what the *South China Morning Post* called a 'deepening economic alliance'.[24] Xi and Putin met in Russia on Wednesday 5 June 2019, the day before the formal opening of the St. Petersburg International Economic Forum; Xi was the honoured guest, but the United States had withdrawn in protest at the detention of executives of the equity investment firm Baring

Vostok and the arrest of its founder, Michael Calvey, over disputed allegations of fraud. Sino-Russian discussions at the forum focused on trade and investment, which had already increased considerably, particularly with greater Russian energy exports to China.

In advance of the forum, Xi Jinping presented two pandas to the Moscow zoo, a powerful symbol of the importance attached by Beijing to the relationship; opened a new Chinese car factory in the Russian capital; and accepted an honorary degree. In return, Putin greeted Xi as his 'dear friend' and made a point of praising China's Belt and Road Initiative, Xi Jinping's signature policy, in spite of known Russian concerns at potential conflicts with Russia's traditional spheres of influence. The semi-official *Global Times* reported from Beijing that,

> Xi called Putin his 'best and bosom friend' and said that he has had closer interactions with President Putin 'than with any other foreign colleague'. In some of the most memorable moments, the two leaders honored each other with the highest medals of their countries, watched an ice hockey match between Chinese and Russian children, and cooked traditional Chinese and Russian pancakes. Over the past six years, Xi has met Putin nearly 30 times in an unusually vigorous streak of head-of-state diplomacy.[25]

The relationship between the two leaders was evolving into a long-term strategic partnership rather than, as had been widely assumed, a 'short-lived marriage of convenience', in the words of the *Financial Times*.[26]

China and Japan

The 'normalisation' of Sino-Japanese relations in the 1970s could not take place until the thaw between China and the United States, as befitted Japan's status as a junior partner in the historical anti-Communist alliance in Asia. The San Francisco Peace Treaty signed on 28 April 1952 at the formal close of the post-war occupation by the allies, and the US-Japan Mutual Security Treaty that was concluded in 1960, committed Japan to the American cause: Tokyo also signed a peace treaty with the Nationalist government on Taiwan. In practice, Japan operated an informal and undeclared two-China policy as it contrived to keep its economic relations and political alliances separate. Japan traded with the PRC, signed non-governmental agreements on commerce and fisheries, and became involved in what the Chinese side termed 'people's diplomacy', primarily the exchange of cultural delegations. Between 1958 and 1971, Beijing made regular formal protests at the military alliance that it believed had been created against China by the relationship between Japan and the United States and particularly by the stationing of American troops in Japan.

Once the Nixon visit of February 1972 had unblocked diplomatic relations, Japan was in a position to regularise its own relations with China. The Chinese Premier Zhou Enlai and his Japanese counterpart, Tanaka Kakuei, came to an agreement in 1972 (the Zhou–Tanaka statement) that formed the basis for progress towards full normalisation. It was not, however, until 1978 – again in line with the timetable established for US-China relations – that China and Japan concluded their Treaty of Peace and Friendship.

Economic relations

The relationship with Japan was to prove vital for China's economic modernisation during the 1980s, when economic issues predominated and political differences were set aside, albeit temporarily. The two states signed a long-term trade agreement in 1978 which resulted in a substantial increase in the volume of reciprocal trade. As a close neighbour and a highly developed economy, Japan was well placed to invest in China's newly modernising industries and also to transfer advanced technology: the Japanese imported iron and steel from China, and in return exported electrical goods and other consumer durables.

One of the firms that benefited from substantial Japanese investment was the Baoshan steel complex in Shanghai; the history of this company illustrates many of the problems faced by Sino-Japanese joint enterprises. A contract for investment and technology transfer to enable the creation of the plant was signed with Nippon Steel in December 1978, but financial retrenchment by the Chinese government led to the Japanese taking heavy losses. The scale and cost of the project came under fire at the meeting of the Chinese Fifth NPC in 1980, and construction of the plant was halted. It was restarted in 1981 and the furnaces were finally lit in 1985, but it operated with a lower output than had originally been planned.

On the political level, Japan was beginning to emerge from the cloud it had been under since the Second World War: Tokyo began to enjoy a higher profile internationally and came under pressure to take a more active role in regional diplomacy and defence. Japan's reluctance to do so was matched by the opposition of other regional powers, especially China, Korea, and other countries occupied by the Japanese military during the Second World War that were deeply suspicious of Tokyo's motives.

Political differences between China and Japan came to a head in the 1980s, although initially they were inextricably linked with economic relations. In 1985 and 1986, Chinese students demonstrated in Beijing against what was described by some commentators in the PRC as Japan's economic invasion of the mainland. The demonstrations spread to other major cities, including Xi'an, Chengdu, and Wuhan. It was clear to anyone travelling in China during the mid-1980s that Japanese products, particularly electrical and electronic goods, had suddenly begun to appear in Chinese shops in vast quantities. They were expensive but popular; their quality and reliability were far greater than that of equivalent Chinese goods at the time, especially radio cassette recorders and cameras. The Chinese government devalued its currency, the renminbi (RMB), by 13.6% in July 1986 in a move designed to stem the flow of imports from Japan and promote Chinese exports: the value of the RMB dropped by 40% against the Japanese yen in the course of a year.[27]

Talking about the war

The major political conflicts between China and Japan were in the context of visits by Japanese politicians to the Yasukuni Shrine and school textbooks. On the face of it, both of these issues appeared peripheral and inconsequential in terms of normal diplomatic relations, but for China, they were regarded as a test of Japan's willingness to distance itself from the attitudes that had led to war and the occupation of China in the 1930s.

In August 1985, on the 40th anniversary of VJ Day (Victory over Japan Day is 12 August, the date of Japan's unconditional surrender in 1945), the Japanese Prime Minister Nakasone Yasuhiro visited the Yasukuni Shrine in Tokyo. The Yasukuni Shrine is a war memorial and Shinto religious complex that was established in 1869 to commemorate all those who had fallen in the conflict to defeat the Tokugawa Shogunate and establish the government of the Meiji Restoration in 1868, which marked the beginning of Japan's great advance to modernisation. The shrine was also created to provide a permanent resting place for the spirits of the war dead in accordance with the tradition of Shinto, Japan's traditional religion. This was not in itself controversial, but soldiers, sailors, and airmen who died in subsequent conflicts, up to and including the Second World War, were also commemorated at the shrine. In 1979, it was revealed that, without any public announcement, the names of 14 individuals who had been convicted at the Tokyo War Crime Tribunal of Class A war crimes during the Second World War had been included in the list of those to be commemorated. This provoked outrage in China and Korea, the two countries which had arguably suffered most from the Japanese occupation, and visits by Japanese prime ministers to the Yasukuni Shrine have been a source of considerable friction ever since. In 1986, such was the furore that Mr. Nakasone did not make a planned visit to the shrine in August. The Yasukuni Shrine has also been the focus of political conflict within Japan as ultra-nationalist groups intent on defending Japan's war record protest if prime ministers do not make annual visits.

A parallel source of conflict was the publication in Japan of history textbooks for schools in which the invasion of China by Japan was played down or even justified. Textbooks play a far greater role in teaching methodology in Japan than they do in the West. In the 1980s, the word of an adopted textbook was law and the teacher would not feel able to deviate from it in the classroom. In a memorable but far from atypical geography lesson in a secondary school in Toyota in 1984, the teacher had the textbook in front of him, as did the pupils: he then wrote out a passage from the book on the blackboard, and then read the same passage aloud to the class. There was no discussion.[28]

China argued that unless the Japanese corrected the false impression that there had been no invasion, their good faith would be in doubt. At the same time, the ultra-nationalist right in Japan insisted that there should be no climb down on the textbooks or on the Yasukuni issue. Right-wing militants who tour the cities in garishly decorated loudspeaker vans are adamant that it was only the Japanese who were militarily aggressive in the 1930s.

Other related issues were the rights claimed by both Taiwan and China to a student hostel that had been set up for Chinese students who were studying in Japan, the vandalism of a memorial to Zhou Enlai by ultra-nationalists in 1987, and the firing of shots at China's consulate in Fukuoka in 1988. China established a museum at Lugouqiao (Marco Polo Bridge) which is just outside Beijing at the location where the 1937 invasion of China began and a memorial in Nanjing to the victims of the massacre that took place there later the same year.

These political differences have not been conclusively resolved, but it is a mark of the closeness between the two countries and particularly the perceived mutual economic interest that after the suppression of the Democracy Movement in Beijing in June 1989 and the flight of foreign businesses fearing that a civil war was about to break out, Japanese business interests were the first to return. Since 1989, this rapprochement has continued. Japanese business continues to play an important role in the economic development of China. Relations between the governments are – on the whole – stable, with occasional crises that still reflect China's unease about Japan's attitude to its role in the Second World War.

In 2007, the 70th anniversary of the 1937 Rape of Nanjing was commemorated by the formal opening of an extended memorial hall in the city of Nanjing dedicated to the victims of the massacre. Until recently, the tone of Chinese discussions of the war, including the documentation in the memorial hall, has been relentlessly negative, but the tenor of the exhibits in the new hall highlights the need for looking forwards as well as backwards, and emphasises the development of peaceful relations between Beijing and Tokyo. The most senior Chinese leaders avoided the commemoration in Nanjing; this was seen as a gesture of reconciliation by Japan.[29]

In December 2007, Japanese Prime Minister Yasuo Fukuda, who had taken office the previous September, held talks with the Chinese Premier Wen Jiabao during his first visit to Beijing. Although the meeting was amicable and emphasised increased bilateral cooperation, it was noted that there was no resolution of one of the major current areas of disagreement between China and Japan, the rights to natural gas fields which are located in the East China Sea between the two countries and are the subject of a dispute over maritime borders. However, in an important gesture to China, Prime Minister Fukuda indicated that he would not visit the Yasukuni Shrine during his term of office. His predecessor, Koizumi Junichiro, had visited the shrine during his time in office, and those visits had led to restrictions on contacts at the highest levels.[30] The visit demonstrated a determination to maintain cordial relationships in spite of some serious differences of opinion.

Diaoyu/Senkaku islands

The archipelago claimed by China and Japan and with separate Chinese (Diaoyu) and Japanese (Senkaku) names lies in the East China Sea, some 200 kilometres to the southwest of Okinawa and northwest of Taiwan. The status of the five main uninhabited islands and associated barren rocks was never resolved in diplomatic negotiations after the Second World War and remains contested. Dozens of minor outcrops are sometimes included in the group. In 2012, the Japanese government bought three of the islets from a private owner, and this occasioned anti-Japanese demonstrations in China, a low point in relations between Beijing and Tokyo.

Although unpopulated, the islands are important as potential sources of under-sea oil. In 2013, China declared an Air Defence Identification Zone over the islands which required all aircraft, including commercial flights, to identify themselves to Chinese controllers. This zone overlapped with one already established by Japan. Potential air conflicts were exacerbated by the increased presence of Chinese and Japanese naval vessels in the surrounding waters.[31]

Xi-Abe relationship

Shinzo Abe, a right-wing conservative nationalist leader of the Liberal Democratic Party, became Prime Minister of Japan on 26 December 2012, six weeks after Xi Jinping's selection as General Secretary of the CCP. Sino-Japanese relations improved as a result of a constructive personal relationship between the two men. In 2010, China had overtaken Japan as the second largest economy in the world. Japan was attempting to extricated itself from dependency on Chinese mineral resources while recognising the need to maintain economic ties with its increasingly powerful neighbour.

As the trade war between Trump's United States and China intensified from 2019, the personal relationship between the leaders of China and Japan was strengthened: although loosely allied to the United States politically, Tokyo also had disagreements with Washington over trade, and Trump's destructive diplomacy had pushed the two former antagonists together. China's Premier Li Keqiang had visited Beijing in May 2018, the first visit at that level for eight years, and in October of the same year, Prime Minister Abe flew to Beijing, the first official visit of a leader since 2011. The visit was low key, but new economic cooperation agreements were signed. Shinzo Abe referred to China as its equal partner rather than its aid donor, a pointed reminder of the part Japan had played in China's economic growth. Xi Jinping was invited to make a state visit to Japan in April 2020 although the invitation prompted criticism in Japan. The visit was postponed in the light of the Covid-19 pandemic.[32]

In August 2020, Shinzo Abe announced his resignation on health grounds. His successor, confirmed in a vote on 14 September, is Yoshihide Suga, who was supported by Abe's faction within the LDP but whose background is quite unlike that of his patrician predecessor. Suga is not from an elite political family, but he has worked his way up to become a respected machine politician focused on domestic issues. He is untried in international relations and great importance will be attached to how he forges a relationship with Xi Jinping.[33]

China and North Korea

By the end of the twentieth century, China had become North Korea's only long-term ally, but this alliance was never an easy one. The first formal diplomatic agreement between the two states was a treaty signed on 11 July 1961 in Beijing by Zhou Enlai and the North Korean leader, Kim Il-sung. It provided for economic cooperation and for either side to come to the assistance of the other in the event of a military attack by an outside power or powers, and enshrined the aspiration of reunifying Korea in a peaceful and democratic manner.[34] This treaty is still in existence and there have been other, undisclosed agreements, but the degree of cooperation between North Korea and China has varied considerably over the years.

Economic collapse

As the North Korean economy deteriorated in the 1990s, the country became increasingly reliant on outside food aid to stave off the threat of famine. China was a major contributor, along with South Korea, Japan, and the two largest donors, the United States and the European Union. The constant threat of a confrontation between Pyongyang and the United States over allegations concerning the production of nuclear weapons and the testing of missile warheads alienated much of the international community and increased North Korea's isolation and its dependence on China.

North Korea has suffered from severe food shortages since the catastrophic natural disasters and famine of 1995. In the spring of 2002, the World Food Programme, which is run by the UN Food and Agriculture Organisation, was predicting that the country had only three months' supply of food remaining and appealed to the international community for increased donations.[35] Pyongyang relaxed the state-controlled system of rationing grain, probably at the prompting of its Chinese advisers, and allowed the introduction of a limited market in some areas in an attempt to alleviate the shortages of rice.

By 2005, China's contribution to food aid for North Korea – wheat, flour, and other grains – had increased dramatically, and Pyongyang had been able to dispense with aid from other sources. International aid agencies were compelled to leave North Korea, and the work of the World Food Programme was severely restricted, in spite of the fact that there were credible reports of another impending famine following in the wake of typhoons and large-scale floods.[36] Pyongyang's dependence on China increased pressure on China by the international community, primarily the United States, to use its influence to persuade the government of Kim Jung-il, who had succeeded his late father Kim Il-sung in 1994, that it should not proceed with its nuclear power and nuclear weapons programme.

Historical ties

The extent and effectiveness of Beijing's influence on Pyongyang has however always been difficult to determine. Some sections of the Korean Party of Labour, the Communist Party that runs North Korea, operated closely with the CCP as early as the 1920s and 1930s, and the close relationship between Beijing and Pyongyang – likened in a classical Chinese analogy to that between the lips and the teeth – was cemented during the Korean War. Although it was a close relationship, it was a fraught one. China was railroaded into the Korean War by a combination of sleight of hand by Kim Il-sung and Stalin's bullying, and the Chinese People's Volunteers (CPV) who fought in Korea suffered enormous losses, estimated at 900,000 killed and injured. Mao Zedong's son, Mao Anying, died in an American bombing raid on the CPV headquarters in December 1950, and as he had been placed by Mao under the personal protection of the leading Chinese field commander, Marshal Peng Dehuai, this was to sour relations between the two men for years to come and was one of the personal causes of the bitter factional disputes within the CCP that led to the Cultural Revolution.

China and North Korea were not defeated in the war, which ended in a stalemate that over 65 years later has still not been formally resolved by a peace treaty. However, both regimes suffered greatly in terms of diplomatic representation and economic investment. China was branded an aggressor and effectively isolated for 30 years. As part of the truce agreement, a demilitarised zone was established between the North and the South, and the United States continues to maintain 35,000 troops in South Korea.

China's attitude toward North Korea is akin to that of someone dealing with a difficult and embarrassing friend or relative. The historical ties between the two make it impossible for China to abandon its neighbour and ally, but Beijing insiders who dealt with Pyongyang were scathing about how demanding and manipulative they found Kim Jung-il, who came to power when his father Kim Il-sung died in July 1994, and his entourage.[37] Kim Jung-il never possessed the authority or power that his father was able to wield, and although he took formal control over the armed forces on the death of his father, the delay in his appointment as state President and General Secretary of the Korean Party of Labour (he was not formally given this post until October 1997) was universally understood to be an indication of the weakness of his position in the Pyongyang elite. Long-standing rumours of a bitter power struggle within the elite were largely substantiated when a senior political theorist, Huang Jang-yop, defected to the South Korean embassy in Beijing in February 1997.

Beijing continued to encourage Kim Jung-il to take the path of economic reform that China had followed so successfully and organised high-profile guided tours of the most dramatic developments in the Shanghai region such as Pudong for him and his senior colleagues. However, apart from limited market reforms in the food supply system, Kim and his officials were reluctant to take that step.

Crisis, 2003

A new phase in the confrontation over Pyongyang's nuclear programme began in October 2002 when the United States accused the North Korean government of having begun the processing of enriched uranium in contravention of an agreement that had been reached in 1994. North Korea claimed (or admitted) that it had a previously undeclared nuclear weapons programme, although there was considerable doubt over whether it actually possessed any functioning nuclear weapons. In reprisal, the United States led a boycott of the supply of oil to North Korea in November 2002. In December of the same year, Pyongyang expelled two inspectors from the International Atomic Energy Authority (the UN regulatory body), and announced in January 2003 its decision to withdraw from the Nuclear Non-Proliferation Treaty. It was announced in February 2003 that the Yongbyon 5-megawatt nuclear power reactor, the main North Korean nuclear plant, and its plutonium reprocessing facility had been reactivated and upgraded.[38]

Since April 2003, Pyongyang has consistently demanded direct talks with Washington to resolve the crisis rather than the six-nation talks process that is preferred by the West because they include the regional powers most directly affected by the North's nuclear programme.[39]

At the end of August 2003, the parliamentary body of North Korea, the Supreme People's Assembly, formally approved a statement by its Foreign Ministry that Pyongyang had no option but to pursue its policy of developing a nuclear deterrent to defend itself against possible pre-emptive nuclear strikes by the United States. However, other sources in Pyongyang indicated that there was still the possibility of negotiation, and as usual with North Korea, the genuine policy direction remained shrouded in mystery. China responded to the increased tension by transferring responsibility for the security of its border with North Korea from the police to the PLA: reports that Beijing had deployed as many as 150,000 troops along the border were nevertheless treated with some scepticism. The United States upgraded its Patriot anti-missile defence system, which is based at the Suwon Air Base south of Seoul in South Korea; the Patriot system is designed to target and destroy incoming ballistic missiles, cruise missiles, and aircraft.[40]

On 19 September 2003, the International Atomic Energy Agency (IAEA) passed a resolution strongly advising North Korea to abandon its nuclear deterrence policy, but a statement from KCNA, the official news agency in Pyongyang, rejected this contemptuously and maintained that it was under no compulsion to comply with the IAEA's instructions since it had withdrawn from the Nuclear Non-proliferation Treaty in January 2003.[41]

On 13 August 2003, as plans were being finalised for a six-nation conference on the nuclear crisis, the Ministry of Foreign Affairs in Pyongyang issued a statement renewing its demands for a non-aggression pact with the United States as a precondition for relinquishing its nuclear ambitions.[42] The conference, with delegates representing North and South Korea, Russia, China, Japan, and the United States, met on 26–27 August in the Diaoyutai State Guest House in Beijing, which had been the venue for many high-level diplomatic negotiations since the establishment of the PRC. The meeting was presided over by the Chinese Foreign Minister Wang Yi, and the pessimistic mood that had prevailed during the preparatory meeting was clearly justified when the meeting concluded without a joint statement and a North Korean spokesman rejected the idea of a further round of meetings.[43]

Continuing confrontation, 2006

A six-party meeting in July 2006 proved as inconclusive as the previous meetings, and there were also signs of further strains in relations between China and North Korea. There have been persistent rumours about North Korea's involvement in money laundering and, more recently, in the counterfeiting of foreign currencies including the US dollar and possibly the Chinese renminbi. After US authorities took action against the Banco Delta Asia, a bank based in Macao which held substantial deposits of money belonging to Pyongyang, Beijing took the unusual step of following suit and froze North Korean bank accounts which were reported to have contained millions of dollars.[44]

Delegates to the 13th meeting of the ASEAN Regional Forum (ARF), which was convened in Kuala Lumpur, Malaysia on 28 July 2006, were hoping to arrange a parallel meeting at this forum during which they would be able to discuss Pyongyang's nuclear plans. However, the North Korean Foreign Minister, Paek Nam-sun, warned that his delegation would walk out if there were any hint of condemnation of Pyongyang's missile tests by ASEAN members. Another spokesman for Pyongyang, Jong Song-il, made it clear that the financial sanctions that had been imposed on North Korea were the main obstacle to discussions at that stage.[45]

On 9 October 2006, North Korea announced that it had carried out a nuclear test. Although there was scepticism in specialist scientific circles about the nature and magnitude of the explosion, it was taken seriously by international bodies. Pressure on China to curb the excesses of its neighbour (and alleged friend and ally) increased. Beijing imposed additional financial restrictions on Pyongyang after the test and the threat of cutting off oil supplies to North Korea was also mooted. China had apparently only been given 20 minutes advance warning of the test.

Wen Jiabao, the Chinese Premier, insisted that diplomacy and dialogue were the only appropriate means to resolve the crisis, and President Hu Jintao dispatched a high-level delegation to Pyongyang, led by Tang Jiaxuan, a former Minister of Foreign Affairs and an experienced and respected diplomat. Although there was no detailed communiqué of the results of this mission, Kim Jung-il is reported to have agreed that North Korea would not test any further nuclear devices: some sources even suggested that he had expressed regret about the consequences of the test to the Chinese team. However, it was also reported that there had been a mass rally of over 100,000 North Koreans in Pyongyang to give support to the nuclear test.[46] Eventually, North Korea did agree to resume its participation in the six-party talks, and the consensus is that this was almost entirely due to China's insistence.[47]

In December 2006, the US government made Pyongyang an offer of economic assistance in exchange for an agreement that North Korea would cease its programme of developing nuclear technology. The offer followed meetings that took place once again in the Diaoyutai State Guesthouse in Beijing and involved the US Assistant Secretary of State, Christopher Hill, and the Deputy Foreign Minister of North Korea, Kim Kye-gwan, in addition to Chinese officials. These proposals, which were far more detailed than previous offers from Washington, included commitments by the United States, Japan, and South Korea to supply further food aid, an agreement on mechanisms for removing the restrictions on North Korean funds that were deposited abroad, and assistance in developing Pyongyang's non-nuclear energy sector.[48]

Koreans in China: minorities and refugees

One factor in relations between North Korea and China that is often overlooked is the existence of an ethnic Korean population living within the borders of the PRC: the existence of a Korean minority in China is hardly surprising, given that the two countries have a common border. The ethnic Korean population of China is approximately two million[49]: most live within the Yanbian Korean Autonomous Prefecture which borders on North Korea, but there are also Koreans living in other parts of China: Beijing is home to a thriving Korean community and has many excellent Korean restaurants. Since the onset of the North Korean famine, steadily increasing numbers of Koreans have been attempting to leave the North and move to China, where, in some cases, they have relatives.

North Koreans who cross the border into the PRC to flee economic hardship and political persecution are considered by the Chinese authorities to be economic migrants: they are treated as illegal immigrants and are under constant threat of deportation. Although China has obligations to refugees under the UN Refugee Convention and Protocol, it claims that these obligations are superseded by an agreement that it has with the government of North Korea in Pyongyang. The contents of this agreement are confidential, but it has been suggested that procedures adopted by Beijing and Pyongyang to deal with cross-border migrations date back to informal attempts to deal with Chinese fleeing into North Korea during the famines that followed the Great Leap Forward in China in 1958. A protocol on border security, signed by the two sides in 1986 but never made public, obliges China to repatriate North Koreans rather than treat them as refugees.[50]

Consequently, China does not permit the UN High Commission for Refugees (UNHCR) and other agencies to have access to North Koreans living within the borders of China. UNHCR, which has maintained an office in Beijing since 1995, argues that many migrants from North Korea are genuine refugees and should be treated as such, but Chinese officials insist that this is an internal problem and UNHCR has complained that it has been obstructed in its attempts to treat these people as refugees.[51]

In spite of these difficulties, the pressure on North Koreans to risk the border crossing into China grew as economic conditions in North Korea deteriorated dramatically, especially in the 1990s, when there was severe famine in the rural areas and the country became dependent on foreign aid. It is difficult to quantify the scale of the migration of refugees from North Korea into China because – for political reasons and motivated by national pride – neither side wishes to admit to the numbers involved, but refugee agencies describe it as a mass exodus. According to a report from the Brookings Institution, a research and policy think tank based in Washington DC, the Chinese government claims that there are 10,000 North Koreans living within the borders of the PRC, whereas the US State Department works on a figure of 30,000–50,000. Even this figure is believed to be a considerable underestimate by NGOs with a special interest in refugees and some of these organisations have put the figure as high as 300,000. China deports refugees back to North Korea on a regular basis: possibly as many as 10,000 annually.[52]

This migration has been complicated by the involvement of South Korean Christians who have assisted in smuggling people across the border, and there have been a number of high-profile cases of North Koreans demanding political asylum in foreign embassies, in particular the Japanese embassy in Beijing. There is a sizeable, and generally disadvantaged, Korean community in Japan which dates back to Japan's colonial adventure in Korea at the beginning of the twentieth century and the migration of Korean labour to Japan. Most of these Japanese Koreans [*zainichi*] were originally from what was then the northern part of colonial Korea, and many of them retain ties with their family members in North Korea.

The authorities in Beijing were so concerned about the possibility of divided loyalties among the Korean community in the northeast of China that they launched an ideological education campaign in September 2003 to remind Koreans living in the Yanbian Korean Autonomous Prefecture that 'their motherland is China'. This was in response to legislation being drafted in South Korea which aimed to extend the rights of Korean nationality to all those who were 'Korean by blood', a policy which Beijing regarded as a direct attempt to undermine the status of Yanbian Koreans as a Chinese national minority. This is taken seriously by Beijing because there are concerns that if the North Korean regime collapses or suffers a military defeat, or if there is an agreement on the peaceful unification of Korea (however unlikely that might seem in the light of the history of conflict between the two Koreas), Korean nationalist opinion might demand the inclusion of Yanbian in an enlarged Korea.[53]

Rapprochement, 2007

In early August 2007, it was announced that the leaders of North and South Korea would meet in Pyongyang from 28–30 August. This was unusual but not unprecedented, since in

2000 Kim Jung-il had met Kim Dae-jung, who as President of South Korea at the time was pursuing a 'sunshine policy' of rapprochement towards his northern neighbour. The 2007 meeting followed protracted confidential negotiations between the two sides, and an international agreement that had been reached to provide aid for North Korea in exchange for disarmament and which had resulted in the closure of the Yongbyon reactor in July 2007. Cynics suggested that one reason for the meeting was an attempt to bolster the chances of the South Korean President Roh Moo-hyun in elections which were due in December 2007. President Roh was nearing the end of his first term of office as President, and polls indicated that he was running second to the opposition Grand National Party which has a hard-line approach to North Korea.

After the three-day meeting, the two sides issued a declaration in which they called for an international conference which would conclude with a treaty to take the place of the armistice, still the only formal conclusion to the Korean War. Parallel negotiations included discussions on continued nuclear decommissioning, cross-border freight transport, and fishing in the disputed western maritime borders. Although the summit was greeted with relief and a degree of enthusiasm, it was not at all clear whether any substantive changes had taken place.[54]

At the end of November 2007, there was more optimism about the reduction of tensions between North Korea and the United States than there had been for many years. There were reports that a US diplomat had established an office in Pyongyang to act as liaison officer between the two governments, and that arrangements were being made for others to join him in preparation for the anticipated normalisation of diplomatic relations.[55] There were also rumours that changes in the government of North Korea were imminent. Intelligence from Pyongyang suggested that Jang Song-taek, the brother-in-law of the Dear Leader Kim Jong-il, had been appointed head of Pyongyang's security service. Korean analysts view Jang as less narrow minded and more outward looking than most of the Pyongyang leadership, and this is attributed to his extensive overseas experience. He has a reputation as an economic reformer, one of a minority within the North Korean elite, and was reported to have been directing a project to create a Chinese-style special economic zone close to the country's border with the PRC.[56]

Regular rail links between North and South Korea began on 12 December 2007. Initially, these only involved freight trains, and although there were hopes that people would be able to cross the border by rail in the future, there were no announcements of immediate plans to resume passenger services. The economies of both Koreas stand to gain considerably from this traffic.[57]

By the end of 2007, it was beginning to be assumed that, after decades of recurrent crises, the normalisation of relations between North Korea and its former adversaries was finally becoming a reality. In early December, US President George W. Bush wrote a personal letter to Kim Jung-il urging the North Korean government to honour undertakings that it had made in the six-party negotiations and reveal full details of their nuclear programmes. A positive reply was received by the White House. This was a verbal rather than a written response, and it was not immediately clear whether it had come from Kim personally, but this unprecedented direct contact was treated as further evidence of normalisation.[58] In January 2008, Pyongyang missed a crucial deadline for declaring details of its nuclear programme, and it appeared that it was business as usual.

Kim Jong-un

Kim Jong-il died suddenly on 17 December 2011, reportedly from a heart attack. He was succeeded by his second son, Kim Jong-un who was 27 years old. Kim Jong-il's first-born,

Kim Jong-chul, was passed over for the succession and a half-brother, Kim Jong-nan, was later assassinated in a bizarre February 2017 attack at Kuala Lumpur International Airport in Malaysia. Kim Jong-un's succession was neither automatic nor smooth; he did not acquire the chairmanship of the Korean Workers Party and the State Affairs Commission until, respectively, May and June 2016. He dealt ruthlessly with opponents, within and outside his family.

On 12 December 2012, Pyongyang launched a rocket carrying an earth observation satellite. This was condemned by the UN Security Council on the grounds that it violated the prohibition on North Korean ballistic missile tests, since the rocket technology was almost identical. Beijing acknowledged that it did not have sufficient leverage to prevent North Korea from continuing with its test programme and opposed new international sanctions so as not to weaken its position.[59]

Kim-Moon talks, Trump and Putin summits, 2018–2019

After the US presidential elections of 2016, China's relations with the Koreas were overshadowed by exaggerated expectations of progress when direct talks between President Trump and Kim Jung-un were arranged for 12 June 2018. Media coverage of their summit meeting in Singapore was intense, as it was the first face-to-face meeting between the leaders of the United States and North Korea, but it yielded few concrete results; neither did subsequent visits to North Korea by US Secretary of State Mike Pompeo.[60]

A second attempt at a summit agreement failed when a meeting on 27–28 February 2019, this time in Hanoi, broke down after unrealistic expectations on the denuclearisation of the Korean peninsula. In a caustic analysis, a commentator argued in *South China Morning Post* that,

> As the self-proclaimed 'great negotiator', Trump botched this summit by underestimating Kim and thinking he could bamboozle him into making a deal. It seemed like Trump was willing to lower the non-proliferation threshold to secure a win, but in the end it was Kim who showed that he would rather suffer the consequences of punishing sanctions than give up his 'treasured sword'. But let's be clear, the summit ultimately failed because sufficient groundwork was not done beforehand to arrive at a mutual understanding on the basic parameters and a framework of understanding as to what both parties were willing to offer or give up.[61]

Neither was it satisfactory for the North Koreans. At the end of May 2019 came rumours of a purge of North Korean officials connected with the failed Trump summit. Unconfirmed reports in the South Korean press, which does not have a good reputation for accuracy, indicated that Kim Hyok-chol, one of the key participants, had been executed and others, including the interpreter, had either been executed or committed to forced labour camps and 'ideological education'. Kim Yo-jong, younger sister of Kim Jong-un who had appeared supportive of the talks, was reported to be 'lying low'. The failure of the talks was an embarrassment for Pyongyang.[62]

In April 2019, Kim Jong-un met Russian President Vladimir Putin for the first time. For Putin, this was an opportunity to upstage the Americans and bolster the status of Russia in international talks over Korea. For Kim, it was an occasion to discuss Pyongyang's need for financial assistance and the response of the two countries to their shared problems of dealing with Western sanctions. Putin briefed Xi Jinping on his summit with Kim during the Belt and Road Forum later that month: keeping China informed was essential for Putin's relations with North Korea.[63]

Negotiations on Pyongyang's international position continued with direct and indirect talks with Seoul, and meetings of Kim Jong-un and Moon Jae-in, who played a pivotal role in the complex multi-lateral negotiations but kept a deliberately low profile. With the increased involvement of the United States and the upcoming G20 summit in Osaka on 28–29 June 2019, it became essential for Beijing to reassert its status as North Korea's main ally. Xi Jinping travelled to Pyongyang on 20 June for a brief but well-publicised state visit; this was his first to North Korea, even though he had been in power for seven years. Xi's visit helped to build momentum for the reopening of the peace process on the Korean peninsula.

Unwilling to be outdone by the Chinese, and with his 2020 electoral prospects in mind, Donald Trump staged a brief photo opportunity in North Korea – or at least a few steps across the demilitarised zone – and a meeting with Kim Jong-un on 30 June in the wake of the G20 summit. This encounter had been brokered by President Moon Jae-in of South Korea, who had also met Xi Jinping at the summit. The Trump trip was performance art rather than serious diplomatic negotiations, and he was not accorded the state visit that Xi had enjoyed, but it permitted the resumption of talks that had stalled after the Hanoi summit of February 2019. Moon maintained a low profile and allowed Trump to take the credit; officially, Pyongyang insisted that Seoul should not interfere with its talks with Washington, but there was no doubt that Moon and Xi had played key roles in putting peace talks back on track.[64] The irrelevance of the Trump visit to serious negotiations was highlighted on 3 July when the North Korean delegation to the United Nations reverted to the previous antagonistic rhetoric, accusing Washington of being 'hell-bent on hostile acts' and 'obsessed with sanctions'.[65]

In 2020, the international relations of North Korea were overshadowed by the mysterious disappearances of Kim Jong-un, notably his failure to attend national celebrations of the birthday of his grandfather Kim Il-sung the founding leader of the regime. These absences, the first of at least three weeks, and the second of 20 days following May Day, prompted speculation about Kim's health, but he reappeared for a meeting of the Workers' Party's Central Military Commission. A communiqué from the meeting was issued on 23 May in response to suggestions that the United States was seriously considering the resumption of nuclear testing. The North Koreans decided to increase their nuclear deterrence capabilities – including the firepower of the artillery, the main threat to the South Korean capital, Seoul – and discussed putting the military on high alert. This strategy was reinforced by the appointment of Ri Pyong-chol as Vice-Chairman of the Commission and the promotion to vice-marshal of 70 generals, including Pak Jong-chun, an artillery and missile specialist.[66]

Persistent rumours about Kim's health and grip on power were reinforced by announcements in August 2020 that he had devolved certain political responsibilities to aides, notably to his younger sister, Kim Yo-jong, 'to reduce his stress levels'. Nevertheless, later that month, he chaired meetings of the Central Committee and then the Politburo of the Korean Workers' Party. These focused on the challenges posed to Pyongyang by the Covid-19 virus and a failure of economic planning. Trade with China, a key factor in North Korea's economic survival, had decreased by more than 20% in July 2020, largely because of border closures in response to the virus.[67] Nevertheless, the continuing impact of sanctions imposed by the United Nations and the United States meant that Pyongyang was increasingly dependent on state aid from Beijing and technically illegal business dealings with Chinese companies.[68]

Overseas Chinese – the politics of diaspora

Ethnic Chinese communities outside China, from Southeast Asia to Europe and the Americas, have played an important role in the development of China's relations with the rest of the world. This role has often been unreported and unrecognised; it has not always been positive, either for China or for the communities of the Chinese diaspora.

The most common modern Chinese term for individuals and communities of ethnic Chinese origin who are resident outside of China is *huaqiao*. It is sometimes considered to be a reference to a bridge between two cultures, as the character for *qiao* is similar to the character for 'bridge'. This is, however, rather fanciful and the *qiao* in *huaqiao* actually refers to an inn or the place of rest for Chinese sojourners who were temporarily away from their native villages for trade or for work – although temporary became permanent in the case of many of these communities. The usual English translation is overseas Chinese, although some prefer Chinese overseas. The term overseas Chinese was not usually applied in the PRC to people resident in Hong Kong and Macao before those territories returned to China, and it is not used for the residents of Taiwan. The preferred term in these cases is *tongbao* [literally, 'born of the same parents' and, by extension, 'compatriots'].

It has been estimated that the total population of overseas Chinese is something of the order of 30 million.[69] Some 80% of these live in Southeast Asia, in both the mainland (Vietnam, Cambodia, Laos, and Thailand) and the island states (Philippines, Indonesia, and Malaysia). There are also significant communities of Chinese origin in the Caribbean, Peru, India, Australia, Canada, the United States, and Europe – including Eastern Europe, where the Chinese-speaking population increased dramatically following the collapse of the Soviet Union in 1991.

The majority of Chinese who live in states such as Malaysia and Indonesia have been settled in their countries of domicile for several generations and have usually taken the nationality of that country. That is also true in North America and much of Europe, but other communities have not yet reached that stage of development.

The majority of the people of the Chinese diaspora trace their origins to the southern coastal provinces of Fujian, Guangdong, Guangxi, and the island of Hainan (now also a province). Their languages and cultures are those of the south rather than the Mandarin-speaking north, and the *lingua franca* in Chinese communities outside China tends to be Cantonese – although many people, especially in Singapore, Malaysia, and Indonesia, speak Hokkien (Fujianese) or Hakka. There has been emigration in every historical period, but it was during the nineteenth and early twentieth centuries that economic pressures and military and political crises in China (notably the Taiping rebellion and its suppression by the Qing armies) precipitated the large-scale emigration of young men.

Many of these travelled initially to the regions that are now part of the states of Malaysia and Indonesia, and settled in towns rather than in the farming areas which were already occupied by local people (known in the Malay language as the *bumiputra*, 'sons of the soil'). Chinese settlers established themselves in industry and commerce rather than agriculture, although they did occasionally become involved in specialist farming enterprises such as the production of rubber or pineapple growing. Distinctive Chinatowns also began to appear. Denied access to most agricultural trades, many Chinese settlers earned their living as itinerant peddlers or village shopkeepers, and over time, they acquired a reputation for business acumen. Their success in business and the wealth and status that it brought them did not always assist them in their relations with the indigenous population: rivalry and envy often led to racial tensions, and at times to inter-communal violence. Initially, Chinese settlers in

Southeast Asia did not assimilate well. In common with other diaspora communities, the earliest arrivals saw themselves as sojourners who assumed that they would return to China once they had made their fortunes. They maintained their own Chinese languages, brought Chinese women over from their home villages to marry (although this was at a later stage in the migration process), and if they could, they educated their children in Chinese-language schools.

Second- and third-generation settlers began to assimilate; they took local names, became proficient in the local tongues (principally the widespread language of administration and commerce which is today known as either *Bahasa Indonesia* or *Bahasa Malaysia* – two national versions of the Malay language), and sent their sons and daughters to local schools where they mixed with the non-Chinese population. When China acquired a Communist government in 1949, the position of the overseas Chinese communities became more troubled and complicated. The mentality of the Cold War created a climate of suspicion and encouraged searches for 'reds under the bed'. Chinese in Malaysia and Indonesia were suspected of being sympathetic to Beijing and therefore to the CCP. Some were indeed prominent in the Communist Party in Malaysia, but even those who were not involved in any political activity were suspect and frequently discriminated against. In Malaysia, there were transfers to special village reservations. In Indonesia, anti-Chinese pogroms as late as 1998 resulted in many deaths and the destruction of Chinese careers and businesses. After riots and the fall of the Indonesian President Suharto, who was suspected of having used inter-communal tensions to bolster his regime, legislation that had discriminated against Chinese Indonesians – especially their use of the written Chinese language – was repealed.

The reform period provided new economic opportunities on the mainland for Chinese entrepreneurs from outside China. Their capital and business prowess were welcomed by the new order that emerged after the death of Mao, and overseas Chinese businesses have been involved in the major economic development projects of the last two decades.

China and India

China and India share the distinction of being the nations that are tipped to be the twin economic powerhouses of the twenty-first century. They are also the world's most populous countries: India has a population of 1.1 billion, which may catch up with or even overtake China's 1.3 billion. Both are predominantly rural societies that are making great strides in their progress towards industrialisation and modernisation. Historically, China owes a major debt to India as the source of one of its core religions, Buddhism. They do not, however, have much in common in terms of political structure or culture, and relations between the two have been difficult since the foundation of the two modern states in the aftermath of the Second World War.

The two states have a common border, but much of it is mountainous and it includes the Himalayas, which are a formidable barrier to communication of any kind, although there are traversable passes and there is a long history of trade and religious pilgrimage across the mountains. The small independent states of Nepal and Bhutan also lie on this border. There are serious disagreements over the demarcation of the borders, the most significant for Sino-Indian relations being two long-standing disputes relating to Aksai Chin in the Jammu and Kashmir region in the west and Arunachal Pradesh (South Tibet to the Chinese) which is in the northeast of India close to Assam and was part of the North East Frontier Agency under the British Raj.

In the 1950s, during the Cold War and the movement for decolonisation, China and India cooperated successfully, and a popular slogan of the time was *Hindi Chini bhai bhai*, 'India and China are brothers'. What became known as the Five Principles of Peaceful Cooexistence, the *panch shila* (also written *panchsheel*) were agreed during negotiations between Zhou Enlai and the Indian Prime Minister Jawaharlal Nehru for the Sino-Indian treaty which was signed in 1954. The essential points of this agreement were peaceful coexistence in spite of different ideological positions, equality, mutual respect, non-aggression, and refraining from interference in the internal affairs of the other party. These idealistic principles were popular and in tune with the spirit of the time, and were widely used in negotiations between other Third World countries.

However, China and India also competed for leadership of the non-aligned Third World, notably during the conference of developing nations that was held in 1955 in the Indonesian city of Bandung. The term non-aligned can only be applied very loosely in this period; the Third World was not exempt from the divisions of the Cold War, and India drew close to Moscow while its regional rival Pakistan became an ally of the United States. As the Sino-Soviet dispute unfolded around 1960, China also formed a strategic alliance with Pakistan to counter the influence of the USSR in Delhi, in spite of Pakistan's close relations with the United States.

From the 1950s to the 1970s, China and India were held up as models for the alternative routes that developing countries could take: Indian democracy or Chinese dictatorship. The differences between the economies of the two states were never as great as their political differences might have suggested: India, like China, had a planned economy with an important role for the state; India did implement a multi-party democracy, however flawed, which China never even attempted.

The simmering border disputes erupted into full-scale conflict in 1962 after complaints by both sides over military incursions into what each considered to be their own sovereign territory in northern Indian territory close to Tibet and Xinjiang. Heavy fighting began in early October of that year, but the armed conflict, although bitterly fought, was short-lived and it came to an end when the Chinese side announced a unilateral ceasefire at the end of November. As a result of its military advances, China had retained its control over Aksai Chin, but it did not take all of the territory that it claimed as its own in the northeast of India. It concluded an agreement with Pakistan, India's rival, on border demarcation and the war came to an end. There have been numerous minor skirmishes in the border region since the ceasefire, but there has been no fighting on the scale of the 1962 conflict.[70]

Although the main border disputes are about Aksai Chin and Arunachal Pradesh, the issue of Tibet has been a major obstacle to the achievement of satisfactory Sino-Indian relations. After China's suppression of the Tibetan rising of 1959, the Dalai Lama had been given asylum in Dharamsala, a town in the northwestern Indian state of Himachal Pradesh. The Dalai Lama intended to return to Tibet in due course, and a Tibetan government in exile was created in Dharamsala: this was regarded by the government of the PRC as unacceptable interference in China's internal affairs and therefore a breach of the Five Principles of Peaceful Coexistence (for further discussion of the Tibet issue, see Chapter 21).

In spite of all these unresolved issues, relations between the two Asian giants have improved gradually and there have been constant discussions on trade and cooperation. The border dispute remains a hard nut to crack: there is still no joint agreement on the implications for border demarcation of the ceasefire line of 1962, although tensions have been reduced since interim agreements were signed in 1993 and 1996. Both sides continue to claim that the other is still occupying territory illegally. India's nuclear tests in May 1998 temporarily destabilised diplomatic relations with Beijing, not least because the Hindu Nationalist BJP (Bharatiya Janata Party) government in New Delhi claimed that the tests were motivated by fears of a nuclear threat from China. Indian Foreign Minister George Fernandes called China 'India's enemy number one'.[71]

When conflict erupted between India and Pakistan over Kashmir in May 1999, both sides appealed to China for support, but China remained neutral in public and appears to have supported international demands for a peaceful solution to a conflict that was potentially perilous since both sides are nuclear states. High-level political and diplomatic visits by Chinese and Indian politicians have continued, and relations have warmed.

Sonia Gandhi, President of the Indian National Congress, which was the dominant party in India's post-BJP ruling coalition, visited China in October 2007 at the invitation of the CCP and its chairman Hu Jintao, and arrived in Beijing just after the CCP's 17th national Congress. Mrs Gandhi, the widow of former Prime Minister Rajiv Gandhi, who was assassinated in 1991, made positive comments about the social and economic development of China during a visit that was intended to strengthen bilateral relations in general, in addition to links between the two political parties. Although published accounts of the meetings between the two sides did not go beyond the usual platitudes, there were reports that their discussions had broached some of the more intransigent issues in Sino-Indian relations, including the border disputes.[72]

Meetings between the Chinese Premier Wen Jiabao and his Indian counterpart Manmohan Singh in December 2005 and January 2008 were productive, and there have also been joint military manoeuvres. China and India have concluded agreements on trade and economic cooperation in fields such as construction, financial services, education, and tourism. Trade is likely to be the key to the relationship between the two states, and fierce competition can be expected, as well as strategic cooperation. In 2006, it was estimated that the total value of bilateral trade was of the order of US$20 billion, and this figure is set to rise significantly.[73]

Relations between China and India remained stable, concerned mainly with economic cooperation and competition, in spite of occasional border clashes and incursions. The most serious of these was in the summer of 2017 at Doklam in disputed territory, claimed by China as part of Tibet, India for Sikkim, and Bhutan. On 16 June, a Chinese military engineer unit began extending a road southward that would potentially give China access to India's northeastern provinces. This construction was resisted by Bhutanese troops, who were rapidly reinforced by Indian military units from Sikkim, in line with 1949 treaty requirements to assist in the defence of Bhutan. The PLA drafted in reinforcements and a standoff lasted until 28 August 2017, when both India and China withdrew their troops. Disagreements remained over ownership and control of the territory, and both India and China reinforced their military presence, notably by the construction of airfields close to the border.[74]

In the summer of 2020, more serious clashes occurred close to the imperfectly demarcated border with Ladakh. India acknowledged that 20 of its soldiers were killed and 76 injured in June. For decades, there had been a tacit agreement that firearms would not be used at the border; most of the Indian casualties were from hypothermia, injuries from stones or makeshift weapons, or falling over ridges or into rivers. China did not admit to casualties. Tensions escalated at the end of August with what Indian sources called 'provocative military movements' on the southern shores of the remote Pangong Tso Lake, which is in territory disputed by the two sides. China blamed India for mobilising more troops in the region, while New Delhi claimed that Beijing was attempting to redraw the international border by force. Live ammunition was used for the first time. The clashes occurred during a meeting of foreign ministers of the SCO in Moscow. Under the auspices of the SCO, Indian and Chinese foreign ministers, Subrahmanyam Jaishankar and Wang Yi, met with the assistance of their Russian counterpart Sergei Lavrov and agreed on a swift 'disengagement' of the armed forces of both sides from the Line of Actual Control.[75]

China and Africa

As China's domestic economy expanded in the 1980s and 1990s, the government began to search for new overseas partners. The PRC required additional markets for its manufactured goods; it also needed inexpensive supplies of raw materials and, above all, energy. Commercial relations were developed with a number of other Third World regions, including the countries of ASEAN and Latin America, but the most interesting – and in many ways, the most controversial – have been China's relations with African states.

China does not have a record of an imperial past in Africa, and this might put it at an advantage in comparison with those Western nations which were former colonial powers on the continent. There is, however, a long history of Chinese contact with Africa. The naval squadrons of the Chinese Muslim Admiral Zhenghe, who explored the Indian Ocean between 1405 and 1433 during the reign of the Yongle Emperor of the Ming dynasty, reached as far as the coast of East Africa. Although these missions were discontinued, trade between China and Africa persisted, as is attested by finds of datable Chinese porcelain at various sites on the Swahili coast. Chinese men were recruited to work as indentured labourers in the gold fields of the Transvaal during the early years of the twentieth century. These early migrants were the basis for the modern Chinese community in South Africa, although it has been augmented by more recent arrivals, some from the PRC but many from Taiwan, including entrepreneurs who set up small businesses. Taiwan and South Africa sustained a diplomatic relationship during the period: South Africa was ostracised by most of the developed world because of its apartheid policies; Taiwan was excluded from the United Nations in 1971 and was constantly searching for political and economic allies.

Tanzania and Zambia Railway

The more recent involvement of the China in Africa began in the 1960s and was essentially part of the PRC's rivalries with both the USSR and Taiwan for political influence on the continent. In 1970, construction began on a railway to link the port of Dar es-Salaam, the largest city in Tanzania and at the time its capital, to the Zambian border, where it would connect with the Zambian railway network.[76] This was a considerable foreign aid project for China, particularly in view of the fact that it was itself at the time a very underdeveloped country. For Tanzania, it provided a much-needed link to the economy of Zambia, which was developing on the basis of vast resources of copper until the price of the metal dropped in the 1970s. The most significant gain for newly independent Zambia was that it would no longer be economically dependent on the regimes of Rhodesia (now Zimbabwe) and South Africa, both of which were dominated by elites of European origin. The Tanzam railway, which in due course also became known as the TAZARA (Tanzania and Zambia Railway Authority) or the Uhuru (freedom) railway, went into operation in 1975. Its economic value has been questioned, but there is no doubt that it had a political value for Beijing as a emblem of China's support for the movement against colonialism in the 1970s.

Oil and construction

By the 1990s, the rhetoric of anti-colonialism and Third World solidarity had given way to hard-headed commercial considerations. Thousands of Chinese workers and managers, mainly in the construction and energy industries, moved to work in African countries such as Angola, Sudan, Zimbabwe, and Zambia in the 1990s. An oversimplified, but not entirely inaccurate, analysis of the relationship is that China acquired valuable raw materials – oil in the case of Sudan and Angola, and valuable minerals from elsewhere – and in return the Africans benefited from the construction or improvement of their infrastructure which was desperately needed. Many Western companies had been reluctant to become involved in development projects in these states, partly because of concerns about human rights and corruption, and partly because of real or perceived risks in regions where there were ongoing insurgencies or countries that have only recently emerged from long and brutal civil wars.

Chinese companies, mostly state-owned, do not have to answer to the same demands for corporate social responsibility that face their counterparts in the West. Life is not easy for the new expatriates, many of whom experience a substantial culture shock in Africa, as did earlier generations of Chinese who came to the continent as diplomats or bearing foreign aid. In many cases, the new Chinese expatriate existence is made tolerable by the creation of residential and social compounds for Chinese engineers and labourers where they can use their own Chinese language, eat their own Chinese dishes, and enjoy their own Chinese entertainment.[77]

Chinese businesses in Africa rarely employ local workers. Not only are almost all managers sent from China, the vast majority of the workforce is also brought in. This has created conflict with local communities, and there have been complaints that Chinese companies do not make a sufficient contribution to the local economies, and in particular to the problems of unemployment that many African countries face.

The similarities between this lifestyle and the concessions created by Westerners in China in the late nineteenth century are striking, but some Chinese expatriates tend to regard themselves almost as commercial aid workers rather than new colonialists. More formally, Li Anshan, a historian of Africa at Beijing University, argues that 'both China and Africa have suffered the ill-effects of the colonial era. This shared experience underlies the ideas of equality and respect for sovereignty that each highlight in their approach to international relations'.[78] This policy of non-interference is far from being a new one, as it dates back to the Five Principles of Peaceful Coexistence that were agreed at the Bandung conference in 1955 as the basis for China's relationship with other Third World countries. It is an important part of Beijing's justification for working with regimes that many in the West criticise as dictatorial.[79]

Beijing Forum on China-Africa cooperation

A government White Paper *China's African Policy* was published by the Ministry of Foreign Affairs in Beijing in January 2006. As part of its strategy of formalising relations between China and the various African states with which it had economic relations, China organised a Forum on China-Africa cooperation in Beijing in November 2006. Representatives of 48 African counties attended, and trade agreements that were reported to be worth over £1 billion were signed; in addition, preferential loans and export credits were promised by President Hu Jintao in his address to the conference. The following year, Hu made official visits to Cameroon, Liberia, Sudan, Zambia, Namibia, South Africa, Mozambique, and the Seychelles to strengthen China's political and economic relationships with those countries.

China has been severely criticised for its close relationship with the Khartoum government in the light of the serious and persistent human rights abuses that have occurred in the Darfur region of Sudan during the civil war that began in 2003. In November 2007, 135 members of the Chinese armed forces were deployed to Dafur as part of a joint peace-keeping mission that had been mounted by the African Union and the United Nations.[80] Rebel forces – that is, armed groups opposed to the Khartoum government – declared that they would not regard the Chinese contingent as neutrals but as supporters of the regime in Khartoum.

China is the largest customer for Sudan's oil, and has been at least since 1999: in return, it has exported, among other commodities, weapons to Sudan and has also contributed to building the infrastructure of the oil industry by developing its exploration, production, and refining technologies. This close relationship is alleged to have been responsible for China's refusal to support international sanctions against the Khartoum government. According to Li Anshan, whose academic analysis is in line with the thinking of the Chinese government on Africa, 'China has consistently opposed economic sanctions in Sudan. China believes the Darfur issue is an issue related to development, where sanctions would only bring more trouble to the region . . . the international community has to give Sudan some time to solve this problem'. He also argued that Chinese aid was tackling the root of the problem: poverty. Representatives of the rebel forces opposed to the Khartoum government did not see it that way and threatened to attack both Chinese military contingents and Chinese companies operating in the region. The influence that China can bring to bear on the Khartoum government is probably overestimated: Beijing is determined to maintain the principle of non-interference in Sudan's internal affairs, and has maintained that it is supplying far fewer armaments than has been alleged.[81]

It remains to be seen whether China can develop economic relations with African countries without turning into a colonial or quasi-colonial power. The prospects are not good. The United States initiated its international relations strategy in the nineteenth and twentieth centuries as a counter to European colonialism, only to become a neo-colonial power in its own right. Japan's attempt to create a Greater East Asia Co-prosperity Sphere, partly on the basis of a promise to drive out the Europeans and Americans, also developed into a colonial system, albeit a short-lived one.

China's international status was evolving rapidly and in December 2007, the World Bank entered into a new relationship with China in connection with its work in Africa. China was a major client of the bank from which it had received significant aid, but following a significant donation by the Export-Import Bank of China, the major international banking arm of the Chinese state, to the World Bank's International Development Association, which targets the poorest communities in the world, China is now regarded as a major donor rather than a recipient.[82]

By 2019, China had become the main trading partner for many African companies but increased competition with India and Russia, among other states. In the northeast of Africa, China has concentrated on extending its Belt and Road Initiative from the Middle East, and the annual summit of the Forum on China-Africa Cooperation in Beijing in September 2018 was well attended by African heads of state and government who heard the Chinese pledge investment of US$60 billion in the continent. Western concern about the sustainability of African countries' debt to China was exacerbated by arrangements for Beijing to take over strategic ports and other facilities in lieu.[83]

Chinese employers, African labour

Experience with the increased number of Chinese enterprises in Africa owned and managed by Chinese organisations led to concerns about the relationship between Chinese management, often isolated in separate communities, and the essentially African workforce. Although there was no doubt about the existence of racialisation of labour in Chinese-run enterprises, this may have been contributed to by African cultural assumptions, as well as Chinese. Official Chinese pressure mitigated the degree of racial discrimination and stereotyping; the government of the PRC, still emerging from its Third World status, encouraged Chinese managers to be sensitive to local cultures.[84]

Africans in Guangzhou

China's image in Africa was tarnished by the treatment of Africans in the southern Chinese city of Guangzhou. The closest large city to Hong Kong, Guangzhou had experienced a remarkable growth in its population of migrant workers and traders, many of them from African countries. In 2012, there were at least 100,000 African migrants in Guangzhou, many of them working in small businesses.[85] By 2014, after strict enforcement of immigration regulations by the Chinese authorities added to problems already created in foreign exchange rates for African currencies, the number had declined and by 2020, there were probably fewer than 5,000 African migrants typically lived in the centre of Guangzhou, many in the district of Xiaobei, which had already been settled by Muslim migrants from Ningxia and Xinjiang, and had mosques which welcomed African Muslims. Businesspeople favoured the Guangyuanxi area just to the north of Guangzhou Railway Station. Tensions between African traders and local people led to many clashes and serious rioting in 2009 and 2012. The depth of ethnic antagonism was revealed with the arrival of the Covid-19 epidemic in 2020. Fear and prejudice turned local Chinese people against the African migrants, and by April, the majority had been evicted from their accommodation and were either sleeping on the streets or forced into quarantine. As the lockdown in Guangzhou was relaxed in June, the migrants struggled to rebuild their businesses, many of them still without satisfactory accommodation.[86]

Notes

1 *Analysis* BBC Radio 4, 21 August 2006.
2 *China Daily* 4 March 2007.
3 Council for Foreign Relations website.
4 Council for Foreign Relations website.
5 *SCMP* 12 May 2019.
6 *Washington Post* 6 May 2019; *SCMP* 29 April, 7, 8, 12 May 2019; BBC News 7 May 2019; *FT* 7, 14 May 2019; *Global Times* 10 May 2019.
7 *SCMP* 8 March 2019; *FT* 8 March 2019.
8 BBC TV *Click* 5 May 2019.
9 *FT* 26 March 2019.
10 BBC News 28 March 2019; *Washington Post* 29 March 2019.
11 *Guardian* 25 April, 4 May 2019.
12 *Sunday Telegraph* 28 April 2019.
13 Embassy of the People's Republic of China, 28 January 2019.
14 www.iiss.org/events/shangri-la-dialogue/shangri-la-dialogue-2019.
15 *Guardian* 29 April 2019.
16 *Washington Post* 18 May 2019.
17 *Guardian* 29 April 2019; *FT* 20, 21 May 2019; *SCMP* 20, 22 May 2019; *Washington Post* 19 May 2019; *Global Times* 20 May 2019.
18 BBC News 29 June 2019; *Wall Street Journal* 29 June 2019.
19 *Guardian* 12 January 2020.

20 *FT* 20 May, 8 June 2020; *Guardian* 14 July 2020.
21 BBC News 14, 15 January 2020; *SCMP* 13, 14, 16 January 2020; *FT* 16, 17, 22 January 2020.
22 Martin Wolf 'A Partial and Defective Truce' *FT* 22 January 2020.
23 *FT* 13 August 2020.
24 *SCMP* 5 June 2019.
25 *Global Times* 6 June 2019.
26 *FT* 3, 6 June 2019; *SCMP* 5 June 2019; *Washington Post* 6 June 2019.
27 Stanley Rosen 'China in 1986: A Year of Consolidation' *Asian Survey* Vol. 27, No. 1, A Survey of Asia in 1986: Part I (Jan., 1987), pp. 35–55.
28 Toyota, September 1984, witnessed by the author.
29 *FT* 14 December 2007.
30 BBC News 28, 30 December 2007.
31 *SCMP* 21 February 2019.
32 *Japan Times* 25 January, 2 March 2020; *New York Times* 26 October 2018.
33 *FT* 2 September 2020.
34 *Peking Review* Volume 4, no. 28, p. 5.
35 BBC News Online 10 April 2002.
36 Mure Dickie 'China's Food Aid to North Korea Soars' *FT* 21 July 2006.
37 Personal communication to the author.
38 BBC News Online 24 April 2003.
39 BBC News Online 30 September 2003.
40 BBC News Online 15, 16 September 2003.
41 BBC News 23 September 2003.
42 BBC News 13 August 2003.
43 BBC News 30 August 2003.
44 *FT* 26 July 2006.
45 BBC News 30 July 2006.
46 Richard McGregor 'China's PM Urges Dialogue to Defuse Nuclear Crisis' *FT* 21, 22 October 2006; *SCMP* 20 October 2006.
47 *FT* 2 November 2006.
48 *New York Times* 6 December 2006.
49 Choi Woo-Gil 'The Korean Minority in China: The Change of Its Identity' *Development and Society* Vol. 30, No. 1 (June 2001), pp. 119–141.
50 *The Invisible Exodus: North Koreans in the People's Republic of China* Human Rights Watch New York, November 2002, pp. 29–30.
51 *North Korean Refugees in China and Human Rights Issues: International Response and U.S. Policy Options* Congressional Research Service Washington, DC, 26 September 2007, pp. 10–12.
52 'Human Rights and the North Korea Refugee Crisis' Brookings Institution, 25 October 2007.
53 *Mainichi Shimbun*, Tokyo in BBC Monitoring 19 September 2003.
54 BBC News 8 August 2007, 4 October 2007.
55 *Bloomberg*, Seoul, 26 November 2007.
56 *FT* 24, 25 November 2007.
57 BBC News 11 December 2007.
58 BBC News 14 December 2007.
59 *SCMP* 13 December 2012.
60 Beyza Unal 23 'US – North Korea Summit Statement Lacks Definition' Chatham House Expert Comment, 23 June 2018.
61 Srini Sitaraman 'Trump-Kim Summit 2019: A Meeting of "Two Stubborn Toddlers" Hoping to Play each other for Suckers?' *SCMP* 1 March 2019.
62 *SCMP* 31 May 2019; *Guardian* 31 May 2019; BBC News 31 May 2019.
63 'Russia-North Korea Summit: Five Key Questions Answered' Chatham House website, 26 April 2019.
64 *SCMP* 30 June 2019; *Guardian* 21, 30 June 2019.
65 BBC News 4 July 2019.
66 *SCMP* 24 May 2020; *New York Times* 24 May 2020; *The Diplomat* 24 April 2020.
67 BBC News 20, 26 August 2020; Ankit Panda 'North Korea Comes to Terms with Internal and External Challenges' *The Diplomat* 25 August 2020.

68 *FT* 10 September 2020.

69 Dudley L. Poston, Jr. and Mei-YuYu 'The Distribution of the Overseas Chinese in the Contemporary World' *The International Migration Review* Vol. 24, No. 3 (Autumn, 1990), pp. 480–508.

70 V.B. Karnik (ed.) *China Invades India: The Story of Invasion against the Background of Chinese History and Sino-Indian Relations* Bombay: Allied Publishers, 1963.

71 BBC News 21 April 2003.

72 *Hindustan Times* 26 October 2007.

73 Xinhua 16 December 2005; BBC News 14 January 2008; Xinhua 14 January 2008; *China Daily* 22 November 2006.

74 *The Diplomat* 30 August 2017; BBC News 5 July 2017, 26 January 2018.

75 BBC News 1 September 2020; Abhijnan Rej 'China Attempts to Shift Its Boundary with India in Ladakh': Again *The Diplomat* 31 August 2020; *Hindustan Times* 31 August 2020; *New York Times* 8 September 2020; *The Economic Times* (Mumbai) 10 September 2020; *Guardian* 11 September 2020; *SCMP* 11 September 2020.

76 In 1996, the National Assembly of Tanzania was transferred to the city of Dodoma, which was designated the new capital; Dar es-Salaam remains the administrative and the economic heart of the country.

77 Alec Russell 'The New Colonialists' *Financial Times Magazine* 17–18 November 2007.

78 Li Anshan 'China and Africa: Policy and Challenges' *China Security* 3, no. 3 (Summer 2007), pp. 69–93.

79 Philip Snow *The Star Raft: China's Encounter with Africa* London: Weidenfeld and Nicolson, 1988.

80 AFP 25 November 2007.

81 *FT* 23, 24 February 2008.

82 *FT* 19 December 2007; The website of the Export-Import Bank is at http://english.eximbank.gov.cn/profile/introduction.jsp.

83 Alex Vines 'Global Engagement with Africa Continued to Surge in 2018', Chatham House Expert Comment, 8 January 2019.

84 Barry Sautmann and Yan Hairong 'The Discourse of Racialisation of Chinese Labour and Chinese Enterprises in Africa' in Michael Dillon (ed.) *Chinese Minorities at Home and Abroad* London: Routledge, 2017, pp. 71–90.

85 Danny Vincent 'Africans in China: We Face Coronavirus Discrimination' BBC News, Hong Kong, 17 April 2020.

86 BBC News 24 April 2020; Reuters 26 June 2020.

27 China and the world 2

Neighbours to the west

China's relations with its immediate neighbours to the west, and to a certain extent with the states of the Islamic Middle East with which those states have close cultural and religious ties, were rekindled in the 1990s after the fall of the Soviet Union. Strictly speaking, the states on the other side of the Inner Asian frontier were not new neighbours; they had always been there. During the Cold War and the Sino-Soviet dispute, contact with China was so limited that when the borders reopened in the 1990s, diplomatic relationships had to be rebuilt almost from first principles.

Central Asia

China's closest neighbours on its western and northwestern borders are the Central Asian states of the former Soviet Union. The collapse of the USSR in 1991 and the creation of the new independent sovereign states of Kazakhstan, Kyrgyzstan, and Uzbekistan produced significant changes in political relations across China's Inner Asian frontiers. It was essential for China to forge diplomatic relations with the new states; discussions on long-standing border demarcation issues and troop reduction began almost immediately. Commercial and political relations developed swiftly, and the impact on the Xinjiang Uyghur Autonomous Region, which is that part of China nearest to Central Asia (or alternatively, that part of Central Asia currently under Chinese rule), was particularly dramatic. The border routes across the mountains were opened to trade for the first time in over 30 years: informally they opened at once but officially they were authorised from 1992 onwards. Families and communities which had enjoyed little contact for many years renewed their acquaintances, and trade developed at a rapid pace.

The new links were not restricted to commerce. Religious – that is, Islamic – connections were also renewed, and there were exchanges of political ideas. The emergence of independent Turkic Islamic states in the vicinity was immensely attractive to Uyghurs, who looked to them for assistance in their own bid for independence. Initially, there was some support for an independent East Turkestan from other Turkic states, including Turkey, but as China's confidence in dealing with its Central Asian neighbours grew, Beijing made it perfectly clear that this support would be treated as unwarranted interference in China's internal affairs and would not be tolerated. Beijing negotiated with the stick of its overwhelming military superiority and the carrot of lucrative trade and energy deals, persuading the Central Asian states that they should curb any political activities on behalf of Uyghurs in China by their own Uyghur communities, which were particularly important in Kyrgyzstan and Kazakhstan. The new Central Asian governments complied readily, partly because they were concerned about the threat to their own stability from political Islamist movements (particularly in Uzbekistan and Kyrgyzstan). The demise of Communist regimes in Central Asia had not led to the hoped-for democratisation of the region but to the emergence of authoritarian governments, based partly on pre-Soviet clan and regional ties and partly on Soviet political culture. Although there was still distrust of China, they shared many common values and a common political idiom.

Nevertheless, these changes fuelled expectations in Xinjiang that the establishment of an independent East Turkestan state was imminent and there were confrontations, including rioting and raids on institutions associated with the Chinese state throughout the region. These included bus bombings in Urumqi in 1992, an explosion in Kashgar in 1993, and, in 1995 and 1997, serious disturbances in Yining (its Chinese name, but Ghulja in Uyghur), the site of the government of the Eastern Turkestan Republic of the 1940s. Many lives were lost when police and the military suppressed the 1997 disturbances.[1] More details on these and later developments can be found in Chapter 22.

Beijing's response to this deepening conflict was to launch a Strike Hard Campaign throughout Xinjiang in 1996. It also put pressure on the governments of neighbouring Central Asian states to compel them to prevent any separatist activity that could be construed as anti-Chinese from taking place within their borders. The governments of Kazakhstan and Kyrgyzstan both complied, partly because of political and economic pressure from China, but also because they perceived a common menace from Islamist political movements. Some Uyghur activists in their territories were returned to China for arrest and trial, and severe restrictions were placed on the press and political activities in the Uyghur minority communities in Kazakhstan and Kyrgyzstan. This awkward alliance formed the basis for the SCO (see in what follows).

Kazakh and Kyrgyz residents of Xinjiang are from the same ethnic background as their counterparts in Kazakhstan and Kyrgyzstan. There are sizeable minority Uyghur communities in both of these former Soviet Central Asian republics: the Uyghurs are closely related to the Uzbeks of Uzbekistan, and there are Uzbek communities in other parts of Central Asia, including Xinjiang. The Uyghur and Uzbek languages are extremely close (effectively two forms of the same language), and the two peoples share a common literary and cultural tradition. Many independent scholars consider that they are essentially the same people, although both Uyghurs and Uzbeks prefer to maintain the distinction between their languages and communities.

Although Xinjiang is firmly under the administrative control of China, the most important social and cultural bonds of the Uyghurs are with the Turkic peoples to the north and west in former Soviet Central Asia. These bonds were severed during the Sino-Soviet dispute which began in the early 1960s. The mass migration of Kazakhs, Uyghurs and others from northwestern Xinjiang into Kazakhstan in 1962 prompted China to seal its borders; contact between China and its western neighbours was minimal for decades. Mikhail Gorbachev's ill-fated visit to Beijing during the protests in Beijing by students and citizens that were suppressed by the PLA on 4 June 1989 was intended to repair this rift, but it was not until the collapse of Soviet power in 1991 that the borders were reopened and the divided communities began to communicate with each other.

In post-Soviet Central Asia, the interests of Russia and China are far from identical, but as both face competition from the United States, they have evolved a mutual accommodation with policies that are often complementary and cooperative. Russia had an early advantage, as Russian was the main administrative language of all the former Soviet states, but China has since become their leading trading partner. Beijing has since consolidated its dominant position with dramatic increases in arms sales to the region and a physical presence by taking the lead in frequent military exercises.[2]

Shanghai Co-operation Organisation

As China developed new forms of political relations with its Central Asian neighbours, bilateral meetings on border and trade issues were deemed inadequate to deal with the rapidly changing geopolitical environment. Political Islam became more and more influential in Afghanistan and Tajikistan, and was viewed by the new governments of Uzbekistan and Kyrgyzstan as a serious threat to their authority. In spite of their great differences, all regional powers recognised a common interest in combating this threat to the stability of the region.

The first meeting of what was to become a major regional grouping took place in Shanghai in 1996 when the foreign ministers of China, Russia, Kazakhstan, Kyrgyzstan, and Tajikistan met to discuss common concerns. An agenda was constructed around border security, combating insurgent Islamic forces, and the smuggling of Islamic literature, weapons, and narcotics. The grouping, which planned to meet on a regular basis, was initially referred to as the Shanghai Five but was renamed the Shanghai Co-operation Organisation in June 2001 when Uzbekistan was admitted. The brand-new name was sufficiently flexible to allow for the admission of other members. Pakistan, the only other state seriously considered for membership, was not permitted to join at that time because of concerns about the government's relationship with political Islamist groups. At the Astana SCO summit on 9 June 2017, Pakistan was admitted, as was India. Other regional states that enjoyed observer status were Mongolia, Afghanistan, Belarus, and Iran, which has unsuccessfully applied for full membership.

The SCO has maintained a low profile with the exception of summit meetings of the Heads of State Council. The 11th Prime Minister's meeting of the SCO in Bishkek on 4 December 2012 was attended by China's Premier, Wen Jiabao, who expressed the hope that the organisation would become more dynamic. Security concerns and Islamist radicalism remained the highest priority. Economic cooperation, often involving Chinese funding, is one aspect that the SCO publicises, but details of cooperation in policing and other security matters are rarely discussed openly. The SCO is also responsible for joint military exercises, some of them under the name 'Peace Mission', biennial multi-national exercises: the fifth of these culminated in the Chelyabinsk region of Russia just to the east of the Urals. As the SCO met in July 2020, analysts questioned whether the common security interests of the member states would be outweighed by economic competition between China's Belt and Road Initiative and Russia's Eurasian Economic Union.[3]

Western Development

Beijing's strategy in dealing with the problem of ethnic separation in Xinjiang since the early 1990s has been twofold. On the one hand, there has been the severest repression of any unofficial religious activity and any political activity that could be classified as separatist. On the other hand, there has been a recognition that poverty and underdevelopment lie at the root of the region's social problems, and programmes to alleviate this poverty have been initiated from time to time.

The decision to tackle the problem of the relative underdevelopment in the whole of China's western provinces led to the policy of the Great Development of the Western

Regions [*Xibu da kaifa*], which was launched in 2000 in Chengdu, the capital of Sichuan province. The Western Development policy was targeted at the whole of the west of China, not just Xinjiang, and this includes Ningxia, Gansu, Qinghai, Sichuan, and also Tibet. The Western Development policy and its successor, the Belt and Road Initiative, are covered in Chapters 12–13.

US bases in Kyrgyzstan after 11 September 2001

China reacted to the 11 September 2001 attacks on New York and the Washington, DC area by restricting the access of foreigners to Xinjiang, which has a 70-kilometre border with Afghanistan, and declared that separatism in Xinjiang was a terrorist phenomenon that China should be given *carte blanche* to deal with as the authorities saw fit. This provoked international concern in human rights circles, including the office of the UN High Commissioner for Human Rights, Mary Robinson, and although the anti-terrorist rhetoric has remained, China has done very little new to suppress separatism but has continued the policies it began in 1996 with the Strike Hard Campaign. China used the cover of the 'war against terrorism' to clamp down on Islam in Xinjiang.

During the Cold War, the presence of US troops in Central Asia this was completely unthinkable, as it was under the absolute control of the USSR. After 1991, Russia continued to take the view that it was the only outside power with a legitimate interest in the region, consequent on its inclusion in the Shanghai Co-operative Organisation. Initially, Central Asian states were also reluctant to accept US and allied troops.

After the 11 September 2001 attacks, the administration of US President George W. Bush embarked on an unusual bout of diplomatic activity with the aim of establishing military bases for the first time ever in a number of the countries of former Soviet Central Asia. The Central Asian states are situated just to the north of Afghanistan, close to those areas in which the remnants of the Al Qaeda organisation were believed to have gone to ground. Mounting operations from the north avoided the political difficulties associated with basing US military forces inside Pakistan, where there was considerable sympathy for the ousted Taliban and its Al Qaeda allies among the poorer sections of the rural population. This unprecedented move by the US government and military had profound implications for regional stability in an area where post-Soviet dictatorships and radical Islamist movements appeared to be the only political options available to communities searching for national identities and economic stability. The US presence in Central Asia posed a particular challenge for China, which had come to regard the region as its own back yard, and in which it exerted considerable influence.

The initial deployment of 200 US servicemen arrived at Manas airport outside the Kyrgyzstan capital, Bishkek, on 25 December 2001 to establish a base.[4] It had been agreed that airfield security would be the joint responsibility of US and Kyrgyz forces, with US troops guarding the outer perimeter.[5] The Kyrgyz Defence Minister and Foreign Minister visited the base on 14 January 2002, and the First Deputy Interior Minister welcomed the presence of US troops in his country and suggested that members of the coalition might have a long-term future in Kyrgyzstan 'if the situation in the region deteriorates'.[6] A high-level delegation of US senators, led by the senior Democrat Thomas Daschle, visited Bishkek for discussions on the situation in Afghanistan and the future of US-Kyrgyz relations and inspected US troops stationed at the airfield.[7] Although the initial agreement for the US presence was for one year, local commentators suggested at the time that it was likely to last much longer than this.

The first ever programme of US-Kyrgyz joint military exercise, code-named Black Knight, began on 5 February 2002 in the Chonkurchak district about 30 kilometres outside Bishkek. The US military provided ten instructors from detachments of special forces troops. Key units of the Kyrgyz armed forces, including 'special subdivisions of the Kyrgyz Defence Ministry and the National Guard' and the National Border Service, underwent specialist training in counter-terrorist operations and mountain warfare. This included landing in combat zones, surveillance, and reconnaissance, ambush tactics and the evacuation of wounded personnel, and training was carried out in poor mountain weather conditions. Specific counter-terrorist training included combat operations in populated areas, dealing with the taking of hostages and techniques for clearing buildings. Although the Kyrgyz armed forces are generally regarded as poorly trained and inexperienced in comparison with their US counterparts, these units included troops with combat experience against armed groups associated with the Islamic Movement of Uzbekistan, which had penetrated the Batken region of southern Kyrgyzstan in 1999 and 2000. US officers were highly critical of the lack of organisation of the Kyrgyz units and claimed that their Kyrgyz counterparts had learned to be more professional as a result of the exercises.[8]

A radio station in Bishkek announced on 25 February that the first stage of the exercises had ended; by March 2002, it was estimated that approximately 1,500 US or coalition troops were based at Manas airfield.[9] Visiting journalists pointed out that the level of US investment in the infrastructure and the potential economic benefits to Kyrgyzstan were indicative of planning for a long-term US presence in the region.[10] In fact, US troops were withdrawn gradually as Washington reduced its military commitments in Afghanistan and the last US facility, the Transit Centre at Manas airbase, finally ceased operation in June 2014.[11]

Kazakhstan

Discussions on the establishment of a US military presence on Kazakhstan also began in January 2002.[12] Kazakhstan is less useful as a forward base for operations against Al Qaeda, as it does not share a common frontier with Afghanistan and its military airfields are reported to have deteriorated severely since independence. However, it is the largest Central Asian state, and it is both politically stable and the most Westernised – or more accurately, Russified – of all the Central Asian countries: it is not involved in the same kind of conflict with radical Islamist movements that affects Kyrgyzstan and Uzbekistan. The degree of US military involvement in Kazakhstan remains somewhat shrouded in mystery, but *The Times* of London reported that a special forces unit of the US Army had been training soldiers of the Kazakh Mountain Chasseur battalion in counter-terrorist techniques since February.[13]

Since 1991, China had been ruled by Nursultan Nazarbayev; he stepped down suddenly in March 2019 and was immediately succeeded as Acting President by Kassym-Jomart Tokayev, who had been Speaker of the parliament. The speed of the handover shocked many in Kazakhstan, and there were protests against political repression and illegal detentions during the presidential election process in which Tokayev, who had been nominated by Nazarbayev was elected with 71% of the votes. Little change was expected in Kazakhstani politics; one of Tokayev's first acts was to rename the capital Astana as Nur-Sultan, in honour of his predecessor.[14]

On 14 April 2020, the Chinese ambassador to Kazakhstan was summoned to the Foreign Ministry in the renamed capital Nur-Sultan to answer a protest about an article entitled 'Why Kazakhstan is eager to return to China' that had been published on the Sohu website. Sohu is independent and does not represent Chinese government policy, but the reaction of the

Kazakhstan authorities reflected the concern felt in Kazakhstan – and elsewhere in Central Asia – about China's intention. By 2020, China had become a key player in the region. Beijing's Good Neighbour policy, initiated after the breakup of the Soviet Union, had evolved into economic relationships; Chinese aid and investments benefited the Kazakhs and others, far more than did Russia's equivalent. In addition, Kazakhstan was crucial to Xi Jinping's Belt and Road Initiative that envisaged links with Europe across Central Asia. In spite of these practical advantages, the size and power of an economically dominant China reawakened anxieties about China as an ancient adversary of Islam and the Turkic people, amounting almost to Sinophobia. This was reinforced by China's draconian repression in Xinjiang, which has a border with Kazakhstan. Some Kazakh families have relations on both sides of the border.[15]

China and the Middle East

Connections between the Middle East and China date back at least to the sixth century AD. Traders and diplomats from what is usually referred to as Arabia, but almost certainly included the Persian-speaking world, appeared in China as early as the Tang dynasty (618–907), entering the country by two main routes, overland across Central Asia by what was later to become known as the Silk Route, or Silk Road, and by sea into southeastern China, now sometimes called the Spice Route; most of its travellers were merchants seeking spices from the islands of Southeast Asia. Some of these traders settled in the port cities of the southeastern coast, in particular Quanzhou, Changzhou, and Guangzhou (Canton), which all became important commercial centres. In the Muslim cemetery in Quanzhou, it is still possible to see gravestones with inscriptions in Arabic, Persian, and Chinese, commemorating settlers from Yemen, Persia, and Central Asia who died and were buried there.[16] The Tang dynasty capital, Chang'an, known today as Xi'an, had a resident community of diplomats and merchants from the Middle East and Central Asia.

The composition of China's population was profoundly affected by the political and social changes brought about by the Mongol conquests of East and Central Asia in the thirteenth century. On their expeditions westward to conquer Central Asia, the armies of Chinggis Khan and his successors sacked major Islamic centres, including Bukhara and Samarkand, and transported sections of the population – including skilled armourers, craftsmen, and enslaved women and children – to China, where they were settled as servants of Mongol aristocrats. When the Mongols established their Yuan dynasty (1260–1368) to rule China, they used Central Asians as border guards, tax collectors, and administrators, finding them more loyal than the Chinese population they had conquered. In the Mongol perception of society in China, Mongols were the elite, but the Muslims from the steppes of Central Asia came next in the hierarchy and were considered superior to both the Chinese population and the non-Chinese minorities of southern China.

The gradual penetration of Islam into China, which reached a high point in the sixteenth and seventeenth centuries, created communities of Muslims, especially in Xinjiang and the northwestern and southwestern regions of China Proper. Unlike the mainstream population of China, they had a natural interest in the Middle East, their spiritual home, and maintained a connection with the region through the *hajj*, whenever this was possible. The distance from Mecca, the difficult terrain, and the cost made the pilgrimage difficult for Muslims from China, and political constraints have added to their isolation, both under the Empire and in modern times.

The PRC was born during the wave of nationalism and decolonisation that followed the Second World War; the new government of China shared many of the concerns and problems of other Third World states. Although the PRC was initially aligned with the USSR and the rest of the Communist bloc, political, doctrinal, and personal conflicts were never resolved during the lifetime of the Soviet Union. China's search for allies steered it towards the Third World, and because of its size and cultural confidence, it gradually came to see itself as a natural leader of those states. This includes relations with the Muslim states of the Middle East, Central Asia and South Asia.

The opening up of Central Asia after the collapse and fragmentation of the Soviet Union in 1991 generated intense competition by Turkey, Iran, and Saudi Arabia – and to a lesser extent (at least initially) – Pakistan for political, economic, and spiritual influence in the region. Because Beijing encouraged these mainly Muslim countries to invest or trade with China, it found it expedient to demonstrate its tolerance of Islam and insist that its Muslim population was able to live and worship in ways that were acceptable to the rest of the world of Islam. While Turkey, as a modernising Muslim nation with a secular government, was an obvious ally, the potential threat of pan-Turkism led China to turn also to the radical Islamic state of Iran as a countervailing force.

In the nineteenth century, the Great Game was the competition between the expanding empires of Russia and Great Britain for hegemony in the heart of Asia. In the late twentieth century, the new Great Game had new players and new prizes, both secular and spiritual.

Turkey

Turkey enjoyed normal diplomatic relations with China, including discussions about economic cooperation – but, conscious of domestic support for pan-Turkism and the potential benefits of a wider Turkic-speaking community, successive governments also took a particular interest in Turkic minorities in China. Isa Yusuf Alptekin (1901–1995), the most prominent Uyghur émigré leader, whose influence in Xinjiang was feared by Beijing in spite of his advanced age, met Turkey's Prime Minister Suleyman Demirel and other senior political figures on a number of occasions. In 1991, Prime Minister Demirel was reported by émigré Uyghurs as having said that he would 'not allow the Chinese to assimilate their ethnic brothers in Eastern Turkestan' and would make representations to the United Nations.[17] Alptekin was received by President Turgut Ozal in 1992, and in an emotional meeting presented the President with a traditional Uyghur coat and cap and an Eastern Turkestani flag, symbolising his handover of the Eastern Turkestani cause to the Turkish President because at 91, he was too old to continue himself. President Ozal is reported to have said,

> I declare that I have taken delivery of the Eastern Turkestani cause. The Turkic republics under former Soviet rule have all declared their independence. Now it is Eastern Turkestan's turn. It is our desire to see the ancient homeland of the Turkic peoples a free country.[18]

Some accounts of these meetings are from émigré Uyghur sources which emphasise the importance of this support, but the Chinese response suggests that they took the exiles very seriously.

Alptekin met government leaders again in Ankara on 22–23 December 1992, to ask them to bring the issue of increased Han Chinese immigration in Xinjiang to the United Nations; the Turkish parliament was also asked to send a mission to Xinjiang to investigate alleged human rights abuses and to report on its findings to the UN Commission on Human Rights.[19] In response, an article in People's Daily in November 1992 claimed that the Turkish President Turgut Ozal and Prime Minister Suleyman Demirel had openly accepted that there should be a Turkic homeland extending 'from the Great Wall of China to the Balkans', and treated Isa Yusuf Alptekin as President-in-exile of East Turkestan.[20] Alptekin died in 1995 at the age of 93, having 'lived out his last days in Istanbul, in a modest flat overlooking the railway line once used by the Orient Express'.[21]

In 1993, Qiao Shi, who was Chairman of the Standing Committee of the NPC and China's most powerful security official at the time, met Turkish visitors including Dorgan Gures (Chief of General Staff) and Nevzat Ayaz (Defence Minister) to discuss defence links.[22] Qiao Shi visited Turkey again in November 1996, and, during talks in Ankara with his opposite number Mustafa Kalemli, made it abundantly clear to the Turkish authorities that the Chinese government was implacably opposed to the activities of separatist movements based in foreign countries, including Turkey. He addressed the Turkish National Assembly on 7 November and praised the Turkish government for its non-interference in China's internal affairs and for restricting the activities of Uyghur separatist organisations in Turkey.[23] The following month, according to reports circulating in Taiwan, Turkey and China signed an agreement on military cooperation, under which Turkey would be able to buy surface-to-surface missiles from China and would acquire a licence to produce them in Turkey with technology transferred from China.[24] Turkish governments have had to perform a delicate balancing act to deal with the incompatible demands of pan-Turkism and trade with China.

In the immediate aftermath of the collapse of the Soviet Union, many Central Asians were interested in the possibility of following a Turkish model of development. The presidents of both Uzbekistan and Kazakhstan declared their intentions of taking 'the Turkish route'. Turkey capitalised on this good will and significant resources were invested in linking the newly emerging former Soviet states with Turkey. Turkish Airlines was one of the first foreign carriers to establish air links with Almaty and the capitals of the other Central Asian states. Turkey provided moral support to the nascent states and offered to educate students from Central Asia, and Turkish television was beamed to the region. Ankara established an agency specifically to coordinate Turkish aid to Central Asia, although in reality, that aid was severely restricted by Turkey's relative lack of financial resources. Turkish President Turgut Ozal organised a summit of the Turkic nations in October 1992, but political and cultural differences between the states and the degree of Russification that had taken place in Central Asia over the previous century and a half made relations and even basic communication far more difficult than either side had expected.[25]

In 1994, the importance attached to relations with Turkey was immediately apparent to visitors to Almaty, then the capital of Kazakhstan. Many academics and government officials were either in Turkey or were about to visit Turkey.[26] The Deputy Prime Minister of Turkey, Bulent Ecevit, after spending a week in China in June 1998, expressed a strong interest in developing economic ties, including joint ventures, and announced that Turkey had established a trade and information centre in Shanghai.[27] Reports from the Taiwanese Central News Agency at the same time claimed that Turkey had granted permanent residence status to about 1,000 Uyghurs who had recently arrived there from Xinjiang to join the 50,000 already in the country.[28]

A previously unknown directive from the office of the Turkish Prime Minister was publicised in February 1999 by the popular Turkish newspaper *Hürriyet* [*Liberty*]. It had been distributed to government organisations during the premiership of the Motherland Party politician Mesut Yilmaz in the 1990s. The burden of the document was to urge ministers and government officials not to take part in any political activities organised by East Turkestan and Uyghur organisations based in Turkey. This was in recognition of Xinjiang's status as part of the territory of the PRC and because the Turkish government conceded that émigré activities were creating difficulties in Turkey's relations with China.[29] The Speaker of the Turkish parliament, Hikmet Cetin, received Li Peng on 5 April 1999 when Li visited Ankara in his capacity as Chairman of the Standing Committee of the NPC, a position seen to be broadly similar to that held by Cetin. The official Chinese news agency, Xinhua, reported that Mr. Cetin reiterated Turkey's opposition to separatist activities, and this was reinforced in a meeting between Li Peng and Prime Minister Bulent Ecevit.[30]

After the repression following the Urumqi riots of 2009, many more Uyghurs were determined to leave Xinjiang because of religious persecution. Those who left avoided the most direct exit route, through Kazakhstan and Kyrgyzstan, because of strict border controls; they travelled southwards through China and into Southeast Asia via Yunnan province, most with the intention of reaching Turkey. This route, pioneered by Chinese people-smugglers, took them through Laos, Cambodia, or Vietnam into Thailand. Hundreds were detained in refugee camps in Bangkok and other parts of Thailand, where many were issued with Turkish passports. A group of 173 Uyghurs, mostly women and children, were released on 30 June 2015 and allowed to travel to Istanbul, where it was agreed that they would be resettled by the Turkish government, either in Istanbul or in the central province of Kayseri, both of which already had established Uyghur communities. The women and children were released after having been held for more than a year on suspicion of illegal entry into Thailand, but male Uyghurs related to these women and children were not released at the same time.

The Ministry of Public Security in Beijing accused the government in Ankara of issuing counterfeit identity documents to some of these Uyghurs to enable them to enter Turkey, and insisted that the refugees were planning to join radical jihadist groups such as Daesh (Islamic State, or ISIS) in Iraq and Syria. Turkey had been experiencing a wave of protests against Chinese repression of the Uyghurs, including the burning of Chinese flags and attacks on Chinese tourists and a Chinese restaurant called Happy China. These attacks were blamed on the Grey Wolves, a paramilitary group associated with the extreme right-wing Nationalist Movement Party (Milliyetçi Hareket Partisi, or MHP), but the organisation denied that its members had been involved.[31]

In common with most other Muslim-majority states, the Turkish government was criticised for its slowness to respond to the mass detention of Xinjiang's Uyghurs in concentration camps. In February 2019, the Ministry of Foreign Affairs in Ankara finally issued a statement condemning the incarcerations. This followed mass protests in Turkey in support of the Uyghurs and came shortly before local elections in Turkey. Ankara's protest provoked a sharp rejoinder from Beijing, but relations between the two states continued as before. Economic interests, especially the prospect of gains from the Belt and Road Initiative, once again took precedence over human rights concerns.[32]

Iran

Cooperation between Iran and China on atomic energy projects was confirmed in 1991,[33] and a delegation from the Iranian Centre for Strategic Research visited China in November of that year.[34] Higher-level visits took place, by the speaker of the Iranian Majlis, the parliament, in December of the same year[35] and by the Foreign Minister Ali Akbar Velayati in April 1992.[36] Arms sales by China to Iran were controversial: Chinese official sources consistently played them down or even denied that they took place at all, but there is general agreement that tanks, artillery, surface-to-air missiles, fighter aircraft, and a nuclear reactor were sold to Tehran during this period.[37] Iran bought Silkworm missiles from China and there were regular reports of visits by high-ranking Iranian military officials to China. Qin Jiwei travelled to Tehran at the end of October 1992; this was the first visit made by a Chinese Foreign Minister since the 1979 revolution in Iran. Qin had meetings with President Rafsanjani and the Iranian Minister of Defence.[38]

Iranian President Ali Akbar Hashemi Rafsanjani visited China in September 1992 after the Non-Aligned Movement conference in Jakarta. After meeting central government leaders in Beijing and signing a nuclear cooperation agreement,[39] he met Tomur Dawamat, the regional government chairman in Urumqi, for discussions on economic, commercial, scientific, technological, and cultural exchanges, including talks on joint Xinjiang-Iran projects, rail links via Kyrgyzstan and Tajikistan, and a new air route.[40] President Rafsanjani visited Kashgar on Friday 11 September and led afternoon prayers in the Heytgar (Id Gah) Mosque. Crowds of Uyghur, Kazakh, Kyrgyz, and Hui Muslims waited for him outside the mosque, and when he walked briefly around the square after the service, there was tremendous applause from the mainly Muslim onlookers, in spite of a massive police presence.[41]

Controversy over China's arms sales to Iran was renewed in August 1993 when the 19,000-tonne freighter *Yinhe* en route from China to Dubai – and under suspicion of carrying chemicals which could be used in the manufacture of nerve and mustard gas, and similar chemical weapons – was shadowed by the US Navy destroyer *USS Chandler* through the Gulf of Hormuz. After initially refusing to allow the ship to be searched, the Chinese authorities changed their minds when it was refused permission to dock in Dubai, and the *Yinhe* changed course for Saudi Arabia.[42] The *Yinhe* was subsequently found not to have been carrying the chemicals alleged by the US authorities, but Washington declined to pay the compensation demanded by Beijing in respect of the delay.

The Iranian newspaper *Jomhuriyat-e Eslami* [*Islamic Republic*] carried a report on the suppression of the Yining disturbances in February 1997 and criticised China's policies as an attempt to separate Xinjiang's Muslims from their co-religionists across the borders.[43]

As China's economy has developed, its energy needs have become increasingly important – and this has influenced its political relationships with oil-producing countries, including Iran. An initial agreement on the supply of oil and gas by Iran to China valued at US$70 billion was concluded in October 2004 by the China Petroleum and Chemical Corporation, Sinopec. Under the terms of this agreement, China agreed to invest in the development of the major Yadavaran oil field in the southwest of Iran in return for guaranteed supplies of crude oil and liquefied natural gas. Towards the end of 2007, a further agreement worth another US$2 billion was signed. China does not feel obliged to comply with sanctions against Iran that have been put in place by the United States and its allies.[44]

China's reliance on oil supplies from Iran became problematic as the United States attempted to isolate the Islamic Republic and subjected it to sanctions. China continued to import oil from Iran, but hedged its bets by transferring some of its demand to Saudi Arabia. As the United States also escalated its trade and diplomatic war with China, Beijing and Tehran became closer partners and Chinese companies replaced Western businesses deterred form working in Iran because of US sanctions. China continued to invest heavily in Iran, which was a crucial node in the Belt and Road Initiative transport network and one that did not pass through Russian territory.[45] Tehran did not publicly criticise China's mass detention of Uyghurs in Xinjiang.

As the engagement of the United States in the Middle East waned during the Trump presidency, Chinese involvement increased, driven by its need for oil and facilitated through the One Belt One Road strategy (see Chapter 13).[46]

China and Pakistan

Relations between China and the individual states of South Asia are complex. China has been in a constant state of tension with India since the war of 1962 over territorial disputes, especially concerning the Aksai Chin region of Kashmir and parts of Arunachal Pradesh in northeastern India. These tensions have been further exacerbated by India's willingness to provide a haven for the exiled Tibetan spiritual leader, the Dalai Lama, and his followers in Dharamsala. These considerations led the Communist PRC towards a curious alliance with India's main political rival since independence in 1947, the Islamic Republic of Pakistan. During the Cold War, New Delhi was close to the Soviet Union, with which China was increasingly estranged, while Pakistan generally enjoyed amicable relations with the United States.

Pakistan and China agreed to open the Khunjerab Pass to border trade from 1 May 1993.[47] On 25 August 1993, the United States imposed sanctions on China and Pakistan after months of enquiries into allegations that China had supplied Pakistan with components for the M-11 missile in violation of international agreements, principally the Missile Technology Control Regime (MTCR): China is not a member, but has agreed to follow its guidelines. The cost to China of these sanctions was of the order of US$500 million. The M-11 missiles have a range of 300 miles and a payload of half a tonne, which would have a serious effect on the balance of power in the region. Defence analysts believed that the missile would enable Pakistan to hit targets in India, Iran, and the former Soviet Union, but within the US intelligence and defence establishment, there were disagreements on the precise level of threat posed. Both China and Pakistan initially denied that any transfer of missile technology had taken place, Pakistan later claiming that the last shipment had been in February 1992. Technically, the missiles may have been just outside the parameters of the MTCR which restricts the transfer of missiles with a range of over 187.5 miles since the range of the M-11 is 190 miles. China's response to the sanctions was a firm rebuttal of the accusations. Deputy Foreign Minister Liu Huaqiu lodged a firm protest in a meeting with the US Ambassador Stapleton Roy and alleged that 'This naked hegemonic act has brutally violated the basic norms governing international relations'. He argued that China was not violating the terms of the Missile Technology Control Regime but that US sanctions left China 'with no alternative but to reconsider its commitment to MTCR'.[48]

On 25 August 1993, Washington announced sanctions, including a restriction on the transfer of satellite and other advanced technology for two years. China did not sign the agreement on MCTR, but had said early in 1992 that the guidelines would be respected as part of an agreement on the removal of earlier US sanctions imposed after the crackdown on the Democracy Movement in June 1989. Defence analysts in Beijing argued that the arms sales to Pakistan did not break international rules, as they were only designed for short-range use. The PRC indicated a sense of injustice, contrasting its own arms sales policy to what it claimed was a grave threat to Chinese security when the United States sold 150 fighter aircraft to Taiwan in 1992. Arms sales were an important source of foreign currency for China, although they dropped from an estimated annual value of US$4.7 billion in 1987 to US$100 million in 1992.[49]

China and Pakistan signed an agreement in Rawalpindi on 4 December 1993, under which China agreed to provide Pakistan with credit facilities for the procurement of defence equipment. At the same time, Li Ruihuan, a member of the Standing Committee of the Politburo of the CCP and Chairman of the advisory body, the CPPCC, visited Islamabad with a high-level delegation and stayed there for a week. General Zhang Wannian, Chief of the General Staff of the PLA, also toured the Afghan-Pakistan border and the Khyber Pass and reiterated China's support for Pakistan.

Pakistan TV, broadcasting from Islamabad on 3 July 1997, carried a response from the Pakistani Foreign Office to concerns raised about the deployment of Indian missiles on the border and the test of a Hatf missile. It insisted that nuclear cooperation between Pakistan and China was purely for peaceful civilian use of the technology, and that there were no military implications. Reports from the United States clearly indicated that the CIA continued to believe that China was providing considerable technical assistance to the nuclear weapons programmes of both Pakistan and Iran.[50]

The question of Xinjiang was rarely raised publicly in discussions between political leaders of the two countries, even though there is a close trading connection between towns such as Kashgar in southern Xinjiang and Pakistan via the Karakorum Highway. Pakistan is also one of the sources of copies of the Qur'an and other Islamic materials coming into Xinjiang, either directly or as a gateway for materials coming from Afghanistan or further west.

General Pervez Musharraf – at the time chairman of the Joint Chiefs of Staff Committee of the Pakistan armed forces, but later to take over the government of Pakistan in a coup d'état and have himself designated Chief Executive – visited China in May 1999 as the guest of the Chief of the General Staff of the Chinese PLA, General Fu Quanyou. He also met President Jiang Zemin, who reaffirmed China's 'friendship in adversity' with Pakistan and stressed the importance of military ties between the two countries.[51]

Pakistan's Prime Minister, Nawaz Sharif, made a state visit to China in June 1999, but decided to return to Pakistan early in view of the growing tension between India and Pakistan over the Kashmir issue.[52] It was later revealed in the Urdu language newspaper The Daily Jang, published in Rawalpindi, that during these talks, the Chinese government agreed to supply Pakistan with 80 F-7 fighter aircraft as an emergency measure. The F-7 was one of the most up-to-date aircraft in China at the time and had previously been used exclusively by the PLA Air Force: the first examples were due to be delivered to the Pakistan Air Force in August 1999, during an official visit to Beijing by the Chief of Staff of the Pakistan Air Force.[53]

The initial response of the authorities in Beijing to the 1999 military coup in Pakistan was to adopt a wait-and-see policy: there were diplomatic comments about maintaining stability in the sub-continent and the long-term prospects for improving trade between China and Pakistan. Stability was what mattered to Beijing, rather than the nature of the regime in Islamabad or whether it was military or democratic; that is consistent with Beijing's policy towards other Third World countries since 1949. The added tension between India and Pakistan did not cause China any real problems, and indeed made Pakistan a more reliable ally. A military government in Pakistan was a positive asset for weapons sales.

Because separatism and unrest in Xinjiang were major preoccupations of Beijing since the mid-1990s, there were serious concern that any instability in Pakistan could cause an upsurge in support for political Islam and a consequent boost for Islamic insurgents in Xinjiang. The role of the Pakistani military was complex. On the one hand, there was considerable support for militant political Islam within its ranks and sympathy for the Taliban in Afghanistan, particularly from elements in Pakistan's military intelligence community. On the other hand, a long-term commitment to a stable Pakistani state was threatened by Islamist militancy. In spite of its alliance, the Foreign Ministry in Beijing lodged formal diplomatic protests with Islamabad over the alleged combat training of Uyghurs in Afghanistan by members of the Pakistani security forces. China claimed that it had extracted this information from a group of Uyghurs who had been arrested and interrogated by the Chinese police after they had crossed from Pakistan back into Xinjiang.

*

In October 2008, Asif Ali Zardari made his first visit to China as head of state; financial assistance was at the head of his shopping list. He sought a soft loan – at below market interest rates – of between US$500 million and US$1.5 billion and also the supply of nuclear reactors, stressing that they were to generate nuclear power for civilian purposes, although Pakistan is one of the nine states to have declared its possession of nuclear weapons. Pakistan already had a nuclear reactor in Punjab supplied by China, and another under construction. As a quid pro quo, it was understood that within five years, Pakistan would complete the purchase of military equipment including additional JF-17 multi-role fighters – Pakistan already had eight – and that this would involve joint production. Sino-Pakistan relations remained important to Beijing, according to Sun Shihai of the CASS South Asia Research Centre, despite China's improved ties with India. In February 2020, the *Dacuiyun*, a Hong Kong-flagged Chinese vessel bound for Karachi, was detained in the Gujarat port of Kandla. It had failed to declare an autoclave in its cargo that could be used in ballistic missile technology. The Indian authorities seized the autoclave and made a formal diplomatic protest to China that it had contravened MTCR guidelines. This incident renewed concerns about the close nuclear partnership of China and Pakistan.[54]

In 2018, Pakistan's financial situation was once again a cause for concern, this time for the new government of Imran Khan, who had taken office on 18 August. The Pakistani rupee had lost 20% of its value against the US dollar since the last quarter of 2017 and had sunk to a new low in July 2018. In order to prevent further devaluation of the Pakistani rupee and strengthen its reserves of foreign exchange, Islamabad secured the promise of a loan from Beijing of some US$2 billion, although the details of the loan were not made public by either party. This agreement was complicated because Islamabad was in the process of negotiating with the IMF for a separate loan of between US$7 and US$8 billion. Chinese state-run banks had also been lending US$4 billion to Islamabad during the year ending June 2017.

Beijing was committed to investments believed to be worth US$60 billion in Pakistani energy, transport, and other infrastructure projects as part of the China-Pakistan Economic Corridor which is a key component of China's Belt and Road Initiative (for which see Chapter 13). The complex arrangements with Beijing were controversial because of Pakistan's other international associations: the United States, another key ally of Pakistan, objected to the IMF loan on the grounds that it would enable Islamabad to repay its loans to Beijing; financial support for Pakistan was also secured from Saudi Arabia and the United Arab Emirates.[55]

The decision to establish the China-Pakistan Economic Corridor in November 2014 was intended to solidify Pakistan's strategic relationship with China. The project, which was associated closely with the Pakistani military, became mired in allegations of corruption and malpractice by Chinese energy producers, some of which were alleged to have grossly inflated their setting-up costs and have been vastly overpaid for their involvement.[56]

The Afghan connection

There were persistent rumours that the Chinese military had sent a group of Uyghurs for combat training in Afghanistan as part of an alliance against the Soviet Union's offensive between 1979 and 1989; it has not been possible to confirm this from independent sources. While it might have seemed a good idea to build up Chinese credibility in Islamic Central Asia during the Sino-Soviet dispute, if the Chinese did send this group, it must in retrospect have seemed a bad decision when Uyghur militancy began to develop in Xinjiang. In 1998,

Chinese officials were reported as having said: 'We closely follow developments in Afghanistan where Islamic fundamentalism is strong. This is very dangerous for Xinjiang'.[57]

Ahmad Baghlan, a leader of the separatist movement in Xinjiang, was reported to have escaped from Xinjiang in late November 1998 and to have reached Badakhshan in Afghanistan after travelling through the mountainous border region of Wakhan. His flight followed the arrest and brief detention of another separatist leader, Abdul Rasul, after he was due to give a press conference in Islamabad to protest against what he claimed was a decision not to allow Muslims from Xinjiang to participate in the *hajj* pilgrimage to Mecca.[58]

China and the Taliban – or its government, formally known as the Islamic Emirate of Afghanistan – concluded a military agreement on 10 December 1998. China agreed to train military pilots, and in return, the Taliban allowed Chinese scientists to examine unexploded American cruise missiles that had landed in Afghanistan.[59] Both Washington and Moscow objected to this and tried to persuade China to cut its ties with the Taliban: a UN embargo on the sale of arms – and in particular, the monitoring of arms supplies from Pakistan – due to come into force in December 2000 was being prepared. China agreed not to veto this embargo, and in return, American diplomats in Beijing supplied information to Chinese military intelligence about Uyghurs working with the Taliban and on drugs and weapons alleged to have been imported into Xinjiang from Afghanistan.[60]

In October 2001, following the invasion of Afghanistan by coalition forces led by the United States, reports began to emerge that a number of Uyghurs had been captured during the fighting, particularly in the operation by the Northern Alliance, a coalition opposed to the Taliban, to capture the city of Mazar-e Sharif with the support of US forces. It was alleged that these Uyghurs had been working with Al Qaeda or the Taliban, although no evidence was ever produced. It subsequently emerged that the United States was holding 22 Uyghurs without charge in the Guantanamo Bay prison camp in Cuba.

In May 2006, five of those detained were cleared of any association with terrorist activities and released. Their release was delayed in part because they could not be repatriated to China, where they would almost certainly have faced the death penalty. After prolonged international negotiations, they were granted political asylum in Albania, which has a Muslim majority; statistics of religious affiliation are disputed. Albania was avowedly atheist under the Enver Hoxha regime, and the post-Communist republic of Albania is officially secular.

Contacts between Taliban and Chinese officials continued. After high-level meetings in Beijing in 2020, the Chinese government agreed to fund major energy and infrastructure projects in the areas of Afghanistan controlled by the Taliban – initially, much-needed roads – in return for a commitment to lasting peace in the region.[61]

Notes

1 Xu Yuqi *Xinjiang fandui minzu fenliezhuyi douzheng shihua (History of the Struggle against Separatism in Xinjiang)* Urumqi: Xinjiang Peoples Publishing House, 1999.
2 Ian J. Lynch 'What Are the Implications for China's Growing Security Role in Central Asia?' *The Diplomat* 3 June 2020.
3 Eleanor Albert 'The Shanghai Co-Operation Organisation: A Vehicle for Cooperation or Competition' *The Diplomat* 21 June 2019.
4 Public Education Radio TV, Bishkek (BBC Monitoring) 25 December 2001.
5 *Argumenty i fakty Kyrgyzstan* (BBC Monitoring) 9 January 2002.
6 *Vecherny Bishkek* 14 December 2001, 15 January 2002 (BBC Monitoring)
7 Kabar News Agency Bishkek (BBC Monitoring) 10 January 2002.

8 Interfax Moscow 15 February 2002; *Kyrgyz Public TV* 15, 20, 25 February 2002 (BBC Monitoring).
9 *Economist* 23 March 2002.
10 *Los Angeles Times* April 2002.
11 *Komsomolskaya Pravda v Kyrgyzstane*, Bishkek 18 January 2002 (BBC Monitoring); Akhilesh Pillalamari 'The United States Just Closed its Last Base in Central Asia' *The Diplomat* 10 June 2014.
12 Kazakh TV, Almaty 18 January 2002 (BBC Monitoring).
13 *The Times*, London, 30 March 2002.
14 Algerim Toleukhanova 'Kazakhstan on the Edge' *The Diplomat* 1 June 2020.
15 'Kazakhstan Summons Chinese Ambassador in Protest over Article' Reuters 14 April 2020; Sebastien Peyrouse 'Understanding Sinophobia in Central Asia' *The Diplomat* 1 May 2020.
16 Chen Dasheng (ed.) *Quanzhou Yisilanjiao shike (Islamic Inscriptions of Quanzhou)* Fuzhou: Ningxia and Fujian People's Publishing House, 1984.
17 *Eastern Turkestan Information* 1, no. 4, November 1991.
18 *Eastern Turkestan Information* 2, no. 2, March 1992.
19 *Eastern Turkestan Information*, Munich, December 1992.
20 *Renmin Ribao* (People's Daily) 17 November 1992, cited in *Eastern Turkestan Information*. The edition of *Renmin Ribao* of that date circulated within China does not contain such an article, but it is possible that it appeared in the overseas edition, which has not been available for consultation.
21 Nicole and Hugh Pope *Turkey Unveiled: Ataturk and after* London: John murray, 1997, p. 284.
22 BBC Monitoring 19 April 1993.
23 BBC Monitoring 5 November 1996.
24 BBC Monitoring 23 December 1996.
25 Pope op. cit. 1997.
26 Author's meetings with members of the Institute of Oriental Studies and Institute of Uyghur Studies of the Kazakhstan Academy of Sciences Almaty, Kazakhstan, September 1994.
27 Xinhua News Agency (BBC Monitoring) 6 June 1998.
28 BBC Monitoring 9 June 1998.
29 BBC Monitoring 10 February 1999.
30 BBC Monitoring 7, 9 April 1999.
31 Radio Free Asia 27 March, 1 July 2015; BBC News 9 July 2015; *SCMP* 10 July 2015; *Global Times* 11 July 2015.
32 *SCMP* 16 February 2019; Shannon Tiezzi 'Why Is Turkey Breaking Its Silence on China's Uyghurs?' *The Diplomat* 12 April 2019.
33 BBC Monitoring 9 November 1991.
34 BBC Monitoring 23 November1993.
35 BBC Monitoring 17, 20 December 1991.
36 BBC Monitoring 14 April 1992.
37 *Far Eastern Economic Review* 3 December 1992.
38 *China Quarterly* March 1993, p. 205.
39 *China Daily* 11 September 1992; BBC Monitoring 11, 12, 15 September 1992.
40 *Eastern Turkestan Information* October 1992; *China Daily* 10 September 1992.
41 Personal observation by the author, Kashgar, 11 September 1992. There were no reports in the Chinese media of Rafsanjani's Kashgar visit although his discussions in Beijing and Urumqi were fully reported in the press and on television in the Chinese and Uyghur language programmes of Xinjiang Television (personal observation).
42 *Independent* 25 August 1993.
43 BBC Monitoring 21 February 1997.
44 *China Daily* 31 October 2004; *FT* 9 December 2007.
45 John Calabrese 'China-Iran Relations: The Not-So-Special "Special Relationship"' *China Brief* 20, no. 5 (16 March 2020); Bonnie Girard 'China's Iran Dilemma' *The Diplomat* 11 January 2020.
46 *FT* 10 September 2020.
47 BBC Monitoring 26 April 1993.
48 Reuters 27 August 1993.
49 Robert Pear 'U.S. Sales of Arms to the Third World Declined by 22% Last Year' *New York Times* 21 July 1992.
50 BBC Monitoring 5 July 1997.
51 BBC Monitoring 25, 26, 27 May 1999.

52 BBC Monitoring 30 June 1999.
53 BBC Monitoring 19, 21 August 1999.
54 *FT* 13 October 2008; Sanjana Gogna and Nasima Khatoon 'The China-Pakistan Nuclear Nexus: How Can India Respond?' *The Diplomat* 27 March 2020.
55 *FT* 1 January 2019.
56 Hussain Haqqanin 'Pakistan Discovers the High Cost of Chinese Investment' *The Diplomat* 18 May 2020.
57 BBC Monitoring 22 April 1998.
58 BBC Monitoring 27 November 1998.
59 BBC Monitoring 12 December 1998.
60 *Far Eastern Economic Review* 30 November 2000.
61 *FT* 9 September 2020.

Part 7

Prospects

Struggle between two new lines

28 After Xi

Harmonious society or new authoritarianism?

The transition from Hu Jintao's vision of a 'harmonious society' to Xi Jinping's authoritarian insistence on homogeneity was dramatic and unexpected, but did not resolve underlying problems that determine long-term developments in China. At the heart of these problems is the uneasy alliance between the CCP, the PRC it controls, and the market economy that has expanded beyond the developed coastal regions to the poorer interior. The question of how this relationship will evolve could be posed to the CCP leadership in terms of the classic Marxist analysis of conflict between the economic base and the social and cultural superstructure, but it rarely is.

In the early phase of its drive for economic reform, in the 1980s and 1990s, the CCP leadership insisted that it was creating an exclusively Chinese type of socialism, 'socialism with Chinese characteristics' in the official terminology. On closer inspection, this concept never amounted to much more than rhetoric, as the Communist state attempted to manage a modern capitalist economy. Communist or socialist ideology is not a significant factor in twenty-first–century China; half-hearted attempts to invoke the spirit of Yan'an, the self-sacrificing soldier Lei Feng, or the model official Jiao Yulu that were revived during the 1990s disappeared below the horizon, although Lei Feng had been resurrected in Shanghai in 2018 to encourage young Chinese to volunteer in social projects.[1]

The political culture of Marxism-Leninism, which degenerated into the cult of Mao, was gradually and surreptitiously replaced by expressions of patriotism or nationalism after the Chairman's death. These were complemented by regular recourse to exhortations to social harmony and conflict avoidance drawn from conservative Confucianism. The success of the economy is all-important; in the 1990s, it was common when discussing problems of democracy with people in China to be told that they were not concerned whether China achieved 'political democracy' – which they were not offered – as long as there was 'economic democracy' – which many, but not all, could achieve. What mattered was the possibility of earning a reasonable living in whichever way that they chose.

Part of the reason for these changes in attitude is the emergence of new social groupings. Over recent decades, an elite group of technocrats emerged as the most important political force. Many of its members were at least partially educated abroad, and they are deeply committed to modernisation and positioning China as the second – if not the first – global economic power. These men and women are often – although by no means exclusively – the children of senior Party, military, and government officials. Many are highly sceptical of political theories, especially socialism or Marxism, even if they are prepared to parrot trite political phrases and are more interested in Western management techniques and economic principles: books on these topics fill the bookshops in the main cities. This lack of ideological commitment has not prevented many of them from joining the CCP and paying lip service to the traditions of the CCP.

Another social group emerged in the 1980s: the *getihu*, or individual entrepreneurs, a *nouveau riche* class originally derided for their social pretensions. *Getihu* were banned from operating their businesses during Mao's lifetime. Most started with small firms, but many became extremely wealthy, even by Western standards; by the twenty-first century, the life-styles of some were barely distinguishable from their counterparts in the West. The relation-ship between this new business class, the political technocrats, and the existing Party elite is still evolving. The middle class has not yet attempted to exercise political power indepen-dently of the CCP, and it has been an important factor in the emergence of one of China's major problems: corruption.

Peaceful development and a harmonious society

On 22 December 2005, three years into Hu Jintao's term of office as CCP General Secretary, the Information Office of the State Council issued a White Paper on the future develop-ment of China. The watchwords of the document were 'peaceful development', 'harmony' and 'prosperity', and the authors attempted to systematise a debate that had been underway within the political elite of the PRC for some years. Although it had echoes of both Nikita Khrushchev's policies of peaceful coexistence in the Soviet Union of the 1950s and Zhou Enlai's negotiations for the Five Principles of Peaceful Coexistence in China's relations with Third World countries of the same era, it was presented as a new and modern approach to China's development and its relationship with the outside world.[2]

Central to this approach is the successful development of the economy and the creation of a 'moderately prosperous society' [*xiaokang shehui*]. The term *xiaokang* did not appear much in public in the PRC before the late 1990s, although it was used by Deng Xiaoping as a long-term aim of the Four Modernisations. It has a distinguished historical pedigree in traditional Confucian discourse, where it described a period of peace and prosperity under the (mostly mythical) ancient kings that immediately preceded a utopia of Datong (Great, or Universal, Harmony). *Xiaokang* was resurrected for the Hu Jintao and Wen Jiabao period, and is also translated as 'comfortably off' or 'basically well off' – not necessarily very wealthy, but certainly not poor. The Chinese leadership may have had in mind the generally affluent and middle class (as they see themselves) population of their economically successful, and fellow Confucian, neighbour, Japan. The *xiaokang* approach and Hu's ambition to build a 'harmonious society' [*hexie shehui*] is the antithesis of the class conflict approach to social change that characterised the CCP under Mao Zedong (see Chapter 4).

President Hu Jintao, in a speech to leading members of the CCP at the Central Party School – the training ground for the next generation of the CCP leadership – on Monday 25 June 2007, reaffirmed his commitment to the spreading of wealth and tackling corruption as the main tasks for the CCP if it were to achieve this goal of a 'comfortably off' society by 2020. The extension of social services, particularly health and education, to the 800 mil-lion residents of rural China, many of whom are still desperately poor, was identified as a crucial part of this strategy. Hu also accepted that the struggle against corruption was going to be a long haul, and that the road to success would be extremely complex and fraught with difficulties.

In addition to senior figures from the Party centre, the meeting was attended by senior officers of the military and security services, and by delegates from regional and provin-cial Party and government organisations. In keeping with his track record of caution on political reform, Hu warned that any reform of the political system would have to keep pace with economic and social development, which he once again identified as the highest priority for China in the twenty-first century. While conceding that participation in the decision-making process could be improved by opening up new channels for consultation and that the rule of law was essential, he insisted that the leading role of the CCP must be maintained; this effectively ruled out political reform and the extension of Western-style democracy.

The session was not open to foreign journalists, but it was reported in *People's Daily* the following day. Hu Jintao's speech was clearly intended to set the tone for political discussions in the run-up to the CCP's 17th quinquennial conference.[3] The congress, which took place in October 2007 and was reported by the international media more widely and in more depth than most previous party congresses, was notable for the complete absence of policy changes. The CCP emphasised its continuing commitment to economic growth, but there was no mention of reforms to the political system.

New authoritarianism: the 'two sessions', 2019 and 2020

It was at that 17th CCP Congress that Xi Jinping emerged as the future leader of China to follow Hu's scheduled retirement in 2012. It was widely believed that a planned and smooth change of leadership over the following five years would result in continuity in policies and continuing rule by the CCP. As has been demonstrated in Chapter 6, the Xi Jinping administration, which began on 15 November 2012, did not favour smoothness and continuity. Continuing rule by the CCP was ensured, but continuity of policies – or rather, the political style – was not. The drastic change in direction and approach after 2012 surprised and dismayed many commentators in China and across the wider world.

The 'two sessions' of the NPC and the Chinese People's Political Consultative Conference for 2020 were due to take place in March; in common with many major and minor events across the world, they were delayed because of the outbreak of Covid-19. They opened, respectively, on 22 May and 21 May. Both meetings were truncated in comparison with the most previous occasions, and health precautions included testing the delegates for infection and isolating them as far as possible.

Li Keqiang's work report to the 2020 NPC reflected the unprecedented challenges posed by the pandemic. In 2019, he had proposed a target of 6–6.5% for growth in the GDP to be achieved by boosting employment and cutting taxes and business costs. In 2020, for the first time ever, no growth target was set. This was primarily because of the uncertainties created by the pandemic, but also reflected the unpredictability of international trade in the light of the trade war with the United States. Premier Li did, however, announce an increase in expenditure on the military. The official figures for the defence budget, which tend to be mistrusted by independent analysts, recorded an increase of 6.6% over the 2019 level. China has increased its defence spending continuously for 20 years, but the 2020 figure was the lowest annual increase during that period. The biggest surprise in the 2020 work report was the announcement, without prior warning, of the government's intention to introduce national security legislation for Hong Kong, in contravention of the Joint Declaration of 1984 (as discussed in Chapter 24).[4]

At the time of writing, in the spring of 2021, China is still recovering from the impact of the coronavirus and dealing with new localised outbreaks, including one in the Fengtai district of Beijing. Looking to the future, the main concerns will be for the Chinese leadership, the people of China, and the world as it interacts with China: the growth and stability of the economy, the need to prevent competition in trade and political rhetoric from becoming a military standoff or conflict with the United States, and a successful resolution of the relationship between Hong Kong and Beijing, a relationship that has serious implications for the government and people of Taiwan.

Notes

1 Observations by the author in Shanghai, 2018.
2 'China's Peaceful Development Road' (full text of government white paper) *People's Daily* 22 December 2005.
3 *Guardian*; BBC News 26 June 2007.
4 *SCMP* 5 March 2019, 22 May 2020.

Abbreviations

CC	Central Committee
CCP	Chinese Communist Party
CPPCC	Chinese People's Political Consultative Conference
GMD	Guomindang, Nationalist Party in pinyin used in the PRC
KMT	Kuomintang, Nationalist Party in older romanisation preferred in Taiwan
NPC	National People's Congress
PRC	People's Republic of China
RMB	Renminbi (people's currency)
RMRB	*Renmin ribao* [*People's Daily*]
SCO	Shanghai Cooperation Organisation
XPCC	Xinjiang Production and Construction Corps

Glossary of selected Chinese terms

baihua qifang, baijia zhengming   let 100 flowers bloom and 100 schools of thought contend
baomu   maid, housemaid, au pair
Beijing wanbao   *Beijing Evening News*
Beijing tuhua   Beijing local dialect
Cankao xiaoxi   *Reference News*
Cankao ziliao   *Reference Material*
Changjiang Yangzi or Yangze,   literally 'long river'
chuanbo meijie   mass media
chujia   marriage when applied to a woman, literally 'to leave the family'
cunmin weiyuanhui   villager committees
da yuejin   Great Leap Forward
danwei   work unit, e.g. factory, office, hospital, school
Daoist   Taoist
dibao   urban minimum living standard guaranteed income
douzheng   struggle
fabi   legal currency, last currency of Nationalist regime
Falungong   a neo-Buddhist religious movement, literally 'exercise of the wheel of the law'
funǚ gongzuo, woman-work, CCP work for and with women
gaige kaifang   reform and opening
getihu   small entrepreneurs, literally 'individual households'
Gong'anbu   Ministry of Public Security
Gong'anju   Bureau of Public Security, police
Gongchanzhuyi qingnian tuan   Communist Youth League
gongkai   open or public, in contrast to *neibu*
Gongnong hongjun   Workers' and Peasants' Red Army
Guangming Ribao Guangming Daily,   a national newspaper. *Guangming* means 'light' or
    'bright', but the paper is invariably referred to by its Chinese name, even by foreigners
guanhua   official language, Mandarin, during the imperial era
guanxi   connections
Guiyidao   the Way of Returning to, or Following, the One, a Daoist organisation
guochi   national humiliation
Guomindang   Nationalist Party – Kuomintang is an older spelling
Guowuyuan   State Council
guxiang   ancestral home
Han   the majority Chinese population
heping jiefang   peaceful liberation

hexie shehui   harmonious society

huang   yellow, but covers a wider spectrum and includes light to medium browns

huaqiao   overseas Chinese, member of the Chinese diaspora

hukou   household registration system

Jiangnan   southern China, that is south [*nan*] of the Yangzi River [*jiang*]

jidu jiao   Protestant Christianity

jihua shengyu   planned birth policy, the official name for the one-child policy

juyou zhongguo tese de shehuizhuyi   socialism with Chinese characteristics

kexue fazhan guan   Scientific Development outlook

Kuomintang   see *Guomindang*

Kuo-yu (*guoyu*)   Usual name in Taiwan for Standard Chinese, *putonghua*

laobaixing   the mass of the population, literally the 'old hundred names' used both affectionately and patronisingly

laogai   reform through labour; labour camps

laojiao   education through labour; labour camps for administrative detention without trial

lifayuan   Legislative Yuan (Taiwan legislative body)

madrasa   (Arabic) Qur'anic schools

mangliu   mobile or floating population

minhang   abbreviation for *Zhongguo minyong hangkong zongju* [CAAC, Civil Aviation Administration of China]

Minnan   Southern Min language spoken in the south of Fujian province and in Taiwan

minquan   people's power

minzheng bu   Ministry of Civil Affairs

Nanfang ribao Southern Daily,   the main Guangdong provincial newspaper

neibu   internal, the opposite of *gongkai*

nongcun shehuizhuyi gaochao   High Tide of Socialism in the Countryside

nongmin shengchan hezuoshe   agricultural producers' cooperatives, APCs

nongye shengchan zeren zhi   Responsibility System for Agricultural Production

putonghua   Standard Chinese, Mandarin

qigong   breathing exercises

qing   dark blue, green, or even nearly black.

Quanguo renmin daibiao dahui   National People's Congress

Renmin gongshe   People's Communes

Renmin Ribao   People's Daily

renminbi   RMB people's currency; the basic unit is the yuan

renquan   human rights

san cong   three obediences of women to father, husband, and son

shangfan   petition

shaoshu minzu   minority nationalities

shaoxiandui   Young Pioneers

Shengwulian,   Hunan Province Revolutionary Great Alliance Committee, Cultural Revolution organisation

shenzhou   sacred territory, China

tianming   Mandate of Heaven

tianzhu jiao   Roman Catholic Christianity

tie fanwan   iron rice bowl

tongbao   compatriot, Chinese living in Taiwan and Hong Kong

tudi gaige   land reform

wailai gong   migrant labour

xiahai   cast into the sea of people forced into private employment or business

xiang   township administrations

xiaokang   shehui comfortably off (moderately prosperous) society

xiejiao   heterodox beliefs, cults

xinfang   letter or complaint and visit petition

Xinhua   New China. New China News Agency, NCNA

Yidai yilu   One Belt One Road initiative

yin, yang   complementary male and female elements

Yiguandao   Way of Pervading Unity, Daoist organsiation

yundong   mass political movements or campaigns

zhengzhi ju   Politburo, standard Russian abbreviation for Political Bureau

zhibian qingnian   young people supporting the border regions

Zhigongdang   Chinese Party for Public Interest, legal minority party in the PRC

zhishi qingnian   educated young people

zhi*xian*   magistrate

Zhongguo gongchandang   Chinese Communist Party

Zhongguo minyong hangkong zongju   CAAC Civil Aviation Administration of China

Zhongguo renmin jiefang jun   Chinese People's Liberation Army

Zhongguo renmin yinhang   People's Bank of China

Zhongguo Xizang   Chinese Tibet

Zhongnanhai   Walled area immediately to the west of the Imperial Palace (Forbidden City) in Beijing, where senior members of the CCP and government live and work. China's Kremlin.

zhongshan zhuang   High-collared Sun Yat-sen jacket, often called the Mao jacket

Zhou Enlai hua zhuan   *Illustrated Biography of Zhou Enlai*

Zhu de huifu   Lord's Recovery, an independent Protestant church

zichanjieji ziyouhua   bourgeois liberalisation – target of campaign in the 1980s

zuguo   motherland – a more accurate translation would be 'ancestral homeland'

Biographical notes

Bo Xilai (1949–)
Son of Bo Yibo, senior adviser to Deng Xiaoping. Bo Xilai was Minister of Commerce and CCP Secretary of Chongqing. Convicted in September 2013 of bribery, abuse of power, and embezzlement, he was sentenced to life imprisonment.

Chen Boda (1904–1989)
Mao Zedong's political adviser, speech writer, and editor from the Yan'an period. Member of CCP Politburo and editor of theoretical journal *Red Flag*. Leader of the Cultural Revolution group and ally of Lin Biao.

Chen Shui-bian (1950–)
President of Republic of China (Taiwan), elected 2004, and leader of the pro-independence Democratic Progressive Party until January 2008.

Chen Yun (1905–1995)
CCP economic supremo and influential figure in the economic modernisation of China in the post-Mao period. A veteran of the Long March and an economic planner trained in the Soviet Union, he opposed China's move away from the planned economy.

Chiang Kai-shek (1887–1975)
Leader of the Kuomintang (Guomindang) and President of the Republic of China on the mainland from 1928–1949, and on Taiwan until his death. After being defeated in the Civil War of 1946–1949, he presided over the beginnings of the Taiwanese economic miracle with financial support from the United States, but ruled the island under conditions of martial law, never losing sight of his main political goal: the reconquest of the mainland.

Deng Xiaoping (1904–1997)
General Secretary of the CCP in 1956, associated with the pragmatic and managerial policies of Liu Shaoqi rather than the revolutionary romantic approach of Mao and purged during the Cultural Revolution. Returned as Deputy Premier after the Cultural Revolution, but was forced to step down after the 1976 Tian'anmen Incident. Returned to power after the fall of the Gang of Four and spearheaded the drive for economic reform.

Fei Xiaotong (1910–2005)
Pioneer of social anthropology in China after training under Bronislaw Malinowski at the London School of Economics. His books *Peasant Life in China* and *Earthbound China* are classic accounts of rural life in China before the Second World War. He was also active in the Democratic League and a delegate to the Chinese People's Consultative Conference, and held senior posts in the Chinese Academies of Sciences and Social Sciences.

Hu Jintao (1952–)
President of People's Republic of China since 2003 and concurrently Chairman of CCP and Central Military Commission.

Hu Qiaomu (1912–1992)
Editor of Mao Zedong's *Selected Works* and speechwriter to the Chairman.

Hu Shi (1891–1962)
Scholar of Chinese literature and philosophy, May Fourth Movement activist and supporter of writing in the vernacular. Hu rejected Marxism in favour of a pragmatic liberal approach, gravitated towards the GMD and was the ambassador in Washington from 1938–1942. He settled in Taiwan and became head of Academia Sinica in 1958, but quarrelled with Chiang Kai-shek over censorship and democracy.

Hu Yaobang (1915–1989)
Secretary General of the CCP from 1982–1987, dismissed after student demonstrations and replaced by Zhao Ziyang. Death on 5 April 1989 generated further demonstrations by students, which led to the Democracy Movement.

Hua Guofeng (1921–2008)
Caretaker Chairman of the CCP after the death of Mao Zedong. He was closely associated with ultra-leftists; ordered the arrest of the Gang of Four but lost power to Deng Xiaoping.

Jiang Qing (1914–1991)
Wife of Mao Zedong and leading member of the Gang of Four. With an acting background in the Shanghai film industry, she used her power base in the city to support Mao's leftist position during the Cultural Revolution and became a leading member of the Cultural Revolution Group and the Politburo. Arrested in 1976, she was tried with the other members of the Gang of Four and sentenced in 1981 to death with a two-year stay of execution. She apparently committed suicide.

Jiang Zemin (1926–)
CCP General Secretary and Chairman in the third generation of leaders and President of the PRC from 1993–2003. He is remembered for his policy of encouraging entrepreneurs to join the CCP.

Jiao Yulu (1922–1964)
A model county Party Secretary who was heroically devoted to the people and was the subject of a hagiographical film in 1990.

Kang Sheng (1899–1975)
The CCP's internal security supremo for much of his career and closely associated with the Cultural Revolution Group. He was posthumously stripped of all his Party posts and blamed for the deaths and persecution of many senior CCP members during the Cultural Revolution.

Kim Jong-un (1984–)
Son of Kim Jong-il and grandson of Kim Il-sung. Leader of North Korea from December 2011 but not confirmed as chairman of the Korean Workers Party and the State Affairs Commission until 2016.

Lam, Carrie (1957–)
Carrie Lam Cheng Yuet-ngor became the fourth Chief Executive of Hong Kong on 1 July 2017. She became prominent during the disputes with Beijing that led to demonstrations and confrontations with police from June 2019 and for aligning Hong Kong with Beijing's policies.

Lee Teng-hui (1923–2020)
President of Taiwan and previously Mayor of Taipei and Governor of Taiwan province. First native Taiwan-born politician to achieve high office under the KMT Outspoken supporter of formal independence for Taiwan, retired from office and joined Taiwan Solidarity Union.

Lei Feng (1939–1962)
Soldier and model Communist who died on duty when he was hit by a falling telegraph pole. His posthumously published diaries, embellished by the PLA's propaganda department, were used to present him as a model young Communist. Memory resurrected for volunteer campaign in twenty-first century.

Li Hongzhi (1951?–)
Founder of Falungong. Reputed to have been a member of the PLA, he left China in 1998 to settle in the United States after the suppression of Falungung by the government.

Li Keqiang (1955–)
Economist and former head of Communist Youth League who became Premier of the PRC in 2013.

Lin Biao (1901–1971)
Marshal of the PLA and Minister of Defence in 1959 after dismissal of Peng Dehuai. Backed Mao in the Cultural Revolution and was designated Mao's successor after the Ninth Party Congress in 1969. Died mysteriously in an airplane crash in 1971 amid allegations that he had tried to stage a military coup to overthrow Mao.

Liu Binyan (1925–2005)
Campaigning journalist and dissident member of the CCP. He was exiled from China in 1989 and lived in the United States.

Liu Shaoqi (1898–1969)
Chairman of the People's Republic of China from 1959–1969 and Top Party-Person Taking the Capitalist Road during the Cultural Revolution. His machine politics and pragmatism contrasted with Mao's revolutionary romanticism, and he died after prolonged ill treatment by Party inquisitors.

Ma Ying-jeou (1950–)
Taiwan KMT chairman and candidate in 2008 presidential election.

Mao Zedong (1893–1976)
Most prominent leader of the CCP, Party chairman from 1943 and the instigator of the Great Leap Forward and the Cultural Revolution. Mao was famed for his advocacy of guerrilla warfare and for his recognition of the importance of the peasantry for China's revolution. In office, he was impatient with pragmatism and gradual change, and he has been held responsible for millions of deaths that have been attributed directly or indirectly to his policies.

Panchen Lama
Senior Tibetan Lama considered by some to possess higher spiritual authority than the Dalai Lama, by others to be the second-hightst ranking lama. Panchen Lamas have often been under the influence of the Chinese court. The tenth Panchen Lama, Choekyi Gyaltsen, lived in Beijing from 1959 until his early and unexpected death in 1989, and he was accused by some Tibetans of having betrayed their cause. In a dispute over the eleventh incarnation, one candidate has been named by the Dalai Lama and another by the PRC religious authorities.

Peng Dehuai (1898–1974)
Minister of Defence from 1954–1959. Peng had spoken out courageously against the Great Leap Forward because of the threat to China's economic development and the future of the armed forces. Conflict with Mao Zedong came to a head at the Lushan Plenum of 1959, and he was purged. He was arrested during the Cultural Revolution and died in prison.

Sun Yat-sen (1866–1925)
Leading advocate of early Chinese Republic who served briefly as First President before being ousted by Yuan Shikai. His *Three People's Principles* [*Sanmin zhuyi*] remains influential among Nationalists, and he is also acknowledged as the founding father of the Republic by the CCP.

Tang Jiaxuan (1938–)
Minister of Foreign Affairs 1998–2003, member of State Council and influential figure in China's diplomacy.

Tsang, Donald (1944–)
Chief Executive of Hong Kong SAR since 2005 and previously Financial Secretary before the handover and Chief Secretary in 2001.

Tsai Ing-wen (1956–)
Academic lawyer, civil servant, and politician. Leader of the Democratic Progressive Party and since 2016, first female President, Republic of China (Taiwan).

Tung Chee-hwa (1937–)
Hong Kong businessman with close connections to Beijing and first Chief Executive of Hong Kong on its return to China in 1997. His administration was unpopular, and he resigned in 2005 before the end of his second term of office; he became a deputy chairman of the Chinese People's Political Consultative Conference.

Wang Hongwen (1935–92)
Former Shanghai cotton mill security guard and founder of the Shanghai Workers Revolutionary General Headquarters during the Cultural Revolution. He became Vice-Chairman of the CCP in 1975, but fell from grace with the other members of the Gang of Four and was sentenced to life imprisonment.

Wen Jiabao (1942–)
Premier of the State Council from 2003–2013. A trained geologist, with administrative experience in Gansu province, Wen was known for his approachable manner and interest in popular issues such as the environment, poverty, and corruption.

Wu Han (1909–1969)
Respected historian and writer and Deputy Mayor of Beijing whose play *Hai Rui Dismissed* was the first target of the radicals in the Cultural Revolution. He died after severe ill treatment in prison.

Wu Yi (1938–)
Deputy Premier of the State Council and the most senior woman politicians in China. She trained as an engineer, and is respected for her economic competence and diplomacy.

Xi Jinping (1953–)
Member of the Standing Committee of the Politburo from the 17th CCP Congress in 2007 and succeeded to Hu Jintao as General Secretary of the CCP and President in 2012.

Yao Wenyuan (1931–2005)
Shanghai radical and literary critic whose article on Wu Han's play initiated the debate that launched the Cultural Revolution. He was sentenced to 20 years imprisonment as one of the Gang of Four.

Zeng Qinghong (1939–)
Vice-President of the PRC and widely tipped as a successor to Hu Jintao as President until his retirement from the Central Committee in 2007. He was effectively the head of the Shanghai faction in the CCP after the retirement of Jiang Zemin.

Zhang Chunqiao (1917–2005)
Shanghai journalist and director of propaganda for the city's Party Committee in the 1960s. Supporter of Jiang Qing's drive to revolutionise opera and film and initiator of the Shanghai Commune. Chairman of the Shanghai Revolutionary Committee in 1967 and as one of the Gang of Four, sentenced to death with a two-year stay of execution.

Zhao Ziyang (1919–2005)
CCP Secretary General and Premier until his removal in 1989 after the suppression of democracy demonstrations in Tian'anmen Square on 4 June. Remained under house arrest until his death.

Zhou Enlai (1898–1976)
First Premier of the PRC. Urbane but ruthless, he maintained his position in the hierarchy throughout the Cultural Revolution. Widely regarded as a pragmatist and a statesman, he was respected for having saved the lives and careers of many senior Party figures during the turmoil of the 1960s.

Further reading

Since China opened to the world in the 1980s, the steady flow of books charting its rise has become a veritable avalanche. Thousands of titles are available; inevitably, they are of varying quality and reliability. Most English-language books on this list have been published since 2010; they are either books that I know, or by authors with an established scholarly reputation. Many books published before 2010 remain of value and some have never been superseded: a few of these classic accounts are therefore included.

Historical background and general analysis

Kerry Brown *China* London: Polity, 2020.
Michael Dillon *China: A Modern History* London: I. B. Tauris, 2010.
Michael Dillon *Deng Xiaoping: The Man who Made Modern China* London: I. B. Tauris, 2015.
Michael Dillon *Zhou Enlai: The Enigma Behind Chairman Mao* London: I. B. Tauris, 2020.
Elizabeth C. Economy *The Third Revolution: Xi Jinping and the New Chinese State* New York: Oxford University Press, 2018.
Carl Minzner *End of an Era: How China's Authoritarian Revival is Undermining Its Rise* New York: Oxford University Press, 2018.
Zheng Yongnian, and Lance L. P. Gore *China Entering the Xi Jinping Era* London: Routledge, 2015.

Politics

Kerry Brown *CEO, China: The Rise of Xi Jinping* London: I.B. Tauris, 2016.
Willy Wo-Lap Lam *The Fight for China's Future: Civil Society vs. The Chinese Communist Party* London: Routledge, 2019.
Julia Lovell *Maoism: A Global History* London: Bodley Head, 2019.
Bruno Maçães *Belt and Road: A Chinese World Order* London: Hurst, 2018.
Roderick MacFraquhar, and Michael Schoenhals *Mao's Last Revolution* Cambridge: Belknap Press of Harvard University Press, 2006.
Richard McGregor *The Party: The Secret World of China's Communist Rulers* London: Penguin, 2011.
Tony Saich *Government and Politics of China* (4th ed.) London: Palgrave, 2015.
Philip Short *Mao: A Life* London: Hodder and Stoughton, 1999.
Michael Yahuda *The International Politics of the Asia-Pacific 1945–1995* (4th and Revised ed.) London: Routledge, 2019.

Economy

Michel Aglietta, and Guo Bai *China's Development: Capitalism and Empire* London: Routledge, 2014.
Cheng Jin (ed.) *An Economic Analysis of the Rise and Decline of Chinese Township and Village Enterprises* London: Palgrave Macmillan, 2017.
Barry Naughton *The Chinese Economy: Adaptation and Growth* (2nd ed.) Cambridge: MIT Press, 2018.

Society

Chen Guidi, and Wu Chuntao *Will the Boat Sink the Water: The Life of China's Peasants* London: Public Affairs, 2006.
Jennifer Hubbert *China in the World: An Anthropology of Confucius Institutes, Soft Power, and Globalisation* Honolulu: University of Hawai'i Press, 2020.
Ian Johnson *Wild Grass: China's Revolution from Below* London: Penguin, 2004.
Ian Johnson *The Souls of China: The Return of Religion after Mao* London: Allen Lane, 2017.
Tom Miller *China's Urban Billion: The Story Behind the Biggest Migration in History* London: Zed Books, 2012.
Elizabeth J. Perry (ed.) *Chinese Society: Change, Conflict and Resistance* (Asia's Transformations) Paperback London: Routledge, 2010.

Gregory Scott *Building the Buddhist Revival: Reconstructing Monasteries in Modern China* Oxford: Oxford University Press, 2020.

Kai Strittmatter *We have been Harmonised: Life in China's Surveillance State* London: Old Street, 2019.

Wang Xiufang *Chinese Education since 1976* Jefferson, NC: McFarland, 2010.

Hong Kong and Taiwan

Leo F. Goodstadt *A City Mismanaged: Hong Kong's Struggle for Survival* Hong Kong: Hong Kong University Press, 2019.

Steve Yui-Sang Tsang *A Modern History of Hong Kong* London; New York: I.B. Tauris, 2004.

Kong Tsung-gan *Liberate Hong Kong: Stories from the Freedom Struggle* Broadway, NSW: Mekong, 2020.

Tibet, Xinjiang and Inner Mongolia

Robert Barnett *Lhasa: Streets with Memories* (Asia Perspectives: History, Society and Culture) New York: Columbia University Press, 2010.

Gardner Bovingdon *The Uyghurs: Strangers in Their Own Land* New York: Columbia University Press, 2020.

Michael Dillon (ed.) *Chinese Minorities at Home and Abroad* London: Routledge, 2017.

Michael Dillon *Lesser Dragons: China's Ethnic Minorities* London: Reaktion Books, 2018.

Michael Dillon *Xinjiang in the Twenty-First Century: Islam, Ethnicity and Resistance* London: Routledge, 2018.

Michael Dillon *Mongolia: A Political History of the Land and its People* London: I. B. Tauris, 2020.

Melvyn C. Goldstein *The Snow Lion and the Dragon: China, Tibet and the Dalai Lama* Berkeley: University of California Press, 1997.

Dawa Norbu *China's Tibet Policy* Richmond: Curzon Press, 2001.

S. Frederick Starr (ed.) *Xinjiang: China's Muslim Borderland* New York: M.E. Sharpe, 2004.

Tsering Woeser (Author), Robert Barnett (ed.), Susan T. Chen (trans.) *Forbidden Memory: Tibet during the Cultural Revolution* Lincoln, NE: Potomac Books, 2020.

Xiaowei Zang (ed.) *Handbook on Ethnic Minorities in China* Cheltenham: Edward Elgar, 2016.

Selected Chinese language sources

Gao Tian 高天 (ed.) *Zhong Gong Diliudai* 中共第六代 (*Chinese Communist Party: The Sixth Generation*) Hong Kong: Hong Kong Cultural Press, 2010.

Luo Pinghan *Nongcun renmin gongshe shi* (*History of Rural People's Communes*) Fujian renmin chubanshe, 2006.

Ma Ling 马玲 *Wen Jiabao xin zhuan* 温家宝新传 (*New Biography of Wen Jiabao*) Hong Kong: Mingbao, 2008.

Ma Shixiang *Nongye hezuohua yundong shimo: baiming qinlizhe koushu shilu* (*Complete Account of the Agricultural Cooperation Movement: Recorded Oral Testimony of One Hundred Participants*) Beijing: Dangdai Zhongguo, 2012.

Shi Hua 史华 *Hu Wen weiji* 胡温危机 (*The Hu Wen Crisis*) Hong Kong: Hong Kong Cultural Press, 2004.

Tan Tian 谭天 *Shiba da qian de xiaoyan* 十八大前的硝烟 (*Smell of Cordite before the 18th Party Congress*) Hong Kong: New Culture Press, 2010.

Waican bianji bu 外参编辑部 (Editorial Department of Waican Magazine) *Zhong Gong shibada zhi zheng* 中共十八大之争 (*The Struggle for Chinese Communists' Eighteenth Congress*) Hong Kong: Waican Publishers, 2011.

Wu Ming 吴鸣 *Hu Jintao xin gong lǚe* 胡锦涛新攻略 (*Hu Jintao's New Attack*) Hong Kong: Hong Kong Cultural Press, 2007.

Wu Ming 吴鸣 *Xi Jinping zhuan: Zhongguo xin lingxiu* 习近平转：中国新领袖 (*Biography of Xin Jinping: China's New Leader*) Hong Kong: Hong Kong Cultural Press, 2010.

Xia Fei et al. 夏飞 *Taizidang he gongqingtuan: Xi Jinping PK Li Keqiang* 太子党和共青团: 习近平 PK 李克强 (*Crown Prince Party and Communist Youth League Faction: Xi Jinping Competes with Li Keqiang*) Hong Kong: Mirror Books, 2007.

Xu Xiuli, and Wang Xianming (eds.) *Zhongguo jindai xiangcun de weiji yu congjian: geming, gailiang ji qita* (*Crisis and Reconstruction of Rural Society in Modern China: Revolution, Reform and More*) Beijing: Social Science Academic Press, 2013.

Yi Ming 伊铭 *Hu Wen xin zheng* 胡温新政 (*New Politics of Hu and Wen*) Hong Kong: Mirror Books, 2003.

Yu Jie 余杰 *Zhongguo yingdi: Wen Jiabao* 中国影帝：温家宝 (Subtitled in English *China's Best Actor: Wen Jiabao*) Hong Kong: New Century Press, 2010.

Index

11 September 2001 350–1
14K triad 282
17th CCP Congress 53
17th Central Committee 61, 106
18th CCP Congress 61, 62
1992 consensus, Taiwan 304–5
2007–2008 financial crisis 92–3

Abdul Rasul 360
acid rain 230
acupuncture 168
Afghanistan 350, 351, 358, 359–60
Africa and China 341–4
Africans, in Guangzhou 344
Agrarian Reform Law 151
Agricultural Bank of China 107, 118
agricultural development 90
Agricultural Producers' Cooperatives (APCs) 99
Agricultural Reform Law 98
agricultural taxation 103
Ahmad Baghlan 360
AIDS *see* HIV/AIDS
Air Defence Identification Zone 328
Aksai Chin 339, 357
Aksu, riot 253
Albania 360
Alibaba 175, 200
Al Jazeera 202
All-China Federation of Trade Unions 114
All-China Women's Federation 226
almanacs 97
Almaty 354
Alptekin, Isa Yusuf 353, 354
Al Qaeda 254, 260, 261, 350
Anglo-Chinese Convention of 1906 242
Anglo-Japanese Alliance of 1902 13
Angola 342
Anhui 100, 108
anti-corruption campaign 35–6, 80–1
Anti-Rightist Campaign 32, 39, 180
Arbour, Louise 181, 188
Ardern, Jacinta 320
Army Day 33

Arunachal Pradesh 339, 357
ASEAN 144, 331
Asian Development Bank 145
Association for Relations across the Taiwan
    Straits ARATS (PRC) 304
Astana 351
Autonomous regions 7
Aviation 128–9

Bahasa Indonesia 338
Bahasa Malaysia 338
Baidu 200
Baiyunguan, (White Cloud Temple) 205
Balochistan Liberation Army (BLA) 146
Baltic Way 283, 339
Bandung Conference 339, 342
banking 117–25
Banking and Insurance Regulatory
    Commission 124
Bank of China 118
banks, foreign 122–3
baomu 101
Baoshan steel complex, Shanghai 326
Baotou 268
barbarian 11
barefoot doctors 158
barefoot healthcare 168
Baren demonstrations 253
Basic Law, Hong Kong 274–5, 295–6
Bauhinia flag 280
Beida clique 78, 79
Beidaihe meetings 59, 81–2
Beijing dialect (*Beijing tuhua*) 7
Beijing Forum on China-Africa cooperation 342
Beijing-Shanghai Express Railway 126
Beijing University 74, 164–5
Belgrade, Chinese Embassy 317
Belt and Road Initiative 124, 144–8, 252, 256,
    320, 325, 350, 352, 355, 359
Bhutan 338, 340
Big Reference 198
Bishkek 350
black jails 191

Black Knight, exercise 351
blood: contaminated 171–2; illegal sale 75–6
Bo Xilai 29, 55–60, 62
Bo Yibo 56
border clashes, China and India 340
border skirmishes, Soviet Union 1969 17
border(s): China and India 338; demarcation of 338
bound feet 224
bourgeois liberalisation 40, 80
Boxer Rising 205
Bretton Woods 122
brigades, agriculture 152
Buddhism 135, 206–8
Buddhist Association, Chinese 207, 208
Buryats 266
Bush, George W. 248
Business and Professionals Alliance for Hong Kong (BPA) 276
ByteDance 323

cable and satellite TV, international 199
Caijing (*Finance and Economics*) magazine 115
Cai Xia 83
Campaign against Lin Biao and Confucius 40
Campaign for the Suppression of Counterrevolutionaries 38
Cantonese 8, 199
Canton (Guangzhou) Trade Fair 121
capitalist socialism 80
capitals 6
Carson, Rachel, *Silent Spring* 229
Cathay Pacific 283
Cathedral of the Immaculate Conception, Beijing 212
Causeway Bay 284, 287
CCP Central Commission for Discipline Inspection (CCDI) 27, 30, 65, 81, 106, 174, 185
CCP Central Committee Propaganda and United Front Work Department 197
CCP Congresses 29
CCP factions 23, 31, 63
CCP founding conference 13
CCP Leading Group for Dealing with Falungong 216
CCP Organisation Department 26, 30
CCP Propaganda Department 196, 199
CCP Secretariat 30
census, 1953 4
Central Advisory Commission 56
Central Asia 347–9
Central Asia, land border with 4
Central Committee 61, 177
Central Committee and Politburo 29–30
Central Coordination Group for Hong Kong and Macao 281

Central Financial and Economic Committee 120
Central Leading Group for Comprehensively Deepening Reforms 80
Central Military Affairs Commission (CMAC) 25, 28, 34, 36, 49, 50, 63, 64
Central Nationalities Institute 253
Central Nationalities University 258
Central Org Dept 65, 71, 72
Central Party School 28, 83, 366
Central People's Government 24
Central Political and Legal Affairs Commission 83, 292
Central Politics and Law Commission of the CCP 258
Centre for China and Globalisation 147
Chairman of the CCP 24
Chairman of the PRC 25, 44
Chan, Melissa 202
Changjiang or Yangzi (Yangtse) river 5
Changqing gas field 139
Chan Kin-man 276
Chan Tong-kai 289
Chan Wing-tsit 204
Chater Park 292
Chek Lap Kok airport 284
Ch'en, Kenneth 206
Chen Bangzhu 235
Chen Boda 152
Cheng Kejie 30
Chen Liangyu 65, 71
Chen Quanguo, Xinjiang 261–2
Chen Quanguo 248–9
Chen Shui-bian 303–4, 306, 307
Chen Xitong 30
Chen Yun 40, 49
Chen Zu 170
Chiang Ching-kuo 301
Chiang Ching-kuo Foundation 167
Chiang Kai-shek (Jiang Jieshi) 13, 15, 17, 272, 300, 301–2, 315
Chiang Kai-shek Memorial Hall 305
Chief Executive, Hong Kong 276–8
China-Africa Cooperation, Beijing, Forum on 342
China and Japan Treaty of Peace and Friendship 325
China Association for the Promotion of Democracy 32
China Daily 198
China Democratic League 31–2, 197
China Democratic National Construction Association 32
China Democratic Party 32
China Eastern Airlines 129
China Northern Airlines 129
China Northwest Airlines 129
China-Pakistan Economic Corridor 147, 359

China Petroleum and Chemical Corporation, Sinopec 356
China Proper 135, 136
China Qigong Scientific Research Association 214
China's *gulag* 186, 189
China Southern Airlines 129
China Southwest Airlines 129
China-Taiwan relations 304
Chinatowns 337
China Youth Daily 31, 72, 198
Chinese Academy of Social Science 89, 131
Chinese Buddhist Association 207, 208
Chinese Catholic Patriotic Association 211
Chinese Central Television (CCTV) 199
Chinese characters 8
Chinese Communist Party (CCP) 26–31; in power 10
Chinese Daoist Association 205
Chinese expatriates in Africa 342
Chinese Family Planning Association 227
Chinese Foundation for the Development of Human Rights 187
Chinese Industrial Cooperatives (Indusco or Gung Ho) 105
Chinese Islamic Academy 255
Chinese Islamic Association 254
Chinese language 158, 162
Chinese National Administration for the Protection of State Secrets 200
Chinese National Petroleum Corporation (PetroChina) 234
Chinese Party for the Public Interest (Zhigongdang) 32
Chinese Peasants' and Workers' Democratic Party 32
Chinese People's Political Consultative Conference 26, 174, 204, 206, 209, 235, 245, 367
Chinese Peoples' Volunteers 33, 322
Chinese Society for Human Rights 187
Chinese Tibet 241
Chinese University 284
Chinese University of Hong Kong 165, 290
Chinese values, Asian values 186–7
Chongqing 14, 55, 131
Chongqing model 55–7, 62
Chongqing Steel Mill 114
Chow, Agnes 284
Christianity, Orthodox 209
Christianity, Protestant 209–11
Christianity, Roman Catholic 209
Chu Yiu-ming, Reverend 276
churches, overseas 213
City University 290
Civic Party (CP) 276
Civic Square 279
Civil Aviation Administration of China) (CAAC) 129
Civil Human Rights Front 293

civil society 79; labour organisations 115
Civil War 15, 33, 44, 49, 97, 98, 272, 300, 315
Cixi, Empress Dowager 11
CMAC *see* Central Military Affairs Commission (CMAC)
coal mining 268
Cohen, Jerome 181
Cold War ix, x, 300, 357, 338, 339
collective leadership 62
collectivisation 16, 106, 107, 151–2
colonial power in Africa, China 342
colonisation 10
Combined Tactics Training Base 38
COMECON (Council for Mutual Economic Assistance) other way round? 112, 121
Comintern 13
command economy 113
Commission for Law-based Governance 185
Commission for Political and Legal Affairs 185
Commission on Discipline Inspection (CCDI) 56
Common Programme 180
communes 118
Communist Party of the Soviet Union (CPSU) 13, 23
Communist Youth League (CYL) 31, 65, 71; and Li Keqiang 74–5
community dialogue 287–91
compradors 12
Comprehensive Nuclear Test Ban Treaty (CTBT) 231
compulsory education 141, 162
Confucianism 155, 158, 160, 186
Confucius Institutes 167–8
Connaught Road 282
conscription 37–8
Constitution of the PRC 23–5, 180
contaminated blood 171–2
contract responsibility system 113
convenience police posts 249, 262
cooperatives 98–100, 152
core curriculum 166
Coronavirus (COVID 19) 173–6
corruption 106, 366
counter-revolutionaries, suppression of 207
court cases, reporting of 183
COVID-19 94, 294, 296, 308, 323, 344, 367
criminal law 181
crown prince 64
cult of Mao 365
cultural Christianity 211
Cultural Revolution 16, 24, 29, 32, 39–40, 56, 65, 91, 137, 161, 164, 180, 186, 203, 207, 209, 218, 219, 244, 252, 254, 267, 275, 316
currency: liberalisation 120; revaluation of 94

Daesh (Islamic State, or ISIS) 355
Dai 219
Dalai Lama 241, 242, 243, 244, 245, 248, 339, 357

Dangwai movement, Taiwan 302, 304
danwei 128, 154
Daodejing 204
Daoism 204–6, 229
Darfur 342
Davos 2019 144
death penalty 188–9
debt trap 145, 146
decentralisation, communes 100
deforestation 230
democracy: in Hong Kong 275–6; inner Party 72
Democracy Movement 18, 33, 49, 75, 78, 245, 327
Democratic Alliance for the Betterment and
    Progress of Hong Kong (DAB) 276
Democratic Management Committees 249
Democratic Party (DP) 23, 31–2, 276
Democratic Progressive Party, Taiwan 302
Democratic Republic of Chinese Taiwan 301
demonstrations: June 12 278–80; led by monks
    of Drepung monastery 245
Deng Xiaoping 1617 28, 40, 49, 62, 100, 131,
    161, 180, 273, 324; 1992 Southern Tour 80;
    reforms 126; theory 132
Development Research Centre of the State
    Council 101
Dharamsala 241, 244, 339
Diaoyu 328
dictatorship of people's democracy 17
Diocesan Girls' School, Hong Kong 284
dissent 185, 191–2
Document No. 7 254
Document No. 9 79–80
double burden system 50
double-linked households 249; management
    system 262
Drepung monastery demonstrations 245
dual price system 113
dust storms 133

Early Rain Covenant Church 211
Eastern Lightning 211
Eastern Turkestan Islamic Movement (ETIM)
    258, 260
Eastern Turkestan People's Party 32
Eastern Turkestan Republic 348
East Turkestan 347, 355
East Turkestan Islamic Party (ETIP) 253, 260
Ecevit, Bulent 355
ecological migration 268
economic democracy 365
economic growth 89–95
educated youth 137
education 134, 158–68; and the CCP 160–8;
    compulsory 141, 162; through labour 80, 190;
    Xi Jinping era 165–7
educational reform, 1980s and 1990s 161
Eighth Route Army 15, 33
elders 56

Empress Dowager Cixi 11
endemic diseases 168
entrepreneurs in CCP 115
environment 133, 134, 229–37
environmental NGOs 235
environmental protection measures 141
Epoch Times 215
ethnic minorities 203–22, 216–20, 266
Eurasian Economic Union 144
European Commission 319
European Union 145
Evans, Sir Richard 274
Examination Yuan 306
Exclusive Brethren 210
Executive Yuan 306
extradition bill 277–8, 286
Extra-Party Movement, Taiwan 301
ExxonMobil 139

F-7 fighter aircraft 358
fabi (legal currency) 117
Falungong 197, 211, 213–16
famine(s) 16; North Korea 329
Fang Lizhi 40
Fei Xiaotong 97
Fengtai district, Beijing 184, 367
Fengyang County, Anhui province 100, 107
fifth generation 61–86
finance 117–25
financial crisis, 2007–2008 92–3
Financial Times 202
First United Front (1923–1927) 13
First World War (1914–1918) 13
fiscal decentralisation 103
Five-Anti Campaign 38–9
Five Classics 159
five demands 282
Five Principles of Peaceful Coexistence 339, 366
Five-Year Plan(s) 26, 91; Tenth 48
floating peg, currency 120
foreign banks 122–3
Foreign Correspondents' Club of China 201
foreign exchange 120
foreign Exchange Certificates (FECs) 117
foreign investment in China 123
foreign media 201–2
Foreign Ministry 314
foreign trade 117–25
Formosa 300
Formosa or Kaohsiung incident 302, 304
Four Basic Principles 17
Four Books 159
Four Modernisations 17, 121, 164, 366
Four Olds 207
fourth-generation leadership 48–54
Free China 300–1
freedom of the press 80
Freezing Point (*Bingdian*) 72, 198

Friendship Stores 117
Fudan University, Shanghai 165
Fu Guohao 282
Fujian 64, 70, 300, 337
Fujianese, Hokkien language 8
Fu Quanyou 358
further and higher education 164–5

G20 summit 145, 322; Osaka, June 2019 322
Gandhi Sonia 340
Gan Junqiu, Joseph 213
Gansu 209; Tibetan-speaking communities 243
Gao Feng 96
Gao Gang 66, 68
gaogan zidi 23, 28
Gao Yaojie 172
Gao Yu 79
Gao Zhisheng 191
GDP 89, 94
gender 223–8
General Agreement on Tariffs and Trade
    (GATT) 122
General Secretary of the CCP 24, 83
generations of leadership in the PRC 48–54
Geng Biao 70, 71
ger 267
getihu 366
Ghulja 253, 254, 348
Global Times 198, 282
globalisation 79, 201
Golmud 247
gongkai (open or public newspapers) 183
Gong Pinmei, Bishop of Shanghai 212
Gong Xiangrui 78
Google 322
Gorbachev, Mikhail 324
Government Communications Headquarters
    (GCHQ) 320
Grantham, Sir Alexander 272
Great Development of the Western regions 255
Greater Bay Area 5, 124
Great Firewall of China 200
Great Game 353
Great Khingan (Xing'an) range 6
Great Leap Forward 15, 39, 56, 91, 152, 154,
    205, 219, 244, 313
Grey Wolves 355
Gross Domestic Product (GDP) 6
Guan Haixiang 56
Guangdong 69, 104, 337; model 56, 62
Guangdong-Hong Kong-Macao Greater Bay
    Area 5, 124
Guangming Daily 196–7
Guangxi Zhuang Autonomous Region 132,
    177, 337
Guangzhou 13
guanxi 27, 31, 181
Gui Minhai 191

Guiyidao (Way of Returning to the One) 205
Gu Junshan 35
Gu Kailai 55
Guo Boxiong 36, 81
Guomindang (Kuomintang or Nationalist Party)
    12, 13, 77, 126, 272, 299
Guo Quan 33
Guo Shengkun 292
Gwadar 146

Hada 267–9
Haifeng 42, 43
Hailufeng Soviet 43
Hainan 317, 337
hajj 209, 352
Hakka 8, 224, 337
Hakluyt & Company 57
Han 136
Han Chinese 11, 216
Hanban 167, 168
handicraft industries 97
Han Dingxiang 212
Han dynasty 206
Han Kuo-yu 308
Han Zheng 30, 279, 281, 289–90
Harbin water pollution 233–5
harmonious society 52–3, 365–8
Harrison, Harry 279
Hatf missile 358
Healthy China 2030 173
Hefei 165
He Guoqiang 65, 71
Henan province 75–6, 171
Hepatitis B 172
herding 268, 269
heterodox cult (*xiejiao*) 215
Heytgar (Id Gah) Mosque 356
Heywood, Neil 55, 57–9
higher education 164–5
higher-level producers' cooperatives (HPCs) 99
high-speed trains 53, 126, 127
High Tide of Socialism in the Countryside 99
hijab 255, 258
Hikmet Cetin 355
Hindi Chini bhai bhai 339
Hindu Nationalist BJP (Bharatiya Janata Party)
    government 340
historical nihilism 80
history textbooks 327
HIV/AIDS 169, 171, 172
Hizb al-Islami al-Turkestani (HAAT) 260
Hogg, Rupert 283
Hokkien (Fujianese) language 8, 337
Hong Kong 12, 196, 271–98, 337, 367
Hong Kong and Macao Affairs Office 281,
    285–6, 295
Hong Kong district elections 291
Hong Kong Federation of Trade Unions (FTU) 276

Hong Kong Ferry Terminal 294
Hong Kong Government Information Services
    Department 295
Hong Kong Human Rights and Democracy
    Act 287
Hong Kong Mass Transit Railway (MTR) 128
Hong Kong Polytechnic University (PolyU)
    290–1
Hong Kong Stock Exchange 119
Hong Kong University 165
Hong Kong University of Science and
    Technology 165, 290
Hong Kong Way 283–5
Hong Kong-Zhuhai-Macao Bridge 294
household registration system (*hukou*) 101,
    153–7, 184
Household Responsibility System 17, 100, 106
HSBC 123–4
Huang Qifan 57
Huanghe (Yellow River) 4–5
Huangpu (Whampoa) Military Academy 13, 74
Huawei electronics company 319–23
Hu Chunhua 269
Hui Muslims 208, 218–19, 252
Hu Jintao 29, 31, 48–54, 64, 71, 77, 106, 108,
    161, 220, 234, 332, 365, 366
Hu Jiwei 197
hukou see household registration system (*hukou*)
Hu Qiaomu 40
Hu Yaobang 18, 24, 30, 49, 51–2, 69, 195, 197,
    245, 324
human rights 179–94
Human Rights Watch 27, 184, 187, 293
Hundred Flowers Movement 32, 39
Hunt, Jeremy 280
hyperinflation 91

ideology 79
Ilham Tohti 259–60
Ili region 253
illiteracy 160
imams 255
Imran Khan 359
Independent Commission Against Corruption
    (ICAC), Hong Kong 273
Independent Police Complaints Council 283, 286–7
India: and China 338–41; population 338
Indian National Congress 340
Indonesia 337
Industrial and Commercial Bank of China 118
industrial development 90, 96, 220
industrialisation 96, 220
industrial pollution 229
infrastructure, modernisation 133, 134
Inner Asian frontiers 347
Inner Mongolia 38, 266–70; disturbances May
    2011 268–70
Inner Mongolian People's Party 267

Internal Reference 198
International Atomic Energy Authority (IAEA)
    330, 331
International Bank for Reconstruction and
    Development 122
international cable and satellite TV 199
International Covenant on Civil and Political
    Rights 181
International Labour Organisation 105
International Monetary Fund (IMF) 122
international relations 313–62
internet 200
internment camps 262–3
Interpol 81
Iran 355–6; China arms sales to 356
iron rice bowl 113
Islam 135, 208–9, 352
Islamic Emirate of Afghanistan 360
Islamic marriage contract, *nikah* 255
Islamic Movement of Uzbekistan 351
Islamist movements 348

Jahriyya 252
Jang Song-taek 334
Japan 186, 366; China 325–9
Japanese invasion of China 14–15, 126, 140, 271
Jeep attack, Tian'anmen Square, October 2013
    258–9
Jiang Chaoliang 174
Jiang Qing 17
Jiang Xingchang 189
Jiangxi Soviet 14, 98
Jiang Zemin 26, 28, 29, 31, 34, 48, 49, 115, 131,
    139, 358
Jiao Yulu 365
jihadist groups 261
Jingdezhen 97, 229
Jinggangshan 14
Jinuo 217
Jiujingzhuan Relief Service Centre 184
Jiusan (3 September) Society 32
Johnson, Boris 322
Johnson, Ian 206
Joint Hong Kong 274
Joint State-Private Bank 118
joint-venture companies 121
Jokhang temple 246, 248
journalists 200–1
judicial reform 185
Judicial Yuan 306
Juncker, Jean-Paul 145
June 12 demonstrations 278–80
Junior Police Officers' Association, Hong Kong
    293
Juzan (Chü-tsan) 207

Kalmyks 266
Kang Sheng 68

Kaohsiung 308
Karakash (Moyu) 258
Karmapa Lama 246
Kashgar 136, 192, 257, 348
Kazakhstan 256, 347, 351–2
key schools 163
Khabarovsk 235
Khotan 257, 261
Khrushchev, Nikita 366
Khufiyya 252
Khunjerab Pass 357
Kim Dae-jung 334
Kim Il-sung 329
Kim Jong-chul 335
Kim Jong-nan 335
Kim Jong-un 334–6
Kim-Moon talks 335–6
Kim Yo-jong 336
Kissinger, Henry 317
Korean Party of Labour 329, 330
Koreans in China 332–3
Korean War 15, 33, 91, 98, 300, 316, 322,
    330, 334
Kuhn, Robert 49
Kunming 259
Kuomintang *see* Guomindang (Kuomintang
    or Nationalist Party)
Kyrgyzstan 347, 351

labour: camps 186; mobility 155; movement
    114–15
Ladakh 340
Lai, Jimmy Chee-Ying 295, 296
Lam, Carrie 276
Lam, Willy 53, 61–2, 63
Lama Buddhism 267
Land Administration Law of August 1998 100
landlords 151
land reform 15, 98, 101–2, 151–2, 207
Lanzhou 231, 253
laogai (reform through labour) camps 182
laojiao (education through labour) camps 182
Larung Gar 249
Lattimore, Owen 316
law 179–94
Lee, Martin 295
Lee Kuan-yew 77
Lee Teng-hui 301, 303
Lee Wen Ho 317–18
legal code 179
Legal Daily (Fazhi ribao) 197
legal system, traditional 179
Legco (Legislative Council), Hong Kong 275,
    277, 280–1, 288, 295, 296
Legislative Yuan 303, 305–6
Leibold, James 219
Lei Feng 365

Lei Yang 84
Leung, C.Y. (Leung Chun-ying) 276
Leung Tin-kei, Edward 277
Lhasa, PLA troops garrisoned 243
Liaison Office of the Central People's
    Government in Hong Kong 196, 293
Li Anshan 342
Liaoning province 76–9
Liberal Democratic Party, Japan 328–9
Liberal Party, Hong Kong 276
Li Changshou, Witness Lee 210
Lien Chan 77, 304
Li Fei 280
Li Hongzhi 214
Li Keqiang 30, 65, 73–9, 174, 175, 328, 367
Lin Biao 16, 40, 45. 273, 314
Ling Jihua 81
Lin Zuluan 44
Li Peng 355
Li Ruihuan 357
Li Shan, Father Joseph 212
literati 158
little emperors 176
Little Flock 210
Liu Binyan 197
Liu He 319, 323
Liu Huaqiu 357
Liu Quanxi 172
Liu Shaoqi 16, 17, 24
Liu Xiaoming 281, 320–1
Liu Yandong 167
Liu Zhidan 66–9
liuzhi system 27–8
Living Buddhas 249–50
Li Wenliang 174
Li Yuanchao 74
Li Zhanshu 30
Li Zhi 257
Local Church 210
local competitive economies 134
Lockheed EP-3E Aries II signals reconnaissance
    aircraft 317
loess soil 4
Long March 48
Lop Nor 231
Lord's Recovery Church 210
Lufeng 42, 43
Lugouqiao (Marco Polo Bridge) 327
lunar-solar calendar 97
Luntai 259
Luo Huining 293
Luoyang 206
Lushan Plenum 67
Lu Shouwang 213

M-1 missile 357
Macao 276, 337

Macartney Embassy, 1793 11
MacLehose, Sir Murray 273
Madsen, Richard 216
Maglev (magnetic levitation) railway 128
Ma Guoqiang 174
Mahathir Mohammed 187
Maitreya, Buddha of the future 206
Ma Jiantang 93
Malaysia 145, 146, 187, 337
Mallet, Victor 202
Manas airfield 350, 351
Manchus 10–11, 217, 218
Mandarin 7, 300
Mandate of Heaven 11
Mao Anying 330
Mao jacket 50
Mao Zedong viii, 14, 15–16, 44–6, 56, 62, 99,
    152–3, 171, 207, 313, 330, 366
Mao Zedong Thought 80, 161
Mao: The Unknown Story 45–6
Maoism 28, 45
Maralbashi County 259
Ma Rong 219
marriage 223–4
Marriage Reform Law of 1950 225
Martial Law 302–3; Taiwan 302–3
Marxism-Leninism 365
Marxism-Leninism-Mao Zedong Thought 14,
    17, 28
mass incidents 105
mass media 195–202
May, Theresa 320
May Fourth Movement 13
Ma Ying-jeou 306–7
Mazar-e Sharif 360
Mazars 252
Mazu 44
McCarthy period 316
McDonald, Sir Simon 281
media, foreign 201–2
media, new 200
medical insurance 169; for countryside 169, 170–1
medicine: reform era 169; traditional 158, 168
Meng Hongwei 81
Meng Jianzhu 59, 185, 258
Meng Wanzhou 123, 319
Metro Beijing 198
Metro Shanghai 198
middle class 366
Middle East and China 352–6
migration 153–4, 135–8, 348
migrant population 135, 138
migrant workers 103
Military Affairs Commission *see* Central
    Military Affairs Commission (CMAC)
Military Service Law 37
minimum living standard guarantee 115

Ministry of Civil Affairs 41
Ministry of Commerce 96
Ministry of Education 162
Ministry of Finance 118
Ministry of Justice 180
Ministry of Public Security 35, 59, 105, 190
minority(ies): nationalities (*shaoshu minzu*) 217;
    religious and ethnic 203–22
Missile Technology Control Regime (MTCR) 357
missionaries 159, 316
Modern Buddhism 207
monasteries 205
Mong Kok 279, 281, 283, 286, 292
Mongol conquests 352
Mongolia 147, 266
Mongolian 11; Buddhism 208; language 269–70;
    People's Republic 266
Mongols 217–18
Moon Jae-in 336
mosques 255
moxibustion 168
MTR 288, 292
multi-party elections 79
municipalities 7
Musharraf, Pervez, General 358
mutual aid teams 98–100
Myanmar 145

Nakasone Yasuhiro 326
Nakhi (Naxi) 219
Nanjing 14
Naqshbandiyya 252
National Assembly 302, 305
National Bureau of Statistics 89, 93
National Cyber Security Centre 320
National Day 288
National Development and Reform Commission
    92, 127, 139, 156
national expressways 127
national flag 24
national humiliation 313
National Intelligence Law 319
National Liberation Front, Vietnam 316
National People's Congress 24–6
National Radio and Television Administration 195
National Security Commission 80
national security legislation 295–6
National Supervisory Commission 25
Nawaz Sharif 358
Naxalite insurrection 45
Nazarbayev Nursultan 351
Nehru, Jawaharlal 244
neibu (internal newspapers) 183
Neighbourhood Committees 175
neoliberalism 79
Nepal 145, 338
new authoritarianism 365–8

new bureaucratic capitalism 80
New China 15
New China News Agency 196
New Culture Movement 13
New Democracy 23, 24
New Democracy Party 33
New Fourth Army 15, 33
New Life Movement 160
new media 200
new socialist countryside 102
newspapers 196–8; daily provinces have their
   own 197; internal 198; national 195; state-
   controlled 197
New Tang Dynasty Television 215
New Territories 273
New Zealand 320
Ni Duosheng, Watchman Nee 210
nine-year compulsory education system 161–3
Ningxia 209
Nixon Doctrine 314, 316–17
Nixon China visit February 1972 317, 325
nomadic herders 266–8
nomenklatura 30
non-aligned Third World 339
North Atlantic Treaty Organisation 317
Northern Expedition 13, 114
North Korea 316, 333; and China 329–36
nouveau riche 154, 366
Nowak, Manfred 181
NPC 174–5, 188, 367
Nur Bekri 256
Nur-Sultan 351

Obama, President Barack 318
Occupy Central movement 276–7
Office for Restructuring the Economic System 92
oil: and construction, Africa 341–2; and gas
   pipelines 138–40; supplies from Iran 356
oilfields, northern Xinjiang 256
old China hands 315
Old Town God Temple, Shanghai 216
Olympic Games 156, 184, 230
One China 51, 306, 318
one country, two systems 274, 294, 308
one-child policy 80, 176–7, 226, 227
O'Neill, Jim 93
Open Brethren 210
Open Constitution (*Gong meng*) Initiative 184
Opium War 11–12, 271
opposition parties 32
Organic Law of People's Courts 180
Organic Law on Village Committees 42
Organised Crime and Triad Bureau,
   Hong Kong 281
Orthodox Christianity 209
Osama bin Laden 261
Outer Mongolia 266

Overseas Chinese 337–8
overseas churches 213
Ozal, Turgut 353

Pakistan 145, 146, 358; and China 357–9
Pak Jong-chun 336
Pamirs 6
Pan-Blue coalition 306
Panchen Lama 244, 245–6
pan-Democrats 278
Pan-Green coalition 306–7
pan-Turkism 354
Pan Yue 236
Paris Club 147
Parker, Andrew, head of United Kingdom
   Security Service (MI5) 322
Party branches 29
Party elders 28
Party History Research Centre 29
passports, confiscation 262
Patriot anti-missile defence system 331
Patten, Chris 275
peaceful development 366
Pearl River Delta 5
Peasant Associations 42
Peasant Burden Reduction Group 41
peasant protest 45, 103–5
Peasant Rights Preservation Committee 41
Pence, Mike 318
Pengcheng 206
Peng Dehuai 67, 68, 330
Peng Liyuan 70
Peng Zhen 40
People First (*Qinmin*) Party 308
People's Bank of China 90, 117, 120, 174
People's Communes 17, 32, 41, 97, 98–100,
   102, 108, 152–3
People's Congresses 24
People's Construction Bank of China 118
People's Courts 182
People's Daily (*Renmin Ribao*) 44, 196–8
People's Liberation Army (PLA) 15, 33–8
People's Tribunals 180
People's Armed Police (PAP) 16, 35, 36–7, 136,
   242–3, 282, 285
personality cult 83
petitioning 183–4
PetroChina 139
phase one trade deal with USA 323
picking quarrels and provoking trouble 191
pivot towards Asia 318
planned birth (*jihua shengyu*) 176
planned economy 91–2, 126
Plymouth Brethren 210
Politburo Standing Committee 279
political birthdays 82
political campaigns 15, 23, 38–9

Political Islam 349, 358
political prisoners 188
pollution 230, 233, 269
PolyU, Hong Kong Polytechnic University 291
Pompeo, Mike 335
Pope Benedict XVI 211, 212
Pope Francis 213
Pope John Paul II 211, 212
population of China 4, 90, 134, 153–4
Potala palace 243
poverty 90, 91, 133, 140–1
PRC Liaison Office, Hong Kong 282, 295
princeling 63–6
prison camps 190
Prisoner of the State: The Secret Journal of Premier Zhao Ziyang 52
prisons 182–3, 186, 190–1
private cars 128
private education 163–4
private sector growth 115
privatisation 79, 113
Procuratorate 25
pro-democracy movement 291, 295
Production Brigade 66
prosperity 366
Protestant Christianity 209–11
provinces 7
public executions 189
public health 134
public order disturbances 105
Public Security Bureau 32, 156
Putin, Vladimir 83, 324–5, 335
putonghua (standard Chinese, Mandarin) 7, 163
Pyongyang, nuclear programme 330, 331

qadi judges 255
Qian Qichen 304
Qiao Shi 354
qigong 214
Qing dynasty 10–11
Qinghai 136, 190, 243, 246
Qinghai-Tibet railway 141, 246–7
Qinghua (Tsinghua) University 50, 78, 165
Qinghua clique 63, 79
Qiushi 185
QR codes 175
Qur'an 255, 262

Rafsanjani, Ali Akbar Hashemi 356
railways 126–7
Ramadan 228, 262
Rape of Nanjing 327
rare earth minerals 322
Reclaim Hong Kong, the revolution of our time 277
red culture 56
Red Guards 32, 253

red tourism 129
re-education through labour 262–3
Reference Material 198
Reference News 198
reform and opening 17, 80, 107, 121, 314
reform through labour (*laogai*) 137, 190
regional autonomy 140–2
Regional Autonomy for Ethnic Minorities in China, a White Paper 140
Religious Affairs Bureau 203, 254
religious freedom 203, 254–5
religious minorities 203–22
religious movements 203–4
Renmin University of China 165
renminbi 94, 117, 120
Ren Zhiqiang 83
Republic of China 299, 305, 308, 314
requisition of land 269
residential surveillance at a designated location 191
Responsibility System 100, 108, 109, 153
Restaurants: classified as 'blue' 292; classified as 'yellow' 292
Revolution of 1911 12
Revolutionary Committee(s) 32, 100; of the Guomindang 31
revolutionary diplomacy 314
revolutionary films 56
Ri Pyong-chol 336
roads 127–8
Robinson, Mary 350
Rocket Force 36
Roh Moo-hyun 334
Roman Catholic Christianity 209, 211–13
Roth, Kenneth 293
Royal Dutch Shell 139
Rural Cooperative Medical Care 170
rural economy 96–111
rural governance 106–7
rural society 151–7
rural-urban migration 100–1
Russia, relations with China 323–5
Russian language 160

San Francisco Peace treaty 325
SARS 169, 171, 173, 233
Sartre, Jean-Paul 45
Scientific Development outlook 52–3
SCO *see* Shanghai Cooperation Organisation
Second Beijing Forum 146
Second United Front 14, 33
semi-colonialism 12, 313
Sendero Luminoso (Shining Path) 45
Senkaku 328
Seriqbuya 259
Service, John 316
service sector 129

Seventeen Point Agreement 243, 244, 245
sexual harassment 227
Sha Zukang 315
shadow banking 124
shangfang (visit to superiors) 184
Shanghai 71, 139
Shanghai (Wu) language 8
Shanghai Clique 31, 48, 63, 71
Shanghai Cooperation Organisation 340, 349
Shanghai Party Committee 65
Shanghai Stock Exchange 119
Shaoguan 256
Shatin 281, 292
Shengwulian, Hunan Province Revolutionary
    Great Alliance Committee 32
Shenzhen 278, 282, 294
Shenzhen Stock Exchange 119
Shigatse 243
Shinkansen Bullet Train 126
Shinzo Abe 328
Shouters 210
shuanggui system 27–8, 30
Sichuan 169–70, 243
Sikkim 340
Silk Road 144, 352
Silkworm missiles 356
simplified script 8
Singapore 337
Singh, Manmohan 340
Sinocentrism 147
Sino-Soviet relations 137, 314
smoking 171
social control 155
social credit 192–3
social imperialism 316
socialisation of industry 115
socialism with Chinese characteristics 80, 187, 365
social welfare 141
soil erosion 233
Songhua River 230, 234
Soong Chu-yu, James 304, 308
Sound of Hope radio station 215
South China Morning Post 278
Southern Metropolitan Daily (*Nanfang dushi
    ribao*) 197
Southern Mongolia 267
Southern Mongolian Human Rights Information
    Centre 268
Southern Weekend (*Nanfang zhoumo*) 74, 78, 197
South Korea 316
South Korean Christians 333
South Manchurian Railway 126
Soviet experts 160
Soviet Union 91, 98, 160, 267, 313, 324; border
    skirmishes, 1969 17
Special Administrative Region 274, 296
Special Economic Zones 17, 68

Special Rapporteur of the UN Commission on
    Human Rights 181
Special Tactical Squad 284
Spence, Michael 94
Spice Route 352
spiritual pollution 80
spying 317–18
Sri Lanka 145
Stalin 44
Standard Chinese 7
Standing Committee of the NPC 25, 181
Standing Committee of the Politburo 30
State Administration for Religious Affairs 203,
    250, 254
State Administration of Foreign Exchange
    (SAFE) 123
State Administration of Radio, Film and
    Television 195
state capitalism 80
State Chairman (President) 24
State Council 24, 26, 118
State Development Bank 77
State Development Planning Commission 92
State Education Commission 162
State Environmental Protection Agency 230–6
State Family Planning Commission 176–7
State-owned Assets Supervision and
    Administration Commission (SASAC) 115
state-owned enterprises (SOE) 112–15
State Planning Commission 91, 92
state secrets 200
State Statistical Bureau 91
stock exchanges 119–20, 319
stock market 119–20
Straits Exchanges Foundation SEF (Taiwan) 304
Strategic Support Force 36
Strayer, Robert, Deputy Assistant Secretary, US
    Department of State 321
Strike Hard Campaign 348, 350; in Xinjiang 254
Sudan 342
Sufi tomb culture 252–3
Suga Yoshihide 328–9
Suharto, President 338
Suleyman Demirel 353
sulphur dioxide 230
Sun Chunlan 175
Sunflower Movement, Taiwan 306
sunshine policy, Korea 334
Sun Yat-sen 12, 50, 186, 217, 232
Supreme People's Court 25, 181, 184, 189, 199
surveillance 192–3, 249, 262
Suzhou 97
Swire, Merlin 283

Tai, Benny 276
Taiwan ix, 15, 51, 122, 277, 289, 299–309,
    314, 327

Taiwan Democratic Self-Government League 32
Taiwan, membership of United Nations 305
Taiwan, post-war economy 299–300
Taiwan Solidarity Union (TSU) 303
Taliban 358
Tamar Park 287
Tanaka Kakuei 325
Tang dynasty 206
Tang Jiaxuan 332
Tang Kin-wing, Augustus 283
Tang Ping-keung, Chris 292
Tangshan 17, 35
Tanzania and Zambia Railway 341
Taoyuan 304
tariffs 319
Tarim Basin 139
Tartars 217
Tashilunpo Monastery 243, 244
technocrats 365
television and radio 199
temples 205
Tencent 175, 200
Tenth Five-Year Plan 48
territorial integrity 12
Terrorism 260–1
Thatcher, Mrs Margaret 274
Thousand Character Classic 159
Three-Anti Campaign 38–9
Three Gorges Dam 5, 133, 136, 231–3
three obediences 223
Three Represents 52–3, 84
three rural issues 134
Three Self Patriotic Movement 209
Tian'anmen 24, 44
Tian'anmen Square 18, 44, 201, 324; Jeep
    attack, October 2013 258–9
Tianshan (Mountains of Heaven) 6
Tibet 187, 241–51; protests and self-immolation
    247–8
Tibetan Autonomous Region 218, 243, 244, 261
Tibetan Buddhism 208, 244, 248
Tibetan Institute of Socialism 250
Tokayev, Kassym-Jomart 351
Tongzhi Restoration 90
torture 189–90
tourism 126–30; domestic 129
township and village enterprises 105–6
trade unions 13
trade war 318–19, 328
transport 126–30
Treaty of Friendship, Alliance and Mutual
    Assistance 313, 323
Treaty of Nanjing 12, 271, 313
Treaty of Versailles 12–13
Trump, Donald 318, 336
Tsai Ing-wen 306, 307, 308–9
Tsang, Erik 295

Tsang, Jasper 279
Tsim Sha Tsui 281
Tsuen Wan 288
Tuen Mun 287
Turkestan Islamic Party (TIP) 260
Turkey 347, 353–5
Twenty-first Century Maritime Silk Road 144
twinning 141
two sessions 367–8

Ulanfu 266–7
Umbrella movement 276–7, 280, 284
UN High Commission for Refugees
    (UNHCR) 333
UN High Commissioner for Human Rights 181,
    188, 350
underground and light rail 128
unequal treaties 12, 313
United Front Work Departments 250
United Kingdom Security Service (MI5) 322
United Kingdom's National Security Council 320
United Nations 243, 314, 315
United States: and China 315–23; -China cold
    war 322; -China Relations Act 2000 318;
    bases in Kyrgyzstan 350
United States Consulate General in Chengdu 56–7
United States Department of Commerce 322
University of Chicago 167
University of Science and Technology, Hefei 165
urban and industrial economy 112–16
urban communes 153
urban insurrections 14
urbanisation 96, 153–4
urban middle class 154
Urumqi 256, 257, 348, 355
Ussuri (Wusuli) river 3
Uyghurs 135, 208, 209, 218, 231, 256, 353
Uyghurs in Turkey 354
Uzbekistan 347
Uzbeks 348

vaccines, counterfeit 172
Vatican, diplomatic relations with Beijing 212
Vietnam 316
village committees 40–4
village economy 96–7
vocational and technical schools 164

Wall Street Journal (*WSJ*) 201
Wan Chai 293
Wang Huiyao 147
Wang Huning 30
Wang Juntao 74
Wang Lequan 257
Wang Lijun 55
Wang Qishan 81, 195
Wang Ruoshui 197

Wang Xiangwei 82, 278, 286
Wang Xiaofang 233
Wang Yang 30, 43, 56, 62
Wang Yi 145, 146, 919, 331
Wang Zhaohua 74
Wang Zhen 136
Wang Zhenchuan 190
Wang Zhimin 293
Wang Zhonglin 175
Wan Li 108
War of Resistance against Japan 14, 66
warlords 12
Watchman Nee 210
water pollution 230
WeChat 200, 280, 323
Wei Fenghe, General 18, 321
Weibo 200, 280
Welch, Holmes 206
Wen Jiabao 48–54, 77, 78, 89, 102–3, 132–5, 170, 220, 233, 234–5, 332, 340
West China Forum 132
West-East Gas Pipeline 139, 141
Western Development 48, 131–43, 349–50
Western Region Development Programme 92
WhatsApp 200
White Lotus 205, 206
White Papers on human rights 187
WHO *see* World Health Organisation (WHO)
Williams, Rowan, Dr. 210
Williamson, Gavin 320
Witness Lee, Li Changshou 210
Wo Shing Wo 282–3
wolf-warrior 232
woman-work, *funu gongzuo* 225
women 223–6
Wong, Joshua 276, 279, 284
work teams 177
Worker Peasant Soldier Student 66
Workers' and Peasants' Red Army 14, 33
World Bank 136, 147, 342
World Food Programme 329
World Health Organisation (WHO) 173, 174, 294
World Trade Organisation (WTO) 50, 51, 96, 119, 121–2, 314
Wu Bangguo 77
Wu language (Shanghai) 8
Wuhan 173–6
Wukan 43–4

Xi Jinping vii–viii, viii–ix, 30, 61–86, 144, 145, 166, 174, 175, 185, 191, 236, 318, 319, 323, 365, 367; address to Central Party School 286; anti-corruption campaign 35–6; military connections 64; opposition to 83
Xi Jinping Thought 25, 29, 166–7
xinfang, letter of complaint 184

Xinhua (New China) news agency 29, 196, 273
Xining 246
Xinjiang 32, 136–8, 187, 190, 192, 208, 209, 218, 231, 248, 252–65, 348, 358, 360
Xinjiang Military Region 137
Xinjiang Production and Construction Corps XPCC (*bingtuan*) 132, 136–8, 253
Xinjiang Uyghur Autonomous Region 252, 347
Xi Zhongxun 64, 65, 66–9
Xu Caihou 36, 81
Xu Lin 167
Xu Wenli 33
Xu Yuling 285
Xu Zhangrun 83

Yan'an 14
Yan Hongyan 68
Yang Guang 285
Yang Jiechi 323
Yangzi (Yangtse or Changjiang) river 5
Yangzi Delta region 70
Yanhuang Chunqiu 195
Yao 219
Yasukuni Shrine 326–7
Yasuo Fukuda 327
Yellow River (Huanghe) 4–5
Yiguandao (Way of Pervading Unity) 205
Yining (Ghulja) 258
Yongbyon nuclear power reactor 330
Yonghegong Lama Temple 208
Youde, Sir Edward 273
Young, Sir Mark 271, 272
Younghusband, Sir Francis 241
Young Pioneer 161–3
Youth Olympic Games 82
Yuan dynasty 11
Yuan Shikai 12, 242
Yuen Long 282–7
Yunnan 219, 355

Zambia 342
Zardar, Asif Ali 359
Zeng Peiyan 132
Zeng Qinghong 48
Zhang Chunxian 261
Zhang Dejiang 57
Zhang Wannian, General 357
Zhang Yesui 145
Zhao Leji 30
Zhao Ziyang 18, 49, 51–2, 69, 195
Zhejiang 70, 72
Zheng Xiaoyu 55
Zhenghe, Admiral 341
Zhengzhou 155, 165
Zhongguoren pan-Chinese identity 220
Zhongnanhai 35, 62, 70
Zhong Nanshan 176

Zhou Enlai 16, 17, 40, 52, 78, 208, 273, 274, 314, 325, 327, 329, 366
Zhou Ji 164
Zhou Nan 274
Zhou Qiang 184
Zhou Xiaochuan 118, 124

Zhou Yongkang 29, 55–60, 80, 81
Zhuangzi 204
Zhu De 17
Zhujiang (Pearl River) 5
Zhu Rongli 50
Zimbabwe 342

Taylor & Francis Group
an **informa** business

Taylor & Francis eBooks

www.taylorfrancis.com

A single destination for eBooks from Taylor & Francis
with increased functionality and an improved user
experience to meet the needs of our customers.

90,000+ eBooks of award-winning academic content in
Humanities, Social Science, Science, Technology, Engineering,
and Medical written by a global network of editors and authors.

TAYLOR & FRANCIS EBOOKS OFFERS:

A streamlined
experience for
our library
customers

A single point
of discovery
for all of our
eBook content

Improved
search and
discovery of
content at both
book and
chapter level

REQUEST A FREE TRIAL
support@taylorfrancis.com

 Routledge
Taylor & Francis Group

 CRC Press
Taylor & Francis Group